Your Study of

The New Testament

Made Easier, Third Edition

Part 3

1 Peter through Revelation

Includes

*Our Savior's Life and Mission
to Redeem and Give Hope*

This is not an official publication of The Church of Jesus Christ of Latter-day Saints. The opinions and views expressed herein belong solely to the author and do not necessarily represent the opinions or views of Cedar Fort, Inc. Permission for the use of sources, graphics, and photos is also solely the responsibility of the author.

ISBN 13: 978-1-4621-4463-1

Published by CFI, an imprint of Cedar Fort, Inc.
2373 W. 700 S., Springville, UT 84663
Distributed by Cedar Fort, Inc., www.cedarfort.com

Library of Congress Control Number: 2022939322

Cover design by Shawnda T. Craig
Cover design © 2022 Cedar Fort, Inc.

Printed in the United States of America

10 9 8 7 6 5 4 3 2 1

Printed on acid-free paper

GOSPEL STUDIES SERIES

Your Study of

The New Testament

Made Easier, Third Edition

Part 3

1 Peter through Revelation

Includes

*Our Savior's Life and Mission
to Redeem and Give Hope*

David J. Ridges

CEDAR FORT
Publishing & Media

CFI
An imprint of Cedar Fort, Inc.
Springville, Utah

Books by David J. Ridges

The Gospel Study Series

- *Your Study of The Book of Isaiah Made Easier, Second Edition*

- *The New Testament Made Easier, Third Edition, Part 1*

- *The New Testament Made Easier, Third Edition, Part 2*

- *The New Testament Made Easier, Third Edition, Part 3*

- *Your Study of The Book of Mormon Made Easier, Part 1*

- *Your Study of The Book of Mormon Made Easier, Part 2*

- *Your Study of The Book of Mormon Made Easier, Part 3*

- *Book of Mormon Made Easier, Family Deluxe Edition, Volumes 1 and 2*

- *Your Study of The Doctrine and Covenants Made Easier, Second Edition, Part 1*

- *Your Study of The Doctrine and Covenants Made Easier, Second Edition, Part 2*

- *Your Study of The Doctrine and Covenants Made Easier, Second Edition, Part 3*

- *The Old Testament Made Easier, Third Edition, Part 1*

- *The Old Testament Made Easier—Selections from the Old Testament, Third Edition, Part 2*

- *The Old Testament Made Easier—Selections from the Old Testament, Third Edition, Part 3*

- *The Old Testament Made Easier—Selections from the Old Testament, Third Edition, Part 4*

- *Your Study of the Pearl of Great Price Made Easier*

- *Your Study of Jeremiah Made Easier*

- *Your Study of The Book of Revelation Made Easier, Second Edition*

Our Savior's Life and Mission to Redeem and Give Hope

Mormon Beliefs and Doctrines Made Easier

The Proclamation on the Family: The Word of the Lord on More than 30 Current Issues

Using the Signs of the Times to Strengthen Your Testimony

Doctrinal Details of the Plan of Salvation: From Premortality to Exaltation

INTRODUCTION

Welcome to the third edition of Your Study of the The New Testament Made Easier. This third edition is a substantial expansion of the second edition and is a three-volume set. It contains numerous additional notes and explanations, plus many additional verses from the Joseph Smith Translation of the Bible, which were not included in the second edition.

In Part 1, we will study the life of our Savior as taught in the Four Gospels—Matthew, Mark, Luke, and John, as found in the King James version of the Bible as published and used by The Church of Jesus Christ of Latter-day Saints. (It is interesting to note that only 31 days of the Savior's life and ministry are covered in the Four Gospels.) Part 2 and a portion of Part 3 are a study of Acts through Revelation. Parts 1, 2, and 3 include every verse in the New Testament. The remainder of Part 3 consists of the book *Our Savior's Life and Mission to Redeem and Give Hope* by David J. Ridges. It is a pleasant and fairly easy read of the Savior's life and mission to cleanse, heal, and make exaltation available to us. This book makes use of Matthew, Mark, Luke, and John as it helps you better understand and appreciate the Savior's mortal mission and Atonement and how His marvelous, infinite Atonement can fill your life with richness, confidence, and peace.

Note: In Part 1, I have used bold font for many words and phrases in Matthew, Mark, and Luke as an example of ways you might highlight or mark your own scriptures and also to point things out to you for teaching purposes. Beginning with the Gospel of John, I do not use bold, except for occasional emphasis, and particularly to point out the JST changes to Bible verses. By the way, I often use "we" rather than "I" when making my comments. The reason is simple. My parents taught me to avoid "I trouble."

—David J. Ridges

THE JST REFERENCES IN
STUDY GUIDES BY DAVID J. RIDGES

Note that some of the JST (The Joseph Smith Translation of the Bible) references I use in my study guides are not found in the King James English-speaking edition of the Bible, published by the Church, in the footnotes or in the Joseph Smith Translation section in the reference section in the back. The reason for this, as explained to me while writing curriculum materials for the Church, is simply that there is not enough room to include all of the JST additions and changes. As you can imagine, as was likewise explained to me, there were difficult decisions that had to be made by the Scriptures Committee of the Church as to which JST contributions were included and which were not.

The Joseph Smith Translation of the Bible in its entirety can generally be found in or ordered through bookstores or online. It was originally published under the auspices of the Reorganized Church of Jesus Christ of Latter Day Saints in Independence, Missouri. The version of the JST that I prefer to use is a parallel column version, *Joseph Smith's "New Translation" of the Bible*, published by Herald Publishing House, Independence, Missouri, in 1970. This parallel column version compares the King James Bible with the JST side by side and includes only the verses that have changes, additions, or deletions made by the Prophet Joseph Smith.

By the way, some members of the Church have wondered whether or not we can trust the JST since it was published by a breakaway faction from our Church. They worry that some changes from Joseph Smith's original manuscript might have been made to support doctrinal differences between us and the RLDS Church. This is not the case. Many years ago, Robert J. Matthews of the Brigham Young University Religion Department was given permission by leaders of the RLDS Church to go to their Independence, Missouri, headquarters and personally compare the original JST document word for word with their publication of the JST. Brother Matthews was thus able to verify that they had been meticulously true to the Prophet's original work.

CONTENTS

DEDICATION

To my wife and eternal companion, Janette,
who has encouraged and supported me
every step of the way.

FOREWORD

In many years of teaching in the Church and for the Church Educational System, I have found that members of the Church encounter some common problems when it comes to understanding the scriptures. One problem is understanding the language of the scriptures themselves. Another is understanding symbolism. Another is how best to mark scriptures and perhaps make brief notes in them. Yet another concern is how to understand what the scriptures are actually teaching. In other words, what are the major messages being taught by the Lord through His prophets?

This study guide is designed to address each of the concerns mentioned above for 1 Peter through Revelation in the New Testament.

The format is intentionally simple, with some license taken with respect to capitalization and punctuation in order to minimize interruption of the flow. The format is designed to help readers to:

- Quickly gain a basic understanding of these scriptures through the use of brief explanatory notes in brackets within the verses as well as notes between some verses.

- Better understand the beautiful language of the scriptures. This is accomplished in this study guide with in-the-verse notes that define difficult scriptural terms.

- Mark their scriptures and put brief notes in the margins that will help them understand now and remember later what given passages of scripture teach.

- Better understand the symbolism of the parables of Jesus as well as many other passages where symbolism is used.

- Get a feel for the background and setting in which events and teachings take place. A basic understanding of Jewish culture in the days of the Savior is vital. Notes between verses help with these issues.

Over the years, one of the most common expressions of gratitude from my students has been, "Thanks for the notes you had us put in our scriptures." This book is dedicated to that purpose.

Sources for the notes given in this work are as follows:

- The standard works of The Church of Jesus Christ of Latter-day Saints.

- Footnotes in the Latter-day Saint version of the King James Bible.

- The Joseph Smith Translation of the Bible.

- The Bible Dictionary in the back of the Latter-day Saint version of the Bible.

- Various dictionaries.

- *Strong's Exhaustive Concordance of the Bible*, shown as [*Strong's* # or Strong's #].

- Various student manuals provided for our institutes of religion, including the New Testament student manual, Religion 211, *The Life and Teachings of Jesus and His Apostles*.

- James E. Talmage, *Jesus the Christ*, Deseret Book, 1982.

- Various translations of the Bible, including the Martin Luther edition of the German Bible, which Joseph Smith said was the most correct of any then available.

- *Doctrinal New Testament Commentary*, volumes 1, 2, and 3, by Apostle Bruce R. McConkie.

- *Teachings of the Prophet Joseph Smith*, 1976.

- *Understanding the Book of Revelation*, by Jay A. Parry and Donald W. Parry.

- *New International Version of the Bible*, Zondervan Publishing House, 1984.

- Other sources as noted in the text and in the "Sources" section.

I hope that this study guide will serve effectively as a "teacher in your hand" to members of the Church as they seek to increase their understanding of the writings and teachings of the New Testament. Above all, if this work serves to bring increased understanding and testimony of the Atonement of Christ, all the efforts to put it together will have been far more than worth it. A special thanks goes to my wife, Janette, and my children who have encouraged me every step of the way.

THE FIRST EPISTLE GENERAL OF
PETER

The Apostle Peter became the president of the Church after the Savior was taken up into heaven. Most Bible scholars believe that he wrote this letter from Rome, sometime around AD 63 or AD 64. It is a general epistle [*letter*] addressed to members of the Church in many locations. At this time in Christian history, Nero, emperor of Rome, was undertaking severe persecutions of the Christians. In this letter, Peter, as the leader of the Church, prepares the Saints to endure much persecution and trouble by reminding them who they are, a "chosen generation" with a "royal priesthood." He reminds them that they were chosen in the premortal life to come to earth and become members of the Lord's Church and that because of this heritage, they can be strong and remain faithful at all costs. Peter's writings are of particular interest to Latter-day Saints because, among other things, he clearly teaches premortal life and foreordination (1 Peter 1:2), work for the dead (1 Peter 3:18–21), and also he teaches about making one's calling and election sure (2 Peter 1:10.)

FIRST PETER 1

In this chapter, Peter teaches the doctrine of foreordination and the bright hope for the future that the Atonement of Christ brings to the faithful.

1 PETER, an apostle of Jesus Christ, to the strangers [*members of the Church who are exiles from society*] scattered throughout Pontus, Galatia, Cappadocia, Asia, and Bithynia,

2 Elect [*chosen, foreordained*] according to the foreknowledge of God the Father [*the knowledge which the Father has about us from our premortal life with Him*], through sanctification of the Spirit [*through the guidance of the Holy Ghost*], unto obedience and sprinkling of the blood of Jesus Christ [*to the point of being blessed and cleansed by the Atonement of Christ*]: Grace unto you, and peace, be multiplied.

The Prophet Joseph Smith taught about God's foreknowledge of us, mentioned in verse 2, above. We often refer to this in conjunction with the doctrine of foreordination (being chosen and foreordained in our premortal life to come to earth and carry out certain responsibilities in the Lord's work here.) The Prophet taught, "Every man who has a calling to minister to the inhabitants of the world was ordained to that very purpose in the Grand Council of

1

heaven before this world was. I suppose I was ordained to this very office in that Grand Council." (*Teachings of the Prophet Joseph Smith*, p. 365.) Apostle Bruce R. McConkie also taught concerning this doctrine. He said, "To bring to pass the salvation of the greatest possible number of his spirit children, the Lord, in general, sends the most righteous and worthy spirits to earth through the lineage of Abraham and Jacob. This course is a manifestation of his grace or in other words his love, mercy, and condescension toward his children. This election to a chosen lineage is based on preexistent worthiness and is thus made 'according to the foreknowledge of God.' (1 Pet. 1:2.) Those so grouped together during their mortal probation have more abundant opportunities to make and keep the covenants of salvation, a right which they earned by preexistent devotion to the cause of righteousness. As part of this election, Abraham and others of the noble and great spirits were chosen before they were born for the particular missions assigned them in this life. . . . (Abraham 3:22–24; Rom. 9.) Actually, if the full blessings of salvation are to follow, the doctrine of election must operate twice. First, righteous spirits are elected or chosen to come to mortality as heirs of special blessings. Then, they must be called and elected again in this life, an occurrence which takes place when they join the true Church. (D&C 53:1.) Finally, in order to reap eternal salvation,

they must press forward in obedient devotion to the truth until they make their 'calling and election sure' (2 Pet. 1), that is, are 'sealed up unto eternal life.' (D&C 131:5.)" (McConkie, *Mormon Doctrine*, pp. 216–17.)

3 Blessed [*praised*] be the God and Father of our Lord Jesus Christ, which according to his abundant mercy hath begotten us again [*has given us spiritual rebirth, in other words, we are "born again"*] unto a lively hope [*unto a joyful and confident expectation of eternal salvation:* Strong's *#1680; compare also with 2 Nephi 31:20 where Nephi calls this "a perfect brightness of hope"*] by the resurrection of Jesus Christ from the dead,

4 To an inheritance [*exaltation, being "heirs of God, and joint-heirs with Christ"; Romans 8:17*] incorruptible [*eternal*], and undefiled [*pure*], and that fadeth not away, reserved in heaven [*celestial glory*] for you,

5 Who are kept [*preserved*] by the power of God through faith [*if they keep the commandments*] unto salvation [*exaltation*] ready to be revealed in the last time [*prepared to receive exaltation on final Judgment Day; compare with* Strong's *#2078*].

The word "salvation," as used in verse 5, above, with very few exceptions in the scriptures, means "exaltation."

6 Wherein ye greatly rejoice [*which you can look forward to with great*

joy], though now for a season [*during the coming days*], if need be, ye are in heaviness [*you may be burdened down*] through manifold temptations [*because of trials and afflictions; see 1 Peter 1:6, footnote b*]:

> Peter, as a prophet of God, is warning the members of the Church that very difficult times are coming, during which they will be severely persecuted. He strengthens them by giving them perspective, reminding them of the glorious reward of exaltation which awaits the faithful in eternity.

7 That the trial [*testing*] of your faith, being much more precious than of gold that perisheth [*faith is much more precious than gold*], though it be [*even though your faith is*] tried with fire [*is tested by severe troubles*], might be found unto praise and honour and glory [*might be found strong and worthy of God's praise and respect and worthy of your exaltation*] at the appearing of Jesus Christ:

8 Whom having not seen, ye love; in whom, though now ye see him not, yet believing [*having faith in Christ*], ye rejoice with joy unspeakable and full of glory: [*In other words, you love Christ, whom you have not seen. The faith which you have in Him brings you inexpressible and glorious joy.*]

9 Receiving the end of your faith, even the salvation of your souls [*the end goal of your faith will be exaltation*].

JST 1 Peter 1:9

9 Receiving the **object** of your faith, even the salvation of your souls.

10 Of which salvation the prophets have enquired and searched diligently, who prophesied of the grace that should come unto you: [*The prophets of old studied diligently and asked God many questions about salvation.*]

JST 1 Peter 1:10

10 **Concerning which salvation the prophets who prophesied of the grace bestowed upon you**, inquired and searched diligently;

11 Searching what, or what manner of time the Spirit of Christ which was in them did signify [*following the promptings of the Spirit*], when it testified beforehand the sufferings of Christ [*when it testified to them about the Atonement of Christ, before it happened*], and the glory that should follow

JST 1 Peter 1:11

11 Searching what **time, and what manner of salvation** the Spirit of Christ which was in them did signify, when it testified beforehand the sufferings of Christ, and the glory which should follow.

The "Spirit of Christ," as used in verse 11, above, can refer to the Holy Ghost or the Spirit of Christ or both. See McConkie, *Doctrinal New Testament Commentary*, Vol. 3, pp. 286–87. We know from D&C 84:45–47, that the Spirit of Christ [*which many people refer to as our "conscience," but which is far more than that*] "giveth light to every man that cometh into the world;" and that "every one that hearkeneth to the voice of the Spirit cometh unto God, even the Father." From this we understand that the Spirit of Christ works with all people to help them eventually come into the true Church so that they can receive the Gift of the Holy Ghost (which is a far more powerful influence) which will testify to them of the Father and Son and will teach them and testify to them of all things necessary for exaltation.

12 Unto whom [*referring to the prophets spoken of in verses 10 and 11*] it [*the gospel of Christ which leads to salvation*] was revealed, that not unto themselves, but unto us they did minister [*teach and prophesy*] the things, which are now reported [*taught*] unto you by them [*the Apostles and missionaries*] that have preached the gospel unto you with the Holy Ghost [*by the power of the Holy Ghost*] sent down from heaven; which things the angels desire to look into [*even the angels want to learn as much as possible about these things*].

13 Wherefore gird up the loins of your mind [*prepare your minds to handle the coming trials and persecutions*] be sober [*be serious about living righteously; circumspectly;* Strong's *#3225*], and hope to the end [*keep your hopes high so that you can reach the goal of exaltation*] for

the grace that is to be brought unto you [*which exaltation will be given you*] at the revelation of Jesus Christ [*when Christ shows forth His power to all*];

14 As obedient children [*keep your hopes high through being obedient followers of Christ*], not fashioning yourselves according to the former lusts in your ignorance [*not returning to your former lifestyles before you were converted and repented*]:

15 But as he [*God*] which hath called you is holy, so be ye holy in all manner of conversation [*conduct;* Strong's *#0391*];

16 Because it is written [*in Leviticus 11:44–45*], Be ye holy; for I am holy.

17 And if ye call on the Father, who without respect of persons [*who, without prejudice; in other words, who is fair and impartial*] judgeth according to every man's work, pass the time of your sojourning here in fear [*spend your time here in mortality with high respect for God*]:

18 Forasmuch as ye know [*since you know*] that ye were not redeemed with corruptible [*temporary, perishable*] things, as [*like*] silver and gold, from your vain [*unsuccessful as far as salvation is concerned;* Strong's *#3152*] conversation [*lifestyle;* Strong's *#0391*] received by tradition from your fathers;

19 But [*rather*] with the precious blood of Christ, as of a lamb [*like a sacrificial lamb*] without blemish

and without spot [*who was perfect*]:

20 Who [*Christ*] verily was fore-ordained before the foundation of the world [*was called to be our Savior in premortality; see Moses 4:1–3 and Abraham 3:27*], but was manifest [*came to earth*] in these last times [*recent times*] for you,

21 Who by him [*Christ*] do believe in God [*Heavenly Father*], that raised him [*Christ*] up from the dead, and gave him [*Christ*] glory; that your faith and hope might be in God [*the Father*]. [*In other words, Jesus came to you and was glorified by the Father so that you could have truth and correct understanding about Heavenly Father.*]

22 Seeing [*since*] ye have purified your souls in [*by*] obeying the truth through the Spirit [*with the help of the Holy Ghost*] unto unfeigned [*genuine*] love of the brethren, see that ye love one another with a pure heart fervently [*deeply*]:

23 Being born again [*having been spiritually reborn*], not of corruptible seed [*not by mortal parents, or doctrines or philosophies*], but of incorruptible [*rather a rebirth that can last forever*], by the word of God [*through the gospel of Christ*], which liveth and abideth for ever [*which lasts eternally*].

24 For all flesh is as grass [*mortal life is very temporary*], and all the glory of man as the flower of grass [*like blossoms which soon fade away and die*]. The grass withereth, and the flower [*blossoms*] thereof falleth away: [*Compare this with Isaiah 40:6–8.*]

25 But the word of the Lord endureth [*lasts*] for ever. And this is the word which by the gospel is preached unto you.

FIRST PETER 2

Peter will now remind these Saints what they must do in order to be "born again," in other words, what they must do in order to become spiritual and worthy for exaltation.

1 WHEREFORE [*and so,*] laying aside all malice [*evil intentions toward others*], and all guile [*deceptiveness; Strong's #1388*], and hypocrisies, and envies [*jealousies*], and all evil speakings [*slandering, gossiping*],

2 As newborn babes [*be like newborn babies*], desire the sincere milk of the word [*seek to be nourished by the simple basics of the gospel*], that ye may grow thereby [*so that you can grow up in the gospel*]:

3 If so be ye have tasted that the Lord is gracious [*I hope you have noticed that the Lord is kind, merciful and gracious*].

Next, Peter will compare Christ to a large, solid rock, or foundation upon which we can safely build. He will also invite these Saints to become "rock solid" in their faithfulness to God and to become solid foundations for others to rely on as they come to Christ.

4 To whom coming, as unto a living stone [*as you come to Christ, which is like coming to a living foundation*], disallowed indeed of men [*who was rejected by worldly men*], but chosen of God [*but was God's chosen Son*], and precious,

5 Ye also, as lively stones [*as foundations who are alive spiritually*], are built up a spiritual house [*are being built up spiritually*], an holy priesthood [*you are a holy priesthood*], to offer up spiritual sacrifices [*and you are sacrificing whatever is necessary in order to become spiritually in tune with God*], acceptable to God by Jesus Christ [*you are becoming acceptable to the Father through the Atonement of Christ*].

6 Wherefore also it is contained in the scripture [*this is the purpose of Isaiah 28:16, which says*], Behold, I lay in Sion [*Zion*] a chief corner stone [*Christ*], elect [*foreordained in premortality*], precious: and he that believeth on him [*Christ*] shall not be confounded [*confused, disappointed, or stopped in progressing to exaltation*].

7 Unto you therefore which believe he is precious [*to you who believe in Christ, He is precious, dear, tender, and loving*]: but unto them which be disobedient [*who do not keep the commandments*], the stone [*Christ*] which the builders [*the Jews*] disallowed [*rejected*], the same [*Christ*] is made [*has been made*] the head of the corner [*the ruler over all things*],

8 And a stone of stumbling, and a rock of offence, even to them which stumble at the word, being disobedient: whereunto also they were appointed.

The JST combines and changes verses 7 and 8 as follows:

JST 1 Peter 2:7–8

Unto you therefore **who** believe, he [*Christ*] is precious; but unto them **who are** disobedient, **who stumble at the word** [*Christ's gospel*] **through disobedience** [*because of disobedience*], **whereunto they** were appointed [*they were invited to live the gospel*], a stone of stumbling [*to them the gospel gets in their way*], and a rock of offense [*and is offensive to them*]. **For** the stone [*Christ*] which the builders [*the Jews and anyone who rejects Christ*] disallowed [*rejected*], is **become** the head of the corner.

Next, in verse 9, Peter uses powerful, symbolic, and beautiful language to describe who the faithful Saints are. We are included in this description if we too are striving to be righteous.

9 But ye are a chosen generation [*a people chosen to carry the blessings of the gospel and the priesthood to all people; see Abraham 2:9*], a royal priesthood [*we have the Melchizedek Priesthood of God, with all its saving ordinances, which can ultimately make us "royalty," in other words kings and queens in exaltation*], an holy nation [*a holy people*], a peculiar people [*a special posses-*

sion of the Lord; see 1 Peter 2:9, footnote f, in our Bible]; that ye should shew forth [tell everyone; declare abroad; Strong's #1804] the praises of him [God] who hath called you out of darkness [spiritual darkness] into his marvellous light [into the marvelous light of the gospel] :

JST 1 Peter 2:9

9 But ye are a chosen generation, a royal priesthood, **a** holy nation, a peculiar people; that ye should **show** forth the praises of him who hath called you out of darkness into his marvelous light;

10 Which in time past were not a people [before you received the gospel and joined the Church, you were not a part of this group of chosen people], but are now the people of God: which had not obtained mercy, but now have obtained mercy.

11 Dearly beloved, I beseech [urge] you as strangers and pilgrims [as temporary inhabitants of this earth here in mortality; see note in Hebrews 11:13 in this study guide], abstain from fleshly lusts [do not give in to physical appetites and passions], which war against the soul [which threaten your exaltation];

12 Having your conversation; honest among the Gentiles [nonmembers of the Church]: that, whereas they speak against you as evildoers [that even though they accuse you of being wicked], they may by your good works, which they shall behold, glorify God in the day of visitation [so that they can, through your good example, be converted and be among the righteous who will join with the Lord and praise Him when He comes].

JST 1 Peter 2:12

12 Having your **conduct** honest among the Gentiles; that, whereas they speak against you as evildoers, they may by your good works, which they shall behold, glorify God in the day of visitation.

There are some, who for religious reasons, refuse to submit to Kings, presidents, government or civic leaders, and so forth. They would do well to follow Peter's counsel here in the next verses. Allegiance to government authority is very necessary for law and order and to prevent anarchy and chaos. See D&C 134 for more about the Lord's counsel on this matter.

13 Submit yourselves to every ordinance [government, institution; Strong's #2937] of man for the Lord's sake: whether it be to the king, as supreme [as the supreme authority];

14 Or unto governors, as unto them [as well as to those] that are sent by him [the governor] for the punishment of evildoers [those who break the law], and for the praise of them that do well.

15 For so is the will of God [this is the will of God], that with well doing [good behavior] ye may put to silence the ignorance of foolish men:

16 As free [*as free people*], and not using your liberty for a cloke of maliciousness [*not misusing your freedom as a cover-up for evil deeds*], but as the servants of God [*use your liberty as becomes servants of God*].

17 Honour all men [*show proper respect to all people*]. Love the brotherhood [*show love to all members of the Church*]. Fear [*show reverence to, respect;* Strong's #5399] God. Honour the king [*show proper respect to political authorities*].

18 Servants, be subject to your masters with all fear [*reverence for one who has authority over you;* Strong's #5401]; not only to the good and gentle, but also to the froward [*also toward masters who are crooked, wicked;* Strong's #4646].

19 For this is thankworthy [*commendable; worthy of being rewarded by God;* Strong's #5485], if a man for conscience toward God [*because of his belief in God*] endure grief, suffering wrongfully [*innocent of wrongdoing*].

20 For what glory is it [*what special honor should you receive*], if, when ye be buffeted [*if, when you are made to suffer*] for your faults [*for your own sins and mistakes*], ye shall take it patiently? but if, when ye do well [*when you are living righteously*], and suffer for it, ye take it patiently, this is acceptable with God.

21 For even hereunto were ye called [*when you joined the Church, you were, in effect, called to suffer persecution*]: because Christ also suffered for us [*just as Christ suffered for being righteous*], leaving us an example, that ye should follow his steps:

22 Who [*Christ*] did no sin, neither was guile [*deception*] found in his mouth:

23 Who, when he was reviled [*mocked and insulted*], reviled not again [*did not retaliate*]; when he suffered, he threatened not; but committed himself to him [*the Father*] that judgeth righteously:

24 Who [*Christ*] his own self [*all alone*] bare [*took*] our sins in his own body [*took our sins upon Himself*] on the tree [*on the cross*], that we, being dead to sins [*when we repent*], should live unto righteousness [*will be spiritually reborn and brought back unto God*]: by whose stripes [*the painful welts on the Savior's back as a result of the scourging He was given before He was crucified*] ye were healed [*you were forgiven and healed through the punishment which Christ took for your sins*].

25 For ye were as [*like*] sheep going astray; but are now returned unto the Shepherd and Bishop [*overseer, guardian;* Strong's #1985] of your souls [*but through the Atonement, you have now returned to the Good Shepherd (Christ) who is the Overseer, the Guardian, of your souls*].

FIRST PETER 3

This chapter contains the marvelous and comforting doctrine that the gospel is taught to the spirits of the dead in the spirit world. This is very significant doctrine and ties in with 1 Corinthians 15:29 which mentions baptism for the dead. It also ties in with 1 Peter 4:6 which teaches that after they have been taught the gospel, the dead will be judged by the same standards by which we will be judged. So far in his epistle (letter), Peter has given the members of the Church much counsel regarding humbly submitting to the Savior as well as submitting to governments and government leaders, masters, and so forth. As noted in Ephesians 5:21 in this study guide, the word "submit" carries with it the connotation of "voluntary cooperation" rather than slave-like subservience. You may wish to review the notes given for Ephesians 5:21–33 as you read Peter's counsel to wives in the next several verses.

1 LIKEWISE [*just as I counseled your husbands to humbly submit to Christ and their leaders*], ye wives, be in subjection to [*voluntarily submit; cooperate with;* Strong's *#5293*] your own husbands; that [*so that*], if any obey not the word [*if they are not living the gospel*], they also may without the word [*without understanding the gospel*] be won [*won over to the gospel*] by the conversation of the wives;

JST 1 Peter 3:1

1 Likewise, ye wives, be in subjection to your own husbands; that, if any obey not the word, they also may without the word be won by the **conduct** of the wives;

2 While they behold your chaste conversation coupled with fear [*coupled with the respect they will have for you*].

JST 1 Peter 3:2

2 While they behold your chaste **conduct** [*in other words, when they see your righteous conduct*] coupled with fear.

3 Whose adorning [*beauty*] let it not be that outward adorning of plaiting [*braiding*] the hair, and of wearing of gold [*wearing costly jewelry*], or of putting on of apparel [*or in the type of clothing you wear*]; [*In other words, let your true beauty not depend on hairstyles, jewelry, clothing styles, etc.*]

JST 1 Peter 3:3

3 **Let your adorning be not** that outward adorning of plaiting the hair, and wearing of gold, or putting on of apparel;

4 But let it be the hidden man of the heart [*let your true beauty be the hidden beauty that dwells in the heart*], in that which is not corruptible [*in qualities and character traits which have eternal value*], even the ornament of [*beauty, such as*] a meek and quiet spirit [*a self-controlled and peaceful nature*],

which is in the sight of God of great price [*of great value*].

5 For after this manner [*this is the way*] in the old time [*in times past*] the holy women also [*the women who were true Saints*], who trusted in God, adorned [*beautified*] themselves, being in subjection unto [*respecting and cooperating with*] their own husbands:

JST 1 Peter 3:5

5 For after this manner **in old times** the holy women, who trusted in God, adorned themselves, being in subjection unto their own husbands;

6 Even as Sara [*even as Sarah did when she*] obeyed Abraham, calling him lord [*when she treated him with respect and reverence; Strong's #2962*]: whose daughters [*descendants*] ye are, as long as ye do well [*as long as you live the gospel*], and are not afraid with any amazement [*and do not give in to fears and pressures of the world*].

Peter pays Sarah a very high compliment in verse 6, above. The phrase, "whose daughters ye are," is symbolic of exaltation. "Daughters of" means "followers of" in the same way that "sons of" means "followers of." See Mosiah 5:7 where "sons" and "daughters" are symbolic words meaning "exalted."

7 Likewise [*in the same way*], ye husbands, dwell with them [*live with your wives*] according to knowledge [*according to what God has taught; footnote b in our Bible for 1 Peter 3:7 which refers us to D&C 121:41–42 which includes persuasion, patience, gentleness, meekness, genuine love, kindness, pure knowledge, no hypocrisy, and no deception*], giving honour unto [*showing respect to*] the wife, as unto the weaker vessel, and as being heirs together of the grace of life; that your prayers be not hindered [*otherwise, bad behavior toward your wives will get in the way of your prayers to God*].

The phrase "as unto the weaker vessel" in verse 7, above, does not agree with the teachings of our prophets today. They clearly teach that "fathers and mothers are obligated to help one another as equal partners" in The Family: A Proclamation To The World, given September 23, 1995. Thus, we are left to conclude that either Peter's statement was not properly translated or that it reflected cultural tradition of his time rather than the eternal status of women.

8 Finally, be ye all of one mind [*be united*], having compassion one of another, love as brethren, be pitiful [*full of compassion; Strong's #2155*], be courteous:

9 Not rendering [*returning*] evil for evil, or railing [*insult*] for railing: but contrariwise blessing [*doing just the opposite, thus blessing each other*]; knowing that ye are thereunto called [*knowing that you have been called by Christ*], that ye should inherit a blessing [*to inherit the blessings of eternal life*].

10 For he that will love life, and see good days, let him refrain his tongue from evil, and his lips that they speak no guile [*no deception;* Strong's #*1388*]:

11 Let him eschew [*avoid*] evil, and do good; let him seek peace, and ensue it [*do his best to achieve it*].

12 For the eyes of the Lord are over [*upon*] the righteous, and his ears are open unto their prayers: but the face of the Lord is against them that do evil.

13 And who is he that will harm you [*who can do you any permanent harm, eternally*], if ye be followers of that which is good?

14 But and if ye suffer for righteousness' sake [*because of being righteous*], happy are ye: and be not afraid of their terror [*don't fear their threats*], neither be troubled;

15 But sanctify the Lord God [*make the Lord God the top priority*] in your hearts: and be ready always to give an answer to every man that asketh you a reason of the hope that is in you with meekness and fear [*be ready to humbly and respectfully tell anyone about the gospel, who asks you why you are so optimistic and happy*]:

JST 1 Peter 3:15

15 But sanctify the Lord God in your hearts; and be ready always to give an answer **with meekness and fear** to every man that asketh **of** you a reason **for** the hope that is in you:

16 Having a good conscience [*having a clear conscience*]; that, whereas they speak evil of you, as of evildoers [*when they accuse you of being evil*], they may be ashamed [*they will be put to shame*] that falsely accuse your good conversation in Christ.

JST 1 Peter 3:16

16 Having a good conscience; that, whereas they speak evil of you, as of evildoers, they may be ashamed that falsely accuse your good **conduct** in Christ.

17 For it is better, if the will of God be so [*if it is in harmony with God's will that you suffer*], that ye suffer for well doing, than for evil doing [*that you suffer for doing good rather than for doing evil*].

Next, Peter uses the Savior as the supreme example of one who suffered for doing good. In so doing, he teaches tremendous doctrine about work for the dead.

18 For Christ also hath once suffered for sins [*suffered once and for all for all sins; compare with 2 Nephi 9:21–22*], the just for the unjust [*the Perfectly Righteous One suffered for the guilty ones (all of us)*], that he might bring us to God [*so that He could bring us to exaltation in the presence of the Father*], being put to death in the flesh [*having His mortal body crucified*], but quickened [*resurrected*] by the Spirit:

JST 1 Peter 3:18

18 **For Christ also once suffered for sins, the just for the unjust, being put to death in the flesh, but quickened by the Spirit, that he might bring us to God**.

19 By which also he went and preached unto the spirits in prison; [*In other words, for the same cause, offering people exaltation, Christ also went and preached to the spirits in prison in the spirit world.*]

JST 1 Peter 3:19

19 **For** which **cause** also, he went and preached unto the spirits in prison;

20 Which sometime were disobedient, when once the longsuffering of God waited in the days of Noah, while the ark was a preparing [*while the ark was being prepared*], wherein few, that is, eight souls were saved by water. [*Those in the spirit prison included those who had been wicked in the days of Noah and who were drowned in the flood. Only eight people were saved on Noah's ark.*]

JST 1 Peter 3:20

20 **Some of whom** were disobedient **in the days of Noah**, **while** the long-suffering of God waited, while the ark was preparing, wherein few, that is, eight souls were saved by water.

We know from D&C 138:18–20 and 29–30 that the Savior only appeared to the righteous in the spirit world. He organized a great missionary force among the righteous who were then sent to the spirit prison to teach the gospel to those spirits. We also know from Moses 7:27 that many people were converted by Noah and were taken up to join the City of Enoch before the flood occurred.]

21 The like figure [*the flooding of the earth by water, mentioned at the end of verse 20, above, is symbolic of baptism*] whereunto even baptism doth also now save us [*baptism, even now, opens the door to our being saved*] not the putting away of the filth of the flesh [*we are not referring to physically washing dirt off of our bodies*], but the answer of a good conscience [*rather to having a clear conscience*] toward God,) by the resurrection of Jesus Christ [*through the Atonement of Christ*]:

22 Who is gone into heaven, and is on the right hand of God [*the Father*]; angels and authorities and powers being made subject unto him [*Christ*].

FIRST PETER 4

Without the help of the JST, people could misinterpret verse 1, below, as saying that Christ "ceased from sin," thus implying that the Savior was not perfect. Such is not the case. As you will see, next, in verse 1, the JST takes the last phrase from verse 1 and adds it to verse 2. The Prophet Joseph Smith also makes significant changes in verse 2.

1 FORASMUCH [*since*] then as Christ hath suffered for us in the flesh, arm yourselves likewise with the same mind [*strive to think like Christ thinks*]: for he that hath suffered in the flesh hath ceased from sin;

JST 1 Peter 4:1

1 Forasmuch then as Christ hath suffered for us in the flesh, arm yourselves likewise with the same mind;

Did you notice that in the JST, Joseph Smith deleted the last phrase of verse 1, above, as it stands in the Bible? As you look carefully at it, you will probably come to the conclusion that it really does not make sense and does not belong in the Bible. This is a rather major change in the JST.

2 That he no longer should live the rest of his time in the flesh to the lusts of men, but to the will of God.

JST 1 Peter 4:2

2 **For you who have suffered in the flesh** [*here in mortality*] **should cease from sin** [*should repent*], **that you no longer the rest of your time in the flesh** [*so that for the rest of your mortal lives*], **should live to the lusts of men** [*you no longer give in to the worldly passions of mortal men*], but to the will of God.

The JST change from "we" to "ye" in verse 3, next, takes away the implication that Peter lived a wicked lifestyle before he was converted and followed the Savior.

3 For the time past of our life may suffice us to have wrought the will of the Gentiles, when we walked in lasciviousness [*all kinds of sexual immorality*], lusts [*uncontrolled passions*], excess of wine [*drunkenness*], revellings [*wild parties;* Strong's *#2970*], banquetings [*carousing;* Strong's *#4224*], and abominable idolatries [*wicked idol worship*];"]

JST 1 Peter 4:3

3 For the time past **of life** may **suffice to** have wrought the will of the Gentiles [*you have spent enough time in the past living like people who don't know the gospel*], when **ye** walked in lasciviousness, lusts, excess of wine, revellings, banquetings, and abominable idolatries;

4 Wherein they [*the Gentiles, non-Christians*] think it strange that ye run not with them to the same excess of riot [*don't understand why you won't participate in their wicked lifestyle anymore*], speaking evil of you [*and so they mock and criticize you*]:

JST 1 Peter 4:4

4 Wherein they **speak evil of you, thinking it strange that you run not with them to the same excess of riot**;

5 Who [*the wicked who continue in this wicked lifestyle*] shall give account to him [*God*] that is ready to judge the quick [*the*

living; Strong's *#2198*] and the dead.

6 For for this cause was the gospel preached also to them that are dead [*this is the reason that the gospel is being taught to the dead in the spirit world prison*], that they might be judged according to men in the flesh [*so that they can be judged by the same standards as mortal people who are taught the gospel*], but live according to God in the spirit [*and can accept the gospel and become spiritually alive*].

JST 1 Peter 4:6

6 **Because of this, is** the gospel **preached to** them **who** are dead, that they might be judged according to men in the flesh, **but live in the spirit according to the will of God**.

7 But the end of all things is at hand [*But for you, this is the time to prepare to meet God; compare with Alma 34:32–33*]: be ye therefore sober [*serious-minded and self-controlled;* Strong's *#4993*], and watch unto prayer [*watch yourselves so that you can pray successfully*].

JST 1 Peter 4:7

7 But **to you**, the end of all things is at hand; be ye therefore sober, and watch unto prayer.

Joseph Smith made a very important change in verse 8, next, namely, that charity does not cover up many sins, rather, it prevents many sins.

8 And above all things have fervent

[*continuous;* Strong's *#1618*] charity among yourselves: for charity shall cover the multitude of sins.

JST 1 Peter 4:8

8 And above all things have fervent charity among yourselves; for charity **preventeth** a multitude of sins.

9 Use hospitality one to another without grudging [*without murmuring*].

10 As every man hath received the gift [*since you have received various spiritual gifts; compare with D&C 46:11–12*], even so minister the same one to another [*use them to help each other*], as good stewards of the manifold grace of God [*as good stewards of the grace of God which is demonstrated in so many different ways*].

11 If any man speak, let him speak as the oracles of God [*In other words, teach under the direction of the Spirit*]; if any man minister, let him do it as of [*according to*] the ability which God giveth: that God [*the Father*] in all things may be glorified through Jesus Christ, to whom be praise and dominion for ever and ever. Amen.

JST 1 Peter 4:11

11 If any man speak, let him speak as **an oracle** of God; if any man minister, let him do it as of the ability which God giveth; that God in all things may be glorified through Jesus Christ; to whom be praise and dominion forever and ever. Amen.

12 Beloved, think it not strange concerning the fiery trial which is to try you [*do not be surprised at the severe trials that are coming upon you*], as though some strange thing happened unto you [*as if such trials were something new for the righteous*]:

13 But rejoice, inasmuch as ye are partakers of Christ's sufferings [*take comfort that you are able to join Christ in suffering because of righteousness*]; that, when his glory shall be revealed [*that when Christ rules over all things here*], ye may be glad also with exceeding joy [*you can rejoice with Him that all wickedness is gone*].

14 If ye be reproached [*mocked*] for the name of Christ [*because you have taken the name of Christ upon you*], happy are ye; for the spirit of glory and of God resteth upon you: on their part he is evil spoken of [*the wicked speak evil of God*], but on your part he is glorified [*but you glorify God*].

Next, Peter again reminds the Saints that it is one thing to suffer because you are trying to be righteous, but quite another thing to suffer because you are wicked.

15 But let none of you suffer as a murderer, or as a thief, or as an evildoer, or as a busybody in other men's matters.

16 Yet if any man suffer as a Christian [*because he is a follower of Christ*], let him not be ashamed; but let him glorify God on this behalf [*because of it*].

17 For the time is come that judgment must begin at the house of God [*the time has come when great trials and tribulation will come upon the members of the Church*]: and if it first begin at us [*and if it starts with us*], what shall the end be of them that obey not the gospel of God [*imagine what will happen to the wicked who deserve punishment because they reject the gospel*]?

18 And if the righteous scarcely be saved [*and if it is hard for the righteous to be saved*], where shall the ungodly and the sinner appear [*can you imagine where the wicked fit into the picture*]?

19 Wherefore let them that suffer according to the will of God commit the keeping of their souls to him in well doing [*through doing good*], as unto a faithful Creator [*as one who can be completely trusted*].

FIRST PETER 5

Peter finishes this letter by reminding the local priesthood of their responsibility to take care of the members under their care. He teaches them that one of the most important ways of leading is to be a good example. He also counsels younger members to show respect for their leaders and to follow them.

There are no JST changes for this chapter.

1 THE elders [*Melchizedek Priesthood holders, local leaders of the*

Church] which are among you I exhort [counsel], who am also an elder, and a witness of the sufferings of Christ [and as a witness who personally saw the suffering of the Savior], and also a partaker of the glory that shall be revealed [and as one who has partaken of the gospel]:

2 Feed the flock [nourish the members of the Church] of God which is among you [of God, who is among you; compare with D&C 38:7 wherein the Savior says "But behold, verily, verily, I say unto you that mine eyes are upon you. I am in your midst and ye cannot see me;"], taking the oversight thereof [supervising the work of the Lord], not by constraint [not because you are obligated to], but willingly; not for filthy lucre [not for money], but of a ready mind [but willingly];

3 Neither as being lords over God's heritage [not as masters or bosses], but being ensamples to the flock [but as good examples to your members].

4 And when the chief Shepherd [Christ] shall appear, ye shall receive a crown of glory that fadeth not away [you will receive a crown of exaltation which will never end].

5 Likewise, ye younger [you younger members], submit [respect; cooperate; Strong's #5293] yourselves unto the elder [cooperate with your leaders]. Yea, all of you be subject one to another [cooperate with one another], and be clothed with humility: for God resisteth [opposes] the proud, and giveth grace to the humble.

6 Humble yourselves therefore under the mighty hand of God, that he may exalt you [give you exaltation] in due time:

7 Casting all your care upon him; for he careth for you.

8 Be sober, be vigilant [be watchful]; because your adversary the devil, as a roaring lion, walketh about, seeking whom he may devour:

9 Whom resist stedfast in the faith [resist the temptations from the devil by carefully living the gospel], knowing that the same afflictions are accomplished in your brethren that are in the world [knowing that other members of the Church throughout the world are going through similar troubles.]

10 But the God [may the Father] of all grace [of all mercy, kindness, forgiveness, and salvation], who hath called us unto his eternal glory [to celestial exaltation] by [through] Christ Jesus, after that ye have suffered a while [after you have passed the test], make you perfect [bring you into exaltation], stablish [make you firm in the gospel], strengthen, settle you [make you well-grounded in the gospel; Strong's #2311].

11 To him [the Father] be glory and dominion for ever and ever. Amen.

12 By Silvanus, a faithful brother unto you, as I suppose, I have written briefly, exhorting, and testifying that this is the true grace of

God wherein ye stand. [*I have sent this letter to you with the help of Silvanus, a faithful member of the Church.*]

13 The church that is at Babylon [*probably meaning that Peter was writing from Rome, where members of the Church are being particularly severely persecuted*], elected together with you [*chosen by God to spread His gospel abroad, as you are*], saluteth [*greets*] you; and so doth Marcus [*Mark, who later wrote the Gospel of Mark*] my son [*my son in the gospel*].

14 Greet ye one another with a kiss of charity. [*Joseph Smith replaced the word "kiss" with "salutation" in several other places, for instance, 1 Thessalonians 5:26*]. Peace be with you all that are in Christ Jesus [*who have taken upon you the name of Jesus Christ*]. Amen.

THE SECOND EPISTLE GENERAL OF
PETER

Second Peter seems to have been written after the persecutions heaped upon the Christians by Nero, Emperor of Rome, had died off somewhat (see notes at the beginning of First Peter, in this study guide). Consequently, many Bible scholars set the approximate date of this letter to be around AD 65 to AD 68, shortly before Peter's death. It was apparently written to the same general audience of Saints to whom First Peter was written. See Bible Dictionary under "Peter, Epistles of." Some scholars believe it was written from Rome. It seems that the real danger to the Church at this time is internal apostasy. Peter is the President of the Church and as such, strengthens the members by teaching them how to make their calling and elections sure (chapter 1), how to avoid personal apostasy by recognizing false teachings and apostate doctrines being taught by some members of the Church (chapter 2), and by warning them not to get caught up in false teachings about the Second Coming (chapter 3.)

SECOND PETER 1

The Prophet Joseph Smith said that "Peter penned the most sublime language of any of the apostles." See *History of the Church*, Vol. 5, p. 392. Certainly, this chapter is a wonderful example of the "sublime language" of this humble and powerful Apostle of the Lord. In it, Peter teaches the Saints how to become Christ like, thus making their callings and elections sure, in other words, how to make sure that they attain exaltation.

1 SIMON Peter, a servant and an apostle of Jesus Christ, to them [to members of the Church] that have obtained like precious faith with us [who have obtained the same precious faith in Christ which we have] through the righteousness of God [the Father] and our Saviour Jesus Christ:

Next, in verse 2, Peter emphasizes that knowledge about the Father and about Jesus Christ is power. Joseph Smith said "Knowledge is the power of salvation." (Teachings of the Prophet Joseph Smith, p. 306—you may wish to read pp. 304–306.) This ties in with D&C 131:6 which says, "It is impossible for a man to be saved in ignorance" meaning ignorance of the gospel.

2 Grace and peace be multiplied unto you through the knowledge of God, and of Jesus our Lord,

3 According as his divine power hath given unto us all things that pertain unto life and godliness [God has taught us everything we need to gain exaltation and to become gods], through the knowledge of him [the Father] that hath called us to glory and virtue [who has called us by His Son Jesus Christ to join Him in eternal glory and righteousness]:

4 Whereby are given unto us exceeding great and precious promises [through the teachings we have been given, we receive the promises of exaltation]: that by these ye might be partakers of the divine nature [that through these teachings and promises you can become like God], having escaped [overcome] the corruption [wickedness] that is in the world through lust [which comes from uncontrolled worldly passions].

Next, Peter will give a detailed set of steps which can lead to making our "calling and election sure" (verse 10). First, though, we need a very basic explanation of what the phrase "calling and election made sure" means. In its most basic sense, it means to "make our exaltation certain." Exaltation means becoming like our Father in Heaven (D&C 76:95) through entering into the highest degree of glory in the celestial kingdom (D&C 131:1–4), becoming gods, having our own spirit offspring (D&C 132:19–20), creating worlds for them, and making exaltation available to them in the same way our Father has made it available to us. Our Father in Heaven "calls" all of His children to make themselves worthy to return to Him in exaltation, through the gospel of His Son, Jesus Christ. Those of His children who heed this "calling" and do all they can to make themselves worthy are cleansed and qualified by the Atonement, "after all they can do" (2 Nephi 25:23), to be "elected by God" to enter exaltation. Thus, they are "called" by their Father to return to Him. If they follow the course requirements for exaltation, they are eventually "elected" by Him to receive it.

Technically, the Father has turned it over to the Savior to be our final judge. "The Father judgeth no man, but hath committed all judgment unto the Son" (John 5:22.) Thus, when the Savior "elects" or "votes" for you to enter exaltation, you are in! Another way to put it is this: "Calling and election" is another way of saying "exaltation." If we live righteously and repent and use the Atonement completely, we make our exaltation "sure" or "certain." Peter gives us instructions on how to do this, in verses 5–12. You may wish to pay special attention to how he sequenced these attributes and how they build off each other.

5 And beside this, giving all diligence, add to your faith virtue [*moral goodness; chastity; purity*]; and to virtue knowledge [*knowledge of the gospel; see verse 3*];

6 And to knowledge temperance [*self-control*]; and to temperance patience; and to patience godliness [*Christ-like attributes; reverence toward God*];

7 And to godliness brotherly kindness; and to brotherly kindness charity [*see 1 Corinthians 13*].

8 For if these things be in you, and abound [*if these attributes are thoroughly ingrained in your personality and your life*], they make you that ye shall neither be barren [*unproductive*] nor unfruitful in the knowledge of our Lord Jesus Christ [*they will produce the highest possible results of the gospel, namely, exaltation*]. [*In other words, you will be on your way to exaltation.*]

9 But he that lacketh these things is blind [*spiritually blind*], and cannot see afar off [*and has no wisdom*], and hath forgotten that he was purged [*cleansed*] from his old sins.

10 Wherefore the rather, brethren, give diligence [*therefore, be all the more anxious*] to make your calling and election sure: for if ye do these things, ye shall never fall: [*In other words, if you do these things, you can plan on obtaining exaltation.*]

11 For so [*thus*] an entrance [*into exaltation*] shall be ministered [*given*] unto you abundantly [*with all the promised blessings*] into the everlasting kingdom [*celestial exaltation*] of our Lord and Saviour Jesus Christ.

12 Wherefore I will not be negligent to put you always in remembrance of these things [*this is why I will keep emphasizing these things to you*], though ye know them [*even though you already know them*], and be established in the present truth [*and are already living them*].

13 Yea, I think it meet [*necessary*], as long as I am in this tabernacle [*as long as I live*], to stir you up by putting you in remembrance [*to keep reminding you of these things*];

14 Knowing that shortly I must put off this my tabernacle [*knowing that*

I will soon die], even as our Lord Jesus Christ hath shewed me [*in the way which the Lord Jesus Christ showed me I would die*].

According to John 21:18–19, we understand that the Savior told Peter that he, too, would be crucified because of his faithfulness to the gospel. Tradition has it that Peter was crucified upside down in Rome as early as AD 64 or as late as AD 68.

15 Moreover I will endeavour [*attempt*] that ye may be able after my decease [*after my death*] to have these things always in remembrance.

16 For we have not followed cunningly devised fables [*cleverly made up false doctrines*], when we made known unto you the power and coming of our Lord Jesus Christ, but were eyewitnesses of his majesty [*we (Peter, James, and John) saw the Savior personally, including His glory when He was transfigured; see verses 17–18*].

17 For he received from God the Father honour and glory, when there came such a voice to him from the excellent glory, This is my beloved Son, in whom I am well pleased [*see Matthew 17:1–5*].

18 And this voice which came from heaven we heard, when we were with him in the holy mount [*the Mount of Transfiguration*].

19 We have also a more sure word of prophecy [*See D&C 131:5*]; whereunto ye do well that ye take heed [*to which you would be wise to pay close attention*], as unto a light that shineth in a dark place [*as if it were a light lighting the way for you through the darkness*], until the day dawn [*until the morning comes*], and the day star arise in your hearts:

JST 2 Peter 1:19

19 We have therefore a more sure knowledge of the word of prophecy, to which word of prophecy ye do well that ye take heed, as unto a light which shineth in a dark place, until the day dawn, and the day star arise in your hearts;

Bruce R. McConkie explained the phrase "until the day dawn, and the day star arise in your hearts" in verse 19, above, as follows: "Until the Second Coming of the Lord; until the Millennial day dawns; until the day when 'the root and the offspring of David' who is 'the bright and morning star' (Rev. 22:16) shall reign personally on earth and be the companion, confidant, and friend of those whose calling and election is sure and who are thus called forth as 'kings and priests' to live and 'reign on earth' (Rev. 5:10) with him a thousand years." (Bruce R. McConkie, *Doctrinal New Testament Commentary*, 3 vols. [Salt Lake City: Bookcraft, 1965–1973], Vol. 3, p. 355.)

20 Knowing this first, that no prophecy of the scripture is of any private interpretation. [*In other words, you must not twist the meaning of the scriptures to suit your own purposes.*]

JST 2 Peter 1:20

20 Knowing this first, that no prophecy of the scriptures is **given of any private will of man**.

21 For the prophecy [*scriptures which include prophecies*] came not in old time [*in ancient times*] by the will of man: but holy men [*prophets*] of God spake [*spoke*] as they were moved [*inspired*] by the Holy Ghost.

SECOND PETER 2

As mentioned in the general introduction to Second Peter, above, it appears that many false doctrines were working their way into the Church at the time Peter wrote this epistle (letter.) In this chapter, Peter warns the Saints about such things. He will use strong language as he condemns the wicked practices found among unrighteous people.

1 BUT there were false prophets also among the people [*in the past; see 2 Peter 1:21, above*], even as there shall be false teachers among you, who privily [*secretly; cunningly;* Strong's #3919] shall bring in damnable heresies [*false doctrines which will make you lose eternal life;* Strong's #0684], even denying the Lord that bought them, and bring upon themselves swift destruction.

JST 2 Peter 2:1

1 But there were false prophets also among the people, even as there shall be false teachers among you who privily shall bring in **abominable** heresies, even denying the Lord that bought them, and bring upon themselves swift destruction.

2 And many shall follow their [*the teachers of false doctrines in verse 1, above*] pernicious [*evil, destructive*] ways; by reason of whom the way of truth shall be evil spoken of [*which will cause the true gospel of Christ to be referred to as false*].

3 And through covetousness [*because of greed and desire for worldly gain*] shall they with feigned [*pretended*] words make merchandise of you [*take advantage of you*]: whose judgment now of a long time lingereth not, and their damnation slumbereth not [*they will soon be caught up with by the judgments and punishments of God*].

JST 2 Peter 2:3

3 And through covetousness shall they with feigned words make merchandise of you; whose judgment now of a long time lingereth not, and their **destruction** slumbereth not.

4 For if God spared not the angels that sinned [*the one third who were cast out as a result of the war in heaven; see Revelation 12:4 and 7–9*], but cast them down to hell, and delivered them into chains of darkness, to be reserved unto judgment;

5 And spared not the old world [*and punished the wicked at the time of Noah and the flood*], but

saved Noah the eighth person [*one of the eight people who survived the flood by entering the ark; see 1 Peter 3:20*], a preacher of righteousness, bringing in the flood upon the world of the ungodly [*the wicked*];

6 And turning the cities of Sodom and Gomorrha into ashes condemned them with an overthrow [*with complete destruction*], making them an ensample [*example*] unto those that after should live ungodly [*as an example to the wicked who came along later*];

7 And delivered just Lot [*and only saved Lot from the destruction of Sodom and Gomorrah*], vexed with [*oppressed, offended by*] the filthy conversation [*filthy behavior; Strong's #0391*] of the wicked:

8 (For that righteous man dwelling among them, in seeing and hearing, vexed his righteous soul from day to day with their unlawful [*evil*] deeds;)

9 The Lord knoweth how to deliver the godly out of temptations, and to reserve the unjust [*the wicked*] unto the day of judgment to be punished:

10 But chiefly [*mainly*] them [*the wicked*] that walk after the flesh in the lust of uncleanness [*who live lustful and evil lives*], and despise government [*hate rules and regulations*]. Presumptuous [*boastful, daring; Strong's #5113*] are they, selfwilled [*arrogant: Strong's #0829*], they are not afraid to speak

evil of dignities [*of angels; of the things of God;* Strong's *#1391*].

11 Whereas angels, which are greater in power and might [*than the wicked men spoken of in the above verses*], bring not railing accusation against them [*do not lower themselves to rant and rave, like the wicked themselves do against the righteous, (see verse 12, next)*] before the Lord [*in the presence of the Lord*].

12 But these [*the wicked*], as natural brute beasts [*are like animals who follow their base instincts*], made to be taken and destroyed, speak evil of the things [*things of righteousness*] that they understand not; and shall utterly perish in their own corruption [*will cause their own destruction; see Mormon 4:5*];

13 And shall receive the reward of unrighteousness [*and will receive the punishment which comes to the wicked*], as they that count it pleasure to riot [*live riotously*] in the day time [*in broad daylight; in other words, they take evil satisfaction in flaunting their wickedness in public*]. Spots they are and blemishes [*they are defects and blemishes on society*], sporting [*amusing*] themselves with their own deceivings [*cunning deceptiveness*] while they feast with you [*even while associating with you*];

14 Having eyes full of adultery [*always lusting after women and looking for opportunities to break*

the law of chastity], and that cannot cease from sin; beguiling unstable souls [*seducing insecure people*]: an heart they have exercised with covetous practices [*their hearts are filled with evil greed*]; cursed children [*immature people who are bringing the punishments of God upon themselves*]:

15 Which have forsaken the right way [*who have left the gospel*], and are gone astray [*and have strayed away*], following the way of Balaam [*see Numbers 22*] the son of Bosor, who loved the wages of unrighteousness [*was trying to profit from wickedness and going against the Lord*];

16 But was rebuked for his iniquity: the dumb ass [*the donkey who normally could not talk*] speaking with man's voice forbad the madness of the prophet [*told Balaam not to do what he was foolishly planning to do*].

17 These are wells without water [*the wicked are like empty wells, they produce nothing of value to others*], clouds that are carried with a tempest [*they have nothing to anchor them and are blown all around by their evil lusts*]; to whom the mist of darkness is reserved for ever [*eternal punishments in hell are being prepared for them; compare with D&C 19:3–12*].

18 For when they [*the apostates, false teachers and wicked people spoken about in the above verses*] speak great swelling words of vanity [*long, empty speeches which draw attention to themselves*], they

allure through the lusts of the flesh [*they use lustful physical desires to attract*], through much wantonness [*especially sexual passions*], those that were clean escaped from them who live in error [*who had successfully gotten away from them and their wicked lifestyles*]; [*In other words, wicked people are quite successful at deceiving and destroying others, who would normally not join in wickedness, through the use of pornography and lustful living.*]

19 While they promise them liberty [*while they promise them freedom from rules and regulations, commandments, etc.*], they themselves are the servants of corruption [*they themselves are enslaved by their own wickedness*]: for of whom a man is overcome, of the same is he brought in bondage. [*In other words, whatever overpowers a person becomes his or her master.*]

20 For if after they have escaped the pollutions [*wickedness*] of the world through the knowledge of the Lord and Saviour Jesus Christ [*through the Atonement of Christ*], they are again entangled therein, and overcome [*they get tangled up in sin again and are overpowered by it*], the latter end is worse with them than the beginning [*they are worse off than they were before they repented the first time; compare with D&C 82:3 and 7*].

21 For it had been [*would have been*] better for them not to have known the way of righteousness,

than, after they have known it, to turn from the holy commandment delivered unto them.

22 But it is happened unto them according to the true proverb [*but what has happened to them is just like the old saying in Proverbs 26:11, which says*], The dog is [*has*] turned to [*is eating*] his own vomit again; and the sow [*pig*] that was washed [*was clean*] to [*has returned to*] her wallowing in the mire.

SECOND PETER 3

In this chapter, Peter will prophesy that when the time of the Second Coming is getting near, many will scoff at it and will not believe in it. He will teach that the Second Coming will catch many people off guard, reminding them that the same attitude prevailed at the time of the flood. He will teach that one day in heaven is a thousand years here on earth. He will give additional details about the Second Coming and the beginning of the Millennium. The JST (The Joseph Smith Translation of the Bible) will be tremendously helpful to us in understanding this last chapter of Peter's second letter to the Saints. Joseph Smith made changes to all but one verse (verse 14). In some cases, the changes are minor wording changes (or even punctuation changes, as in verse 16, where a semicolon is replaced by a comma), but the changes in other verses are crucial to correct understanding of Peter's message.

1 THIS second epistle [*letter*], beloved, I now write unto you; in both which I stir up your pure minds by way of remembrance [*in which I am going to remind you of several important things*]:

JST 2 Peter 3:1

1 This second epistle, beloved, I now write unto you; **in which I** stir up your pure minds by way of remembrance;

2 That ye may be mindful of [*remember*] the words which were spoken before [*in times past*] by the holy prophets, and of the commandment of [*and I am going to remind you about the commandments you have received from the Savior through*] us the apostles of the Lord and Saviour:

3 Knowing this first, that there shall come in the last days scoffers [*mockers of righteousness*], walking after their own lusts [*who make their own rules and live in wickedness*],

JST 2 Peter 3:3

3 Knowing this first, **that in the last days there shall come scoffers,** walking after their own lusts.

4 And saying, Where is the promise of his coming [*where is this much talked about Second Coming*]? for since the fathers [*ancestors*] fell asleep [*died*], all things continue [*everything keeps right on going*] as they were from the beginning of the creation. [*In other words, they have been talking about this*

"Second Coming" since way back, and nothing has happened. Life keeps right on going. There is nothing to worry about.]

JST 2 Peter 3:4

Denying the Lord Jesus Christ, and saying, Where is the promise of his coming? for since the fathers fell asleep, all things **must continue as they are, and have continued as they are** from the beginning of the creation.

Next, Peter will remind them that people didn't expect the flood to happen either.

5 For this they willingly are ignorant of [*there is one thing that they are intentionally ignoring*], that by the word of God the heavens were of old, and the earth standing out of the water and in the water: [*In other words, they are ignoring the fact that God created the earth and that when He says something will happen, it will happen!*]

JST 2 Peter 3:5

5 For this they willingly are ignorant of, **that of old the heavens, and the earth standing in the water and out of the water, were created by the word of God**;

6 Whereby the world that then was, being overflowed with water, perished: [*In other words, when God gave the "word," the earth was flooded and the wicked perished.*]

JST 2 Peter 3:6

6 **And by the word of God**, the world that then was, being overflowed with water, perished;

7 But the heavens and the earth, which are now [*which currently exist*], by the same word [*by that same power*] are kept in store [*are preserved*], reserved unto fire against the day of judgment and perdition [*utter destruction;* Strong's #0684] of ungodly men.

JST 2 Peter 3:7

7 But the heavens, and the earth which are now, **are kept in store by the same word**, reserved unto fire against the day of judgment and perdition of ungodly men [*being saved until it is time to burn the wicked*].

8 But, beloved, be not ignorant of this one thing, that one day [*in heaven*] is with the Lord as a thousand years [*on earth*], and a thousand years [*on earth*] as one day [*is as one day in heaven*]. [*In other words, what seems like a long time to us on earth is just a short time in heaven. The point is that even though wicked men claim that it has been "forever" that prophets have been saying that Jesus will come again, and so it is just an empty threat, yet it surely will come, and it will be just a "little while longer" in the Lord's time system.*]

JST 2 Peter 3:8

8 **But concerning the coming of the Lord, beloved, I would not have you ignorant of this one**

thing, that one day is with the Lord as a thousand years, and a thousand years as one day.

9 The Lord is not slack [*being slow,* Strong's *#1019*] concerning his promise, as some men count slackness [*like some people think*]; but is longsuffering to us-ward [*In other words, He is very patient, giving us plenty of time to repent*], not willing that any should perish [*He doesn't want any of us to be destroyed*], but that all should come to repentance [*rather, He wants everyone to repent*].

JST 2 Peter 3:9

9 The Lord is not slack concerning his promise **and coming**, as some men count slackness; **but long-suffering toward us**, not willing that any should perish, but that all should come to repentance.

Notice in the JST of verse 10 that Joseph Smith points out that only "corruptible" things (people and things which deal with and represent evil and wickedness) will be burned. The verse, as it stands in our Bible, would lead the reader to believe that everything on the earth ("the works that are therein") will be destroyed by the burning which accompanies the Second Coming.

10 But the day of the Lord will come as a thief in the night [*the wicked will be caught off guard*]; in the which [*at which time*] the heavens shall pass away with a great noise, and the elements shall melt with fervent heat, the earth

also and the works that are therein shall be burned up.

JST 2 Peter 3:10

10 But the day of the Lord will come as a thief in the night, in the which the heavens shall **shake, and the earth also shall tremble, and the mountains shall melt, and pass away with a great noise, and the elements shall be filled with fervent heat; the earth also shall be filled, and the corruptible works which are therein** shall be burned up.

D&C 106:4 teaches us that the wicked will be caught off guard by the Second Coming; however, D&C 106:5 teaches us that the righteous will be expecting the Second Coming and thus will not be caught off guard when it actually happens.

11 Seeing then that all these things shall be dissolved, what manner of persons ought ye to be in all holy conversation and godliness, [*In other words, since all these wicked people and evil things, which could include pornography, Satanic rites, evil literature, evil media, etc., are going to be destroyed, what kind of people do you think you ought to be?*]

JST 2 Peter 3:11

11 **If then all these things shall be destroyed**, what manner of persons ought ye to be in **holy conduct** and godliness,

12 Looking for and hasting unto the coming of the day of God,

wherein the heavens being on fire shall be dissolved, and the elements shall melt with fervent heat?

JST 2 Peter 3:12

12 Looking unto, and preparing for the day of the coming of the Lord wherein the corruptible things of the heavens being on fire, shall be dissolved, and the mountains shall melt with fervent heat?

13 Nevertheless we, according to his promise, look for new heavens and a new earth, wherein dwelleth righteousness. [*In other words, we are looking forward to the Millennium and the celestial kingdom.*]

JST 2 Peter 3:13

13 Nevertheless, **if we shall endure, we shall be kept** [*preserved*] according to his promise. **And we look for a** new heavens, and a new earth wherein dwelleth righteousness.

14 Wherefore, beloved, seeing that ye look for such things, be diligent that ye may be found of [*by*] him [*Christ*] in peace, without spot, and blameless [*having been cleansed by His Atonement*].

15 And account [*keep in mind*] that the longsuffering of our Lord is salvation; even as our beloved brother Paul also according to the wisdom given unto him hath written unto you; [*In other words, keep in mind what Paul wrote you about how the Lord is so patient and gives us plenty of time to work out our salvation.*]

JST 2 Peter 3:15

15 And **account, even as our beloved brother Paul** also, according to the wisdom given unto him, hath written unto you, **the long-suffering and waiting of our Lord, for salvation.**

16 As also in all his epistles [*Paul's letters*], speaking in them of these things; in which are some things hard to be understood [*some of Paul's writings are hard to understand*], which they that are unlearned and unstable wrest [*and so some who do not know the gospel very well or who are not committed to the Church misinterpret and twist what Paul wrote*], as they do also the other scriptures [*just like they do other scriptures*], unto their own destruction [*which will lead to their destruction*].

JST 2 Peter 3:16

16 As also in all his epistles, speaking in them of these things, in which are some things hard to be understood, which they **who** are unlearned and unstable wrest, as they do also the other scriptures, unto their own destruction.

17 Ye therefore, beloved, seeing ye know these things before [*ahead of time because of prophecies*], beware lest ye also, being led away with the error of the wicked [*mistakes in interpreting the scriptures*], fall from your own stedfastness [*from your faithfulness in the Church*].

JST 2 Peter 3:17

17 Ye therefore, beloved, seeing ye **know before the things which are coming**, beware lest ye also being led away with the error of the wicked, fall from your own steadfastness.

18 But grow in grace, and in the knowledge of our Lord and Saviour Jesus Christ. To him be glory both now and for ever. Amen.

JST 2 Peter 3:18

18 But grow in grace **and the** knowledge of our Lord and Savior Jesus Christ. To him be glory both now and for ever. Amen.

THE FIRST EPISTLE OF
JOHN

Bible scholars do not know when this letter was written, but many believe it was written around AD 96. This epistle was written by the Apostle John, who, with Peter and James, served as the First Presidency of the Church after the Savior was taken up into heaven. John wrote five of the books which are contained in our New Testament, namely, The Gospel of John, First John, Second John, Third John, and The Book of Revelation. This great Apostle was translated and is still on earth, helping with the work of the Lord (see D&C 7). In 1831, Joseph Smith told the early members of the Church that John was, at that time, working with the lost ten tribes, getting them ready for their return (see *History of the Church*, Vol. 1, p. 176.) John was with Peter and James when they gave Joseph Smith and Oliver Cowdery the Melchizedek Priesthood (see D&C 27:12.)

FIRST JOHN 1

It seems that by the time this letter was written, many Christians were beginning to doubt that Jesus had actually been born into a mortal body and that He had actually lived as a mortal being on earth. They were teaching that such could not be the case because God is holy and certainly would not lower Himself to be so closely associated with unclean mankind. Thus, they were teaching that the birth, baptism, mortal mission, suffering in the Garden of Gethsemane, crucifixion, resurrection, and ascension into heaven did not literally happen, because such things could not actually happen to God. John, who was an eyewitness to the Savior's mortal mission, Atonement, resurrection, and ascension bears strong witness that these things did literally happen.

1 THAT which was from the beginning, which we have heard, which we have seen with our eyes, which we have looked upon, and our hands have handled, of the Word of life;

JST 1 John 1:1

1 **Brethren, this is the testimony which we give of** that which was from the beginning [*in other words, Jesus Christ*], which we have heard [*to whom we have personally listened*], which we have seen with our eyes, which we have looked upon, and our hands have handled [*whom we have personally touched*], of the Word of life;

2 (For the life was manifested [*Christ was here on earth*], and we have seen it [*Him*], and bear witness [*and testify of Him*], and shew unto you [*point out to you*] that eternal life, which was with the Father, and was manifested [*clearly shown*] unto us;)

3 That [*the things*] which we have seen and heard declare we unto you, that [*so that*] ye also may have fellowship with us [*so that you may join with us*]: and truly our fellowship is with the Father [*and indeed we have joined with the Father*], and with his Son Jesus Christ.

4 And these things write we unto you, that your joy may be full.

5 This then is the message which we have heard of him [*which we have heard from the Father through Christ*], and declare unto you, that God is light, and in him is no darkness at all [*as Jesus said, "I am the light of the world; he that followeth me shall not walk in darkness, but shall have the light of life"; John 8:12*].

6 If we say that we have fellowship with him [*if we claim that we worship the Father*], and walk in darkness, we lie, and do not the truth:

7 But if we walk in the light, as he is in the light, we have fellowship one with another [*we are truly united as brothers and sisters in the gospel*], and the blood of Jesus Christ his Son cleanseth us from all sin.

8 If we say that we have no sin [*if we say that we are perfect*], we deceive ourselves, and the truth is not in us.

9 If we confess our sins [*and repent*], he is faithful and just [*fair*] to forgive us our sins, and to cleanse us from all unrighteousness.

10 If we say that we have not sinned, we make him a liar [*because He said we all need to repent of sins; see D&C 49:8*], and his word is not in us.

FIRST JOHN 2

In this chapter, we are reminded that Jesus Christ is our Advocate with the Father (see similar verses in D&C 45:3–5). We are given counsel for daily living of the gospel and avoiding those who fight against the teachings of Christ (antichrists.)

1 MY little children, these things write I unto you, that ye sin not [*I am writing this to you to help you avoid sinning*]. And if any man sin, we have an advocate with the Father, Jesus Christ the righteous [*compare with D&C 45:3–5*]:

JST 1 John 2:1

1 My little children, these things write I unto you, that ye sin not. **But** if any man sin **and repent**, we have an advocate with the Father, Jesus Christ the righteous;

2 And he is the propitiation [*the Atonement*] for our sins: and not for ours only, but also for the sins of the whole world.

3 And hereby we do know that we know him, if we keep his commandments [*here is how you demonstrate that you know Him, you keep His commandments*].

4 He that saith, I know him, and keepeth not his commandments, is a liar, and the truth is not in him.

5 But whoso keepeth his word [*keeps His commandments*], in him verily is the love of God perfected [*the love of God as shown in the gospel will work with him until he reaches exaltation*]: hereby know we that we are in him [*and this is how we ourselves know that we are in harmony with God*].

6 He that saith he abideth in him [*he who claims to follow Christ*] ought himself also so to walk, even as he walked [*ought to follow in Christ's footsteps*].

7 Brethren, I write no new commandment unto you, but an old commandment which ye had from the beginning. The old commandment is the word which ye have heard from the beginning.

JST 1 John 2:7

7 Brethren, I write **a new** commandment unto you, **but it is the same commandment** which ye had from the beginning [*which you have had all along*]. The old commandment is the word which ye have heard from the beginning.

8 Again, [*I repeat*] a new commandment I write unto you, which thing is true in him and in you: because the darkness is past, and the true light now shineth.

JST 1 John 2:8

8 Again, a new commandment I write unto you, which thing **was of old ordained of God** [*which is what God gave us long ago*]; **and** is true in him, and in you; because the darkness is past **in you** [*you have repented and changed and the spiritual darkness has left you*], and the true light now shineth.

9 He that saith he is in the light [*someone who claims to be a faithful member of the Church*], and hateth his brother, is in darkness even until now [*is still in spiritual darkness*].

10 He that loveth his brother abideth in the light [*is living as Christ would have him live*], and there is

none occasion of stumbling in him [*and there is nothing holding him back*].

11 But he that hateth his brother is in darkness [*is living in spiritual darkness*], and walketh in darkness, and knoweth not whither he goeth [*and does not realize where he is heading*], because that darkness hath blinded his eyes [*because he has become spiritually blind and insensitive*].

12 I write unto you, little children, because your sins are forgiven you for his name's sake [*because little children are not accountable for sins because of Christ's Atonement; see Mosiah 3:16; D&C 29:46–47*].

13 I write unto you, fathers, because ye have known him [*Christ*] that is from the beginning. I write unto you, young men, because ye have overcome the wicked one [*because you have overcome the temptations of the devil*]. I write unto you, little children, because ye have known the Father.

14 I have written unto you, fathers, because ye have known him [*Christ*] that is from the beginning. I have written unto you, young men, because ye are strong, and the word of God abideth in you [*and you are living the gospel*], and ye have overcome the wicked one.

15 Love not the world, neither the things that are in the world [*don't become involved in worldly wickedness*]. If any man love the world [*participates in the wickedness of*

worldly people*], the love of the Father is not in him [*the Father cannot bless him as he would like to; see "Divine Love" by Elder Russell M. Nelson of the Quorum of the Twelve Apostles,* Ensign, *February 2003, pp. 20–25*].

JST 1 John 2:15

15 Love not the world, neither the things that are **of** the world. If any man love the world, the love of the Father is not in him.

16 For all that is in the world, the lust of the flesh, and the lust of the eyes, and the pride of life, is not of the Father, but is of the world. [*In other words, all of the wickedness in the world does not come from the Father, rather comes from other sources.*]

JST 1 John 2:16

16 For all in the world that is of the **lusts of the flesh,** and the lust of the eyes, and the pride of life, is not of the Father, but is of the world.

17 And the world passeth away [*the wicked and the wickedness on the world will be done away with at the Second Coming and again after the little season at the end of the Millennium; see D&C 5:19 and 88:111–14*], and the lust thereof: but he that doeth the will of God abideth for ever [*will attain the celestial kingdom and will live on earth forever when it becomes their celestial kingdom; see D&C 130:9–11*].

18 Little children, it is the last time [*we know that the church which*

Christ established is entering its last days, because the great apostasy is underway; compare with 2 Thessalonians 2:1–3]: and as ye have heard that antichrist [*false prophets; see 2 Peter 2:18, footnote a*] shall come, even now are there many antichrists [*apostates and false prophets*]; whereby [*this is how*] we know that it is the last time.

19 They went out from us [*many of them were members of the Church*], but they were not of us [*but they were not faithful*]; for if they had been of us [*if they had been faithful*], they would no doubt have continued with us: but they went out, that they might be made manifest that they were not all of us [*they left us and it has become obvious that they were apostates*].

20 But ye have an unction [*an anointing; Strong's #5545; in other words, you have the Gift of the Holy Ghost; see McConkie, Doctrinal New Testament Commentary, Vol. 3, p. 383*] from the Holy One [*given to you by Christ*], and ye know all things [*and you have a testimony of what I am telling you*].

21 I have not written unto you because ye know not the truth, but because ye know it, and that no lie is of the truth [*no lie can be part of truth*].

22 Who is a liar but he that denieth that Jesus is the Christ? He is antichrist, that denieth the Father and the Son.

23 Whosoever denieth the Son, the same hath not the Father [*will not be accepted by the Father*]: [*but*] he that acknowledgeth the Son hath the Father also.

24 Let that therefore abide in you, which ye have heard from the beginning [*stand firm and steadfast in what you heard originally from us*]. If that which ye have heard from the beginning shall remain in you, ye also shall continue in the Son, and in the Father [*you will continue faithful to the Savior and the Father*].

JST 1 John 2:24

24 Let that therefore abide in you, which ye have heard from the beginning. If that which ye have heard from the beginning shall remain in you, ye **shall continue** in the Son, and **also** in the Father.

25 And this is the promise that he hath promised us, even eternal life [*exaltation*].

26 These things have I written unto you concerning them [*false prophets and teachers*] that seduce [*deceive*] you.

27 But the anointing [*see verse 20, above*] which ye have received of him [*from Christ*] abideth in you [*you have the Gift of the Holy Ghost*], and ye need not that any man teach you [*and you have no reason to be led astray by false teachings*]: but as the same anointing teacheth you of all things [*but since the Holy Ghost teaches you all things; John 14:26*],

and is truth, and is no lie, and even as it hath taught you, ye shall abide in him [*do as the Holy Ghost teaches you and remain true to Christ*].

28 And now, little children, abide in him [*remain true to Christ*]; that, when he shall appear, we may have confidence, and not be ashamed before him [*in His presence*] at his coming.

29 If ye know that he is righteous, ye know that every one that doeth righteousness is born of him [*is "born again" and becomes a "son" or "daughter" of Christ; compare with Mosiah 5:7*].

FIRST JOHN 3

One of the first things John teaches in this chapter, as he continues to bear witness that Jesus Christ literally did come and dwell on earth and minister in the flesh, is that if we strive to be righteous and live the gospel, we can literally become like Him (verse 2).

1 BEHOLD [*consider*], what manner of [*kind of*] love the Father hath bestowed upon us, that we should be called the sons of God: [*In other words, consider the incredible love which the Father has given us, to allow us to someday become like He is, in other words, to be exalted. The terms "sons of God" and "daughters of God" are scriptural terms which mean exaltation; see Mosiah 5:7 and D&C 76:24.*] therefore the world knoweth us not [*worldly people don't understand us*], because it knew him not

[*because they don't understand the Father*].

Verse 2, next, teaches very clearly that we can become like Christ, just as Paul taught in Romans 8:17.

2 Beloved, now are we the sons of God [*followers of Christ, who will be exalted if we remain faithful*], and it doth not yet appear what we shall be [*and we don't understand everything about exaltation*]: but we know that, when he [*Christ*] shall appear, we shall be like him; for we shall see him as he is.

3 And every man that hath this hope in him [*everyone who hopes for exaltation*] purifieth himself, even as he [*Christ*] is pure.

4 Whosoever committeth sin transgresseth also the law: for sin is [*defined as*] the transgression of the law.

5 And ye know that he [*Christ*] was manifested [*sent*] to take away our sins; and in him is no sin [*and that He was perfect*].

6 Whosoever abideth in him [*whoever is faithful to Christ*] sinneth not: whosoever sinneth hath not seen him, neither known him [*whoever commits sin and does not repent, does not understand Christ's teachings*].

JST 1 John 3:6

6 Whosoever abideth in him sinneth not; whosoever **continueth in sin** hath not seen him, neither known him.

7 Little children, let no man deceive [*fool*] you: he that doeth righteousness is righteous, even as he is righteous [*he who follows Christ becomes righteous, just like Christ is righteous*].

8 He that committeth sin is of the devil; for the devil sinneth from the beginning. For this purpose the Son of God was manifested [*came to earth*], that he might destroy the works of the devil.

JST 1 John 3:8

8 He that **continueth** in sin is of the devil; for the devil sinneth from the beginning. For this purpose the Son of God was manifested, that he might destroy the works of the devil.

9 Whosoever is born of God doth not commit sin; for his seed remaineth in him: and he cannot sin, because he is born of God.

JST 1 John 3:9

9 Whosoever is born of God doth not **continue in** sin; **for the Spirit of God remaineth** in him; and he cannot **continue in** sin, because he is born of God, **having received that holy Spirit of promise** [*the gift of the Holy Ghost*].

10 In this the children of God are manifest, and the children of the devil [*this is how you can tell the true followers of God from the followers of the devil*]: whosoever doeth not righteousness is not of God, neither he that loveth not his brother.

11 For this is the message that ye heard from the beginning [*this is what the gospel is all about*], that we should love one another.

12 Not as Cain, who was of that wicked one [*who was inspired by Satan; see Moses 5:18–33*], and slew his brother [*Abel*]. And wherefore slew he him [*and why did he kill him*]? Because his own works were evil, and his brother's righteous.

13 Marvel not [*don't be surprised*], my brethren, if the world hate you [*if worldly, wicked people hate you*].

14 We know that we have passed from death [*from being spiritually dead*] unto life [*to being spiritually alive*], because we love the brethren [*because we love one another*]. He that loveth not his brother abideth in death [*remains spiritually dead*].

15 Whosoever hateth his brother is a murderer [*in his heart*]: and ye know that no murderer hath eternal life abiding in him.

16 Hereby perceive we the love of God, [*In other words, this is how we know that Christ loved us*] because he laid down his life for us: and we ought to lay down our lives for the brethren [*for each other*].

JST 1 John 3:16

16 Hereby perceive we the love of **Christ**, because he laid down his life for us; and we ought to lay down our lives for the brethren.

17 But whoso hath this world's good [*but a person who has plenty*], and seeth his brother have need [*and sees that his brother is in need*], and shutteth up his bowels of compassion from him [*and refuses to feel compassion toward him*], how dwelleth the love of God in him [*how could he have Christ-like love in his heart*]?

18 My little children, let us not love in word, neither in tongue [*let us not merely claim that we have Christ-like love*]; but in deed and in truth [*but let us show it through our good works*].

JST 1 John 3:18

18 My little children, let us not love in word, neither in tongue **only**; but in deed and in truth.

19 And hereby [*and if we do this*] we know that we are of the truth [*that we are genuine in the gospel*], and shall assure our hearts before him [*and we will have confidence someday in the presence of the Lord*].

20 For if our heart condemn us [*if the content of our heart condemns us*], God is greater than our heart, and knoweth all things [*God knows what is in our heart*].

21 Beloved, if our heart condemn us not [*if our heart is clean and pure*], then have we confidence toward God [*then we can approach God in confidence*].

22 And whatsoever we ask, we receive of him, because we keep his commandments, and do those things that are pleasing in his sight. [*In other words, if we are keeping His commandments, we can have faith when we pray and thus receive the blessings we need, provided it is in harmony with His will. See D&C 46:30 and 50:30 where it tells us that if we are pure before God, the Holy Ghost will tell us what we can ask for in prayer and thus we will receive what we ask for.*]

23 And this is his [*the Father's*] commandment, That we should believe on the name of his Son Jesus Christ, and love one another, as he gave us commandment [*like He commanded us to*].

24 And he that keepeth his commandments dwelleth in him, and he in him [*is close to Him and He is close to them*]. And hereby we know that he abideth in us, by the Spirit which he hath given us [*the way we can tell if God is close to us is that it will be manifest to us by the Holy Ghost*].

FIRST JOHN 4

Next, the Apostle John gives counsel to the Saints about detecting false spirits and false doctrine. You may wish to read D&C 129 also, with respect to detecting false spirits.

1 BELOVED, believe not every spirit [*don't believe everything you hear*], but try the spirits whether they are of God [*test the doctrines and spirits to see if what*

you are hearing is in harmony with the gospel]: because many false prophets are gone out into the world [*because there are many false prophets around*].

2 Hereby know ye [*here is how you can recognize*] the Spirit of God: Every spirit that confesseth [*testifies*] that Jesus Christ is come in the flesh [*that Jesus Christ literally was born into mortality*] is of God:

As mentioned in the general introduction to First John, one of the "false spirits" or false doctrines at the time John wrote this letter was the teaching that Christ, as a God, could not possibly have literally been born into a mortal body, because God would not lower Himself to associate so closely with corrupt mankind. Thus, John, in verse 2, above, states very clearly that one way to tell the difference between false teachers and those who teach truth is to listen to see if they bear testimony that Jesus literally came to earth in a mortal body.

3 And every spirit that confesseth not [*all who do not testify*] that Jesus Christ is come in the flesh is not of God: and this is that spirit of antichrist [*deceivers, false prophets, false teachers; compare with 2 John 1:7*], whereof ye have heard that it should come; and even now already is it in the world [*you have heard that the time would come when there are many antichrists (deceivers) and that time has come*].

JST 1 John 4:3

And every spirit that confesseth not that Jesus Christ is come in the flesh is not of God; and this is that spirit of antichrist, whereof ye have heard that it should come; and even now **it is already** in the world.

4 Ye are of God, little children, and have overcome them [*teachers of false doctrines*]: because greater is he [*God*] that is in you, than he [*the false teacher*] that is in the world.

5 They [*antichrists, false teachers*] are of the world [*are worldly*]: therefore speak they of the world, and the world [*worldly and wicked people*] heareth them [*listen to them*].

6 We are of God [*we are in tune with God*]: he that knoweth God heareth us [*people who are spiritually in tune listen to us*]; he that is not of God heareth not us [*will not listen to our message*]. Hereby know we [*this is how we tell the difference between*] the spirit of truth, and the spirit of error.

7 Beloved, let us love one another: for love is of God; and every one that loveth is born of God [*has the Spirit with them and is "born again"*], and knoweth God.

8 He that loveth not [*who doesn't love his fellow men*] knoweth not God; for God is love.

9 In this was manifested [*demonstrated, made clear*] the love of God toward us, because that God sent his only begotten Son into

the world, that we might live [*that we might be born "spiritually" and have eternal life*] through him [*Christ*].

10 Herein is love [*the love the Father has for us is shown by this*], not that we loved God, but that he loved us, and sent his Son to be the propitiation [*sacrifice; Atonement*] for our sins.

11 Beloved, if God [*the Father*] so loved us, we ought also to love one another.

12 No man hath seen God at any time. If we love one another, God dwelleth in us, and his love is perfected in us.

JST 1 John 4:12

12 No man hath seen God at any time, **except them who believe.** If we love one another, God dwelleth in us, and his love is perfected in us.

13 Hereby know we that we dwell in him, and he in us, because he hath given us of his Spirit [*the Holy Ghost tells us when we are in harmony with God*].

14 And we have seen and do testify that the Father sent the Son to be the Saviour of the world.

15 Whosoever shall confess [*accept*] that Jesus is the Son of God, God dwelleth in him, and he in God.

16 And we have known [*felt*] and believed the love that God hath to us. God is love; and he that dwelleth in love dwelleth in God, and God in him.

17 Herein is our love made perfect [*this is how our love becomes Christ-like love*], that we may have boldness [*confidence in the presence of God*] in the day of judgment: because as he is, so are we in this world [*because we have become clean through the Atonement*].

18 There is no fear [*of God*] in love; but perfect love casteth out fear: because fear hath torment [*fear of God comes from a guilty conscience*]. He that feareth is not made perfect in love.

19 We love him, because he first loved us.

20 If a man say, I love God, and hateth his brother, he is a liar: for he that loveth not his brother whom he hath seen, how can he love God whom he hath not seen?

21 And this commandment [*see Matthew 22:37–39*] have we from him, That he who loveth God love his brother also.

FIRST JOHN 5

As John concludes this letter, he, in effect, defines the term "born again."

1 WHOSOEVER [*whoever*] believeth that Jesus is the Christ is born of God [*experiences spiritual rebirth; compare with Alma 5:14*]: and every one that loveth him [*Heavenly Father*] that begat [*who is the Father of Jesus*] loveth

him [*Jesus*] also that is begotten of him [*who is Heavenly Father's Son*].

2 By this we know that we love the children of God [*our fellow beings*], when we love God, and keep his commandments [*compare with John 14:15 where the Savior said, "If ye love me, keep my commandments"*].

3 For this is the love of God, that we keep his commandments: and his commandments are not grievous [*are not difficult to keep, are not a burden*].

4 For whatsoever is born of God overcometh the world [*anyone who experiences spiritual rebirth successfully overcomes the evils and temptations of the world*]: and this is the victory that overcometh the world, even our faith [*and it is our faith in Christ which enables us to successfully overcome the world*].

5 Who is he that overcometh the world, but [*can anyone successfully overcome the temptations of the world except*] he that believeth that Jesus is the Son of God?

Next, the Apostle John uses the terms "water," "blood," and "Spirit" both literally and symbolically. You may wish to read Moses 6:59–60 in which this symbolism is also used. Basically, each of us, including the Savior, literally came into this world by the process of physical birth, which involved "water" (in the womb,) "blood" (involved in the birth process,) and "spirit" (our spirit bodies gave life to our physical, mortal bodies.) Symbolically, in order to be "born again," this time spiritually, we must be baptized by "water." We must receive the "Spirit," the Gift of the Holy Ghost." And we are saved from our sins, through repentance, by the "blood" of Christ. Note also the literal application to the Savior's crucifixion itself, wherein His spirit left His body when He was finished on the cross (John 19:30) and blood and water came forth from the wound in His side when the soldier pierced His side (John 19:33–34.)

6 This [*Christ*] is he that came by water and blood [*who was born into a mortal body by the birth process*], even Jesus Christ; not by water only, but by water and blood. And it is the Spirit [*the Holy Ghost*] that beareth witness, because the Spirit is truth [*the Holy Ghost guides us to the truth in all things; see John 16:13*].

7 For there are three that bear record in heaven, the Father, the Word [*Christ, the Son*], and the Holy Ghost: and these three are one [*work in complete unity and harmony with each other*].

8 And there are three that bear witness in earth [*there are three things here on earth which show us the way to salvation and enable us to achieve it, namely*], the Spirit [*the Holy Ghost*], and the water [*baptism*], and the blood [*the blood of Christ*]: and these three agree in one [*bring us into unity and harmony with God*].

9 If we receive the witness [*accept the testimony*] of men [*who bring us the gospel message*], the witness of God is greater [*we will receive a greater testimony from God*]: for this [*the testimony given by the Holy Ghost; see verse 6*] is the witness of God [*from the Father*] which he hath testified of his Son.

10 He that believeth on the Son of God hath the witness in himself [*receives the testimony of the Holy Ghost into his soul; see Joseph Smith's correction of 1 Corinthians 12:3 in which he says, "no man can know that Jesus is the Lord, but by the Holy Ghost"* (*Teachings of the Prophet Joseph Smith, p. 223*)]: he that believeth not God hath made him a liar [*anyone who rejects the testimony of Christ given them by the Holy Ghost, is, in effect, calling God a liar*]; because he believeth not the record [*the testimony given by the Holy Ghost*] that God [*the Father*] gave of his Son.

11 And this is the record [*what the Holy Ghost witnesses to us*], that God hath given to us eternal life [*that the Father has made exaltation available to us*], and this life is in his Son [*and this exaltation comes to us through Jesus Christ*].

12 He that hath the Son hath life [*he who is faithful to Christ receives exaltation*]; and he that hath not the Son of God hath not life [*he who is not faithful to Christ does not receive exaltation*].

13 These things have I written unto you that believe on the name of the Son of God; that ye may know

that ye have eternal life [*that you can achieve exaltation*], and that ye may believe on the name of the Son of God.

JST 1 John 5:13

13 These things have I written unto you that believe on the name of the Son of God; that ye may know that ye have eternal life, and that ye may **continue to** believe on the name of the Son of God.

14 And this is the confidence that we have in him [*the assurance we receive from the Father*], that, if we ask any thing according to his will [*D&C 46:30; 50:30*], he heareth us [*he will give it to us*]:

15 And if we know that he hear us, whatsoever we ask [*if it is "according to His will" (verse 14, above)*], we know that we have the petitions [*things we were asking*] that we desired of him.

Next John indicates that there is such thing as sin which cannot be forgiven. He refers to this as "sin unto death." You may wish to read D&C 76:31–35 where it reviews the sins which would lead one to become a son of perdition. You may also wish to read D&C 42:18, 76:103 and Revelation 22:15 wherein it indicates that first degree murder is unforgivable in the sense that such murderers will go to the telestial kingdom.

16 If any man see his brother sin a sin which is not unto death, he shall ask, and he shall give him

life for them that sin not unto death [*forgiveness, through repentance, is available except for unforgivable sins*]. There is a sin unto death: I do not say that he shall pray for it [*pray for forgiveness from it*].

17 All unrighteousness is sin: and there is a sin not unto death [*there are sins which can be forgiven*].

18 We know that whosoever is born of God sinneth not; but he that is begotten of God keepeth himself, and that wicked one toucheth him not.

JST 1 John 5:18

We know that whosoever is born of God [*anyone who is "born again"*] **continueth not in sin**; but he that is begotten of God [*who is "born*

again"] **and keepeth himself** [*and is always on guard against committing sin;* Strong's #5083], that wicked one **overcometh** him not [*Satan will not overcome him*].

19 And we know that we are of God [*are following God*], and the whole world lieth in wickedness.

20 And we know that the Son of God is come [*came to earth*], and hath given us an understanding, that we may know him [*the Father*] that is true, and we are in him [*and we are following Christ*] that is true, even in his Son Jesus Christ. This is the true God, and eternal life [*and this is how we gain exaltation*].

21 Little children, keep yourselves from idols [*avoid idol worship*]. Amen.

THE SECOND EPISTLE OF
JOHN

This brief letter by John seems to be an intimate note to family members, perhaps even to his wife and children. We don't know for sure. It was probably written about the same time as First John, but, again, Bible scholars don't know for sure.

There are no JST changes for this book.

SECOND JOHN 1

In this chapter, John briefly teaches the great value of striving to live

the gospel of Jesus Christ. He also warns against being influenced by or even agreeing with those who teach things against the true gospel.

1 THE elder [*John*] unto the elect lady and her children, whom I love in the truth; and not I only, but also all they [*the faithful members of the Church*] that have known the truth;

2 For the truth's sake, which dwelleth in us, and shall be with us for ever.

3 Grace be with you, mercy, and peace, from God the Father, and

from the Lord Jesus Christ, the Son of the Father, in truth and love.

4 I rejoiced greatly that I found of thy children walking in truth [*I am grateful that your children are living the gospel faithfully*], as we have received a commandment from the Father [*according to the commandments we have received from Heavenly Father*].

5 And now I beseech thee [*I urge you*], lady, not as though I wrote a new commandment unto thee [*not as if I were telling you anything you don't already know*], but that which we had from the beginning, that we love one another.

6 And this is love [*this is what truly helps us love one another, namely*], that we walk after his commandments [*keeping His commandments*]. This is the commandment, That, as ye have heard from the beginning, ye should walk in it [*keep it*].

7 For many deceivers are entered into the world, who confess not that Jesus Christ is come in the flesh [*there are many false prophets and false teachers in the world now who do not accept the fact that Jesus Christ came to us in a mortal body*]. This is a deceiver and an antichrist [*such people are deceivers and apostates; see 1 John 2:18, footnotes a and b*].

8 Look to yourselves [*watch out*], that we lose not those things which we have wrought [*already accomplished in the gospel*], but that we receive a full reward [*exaltation*].

9 Whosoever [*anyone who*] transgresseth, and abideth not [*does not remain faithful*] in the doctrine of Christ, hath not God [*does not have God in their lives*]. He that abideth in the doctrine of Christ, he hath both the Father and the Son [*he will obtain the full blessings promised to the faithful by the Father and the Son*].

10 If there come any unto you, and bring not this doctrine [*if any people come to you and their teachings are not in harmony with what Christ taught*], receive him not into your house, neither bid him God speed [*don't have anything to do with them*]:

11 For he that biddeth him God speed is partaker of his evil deeds [*if you lead him to believe that you agree with what he is teaching, you are a partner with him in his evil work*].

12 Having many things to write unto you, I would not write with paper and ink: but I trust to come unto you, and speak face to face [*I have many more things to say which I want to tell you in person, rather than writing them in this letter*], that [*so that*] our joy may be full.

13 The children of thy elect sister greet thee. Amen.

THE THIRD EPISTLE OF
JOHN

In this brief letter, John commends a member of the Church named Gaius for the good work he has accomplished.

There are no JST changes for this book.

THIRD JOHN 1

In this chapter, John compliments Gaius, as mentioned above, but also warns against getting involved with or even believing and following those whose example and teachings oppose the Church.

1 THE elder [*John*] unto the well-beloved Gaius, whom I love in the truth.

2 Beloved, I wish above all things that thou mayest prosper and be in health, even as thy soul prospereth [*I wish you prosperity and health to match your spiritual prosperity*].

3 For I rejoiced greatly, when the brethren came and testified of the truth that is in thee, even as thou walkest in the truth [*I rejoiced when I received word from the brethren that you are faithfully living the gospel*].

4 I have no greater joy than to hear that my children walk in truth.

5 Beloved, thou doest faithfully whatsoever thou doest to the brethren, and to strangers [*you perform faithful service to our traveling elders as well as nonmembers*];

6 Which have borne witness of [*who have told me about*] thy charity before the church: whom if thou bring forward on their journey after a godly sort, thou shalt do well [*and it would be wonderful if you would continue helping them on their way in their missionary travels and so forth*]:

7 Because that for his name's sake they went forth, taking nothing of the Gentiles [*because they are in the service of God and they do not receive assistance from nonmembers*].

8 We therefore ought to receive such [*we ought to be hospitable to them*], that we might be fellowhelpers to the truth [*so that we, ourselves, are involved in helping spread the gospel*].

9 I wrote unto the church [*I wrote to the ward there*]: but Diotrephes, who loveth to have the preeminence among them, receiveth us not [*but Diotrephes, who thinks himself to be a very important person, rejected us*].

It would appear that Diotrephes was a Gentile convert to the

Church who held a powerful political position in the community and who had been called to be a leader in one of the wards but who now had gone into apostasy. See *Strong's* #1361.

10 Wherefore, if I come, I will remember his deeds which he doeth, prating against us [*making false accusations against us:* Strong's #5396] with malicious [*vicious*] words: and not content therewith [*it is not enough in his mind to speak evil against us, but in addition*], neither doth he himself receive the brethren [*he will not allow the Lord's servants to come to him*], and forbiddeth them that would [*but he also forbids the members in his area to welcome them*], and casteth them out of the church [*and has them cast out of the church*].

11 Beloved, follow not [*do not get involved with*] that which is evil, but that which is good. He that doeth good is of God [*is in harmony with God*]: but he that doeth evil hath not seen God [*compare with JST 1 John 4:12; see 1 John 4:12, footnote a*].

12 Demetrius hath good report [*has a good reputation*] of all men, and of the truth itself: yea, and we also bear record; and ye know that our record is true.

13 I had many things to write, but I will not with ink and pen write unto thee:

14 But I trust I shall shortly see thee, and we shall speak face to face. Peace be to thee. Our friends salute [*greet*] thee. Greet the friends by name.

THE GENERAL EPISTLE OF
JUDE

Jude identifies himself as the "brother of James" (see verse 1, below). Thus, it appears quite possible to some Bible scholars that Jude was the "Juda," who was one of Jesus' half-brothers, spoken of in Mark 6:3. In his epistle (letter), Jude warns members of the Church to beware of people who claim to be Christians but who were giving in to sexual immorality which was widely accepted in the culture in which they lived. Jude also uses the term "first estate," which we use often in our doctrinal discussions concerning our premortal life and the war in heaven. Jude also mentions something not mentioned elsewhere in scripture, namely an event in which Michael (Adam) and Satan contend "over the body of Moses." See Bible Dictionary, p. 719, under "Jude, Epistle of."

JUDE 1

Watch for important doctrinal concepts in this chapter, such as "first estate" (verse 6), which is an important reference to our premortal existence (along with Jeremiah 1:5). As you may be aware, most Christian ministers do not teach that we had a premortal existence before coming to earth. So, if you have a Christian friend who is not aware of this, you might use Jeremiah 1:5 and Jude 1:6 to get them interested in learning more about it.

1 JUDE, the servant of Jesus Christ, and brother of James, to them that are sanctified [*in process of being made worthy to enter celestial glory*] by God the Father, and preserved in [*in process of being saved by*] Jesus Christ, and called [*called by the Father to come unto him through Jesus Christ*]:

JST Jude 1:1

1 Jude, the servant of **God, called of Jesus Christ**, and brother of James; to them **who** are sanctified **of the Father**; and preserved in Jesus Christ;

2 Mercy unto you, and peace, and love, be multiplied.

3 Beloved, when I gave all diligence to write unto you of the common salvation, it was needful for me to write unto you, and exhort [*warn*] you that ye should earnestly contend [*stand up*] for the faith [*gospel*] which was once

[*originally*] delivered unto the saints. [*In other words, there is much apostasy that is creeping into the Church and we must stick to the original teachings of the Savior and Apostles.*]

4 For there are certain men crept in unawares [*who have infiltrated the Church*], who were before of old ordained to this condemnation [*who are those spoken of in the scriptures who will be condemned for what they are doing*], ungodly [*wicked*] men, turning the grace of our God into lasciviousness [*turning from the gospel to sexual immorality*], and denying the only Lord God, and our Lord Jesus Christ [*and thus rejecting the only One who can save them*].

5 I will therefore put you in remembrance [*remind you*], though ye once knew this [*though you have already been taught this*], how that the Lord, having saved the people out of the land of Egypt, afterward destroyed them that believed not [*wicked Pharaoh and his armies were drowned in the Red Sea*].

6 And the angels [*the wicked spirits, in other words, the one third (Revelation 12:4)*] which kept not their first estate [*who did not earn the right to be born on earth, into this "second estate" (Abraham 3:26)*], but left their own habitation [*rejected the opportunity to have physical bodies of their own*], he [*God*] hath reserved in everlasting chains [*they will be sons of perdition forever*] under darkness [*in total spiritual darkness*] unto the

judgment of the great day [*as their final judgment*].

The phrase "left their own habitation" in verse 6, above, in Greek, means that they do not have a physical body as a dwelling place for the spirit. Joseph Smith used the word "habitation" in teaching that Satan will not have a physical body. He said, "The punishment of the devil was that he should not have a habitation like men." In referring to the privilege spirits have of obtaining physical bodies, Joseph Smith said that the spirits "who kept not their first estate" do not receive physical bodies. *Teachings of the Prophet Joseph Smith*, pp. 305–306.

7 Even as [*just like*] Sodom and Gomorrha, and the cities about them in like manner, giving themselves over to fornication [*sexual immorality*], and going after strange flesh [*homosexuality; see Jude 1:7, footnote c, in our Bible*], are set forth for [*are given as*] an example, suffering the vengeance of eternal fire.

8 Likewise also these filthy dreamers [*people who do not face reality*] defile the flesh [*pollute their bodies*], despise dominion [*despise being ruled by God, Priesthood leaders, etc.*], and speak evil of dignities [*and mock God, angels, Church leaders, and so forth*].

9 Yet Michael [*Adam*] the archangel, when contending with the devil he disputed about the body of Moses [*see note in the introduction to this chapter, above*], durst not bring against him a railing [*slanderous;* Strong's #0988] accusation, but said, The Lord rebuke thee.

Joseph Smith spoke of Moses not "railing" against the devil when he said, "The spirits of good men cannot interfere with the wicked beyond their prescribed bounds, for Michael, the Archangel, dared not bring a railing accusation against the devil, but said, 'The Lord rebuke thee, Satan.'" See *History of the Church*, vol. 4, pp. 575–76.

10 But these [*such people, filthy dreamers in verse 8, above*] speak evil of those things [*gospel truths and commandments*] which they know not [*which they do not understand or which they intentionally reject*]: but what they know naturally [*as carnal, sensual, and devilish, "natural men;" see Mosiah 3:19*] as brute beasts [*like animals*], in those things they corrupt [*destroy*] themselves.

11 Woe unto them! for they have gone in the way of Cain [*who opposed God and killed Abel; see Moses 5:16–33*], and ran greedily after the error of Balaam [*Numbers 22*] for reward, and perished in the gainsaying [*rebelling against God*] of Core [*Korah, who rebelled against Moses as recorded in Numbers 16*].

12 These are spots [*blemishes*] in your feasts of charity, when they feast with you, feeding themselves

without fear [*with no qualms; boldly, as if they belonged among the righteous;* Strong's #0870]: clouds they are without water [*they are like clouds that don't carry rain to benefit others*] carried about of winds [*blown every which way by the winds of passion and greed*]; trees whose fruit withereth, without fruit [*they are barren trees*], twice dead [*they are already dead spiritually and will die physically and be condemned*], plucked up by the roots;

13 Raging waves of the sea [*dangerous like wild crashing waves*], foaming out their own shame [*foaming at the mouth with their shameful wickedness*]; wandering stars, to [*for*] whom is reserved the blackness of darkness [*of hell*] for ever.

Jude next quotes a prophecy given by Enoch, which does not appear elsewhere in scripture except perhaps a brief reference in Moses 7:65.

14 And Enoch also, the seventh [*generation*] from Adam, prophesied of these [*about these kinds of wicked people*], saying, Behold, the Lord cometh with ten thousands of his saints [*at the Second Coming*],

15 To execute judgment upon all, and to convince all that are ungodly [*wicked*] among them of all their ungodly deeds which they have ungodly [*wickedly*] committed, and of all their hard [*wicked*] speeches which ungodly sinners have spoken against him.

16 These are murmurers, complainers, walking after their own lusts [*living in wickedness*]; and their mouth speaketh great swelling words [*they give long, empty explanations in which they attempt to justify their wickedness*], having men's persons in admiration [*they are admired by wicked people*] because of advantage [*because they stand to gain from the admiration of others*].

17 But, beloved, remember ye the words which were spoken before [*in the past*] of [*by*] the apostles of our Lord Jesus Christ;

18 How that they told you there should [*would*] be mockers in the last time [*in the last days*], who should walk after their own ungodly lusts [*wicked desires and passions*].

19 These be they who separate themselves [*who leave the Church*], sensual [*involved in sexual immorality*], having not the Spirit [*who have become insensitive to the Spirit*].

20 But ye, beloved, building up yourselves on your most holy faith, praying in the Holy Ghost [*as directed by the Holy Ghost; see 1 John 5:14; D&C 46:30 and 50:30*],

21 Keep yourselves in the love of God, looking for the mercy of our Lord Jesus Christ [*using the Atonement of Christ*] unto [*which leads to*] eternal life [*exaltation*].

22 And of some have compassion, making a difference [*show

compassion to those who need it, thus making a difference in their lives]:

23 And others save with fear, pulling them out of the fire [saving their souls from punishment]; hating even the garment spotted by the flesh ["Touch not their unclean things." (Alma 5:57)].

24 Now unto him [Christ] that is able to keep you from falling, and to present you faultless before the presence of his [the Father's] glory with exceeding joy [compare with D&C 45:3–5],

25 To the only wise God our Saviour, be glory and majesty, dominion and power, both now and ever. Amen.

THE REVELATION
OF ST JOHN THE DIVINE

The book of Revelation is often referred to as "the Apocalypse," which is a Greek word meaning "a revelation" or an "unveiling or uncovering of that which is hidden." The Prophet Joseph said, "The book of Revelation is one of the plainest books God ever caused to be written" (Teachings of the Prophet Joseph Smith, p. 290). This statement by the Prophet is a reminder that this marvelous book of scripture can be understood. In fact, we are greatly blessed to have much inspired help as we seek to understand the Revelation of John. Elder Bruce R. McConkie, of the Quorum of the Twelve Apostles, said the following:

"As a matter of fact, we are in a much better position to understand those portions of Revelation which we are expected to understand than we generally realize. Thanks be to the interpretive material found in sections 29, 77, 88, and others of the revelations in the Doctrine and Covenants; plus the revisions given in the Inspired Version of the Bible [the Joseph Smith Translation of the Bible]; plus the sermons of the Prophet; plus some clarifying explanations in the Book of Mormon and other latter-day scripture; plus our overall knowledge of the plan of salvation—thanks be to all of these things (to say nothing of a little conservative sense, wisdom and inspiration in their application), the fact is that we have a marvelously comprehensive and correct understanding of this otherwise hidden book." (Bruce R. McConkie, Doctrinal New Testament Commentary, 3 vols. [Salt Lake City: Bookcraft, 1965–1973], 3: 431.)

One of our real advantages in studying the Book of Revelation is that we recognize that it presents the Plan of Salvation, especially as seen against the background of the last days, when evil and wickedness will finally come to an end as the Millennium is ushered in by the Second Coming of the Savior. Since we have been taught the Plan of Salvation, we are in a much better position to understand Revelation than others who are not familiar with the restored gospel.

The JST makes changes in over 80 verses of the Book of Revelation, and thus becomes one of our most valuable keys for understanding John's writings in this book of the New Testament.

Still, for many members of the Church, the Book of Revelation is somewhat intimidating when it comes to reading it and trying to understand it. Therefore, as is the case elsewhere in this study guide, our notes will be rather simple, brief, and straightforward, allowing you to concentrate mostly on the scriptures themselves. It is hoped that you will mark your own scriptures, whether electronic or paper copies, and make many notes so that your study of Revelation will bless you throughout your life.

Background

The Book of Revelation was written by the Apostle John. According to most Bible scholars, it was written about AD 95. He was the brother of James and was one of the original Twelve Apostles called by Jesus. He came to be known as John the Beloved because of the special fondness Jesus felt for him (John 13:23). He was in the presidency of the early Church with Peter and James. He is the author of the Gospel of John, the three epistles of John, and the book of Revelation. He was given the special privilege of being allowed to live on the earth as a translated being until the Savior's Second Coming. (See John 21:21–23; D&C 7.) Little more is recorded of his life except for the brief mention in Revelation of his being on the isle of Patmos (Revelation 1:9), to which he was, according to tradition, banished during the wave of Christian persecution under the emperor Domitian. In 1831 the Prophet Joseph Smith indicated that John was then laboring among the lost ten tribes. (See HC 1:176.)

Revelation chapters 1–3 deal mainly with John's day. Chapters 4–22 deal mainly with the future, including our day, and include glimpses back into premortality as well as visions of the last days, the Second Coming, the Millennium, and celestial glory.

Symbolism

The use of symbolism in the Book of Revelation is one of several things which make it hard for us to understand. While we use much symbolism in our own culture, the symbolism used by John is difficult for us because we are not familiar with the culture of his day.

One of the great things about symbolism is that it is "infinitely deep," meaning that through symbolism, the Holy Ghost can teach you one thing during one reading of a verse or set of verses, then, the next time your read the same thing, you can be given a different message. For instance, suppose you are reading Revelation 1:18 where the Savior says "I . . . have the keys of hell and of death." The symbolism used is "keys," meaning the power to lock up or unlock, to condemn or to set free. During this reading of this verse, the Holy Ghost impresses your mind that the Savior is our final Judge and can, if necessary, smite wicked people and transfer them to hell in order to cleanse the earth and free it from their wicked influence. Thus, in your heart, you say to yourself, "I'd better be good!" However, the next time you read this verse, with its symbolism of "the keys of hell and of death," your mind is on personal progress and improvement. This time, the Holy Ghost whispers that the Savior has the "keys," through His Atonement, to free you from hell and from spiritual death. Thus, you are impressed and encouraged to repent and accept the cleansing and healing power of the Atonement in your own life.

The list of symbols on the following two pages can be helpful in understanding the scriptures.

SYMBOLISM OFTEN USED IN THE SCRIPTURES

COLORS

white	purity; righteousness; exaltation (Example: Rev. 3:4–5)
black	evil; famine; darkness (Example: Rev. 6:5–6)
red	sins; bloodshed (Example: Rev. 6:4; D&C 133:51)
blue	heaven; godliness; remembering and keeping God's commandments (Example: Numbers 15:37–40)
green	life; nature (Example: Rev. 8:7)
amber	sun; light; divine glory (Example: D&C 110:2, Rev. 1:15, Ezek. 1:4, 27; 8:2)
scarlet	royalty (Example: Dan. 5:29; Matt. 27:28–29)
silver	worth, but less than gold (Example: Ridges, *Isaiah Made Easier*, Isa. 48:10 notes)
gold	the best; exaltation (Example: Rev. 4:4)

BODY PARTS

eye	perception; light and knowledge
head	governing
ears	obedience; hearing
mouth	speaking
hair	modesty; covering
members	offices and callings
heart	inner man; courage
hands	action, acting
right hand	covenant hand; making covenants
bowels	center of emotion; whole being
loins	posterity; preparing for action (gird up your loins)
liver	center of feeling
reins	kidneys; center of desires, thoughts
arm	power
foot	mobility; foundation
toe	associated with cleansing rites (Example: Lev. 14:17)

nose	anger (Example: 2 Samuel 22:16; Job 4:9)
tongue	speaking
blood	life of the body
knee	humility; submission
shoulder	strength; effort
forehead	total dedication, loyalty (Example: Rev. 14:1 [loyalty to God]; Rev. 13:16 [loyalty to wickedness, Satan])

NUMBERS

1	unity; God
3	God; Godhead; A word repeated 3 times means superlative, "the most" or "the best." (See Isa. 6:3)
4	mankind; earth (See Smith's Bible Dictionary, p. 456) (Example: Rev. 7:1. Four angels over four parts of the earth)
7	completeness; perfection. When man lets God help, it leads to perfection. (man + God = perfection) $4 + 3 = 7$
10	numerical perfection (Example: Ten Commandments, tithing); well-organized (Example: Satan is well-organized, Rev. 13:1)
12	divine government; God's organization (Example: JST Rev. 5:6)
40 days	literal; sometimes means "a long time" as in 1 Samuel 17:16
forever	endless; can sometimes be a specific period or age, not endless (see *BYU Religious Studies Center Newsletter*, Vol. 8, No. 3, May 1994)

OTHERS

horse	victory; power to conquer (Example: Rev. 19:11; Jer. 8:16)
donkey	peace (Example: Christ came in peace at the Triumphal Entry; Matthew 21:1–10)
palms	joy; triumph, victory (Example: John 12:13; Rev. 7:9)
wings	power to move, act etc. (Example: Rev. 4:8; D&C 77:4)
crown	power; dominion; exaltation (Example: Rev. 2:10; 4:4)
robes	royalty; kings, queens; exaltation (Example: Rev. 6:11, 7:14; 2 Ne. 9:14; D&C 109:76; 3 Ne. 11:8)

REVELATION 1

As mentioned in the introductory material above, chapters 1–3 deal mainly with things in John's day, while chapters 4–22 deal mainly with the future, including our day.

1 The Revelation of Jesus Christ, which God gave unto him, to show unto his servants things which must shortly come to pass; and he sent and signified it by his angel unto his servant John [*This is an example of what is known as "divine investiture" when an angel speaks directly for Christ. See, for example, Revelation 19:9–10.*]:

JST Revelation 1:1

1 The Revelation of **John, a servant of God**, which **was given unto him of Jesus Christ**, to show unto his servants things which must shortly come to pass, **that** he sent and **signified by** his angel unto his servant John,

Divine Investiture

Often in the scriptures, without so indicating, the Savior speaks for the Father (example: D&C 29:1, 42, 46), the Holy Ghost speaks for the Savior (example: Moses 5:9), an angel speaks for the Savior (example: Revelation 1:1), and so forth. This is known as "divine investiture." Apostle Joseph Fielding Smith explained this divine investiture of authority as follows: "In giving revelations our Savior speaks at times for himself; at other times for the Father, and in the Father's name, as though he were the Father, and yet it is Jesus Christ, our Redeemer who gives the message. So, we see, in Doctrine and Covenants 29:1, that he introduces himself as 'Jesus Christ, your Redeemer,' but in the closing part of the revelation he speaks for the Father, and in the Father's name as though he were the Father, and yet it is still Jesus who is speaking, for the Father has put his name on him for that purpose." (*Doctrines of Salvation*, 3 vols., edited by Bruce R. McConkie [Salt Lake City: Bookcraft, 1954–56], Vol. 1, p. 27.)

Apostle Jeffrey R. Holland also explained divine investiture. "Christ can at any time and in any place speak and act for the Father by virtue of the 'divine investiture of authority' the Father has given him. (Jeffrey R. Holland, *Christ and the New Covenant: The Messianic Message of the Book of Mormon* [Salt Lake City: Deseret Book, 1997], 183–84.)

2 Who [*John*] bare record of the word of God, and of the testimony of Jesus Christ, and of all things that he [*John*] saw.

JST Revelation 1:2

2 Who **bore** record of the word of God, and of the testimony of Jesus Christ, and of all things that he saw.

3 Blessed is he that readeth, and they that hear the words of this prophecy, and keep those things

which are written therein: for the time is at hand.

JST Revelation 1:3

3 Blessed **are they who read**, and they **who hear and understand** the words of this prophecy, and keep those things which are written therein, for the time **of the coming of the Lord draweth nigh**.

4 John to the seven churches [*to the leaders of the seven "branches" or "wards" of the Church*] which are in Asia [*modern day western Turkey*]: Grace be unto you, and peace, from him [*Christ*] which is, and which was, and which is to come; and from the seven Spirits which are before his throne;

JST Revelation 1:4

4 **Now this is the testimony of** John to the seven **servants who are over the seven churches** in Asia. Grace unto you, and peace from him **who** is, and **who was**, and **who** is to come; **who hath sent forth his angel from before his throne, to testify unto those who are the seven servants** [*leaders, such as bishops or branch presidents*] **over the seven churches** [*wards or branches*].

5 And from Jesus Christ, who is the faithful witness, and the first begotten of the dead [*the first resurrected*], and the prince of [*the leader over*] the kings of the earth. Unto him [*Christ*] that loved us, and washed us from our sins in his own blood [*the Atonement*],

Notice that the JST puts the rest of verse 5 with verse 6.

JST Revelation 1:5

5 **Therefore, I, John, the faithful witness, bear record of the things which were delivered me of the angel, and from Jesus Christ** the first begotten of the dead, and the Prince of the kings of the earth.

The phrase, "washed us from our sins in his own blood," in verse 5, above is symbolic of being cleansed by the Atonement of Jesus Christ. It is interesting to note the cleansing role of blood in our own physical bodies. It constantly cleans out the toxins from each individual cell, and thus continually gives each cell newness of life.

6 And hath made us kings and priests [*terms referring to exaltation*] unto God [*Heavenly Father*] and his Father; to him be glory and dominion for ever and ever. Amen.

JST Revelation 1:6

6 **And unto him who loved us, be glory; who washed us from our sins in his own blood**, and hath made us kings and priests unto God, **his Father**. To him be glory and dominion, for ever and ever. Amen.

Bruce R. McConkie explains verse 6, above, as follows: "If righteous men have power through the gospel and its crowning ordinance of celestial marriage to become kings and priests to rule in exaltation forever, it follows that the women by their side (without whom they cannot attain exaltation) will be queens and priestesses (Rev. 1:6; 5:10). Exaltation grows out of the eternal union of a man and his wife. Of those whose marriage endures in eternity, the Lord says, 'Then shall they be gods' (D&C 132:20); that is, each of them, the man and the woman, will be a god. As such they will rule over their dominions forever." (Bruce R. McConkie, *Mormon Doctrine*, 2nd ed. [Salt Lake City: Bookcraft, 1966], 613.)

7 Behold, he [*Christ*] cometh with clouds [*symbolic of the presence of the Lord; see Exodus 13:21 and Exodus 19:9*]; and every eye shall see him, and they also which pierced him [*even those who participated in his crucifixion will see him at the Second Coming; see Orson Pratt, Journal of Discourses, Vol. 18, p. 170*]: and all kindreds [*the wicked*] of the earth shall wail because of him. Even so, Amen.

JST Revelation 1:7

7 **For** behold, he cometh **in the** clouds **with ten thousands of his saints in the kingdom, clothed with the glory of his Father**. And every eye shall see him; and **they who** pierced him, and all kindreds of the earth shall wail because of him. Even so, Amen.

8 I am Alpha and Omega [*the beginning and ending letters of the Greek alphabet*], the beginning and the ending, saith the Lord, which is, and which was, and which is to come, the Almighty [*In other*

words, I have been involved with you since the beginning, premortality and creation, and I will be around at the end of the earth as I judge you and finish all things the Father has asked Me to do].

JST Revelation 1:8

8 **For he saith,** I am Alpha and Omega, the beginning and the ending, **the Lord, who** is, and **who** was, and **who** is to come, the Almighty.

Having set the stage now, John proceeds to tell us what the circumstances in his life were at the time he received this revelation.

9 I John [*the Beloved Apostle*], who also am your brother, and companion in tribulation [*I've got problems too; I understand you*], and in the kingdom and patience of Jesus Christ, was in the isle that is called Patmos [*he was in a prison colony just off the west coast of Turkey, just below the island of Samos; (see E 2 on map 13 of your Bible or Map 22 in the 1989 LDS Bible for the location of Samos), then put a dot just under Samos and label it Patmos*], for the word of God, and for the testimony of Jesus Christ [*I am in prison because I wouldn't stop teaching and living the gospel*].

10 I was in the Spirit on the Lord's day [*Sunday, Acts 20:7*], and heard behind me a great voice, as of a trumpet,

Trumpet is used often in the scriptures to represent a clear, easy to recognize message from God, just as a trumpet is a clear, easy-to-recognize musical instrument for us today.

Revelation 19:10 informs us that an angel is speaking for Jesus Christ here. As mentioned earlier, this is known as "divine investiture."

11 Saying, I [*Christ*] am Alpha and Omega, the first and the last: and, What thou seest, write in a book, and send it unto the seven churches [*"wards" or "branches"*] which are in Asia [*western Turkey today*]; unto Ephesus, and unto Smyrna, and unto Pergamos, and unto Thyatira, and unto Sardis, and unto Philadelphia, and unto Laodicea [*listed in geographical order*].

12 And I turned to see the voice that spake with me. And being turned, I saw seven golden candlesticks [*representing the seven "wards" or "branches"*];

Symbolism is involved here and carries an important message. Gold symbolizes the best, i.e., the true gospel. Candlesticks don't give light, rather, they carry the source of light, which is Christ and His gospel, to the world.

JST Revelation 1:12

12 And I turned to see **from whence the voice came** that spake to me; and being turned, I saw seven golden candlesticks;

13 And in the midst [*D&C 38:7 reminds us that Christ is often in*

our midst] of the seven candlesticks one like unto the Son of man [*Christ*], clothed with a garment down to the foot, and girt about the paps [*breast, chest*] with a golden [*symbolic of the best, celestial*] girdle.

The phrase "one like unto the Son of man" in verse 13, above, needs explaining. The question is, why don't they just say "Jesus Christ," rather than using an oblique reference to Him? In order to keep the commandment "Thou shalt not take the name of the Lord thy God in vain;" (Exodus 20:7), the Jews developed rules and standard practices which kept them far away from taking the name of the Lord in vain. For instance, rather than saying the Lord's name directly, they would use an indirect reference such as "one like unto," and then the name. Thus, they avoided even coming close to breaking the commandment. There are many examples of this practice of showing reverence and respect toward the name of Deity. For instance, see Daniel 3:25, 7:13; Revelation 14:14; Abraham 3:27; 1 Nephi 1:8.

The phrase "Son of man," in reference to Christ in verse 13, above, and elsewhere in the scriptures is explained in Moses 6:57 as follows: ". . . in the language of Adam, Man of Holiness is his name, and the name of his Only Begotten is the Son of Man, even Jesus Christ. . . " In other words, "Man of Holiness" refers to Heavenly Father. Jesus is, therefore, the "Son of Man of

Holiness," which, in the Bible, is shortened to "Son of man."

14 His head and his hairs were white like wool, as white as snow; and his eyes were as a flame of fire [*this is similar to the description of the Savior in D&C 110:3*];

It is interesting to notice that the word "wool" and the phrase "white as snow," used in verse 14, above, are also used in Isaiah 1:18 in describing the power of the Atonement to cleanse and heal from sin. Isaiah 1:18 says, "Come now, and let us reason together, saith the LORD: though your sins be as scarlet, they shall be as white as snow; though they be red like crimson, they shall be as wool." The use here is no doubt a tie-in with Isaiah 1:18 and a reminder to us of the power of the Atonement.

15 And his feet like unto fine brass, as if they burned in a furnace; and his voice as the sound of many waters.

16 And he had in his right hand [*covenant hand*] seven stars [*the leaders of the seven "wards"; stars are symbolic. We rely on them, like we rely on our Church leaders, to guide us through darkness to our desired destination.*]: and out of his [*Christ's*] mouth went a sharp twoedged sword [*perhaps symbolic of the fact that the Savior can both defend the righteous and destroy the wicked; see 2:16. It is our choice. Also, a two edged sword, representing the word of*

God as in JST Rev. 19:15, can cut quickly through falsehood and error.]: and his countenance was as the sun shineth in his strength.

JST Revelation 1:16

16 And he had in his right hand seven stars; and out of his mouth went a sharp two-edged sword; and his countenance was as the sun **shining** in his strength.

Next, in verse 17, John tells us how seeing the resurrected Savior (see heading to this chapter in your Bible) affected him at this moment.

17 And when I [*John*] saw him, I fell at his feet as dead [*completely overwhelmed*]. And he laid his right hand [*covenant hand; symbolizing that via making and keeping covenants, we can feel at ease in Christ's presence*] upon me, saying unto me, Fear not; I am the first and the last [*i.e., I am Jesus Christ your Savior; you don't need to be afraid of Me.*]:

18 I am he that liveth, and was dead [*I have been literally resurrected!*]; and, behold, I am alive for evermore [*I will continue to live forever*], Amen; and have the keys of hell and of death [*i.e., I overcame all things and thus have all power to save you; I am fully qualified to be your Savior*].

19 Write the things which thou hast seen, and the things which are, and the things which shall be hereafter [*write this vision down*];

The angel, speaking for Christ, now explains to John some of the imagery used so far in the vision.

20 The mystery of the seven stars which thou sawest in my right hand, and the seven golden candlesticks. The seven stars are the angels of the seven churches [*wards or branches*]: and the seven candlesticks which thou sawest are the seven churches.

JST Revelation 1:20

20 **This is** the mystery of the seven stars which thou sawest in my right hand, and the seven golden candlesticks. The seven stars are the **servants** [*leaders, presiding elders*] of the seven churches; and the seven candlesticks which thou sawest are the seven churches.

REVELATION 2

The Savior here and in chapter 3 gives personal messages through John the Revelator to the Saints in the various "wards" or "branches" spoken of in Revelation 1:11, which were located in what is known as western Turkey, today. Watch for symbolism representing the celestial kingdom at the end of each of these messages.

The first message is the Savior's message to the members of the Ephesus "ward" in verses 1–7, next.

1 Unto the angel [*presiding elder, leader*] of the church ["*ward*"] of Ephesus write; These things saith he [*Christ*] that holdeth the seven stars ["*branch presidents*" or "*bishops*"; the Savior similarly helps our church leaders today*] in his right hand [*covenant hand*], who walketh in the midst of the seven golden candlesticks [*the Savior is in our midst, D&C 38:7; He is not an absentee Savior*];

JST Revelation 2:1

1 Unto the **servant** of the church of Ephesus write; These things saith he that holdeth the seven stars in his right hand, who walketh in the midst of the seven golden candlesticks;

In the next few verses, the Savior will first compliment these Saints and then express some concerns to them.

2 I know thy works, and thy labour, and thy patience, and how thou canst not bear them which are evil: and thou hast tried [*tested*] them which say they are apostles, and are not, and hast found them liars [*you have faced issues and dealt properly with apostates among you*];

3 And hast born, and hast patience, and for my name's sake hast laboured, and hast not fainted [*you haven't given up when the going was difficult*].

4 Nevertheless I have somewhat against thee [*I have a serious concern*], because thou hast left thy first love [*i.e., your enthusiasm for the gospel when you were first converted; now you are diminishing in zeal and getting weak in the faith*].

5 Remember therefore from whence thou art fallen, and repent, and do the first works [*return to your former level of commitment and enthusiasm*]; or else I will come unto thee quickly, and will remove thy candlestick out of his place, except thou repent [*your "ward" will die out much faster than you might think possible, if you don't repent*].

6 But this thou hast [*here is another compliment, something you are doing right*], that thou hatest the deeds of the Nicolaitans [*D&C 117:11; people who want the prestige of Church membership but who are not fully committed to the gospel; they secretly want to follow the ways of the world*], which I also hate.

7 He that hath an ear, let him hear what the Spirit saith unto the churches [*listen carefully to the promptings of the Holy Ghost who teaches and warns members of the Church constantly*]; To him that overcometh will I give to eat of the tree of life, which is in the midst of the paradise of God. [*Celestial glory is the reward of the righteous. Perhaps this reflects back to Lehi's dream in 1 Nephi 8. Also note that the Nicolaitans in verse 6 of Rev. 2 seem to tie in with the "great and spacious building" in 1 Nephi 8:26–27 while verse 5 above might tie in with 1 Nephi 8:25, where members have tasted the gospel but then let peer pressure make them ashamed of it.*]

Next, the Savior gives John a message for the Saints in Smyrna.

8 And unto the angel [*presiding elder*] of the church ["*ward*"] in Smyrna write; These things saith the first and the last [*the Savior*], which was dead, and is alive [*is resurrected*];

JST Revelation 2:8

8 And unto the **servant** of the church in Smyrna write; These things saith the first and the last, which was dead, and is alive;

9 I know thy works, and tribulation, and poverty, [*but thou art rich; i.e., you are well-off because you have the gospel*] and I know the blasphemy of them which say they are Jews [*who claim to be "the chosen people of the Lord"*], and are not [*i.e., they are not faithful and have rejected Christ and are persecuting the Saints in Smyrna*], but are the synagogue of Satan [*the church of the Devil; 1 Nephi 14:10; 1 Nephi 13:6–9*].

10 Fear none of those things which thou shalt suffer [*you will have some suffering as part of your "curriculum" here on earth, but don't fear it*]: behold, the devil shall cast some of you into prison, that ye may be tried [*tested*]; and ye shall have tribulation ten days [*perhaps meaning a short time compared to eternity*]: be thou faithful unto death [*endure to the end*], and I will give thee a crown of life [*you will be a god in exaltation*].

11 He that hath an ear [*he who is willing to listen*], let him hear what

the Spirit saith unto the churches; He that overcometh [*who overcomes evil through the Atonement of Christ*] shall not be hurt of the second death [*will not suffer spiritual death and be cut off from the presence of God forever; in other words, you will receive a celestial reward*].

The next message from the Savior goes to the Saints in Pergamos.

12 And to the angel [*leader*] of the church [*"ward"*] in Pergamos [*a center for Roman emperor worship*] write; These things saith he [*Christ*] which hath the sharp sword with two edges [*Rev. 1:16*];

JST Revelation 2:12

12 And to the **servant** of the church in Pergamos write; These things saith he which hath the sharp sword with two edges;

13 I know thy works, and where thou dwellest [*I know your situation*], even where Satan's seat is [*you live in an area where evil and false religion is very strong*]: and thou holdest fast my name [*and are remaining faithful to the covenants you made when you took My name upon you*], and hast not denied my faith [*a compliment*], even in those days wherein Antipas was my faithful martyr [*gave his life for the gospel*], who was slain among you, where Satan dwelleth [*where Satan has great power over many*].

14 But I have a few things against thee [*I have some concerns about you*], because thou hast there them

that hold the doctrine of Balaam [*priestcraft; preaching for popularity, money, and approval of men; see Numbers 22*], who taught Balac to cast a stumblingblock before the children of Israel, to eat things sacrificed unto idols [*participating in idol worship*], and to commit fornication [*sexual immorality used as part of idol worship in many Bible cults; "fornication" can also mean breaking covenants, intense and total disloyalty to God. See Jer. 3:8, Rev. 14:8; also see Bible Dictionary under "Adultery"*].

15 So hast thou also them that hold the doctrine of the Nicolaitans [*some members of the Church in your area are thinking like Nicolaitans; see verse 6, above*], which thing I hate.

16 Repent; or else I will come unto thee quickly, and will fight against them with the sword of my mouth [*the two edged sword in 1:16 can destroy the wicked as well as protect the righteous*].

17 He that hath an ear, let him hear what the Spirit saith unto the churches; To him that overcometh [*who overcomes sin and evil through repentance and the Atonement*] will I give to eat of the hidden manna [*i.e., nourishment from heaven*], and will give him a white stone [*symbolic of celestial glory, D&C 130:11*], and in the stone a new name [*symbolic of celestial glory; see also Rev. 3:12*] written, which no man knoweth saving he that receiveth it [*a key word, D&C 130:11*].

JST Revelation 2:17

17 He that hath an ear, let him hear what the Spirit saith unto the churches; To him that overcometh will I give to eat of the hidden manna, and will give him a white stone, and in the stone a new name written, which no man knowest saving he that receiveth it.

Isaiah mentions "a new name, which the mouth of the Lord shall name" in Isaiah 62:2. Additional information about the term "new name," as used in verse 17, above, is given in the Doctrine and Covenants. According to D&C 130:10–11, a "white stone" is given to each of those who attains the celestial kingdom. In D&C 130:11, the "new name" is "the key word" used in conjunction with celestial glory.

Brigham Young explained the term "key word," in conjunction with temple endowments, as follows: "Your endowment is, to receive all those ordinances in the house of the Lord, which are necessary for you, after you have departed this life, to enable you to walk back to the presence of the Father, passing the angels who stand as sentinels, being enabled to give them the key words, the signs and tokens, pertaining to the holy Priesthood, and gain your eternal exaltation in spite of earth and hell." (Discourses of Brigham Young, p. 416.)

It is interesting to note that people anciently had new names given them upon making additional covenants with the Lord. Examples include Abram, whose name was changed to Abraham when he made covenants of exaltation with the Lord (Genesis 17:5.) In the heading to JST Genesis 17, the term "new name" appears again as "Abram's new name." Likewise, Sarai's name was changed to Sarah (Genesis 17:15–16.) Jacob's name was changed to Israel (Genesis 32:28.) Saul's name was changed to Paul (Acts 13:2–3, 9 and 13.) King Mosiah promised his people another name if they would be diligent "in keeping the commandments of the Lord" (Mosiah 1:11). The name he gave them was the name of Jesus Christ (Mosiah 5:8 and 11) which is the name through which we receive exaltation if worthy (see Mosiah 5:7.)

Robert L. Millet spoke of this name which King Benjamin gave his people as follows: "As members of the family of Christ, they were required to take upon them a new name, the name of Christ; they thereby became Christians in the truest sense of the word and were obligated by covenant to live by the rules and regulations of the royal family, to live a life befitting the new and sacred name they had taken." (Robert L. Millet, *Alive in Christ: The Miracle of Spiritual Rebirth* [Salt Lake City: Deseret Book, 1997], p. 77.)

Next, the Lord gives John a message for the members in Thyatira.

18 And unto the angel [*leader*] of the church in Thyatira write; These things saith the Son of God, who hath his eyes like unto a flame of fire, and his feet are like fine brass;

JST Revelation 2:18

18 And unto the **servant** of the church in Thyatira write; These things saith the Son of God, who hath his eyes like unto a flame of fire, and his feet are like fine brass;

19 I know thy works, and charity, and service, and faith, and thy patience, and thy works [*a compliment*]; and the last to be more than the first [*in effect, your recent works are greater than your previous works, in other words, you continue to progress in living the gospel*].

20 [*A concern:*] Notwithstanding I have a few things against thee, because thou sufferest [*you allow*] that woman Jezebel, which calleth herself a prophetess, to teach [*major message: There are limits as to what you can tolerate in the Church. You leaders shouldn't allow her to do this teaching in your congregation.*] and to seduce my servants to commit fornication [*can be literal; also means apostasy, total disloyalty—see Rev. 14:8; Bible Dictionary under "Adultery"*], and to eat things sacrificed unto idols [*i.e., participating in idol worship*].

21 And I gave her space to repent of her fornication [*she had plenty of chances to repent*]; and she repented not.

JST Revelation 2:21

21 And I gave her space to repent of her **fornications**; and she repented not.

22 Behold, I will cast her into a bed, and them [*her followers*] that commit adultery [*who are in apostasy*] with her into great tribulation, except [*unless*] they repent of their deeds.

JST Revelation 2:22

22 Behold, I will cast her into **hell**, and them that commit adultery with her into great tribulation, except they repent of their deeds.

23 And I will kill her children [*followers*] with death [*spiritual death*]; and all the churches ["*wards*"] shall know that I am he which searcheth [*knows*] the reins [*kidneys, loins; symbolically the center of thoughts and desires, i.e., the inner person*] and hearts: and I will give unto every one of you according to your works.

24 But unto you [*the presiding officer*] I say, and unto the rest in Thyatira, as many as have not this doctrine [*who haven't become followers of Jezebel*], and which have not known the depths of Satan [*haven't gone deep into apostasy*], as they speak; I will put upon you none other burden [*i.e., I will not express any other concerns about you at this time; just work on this one*].

25 But that which ye have already [*the things in which you are being*

faithful] hold fast till I come [*endure to the end*].

26 And he that overcometh, and keepeth my works unto the end, to him will I give power over the nations [*celestial reward; i.e., they will become gods, D&C 132:20*]:

JST Revelation 2:26

26 And **to him who** overcometh, and keepeth my **commandments** unto the end, will I give power over **many kingdoms**;

27 And he [*those who overcome all things and become gods*] shall rule them [*nations, i.e., future worlds; D&C 132:20*] with a rod of iron [*the word of God—see JST below, also, 1 Nephi 11:25*]; as the vessels [*clay pots*] of a potter shall they be broken to shivers [*broken to bits, if they are disobedient*]: even as I received of my Father [*just as is the case with Me and My work on this earth*].

JST Revelation 2:27

27 And he shall rule them with **the word of God** [*in other words, will use the same plan of salvation as that used for us by our Heavenly Father*]; **and they shall be in his hands as the vessels of clay in the hands of a potter; and he shall govern them by faith, with equity and justice,** even as I received of my Father.

28 And I will give him [*the righteous in verse 26*] the morning star [*the brightest, best, symbolic of exaltation*].

29 He that hath an ear, let him hear what the Spirit saith unto the churches [*i.e., pay close attention and obey what I say to you through the Holy Ghost*].

REVELATION 3

As the revelation and vision continue, John is given messages from the Savior to three more units of the Church, namely Sardis, Philadelphia, and Laodicea. Among other things in this chapter, we are taught about the book of life (verse 5) and the fact that worthy people can become gods (verse 21).

1 And unto the angel [*presiding officer*] of the church [*"ward"*] in Sardis write; These things saith he [*the Savior*] that hath the seven Spirits of God, and the seven stars; I know thy works, that thou hast a name that thou livest [*i.e., you have a reputation for being good*], and art dead [*see JST change below*].

JST Revelation 3:1

1 And unto the **servant** of the church in Sardis, write; These things saith he **who** hath the seven **stars, which are the seven servants of God** [*in other words, the Savior is holding the seven "bishops" of the seven "wards" in the hollow of His hand; He is directing them*]; I know thy works, that thou hast a name that thou livest, and art **not** dead [*in effect, you still have some spirituality left—see verse 2, next*].

2 Be watchful, and strengthen the things which remain, that are ready to die: for I have not found thy works perfect before God. [*An understatement of concern!*]

JST Revelation 3:2

2 Be watchful **therefore**, and strengthen **those who** remain, **who** are ready to die [*spiritually*]; for I have not found thy works perfect before God.

3 Remember therefore how thou hast received and heard [*the gospel*], and hold fast [*keep your commitments*], and repent. If therefore thou shalt not watch, I will come on thee as a thief [*unexpectedly;* Strong's *#2240*], and thou shalt not know what hour I will come upon thee.

4 Thou hast a few names [*you have a few members*] even in Sardis which have not defiled their garments [*a compliment; you still have a few righteous members*]; and they shall walk with me in white [*symbolic of exaltation*]: for they are worthy.

5 He that overcometh [*he who overcomes sin through Christ's Atonement*], the same shall be clothed in white raiment [*white clothing; symbolic of exaltation*]; and I will not blot out his name out of the book of life, but I will confess [*acknowledge, praise*] his name before my Father [*as in D&C 45:3–5*], and before his angels [*i.e., they will receive celestial reward*].

The term "book of life" referred to in verse 5, above, is referred to as the "Lamb's Book of Life" in D&C 132:19. It represents the records kept in heaven in which the names of those worthy of exaltation are written. See McConkie, *Mormon Doctrine*, second edition, 1966, p. 97.

6 He that hath an ear, let him hear what the Spirit saith unto the churches.

7 And to the angel [*presiding officer*] of the church in Philadelphia write; These things saith he [*Christ*] that is holy, he that is true, he that hath the key of David [*Isaiah 22:22; i.e., power to command and be obeyed; who holds the priesthood keys of exaltation*], he that openeth, and no man shutteth; and shutteth, and no man openeth [*i.e., Christ's Atonement can set us free from death and hell, in spite of Satan's efforts against us, or He can condemn us on Judgment Day*];

JST Revelation 3:7

7 And to the **servant** of the church in Philadelphia write; These things saith he that is holy, he that is true, he that hath the key of David, he that openeth, and no man shutteth; and shutteth, and no man openeth;

8 I know thy works: behold, I have set before thee an open door [*I have prepared the way for you to come unto Me*], and no man can shut it [*no man can stop you*]: for thou hast a little strength, and hast kept my word [*i.e., you are improving, and you are keeping your commitments to Me*], and hast not

denied my name [*and you have not rejected Me*].

9 Behold, I will make them of the synagogue of Satan [*the church of the Devil, 1 Nephi 14:10; Rev. 2:9*], which say they are Jews [*i.e., claim to be covenant people*], and are not, but do lie [*through their personal wickedness*]; behold, I will make them to come and worship before thy feet [*you will be exalted and have power over them; see D&C 132:20*], and to know that I have loved thee [*I have been privileged to bless you because of your righteousness; see* Ensign, *Feb. 2003 article "Divine Love" by Elder Russell M. Nelson, pp. 20–25*].

10 Because thou hast kept the word of my patience [*i.e., you have patiently kept your commitments, Heb. 10:36*], I also will keep thee from the hour of temptation [*help and protect you during temptation*], which shall come upon all the world, to try [*test*] them that dwell upon the earth.

11 Behold, I come quickly [*not "soon," rather, when I do come, it will be "quickly" (see Strong's #5035) and the wicked will not have time to repent and escape*]: hold that fast which thou hast [*keep your commitments*], that no man take thy crown [*exaltation*].

Notice the various ways exaltation is described in verse 12, next.

12 Him that overcometh will I make a pillar in the temple of my God [*you will receive exaltation in my "temple," in other words, in the celestial kingdom; see Revelation 21:22*], and he shall go no more out [*exaltation lasts forever*]: and I will write upon him the name of my God [*symbolism meaning he will belong to God, i.e., exaltation; Rev. 14:1, 22:4*], and the name of the city of my God, which is new Jerusalem [*i.e., your eternal "address" will be New Jerusalem, Celestial Kingdom*], which cometh down out of heaven from my God: and I will write upon him my new name [*symbolic of celestial glory, D&C 130:11*].

JST Revelation 3:12

12 Him that overcometh will I make a pillar in the temple of my God, and he shall go no more out; and I will write upon him the name of my God, and the name of the city of my God, **this** is New Jerusalem, which cometh down out of heaven from my God; and I will write upon him my new name.

The phrase "new name" has meaning understood only by endowed members of the Church of Jesus Christ of Latter-day Saints. See the note after Revelation 2:17 in this study guide.

13 He that hath an ear, let him hear what the Spirit saith unto the churches.

To this next "ward" or "branch" of the Church, the Savior expresses only "concerns." From what Christ tells them, we should learn that one of the most serious concerns of all is indecision about whether or not to be completely committed to God.

14 And unto the angel [*presiding officer*] of the church of the Laodiceans write; These things saith the Amen [*Christ*], the faithful and true witness, the beginning [*the firstborn spirit child of our Heavenly Father, Colossians 1:15*] of the creation of God [*the Father*];

JST Revelation 3:14

14 And unto the **servant** of the church of the Laodiceans write; These things saith the Amen, the faithful and true witness, the beginning of the creation of God;

15 I know thy works, that thou art neither cold nor hot [*i.e., you won't make a commitment or take a stand*]: I would [*wish that*] thou wert cold or hot.

16 So then because thou art lukewarm [*you won't make a solid commitment*], and neither cold nor hot, I will spue [*vomit; see Rev. 3:16, footnote b in our Bible*] thee out of my mouth [*i.e., I will reject you*].

17 Because thou sayest, I am rich, and increased with goods [*I have lots of worldly possessions;* Strong's *#4147*], and have need of nothing [*you are materialistic*]; and knowest not that thou art wretched, and miserable, and poor, and blind, and naked [*you don't realize how spiritually poor you really are!*]:

Next, the Savior explains how such people can repent. This counsel applies to all of us.

18 I counsel thee to buy [*through your actions*] of me gold [*symbolic of the best, i.e., the gospel, the Atonement, exaltation*] tried in the fire [*proven to be good*], that thou mayest be [*truly*] rich; and white raiment [*buy white robes; symbolic of purity and exaltation*], that thou mayest be clothed, and that the shame of thy nakedness do not appear [*i.e., you need to repent and be clothed with righteousness, so you do not stand naked, i.e., without excuse for your sins, and embarrassed on Judgment Day*]; and anoint thine eyes [*prepare your spiritual eyes*] with eyesalve, that thou mayest see. [*Eye salve often hurts at first and then heals; so also with the Holy Ghost. His counsel sometimes hurts at first, but when heeded, it heals.*]

19 As many as I love, I rebuke and chasten [*D&C 95:1*]: be zealous [*pursue the "gold" in verse 18 earnestly;* Strong's *#2206*] therefore, and repent.

Perhaps you have seen paintings depicting verse 20, next. If so, did you notice that the artist did not put a doorknob on the outside of the door? It is symbolic of the fact that the Savior knocks, but we must let Him in to our hearts and lives.

20 Behold, I [*the Savior*] stand at the door [*your door; your life*],

and knock [*waiting humbly*]: if any man hear [*pay attention to*] my voice, and open the door [*we have the agency to or not to*], I will come in to him, and will sup [*eat the evening meal; can be symbolic of the Last Supper, sacrament; in other words, making covenants*] with him, and he with me.

"Throne," as used in verse 21, next, symbolizes exaltation, in other words, attaining the highest degree of glory in the celestial kingdom and becoming gods. See D&C 132:20.

21 To him that overcometh [*overcomes wickedness and temptation*] will I grant to sit with me in my throne [*i.e., we will be joint-heirs with Christ (Romans 8:17), exalted*], even as I also overcame, and am set down with my Father in his throne [*compare with D&C 76:107–108*].

22 He that hath an ear, let him hear what the Spirit saith unto the churches.

REVELATION 4

As mentioned previously, chapters 1–3 of Revelation deal mainly with John's day. Starting with this chapter, John will primarily be shown things which will take place in the future. Verse 1 specifically says that John will now be shown the future.

Among other things, he will be shown Heavenly Father seated on His throne of power and glory.

1 After this I [*John*] looked, and, behold, a door was opened in heaven: and the first voice which I heard was as it were of a trumpet [*a clear, definite sound whose source is unmistakable, and whose message is clear*] talking with me; which said, Come up hither, and I will shew [*pronounced "show"*] thee things which must be hereafter [*now we will talk about the future*].

JST Revelation 4:1

1 After this I looked, and behold, a door was opened **into** heaven; and the first voice which I heard was as it were of a trumpet talking with me; which said, Come up hither, and I will **show** thee things which must be hereafter.

Did you notice the JST change? It changes "opened in heaven" to "opened into heaven," giving the sense that John was invited to look into heaven, where he will see the Father.

2 And immediately I was in the spirit: and, behold, a throne was set in heaven, and one [*Heavenly Father, see 5:7*] sat on the throne.

John now uses highest descriptive terms, superlatives, precious jewel stones, and so forth in attempting to describe the Father.

3 And he that sat [*upon the throne*] was to look upon like a jasper and a sardine stone [*a very hard, deep orange-red jewel stone symbolic of something one would look upon*

with total awe and wonder]: and there was a rainbow [*depicting glory and beauty*] round about the throne, in sight like unto an emerald.

JST Revelation 4:3

3 And he that sat **there** was to look upon like a jasper and a sardine stone; and there was a rainbow round about the throne, in sight like unto an emerald.

The JST changes for verse 4, next, are doctrinally very significant because they show that faithful Saints can become gods, rather than existing eternally as angels.

4 And round about the throne were four and twenty seats: and upon the seats I saw four and twenty elders [*faithful elders from the seven "wards" mentioned in Rev. 1:11 who had died; see D&C 77:5*] sitting, clothed in white raiment [*white robes; Strong's #2440; symbolic of exaltation*]; and they had on their heads crowns [*symbolic of authority and power*] of gold [*gold represents the best, i.e., exaltation*].

JST Revelation 4:4

4 And **in the midst of the throne** [*symbolizing becoming "joint heirs" with God, rather than forever being "on-the-outside-looking-in" worshipers*] were four and twenty seats [*thrones; symbolic of royalty, in other words, exaltation—see Revelation 3:21*]; and upon the seats I saw four and twenty elders sitting, clothed in white raiment, and

they had on their heads crowns **like** gold.

5 And out of the throne proceeded lightnings and thunderings [*symbolic of God's presence, as on Mt. Sinai; Exodus 20:18*] and voices: and there were seven lamps of fire [*the seven leaders of the seven "wards"*] burning [*shining*] before the throne [*in front of the throne of the Father*], which are the seven Spirits of God.

JST Revelation 4:5

5 And out of the throne proceeded lightnings and thunderings and voices; and there were seven lamps of fire burning before the throne, which are the seven **servants** of God [*in other words, the presiding officers of the seven "wards" mentioned in Revelation 1:4*].

6 And before [*in front of*] the throne there was a sea of glass [*the celestialized earth; see D&C 77:1, 130:9*] like unto crystal: and in the midst of the throne, and round about the throne, were four beasts [*see D&C 77:2–3*] full of eyes [*representing light and knowledge; D&C 77:4*] before and behind [*in front and back*].

JST Revelation 4:6

6 And before the throne there was a sea of glass like unto crystal; and in the midst of the throne **were the four and twenty elders;** and round about the throne, were four beasts full of eyes before and behind.

Did you notice the clear distinction in JST verse 6 above

between where the 24 elders were and where the four beasts were? The 24 elders were in the "midst of the throne," symbolizing exaltation, being "joint heirs with Christ" (Romans 8:17). The 4 beasts were "round about the throne," symbolizing that animals can be in the presence of God but cannot receive exaltation. It is reserved for the "offspring of God" (Acts 17:28–29), which we are.

7 And the first beast was like a lion, and the second beast like a calf, and the third beast had a face as a man, and the fourth beast was like a flying eagle [*D&C 77:4*].

8 And the four beasts had each of them six wings [*representing power to move, act, etc. in the service of God; D&C 77:4*] about him; and they were full of eyes within [*full of knowledge; D&C 77:4*]: and they rest not day and night [*never stop being loyal to God*], saying, Holy, holy, holy [*in Hebrew culture, repeating something three times makes it the highest superlative, i.e., the very best*], Lord God Almighty [*Elohim*], which was, and is, and is to come [*i.e., is eternal*].

9 And when those beasts give glory and honour and thanks to him [*the Father*] that sat on the throne, who liveth for ever and ever [*indicating that all created things respect and worship the Father*],

JST Revelation 4:9

9 And when those beasts give glory and honor and thanks to him that **sits** on the throne, who liveth forever and ever,

10 The four and twenty elders fall down before him that sat on the throne, and worship him that liveth for ever and ever [*i.e., these faithful elders are eternally loyal to God*], and cast their crowns before the throne [*show submission and respect to the Father and His authority*], saying,

JST Revelation 4:10

10 The four and twenty elders fall down before him that **sits** on the throne, and worship him that liveth forever and ever, and cast their crowns before the throne, saying,

11 Thou art worthy, O Lord, to receive glory [*praise; Strong's #1391*] and honour and power: for thou hast created all things, and for thy pleasure [*according to Thy will; Strong's #2307*] they are and were created.

REVELATION 5

Chapter five is the most complete description we have in the scriptures of the premortal council wherein Christ was chosen to be our Savior and Redeemer. Most Christian religions do not believe in a premortal life. If someone is willing to believe the Bible, this chapter, in conjunction with Job 38:4–7, and Jeremiah 1:5, presents a chance to help them understand that we did, indeed, live before we came to earth.

This chapter also contains one of the greatest collections of significant symbolic words and phrases anywhere in the scriptures. You may find it helpful to become familiar with these. A partial list follows:

Symbolic words and Phrases

Verse 1

right hand: covenant hand

him that sat on the throne: Heavenly Father (see verse 7)

a book: the Father's plan for us to be sent to this mortal world (Note that in Revelation 10:2, 8–10, "book" is a mission for John, see D&C 77:14, thus, "a book" can also be symbolic here of Christ's mission to be our Redeemer.)

written within and on the backside: a complete plan **sealed with seven seals:** the 7000 years of the earth's mortal existence (see D&C 7:7)

Verse 2

a strong angel: a mighty angel (we don't know who this is)

Who is worthy to open the book, and loose the seals thereof? Who can carry out the Father's plan for us?

Verse 3

neither to look thereon: No one could even come close to being our Savior and carrying out the Father's plan.

Verse 4

read the book: carry out the Father's plan for us

Verse 5

the Lion of the tribe of Juda: Christ (Jesus was from the tribe of Judah. See Heb. 7:14)

the Root of David: Christ (see Revelation 22:16)

hath prevailed: can carry out the Father's plan

Verse 6

in the midst: the central focus

a Lamb: Christ; symbolic of being sacrificed

as it had been slain: The Atonement worked for us even in premortality, as if it had already been accomplished. See Elder Jeffery R. Holland, General Conference, Oct. 1995. See also quote in the Institute of Religion's New Testament student manual, published in 1978, p. 336.

seven horns (JST "twelve horns"): Horn symbolizes power. See scriptural examples in Topical Guide, p. 218, under "horn."

seven (JST "twelve") Spirits of God sent forth into all the earth: Twelve Apostles

eyes: light and knowledge, see D&C 7:4

Verse 7

he came and took the book: Jesus accepted the mission to be our Savior.

out of the right hand of him that sat upon the throne: Jesus covenanted with the Father

1 And I saw in the right hand [*the covenant-making hand*] of him [*the Father; 5:7*] that sat on the throne a book [*containing the Father's plan; also a specific mission for Jesus*] written within [*on the inside*] and on the backside, sealed with seven seals [*containing information about the 7,000 years of the earth's temporal existence; see D&C 77:7*].

JST Revelation 5:1

1 And I saw in the right hand of him that **sits** on the throne a book written within and on the back side, sealed with seven seals.

We use Rev. 10:2, 8–9 plus D&C 77:14 to show us that "book," as used in verse 1, above, is symbolic of a mission or stewardship.

2 And I saw a strong angel [*one high in authority*] proclaiming with a loud voice, Who is worthy to open the book, and to loose the seals thereof [*i.e., who can carry out the Father's plan of salvation, including the Atonement, for us*]?

JST Revelation 5:2

2 And I saw a strong angel, **and heard him** proclaiming with a loud voice, Who is worthy to open the book, and loose the seals thereof?

3 And no man [*no common man*] in heaven, nor in earth, neither under the earth, was able to open the book, neither to look thereon [*i.e., there was no one to carry out the Father's plan and perform the Atonement; this was a dramatic moment in the vision (a very effective teaching technique) which created the "need" to know in John's mind*].

4 And I [*John*] wept much [*John has become deeply emotionally involved in the vision*], because no man was found worthy to open and to read the book, neither to look thereon [*none of God's spirit children was even close to being worthy or able to carry out the Father's plan or perform the Atonement*].

5 And one of the elders [*mentioned in Rev. 4:4*] saith unto me, Weep not: behold [*look!*], the Lion of the tribe of Juda [*Christ*], the Root of David [*Christ*], hath prevailed to open the book, and to loose the seven seals thereof. [*Jesus Christ can do it!*]

6 And I beheld [*I looked*], and, lo, in the midst of the throne and of the four beasts, and in the midst of the elders, stood a Lamb [*Christ*] as it had been slain [*symbolic of Christ's atoning blood, shed for us*], having seven horns and seven eyes, which are the seven Spirits of God sent forth into all the earth.

JST Revelation 5:6

6 And I beheld, and, lo, in the midst of the throne and of the four beasts, and in the midst of the elders, stood a Lamb as it

had been slain, having **twelve** horns and **twelve eyes**, which are the **twelve servants** of God [*symbolic of the Twelve Apostles*], sent forth into all the earth.

If you will refer back to the symbolism notes included at the beginning of Revelation, in this study guide, you will note that the number 12 symbolizes God's divine organization here on earth.

7 And he [*Christ*] came and took the book [*i.e., accepted the calling*] out of the right hand [*covenant hand*] of him [*Elohim*] that sat upon the throne [*in other words, Jesus Christ made a covenant with the Father to be the Redeemer*].

Next, In verses 8–14, John beautifully describes all of heaven praising Christ for His willingness to perform the Atonement and be our Redeemer, thus carrying out the Father's plan.

8 And when he [*Christ*] had taken the book, the four beasts and four and twenty elders fell down before the Lamb, having every one of them harps [*harps symbolize being in the presence of God in biblical culture*], and golden vials [*containers*] full of odours [*incense; symbolic of prayers which rise up to God*], which are the prayers of saints.

The phrase "they sung a new song," in verse 9, next, is a scriptural phrase which means, in effect, that they could now rejoice over something that they could not rejoice about before.

In other words, they can now sing praises to our Redeemer, whereas, they couldn't before. They can now rejoice about blessings of the Atonement which are now available which were not available before. Another example of "new song" can be found in D&C 84:98–102, where a "new song" can be sung about the Millennium which has finally come.

9 And they sung a new song, saying, Thou [*Christ*] art worthy to take the book [*see verse 1, i.e., the mission to be the Savior and work out the Father's plan*], and to open the seals thereof [*and to carry out the work planned for each of the 1,000 year periods of the earths temporal history*]: for thou wast slain [*speaking of the Atonement as if it were already accomplished*], and hast redeemed us to God [*brought us to the Father*] by thy blood out of every kindred, and tongue, and people, and nation [*the gospel covenants are for all peoples of the world; the Pharisees of Jesus' day didn't like this concept because they felt that the Jews were superior to all other people and, consequently, all other people would be "second class" citizens in heaven*];

10 And hast made us unto our God kings and priests [*celestial glory; see Rev. 1:6*]: and we shall reign on the earth [*both during the Millennium (Rev. 20:4) and when it becomes the celestial kingdom; see D&C 132:20*].

11 And I beheld, and I heard the

voice of many angels round about the throne [*of the Father; see Rev. 4:2 and 5:1*] and the beasts and the elders: and the number of them was ten thousand times ten thousand [*a hundred million*], and thousands of thousands [*plus millions more*];

> The emphasis in verse 11, above, that there will be a great number of people in the celestial kingdom is very comforting. You may wish to cross-reference verse 11 with Revelation 7:9 and also with D&C 76:67 in which we learn that there will be "innumerable" people in celestial glory. This is not surprising when we consider the missionary work that is being done in the spirit world as well as the fact that "all children who die before they arrive at the years of accountability are saved in the celestial kingdom of heaven." See D&C 137:10.

12 Saying with a loud voice, Worthy is the Lamb [*Christ*] that was slain to receive power, and riches, and wisdom, and strength, and honour, and glory, and blessing.

13 And every creature which is in heaven [*birds, etc.*], and on the earth, and under the earth [*animals that burrow underground*], and such as are in the sea [*fish, etc.*], and all that are in them, heard I saying, Blessing, and honour, and glory, and power, be unto him [*the Father*] that sitteth upon the throne, and unto the Lamb [*Christ*] for ever and ever [*all animals, birds, fish, etc., will be resurrected too as a result of Christ's Atonement; see D&C 29:23–24*].

14 And the four beasts said, Amen ["*We agree.*"]. And the four and twenty elders fell down and worshipped him that liveth for ever and ever.

REVELATION 6

This is one of the most famous and well known chapters in the Book of Revelation. In it, the Lamb, Christ, opens six of the seven seals mentioned in Revelation 5:1. Joseph Smith tells us, in D&C 77:7, that each of the seals represents one thousand years of the earth's temporal or mortal existence. We understand this to mean that the earth has a total of 7,000 years from the time of the Fall of Adam and Eve to the end of the "little season" at the end of the Millennium (see D&C 77:6). It is important to remember that we do not know the exact date of Adam's Fall (see Bible Dictionary under "Chronology," p. 635, where it says, "Many dates cannot be fixed with certainty.") Thus, we cannot tell exactly where we are in relation to the 7,000 years.

In Revelation, chapter 6, we are given a very, very brief overview of each of the first six thousand year periods of the earth's temporal existence. In the following chapters of Revelation, many more details will be given, which are to be fulfilled near the end of the sixth thousand year period and in the beginning of the seventh thousand year period, before the Savior's Second Coming (see D&C 7:12–13).

The fact that the Lamb, the Savior, opens the seals is symbolic of the fact that Christ is in charge of things here on earth, under the Father's direction, and is carrying out the Father's plan as shown in Revelation, chapter five [*see notes for Revelation 5:1–4 and 5:5–7*]. There are four "horsemen" in this chapter, which are rather famous among Christians who study their Bibles. With the aid of symbolism given in the introduction of Revelation in this study guide, we can see major insights and descriptions given for each of these one thousand year periods as summarized in the following chart:

Verses 1–2
The First Thousand Years
(ca. 4,000 to 3,000 BC):

"White" is symbolic of righteousness, purity, etc., and "horse" is symbolic of victory, might, triumph, etc. Thus, there is a great triumph of righteousness during the first thousand years. We don't know who this horseman is, but two good possibilities would be Adam and Enoch.

Verses 3–4
The Second Thousand Years
(ca. 3,000 to 2,000 BC):

A red horse could symbolize the triumph of war, bloodshed, etc., possibly representing the wickedness during Noah's day. This horseman has a "great sword," representing terrible destruction.

Verses 5–6
The Third Thousand Years
(ca. 2,000 to 1,000 BC):

A black horse and its rider could symbolize evil, spiritual darkness, etc., as well as the blackness and depression which accompanies famine. This period of the earth's history would include the days of Abraham, Joseph in Egypt, and the years of captivity in Egypt for the children of Israel. Famine was a major aspect of life during this one thousand year period. Abraham's brother, Haran, starved to death during this period (see Abraham 2:1). In fact, the rider of the black horse is holding "a pair of balances in his hand" which can be symbolic of famine and can represent that every morsel of food must be carefully measured out during times of famine (see Leviticus 26:26). Additional famine symbolism is found in the phrases "A measure of wheat for a penny," and "three measures of barley for a penny." Here, a "penny" represents a day's wages (see Matt. 20:2) and a "measure of wheat" is about one quart (see McConkie, *Doctrinal New Testament Commentary*, Vol. 3, p. 480).

Verses 7–8
The Fourth Thousand Years
(ca. 1,000 to 0 BC):

The fourth horse is pale and its rider is named "Death." "Hell" seems to be following this horseman around and could symbolize that spirit prison is gaining many new inmates during this thousand year period. The pale horse could represent that, after the riders of the red horse and the black horse have taken their toll, not much quality of life remains for those who have chosen wickedness as a lifestyle. It is during this time in history that we see Israel divided by civil war, Assyria carries the lost ten tribes away, Lehi and his family flee Jerusalem, the Babylonians conquer Jerusalem, Daniel is thrown into the lions' den, and the Romans become the rulers of the Holy Land.

The next two 1000-year periods do not involve "horsemen" but do give a very brief overview of events during those times.

Verses 9–11
The Fifth Thousand Years
(ca. AD 0 to 1,000):

The fifth seal would include the Savior's birth, the early Church, the persecutions of the Christians and the beginning centuries of the dark ages. In verses nine through eleven, John was shown early martyrs, members of the church organized by the Savior during His mortal mission who had been killed because they would not deny their testimonies. According to symbolism in verse 11, these righteous Saints were given "white robes" indicating that they had earned exaltation.

Verses 12–16
The Sixth Thousand Years
(ca. AD 1,000 to 2,000):

In these verses, John sees the Savior open the sixth seal, and is shown some signs of the times, including a great earthquake (verse 12). Perhaps, as a result of this earthquake, "every mountain and island were moved out of their places." These and other signs of the times occurring in the sixth seal appear to make the wicked think that the end of the world has come. Whatever the case, events which occur in the sixth seal cause the wicked to wish for anything necessary to prevent them from seeing God. These verses remind us that "wickedness never was happiness" (Alma 41:10), and that the wicked, when faced with the evil and foolishness of their agency choices, will be in great agony.

We will now study Revelation, chapter 6.

1 And I saw when the Lamb [*Christ*] opened one of the seals [*the first one, representing the first thousand years of the earth's temporal existence, i.e., approximately 4,000–3,000 BC; (D&C 77:7)*], and I heard, as it were the noise of thunder, one of the four beasts saying, Come and see.

JST Revelation 6:1

1 And I saw when the Lamb opened one of the seals, **one of the four beasts**, and I heard,

as it were, the noise of thunder, saying, Come and see.

2 And I [*John*] saw, and behold a white horse [*symbolically, white can mean righteousness and horse represents victory*]: and he that sat on him had a bow; and a crown [*authority*] was given unto him: and he went forth conquering, and to conquer [*one possible interpretation could be Adam. Another, Enoch and his victories with the City of Enoch*].

3 And when he [*Christ*] had opened the second seal [*3,000–2,000 BC*], I heard the second beast say, Come and see.

4 And there went out another horse that was red [*bloodshed, war*]: and power was given to him [*perhaps Satan and wicked worldly leaders during the days of Noah*] that sat thereon to take peace from the earth, and that they should kill one another: and there was given unto him a great sword [*representing terrible destruction*].

5 And when he [*Christ*] had opened the third seal [*2,000–1,000 BC*], I heard the third beast say, Come and see. And I beheld [*I looked*], and lo a black horse [*evil, darkness, despair*]; and he that sat on him had a pair of balances [*representing famine; food had to be carefully measured and meted out*] in his hand. [*During this seal, Abraham went to Egypt because of famine; Joseph's brothers later came to him in Egypt because of famine; also, the Israelites were held as slaves in Egypt during this period.*]

6 And I heard a voice in the midst of the four beasts say, A measure [*two U.S. pints*] of wheat for a penny [*a day's wages*], and three measures of barley for a penny; and see thou hurt not [*don't waste*] the oil and the wine [*i.e., terrible famine*].

JST Revelation 6:6

6 And I heard a voice in the midst of the four beasts say, A measure of wheat for a penny, and three measures of barley for a penny; **and hurt not thou** the oil and the wine.

7 And when he [*Christ*] had opened the fourth seal [*1,000–0 BC; Assyrian captivity, ten tribes lost about 722 BC; Babylonian captivity about 588 BC; Daniel in lion's den; Romans take over prior to Christ's birth*], I heard the voice of the fourth beast say, Come and see.

8 And I looked, and behold a pale horse [*not much left of Israel, few righteous people, terrible conditions among the wicked, etc.*]: and his name that sat on him was Death, and Hell followed with him. And power was given unto them over the fourth part [*perhaps meaning not quite as severe destruction as in the wind up scenes of the world in Rev. 9:15*] of the earth, to kill with sword [*military destruction*], and with hunger, and with death [*pestilence, plagues*], and with the beasts of the earth.

9 And when he [*Christ*] had opened the fifth seal [*AD 0–1,000*], I saw

under the altar [*altar represents sacrifice*] the souls of them that were slain for the word of God [*for the gospel*], and for the testimony which they held [*i.e., those who gave their lives for the gospel's sake*]:

10 And they [*the people who had given their lives for the gospel*] cried with a loud voice, saying, How long, O Lord, holy and true, dost thou not judge and avenge our blood on them [*the wicked*] that dwell on the earth [*i.e., when will the wicked get what's coming to them?; the same question is asked by Joseph Smith in D&C 121 and by Habakkuk in Habakkuk 1*]?

11 And white robes [*exaltation; 3:5*] were given unto every one of them [*the righteous martyrs in verse 9*]; and it was said unto them, that they should rest yet for a little season, until their fellowservants also and their brethren, that should be killed as they were, should be fulfilled [*i.e., others would have similar fates throughout earth's remaining history*].

12 And I beheld when he [*Christ*] had opened the sixth seal [*roughly AD 1,000–2,000*], and, lo, there was a great earthquake; and the sun became black as sackcloth of hair [*perhaps meaning black goat's hair used in weaving fabric*], and the moon became as blood [*i.e., great signs in heaven and earth during this period of time*];

13 And the stars of heaven [*perhaps including satellites, airplanes, etc., in our day*] fell unto the earth, even as a fig tree casteth her untimely figs, when she is shaken of a mighty wind.

John now jumps ahead to the Second Coming for a few verses. Caution, do not put the Second Coming in the sixth seal. See headings to Rev. 8 and 9 and D&C 77:13.

14 And the heaven departed as a scroll when it is rolled together; and every mountain and island were moved out of their places [*one continent, one ocean again; D&C 133:22–24, Gen. 10:25*].

JST Revelation 6:14

14 And the **heavens opened as a scroll is opened** when it is rolled together; and every mountain, and island, **was** moved out of **its** place.

15 And the kings [*wicked political leaders*] of the earth, and the great men, and the rich men, and the chief captains, and the mighty men, and every bondman, and every free man [*i.e., all the wicked*], hid themselves in the dens [*caves*] and in the rocks of the mountains [*like Isaiah said the wicked would do at the Second Coming; see Isaiah 2:19, and 2 Nephi 12, verses 10, 19 and 21*];

16 And said to the mountains and rocks, Fall on us, and hide us from the face of him [*the Father; Rev. 5:1, 7, 13*] that sitteth on the throne, and from the wrath [*anger*] of the Lamb [*Christ*]:

17 For the great day of his [*the

Savior's] wrath is come; and who shall be able to stand [*i.e., who will be able to survive the Second Coming*]? [*Answer: those living a terrestrial or celestial lifestyle. D&C 5:19 plus 76:81–85 and 88:100–101 tell us that those who live the wicked lifestyle of telestials, which includes lying, stealing, sexual immorality, and murder (and of course, sons of perdition) will be destroyed by the Savior's glory at the Second Coming and will not be resurrected until after the Millennium is over.*]

REVELATION 7

John now returns to the 6th seal and tells more about it. He will show us that great missionary work will take place during the sixth 1,000 year period of the earth's temporal existence. He will also show that many will eventually be exalted out of all nations. This chapter is perhaps best known for verse 4 in which the 144,000 are mentioned. We will say more about them when we come to that verse.

As we begin with verse 1, it helps to know that "wind," as used in the scriptures, is often symbolic of destruction.

1 And after these things I saw four angels [*with power and authority to save life or destroy, and to oversee the preaching of the gospel to the whole earth; D&C 77:8*] standing on the four corners of the earth, holding the four winds [*north, east, south, and west winds*

which symbolically have power to bless mankind from all directions or cause great destruction from all directions*] of the earth, that the wind should not blow on the earth, nor on the sea, nor on any tree [*i.e., these four angels hold massive destruction back until the restoration and ensuing gathering of the righteous have taken place; see verse 3*].

2 And I saw another angel [*Elias; D&C 77:9; represents several angels with keys, see McConkie, Doctrinal New Testament Commentary, Bookcraft, Inc., 1973, Vol 3, p. 492*] ascending from the east [*"east" typically represents coming from heaven, since the sun, representing celestial glory and heaven, appears first from the east*], having the seal of the living God: and he cried with a loud voice to the four angels, to whom it was given to hurt the earth and the sea [*they are not just destroying angels; they save life too, D&C 77:8*],

JST Revelation 7:2

2 And I saw another angel ascending from the east, having the seal of the living God; **and I heard him cry** with a loud voice to the four angels, to whom it was given to hurt the earth and the sea,

3 Saying, Hurt not the earth, neither the sea, nor the trees [*do not allow the final destructions prior to the Second Coming*], till we have sealed the servants of our God [*the righteous*] in their foreheads [*i.e., the faithful will be gathered to the*

gospel before the final destruction; anciently, some cultures literally marked their foreheads indicating which religion they were loyal to].

4 And I heard the number of them which were sealed: and there were sealed an hundred and forty and four thousand [*these are not the only ones saved; see verse 9*] of all the tribes of the children of Israel.

JST Revelation 7:4

4 **And the** number of them **who** were sealed, **were an hundred and forty and four thousand** of all the tribes of the children of Israel.

Who are the 144,000? Joseph Smith answered this question for us in D&C 77:11. He said that these are high priests, 12,000 out of each of the tribes of Israel, who will "bring as many as will come to the church of the First-born." The "church of the First-born" is the Church of Jesus Christ of Latter-day Saints and often includes the connotation of being exalted. Thus, we see this great group of high priests much involved in the gathering of the righteous spoken of in verses 1–3, above.

5 Of the tribe of Juda were sealed twelve thousand. Of the tribe of Reuben were sealed twelve thousand. Of the tribe of Gad were sealed twelve thousand.

6 Of the tribe of Aser were sealed twelve thousand. Of the tribe of Nepthalim were sealed twelve

thousand. Of the tribe of Manasses were sealed twelve thousand.

7 Of the tribe of Simeon were sealed twelve thousand. Of the tribe of Levi were sealed twelve thousand. Of the tribe of Issachar were sealed twelve thousand.

8 Of the tribe of Zabulon were sealed twelve thousand. Of the tribe of Joseph were sealed twelve thousand. Of the tribe of Benjamin were sealed twelve thousand.

If you look very carefully at verses 5–8, above, you will see that the tribes of Dan and Ephraim are missing. We have no idea why they are left out here and speculation doesn't help. We know for sure that they are not "left out" as far as the Lord's blessings are concerned, because many members of the Church are from the lineage of Ephraim, and quite a number are from the tribe of Dan.

9 After this I beheld, and, lo, a great multitude, which no man could number [*i.e., many more than 144,000 are saved; see also D&C 76:67*], of all nations, and kindreds, and people, and tongues, stood before the throne [*of the Father*], and before the Lamb, clothed with white robes [*symbolic of exaltation*], and palms [*symbolic of joy and triumph, victory*] in their hands;

10 And cried with a loud voice, saying, Salvation to our God [*the Father*] which sitteth upon the throne, and unto the Lamb.

11 And all the angels stood round about the throne, and about the elders and the four beasts [*see notes in chapter 4*], and fell before the throne on their faces [*a way of showing humility and worship in Biblical culture*], and worshipped God,

12 Saying, Amen ["*We agree.*"]: Blessing, and glory, and wisdom, and thanksgiving, and honour, and power, and might, be unto our God for ever and ever. Amen.

John is now invited to become an active participant in the vision, as one of the elders asks him a question about what he has just seen. Notice his wise and careful answer.

13 And one of the elders answered [*asked a question*], saying unto me [*John*], What are these which are arrayed in white robes? and whence came they [*i.e., who are the people dressed in white in verse 9*]?

14 And I said unto him, Sir, thou knowest [*please tell me*]. And he said to me, These are they which came out of great tribulation [*trials and persecutions*], and have washed their robes [*had their sins cleansed by the Atonement of Christ; something each of us must do in our own lives, i.e., symbolic of repentance, obedience*], and made them white [*i.e., become clean*] in the blood of the Lamb [*i.e., the Atonement can cleanse completely; compare with Isaiah 1:16–18*].

15 Therefore are they [*this is the reason they are*] before the throne of God [*they are in celestial glory*], and serve him day and night [*keep His commandments day and night*] in his temple: and he that sitteth on the throne shall dwell among them.

16 [*John now briefly and beautifully describes some benefits of celestial glory.*] They shall hunger no more, neither thirst any more; neither shall the sun light on them, nor any heat.

17 For the Lamb [*the Savior*] which is in the midst of the throne shall feed them, and shall lead them unto living fountains of waters: and God shall wipe away all tears from their eyes [*the final state of the righteous; in other words, it is worth repenting and returning to God's presence!*].

REVELATION 8

Many people think that the Savior's Second Coming will occur at the end of the sixth seal. According to the Lord, this is not so. In D&C 77:12, Joseph Smith tells us that the things prophesied in Revelation, chapter 8, will happen "in the beginning of the seventh thousand years," before the coming of the Lord. Indeed, we who live in the last days live in a day when prophecies are being fulfilled all around us. It is a glorious time to be alive, a time when testimonies can be strengthened by observing the fulfillment of many ancient prophecies known as the signs of the times, which will lead up to the actual Second Coming of the Lord.

Let's watch now and see some of the things that will take place early in the seventh seal, before the Savior comes to usher in the Millennium.

1 And when he had opened the seventh seal [*roughly AD 2,000–3,000*], there was silence in heaven about the space of half an hour.

This "silence" is also mentioned in D&C 88:95. We have not been told yet what this means. So far in the opening of the seals, we have been dealing with the earth's time system. Some people speculate about this half hour of silence and suggest that it might be about 21 years in the Lord's time system, and thus we would be 21 years without revelation. This has no merit, especially in view of Daniel 2:35, 44–45, in which we are assured that this restored Church "shall stand forever" and thus we will have continuous revelation right up to the Second Coming.

2 And I saw the seven angels which stood before God; and to them were given seven trumpets [*perhaps symbolic of perfecting or finishing his work; in Biblical number symbolism, "seven" represents being complete or perfection*].

We will pause to mention an interesting possibility in conjunction with Biblical numerical symbolism. As indicated in the symbolism notes at the beginning of Revelation in this study guide, the number three represents God, and the number four represents man. Therefore, 3 (God) plus 4 (man) equals 7 (perfection), i.e., when man works with God, the result is perfection, ultimately, exaltation.

3 And another angel came and stood at the altar [*worshiped*], having a golden censer [*symbolic of worship*]; and there was given unto him much incense [*incense rises, prayers "rise;" hence incense is symbolic of prayers*], that he should offer it with the prayers of all saints upon the golden altar which was before the throne [*in front of the throne of the Father; see Rev. 4:4 and 5:5; in other words, Saints and angels worship God*].

4 And the smoke of the incense, which came with the prayers of the saints, ascended up [*rose up*] before God out of the angel's hand [*the prayers reached God*].

5 And the angel took the censer, and filled it with fire [*punishments of God*] of the altar, and cast it into the earth [*punishments of God pour out upon the earth early in the seventh seal, before Second Coming*]: and there were voices, and thunderings, and lightnings, and an earthquake [*more signs of the times*].

6 And the seven angels [*in verse 2, above*] which had the seven trumpets [*since "seven" is symbolic of completeness or perfection, this could be symbolic of the completing, perfecting, or finishing of all things necessary before the Second*]

Coming; see D&C 77:12] prepared themselves to sound.

Just a thought about verses 7–12, next. There is much use of symbolism. Symbolism can be understood many ways and thus can present many different messages to us as directed by the Holy Ghost. So it is with the symbolism in these next verses. One could easily look at the damage to earth, trees, grass, sea, rivers, fountains of waters, waters, sun, moon, and stars, as shown in this chapter, and consider it to be prophetic reference to severe ecological damage in the last days prior to the Second Coming.

Another possibility is that one could consider "trees" and "grass" to represent people, as is often the case in the scriptures. If so, the prophetic symbolism here could refer to damage done to people by evil in the last days. We could look at the "rivers," "fountains of waters" and "waters" and consider John 4:10 and 14 wherein the Savior teaches of the "living water" (the gospel, including the Atonement) and its cleansing and refreshing power in our lives. Then we could see prophetic reference to the damage done to the "living water" in people's lives by the wickedness in the last days. Again, we could look at the "sun, moon, and stars" as representing spiritual light from above and the darkening of them as spiritual darkness increases in the last days.

Chapter 8 also mentions hail, fire, blood, and so forth. It is interesting to observe that some of these plagues and pestilences to be poured out upon the earth in the last days, prior to the coming of the Lord, are reminiscent of some which took place in order to prepare the way for Moses and the children of Israel to gain freedom from Egyptian bondage. Revelation chapter 16 contains a number of these plagues also. We will make a brief list of these plagues from both chapters 8 and 16, which lead us to realize that the ten plagues are, in effect, to be repeated in the last days before the Second Coming, and for the same purpose (to serve as a wake up call to repent and be delivered from spiritual bondage).

From Revelation Chapter 8:

Verse 7: **hail and fire** (Exodus 9:23)

Verse 7: **blood** (Exodus 7:17)

Verse 8: **sun. . . darkened** (Exodus 10: 21–22)

From Revelation Chapter 16:

Verse 2: **sores** (Exodus 9:9)

Verse 3: **blood** (Exodus 7:17)

Verse 8: **fire** (Exodus 9:23–24)

Verse 10: **darkness** (Exodus 10:21–22)

Verse 13: **frogs** (Exodus 8:2)

Verse 21: **hail** (Exodus 9:18)

7 The first angel sounded, and there followed hail and fire mingled with blood [*similar to plagues in Egypt whose purpose likewise was to humble the wicked and prepare Israelites for redemption from wickedness*], and they were cast upon the earth: and the third part of trees was burnt up, and all green grass was burnt up [*perhaps indicating that significant amounts of earth's greenery will be destroyed prior to the Second Coming, rain forests razed, acid rain damage, etc.*].

8 And the second angel sounded, and as it were a great mountain burning with fire was cast into the sea: and the third part of the sea became blood [*similar to the plague in Egypt; Exodus 7:17*];

9 And the third part of the creatures which were in the sea, and had life, died; and the third part of the ships were destroyed [*much destruction everywhere*].

10 And the third angel sounded, and there fell a great star [*Lucifer; Isaiah 14:12, D&C 76:25–27*] from heaven, burning as it were a lamp, and it fell upon the third part of the rivers, and upon the fountains of waters [*Satan has counterfeit "living water," i.e., false religions and philosophies*];

11 And the name of the star is called Wormwood [*a very bitter substance; see Bible Dictionary under "Wormwood;" i.e., followers of Satan have a "bitter" fate*]: and the third part of the waters became wormwood; and many men died of the waters, because they were made bitter.

12 And the fourth angel sounded, and the third part of the sun was smitten, and the third part of the moon, and the third part of the stars; so as the third part of them was darkened [*perhaps symbolizing that there would be great spiritual darkness upon the earth in the last days before the coming of the Savior*], and the day shone not for a third part of it, and the night likewise [*perhaps referring in part to spiritual darkness as well as physical darkness caused by burning oil fields, pollution, volcanic ash, etc., in the last days*].

JST Revelation 8:12

12 And the fourth angel sounded, and the third part of the sun was smitten, and the third part of the moon, and the third part of the stars; so **that** the third part of them was darkened, and the day shone not for a third part of it, and the night likewise.

The "one third" used in the above verses might be a symbolic tie in with the "one third" who were cast out with Satan (Rev. 12:4), thus symbolizing their destructive influence upon the earth in the last days.

13 And I beheld, and heard an angel flying through the midst of heaven, saying with a loud voice, Woe, woe, woe, to the inhabiters [*inhabitants*] of the earth by reason of [*because of*] the other voices of the trumpet of the three angels [*in verse 2, above*], which are yet to sound [*i.e., worse is yet to come*]!

REVELATION 9

This chapter continues with prophecies of events which will take place in the seventh seal, prior to the Second Coming.

The JST makes a very significant change to verse 1. As it stands in the Bible, it sounds like Lucifer is given the "key" to the bottomless pit. However, the JST informs us that the key is given to a powerful angel, through whose power and authority limits are placed upon Satan and his kingdom (see verse 4).

1 And the fifth angel sounded, and I saw a star [*Lucifer*] fall from heaven unto the earth: and to him was given the key of the bottomless pit.

JST Revelation 9:1

1 And the fifth angel sounded, and I saw a star fall from heaven unto the earth; and to **the angel** was given the key of the bottomless pit.

In verses 2 and 3, next, we see all of the forces of hell unleashed in the final days before the coming of the Lord. There is much imagery here. We see "the bottomless pit" representing hell, Satan's kingdom, etc. We see "smoke." In a house fire, "smoke" gets into everything and causes much damage. Thus, "smoke," as used here, can be symbolic of evil and wickedness permeating every aspect of society. It arises out of the pit and darkens the light of the sun, reminding us that Satan's goal is to obscure the spiritual light which comes from above and leave us in spiritual darkness. "Locusts" bring to mind one of the plagues in Egypt (Exodus 10:4) and can symbolize seemingly countless hordes of the wicked working their evil designs upon the earth in the last days.

2 And he [*the angel in JST verse 1*] opened the bottomless pit [*allowed Satan to unleash all the forces of hell!*]; and there arose a smoke [*Satan's "dark" influence*] out of the pit, as the smoke of a great furnace; and the sun and the air were darkened by reason of the smoke of the pit [*Satan and his evil hosts have great influence in the last days*].

3 And there came out of the smoke [*Satan's influence; see verse 2*] locusts [*symbolic of countless numbers of wicked in the last days*] upon the earth: and unto them was given power, as the scorpions of the earth have power [*scorpions have power to cause much suffering if people get close enough to them; so also is the case with wickedness*].

It is very important that we know that God has power over Satan and his wicked followers. He sets limits on them, as we see in verse 4, next.

4 And it was commanded them [*Satan and his hosts have limits put upon them by God*] that they should not hurt the grass of the earth,

neither any green thing [*perhaps representing those who are still growing toward heaven*], neither any tree [*protection for the righteous; trees often represent people, for instance Isaiah 10:19*]; but only those men which have not the seal of God in their foreheads [*i.e., Satan only has power to "hurt" the spirituality of the wicked who do not have God's seal, i.e., who are not loyal to God*].

5 And to them [*Satan and his hosts*] it was given that they should not kill them [*the wicked in verse 4 who have not the seal of God in their foreheads*], but that they should be tormented five months [*through this torment, hopefully, some of them would see Satan for what he is and repent*]: and their torment was as the torment of a scorpion, when he striketh a man.

What is the significance of "five months" as seen in chapter nine? Answer: We don't know. We do know that the life cycle of a locust is about five months (see Jay and Donald Parry, *Understanding the Book of Revelation*, p. 118), so it could symbolize that Satan and his evil forces have a limited time, as stated in Revelation 12:12. It could also be a symbolical tie in with the "fifth angel" in verse 1.

6 And in those days [*the last days*] shall men seek death, and shall not find it; and shall desire to die, and death shall flee from them [*some plagues are worse than death*].

7 And the shapes of the locusts were like unto horses [*horse is symbolic of military victory, i.e., Satan had much success; there are almost countless people involved in military actions in the last days*] prepared unto battle; and on their heads were as it were crowns like gold [*Satan's counterfeit rewards of power and wicked temporary glory lead many to follow him*], and their faces were as the faces of [*wicked*] men.

8 And they had hair as the hair of women [*perhaps long hair might cause people in New Testament times to think of Samson's long hair and great strength and his destructive misuse of power; Judges 14–16*], and their teeth were as [*like*] the teeth of lions [*lion is symbolic of great power, i.e., they were able to inflict much damage, destruction*].

9 And they had breastplates [*armor*], as it were breastplates of iron; and the sound of their wings [*airplanes?*] was as the sound of chariots of many horses running to battle [*noises of modern military machinery in action?*].

10 And they had tails like unto scorpions [*modern warfare, tanks, flame throwers, rifles, etc.?*], and there were stings in their tails: and their power was to hurt men five months. [*We don't know for sure what the five months symbolize here or in verse 5. Perhaps it might simply be symmetry tying in with the fifth angel in verse one, thus meaning the "five months" or time spoken of by the fifth angel during which Satan rages in the last days.*]

11 And they had a king [*Satan*] over them, which is the angel of the bottomless pit, whose name in the Hebrew tongue is Abaddon [*ruin, destruction;* Strong's #0003], but in the Greek tongue hath his name Apollyon [*Destroyer;* Strong's #0623].

Moses 5:24 gives another name for Satan. It is "Perdition" which means "utter loss" or "destruction." See also 2 Thessalonians 2:3.

12 One woe is past [*of the three woes spoken of in 8:13*]; and, behold, there come two woes more hereafter.

Just a bit more about the woes spoken of in verse 12, above. In chapter eight, verse 13, John was told that there were "three angels, which are yet to sound," in other words, three more "woes" or plagues to come. Revelation 9, verses 1–11, have described one of the three "woes" for us, which leaves two more to come.

13 And the sixth angel sounded [*still dealing with occurrences in the beginning of the seventh seal, before the Lord comes; see heading to chapter 9 in our Bible*], and I heard a voice from the four horns [*of the altar, see 1 Kings 1:50; symbolic of a place of safety, refuge, protection; in other words, heaven*] of the golden [*heavenly*] altar which is before God [*i.e., he heard a voice from heaven*],

14 Saying to the sixth angel [*the sixth of the seven angels in Rev. 8:2*] which had the trumpet, Loose the four angels [*Satan's angels of destruction; counterfeits of God's four righteous angels in Rev. 7:1; i.e., Satan is the great counterfeiter!*] which are bound [*by God's power*] in the great river Euphrates.

JST Revelation 9:14

14 Saying to the sixth angel which had the trumpet, Loose the four angels which are bound in the **bottomless pit**.

15 And the four angels [*evil angels*] were loosed, which were prepared for an hour, and a day, and a month, and a year, for to slay the third part of men. [*Perhaps one third ties in symbolically with the one third wicked in Rev. 12:4 indicating that Satan and his hosts will devastate a great number of people on earth, just as he did in the war in heaven.*]

16 And the number of the army of the horsemen [*Satan's wicked followers*] were two hundred thousand thousand [*200 million, i.e., innumerable!*]: and I heard the number of them.

JST Revelation 9:16

16 And the number of the army of the horsemen were two hundred thousand thousand; and I **saw** the number of them.

17 And thus I saw the horses [*symbolic of military victory*] in the vision, and them that sat on them [*Satan and his followers*], having breastplates of fire, and of jacinth [*a precious stone, perhaps symbolizing that materialism will lead many to follow Satan; could also*]

mean that misuse of wealth will cause much sorrow and destruction in the last days], and brimstone [molten sulphur; symbolic of destruction]: and the heads of the horses were as the heads of lions [capable of much destruction]; and out of their mouths issued fire and smoke and brimstone [i.e., terrible devastations will occur in the last days].

18 By these three [fire, smoke and brimstone in verse 17, above] was the third part of men killed, by the fire, and by the smoke, and by the brimstone, which issued out of their mouths.

19 For their power is in their mouth [perhaps including, symbolically, the power of the media in the last days to destroy], and in their tails [perhaps referring to "scorpion" in verse 5, which could symbolize military weapons, tanks, flame throwers, missiles, etc.]: for their tails were like unto serpents, and had heads, and with them they do hurt.

20 And the rest of the men which were not killed by these plagues yet repented not [a sad fact] of the works of their hands, that they should not worship devils, and idols of gold, and silver, and brass, and stone, and of wood: which neither can see, nor hear, nor walk [i.e., the remaining wicked went right on with their wicked lifestyles in spite of the destruction all around them]:

21 Neither repented they of their murders, nor of their sorceries [witchcraft, etc.], nor of their for-

nication [sexual immorality], nor of their thefts.

REVELATION 10

This chapter is particularly touching when one realizes that by this time (approximately AD 95) John has long been the only Apostle remaining from the Church which Jesus established in the Holy Land. He was told that he would "tarry" (see John 21:21–23 combined with D&C 7:3), but, as far as we know, nothing had yet transpired with respect to that promise. He is now an old man, likely in his nineties, and a prisoner on the Isle of Patmos. Imagine his feelings when he is told that he would yet prophesy before the nations and carry out a great mission among the people of the earth! We know that he was translated and has not yet died, rather, has continued assisting with the work of the Lord here on earth. He will continue to do so until the Second Coming, at which time he will be resurrected.

1 And I saw another mighty angel [this appears to be the seventh of the angels in 8:2; if so, it might be Adam, the "seventh angel" in D&C 88:106, 110, 112] come down from heaven, clothed with a cloud: and a rainbow was upon his head, and his face was as it were the sun, and his feet as pillars of fire [quite a description of Michael or Adam, if he is the seventh angel spoken of here]:

The "rainbow upon his head" in verse 1, above, could tie in with the "rainbow round about the throne" of the Father, in Rev. 4:3. If so, it might be symbolic of the splendid power of God and of exaltation.

2 And he had in his hand a little book [*a mission for John; see verses 8–10, also D&C 77:14*] open: and he set his right foot upon the sea, and his left foot on the earth [*D&C 88:110; i.e., this angel has a large jurisdiction*],

3 And cried with a loud voice, as when a lion roareth: and when he had cried, seven thunders uttered their voices [*seven angels with seven seals; D&C 88:108–110*].

4 And when the seven thunders had uttered their voices, I [*John*] was about to write: and I heard a voice from heaven saying unto me, Seal up those things which the seven thunders uttered, and write them not [*in other words, they are not yet to be revealed to the world in the scriptures*].

JST Revelation 10:4

4 And when the seven thunders had uttered their voices, I was about to write; and I heard a voice from heaven saying unto me, **Those things are sealed up** which the seven thunders uttered, and write them not.

5 And the angel [*in verses 1 and 2, above*] which I saw stand upon the sea and upon the earth lifted up his hand to heaven,

6 And sware [*promised*] by him that liveth for ever and ever [*spoke with authority from God*], who created heaven, and the things that therein are, and the earth, and the things that therein are, and the sea, and the things which are therein, that there should be time no longer [*that there will be no more delay, in other words, "Let the Millennium begin."*]:

7 But in the days of the voice of the seventh angel, when he shall begin to sound, the mystery [*plans; Strong's #3466*] of God should be finished [*completed; Strong's #5055*], as he hath declared to his servants the prophets.

8 And the voice which I heard from heaven spake unto me again, and said, Go and take the little book [*a mission for John; D&C 77:14*] which is open in the hand of the angel which standeth upon the sea and upon the earth.

9 And I went unto the angel, and said unto him, Give me the little book [*i.e., I accept the mission*]. And he said unto me, Take it, and eat it up [*i.e., "internalize" it, make it a part of you*]; and it shall make thy belly bitter, but it shall be in thy mouth sweet as honey [*being a servant of God to the people has both bitter and sweet aspects*].

10 And I took the little book out of the angel's hand, and ate it up [*"internalized it"; made it a part of me*]; and it was in my mouth sweet as honey: and as soon as I had eaten it, my belly was bitter [*working with stubborn, unrepentant people can sometimes cause indigestion indeed!*].

11 And he said unto me, Thou must prophesy again before many peoples, and nations, and tongues, and kings [*i.e., you have a great mission yet to perform on earth, a very significant and encouraging statement, since John at this time, about AD 95, was banished on the Isle of Patmos in a prison colony. In D&C 7, we are told that John will "tarry" or remain until the Second Coming. In June, 1831, Joseph Smith said "that John the Revelator was then among the ten tribes of Israel . . . to prepare them for their return." See* History of the Church, *vol. 1, p. 176.*]

REVELATION 11

We are not alone in the Christian world in believing that the events of the last days spoken of in this chapter will take place. This chapter is one of the most famous among Christians throughout the world. They, like we, believe that the mission of these two prophets, ending with their martyrdom and being brought back to life, will signify that the Second Coming of the Savior is close. Revelation 11:3 refers to them as "two witnesses" and Revelation 11:10 refers to them as "two prophets." In D&C 77:15, the Prophet Joseph Smith calls them "two prophets." Therefore, we see them as two witnesses, fulfilling the law of witnesses (D&C 6:28) and as two prophets holding the keys to control the elements, etc., as shown in verse 6.

It is interesting to point out several parallels between the ministry of these two prophets and the ministry of the Savior. For instance, Christ's formal mission was carried out in the Holy Land and lasted about three years. The mission of these two prophets in the last days will be to the Holy Land and will last about three years. The Savior is the "light of the world." The two prophets are "candlesticks" (verse 4) which carry the light from the Savior to the world. Jesus demonstrated His power over the elements during His mortal ministry. The two prophets will be given power over the elements during their ministry (verse 6). Christ was crucified when He had completed His mortal mission. The two prophets will be killed after they have completed their mission (verse 7). The wicked rejoiced in the Savior's death. The wicked will rejoice in the slaying of the two prophets (verses 8–10). Jesus was resurrected after three days. The two will be resurrected [*see heading to chapter 11*] after three days. Great destruction accompanied the death of the Savior. Great destruction will accompany the resurrection of the two prophets [*verse 13*]. Many were converted by Christ's resurrection. Many will be converted after the resurrection of these two prophets [*verse 13, last phrase.*]

1 [*John is the only living apostle remaining in the eastern hemisphere at this time. He is told here to see how the Church is doing in his day.*] And there was given me

[*John*] a reed [*a measuring device*] like unto a rod: and the angel stood, saying, Rise, and measure the temple of God, and the altar, and them that worship therein [*i.e., study current conditions among the Saints, see how they "measure up"*].

2 But the court [*the courtyard or temple grounds*] which is without [*outside of*] the temple leave out, and measure it not; for it is given unto the Gentiles [*apostasy is coming*]: and the holy city [*Jerusalem*] shall they tread under foot forty and two months [*perhaps referring to the 42 months spoken of in verse 3. Jerusalem will be downtrodden by Gentiles for hundreds of years. The universal apostasy alluded to here will end in the spring of 1820 when Joseph Smith has his first vision.*]

3 And I will give power unto my two witnesses [*two prophets to the Jews in the last days; D&C 77:15*], and they shall prophesy [*serve, minister, prophesy, etc.*] a thousand two hundred and threescore days [*42 months or 3 1/2 years, about the same length as Christ's ministry*], clothed in sackcloth [*in humility*].

4 These are the two olive trees [*olive trees provide olive oil for lamps so people can be prepared to meet Christ; compare with the parable of the ten virgins in Matthew 25:1–13*], and the two candlesticks [*hold light so people can see clearly*] standing before the God of the earth.

5 And if any man will hurt them [*the two prophets*], fire [*the power of God to destroy*] proceedeth out of their mouth, and devoureth their enemies [*the two prophets will be protected during their mission*]: and if any man will hurt them, he must in this manner be killed [*he will be killed by the power of God; Strong's #1163*].

6 These [*two prophets*] have power to shut heaven [*have the power of God; compare with the Prophet Nephi in Helaman 10:5–10 and 11:1–6*], that it rain not in the days of their prophecy: and have power over waters to turn them to blood, and to smite the earth with all plagues [*to encourage people to repent; to deliver from evil, bondage, as with the plagues in Egypt*], as often as they will.

7 And when they shall have finished their testimony [*ministry*], the beast [*Satan*] that ascendeth out of the bottomless pit [*Rev. 9:1–2*] shall make war against them [*the two prophets*], and shall overcome them, and kill them.

8 And their dead bodies shall lie in the street of the great city [*Jerusalem*], which spiritually is called Sodom and Egypt [*i.e., is very wicked*], where also our Lord was crucified.

9 And they [*the wicked*] of the people and kindreds and tongues and nations shall see their dead bodies three days and an half [*perhaps symbolically tying in with their 3 1/2 year ministry as well as the Savior's three days in the tomb;*]

the Savior was killed, too, by the wicked for trying to save them], and shall not suffer [*allow*] their dead bodies to be put in graves [*many in eastern cultures believed that if the body is not buried, the spirit is bound to wander the earth in misery forever*].

10 And they that dwell upon the earth [*not just people in Jerusalem; implies that knowledge of the death of the two prophets will be known world wide*] shall rejoice over them, and make merry, and shall send gifts one to another [*people all over the world will cheer and send gifts to one another to celebrate the deaths of these two prophets*]; because these two prophets tormented them [*the wicked*] that dwelt on the earth [*implies that these prophets' influence was felt and irritated the wicked far beyond Jerusalem*].

11 And after three days and an half the Spirit of life from God entered into them [*they are resurrected at this time; McConkie,* Doctrinal New Testament Commentary, *Bookcraft, Inc., 1973, Vol. 3, p. 511*], and they stood upon their feet; and great fear fell upon them which saw them.

12 And they [*the wicked who were celebrating*] heard a great voice from heaven saying unto them [*the two slain prophets*], Come up hither. And they ascended up to heaven in a cloud; and their enemies beheld [*saw*] them.

13 And the same hour [*immediately*] was there a great earthquake, and the tenth part of the city fell, and in the earthquake were slain of men seven thousand: and the remnant were affrighted, and gave glory to the God of heaven [*perhaps implying that some of the wicked were converted as was the case with the Savior's resurrection and also when Lazarus was brought back from the dead; if so, the deaths of the two prophets bore immediate fruit in helping some begin returning to God*].

14 The second woe [*Rev. 9:12–21; 10; 11:1–13*] is past [*one more to go; Rev. 8:13*]; and, behold, the third woe [*the burning at the Second Coming*] cometh quickly.

15 And the seventh angel sounded; and there were great voices in heaven, saying, The kingdoms of this world are become the kingdoms of our Lord, and of his Christ [*i.e., Christ will now come to rule and the Millennium will begin*]; and he shall reign for ever and ever.

JST Revelation 11:15

15 And the seventh angel sounded; and there were great voices in heaven, saying, The kingdoms of this world are become the **kingdom** of our Lord, and of his Christ; and he shall reign for ever and ever.

Even though the JST change for verse 15, above consisted only of changing "kingdoms" to "kingdom," the change is doctrinally significant. When the Savior comes to rule and reign on earth for the thousand years, He will have just one kingdom on earth, and it will be a time of unity and peace.

16 And the four and twenty elders [*who had asked how long they must wait for justice to be done upon the wicked; Rev. 6:10*], which sat before God on their seats, fell upon their faces [*a show of humility and respect in Bible culture*], and worshipped God,

17 Saying, We give thee thanks, O Lord God Almighty, which art, and wast, and art to come [*in other words, the Lord is eternal*]; because thou hast taken to thee thy great power [*i.e., have finally taken over*], and hast reigned [*finally will rule the earth, during the Millennium*].

18 And the nations were angry, and thy wrath [*righteous anger at the wicked*] is come, and the time of the dead, that they should be judged, and that thou shouldest give reward unto thy servants the prophets, and to the saints, and them that fear [*respect and honor*] thy name, small and great [*the hardly-known righteous as well as the widely-known righteous*]; and shouldest destroy them [*the wicked*] which destroy [*corrupt*] the earth.

19 And the temple of God was opened in heaven, and there was seen in his temple the ark of his testament [*the ark of the covenant was behind the veil in the Holy of Holies in Israel's temple, and when the high priest passed through the veil into the presence of the ark, it symbolized entering into the presence of God; thus, the symbolism*

here is that the righteous may now enter the presence of the Lord*]: and there were lightnings, and voices, and thunderings, and an earthquake, and great hail [*perhaps this last phrase is a brief review of woes and events leading up to the Second Coming as mentioned in verses 13 and 15 above as well as elsewhere, rather than being a prophesy of things yet to come*].

REVELATION 12

This is the most revised chapter in the JST version of Revelation. The Prophet changed the verse sequence in several places. For your convenience, at the end of this chapter, we will include the entire Joseph Smith Translation of chapter 12.

1 And there appeared a great wonder in heaven; a woman [*the true Church—see JST verse 7*] clothed with the sun, and the moon under her feet [*symbolic of beauty and glory*], and upon her head a crown [*symbolic of power*] of twelve stars [*the twelve Apostles*]:

JST Revelation 12:1

1 And there appeared a great **sign** in heaven, in the likeness of things on the earth; a woman clothed with the sun, and the moon under her feet, and upon her head a crown of twelve stars.

2 And she [*the Church*] being with child [*the kingdom of God—see JST 12:7*] cried, travailing in birth

and pained to be delivered [*labor pains; symbolic of the fact that there are labor and pain involved in bringing forth the kingdom of God*].

JST Revelation 12:2

2 And **the woman** being with child, cried, travailing in birth, and pained to be delivered.

3 And there appeared another wonder in heaven; and behold a great red dragon [*Lucifer; see verse 9*], having seven heads and ten horns, and seven crowns upon his heads [*i.e., Satan has great power, has many "front" organizations behind which he hides*].

4 And his tail drew the third part of the stars of heaven [*1/3 followed Satan in the war in heaven; D&C 29:36*], and did cast them to the earth [*the spirits who followed Lucifer are here on earth!*]: and the dragon [*Satan*] stood before the woman [*the Church*] which was ready to be delivered [*ready to bring forth the kingdom of God*], for to devour her child [*the kingdom of God*] as soon as it was born [*started*].

The JST combines verses 3 and 4, above.

JST Revelation 12:4

4 And there appeared another **sign** in heaven; and behold, a great red dragon, having seven heads and ten horns, and seven crowns upon his heads. And his tail drew the third part of the stars of heaven, and did cast them to

the earth. And the dragon stood before the woman **which was delivered, ready** to devour her child **after** it was born.

5 And she [*the Church; JST 12:3, 7*] brought forth a man child [*the kingdom of God and his Christ; JST 12:7*], who was to rule all nations with a rod of iron [*i.e., during the Millennium (which John has just seen in the vision, 11:15–19), the kingdom of God will be established, and the iron rod (or the word of God), will be in full effect*]: and her child was caught up unto God, and to his throne.

JST Revelation 12:3

3 And she brought forth a man child, who was to rule all nations with a rod of iron; and her child was caught up unto God **and his** throne.

6 And the woman fled into the wilderness [*symbolic of the great apostasy, when the Church was gone for many centuries*], where she hath a place prepared of God, that they should feed her there a thousand two hundred and three-score days.

JST Revelation 12:5

5 And the woman fled into the wilderness, where she **had** a place prepared of God, that they should feed her there a thousand two hundred and three-score **years**.

Did you notice that the JST changes "days" to "years" at the end of the verse?

Remember that the verse numbers in the JST are not always the same as the verse numbers in the Bible. Joseph Smith often added verses that were left out of the Bible or combined verses.

7 And there was war in heaven [*a war of opinions, words, truth, error, light, darkness, and so forth, which continues here on earth today*]: Michael [*Adam*] and his angels [*righteous spirits*] fought against the dragon [*Satan*]; and the dragon fought and his angels [*the evil spirits who followed Satan*],

JST Revelation 12:6

6 And there was war in heaven; Michael and his angels fought against the dragon; **and the dragon and his angels fought against Michael**;

Next, you will see that JST verse 7 combines parts of Bible verses 7 and 8.

8 And prevailed not [*did not win*]; neither was their [*Satan and his followers*] place found any more in heaven.

JST Revelation 12:7

7 And **the dragon** prevailed not **against Michael, neither the child, nor the woman which was the church of God, who had been delivered of her pains, and brought forth the kingdom of our God and his Christ**.

9 And the great dragon was cast out, that old serpent, called the Devil, and Satan, which deceiveth the whole world: he was cast out into the earth, and his angels were cast out with him.

JST Revelation 12:8

8 Neither was **there** place found in heaven **for the great dragon, who** was cast out; that old serpent called the **devil**, and **also called** Satan, which deceiveth the whole world; he was cast out into the earth; and his angels were cast out with him.

10 And I heard a loud voice saying in heaven, Now is come salvation [*in other words, now people will be able to go down to earth and live and choose between good and evil, and thus earn salvation; see 2 Nephi 2:11*], and strength, and the kingdom of our God, and the power of his Christ: for the accuser [*Satan*] of our brethren is cast down, which accused them before our God day and night.

The JST breaks verse 10, above, into two verses.

JST Revelation 12:9–10

9 And I heard a loud voice saying in heaven, Now is come salvation, and strength, and the kingdom of our God, and the power of his Christ;

10 For the accuser of our brethren is cast down, which accused them before our God day and night.

11 And they [*the righteous*] overcame him [*Satan and his evil*] by the blood of the Lamb [*through the Atonement of Christ*], and by the

word of their testimony [*they kept their covenants*]; and they loved not their lives unto the death [*i.e., they were willing to give all to gain exaltation*].

12 Therefore rejoice, ye heavens, and ye that dwell in them. Woe to the inhabiters of the earth [*there will be trouble because Satan is here, and you will have to choose right from wrong under severe pressure*] and of the sea! for the devil is come down unto you, having great wrath [*Satan is really "turning up the pressure"*], because he knoweth that he hath but a short time.

The JST rearranges verses 11–12, above, as follows:

JST Revelation 12:11–12

11 **For they have overcome** him by the blood of the Lamb, and by the word of their testimony; **for** they loved not their **own lives, but kept the testimony even unto death. Therefore, rejoice O heavens, and ye that dwell in them**.

12 **And after these things I heard another voice saying,** Woe to the inhabiters of the earth, **yea, and they who dwell upon the islands of the sea!** for the devil is come down unto you, having great wrath, because he knoweth that he hath but a short time.

13 And when the dragon saw that he was cast unto the earth, he perse-cuted the woman [*the Church; i.e., this is the time of Satan's power*] which brought forth the man child [*the kingdom of God*].

JST Revelation 12:13

13 **For** when the dragon saw that he was cast unto the earth, he persecuted the woman which brought forth the **man-child**.

14 And to the woman were given two wings of a great eagle, that she might fly into the wilderness [*universal apostasy*], into her place, where she is nourished for a time, and times, and half a time [*we don't know what this means; perhaps it could be 1 time plus 2 times plus 1/2 a time, i.e., 3 1/2 times which might symbolically tie in with other uses of 3 1/2, such as in Rev. 11:3 where the Lord preserves the two prophets for three and a half years*], from the face of the serpent [*Satan*].

JST Revelation 12:14

14 **Therefore**, to the woman were given two wings of a great eagle, that she might **flee** into the wilderness, into her place, where she is nourished for a time, and times, and half a time, from the face of the serpent.

15 And the serpent cast out of his mouth water as a flood after the woman [*symbolically, just as flood waters reach and surround everything in their path, so also Satan tries to get to us from every angle*], that he might cause her to be carried away of [*destroyed by*] the flood.

JST Revelation 12:15

15 And the serpent **casteth** out of his mouth water as a flood after the woman, that he might

cause her to be carried away of the flood.

16 And the earth helped the woman [*earth is designed and created to help us return to the Father; all things in it bear witness of Him to us; Moses 6:63*], and the earth opened her mouth, and swallowed up the flood which the dragon cast out of his mouth.

JST Revelation 12:16

16 And the earth **helpeth** the woman, and the earth **openeth** her mouth, and **swalloweth** up the flood which the dragon **casteth** out of his mouth.

17 And the dragon [*Satan*] was wroth [*angry*] with the woman [*the Church*], and went to make war with the remnant of her seed [*the Saints in the last days*], which keep the commandments of God, and have the testimony of Jesus Christ.

JST Revelation 12:17

17 **Therefore**, the dragon was wroth with the woman, and went to make war with the remnant of her seed, which keep the commandments of God, and have the testimony of Jesus Christ.

JST Revelation 12:1–17.

As mentioned above, we are including the complete JST of Revelation, chapter 12, here, in order that you might read straight through it in the order in which Joseph Smith arranged the verses. We have included some notes for teaching purposes.

1 And there appeared a great sign in heaven, in the likeness of things [*symbolic of things*] on the earth; a woman [*the Church, see verse 7*] clothed with the sun [*symbolic of beauty, glory, and power to bring us to exaltation*] and the moon under her feet, and upon her head a crown [*symbolic of power, authority; exaltation*] of twelve stars [*the Twelve Apostles*].

In this imagery, woman brings forth the greatest, highest good. In contrast, in Satan's work, see Revelation 17:1–6 and elsewhere, the woman "the whore of all the earth," (1 Nephi 14:11) brings forth the greatest evil. Perhaps this is symbolic of the power of women, both for good and for evil.

2 And the woman being with child [*verse 7, the kingdom of God and his Christ*], cried, travailing in birth [*labor pains*], and pained to be delivered [*i.e., it requires much pain and effort to establish God's kingdom on earth*].

Some might think that the "man child" in verse 7, next, refers to Christ. Such is not the case. Mary brought forth Christ. The Church did not bring Christ forth. Rather, He brought forth the Church.

3 And she [*the Church, verse 7*] brought forth a man child [*verse 7, the kingdom of God*], who was to rule all nations with a rod of iron [*the word of God, 1 Nephi 11:25*]; and her child [*see verse*

7, the kingdom of God and the righteous Saints who belong to it] was caught up unto God and his throne [i.e., the righteous are eventually taken up to live in celestial glory with God].

4 And there appeared another sign [John is seeing actual events in premortality and on earth in vision] in heaven; and behold, a great red dragon [Satan], having seven heads [symbolic of counterfeiting God's work] and ten [a number often associated with being well-organized] horns [horns are symbolic of power], and seven crowns [Satan has authority in his own realm] upon his heads. And his tail drew the third part of the stars of heaven [a third part of the premortal spirits in our group;], and did cast them to the earth. And the dragon stood before the woman which was delivered [gave birth to the Kingdom of God, verse 7], ready to devour her child [the Kingdom of God, verse 7] after it was born. [Satan has tried to destroy God's work from the beginning.]

Apostle James E. Talmage indicates that there was a certain number of spirits assigned to our group to come to this earth. See Articles of Faith, by James E. Talmage, printed in 1977, p. 194. Thus, we understand the "third part" in verse 4, above, to be a third part of our group of spirits.

5 And the woman fled into the wilderness [symbolic of the great apostasy; the Church is gone for many centuries until the restoration by Joseph Smith],

where she had a place prepared of God, that they should feed [nourish, take care of] her there a thousand two hundred and threescore years.

6 And there was war in heaven [a war of words, ideas, truth, error, loyalties, etc.]; Michael [Adam] and his angels [righteous spirits] fought against the dragon [Satan]; and the dragon and his angels [wicked spirits] fought against Michael;

7 And the dragon [Satan] prevailed not [did not win] against Michael, neither the child [the kingdom of our God], nor the woman [the Church] which was the church of God, who had been delivered of her pains, and brought forth the kingdom of our God and his Christ. [This is a great prophecy that Satan will not ultimately win against Christ and the forces of good.]

8 Neither was there place found in heaven for the great dragon [Lucifer, Satan], who was cast out; that old serpent called the devil, and also called Satan, which deceiveth the whole world; he was cast out into the earth; and his angels were cast out with him. [They are here on earth and in the spirit world prison, tempting, and fighting against that which is good. See Teachings of the Presidents of the Church: Brigham Young, 1997, p. 282. (study course for priesthood and Relief Society)]

9 And I heard a loud voice saying in heaven, Now is come

salvation, and strength, and the kingdom of our God, and the power of his Christ; [*In other words, the earth is set up and "school is in session;" worthy spirits can go down to earth, have opportunities to choose between good and evil, join the kingdom of God via the gospel of Jesus Christ, and gain exaltation because of the Atonement of Christ–see verse 11.*]

10 For the accuser [*Satan*] of our brethren is cast down, which accused them before our God day and night [*continuously*].

11 For they [*the righteous*] have overcome him [*Satan*] by the blood of the Lamb [*using the Atonement of Christ*], and by the word of their testimony [*keeping their covenants*]; for they loved not their own lives, but kept the testimony even unto death [*endured faithful to the end*]. Therefore, rejoice O heavens, and ye that dwell in them [*righteous people bring joy to the inhabitants of heaven*].

12 And after these things I heard another voice saying, Woe to [*a warning, caution to*] the inhabiters of the earth, yea, and they who dwell upon the islands of the sea [*all continents; everybody on earth*]! for the devil is come down unto you, having great wrath, because he knoweth that he hath but a short time [*beware of Satan; he is really "turning up the heat"*].

13 For when the dragon [*Satan*] saw that he was cast unto the earth, he persecuted the woman [*the Church*] which brought forth the man-child [*the kingdom of God—see verse 7*].

The "great eagle" in verse 14, next, could possibly symbolize the role which the United States of America would play in providing a safe place for the Church to start and then grow, when the time was right.

14 Therefore, to the woman were given two wings of a great eagle, that she might flee into the wilderness, into her place, where she is nourished for a time, and times, and half a time, from the face of the serpent [*Satan, who wants to destroy the Church in its infancy, see verse 4*].

15 And the serpent [*Satan*] casteth out of his mouth water as a flood [*a wicked flood of filthiness designed to get into every aspect of life. This may tie in with the "filthy water" in 1 Nephi 12:16*], after the woman [*the Church, verse 7*], that he might cause her to be carried away of the flood [*destroyed by a flood of wickedness*].

16 And the earth helpeth the woman [*example: Moses 6:63, "all things bear witness*], and the earth openeth her mouth, and swalloweth up the flood which the dragon [*Satan*] casteth out of his mouth [*the earth is set up to help us overcome Satan and gain exaltation*].

17 Therefore, the dragon was wroth [*angry*] with the woman [*the Church*], and went to make

war with the remnant of her seed [*the Saints in the last days*], which keep the commandments of God, and have the testimony of Jesus Christ [*who make and keep covenants with God*].

REVELATION 13

This chapter contains one of the most notable and often talked about topics contained in the Bible. It is the mark of the beast, mentioned in verses 16 and 17.

We don't have exact interpretations of many of the things John saw in this chapter. It is easy to get caught up in trying to figure out details and thus miss the rather obvious and simple messages. For instance, we may not know who or what the beast is or what his seven heads and ten horns are. However, it is obvious that evil is being represented in the vision as vicious and destructive, something for us to avoid. The beast's seven heads might represent Satan's attempted counterfeits of God's perfect work since the number seven represents perfection in Bible symbolism. Or the seven heads could represent attempts by Lucifer to confuse us. (For example, which one is really Satan or his front organizations or what?) Or perhaps the seven heads could symbolize Satan's ability to come at us from several different directions, using many different types of temptations. The head wounded, that was then healed in verse 3, could remind us that just when we think we have overcome

Satan's temptations, he bounces back and tries for us again. The important thing is for us to be reminded that Satan is a very capable enemy and we must do all that we can to avoid getting the "mark of the beast" in our foreheads [*verse 16*], i.e., to avoid becoming followers of Satan.

1 And I stood upon the sand of the sea, and saw a beast rise up out of the sea, having seven heads and ten horns [*perhaps symbolizing that Satan is well-organized but not as powerful as Christ's 12 horns, 12 eyes and 12 servants or Apostles in JST 5:6*], and upon his horns ten crowns [*symbolizing power over kingdoms*], and upon his heads the name of blasphemy [*symbolic of total disrespect for God*].

JST Revelation 13:1

1 And I saw another sign, in the likeness of the kingdoms of the earth; a beast rise up out of the sea, and he stood upon the sand of the sea, having seven heads and ten horns; and upon his horns ten crowns; and upon his heads the name of blasphemy.

The phrase "sand of the sea" in the JST, above, reminds us that Satan's kingdom is built upon "sand." As depicted by the Savior in Matthew 7:24–27, sand is not a good foundation upon which to build. It will eventually crumble out from under the "kingdom" and the kingdom will be destroyed.

2 And the beast which I saw was like unto a leopard, and his feet were as the feet of a bear, and his mouth as the mouth of a lion [*i.e., he has great ability to destroy*]: and the dragon [*the devil*] gave him [*Satan's degenerate earthly kingdoms*] his power, and his seat, and great authority.

3 And I saw one of his heads as it were wounded to death; and his deadly wound was healed: and all the world wondered after the beast [*the majority of the world will admire and desire wickedness in the last days*].

4 And they worshipped the dragon [*Satan*] which gave power unto the beast [*representing degenerate earthly kingdoms controlled by Satan; see heading to Revelation 13 in our Bible*]: and they [*the wicked*] worshipped the beast, saying, Who is like unto the beast? who is able to make war with him [*i.e., isn't he wonderful!*]?

5 And there was given unto him a mouth speaking great things and blasphemies [*God allows Satan to wield power that we might be properly tested*]; and power was given unto him to continue forty and two months. [*42 months; a thousand two hundred and threescore days represented the time allocated to the two prophets in Rev. 11:3 to do God's work. Perhaps the use of 42 months again here simply implies that whenever God is doing His work, Satan is allowed to provide opposition at the same time. Such will be the case until the Millennium.*]

6 And he opened his mouth in blasphemy [*mocking God and all that is sacred and good*] against God, to blaspheme his name, and his tabernacle, and them that dwell in heaven [*Satan and his followers will mock all that is sacred on earth and in heaven*].

Some read verse 7, next, and think that all the righteous will eventually be overcome by Satan in the last days. Such is obviously not the case. They need to read verse 8, also, where we see that Satan overcomes those who worship or follow him. In other words, he overcomes those who do not overcome him by following Christ and accessing His Atonement in their lives.

7 And it was given unto him [*allowed him*] to make war with the saints, and to overcome them [*only the unfaithful Saints whose names are not written in the book of life will be overcome; see verse 8*]: and power was given him over all kindreds, and tongues, and nations [*i.e., he is allowed to tempt people everywhere*].

At the risk of being redundant, we will again emphasize that Satan will not overcome all of the righteous. Note that "all," in verse 8, next, refers to those "whose names are not written in the book of the . . . Lamb," as defined in the note following verse 8.

8 And all [*the wicked*] that dwell upon the earth shall worship him, whose names are not written in the

book of life of the Lamb slain from the foundation of the world [*i.e., those who do not follow the Savior are worshiping Satan; compare with Matthew 12:30*].

"The book of life of the Lamb" in verse 8, above, is symbolic of the record kept in heaven which contains the names of those who will be exalted. See D&C 132:19.

9 If any man have an ear, let him hear [*i.e., you would be very wise to heed these warnings about Satan*].

10 He [*the powerful wicked*] that leadeth into captivity shall go into captivity [*the wicked will be destroyed by the wicked; Mormon 4:5; also could mean that the wicked who lead others to the captivity of hell will go into the captivity of hell themselves*]: he [*the wicked*] that killeth with the sword must be [*will be*] killed with the sword. Here is the patience and the faith of the saints [*perhaps meaning that through being surrounded by opposition in the mortal world, the patience and faith of the Saints are developed*].

11 And I beheld another beast coming up out of the earth; and he had two horns like a lamb [*"like a lamb," not "the Lamb," perhaps meaning a powerful "false Christ," a counterfeit by Satan*], and he spake as a dragon [*like Satan; see Rev. 12:9*].

12 And he exerciseth all the power of the first beast before him [*just when you think you've seen Satan*

at his worst, worse will come!*], and causeth the earth and them [*the wicked*] which dwell therein to worship the first beast [*in verse 3, above*], whose deadly wound was healed.

13 And he doeth great wonders [*Satan and his angels can do miracles*], so that he maketh fire come down from heaven on the earth in the sight of men [*a counterfeit of Elijah's miracle, 1 Kings 18:38*],

14 And deceiveth them [*the wicked' and foolish*] that dwell on the earth by the means of those miracles which he had power to do in the sight of the beast; saying to them that dwell on the earth, that they should make an image to [*i.e., worship*] the beast, which had the wound by a sword, and did live. [*In other words, Satan will do all he can to get all people to follow him, to "worship" him by living wickedly in the last days.*]

15 And he had power to give life [*make wickedness attractive*] unto the image of the beast [*which the wicked made in verse 14 by following Satan's instructions*], that the image of the beast should both speak, and cause that as many as would not worship the image of the beast should be killed [*people's "idols" can take over their lives and cause them to die spiritually, as well as physically in wars, plagues, etc. Also, the wicked can cause great trouble, temporarily, for the righteous*].

Verses 16 and 17, next, are an example of the importance

of carefully considering context when interpreting verses of scripture. If one were to read only these verses, the conclusion would be that, in the last days, "all" (verse 16) people will eventually come under the power of Satan and wicked people under his control. This would be very depressing and could cause people to give up hope. However, if we examine other verses in Revelation, we see the truth. For example, read Revelation 14:1, where we see 144,000 with the Father's name in their foreheads, rather than the mark of the beast in their foreheads. Furthermore, in Revelation 20:4, we see righteous people "which had not worshipped the beast, neither his image, neither had received his mark upon their foreheads, or in their hands." Thus we see that "all" (Rev. 13:16) do not come under Satan's control, rather "all" the foolish or wicked do who "wondered after the beast" (verse 3).

Verse 17 implies much of financial bondage in the last days. If we follow the council of the Brethren, we will not come under this bondage. For example, Elder L. Tom Perry counseled: "Live strictly within your income and save something for a rainy day. Incorporate in your lives the discipline of budgeting that which the Lord has blessed you with . . . avoid excessive debt. Necessary debt should be incurred only after careful, thoughtful prayer and after obtaining the best possible

advice. We need the discipline to stay well within our ability to pay. Wisely we have been counseled to avoid debt as we would avoid the plague . . . It is so easy to allow consumer debt to get out of hand. If you do not have the discipline to control the use of credit cards, it is better not to have them. A well-managed family does not pay interest—it earns it. The definition I received from a wise boss at one time in my early business career was 'Thems that understands interest receives it, thems that don't pays it.'. . .Acquire and store a reserve of food and supplies that will sustain life. Obtain clothing and build a savings account on a sensible, well-planned basis that can serve well in times of emergency. As long as I can remember, we have been taught to prepare for the future and to obtain a year's supply of necessities. I would guess that the years of plenty have almost universally caused us to set aside this counsel. I believe the time to disregard this counsel is over. With events in the world today, it must be considered with all seriousness." (L. Tom Perry, *Ensign*, November 1995, p. 36.)

16 And he causeth all [*who follow Satan; the righteous are not part of this group because they have the seal of God in their foreheads as seen in Rev. 7:3*], both small and great, rich and poor, free and bond, to receive a mark in their right hand, or in their foreheads [*symbolically indicating that they are loyal to Satan and the wickedness he sponsors*]:

In the culture of the Bible, "forehead" was symbolic of "loyalty" (see symbolism notes at the beginning of Revelation in this study guide.) Thus we see faithful Jews wearing phylacteries even today (see Bible Dictionary under "Phylacteries") tied to their foreheads, symbolizing loyalty and obedience to their God. Notice also in Revelation 14:1 that there are a 144,000 righteous who have the "Father's name written in their foreheads," which symbolizes loyalty and obedience to the Father.

17 And that no man might buy or sell, save he that had the mark, or the name of the beast, or the number of his name [*Satan exercises great control over economies where the majority are wicked or allow wickedness; the righteous today would do well to follow the counsel of the prophets regarding self-sufficiency and staying out of unnecessary debt, etc.*].

18 Here is wisdom. Let him that hath understanding count the number of the beast: for it is the number of a man; and his number is Six hundred threescore and six [*i.e., 666; we don't yet know what this means*].

REVELATION 14

In this chapter, the Apostle John sees the restoration of the gospel (verses 6–7), then sees the fall of Satan's kingdom (verses 8–11), including the final gathering and the destruction of the wicked (verses 14–20).

1 And I [*John*] looked, and, lo, a Lamb [*Christ*] stood on the mount Sion [*this is representative of many appearances; D&C 133:18–20*], and with him an hundred forty and four thousand [*Rev. 7:4*], having his Father's name written in their foreheads [*i.e., who were loyal to the Father*].

JST Revelation 14:1

1 And I looked, and, lo, a Lamb stood on the mount Sion, and with him **a** hundred forty and four thousand, having his Father's name written in their foreheads.

2 And I heard a voice from heaven, as the voice of many waters [*D&C 110:3*], and as the voice of a great thunder [*symbolic of a voice from heaven as on Sinai; Exodus 19:16–19*]: and I heard the voice of harpers harping with their harps [*in Bible symbolism, harps are symbolic of heaven*]:

3 And they sung as it were a new song [*i.e., one that couldn't be sung before the Millennium and the destruction of the wicked came; see note with Rev. 5:9 in this study guide*] before the throne [*in front of the throne of God*], and before the four beasts, and the elders: and no man could learn that song but the hundred and forty and four thousand [*plus many others as mentioned in Rev. 7:9*], which were redeemed from the earth. [*In other words, only the righteous, those who were saved by the Atonement, could sing the words of the "new song" in the presence of God in celestial splendor, which words applied to them. The words of the*

"new song" are, in effect, given in D&C 84:99–102.]

4 These are they which were not defiled with women [*i.e., they are morally clean*]; for they are virgins [*i.e., pure and clean, keeping the law of chastity; does not mean unmarried*]. These are they which follow the Lamb whithersoever he goeth [*who follow Christ at all costs*]. These were redeemed from among men, being the firstfruits [*the "highest quality fruit"; i.e., those who will attain exaltation*] unto God and to the Lamb.

5 And in their mouth was found no guile [*deceit;* Strong's *#1388*]: for they are without fault [*blameless; without sin, pure and clean because of the Atonement*] before the throne of God.

6 And I saw another angel [*Angel Moroni plus many other angels who helped with the restoration; D&C 128:20–21; 133:36*] fly in the midst of heaven, having the everlasting gospel to preach unto them that dwell on the earth, and to every nation, and kindred, and tongue, and people [*the restoration of the Church*],

7 Saying with a loud voice, Fear [*respect, reverence;* Strong's *#5399*] God, and give glory to him; for the hour of his judgment is come: and worship him that made heaven, and earth, and the sea, and the fountains of waters.

8 And there followed another angel, saying, Babylon [*symbolic of Satan and his earthly kingdom*] is fallen, is fallen, that great city [*Satan's kingdom*], because she made all nations drink of the wine of [*i.e., the results of*] the wrath of her fornication [*fornication as used here includes apostasy (see Bible Dictionary under "Adultery"), disloyalty, all manner of wickedness, breaking of covenants and commitments*].

9 And the third angel followed them, saying with a loud voice, If any man worship the beast and his image [*Rev. 13:14*], and receive his mark in his forehead, or in his hand [*i.e., is a loyal follower of Satan, in other words, is wicked*],

10 The same shall drink of the wine [*results of, i.e., punishments*] of the wrath of God, which is poured out without mixture [*undiluted*] into the cup of his indignation; and he [*the wicked*] shall be tormented with fire and brimstone in the presence of the holy angels, and in the presence of the Lamb [*i.e., will not be able to stand the presence of God; D&C 88:22*]:

11 And the smoke of their torment ascendeth up for ever and ever: and they have no rest day nor night, who worship the beast and his image, and whosoever receiveth the mark of his name [*applies eternally only to the sons of perdition, D&C 76:33; all others will eventually suffer for their own sins, D&C 19:17, and then be redeemed into the telestial kingdom*].

12 Here is the patience of the saints [*when the righteous see the fall of Satan's kingdom as mentioned in*

the above verses, they will see that their patience, in waiting for God to destroy Lucifer's kingdom, has paid off]: here are they that keep the commandments of God, and the faith of Jesus.

13 And I heard a voice from heaven saying unto me, Write, Blessed are the dead which die in the Lord [*i.e., who have lived righteously*] from henceforth: Yea, saith the Spirit, that they may rest from their labours; and their works do follow them [*they will be rewarded for their righteousness*].

14 And I looked, and behold a white cloud [*symbolic of heaven*], and upon the cloud one [*Christ*] sat like unto the Son of man [*Christ*], having on his head a golden crown [*celestial*], and in his hand a sharp sickle [*i.e., it is "harvest" time*].

The phrase "like unto the Son of man" is explained in two notes following Revelation 1:13 in this study guide.

15 And another angel came out of the temple [*where Heavenly Father is; Rev. 3:12; 7:15*], crying with a loud voice to him [*Christ*] that sat on the cloud [*giving instructions to the Savior from the Father*], Thrust in thy sickle, and reap: for the time is come for thee to reap; for the harvest of the earth is ripe [*"the field is white already to harvest;" D&C 6:3, in other words, the Father is telling Christ that it is time for the final gathering, prior to the Second Coming*].

First the righteous are gathered out of all the earth.]

16 And he [*Christ*] that sat on the cloud thrust in his sickle on the earth; and the earth was reaped [*Christ supervised the final gathering of the righteous; compare with D&C 86:7, in which the "wheat" is gathered first, and then the "tares" are burned*].

Now the wicked will be "harvested" and cast into the fire. See verses 18 and 19.

17 And another angel [*the "destroying angel;" see verses 18–20*] came out of the temple [*from the presence of the Father*] which is in heaven, he also having a sharp sickle.

18 And another angel came out from the altar [*i.e., from the presence of the Father*], which had power over fire; and cried with a loud cry to him [*the destroying angel in verse 17*] that had the sharp sickle, saying, Thrust in thy sharp sickle, and gather the clusters of the vine of the earth; for her grapes [*wicked people*] are fully ripe [*ripe in iniquity, thoroughly wicked*].

19 And the angel thrust in his sickle into the earth, and gathered the vine of the earth [*the wicked*], and cast it into the great winepress of the wrath of God [*the destruction of the wicked*].

20 And the winepress was trodden without [*outside of*] the city, and blood came out of the wine-

press, even unto the horse bridles [*in other words, many wicked are destroyed when the Savior comes again*], by the space of a thousand and six hundred furlongs [*the blood ran for over 200 miles in the vision seen by John; symbolic of terrible destruction accompanying the Battle of Armageddon and the Second Coming*].

JST Revelation 14:20

20 And the winepress was trodden without the city, and blood came out of the winepress, even unto the **horses'** bridles, by the space of a thousand and six hundred furlongs.

REVELATION 15

This is a beautiful part of the vision in which John was shown the reward of the righteous who have overcome evil through the Atonement. He sees them on "a sea of glass," representing a celestial world (D&C 77:1 and 130:7) with "harps," symbolizing that they spend the rest of eternity in the presence of God. They are singing "the song of Moses. . . and the song of the Lamb," meaning that they have received the same reward which Moses receives from Christ and His Father, in other words, exaltation. Some of the words they "sing" in verses three and four are contained in our hymn # 267.

There are no JST changes for this chapter.

1 And I saw another sign in heaven, great and marvellous, seven angels having the seven last plagues [*as described in chapters 16, 17, and 18, and which will take place prior to the Millennium*]; for in them is filled up [*concluded*] the wrath of God.

2 And I saw as it were a sea of glass mingled with fire [*celestial glory; D&C 130:7*]: and them [*the righteous*] that had gotten the victory over the beast [*in chapter 13*], and over his image [*13:14*], and over his mark [*13:16–17*], and over the number of his name [*13:17, i.e., the righteous who had overcome all attempts of Satan to trap them*], stand on the sea of glass, having the harps of God [*i.e., they were standing in the presence of God; the harps could symbolize that they were found in "harmony" with God*].

3 And they sing the song of Moses the servant of God [*they sing God's praises like Moses did*], and the song of the Lamb [*Christ*], saying, Great and marvellous are thy works, Lord God Almighty; just and true are thy ways, thou King of saints [*praising God*].

4 Who shall not fear thee, O Lord, and glorify thy name? for thou only art holy: for all nations shall come and worship before thee; for thy judgments are made manifest.

5 And after that I looked, and, behold, the temple [*see Rev. 11:19*] of the tabernacle of the testimony in heaven was opened:

6 And the seven angels came out of the temple, having the seven plagues [*spoken of in verse 1*], clothed in pure and white linen [*i.e., celestial beings; fine linen represents personal righteousness in Rev. 19:8*], and having their breasts girded with golden girdles [*symbolic of the best, celestial*].

7 And one of the four beasts gave unto the seven angels seven golden vials [*representing the final seven plagues*] full of the wrath of God, who liveth for ever and ever.

8 And the temple was filled with smoke [*symbolic of God's glory as on Sinai; Exodus 19:18*] from the glory of God, and from his power; and no man was able to enter into the temple, till the seven plagues of the seven angels were fulfilled [*i.e., millennial conditions won't start until the final seven plagues are finished*].

REVELATION 16

This chapter will review plagues which will sweep the earth, leading up to the Battle of Armageddon and the Second Coming of Christ. A major message here is that there will be widespread destruction before the Millennium. You may also note that there seems to be terrible damage to the ecology of the earth in the last days prior to the Second Coming.

1 And I [*John*] heard a great voice out of the temple [*from heaven*] saying to the seven angels, Go your ways, and pour out the vials of the wrath of God upon the earth [*i.e., start the final plagues*].

2 And the first [*angel*] went, and poured out his vial [*the first plague during the final scenes*] upon the earth; and there fell a noisome [*destructive:* Strong's #2556] and grievous [*evil, devastating;* Strong's #4190] sore upon the men which [*who*] had the mark of the beast [*who were loyal to Satan, evil, wickedness*], and upon them which worshipped his image [*i.e., upon the wicked*].

3 And the second angel poured out his vial [*the second plague*] upon the sea; and it became as the blood [*similar to the plague of blood in Egypt; Exodus 7:20*] of a dead man [*in other words, the waters were polluted, like a corpse*]: and every living soul died in the sea.

4 And the third angel poured out his vial [*the third plague*] upon the rivers and fountains of waters [*springs*]; and they became blood.

5 And I heard the angel of the waters [*the angel who poured the plague upon the waters in verse 4, above*] say, Thou art righteous, O Lord, which art, and wast, and shalt be, because thou hast judged thus [*i.e., this punishment is fair and just because of the wickedness of men*].

6 For they have shed the blood of saints and prophets, and thou hast given them blood to drink [*symbolic of forbidden evils, pollution; in other words, this is the "Law of the Harvest;" what you have*]

"planted", comes back to you at "harvest time" or Judgment Day]; for they are worthy [*they deserve such punishment*].

7 And I heard another out of the altar [*from heaven; Rev. 8:3*] say, Even so, Lord God Almighty, true and righteous are thy judgments. [*In other words, a second witness, according to the law of witnesses, that God is completely fair and just in punishing the wicked.*]

JST Revelation 16:7

7 And I heard another **angel who came out from** the altar **saying**, Even so, Lord God Almighty, true and righteous are thy judgments.

8 And the fourth angel poured out his vial [*plague*] upon the sun; and power was given unto him to scorch men with fire [*perhaps similar to our modern saying, "turn up the heat," to see if we can get some of them to repent*].

9 And men were scorched with great heat [*terrible calamities*], and blasphemed [*mocked*] the name of God, which hath power over these plagues [*God could stop these plagues if men would repent*]: and they repented not to give him glory.

10 And the fifth angel poured out his vial [*the fifth plague*] upon the seat [*headquarters*] of the beast [*Satan*]; and his kingdom was full of [*spiritual*] darkness; and they [*the wicked*] gnawed their tongues for [*because of*] pain [*the wicked will suffer greatly, both physically and spiritually, because they*]

refuse to repent and let Christ's Atonement pay for their sins; D&C 19:15–18],

11 And blasphemed [*mocked*] the God of heaven because of their pains and their sores, and repented not of their deeds [*their wickedness*].

12 And the sixth angel poured out his vial [*the sixth plague*] upon the great river Euphrates [*included in modern-day Iraq and the Persian Gulf*]; and the water thereof was dried up, that the way of the kings of the east might be prepared [*perhaps symbolic of world leaders gathering for the Battle of Armageddon; see verse 16, below*].

13 And I saw three unclean [*evil*] spirits like frogs [*frogs represent unclean spirits in some cultures; perhaps this harks back to the plague of frogs in Egypt, Exodus 8:6, with the same purpose, i.e., to encourage people to repent and obey God*] come out of the mouth of the dragon [*Satan; Rev. 12:9*], and out of the mouth of the beast, and out of the mouth of the false prophet [*i.e., evil spirits are much involved in all Satan-sponsored evil and wickedness*].

14 For they are the spirits of devils, working miracles [*Satan and his evil spirits have much power, although limited by God*], which go forth unto the kings [*wicked political leaders*] of the earth and of the whole world, to gather them to the battle of that great day of God Almighty [*the battle of Armageddon; see verse 16*].

15 Behold, I [*Christ*] come as a thief [*unexpectedly, i.e., will catch the wicked off guard, but not the righteous, D&C 106:4–5*]. Blessed is he that watcheth, and keepeth his garments [*who keeps himself unspotted from the sins of the world (D&C 59:9); who keeps clean via the Atonement*], lest he walk naked [*his wickedness is no longer "covered" by excuses on Judgment Day*], and they see his shame [*embarrassment for his wicked deeds*].

16 And he [*the sixth angel in verse 12?*] gathered them together into a place called in the Hebrew tongue Armageddon [*also called "Megiddo," geographically located in a valley about 60 miles north of Jerusalem in northern Israel, today*].

17 And the seventh angel [*probably Adam; see D&C 88:110 and 112*] poured out his vial [*plague*] into the air; and there came a great voice [*Heavenly Father's voice*] out of the temple of heaven, from the throne, saying, It is done [*the end is here; Rev. 11:15*].

18 And there were voices, and thunders, and lightnings; and there was a great earthquake [*great destruction, perhaps including that caused by putting the land masses back together. D&C 133:23–24*], such as was not since men were upon the earth, so mighty an earthquake, and so great [*final destruction before the Millennium*].

19 And the great city [*Babylon, Satan's kingdom; see middle of this verse*] was divided into three parts [*perhaps meaning 1/3, 1/3, and 1/3, symbolic of Satan and his 1/3 completely dominating the wicked in the last days*], and the cities of the nations fell [*all worldly kingdoms have fallen; "a full end of all nations" (see D&C 87:6)*]: and great Babylon came in remembrance before God [*God "remembered" Babylon*], to give unto her the cup of the wine of the fierceness of his wrath [*gave the wicked the punishments they had earned*].

20 And every island fled away, and the mountains were not found [*geographical changes in conjunction with the Second Coming; D&C 133:22–24*].

21 And there fell upon men a great hail out of heaven, every stone about the weight of a talent [*in Old Testament weight, about 75 pounds; Bible Dictionary, p. 789, but we don't know what a "talent" was in New Testament times*]: and men blasphemed [*mocked and criticized*] God [*they didn't repent*] because of the plague of the hail; for the plague thereof was exceeding great.

REVELATION 17

The description of the final seven plagues is continued here. This is a chapter of Revelation which makes use of many symbols and images introduced previously in the vision. Assuming that you have become somewhat familiar with many of them, studying this part of the vision will be a rather rewarding experience, as far as understanding Biblical symbolism is concerned. In it, we see "the great whore" (Satan, in verse 1) sitting on the "many waters" (representing the wicked in all nations; verse 15). He has been highly successful among the leaders and inhabitants of the earth, and they are "drunk" (out of control) with wickedness (verse 2). The woman in verse 3 is the complete opposite of the woman (the Church) in JST Revelation 12:7, symbolizing Satan's skill at being attractive while blaspheming and prostituting all that is good, pure and righteous. The beast ridden by the woman has "seven heads" and "ten horns" (Revelation 13:1), symbolizing, among other things, Satan's counterfeiting of God's work and his power to attack us from several different directions.

The woman in this chapter has "MYSTERY" (Secret combinations —see footnote 5a) written upon her forehead (forehead here symbolizes loyalty, dedication to Satan's goals) along with several other terms describing Satan's kingdom. In verse 8 we see the wicked, those "whose names were not written in the book of life," astonished that "the beast ... was, and is not," perhaps meaning that Babylon was once powerful, but now is not, i.e., has fallen at the Second Coming. At the end of verse eight, these same wicked are astonished "when they behold the beast that was, and is not, and yet is," perhaps meaning Satan's kingdom was here, but is not here now, yet is still in existence in outer darkness (after the final battle at the end of the Millennium).

In verse 16, the "ten horns" take on additional symbolic identity as parts of Satan's kingdom which "hate the whore and ... make her desolate and naked, and shall eat her flesh, and burn her with fire." In other words, "That great and abominable church, which is the whore of all the earth, shall turn upon their own heads; for they shall war among themselves" (1 Nephi 22:13).

A very comforting prophetic fact in verse 14 is that "the Lamb (Christ) shall overcome them (the wicked, including Satan and his evil spirits)." Thus, those who remain faithful to the Lord are assured that they will be on the winning side.

1 And there came one of the seven angels [*Rev. 15:1*] which had the seven vials [*representing the final seven plagues before the Millennium*], and talked with me [*John*], saying unto me, Come hither; I will shew unto thee the judgment [*punishment*] of the great whore [*a word that means perversion, terrible abuse of that which is good; the great whore is the church or kingdom of the devil; 1 Nephi 14:10–11*], that sitteth upon many waters [*representing peoples and nations of the earth; Rev. 17:15*]:

2 With whom the [*wicked*] kings of the earth have committed fornication [*they have "stepped out" on the true God, have been unfaithful to Him*], and the inhabitants of

the earth have been made drunk [*gone out of control*] with the wine [*symbolizing the attractiveness of Satan's temptations*] of her fornication [*terrible wickedness of all kinds*].

3 So he [*one of the seven angels*] carried me away in the spirit into the wilderness [*the apostate world*]: and I saw a woman [*symbolizing Satan's counterfeits for the true Church which was represented by a righteous woman in JST Rev. 12:1 and 7*] sit upon a scarlet [*symbolic of royalty, governing power*] coloured beast [*the beast is controlled by Satan; Revelation 13 heading*], full of names of blasphemy [*i.e., full of mocking, disrespect for God, sacred things, truth, etc.*], having seven heads and ten horns [*the number, ten, in symbolism represents ordinal perfection, i.e., well-ordered or well organized; in other words, Satan's kingdom is well organized*].

4 And the woman was arrayed [*dressed*] in purple and scarlet colour, and decked with gold and precious stones and pearls [*all symbolic of royalty, wealth, power, glory, materialism, etc., i.e., Satan's kingdom has its "hour of glory" on the earth*], having a golden cup [*counterfeiting God's "best"*] in her hand full of abominations and filthiness [*the things Satan "pours" out upon the earth*] of her fornication:

5 And upon her forehead was a name written, MYSTERY [*secret combinations*], BABYLON THE GREAT [*Satan and his kingdom; Isaiah 14:4 and 12*], THE MOTHER OF HARLOTS [*the "producer of terrible wickedness;" just as a harlot, prostitute, appears desirable to wicked men, so also Satan's ways appear desirable to the wicked*] AND ABOMINATIONS OF THE EARTH.

6 And I saw the woman drunken with the blood of the saints [*i.e., Satan's forces have caused much suffering for the Saints*], and with the blood of the martyrs of Jesus: and when I saw her, I wondered [*marveled; Strong's #2296*] with great admiration [*surprise, astonishment; see Rev. 17:6, footnote c, in our Bible*].

7 And the angel said unto me, Wherefore didst thou marvel [*why were you so astonished*]? I will tell [*explain*] thee the mystery of the woman, and of the beast [*in Revelation 13*] that carrieth her, which hath the seven heads and ten horns.

8 The beast [*Satan and his forces; Rev. 9:1–2*] that thou sawest was, and is not; and shall ascend out of the bottomless pit, and go into perdition [*Rev. 20:1–3; D&C 76:26*]: and they that dwell on the earth shall wonder [*i.e., will be amazed when they see Satan and his forces "trimmed down to size" as told in Isaiah 14:12–16*], whose names were not written in the book of life [*the wicked*] from the foundation of the world [*because of disobedience to the gospel which was established before the foundation of the world*], when they behold

the beast that was, and is not, and yet is [*perhaps meaning Satan was here on earth, is not here anymore, because he is in perdition*].

9 And here is the mind which hath wisdom [*if you have wisdom, you will understand this*]. The seven heads are seven mountains [*could refer to Rome, which persecuted the Saints in John's day; see also notes in verse 18*], on which the woman sitteth.

We don't know the interpretation of many of the following images and events in John's vision.

10 And there are seven kings: five are fallen, and one is, and the other is not yet come; and when he cometh, he must continue a short space.

11 And the beast that was, and is not, even he is the eighth, and is of the seven, and goeth into perdition.

12 And the ten horns which thou sawest are ten kings, which have received no kingdom as yet; but receive power as kings one hour with the beast [*perhaps meaning that they will have very temporary power and glory in Satan's organizations*].

13 These have one mind [*perhaps meaning they are united in evil*], and shall give their power and strength [*i.e., loyalty*] unto the beast.

14 These shall make war with the Lamb [*Christ*], and the Lamb shall overcome them [*a wonderfully comforting statement of fact*]:

for he is Lord of lords, and King of kings: and they that are with him are called, and chosen [*a word meaning "elected" by God for eternal happiness*], and faithful.

As stated in verse 14, above, Christ is "Lord of lords, and King of kings." It is interesting to note that "Lord" with a capital "L" refers to Christ as does "King" with a capital "K." We (hopefully) the righteous, who will rule with Him during the Millennium are the "lords" and "kings," spelled with small "l" and small "k."

15 And he saith unto me, The waters [*verse 1*] which thou sawest, where the whore sitteth, are peoples, and multitudes, and nations, and tongues.

Just as water gets into everything, for instance when a home's basement is flooded, so also the "waters" symbolizing a flood of wickedness in the last days get into all aspects of society.

16 And the ten horns which thou sawest upon the beast, these shall hate the whore, and shall make her desolate and naked, and shall eat her flesh, and burn her with fire [*perhaps a reminder that Satan's followers often turn on each other; Isaiah 49:26*].

17 For God hath put in their [*the wicked*] hearts [*Probably a mistranslation similar to Exodus 4:21 that was corrected in the JST to read "but Pharaoh will harden his heart." God does not inspire people to do evil, rather allows them agency to chose between*

good and evil.] to fulfil his [*Satan's?*] will, and to agree, and give their kingdom unto the beast, until the words of God shall be fulfilled [*i.e., until the Millennium comes and judgment catches up with the wicked*].

18 And the woman which thou sawest is that great city, which reigneth over the kings of the earth [*this city could be Rome in John's day but in a general sense would seem to symbolize "Babylon" or the "church of the devil" as stated in 1 Nephi 14:10–11*].

REVELATION 18

The description of the final seven plagues (described, starting in Revelation 16:1) is continued in this chapter.

Chapter 17 gave considerable detail about Babylon, which is Satan and his wicked earthly kingdom. Now, in chapter 18, John sees the fall of Babylon, described as "the woman . . . that great city" in Revelation 17:18. The actual ancient city of Babylon is used in scripture to symbolize Satan's huge kingdom. Babylon was an enormous city, straddling the Euphrates River and was said to have had walls 335 feet high, 85 feet wide and 56 miles long surrounding the square city (see Bible Dictionary under "Babylon").

One of the sad things in this part of John's vision is that the wicked who "have committed fornication and lived deliciously (in lustful, riotous sin) with her (Babylon)"

will mourn Babylon's downfall, rather than repenting and worrying about their status with God. See verses 10–19. They have no "godly sorrow" as described in 2 Corinthians 7:10.

There are no JST changes for this chapter.

1 And after these things I saw another angel come down from heaven, having great power; and the earth was lightened [*brightened, lit up*] with his glory.

2 And he cried mightily with a strong voice, saying, Babylon the great is fallen, is fallen [*Satan's kingdom on earth has come to an end via the Second Coming*], and is [*has*] become the habitation of [*dwelling place for*] devils, and the hold [*prison; Strong's #5438*] of every foul [*wicked*] spirit, and a cage [*prison; the unrighteous have been "caged" by their wickedness and ultimately "trapped" by Satan*] of every unclean and hateful [*detestable; Strong's #3404*] bird [*i.e., the wicked are destroyed and are turned over to Satan to pay for their own sins; 2 Nephi 12:10, D&C 101:24, 19:17*].

3 For all nations have drunk of the wine [*intentionally and skillfully produced temptations*] of the wrath of her fornication [*i.e., people in all nations of the earth have joined Satan in gross wickedness and disloyalty to God*], and the kings [*leaders, people of power and influence*] of the earth have committed fornication [*symbolic of*]

"stepping out" on God, breaking covenants and promises, extreme disloyalty] with her, and the merchants of the earth are waxed [*have grown*] rich through the abundance of her [*"Babylon's"*] delicacies [*i.e., much wealth has been acquired by exploiting people's wicked and lustful desires*].

4 And I heard another voice from heaven, saying, Come out of her, my people, that ye be not partakers of her sins, and that ye receive not of her plagues [*the righteous are warned not to participate in the gross evils of the last days*].

5 For her sins have reached unto heaven, and God hath remembered her iniquities [*God is fully aware of what is going on and the wicked will be punished*].

6 Reward her even as she rewarded you [*the "law of the harvest"*], and double unto her double according to her works: in the cup which she hath filled fill to her double [*i.e., Babylon's cup of wickedness is completely full, therefore, punish her and her followers accordingly*].

7 How much [*to the degree that*] she hath glorified herself, and lived deliciously [*wickedly, riotously*], so much [*to the same degree*] torment and sorrow give her [*an equation of justice; D&C 1:10*]: for she [*Babylon; the wicked*] saith in her heart [*the wicked fool themselves by thinking . . .*], I sit a queen [*I am untouchable, I have great power*], and am no widow [*i.e., I won't be cut off from support and admiration*], and shall see no sorrow [*I*

won't get caught up with or be punished*].

8 Therefore shall [*this is why*] her plagues come in one day [*i.e., suddenly*], death, and mourning, and famine; and she shall be utterly burned with fire [*the wicked will be burned at the Second Coming, utterly destroyed by the Savior's glory; D&C 5:19*]: for strong [*powerful*] is the Lord God who judgeth her [*God has power over Satan*].

9 And the kings [*powerful, wicked leaders*] of the earth, who have committed fornication [*who have been extremely wicked*] and lived deliciously [*riotously*] with her [*the "whore," Satan's kingdom, Babylon*], shall bewail her [*mourn losing her; Strong's #2799*], and lament for her [*instead of repenting*], when they shall see the smoke of her burning [*i.e., the wicked will be devastated by the destruction of their lifestyle*],

10 Standing afar off for the fear of her torment, saying, Alas, alas, that great city Babylon, that mighty city! for in one hour is thy judgment come [*i.e., the Second Coming will change things quickly; they can't believe how fast she was destroyed!*].

11 And the merchants of the earth shall weep and mourn over her [*rather than repenting*]; for no man buyeth their merchandise any more [*because Satan's kingdom has fallen*]:

12 [*In verses 12 and 13, idolatry and accompanying wickedness are*

described along with materialism.]
The merchandise of gold, and
silver, and precious stones, and of
pearls, and fine linen, and purple,
and silk, and scarlet, and all thyine
wood, and all manner vessels of
ivory, and all manner vessels of
most precious wood, and of brass,
and iron, and marble,

13 And cinnamon, and odours
[*incense*], and ointments, and
frankincense, and wine, and oil,
and fine flour, and wheat, and
beasts [*domestic animals*], and
sheep, and horses, and chariots,
and slaves, and souls of men. [*In
other words, everything Satan does
has the ultimate goal of trapping
the "souls of men."*]

14 And the fruits [*the wickedness*] that thy soul lusted [*sinfully
chased*] after are departed from
thee [*are gone*], and all [*wicked*]
things which were dainty and
goodly [*i.e., which you considered
pleasurable*] are departed from
thee [*are gone*], and thou shalt find
them no more at all [*they are gone
permanently*].

You have no doubt noticed that
repetition is often used in the
scriptures to drive home a point.
What you are seeing in John's
vision here is an example of this
teaching technique.

15 The merchants of these things
[*wickedness*], which [*who*] were
made rich by her [*Babylon*], shall
stand afar off for the fear of her torment, weeping and wailing,

16 And saying, Alas, alas, that great
city [*Babylon, i.e., the wickedness
of the world sponsored by Satan*],
that was clothed in fine linen, and
purple, and scarlet, and decked
with gold, and precious stones, and
pearls!

17 For in one hour [*suddenly*] so
great riches is come to nought
[*destroyed completely*]. And every
shipmaster, and all the company in
ships, and sailors, and as many as
trade by sea, stood afar off,

18 And cried when they saw the
smoke of her burning, saying,
What city is like unto this great
city! [*i.e., we thought Babylon
(verse 21), Satan's kingdom, was
indestructible!*]

19 And they cast dust on their
heads [*a sign of extreme mourning
in New Testament culture and society*], and cried, weeping and wailing, saying, Alas, alas, that great
city, wherein were made rich all
that had ships in the sea by reason
of her costliness! for in one hour
is she made desolate [*our wicked
businesses have been destroyed*].

20 Rejoice over her, thou heaven,
and ye holy apostles and prophets;
for God hath avenged you on her
[*i.e., all you righteous who have
asked how long it will be before
the wicked get what's coming to
them (Habakkuk 1:4, D&C 121:2,
Rev. 6:10) can now rejoice that the
Savior has finally come*].

21 And a mighty angel took up a
stone like a great millstone [*a stone
used to grind wheat, commonly
used to represent the fate of the
wicked; Matthew 18:6*], and cast it

into the sea, saying, Thus with violence shall that great city Babylon [*symbolic of Satan's kingdom and his followers*] be thrown down, and shall be found no more at all.

22 And the voice of harpers, and musicians, and of pipers, and trumpeters, shall be heard no more at all in thee [*Babylon*]; and no craftsman, of whatsoever craft he be, shall be found any more in thee; and the sound of a millstone shall be heard no more at all in thee [*i.e., the destruction of Satan's kingdom will be absolute*];

23 And the light of a candle shall shine no more at all in thee; and the voice of the bridegroom and of the bride shall be heard no more at all in thee [*absolute destruction*]: for [*because*] thy [*Babylon's*] merchants were the great men of the earth; for by thy sorceries [*Satan's deceptions*] were all nations deceived.

24 And in her [*Babylon*] was found the blood of prophets, and of saints, and of all that were slain upon the earth [*i.e., Babylon is guilty as charged*].

REVELATION 19

After witnessing the destruction of Babylon, as shown in chapter 18, John now sees the faithful Saints praising God for His righteous judgment upon the wicked which has prepared the way for the Millennium to begin (verses 1–6). The righteous are invited to the marriage supper of the Lamb (verses

7–9), symbolic in this context of being invited to join the Savior for the Millennium. John sees the glory, power, and authority of the Savior symbolically coming on a white horse (verse 11) to reign as "KING OF KINGS, AND LORD OF LORDS" (verse 16).

Perhaps you have noticed already that things in Revelation are often not given in chronological order. Such is also the case in this chapter. For example, you will see the arrival of the Millennium, but later, in verse 19, you will read about the final wars and battles on the earth before the Millennium.

1 And after these things [*after the destruction of Satan and his kingdom, Babylon, spoken of in Revelation 18*] I [*John*] heard a great voice of much people in heaven, saying, Alleluia [*"Praise ye the Lord," see Bible Dictionary under "Alleluia"*]; Salvation, and glory, and honour, and power, unto the Lord our God [*the righteous rejoice*]:

2 For true [*exactly on the mark*] and righteous are his judgments: for he hath judged the great whore [*Satan's kingdom; D&C 29:21, 1 Nephi 14:10*], which did corrupt the earth with her fornication [*total disloyalty to God, wickedness, breaking covenants*], and hath avenged the blood of his servants at her hand [*has punished the wicked for killing the Saints; Revelation 18:20*].

3 And again they said, Alleluia. And her smoke rose up for ever

and ever [*Babylon's destruction is complete; Rev. 18:18*].

4 And the four and twenty elders [*the 24 faithful Elders from John's day, who had died; Rev. 4:4, D&C 77:5*] and the four beasts [*defined in D&C 77:2–4*] fell down and worshipped God that sat on the throne, saying, Amen; Alleluia.

5 And a voice came out of the throne, saying, Praise our God, all ye his servants [*the righteous*], and ye that fear [*respect*] him, both small and great.

JST Revelation 19:5

5 And a voice came out of the throne, saying, Praise our God, all ye his **saints** [*righteous members of the Church who are firmly on the covenant path*], and ye that fear him, both small and great.

6 And I heard as it were the voice of a great multitude, and as the voice of many waters, and as the voice of mighty thunderings, saying, Alleluia: for the Lord God omnipotent reigneth. [*Finally, the Millennium is here and Jesus is our King!*]

7 Let us be glad and rejoice, and give honour to him: for the marriage of the Lamb is come [*i.e., the Savior has come to join with the righteous for a thousand years*], and his wife [*the Church, the righteous Saints*] hath made herself ready [*i.e., they are prepared for him, they have "oil in their lamps;" Matthew 25:4*].

8 And to her [*the Church, the righteous*] was granted that she should be arrayed in fine linen, clean and white [*dressed in white robes, symbolic of exaltation*]: for the fine linen is the righteousness of saints [*i.e., they are clothed with personal righteousness; the Savior's Atonement can do this for us, after all we can do; 2 Nephi 25:23*].

9 And he [*the angel in Rev. 1:1*] saith unto me [*John*], Write, Blessed are they which are called unto the marriage supper of the Lamb [*i.e., the righteous who are called up to meet and be with the Savior at his coming; D&C 88:96*]. And he saith unto me, These are the true sayings of God [*the angel bears his testimony to John*].

10 And I [*John*] fell at his [*the angel's*] feet to worship him. And he said unto me, See thou do it not: I am thy fellowservant, and of thy brethren that have the testimony of Jesus: worship God [*i.e., don't worship me, worship God; I am one of you, one of the prophets (Rev. 22:9)*]: for the testimony of Jesus is the spirit of prophecy.

JST Revelation 19:10

10 And I fell at his feet to worship him. And he said unto me, See **that** thou do it not; I am thy fellow servant, and of thy brethren that have the testimony of Jesus; worship God; for the testimony of Jesus is the spirit of prophecy.

11 And I saw heaven opened, and behold a white horse [*symbolic of*

the triumph of righteousness]; and he [*Christ*] that sat upon him was called Faithful and True, and in righteousness he doth judge [*the Father turns all judgment over to the Son; John 5:22*] and make war [*destroy the wicked with Satan's kingdom*].

JST Revelation 19:11

11 And I saw heaven opened, and behold a white horse; and he that sat upon him **is** called Faithful and True, and in righteousness he doth judge and make war;

12 His [*Christ's*] eyes were as a flame of fire, and on his head were many crowns [*Christ rules over many kingdoms; D&C 88:50–61*]; and he had a name written [*new name, Rev. 2:17; symbolic of celestial glory; D&C 130:11*], that no man knew, but he himself.

JST Revelation 19:12

12 His **eyes as** a flame of fire; and **he had on his head many crowns**; **and a name** written, that no man knew, **but himself**.

13 And he was clothed with a vesture dipped in blood [*He wore red at his coming, D&C 133:48, symbolic of the blood of the wicked as judgment falls upon them, D&C 133:50–51*] : and his name is called The Word of God [*i.e., Christ; John 1:1*].

JST Revelation 19:13

13 And he **is** clothed with a vesture dipped in blood; and his name is called The Word of God.

14 And the armies which were in heaven [*the hosts of heaven*] followed him upon white horses [*symbolic of righteous victory*], clothed in fine linen [*righteousness; Rev. 19:8*], white and clean.

15 And out of his mouth goeth a sharp sword, that with it he should smite the nations: and he shall rule them with a rod of iron [*the word of God; 1 Nephi 11:25*]: and he treadeth the winepress of the fierceness and wrath of Almighty God [*He destroys the wicked*].

JST Revelation 19:15

15 And out of his mouth **proceedeth the word of God**, and with it he **will** smite the nations; and he **will** rule them with **the word of his mouth;** and he treadeth the winepress **in** the fierceness and wrath of Almighty God.

16 And he hath on his vesture [*robe: Strong's #2440*] and on his thigh [*German Bible: "hip." Symbolic of great slaughter of the wicked at Christ's coming. See Judges 15:8 where a terrible slaughter is described as "smote them hip and thigh with a great slaughter."*] a name written, KING OF KINGS, AND LORD OF LORDS [*i.e., He is Jesus Christ!*].

17 And I saw an angel standing in the sun [*symbolic of power and authority in heaven*]; and he cried with a loud voice, saying to all the fowls that fly in the midst of heaven, Come and gather yourselves together unto the supper of

the great God [*symbolically, many carrion birds are needed to clean up the carcasses of the wicked who will be destroyed in the final wars before the Second Coming*];

18 That ye may eat the flesh of kings [*wicked, influential leaders*], and the flesh of captains, and the flesh of mighty men, and the flesh of horses [*horses are symbolic of military might, weapons of war and destruction*], and of them that sit on them, and the flesh of all men, both free and bond, both small and great [*i.e., all the wicked*].

JST Revelation 19:18

18 That ye may eat the flesh of kings, and the flesh of captains, and the flesh of mighty men, and the flesh of horses, and of them that sit on them, and the flesh **of all who fight against the Lamb, both bond and free**, both small and great.

19 And I saw the beast [*perhaps referring back to Revelation 13:1*], and the [*wicked*] kings of the earth, and their armies, gathered together to make war against him [*Christ; verse 11*] that sat on the horse, and against his army [*the final battles*].

20 And the beast was taken [*conquered*], and with him the false prophet that wrought miracles before him [*Revelation 13:14*], with which he deceived them that had received the mark of the beast [*Revelation 13:16*], and them that worshipped his image [*i.e., his followers; Revelation 13:14*]. These both were cast alive into a lake of fire burning with brimstone [*i.e., you can't imagine how miserable it will be for the wicked; compare with D&C 19:15*].

21 And the remnant [*those wicked who survive the horrible final battles before the Second Coming*] were slain with the sword of him that sat upon the horse, [*i.e., destroyed at the Second Coming*] which sword proceeded out of his mouth: and all the fowls [*the carrion birds in verse 17*] were filled with their flesh [*the carcasses of the slain wicked in verse 18*].

JST Revelation 19:21

21 And the remnant were slain with the **word** of him that sat upon the horse, which **word** proceeded out of his mouth; and all the fowls were filled with their flesh.

REVELATION 20

In this chapter, we see the binding of Satan for the duration of the Millennium. We see the righteous, resurrected Saints reigning with Christ a thousand years. Then we see Satan "loosed a little season" at the end of the thousand-year Millennium, which leads to the battle of Gog and Magog. At the end of this battle, we see the total defeat of the devil and the hosts of the wicked. Finally, we see the last resurrection and final judgment.

1 And I saw an angel come down from heaven, having the key of the bottomless pit and a great chain

in his hand [*i.e., fully equipped to bind Satan*].

JST Revelation 20:1

1 And I saw an angel come down **out of** heaven, having the key of the bottomless pit and a great chain in his hand.

2 And he laid hold on the dragon, that old serpent, which is the Devil, and Satan, and bound him a thousand years [*during the Millennium*],

From verse 2, above, we see that Satan is bound for the duration of the Millennium and is not even allowed to try to tempt the people living on the earth during the thousand years. This doctrine is taught clearly in D&C 101:28.

3 And cast him into the bottomless pit [*the depths of hell*], and shut him up, and set a seal upon him, that he should deceive the nations no more, till the thousand years should be fulfilled [*i.e., are over*]: and after that he must be loosed a little season [*for the Battle of Gog and Magog—see Revelation 20:8, D&C 88:110–15*].

4 And I saw thrones [*symbolic of being joint heirs with Christ; Romans 8:17; i.e., exaltation*], and they [*the righteous*] sat upon them, and judgment was given unto them: and I saw the souls [*resurrected bodies*] of them that were beheaded for the witness of Jesus [*i.e., righteous martyrs*], and for the word of God, and which had not worshipped the beast [*Revelation 13, i.e., who had not followed*

Satan], neither his image [*Revelation 13:14*], neither had received his mark upon their foreheads, or in their hands [*Revelation 13:16*]; and they [*the righteous*] lived and reigned with Christ a thousand years.

5 But the rest of the dead [*the wicked*] lived not again [*were not resurrected*] until the thousand years were finished. This [*the resurrection of the righteous indicated in verse 4—see D&C 88:97–98*] is the first resurrection [*which takes place at the beginning of the Millennium*].

6 Blessed and holy is he that hath part in the first resurrection [*a reference to those who gain celestial glory*]: on such the second death [*spiritual death*] hath no power, but they shall be priests of God and of Christ, and shall reign with him a thousand years.

JST Revelation 20:6

6 Blessed and holy **are they who have** part in the first resurrection; on such the second death hath no power, but they shall be priests of God and of Christ, and shall reign with him a thousand years.

7 And when the thousand years are expired, Satan shall be loosed out of his prison [*D&C 88:111*],

8 And shall go out to deceive the nations which are in the four quarters of the earth, Gog and Magog [*symbolic of wicked nations and their leaders; for a definition of Gog, see Bible Dictionary under*

"Gog," and for Magog, under "Magog"], to gather them together to battle: the number of whom is as the sand of the sea [*i.e., there will be great numbers of wicked during the "little season," after the end of the Millennium*].

9 And they [*the wicked; Gog and Magog*] went up on the breadth of the earth, and compassed the camp of the saints about [*made war against the Saints; D&C 88:112–15*], and the beloved city [*the Lord's kingdom*]: and fire came down from God out of heaven, and devoured them.

10 And the devil that deceived them was cast into the lake of fire and brimstone, where the beast and the false prophet are, and shall be tormented day and night for ever and ever [*Satan and his wicked hosts are cast out forever (D&C 76:32–36, 44–45)*].

11 And I saw a great white throne, and him [*Christ; Rev. 21:5–6*] that sat on it, from whose face the earth and the heaven fled away; and there was found no place for them [*i.e., there will be a new heaven after the Millennium and little season are over, perhaps referring to the fact that "This earth will be rolled back into the presence of God, and crowned with celestial glory."* (Teachings of the Prophet Joseph Smith, Deseret Book, 1977, p. 181)] and new earth; [*not a different one, but a resurrected, glorified, earth as it becomes the celestial kingdom for the righteous from this*

earth; D&C 88:26, 130:9].

12 And I saw the dead, small and great, stand before God; and the books were opened: and another book was opened, which is the book of life: and the dead were judged out of those things which were written in the books, according to their works [*the final judgment*].

13 And the sea gave up the dead which were in it; and death and hell delivered up the dead which were in them [*all the wicked were finally resurrected also; D&C 88:101–102*]: and they were judged every man according to their works.

14 And death and hell were cast into the lake of fire. This is the second death [*only sons of perdition will suffer this forever; D&C 76:36–37*].

15 And whosoever was not found written in the book of life was cast into the lake of fire [*all except sons of perdition are saved at least to some degree, by Christ, into the telestial, terrestrial or celestial kingdoms; D&C 76:37–39, 81–87*].

REVELATION 21

In this chapter, John describes the earth as it attains celestial glory. (See heading to Revelation 21 in your Bible.)This will take place after the end of the Millennium and after the battle of Gog and Magog (D&C 88:111–14), which follows the Millennium. Joseph Smith taught "This earth will be rolled back into the presence of God,

and crowned with celestial glory."
(*Teachings of the Prophet Joseph Smith*, Deseret Book, 1976, p. 181.)

1 And I saw a new heaven and a new earth [*D&C 29:23–24; see also notes for Rev. 20:11*]: for the first heaven and the first earth were passed away; and there was no more sea.

2 And I John saw the holy city, new Jerusalem, coming down from God out of heaven, prepared as a bride adorned for her husband [*i.e., dressed in her finest i.e., celestial*].

3 And I heard a great voice out of heaven saying, Behold, the tabernacle [*physical body*] of God is with men [*i.e., the Savior is literally, physically, here with us*], and he will dwell with them, and they shall be his people, and God himself shall be with them, and be their God [*Christ will dwell with the righteous on the celestialized earth; D&C 130:9*].

Referring to verses 2 and 3, above, we see that, according to Ether 13:8–10, a city called "New Jerusalem" will be built upon the American continent (see also the tenth Article of Faith). Moses 7:22 tells us that this New Jerusalem will be built up by the righteous as they look forward to the coming of Christ. In his vision, John saw "the holy city, new Jerusalem, coming down from God out of heaven" (verse 3). We understand the "new Jerusalem" which John saw here to be a different city than the New Jerusalem described in Ether

and Moses. The "new Jerusalem" seen by John seems to be symbolic of this earth as it is celestialized and as it becomes the abode of the Savior and the righteous Saints forever (see verse 3). Bruce R. McConkie said: "When this earth becomes a celestial sphere 'that great city, the holy Jerusalem,' shall again descend 'out of heaven from God,' as this earth becomes the abode of celestial beings forever. (Rev. 21:10–27.)" (McConkie, *Doctrinal New Testament Commentary*, 3:580–81.)

Verses 4–7, next, are some of my favorite verses of scripture. They are a beautiful reminder that, for the righteous, all of the trials and tribulations we go through on earth as we strive to stay on the covenant path will fade away into the past in light of the great blessings we receive as we enter exaltation in the celestial kingdom.

4 And God shall wipe away all tears from their eyes; and there shall be no more death, neither sorrow, nor crying, neither shall there be any more pain [*a beautiful description of celestial exaltation*]: for the former things [*past troubles*] are passed away.

5 And he [*Christ; Rev. 20:11, 21:6*] that sat upon the throne said, Behold, I make all things new. And he said unto me, Write: for these words are true and faithful [*Christ bears testimony to John of the truthfulness of the things he is seeing and hearing*].

6 And he [*Christ*] said unto me [*John*], It is done [*everything is fulfilled; D&C 1:38*]. I am Alpha and Omega, the beginning and the end. I will give unto him [*the righteous*] that is athirst of the fountain of the water of life freely [*living water; John 4:14*].

7 He that overcometh [*overcomes sin and wickedness*] shall inherit all things [*i.e., will receive exaltation, D&C 132:20*]; and I will be his God, and he shall be my son.

8 But the fearful [*perhaps meaning those who are afraid to do right*], and unbelieving, and the abominable, and murderers, and whoremongers, and sorcerers, and idolaters, and all liars, shall have their part [*will receive their punishment*] in the lake which burneth with fire and brimstone: which is the second death [*an important message for John to give during his remaining ministry on earth*].

9 And there came unto me one of the seven angels [*Revelation 15:1*] which had the seven vials full of the seven last plagues, and talked with me, saying, Come hither, I will shew thee the bride, the Lamb's wife [*there are many possible meanings for this, including the Church, the righteous, the City of Enoch, the celestial city or kingdom described in verses 11–27 of this chapter*].

10 And he carried me away in the spirit to a great and high mountain, and shewed me that great city, the holy Jerusalem [*symbolic of the celestial kingdom*], descending out of heaven from God,

In other words, John is now shown the beauty and glory of the celestial kingdom.

11 Having the glory of God: and her light [*the city's light*] was like unto a stone most precious, even like a jasper stone, clear as crystal;

12 And had a wall great and high [*symbolic of security, safety*], and had twelve [*symbolic of divine government—see symbolism notes at the beginning of Revelation in this study guide*] gates, and at the gates twelve angels, and names written thereon, which are the names of the twelve tribes of the children of Israel:

13 On the east three gates; on the north three gates; on the south three gates; and on the west three gates [*perhaps the use of sets of "three" symbolizes that the whole celestial city or kingdom is blessed with the presence of the Godhead— see symbolism notes referred to above*].

14 And the wall of the city had twelve foundations, and in them the names of the twelve apostles of the Lamb [*perhaps symbolizing that the city is indeed built upon the righteous principles and priesthood covenants taught by the twelve Apostles*].

15 And he that talked with me had a golden reed [*perhaps a celestial measuring device similar to the reed in Revelation 11:1, used here to show John that things indeed "measure up" just as promised*] to measure the city, and the gates thereof, and the wall thereof.

16 And the city lieth foursquare, and the length is as large as the breadth: and he measured the city with the reed, twelve thousand furlongs [*if a furlong is about 220 yards, Bible Dictionary under "Weights and Measures," and the length and breadth are twelve thousand furlongs each, the city which John saw was about 1,500 U.S. miles in length, width and height, or about 3 billion, 375 million cubic miles of living space, perhaps symbolizing to John that there is plenty of glorious living space for the "great multitude" of the righteous which he saw in heaven in Revelation 7:9; see also D&C 76:67*]. The length and the breadth and the height of it are equal.

17 And he [*the angel talking to John in verse 15*] measured the wall thereof, an hundred and forty and four cubits, according to the measure of a man, that is, of the angel.

JST Revelation 21:17

17 And he measured the wall thereof, **a** hundred and forty and four cubits, according to the measure of a man, that is, of the angel.

18 [*John now attempts almost the impossible, i.e., to describe to us the beauty of celestial glory.*] And the building of the wall of it was of jasper: and the city was pure gold, like unto clear glass.

19 And the foundations of the wall of the city were garnished with all manner of precious stones. The first foundation was jasper; the second, sapphire; the third, a chalcedony; the fourth, an emerald;

20 The fifth, sardonyx; the sixth, sardius; the seventh, chrysolite; the eighth, beryl; the ninth, a topaz; the tenth, a chrysoprasus; the eleventh, a jacinth; the twelfth, an amethyst.

21 And the twelve gates were twelve pearls; every several gate was of one pearl: and the street of the city was pure gold, as it were transparent glass.

22 And I saw no temple therein [*a temple is not needed*]: for the Lord God Almighty and the Lamb are the temple of it.

23 And the city had no need of the sun, neither of the moon, to shine in it: for the glory of God did lighten it, and the Lamb [*Christ*] is the light thereof.

24 And the nations of them which are saved [*i.e., the righteous*] shall walk in the light of it: and the kings of the earth do bring their glory and honour into it.

25 And the gates of it shall not be shut at all by day: for there shall be no night there.

26 And they shall bring the glory and honour of the nations into it.

27 And there shall in no wise enter into it any thing that defileth, neither whatsoever worketh abomination, or maketh a lie [*i.e., no unclean thing can enter the kingdom; 3 Nephi 27:19*]: but they which are written in the Lamb's

book of life [*i.e., the righteous who have been made clean through the Atonement of Christ; Alma 34:36*].

REVELATION 22

John's vision draws to a close with symbolism and doctrines which summarize major messages of the Book of Revelation, including that the reward of the righteous is wonderful beyond our ability to comprehend and that the wicked are left out of these priceless blessings.

As we start verse 1, we see that it is a continuation of the description of celestial glory from chapter 21.

1 And he [*one of the seven angels; Revelation 21:9*] shewed me a pure river of water of life, clear as crystal, proceeding out of the throne of God and of the Lamb.

2 In the midst of the street of it [*the celestial city (chapter 21), i.e., celestial glory*], and on either side of the river, was there the tree of life [*1 Nephi 8:10, Revelation 22:14*], which bare twelve manner of fruits, and yielded her fruit every month [*i.e., the benefits of the gospel are not "seasonal," rather continue constantly forever*]: and the leaves of the tree were for the healing of the nations [*what the gospel can do for people*].

3 And there shall be no more curse [*on the earth, Genesis 3:17, which will then be the celestial kingdom, D&C 130:9; 88:25*]: but the throne of God and of the Lamb shall be in it; and his servants shall serve him:

4 And they shall see his face; and his name shall be in their foreheads [*Revelation 3:12; i.e., they have taken His name upon them and kept their covenants, therefore they will be with Him in celestial glory*].

5 And there shall be no night there; and they need no candle, neither light of the sun; for the Lord God giveth them light: and they shall reign for ever and ever [*i.e., they will be Gods; D&C 132:20*].

6 And he said unto me, These sayings are faithful and true [*the angel bears his testimony to John*]: and the Lord God of the holy prophets sent his angel to shew unto his servants the things which must shortly be done [*the vision is now coming to a close and the angel is summarizing for John*].

7 Behold, I [*Christ*] come quickly [*not "soon," rather, when the time is right, He will come suddenly upon the wicked as a thief in the night; D&C 106:4–5*]: blessed is he that keepeth [*obeys*] the sayings of the prophecy of this book.

8 And I John saw these things, and heard them. And when I had heard and seen, I fell down to worship before the feet of the angel [*as mentioned in Revelation 19:10*] which shewed me these things.

9 Then saith he unto me, See thou do it not [*don't worship me*]: for I am thy fellowservant, and of thy brethren the prophets [*I am one of you*], and of them which keep the sayings of this book: worship God.

JST Revelation 22:9

9 Then saith he unto me, See **that** thou do it not; for I am thy fellowservant, and of thy brethren the prophets, and of them which keep the sayings of this book; worship God.

10 And he saith unto me, Seal not the sayings of the prophecy of this book [*i.e., let these things be read*]: for the time is at hand.

11 He that is unjust, let him be unjust still: and he which is filthy, let him be filthy still: and he that is righteous, let him be righteous still: and he that is holy, let him be holy still [*when final judgment comes you will be judged according to what you are*].

12 And, behold, I [*Christ*] come quickly; and my reward is with me, to give every man according as his work shall be.

13 I am Alpha and Omega [*Revelation 1:11*], the beginning and the end, the first and the last [*i.e., I am the "A" and the "Z"; I know the beginning from the end; I was there at the beginning of creation, and I will be there at the end of the earth to judge you; I am in charge of all things under the direction of the Father*].

14 Blessed are they that do his commandments, that they may have right to the tree of life [*spoken of in verse 2*], and may enter in through the gates into the city [*the celestial kingdom*].

15 For without [*i.e., outside of the celestial glory, i.e., telestial glory; see D&C 76:103*] are dogs [*an unclean beast under the law of Moses, perhaps symbolic here of people who refused to make themselves clean through the Atonement*], and sorcerers, and whoremongers [*people who constantly seek opportunities for immorality*], and murderers, and idolaters, and whosoever loveth and maketh a lie [*people who are dishonest, love to lie*].

Next, the Savior bears His testimony to John that He is the Redeemer, about whom the Old Testament prophesied.

16 I Jesus have sent mine angel to testify unto you these things in the churches [*probably the seven churches or "wards" referred to in Rev. 1:11*]. I am the root [*that came out of dry ground, i.e., apostate Judaism, as stated by Isaiah in Isaiah 53:2*] and the offspring of David [*a descendent of David, as prophesied*], and the bright and morning star [*the first and the brightest, i.e., I am the Savior*].

17 And the Spirit [*the Holy Ghost*] and the bride [*the righteous members of the Church; see Rev. 21:2*] say, Come. And let him that heareth say, Come. And let him that is athirst come. And whosoever will, let him take the water of life freely [*an open invitation to all to come unto Christ*].

Perhaps you have run into the argument by other Christians

that our Book of Mormon and other scriptures in addition to the Bible, violate Revelation 22:18. They suggest that nothing should be added to the Bible. Pay close attention to the notes in verses 18–19, next, for the solution to this challenge.

18 For I testify unto every man that heareth the words of the prophecy of this book [*the Book of Revelation, not the whole Bible; John wrote the Gospel of John after he wrote Revelation*], If any man shall add unto these things [*i.e., intentionally twists meanings or adds false doctrines*], God shall add unto him the plagues that are written in this book:

19 And if any man shall take away from the words of the book of this prophecy, God shall take away his part out of the book of life, and out of the holy city, and from the things which are written in this book [*i.e., don't intentionally twist the meanings, delete doctrines, etc., from this book; see also Deuteronomy 4:2*].

20 He which testifieth these things saith, Surely I come quickly. Amen. Even so, come, Lord Jesus.

21 The grace of our Lord Jesus Christ be with you all. Amen.

Sources

Doctrine and Covenants Student Manual, Religion 324 and 325. Salt Lake City: The Church of Jesus Christ of Latter-day Saints, 2001.

Ensign. March 1976 and November 1995.

Hymns of The Church of Jesus Christ of Latter-day Saints. Salt Lake City: The Church of Jesus Christ of Latter-day Saints, 1985.

Improvement Era. Vol. 19.

Journal of Discourses. Vol 18. London: Latter-day Saints' Book Depot, 1854–86.

Parry, Jay A. and Donald W. *Understanding the Book of Revelation.* Salt Lake City: Deseret Book, 1998.

Kimball, Spencer W. *The Miracle of Forgiveness.* Salt Lake City: Bookcraft, 1969.

Life and Teachings of Jesus and His Apostles, The. New Testament student manual, Religion 211. Salt Lake City: The Church of Jesus Christ of Latter-day Saints, 1979.

McConkie, Bruce R. *Doctrinal New Testament Commentary.* 3 vols. Salt Lake City: Bookcraft, 1965–73.

McConkie, Bruce R. *Mormon Doctrine.* 2d ed. Salt Lake City: Bookcraft, 1966.

Millet, Robert L. *Alive in Christ: The Miracle of Spiritual Rebirth.* Salt Lake City: Deseret Book, 1997.

Pratt, Orson. *Masterful Discourses and Writings of Orson Pratt.* Compiled by N. B. Lundwall. Salt Lake City: Bookcraft, 1962.

Smith, Joseph. *History of The Church of Jesus Christ of Latter-day Saints.* Edited by B. H. Roberts. 2d ed. rev., 7 vols., Salt Lake City: The Church of Jesus Christ of Latter-day Saints, 1932–51.

Smith, Joseph. *Joseph Smith's "New Translation" of the Bible* (JST). Independence, Missouri: Herald Publishing House, 1970.

Smith, Joseph. *Lectures on Faith.* Salt Lake City: Deseret Book, 1985.

Smith, Joseph. *Teachings of the Prophet Joseph Smith.* Selected by Joseph Fielding Smith. Salt Lake City: Deseret Book, 1976.

Smith, Joseph F. *Gospel Doctrine: Selections from the Sermons and Writings of Joseph F. Smith.* Salt Lake City: Deseret Book, 1971.

Smith, Joseph Fielding. *Doctrines of Salvation.* Compiled by Bruce R. McConkie. 3 vols. Salt Lake City: Bookcraft, 1954–56.

Strong, James. *The Exhaustive Concordance of the Bible.* Nashville: Abingdon, 1890.

Talmage, James E. *Jesus the Christ.* Salt Lake City: Deseret Book, 1982.

Widtsoe, John A. *Evidences and Reconciliations.* Salt Lake City: Bookcraft, 1943.

Various translations of the Bible, including the Martin Luther edition of the German Bible, which Joseph Smith said was the most correct of any then available.

OUR SAVIOR'S LIFE AND MISSION TO REDEEM AND GIVE HOPE

DAVID J. RIDGES

CONTENTS

———— ∞∞∞ ————

Contents

PREFACE

The Atonement of Jesus Christ is the central focus of the gospel. It is not merely a part of it, nor is it just a very significant part of it. It is the very essence of the Father's plan for us. It is the means by which we can return to the presence of the Father to live with Him forever. It influences every aspect of daily living. There is absolutely no substitute for it. "And moreover, I say unto you, that there shall be no other name given nor any other way nor means whereby salvation can come unto the children of men, only in and through the name of Christ, the Lord Omnipotent" (Mosiah 3:17).

A correct understanding of the Atonement leads to joy and happiness, progress and satisfaction in this life, in spite of troubles and difficulties encountered along the way. Lack of understanding or misunderstanding of the Atonement can lead many to hold onto the effects of past sins unnecessarily. They miss out on the joy, happiness, and personal progress intended for this life (2 Nephi 2:25). Many confess sins and repent, but still don't allow the healing and cleansing of the Atonement to actually work for them.

This book briefly reviews the Savior's premortal roles as the firstborn spirit child of the Father, as the Redeemer chosen in the grand premortal council, as the Creator, and as the God of the Old Testament. Then, His mortal life and ministry will be treated in more detail. The last week of His life will be a major focus as it leads up to His atoning sacrifice and resurrection. Throughout the book, the blessings and influence of the infinite Atonement will be emphasized.

In chapter 15, which deals with the cleansing and healing power of the Atonement, the author will give many examples gleaned from his years as a bishop, stake president, and teacher in the Church Educational System, which illustrate correct understanding as well as misunderstanding of the Atonement, and the effect on individual lives that such perceptions can have.

The Savior's continuing ministry after the resurrection, including His appearance to the Nephites, the appearance with His Father to Joseph Smith, the Restoration, the fact that He is often in our midst, the Second Coming, the Millennium, and His role as our final Judge will also be briefly considered.

It is hoped by the author that this book will help to bring increased understanding and application of the saving principles found in the life and Atonement of the Lord Jesus Christ into the lives of those who read and study its contents.

INTRODUCTION

"To this end was I born" (John 18:37) was the Savior's brief but profound summary of His mortal ministry, culminating with His atoning sacrifice and resurrection. A major goal of this book is to use scripture and commentary to bring greater understanding and appreciation of the Master's steadfast resolve to carry out the Father's Plan. Chronology, which extends far back into the premortal realm, is used to bring the reader along step by step with the Lord toward the fulfilling of His commitment to be the Redeemer. A sense of drama is felt as the time for the final sacrifice of the Son of God draws closer and closer.

There are several different chronologies which list the events in the Savior's mortal mission in order. They do not always agree with each other. Therefore, for the most part, the chronology used in this work is the one given in the "Harmony of the Gospels" found in the Bible Dictionary at the back of the Latter-day Saint edition of the King James Version of the Bible. However, on occasion, the order of events given in the Institute of Religion's New Testament student manual is followed. The title of that manual is *The Life and Teachings of Jesus and His Apostles*, 1979 edition. The division of the Lord's formal mortal ministry into three years, with each of the years beginning and ending at Passover time (New Testament student manual, p. 32) will be used as a general guideline.

In the commentary that I give along the way, I almost always use "we" rather than "I" in order to avoid drawing inappropriate attention to myself.

This is not an official publication of The Church of Jesus Christ of Latter-day Saints. I am solely responsible for my thoughts and commentary as well as for assembling and arranging its content that comes from other specified sources.

I express special appreciation to my wife, Janette, who has completely supported me and provided invaluable help in this endeavor. I also thank the wonderful and skilled editors and staff at Cedar Fort for their vital help in bringing this work to publication.

—David J. Ridges

CHAPTER 1
THE "FIRSTBORN" OF THE FATHER

If we were able to go back in time, way back, unimaginably far back, long before we, ourselves, were born as spirit children of "heavenly parents" (The Family: A Proclamation to the World) in premortality, we would come to the time in which our Father in Heaven was a mortal man, living on an earth similar to the one on which we live, working out His salvation, just as we are now doing on this earth which He has provided for us. He successfully finished up His mortal life and received His exaltation. Joseph Smith taught:

> God himself was once as we are now, and is an exalted man, and sits enthroned in yonder heavens! That is the great secret. If the veil were rent today, and the great God who holds this world in its orbit, and who upholds all worlds and all things by his power, was to make himself visible,—I say, if you were to see him today, you would see him like a man in form—like yourselves in all the person, image, and very form as a man; for Adam was created in the very fashion, image and likeness of God, and received instruction from, and walked, talked and conversed with him, as one man talks and communes with another. (*Teachings of Presidents of the Church—Joseph Smith*, p. 40 [the Melchizedek Priesthood and Relief Society study course for 2008]; see also *TPJS*, p. 345)

> These are incomprehensible ideas to some, but they are simple. It is the first principle of the Gospel to know for a certainty the Character of God, and to know that we may converse with him as one man converses with another, and that he was once a man like us; yea, that God himself, the Father of us all, dwelt on an earth, the same as Jesus Christ himself did; and I will show it from the Bible. (*TPJS*, p. 345–46)

Based on the doctrine taught by the Prophet Joseph Smith, quoted above, an article in the 1971 *New Era* explained again the simple and beautiful doctrine that our Heavenly Father went through the same plan of salvation that we are now privileged to be going through on our earth. The following is a brief excerpt from that article:

> Long before our God began his creations, he dwelt on a mortal world like ours . . . He, with many of his brethren, was obedient to the principles of the eternal gospel [and] they obtained a resurrection and an exaltation on an eternal, celestial world [Brigham Young in *Journal of Discourses*, Vol. 14, p. 71]. Then they gained . . . godhood . . . creating worlds of their own for their own posterity—and on and on. (Nielsen, "People on Other Worlds," par. 41)

THE FIRSTBORN SPIRIT CHILD

Knowing that each of us "is a beloved spirit son or daughter of heavenly parents" (Proclamation on the Family), we can sense that if we were somehow privileged to see that far back to that far distant period of eternity, we would see the joy on their faces and share the sweet feelings in their hearts as they held their own firstborn spirit child in their arms. This son was to become our Savior and Redeemer, Jesus Christ, and was literally "the firstborn of every creature" (Colossians 1:15).

President Joseph F. Smith taught that Jesus Christ was indeed the first of the spirit children born to Heavenly Father.

> Among the spirit children of Elohim, the first-born was and is Jehovah, or Jesus Christ, to whom all others are juniors. (*Improvement Era*, Vol. 19, p. 940; see also *Gospel Doctrine*, p. 70)

Gordon B. Hinckley likewise bore witness that Jesus Christ was the Firstborn of the Father.

> I believe in the Lord Jesus Christ, the Son of the eternal, living God. I believe in him as the Firstborn of the Father and the Only Begotten of the Father in the flesh. I believe in him as an individual, separate and distinct from his Father. I believe in the declaration of John, who opened his gospel with this majestic utterance. (*Faith: The Essence of True Religion*, 23)

The Savior refers to Himself as the "Firstborn."

> 21 And now, verily I say unto you, I was in the beginning with the Father, and am the Firstborn. (D&C 93:21)

Thus, it is clear from the scriptures and the teachings of modern prophets that the Savior was the first spirit child born to our Father in Heaven, after the Father attained His own exaltation.

THE FIRSTBEGOTTEN

Christ is also referred to as the "Firstbegotten," which is a term that means the "first child born to a particular parent."

1 God, who at sundry times and in divers manners spake in time past unto the fathers by the prophets,

2 Hath in these last days spoken unto us by his Son, whom he hath appointed heir of all things, by whom also he made the worlds;

6 And again, when he bringeth in the firstbegotten [*in other words, the Father's firstborn spirit child*] into the world, he saith, And let all the angels of God worship him. (Hebrews 1:1, 2, 6)

Have you noticed in the scriptures that another term for exaltation is "church of the Firstborn"? This is another way of saying "the Church of Jesus Christ," and in this setting, it means those who receive all that the Savior offers, in other words, exaltation. We see this in section 76, verses 54, 67, and 94 of the Doctrine and Covenants. We will include these three verses among several other verses of section 76 which show that the context of "church of the Firstborn" is that of exaltation, in other words, the highest degree in the celestial kingdom.

54 They are they who are the church of the Firstborn.

55 They are they into whose hands the Father has given all things—

67 These are they who have come to an innumerable company of angels, to the general assembly and church of Enoch, and of the Firstborn. (D&C 76:54–55, 67)

The next part of this revelation reminds us that it is through the Atonement of Jesus Christ that we can be made perfect. "Just men," in verse 69, next, are those who have done their best to live the gospel with exactness.

69 These are they who are just men made perfect through Jesus the mediator of the new covenant, who wrought out this perfect atonement through the shedding of his own blood. (D&C 76:69)

The last three verses quoted here clearly show that exaltation is what is being discussed by the Lord in this portion of section 76.

70 These are they whose bodies are celestial, whose glory is that of the sun, even the glory of God, the highest of all, whose glory the sun of the firmament is written of as being typical.

94 They who dwell in his presence are the church of the Firstborn; and they see as they are seen, and know as they are known [*in other words, they are gods, and have all the power that God has*], having received of his fulness and of his grace;

95 And he makes them equal in power, and in might, and in dominion. (D&C 76:70, 94–95)

Elder Brother

Yet another reminder that Jesus Christ is literally the first spirit child born to our Heavenly Father is found in the teachings of Church leaders, past and present, as they refer to the Savior as our "Elder Brother."

An example of this is found in the teachings of Apostle James E. Talmage (1862–1933).

> There is no impropriety, therefore, in speaking of Jesus Christ as the Elder Brother of the rest of human kind. That He is by spiritual birth Brother to the rest of us is indicated in Hebrews: "Wherefore in all things it behooved him to be made like unto his brethren, that he might be a merciful and faithful high priest in things pertaining to God, to make reconciliation for the sins of the people" (Hebrews 2:17). Let it not be forgotten, however, that He is essentially greater than any and all others, by reason (1) of His seniority as the oldest or firstborn; (2) of His unique status in the flesh as the offspring of a mortal mother and of an immortal, or resurrected and glorified, Father; (3) of His selection and foreordination as the one and only Redeemer and Savior of the race; and (4) of His transcendent sinlessness. (*Articles of Faith*, p. 426)

Over the course of premortal eons of time, our Heavenly Father has had untold additional spirit sons as well as spirit daughters born to Him. This includes us. In Acts, the Apostle Paul uses a unique word to refer to us, which separates and differentiates us from the general "creations" of the Lord.

> 28 For in him we live, and move, and have our being; as certain also of your own poets have said, For we are also his offspring.
> 29 Forasmuch then as we are the offspring of God, we ought not to think that the Godhead is like unto gold, or silver, or stone, graven by art and man's device. (Acts 17:28–29)

As you can see, Paul teaches that we are the Father's "offspring." In Hebrews 12:9, Paul teaches that God is the "father of spirits." Thus, we are all literal spirit brothers and sisters of Christ, with Him being the firstborn of all of us as spirit children of the Father. A statement by the First Presidency in the early 1900s confirms that we were literally born to heavenly parents as spirit children.

> Man, as a spirit, was begotten [conceived] and born of heavenly parents, and reared to maturity in the eternal mansions of the Father, prior to coming

upon the earth. (The First Presidency, Heber J. Grant and counselors, "The Mormon View of Evolution")

In summary, Jesus Christ was literally the firstborn spirit child of our Heavenly Father and is thus referred to in the scriptures and in the teachings of the Church as the "Firstborn" and the "Firstbegotten" of the Father. Thus, He is indeed our oldest brother, our "Elder Brother."

CHAPTER 2
CHOSEN TO BE THE REDEEMER IN THE PREMORTAL COUNCIL

THE GRAND PREMORTAL COUNCIL

Each of us "is a beloved spirit son or daughter of heavenly parents" (Proclamation on the Family, para. 2). As premortal spirits, living with our heavenly parents for eons of time, we were taught the gospel and schooled in all the things that would prepare us for the time when we would be sent to earth to continue our progression toward becoming like our Father. This progression would include receiving a mortal physical body so that we could eventually have a resurrected body of flesh and bone, and indeed, a glorified, exalted, resurrected body like Father's (D&C 130:22), if we proved worthy. When it was finally announced that our time to be sent to an earth had arrived, we were overjoyed!

> 4 Where wast thou when I laid the foundations of the earth? declare, if thou hast understanding.
> 5 Who hath laid the measures thereof, if thou knowest? or who hath stretched the line upon it?
> 6 Whereupon are the foundations thereof fastened? or who laid the corner stone thereof;
> 7 When the morning stars sang together, and all the sons of God shouted for joy? (Job 38:4–7)

At a certain stage of our premortal progression, the "Grand Council" was convened during which Jesus was chosen to be the Savior. We all attended. Joseph Smith taught that we all participated in this council and sanctioned the plan of salvation and the choice of Jesus to be the Redeemer.

We were all present and saw the Savior chosen and appointed, and the plan of salvation made and we sanctioned it. (*Words of Joseph Smith*, p. 60)

From another statement of Joseph Smith, we are taught that we, as members of this grand premortal council, voted for the Savior. As we read the Prophet's words, we also come to understand that there was considerable tension and drama during this council when Satan rebelled.

The contention in heaven was—Jesus said there would be certain souls that would not be saved; and the devil said he would save them all, and laid his plans before the grand council, who gave their vote in favor of Jesus Christ. So the devil rose up in rebellion against God, and was cast down, with all who put up their heads for him. (*HC* Vol. 6, p. 314)

As the scene unfolded in which the Firstborn of the Father was chosen to be our Redeemer, we no doubt watched with deep emotion and rapt attention as Satan tried to undermine the Father's plan and take on the role of savior. Perhaps we were startled as he demanded the glory and honor for himself, rather than giving it to the Father. The end result of Lucifer's attempt to change the plan was that he was cast out. Moses described this part of the council:

1 And I, the Lord God, spake unto Moses, saying: That Satan, whom thou hast commanded in the name of mine Only Begotten, is the same which was from the beginning, and he came before me, saying—Behold, here am I, send me, I will be thy son, and I will redeem all mankind, that one soul shall not be lost, and surely I will do it; wherefore give me thine honor.
2 But, behold, my Beloved Son, which was my Beloved and Chosen from the beginning, said unto me—Father, thy will be done, and the glory be thine forever.
3 Wherefore, because that Satan rebelled against me, and sought to destroy the agency of man, which I, the Lord God, had given him, and also, that I should give unto him mine own power; by the power of mine Only Begotten, I caused that he should be cast down;
4 And he became Satan, yea, even the devil, the father of all lies, to deceive and to blind men, and to lead them captive at his will, even as many as would not hearken unto my voice. (Moses 4:1–4)

John the Revelator (the Apostle John) was shown a vision of this grand council in heaven. His account of this premortal gathering of spirits is the most complete anywhere in the scriptures and is an entire chapter dedicated to this topic (Revelation 5). As you read his record of what he saw, you will see that he became deeply involved emotionally and wept much (verse 4) during this vision, until he saw the Savior step forward and say, "Here am I, send me" (Abraham 3:27). We will use Revelation 5:1–9 for our purposes here, and add some commentary for clarification:

1 And I saw in the right hand [*the covenant-making hand*] of him [*the Father; see 5:7*] that sat on the throne a book [*containing the Father's plan; also a specific mission for Jesus*] written within [*on the inside*] and on the backside [*in other words, the plan was complete, no need for or room for additions or changes to it*], sealed with seven seals [*containing information about the seven thousand years of the earth's temporal existence; see D&C 77:7*].

2 And I saw a strong angel [*one high in authority*] proclaiming with a loud voice, Who is worthy to open the book, and to loose the seals thereof [*who can carry out the Father's plan of salvation, including the Atonement, for us*]?

3 And no man [*no common man*] in heaven, nor in earth, neither under the earth, was able to open the book, neither to look thereon [*there was no one to carry out the Father's plan and perform the Atonement; this was a dramatic moment in the vision (a very effective teaching technique) which created the "need" to know in John's mind*].

4 And I [*John*] wept much [*John has become deeply emotionally involved in the vision*], because no man was found worthy to open and to read the book, neither to look thereon [*none of God's spirit children was even close to being worthy or able to carry out the Father's plan or perform the Atonement*].

5 And one of the elders [*mentioned in Revelation 4:4*] saith unto me, Weep not: behold [*look!*], the Lion of the tribe of Juda [*Christ*], the Root of David [*Christ*], hath prevailed to open the book, and to loose the seven seals thereof. [*Jesus Christ can do it!*]

6 And I beheld [*I looked*], and, lo, in the midst of the throne and of the four beasts, and in the midst of the elders [*mentioned in Revelation 4:4*], stood a Lamb [*Christ*] as it had been slain [*symbolic of Christ's atoning blood, shed for us*], having seven horns and seven eyes, which are the seven Spirits of God sent forth into all the earth.

The JST (Joseph Smith Translation of the Bible) changes "seven horns" to "twelve horns." In this case, "twelve" is symbolic of the twelve Apostles, and "horn" symbolizes power.

6 And I beheld, and, lo, in the midst of the throne and of the four beasts, and in the midst of the elders, stood a Lamb as it had been slain, *having twelve horns and twelve eyes, which are the twelve servants of God*, sent forth into all the earth. (JST, Revelation 5:6)

Next, we see the Savior accept the mission to be the Redeemer, during this grand premortal council in which we all participated.

7 And he [*Christ*] came and took the book [*accepted the calling*] out of the right hand [*covenant hand*] of him [*Elohim*] that sat upon the throne [*in other words, Jesus Christ made a covenant with the Father to be the Redeemer*].

Next, John beautifully describes all of heaven praising Christ for His willingness to perform the Atonement and be our Redeemer, thus carrying out the Father's plan for us.

> 8 And when he [*Christ*] had taken the book, the four beasts and four and twenty elders fell down before the Lamb, having every one of them harps [*harps symbolize being in the presence of God in biblical culture*], and golden vials [*containers*] full of odours [*incense; symbolic of prayers which rise up to God*], which are the prayers of saints.

The phrase "they sung a new song," in verse 9, next, is a scriptural phrase which means, in effect, that they could now rejoice over something that they could not rejoice about before. In other words, they can now sing praises to our Redeemer, whereas they couldn't before He was chosen. They can now rejoice about blessings of the Atonement that are now available which were not available before.

> 9 And they sung a new song, saying, Thou [*Christ*] art worthy to take the book [*the mission to be the Savior and work out the Father's plan for us; see verse 1*], and to open the seals thereof [*and to carry out the work planned for each of the thousand-year periods of the earth's temporal history; see D&C 77:6*]: for thou wast slain [*speaking of the Atonement as if it were already accomplished*], and hast redeemed us to God [*brought us back to the Father*] by thy blood out of every kindred, and tongue, and people, and nation [*the gospel covenants are for all peoples of the world*].

In summary, we attended and participated in the premortal council in heaven during which Jesus was chosen to be the Redeemer. When it was announced that our time to come to earth had arrived, we "shouted for joy" (Job 38:7). We saw Satan cast out with those who followed him, after he rebelled (Moses 4:3) and led the opposition during the War in Heaven (Revelation 12:7–9). We wept with the rest of the heavenly hosts over losing him (D&C 76:26).

CHAPTER 3

THE ATONEMENT WORKED
BEFORE IT WAS PERFORMED

Over four hundred years before Christ was born, Enos was astonished by the wonderful cleansing power of the Atonement in his own life, and by how fast his guilt was taken away.

> 6 And I, Enos, knew that God could not lie; wherefore, my guilt was swept away.
> 7 And I said: Lord, how is it done? (Enos 1:6–7)

About 740 BC, Isaiah was overwhelmed by his inadequacies and imperfections when he saw Jehovah (the premortal Christ) in vision and was called by Him to serve as a prophet to wicked Israel. Initially, Isaiah was "undone" (verse 5, quoted next), in other words, completely overwhelmed. He was worried about his "unclean lips" (verse 5), which meant imperfections, sins, inadequacies, and so forth, in his language and culture. However, when the strengthening and enabling power of the Atonement had worked for him, he was ready to serve (verse 8).

> 1 In the year that king Uzziah died I saw also the Lord sitting upon a throne, high and lifted up, and his train filled the temple.
> 5 Then said I, Woe is me! for I am undone; because I am a man of unclean lips, and I dwell in the midst of a people of unclean lips: for mine eyes have seen the King, the LORD of hosts.
> 6 Then flew one of the seraphims unto me, having a live coal in his hand, which he had taken with the tongs from off the altar [*symbolic of the Atonement*]:
> 7 And he laid it upon my mouth, and said, Lo, this [*the Atonement*] hath touched thy lips; and thine iniquity is taken away, and thy sin purged.
> 8 Also I heard the voice of the Lord, saying, Whom shall I send, and who will go for us? Then said I, Here am I; send me. (Isaiah 6:1, 5–8)

How is it that the Atonement of Christ could work before it was performed by the Savior, at the end of His mortal ministry? The answer lies in the fact that it was an infinite Atonement. The scriptures and the teachings of modern prophets speak of this. For example:

> 7 Wherefore, it must needs be an infinite atonement—save it should be an infinite atonement this corruption could not put on incorruption. Wherefore, the first judgment which came upon man must needs have remained to an endless duration. And if so, this flesh must have laid down to rot and to crumble to its mother earth, to rise no more. (2 Nephi 9:7)

> 16 And after they have been scattered, and the Lord God hath scourged them by other nations for the space of many generations, yea, even down from generation to generation until they shall be persuaded to believe in Christ, the Son of God, and the atonement, which is infinite for all mankind—and when that day shall come that they shall believe in Christ, and worship the Father in his name, with pure hearts and clean hands, and look not forward any more for another Messiah, then, at that time, the day will come that it must needs be expedient that they should believe these things. (2 Nephi 25:16)

Joseph Fielding Smith taught that an infinite Atonement was essential in order for the Father's plan to work for us.

> Adam could not atone for his transgression. An infinite atonement was required and only Christ was in a position to fulfil this requirement. (*Answers to Gospel Questions*, Vol. 3, p. 207)

Being "infinite," the Atonement worked for the salvation of individuals, even before it was performed by the Savior on our earth. Adam was comforted by the Lord regarding his transgression in the Garden.

> 53 Behold I have forgiven thee thy transgression in the Garden of Eden. (Moses 6:53)

The Lord instructed Adam to teach his children concerning the Atonement (Moses 6:57–58), and explained what he was to teach them.

> 59 Ye must be born again into the kingdom of heaven, of water, and of the Spirit, and be cleansed by blood, even the blood of mine Only Begotten; that ye might be sanctified from all sin, and enjoy the words of eternal life in this world, and eternal life in the world to come, even immortal glory. (Moses 6:59)

Noah taught the first principles of the gospel to the people in his day, before the Flood, thus inviting them to access the blessings of the Atonement of Christ, just as their ancestors had done.

24 Believe and repent of your sins and be baptized in the name of Jesus Christ, the Son of God, even as our fathers, and ye shall receive the Holy Ghost, that ye may have all things made manifest. (Moses 8:24)

Over seven hundred years before the Savior was born, Isaiah taught the wicked people of his day (described in Isaiah 1:1–17) that they could repent and be forgiven. He used beautiful symbolism to emphasize the cleansing power of the Atonement.

18 Come now, and let us reason together, saith the LORD: though your sins be as scarlet, they shall be as white as snow; though they be red like crimson, they shall be as wool. (Isaiah 1:18)

The Book of Mormon gives many examples of the power of the Atonement to cleanse and heal, before it was actually accomplished by the Savior on this earth. Alma the Elder (Mosiah 18:1), Alma the Younger (Alma 36:18–26), the sons of Mosiah, and a host of others, who lived before the mortal mission of Jesus Christ, were forgiven of their sins long before the Savior suffered in Gethsemane and on the cross.

DID THE ATONEMENT WORK FOR US IN PREMORTALITY?

We might also ask the question as to whether or not the Atonement worked for us in premortality. The answer is, yes. The following quote from Revelation, dealing with the War in Heaven, refers to the Atonement in premortality as well as mortality. We will include a few explanatory notes within the verses.

7 And there was war in heaven: Michael and his angels fought against the dragon; and the dragon fought and his angels,
8 And prevailed not; neither was their place found any more in heaven.
9 And the great dragon was cast out, that old serpent, called the Devil, and Satan, which deceiveth the whole world: he was cast out into the earth, and his angels were cast out with him.
10 And I heard a loud voice saying in heaven, Now is come salvation, and strength, and the kingdom of our God, and the power of his Christ: for the accuser of our brethren is cast down, which accused them before our God day and night.
11 And they [*the righteous premortal spirits*] overcame him [*overcame Satan and his evil teachings and ways*] by the blood of the Lamb [*the Atonement of Christ*], and by the word of their testimony; and they [*righteous mortals*] loved not their lives unto the death. (Revelation 12:7–11)

Referring to premortality, Elder Jeffrey R. Holland taught that the Atonement worked for us there. He said:

> We could remember that even in the Grand Council of Heaven [in the premortal realm] He loved us and was wonderfully strong, that we triumphed even there by the power of Christ and our faith in the blood of the Lamb. ("This Do in Remembrance of Me," *Ensign*, October 1995)

A question which logically arises during this discussion is whether or not we could sin and repent when we were spirits during our premortal life. The answer is, yes. We were given agency there (D&C 29:36), and, obviously, if we were not given the privilege of choosing, we would not have had real agency. But we did have agency and we could choose. Therefore, we did make mistakes, and, in order to change our ways, we needed the Atonement of Jesus Christ with its accompanying gift of repentance and forgiveness in order to progress. This is clearly taught in the New Testament student manual used by the Institutes of Religion of the Church.

> We were given laws and agency, and commandments to have faith and repent from the wrongs that we could do there [in our premortal life]. (*The Life and Teachings of Jesus and His Apostles*, p. 336)

> Man could and did in many instances, sin before he was born. (Smith, *The Way to Perfection*, p. 44, in *The Life and Teachings of Jesus and His Apostles*, p. 336)

Thus, we, as spirit children of God, before we came to earth, had been taught the Father's plan for us to become like Him, as represented in the gospel of Jesus Christ. We had been given agency, and therefore could make choices. With this knowledge and agency, we could make mistakes, repent, and therefore could progress. The Atonement of Christ, as mentioned in the quotes above, worked for us there and enabled us to make progress, just as it does here on earth. Some progressed to the point of being counted among "the noble and great ones" (Abraham 3:22). In many significant ways, our education toward exaltation during our premortal probationary period was quite similar to what it is here on earth, with a major exception—we did not have physical mortal bodies there. We have been well prepared for this mortal existence by the things we learned in our pre-earth life.

Does the Atonement Work for Other Worlds Also?

One more question before we continue to the next chapter. Does the Savior's Atonement work for the other worlds He has created and will yet create for the Father? The answer is yes. When Joseph Smith and Sidney Rigdon were shown the three degrees of glory in vision, they included the answer to this question in what they recorded. Note that in verse 24, referring to all the worlds created by the Savior for the Father and the inhabitants on them, the phrase "begotten sons and daughters unto God" means exaltation.

> 20 And we beheld the glory of the Son, on the right hand of the Father, and received of his fulness;
> 21 And saw the holy angels, and them who are sanctified before his throne, worshiping God, and the Lamb, who worship him forever and ever.
> 22 And now, after the many testimonies which have been given of him, this is the testimony, last of all, which we give of him: That he lives!
> 23 For we saw him, even on the right hand of God; and we heard the voice bearing record that he is the Only Begotten of the Father—
> 24 That by him, and through him, and of him, the worlds are and were created, and the inhabitants thereof are begotten sons and daughters unto God. (D&C 76:20–24)

In summary, the Savior's Atonement has already been blessing us individually for eons of time. And now it continues to bless us during our lives here on earth as it holds forth the invitation to each of us to be cleansed and healed of our sins and return to live with our Father in Heaven, and continue on to become like Him as exalted beings, in other words, as gods (D&C 132:19–20).

DOES THE ASSIGNMENT WORK
FOR OTHER WORLDS ALSO?

CHAPTER 4

THE CREATOR

Jesus Christ, the Redeemer, our Savior, was also the Creator. Under the direction of the Father, He created the earth. This is clearly taught in the scriptures. During a marvelous vision and instruction session with the premortal Jesus Christ, who was generally known in the Old Testament as Jehovah, Moses (who was being prepared to go back to Egypt and lead the children of Israel out of bondage) asked the Savior about the earth and how it came to be. In response, the Savior spoke directly for His Father (a process called "divine investiture"), explaining to Moses that the phrase "word of my power" is another term for the Son of God, and that the Son was the Creator. Jesus spoke of the things He had created on this earth and quoted His Father, saying:

> 32 And by the word of my power, have I created them, which is mine Only Begotten Son, who is full of grace and truth.
> 33 And worlds without number have I created; and I also created them for mine own purpose; and by the Son I created them, which is mine Only Begotten. (Moses 1:32–33)

John taught the same doctrine, that Jesus was the Creator, also using "Word" to refer to the Son of God.

> 1 In the beginning was the Word, and the Word was with God, and the Word was God.
> 2 The same was in the beginning with God.
> 3 All things were made by him; and without him was not any thing made that was made. (John 1:1–3)

The JST version of the above three verses gives additional clarification to what John taught about the Savior as the Creator of the earth. Here, we see another meaning of "Word," namely, "the gospel."

> 1 In the beginning was the *gospel preached through the Son. And the gospel was the word*, and the word was with *the Son, and the Son was with God, and the Son was of God.*
> 2 The same was in the beginning with God.
> 3 All things were made by him; and without him was not anything made which was made. (JST, John 1:1–3)

THE FATHER TOOK OVER WHEN IT WAS TIME TO CREATE MAN

It is interesting to note, as we read the account of the Creation in the scriptures, that Jesus directed the creation of all things, except for the creation of man. When it came time to create Adam and Eve, there was a change in creators. The Father then took over. We will quote from the Institute of Religion *Doctrines of the Gospel Student Manual* where this is explained.

> We know that Jehovah-Christ, assisted by "many of the noble and great ones" (Abr. 3:22), of whom Michael is but the illustration, did in fact create the earth and all forms of plant and animal life on the face thereof. But when it came to placing man on earth, there was a change in Creators. That is, the Father himself became personally involved. All things were created by the Son, using the power delegated by the Father, except man. In the spirit and again in the flesh, man was created by the Father. There was no delegation of authority where the crowning creature of creation was concerned. (McConkie, The Promised Messiah, p. 62, in the *Doctrines of the Gospel Student Manual*, chapter 7)

Let's watch this illustrated in the Genesis account of the Creation. You may wish to read verses 1–25 in Genesis, chapter 1, on your own, which details the creation work of Christ. Keep in mind that, in these verses, "God" means "Jehovah," or "the premortal Jesus Christ." We will pick it up here with verse 26 where you will see Heavenly Father become directly involved, as He says, "Let us make man in our image, after our likeness." One of the reasons that this is such an important observation is that we are not "creations" of God, in the same sense that plants, animals, fish, birds, mountains, streams, and so forth are creations. Rather, we are the Father's "offspring" (Acts 17:28–29), His literal spirit sons and daughters. As such, we have the potential to become like Him, whereas, none of His "creations" have that potential.

26 And God said, Let us make man in our image, after our likeness: and let them have dominion over the fish of the sea, and over the fowl of the air, and over the cattle, and over all the earth, and over every creeping thing that creepeth upon the earth.

27 So God created man in his own image, in the image of God created he him; male and female created he them.

28 And God blessed them, and God said unto them, Be fruitful, and multiply, and replenish the earth, and subdue it: and have dominion over the fish of the sea, and over the fowl of the air, and over every living thing that moveth upon the earth.

29 And God said, Behold, I have given you every herb bearing seed, which is upon the face of all the earth, and every tree, in the which is the fruit of a tree yielding seed; to you it shall be for meat.

30 And to every beast of the earth, and to every fowl of the air, and to every thing that creepeth upon the earth, wherein there is life, I have given every green herb for meat: and it was so.

31 And God saw every thing that he had made, and, behold, it was very good. And the evening and the morning were the sixth day. (Genesis 1:1–31)

President Spencer W. Kimball gave additional insights for the creation of man. He gave some commentary on scriptures he quoted. His commentary is included here in brackets. He said:

It is written:

"And I, God, created man in mine own image, in the image of mine Only Begotten created I him; male and female created I them. [The story of the rib, of course, is figurative.]

"And I, God, blessed them [Man here is always in the plural. It was plural from the beginning.] and said unto them: Be fruitful, and multiply, and replenish the earth, and subdue it, and have dominion over [it]." (Moses 2:27–28.)

And the scripture says:

"And I, God, said unto mine Only Begotten, which was with me from the beginning: Let us make man [not a separate man, but a complete man, which is husband and wife] in our image, after our likeness; and it was so." (Moses 2:26.) What a beautiful partnership! Adam and Eve were married for eternity by the Lord. . . .

"Male and female created he them; and blessed them, and called their name Adam [Mr. and Mrs. Adam, I suppose, or Brother and Sister Adam], in the day when they were created." (Gen. 5:2.)

This is a partnership. Then when they had created them in the image of God, to them was given the eternal command, "Be fruitful, and multiply, and replenish the earth, and subdue it" (Gen. 1:28), and as they completed this magnificent creation, they looked it over and pronounced it "good, very good"—something that isn't to be improved upon by our modern intellectuals; the male to till the ground, support the family, to give proper leadership; the woman to cooperate, to bear the children, and to rear and teach them. It was "good, very good." And that's the way the Lord organized it. This wasn't an experiment. He knew what he was doing. ("The Blessings and Responsibilities of Womanhood," p. 71)

In addition to creating this earth, the Savior has created countless other worlds under the direction of the Father.

15 And worlds without number have I created; and I also created them for mine own purpose; and by the Son I created them, which is mine Only Begotten. (Moses 1:33)

The "purpose" mentioned in verse 15, above, is defined later during that same revelation to Moses.

39 For behold, this is my work and my glory—to bring to pass the immortality and eternal life of man. (Moses 1:39)

Finally, can you imagine the feelings of the Savior as the Father instructed Him to create this world, the one on which we live, knowing that this would be the world upon which He would be born and serve His mortal mission? It would be upon this world that He would suffer for the sins of all (2 Nephi 9:21), be crucified, and be resurrected, thus performing His infinite Atonement. Perhaps there were particularly tender and poignant feelings in His heart as He created this world.

CHAPTER 5

THE FALL

The Atonement cannot be properly understood without an understanding of the Fall. The two go hand in hand. The Fall refers to the partaking of the forbidden fruit by Adam and Eve in the Garden of Eden and their being cast out of the garden into mortal life (Genesis 3). It can be said that they "fell forward." It was a necessary and planned step in the Father's plan of salvation for us. It brought with it physical death and also brought spiritual death (being cut off from the direct physical presence of God). The Atonement of Jesus Christ overcomes physical death for all, through the universal resurrection of the dead (1 Corinthians 15:22). It also makes it possible for those who will to repent and overcome spiritual death and thus return to the physical presence of the Father, to live with Him forever in celestial glory.

While other churches teach that the Fall was a terrible tragedy and brought unfortunate misery upon all mankind, the true gospel teaches that it was good and is a great blessing for all of us. While many churches criticize and even vilify Adam and Eve, especially Eve, for partaking of the forbidden fruit, we honor them and hold them in highest esteem for taking this vital step which opened the door for all of us to come to earth. The fact that the Fall was good and was part of the Father's plan is clearly taught by Lehi in the Book of Mormon as he gives a brief and concentrated overview of the Fall and Atonement. As you read the verses quoted next, note the important points emphasized by the Savior through His prophet, Lehi, including:

- **Work is a part of the plan.**

    19 And after Adam and Eve had partaken of the forbidden fruit they were driven out of the garden of Eden, to till the earth.

20 And they have brought forth children; yea, even the family of all the earth. (2 Nephi 2:19–20)

- **Repentance and resulting personal progress are part of the plan. This life is a test, a "probation," to see how we act away from home. The Fall without the Atonement would lead to our being "lost."**

  21 And the days of the children of men were prolonged, according to the will of God, that they might repent while in the flesh; wherefore, their state became a state of probation, and their time was lengthened, according to the commandments which the Lord God gave unto the children of men. For he gave commandment that all men must repent; for he showed unto all men that they were lost, because of the transgression of their parents. (2 Nephi 2:21)

- **Without the Fall, there would have been no progress.**

  22 And now, behold, if Adam had not transgressed he would not have fallen, but he would have remained in the garden of Eden. And all things which were created must have remained in the same state in which they were after they were created; and they must have remained forever, and had no end. (2 Nephi 2:22)

- **Without the Fall, we would not be here. Without the Fall, there would have been no contrasts, no joy, no misery, no good, no sin. (2 Nephi 2:23)**

  23 And they would have had no children; wherefore they would have remained in a state of innocence, having no joy, for they knew no misery; doing no good, for they knew no sin.

- **The Fall was according to God's plan, "done in the wisdom of him who knoweth all things."**

  24 But behold, all things have been done in the wisdom of him who knoweth all things. (2 Nephi 2:24)

- **The Fall was good, designed to bring joy to us.**

  25 Adam fell that men might be; and men are, that they might have joy. (2 Nephi 2:25)

- **The Atonement redeems us from the Fall. The Fall and the Atonement work together to give us the opportunity to progress. The Fall both enables and also preserves individual agency. Satan wants everyone to be miserable like he is.**

  26 And the Messiah cometh in the fulness of time, that he may redeem the children of men from the fall. And because that they are redeemed from the fall they have become free forever, knowing good from evil; to act for themselves and not to be acted upon, save it be by the punishment of the law at the great and last day, according to the commandments which God hath given.

27 Wherefore, men are free according to the flesh; and all things are given them which are expedient unto man. And they are free to choose liberty and eternal life, through the great Mediator of all men, or to choose captivity and death, according to the captivity and power of the devil; for he seeketh that all men might be miserable like unto himself. (2 Nephi 2:26–27)

OTHERS HAVE LIKEWISE PRAISED ADAM AND EVE

We are not the first on earth to understand that the Fall was good and that the Fall and Atonement go hand in hand. Consequently, we are not the first to praise and honor our original ancestors. Three years before Adam died, the righteous posterity of Adam and Eve met in a large gathering at Adam-ondi-Ahman (about seventy miles northeast of present-day Independence, Missouri) to receive a final blessing from Adam and to praise him (no doubt Eve was included in that praise). They knew him as their grand ancestor and also as Michael, the archangel, who helped create the earth.

> 53 Three years previous to the death of Adam, he called Seth, Enos, Cainan, Mahalaleel, Jared, Enoch, and Methuselah, who were all high priests [*Adam had ordained all of them to the Melchizedek Priesthood—see D&C 107:42–50*], with the residue of his posterity who were righteous, into the valley of Adam-ondi-Ahman, and there bestowed upon them his last blessing.
> 54 And the Lord appeared unto them, and they rose up and blessed Adam, and called him Michael, the prince, the archangel.
> 55 And the Lord [*the Savior*] administered comfort unto Adam, and said unto him: I have set thee to be at the head; a multitude of nations shall come of thee, and thou art a prince over them forever.
> 56 And Adam stood up in the midst of the congregation; and, notwithstanding he was bowed down with age [*according to Bible chronology, he was 927 years old at this point*], being full of the Holy Ghost, predicted whatsoever should befall his posterity unto the latest generation. (D&C 107:53–56)

WERE ADAM AND EVE CURSED?

The answer to this question is no. Unfortunately, many view the Fall as having brought a curse upon both Adam and Eve. Such a view casts a false negative light on the fairness of the work of God. Such people mistakenly tend to use the scriptures that describe the scene right after the partaking of the forbidden fruit to teach that the Fall was a very negative thing, with resulting curses on Eve and also on Adam. They even engage in debates as to who got the worst curse, Adam or Eve. In so doing, they sadly and badly misinterpret the scriptures. The fact is that neither Adam nor Eve was cursed. The Fall was good for them and good for us. It worked in harmony with the Atonement. Satan was cursed and the earth was cursed "for their sake." We will read the relevant verses and add some commentary as we go. First, we see that Satan was cursed.

14 And the Lord God [*the Father*] said unto the serpent, Because thou hast done this, thou art cursed above [*limited more than*] all cattle, and above every beast of the field [*one aspect of this curse is that even "cattle" and "every beast of the field" get a physical body to go with their spirit; Satan will never get a physical body*]; upon thy belly shalt thou go [*Satan will be looked upon as the lowest of the low*], and dust shalt thou eat all the days of thy life [*perhaps meaning that he will always be behind the Savior, in effect, "eating the Savior's dust"; this could also be a play on words, saying, in effect, that Satan will be "eating dust," in other words, associating with mortals, trying to swallow them up in spiritual destruction, but never receive a mortal body himself, one made of the "dust of the ground"—see Moses 3:7*]:

15 And I will put enmity [*a natural dislike, intense distrust, hatred*] between thee [*Satan*] and the woman, and between thy seed [*Satan's followers, including not only those evil spirits who followed him in premortality, but also the wicked who follow him here on earth*] and her seed [*Jesus Christ—see Institute of Religion reference below*]; it [*Christ*] shall bruise thy head [*will triumph over Satan and his kingdom; will have power over Satan*], and thou shalt bruise his heel [*will cause suffering, including causing evil men to crucify the Savior, and also causing pain and sorrow by leading people away from Christ and His gospel, and so forth*]. (Genesis 3:14–15)

Many of the notes supplied in verse 15, above, are taken from the *Old Testament Student Manual: Genesis–2 Samuel* used by the Institutes of Religion.

Since Satan has no body and therefore can have no literal children, his seed are those who follow him, both the one-third he led away in the premortal existence and those who follow his enticements in mortality until they come under his power. The seed of the woman refers to Jesus Christ, who was the only mortal born of an earthly mother and a Heavenly Father.

President Joseph Fielding Smith referred to what the Apostle Paul wrote to the Roman Saints: "Near the close of his epistle to the Roman saints, he said: 'And the God of peace shall bruise Satan under your feet shortly. The grace of our Lord Jesus Christ be with you. Amen.'" [Romans 16:20]

The "God of peace," who according to the scriptures is to bruise Satan, is Jesus Christ. (*Answers to Gospel Questions*, 1:3.)

The promise concerning the bruising of the heel and head means that while Satan (as the serpent) will bruise the heel of the Savior by leading men to crucify him and seemingly destroy him, in actuality that very act of atonement will give Christ the power to overcome the power that Satan has over men and undo the effects of the Fall. Thus, the seed of the woman (Christ) shall crush the head of the serpent (Satan and his kingdom) with the very heel that was bruised (the atoning sacrifice). (p. 41)

WHY DOES IT SOUND LIKE THEY WERE CURSED?

Next, we will read the verses that deal with the consequences of the Fall for Eve, and then for Adam. We will use the account from Moses, in the Pearl of Great Price. First, we will read the verse that deals with Eve. Since this verse is often misunderstood, we will first add incorrect commentary in brackets within the verse that reflects the false view that the Fall was bad and Eve was cursed, and then we will repeat the verse, adding correct commentary that reflects true doctrine, namely, that the Fall was good and Eve was blessed. First, the negative approach. We will overdo it a bit.

Remember, the commentary added to this verse is not true.

22 Unto the woman, I, the Lord God, said: [*Shame, shame on you for disobeying Me. Because of your disobedience*] I will greatly multiply thy sorrow and thy conception [*I will make it hurt badly every time you have a child as a punishment for your disobedience*]. In sorrow thou shalt bring forth children [*as part of your punishment, you will have much of sadness and heartache because of your children*], and thy desire shall be to thy husband [*you will have the status of a servant to your husband*], and he shall rule over thee [*because you started it all by your disobedience in the Garden of Eden, I will make you subject to Adam and he will be your superior*]. (Moses 4:22)

President Spencer W. Kimball spoke of the correct interpretation and understanding of what the Lord said to Eve.

The Lord said to the woman: "… in sorrow thou shalt bring forth children." I wonder if those who translated the Bible might have used the term distress instead of sorrow. It would mean much the same, except I think there is great gladness in most Latter-day Saint homes when there is to be a child there. As He concludes this statement he says, "and thy desire shall be to thy husband, and he shall rule over thee." (Gen. 3:16.) I have a question about the word rule. It gives the wrong impression. I would prefer to use the word preside because that's what he does. A righteous husband presides over his wife and family. ("The Blessings and Responsibilities of Womanhood," p. 72)

Using President Kimball's commentary, given above, and using our understanding of the purposes of God and His "plan of happiness" (Alma 42:8) for us, We will now reread Moses 4:22, adding notes which reflect this understanding. Again, we may overdo it a bit, for purposes of emphasizing the positives of the Fall as a great and vital step in the plan.

22 Unto the woman, I, the Lord God, said: [*Thank you, thank you, thank you!*] I will greatly multiply thy sorrow [*mortality; because of your choice in the Garden of Eden, I can now give you many years in mortality*] and thy conception [*I can send many children into your home*]. In sorrow [*in mortality, with the joys and sorrows,*

pains and distresses which attend it] thou shalt bring forth children, and thy desire [*highest love and loyalty—see Moses 3:24, D&C 42:22*] shall be to thy husband, and he shall rule over thee [*preside, protect, and serve you, as the Savior did His disciples and people*]. (Moses 4:22)

Notice in verse 23, next, that "sorrow" is also used for Adam, as he begins the toil and labor which will be his responsibility and opportunity as he also begins providing for his family in mortal life. This is perhaps another indicator that we can consider "sorrow" to be a partial description of mortality, rather than a description of punishment. The same Hebrew word is used in the Bible (Genesis 3:17) referring to Adam, as was used for Eve (Genesis 3:16), translated as "sorrow" in English. One of the important lessons we can learn from verse 23 is that the ground was cursed for Adam's "sake," in other words, for his blessing and benefit. It will be good for his growth and development to have to work for a living.

23 And unto Adam, I, the Lord God, said: Because thou hast hearkened unto the voice of thy wife [*which was a very wise thing to do*], and hast eaten of the fruit of the tree of which I commanded thee, saying—Thou shalt not eat of it [*unless you choose to become mortal and leave the Garden*], cursed shall be the ground for thy sake [*for your good*]; in sorrow [*in an environment of work, toil, pain, which will be for your benefit*] shalt thou eat of it all the days of thy life. (Moses 4:23)

Again, the point is that the Fall was good. It was vital and good for Adam and Eve. It was vital and good for us. It was the next step in the Father's "plan of salvation" (Alma 42:5) for us and a continuation of opportunities to ultimately become like our Father in Heaven, through the blessings of the Atonement of Jesus Christ.

THE TWO "CONFLICTING" COMMANDMENTS

Understanding the fact that the Fall was good and that it was part of the plan can give rise to some questions, including why Adam and Eve were given two seemingly conflicting commandments. The first commandment was:

28 And God blessed them, and God said unto them, Be fruitful, and multiply, and replenish the earth, and subdue it: and have dominion over the fish of the sea, and over the fowl of the air, and over every living thing that moveth upon the earth. (Genesis 1:28)

And the second commandment, which seems to be in conflict with the first is:

16 And the Lord God commanded the man, saying, Of every tree of the garden thou mayest freely eat:

THE FALL...

17 But of the tree of the knowledge of good and evil, thou shalt not eat of it: for in the day that thou eatest thereof thou shalt surely die. (Genesis 2:16–17)

We know that Adam and Eve were not capable of having children under the conditions in which they lived in the Garden of Eden (2 Nephi 2:23). And without partaking of the forbidden fruit, they could not fulfil the commandment to "multiply, and replenish the earth" (Genesis 1:28). Yet, they were forbidden to partake of the fruit of the tree of knowledge of good and evil (Genesis 2:17), which would cause them to become mortal so that they could have children. Thus we see that they were in a situation in which making a priority choice was absolutely necessary. In a way, this whole scenario is symbolic of our mortal lives. One of the purposes of mortality is to gain practice in the wise use of agency. We find ourselves in constant situations in which we must choose. When we make mistakes, the Atonement allows us to repent and thus keeps the door open for continued practice and improvement based on past experience and current information and understanding. Even choosing not to choose is a choice. Thus, our use of agency is inherently put into motion by the simple fact that we are on earth. And since we don't begin to become accountable until we turn age eight (D&C 29:46–47; 68:25–28), we have some years to be taught the gospel and to practice without penalty.

Now, back to the two "conflicting" commandments. In his teachings on this subject, Apostle Joseph Fielding Smith indicated that there is more to this situation than first meets the eye.

Now this is the way I interpret that: The Lord said to Adam, here is the tree of the knowledge of good and evil. If you want to stay here, then you cannot eat of that fruit. If you want to stay here, then I forbid you to eat it. But you may act for yourself, and you may eat of it if you want to. And if you eat it, you will die. I see a great difference between transgressing the law and committing a sin. (Joseph Fielding Smith, "Fall—Atonement—Resurrection—Sacrament," in *Charge to Religious Educators*, p. 124; quoted in *Doctrines of the Gospel Student Manual*, p. 20)

Just why the Lord would say to Adam that he forbade him to partake of the fruit of that tree is not made clear in the Bible account, but in the original as it comes to us in the Book of Moses [Moses 3:17 adds "nevertheless, thou mayest choose for thyself, for it is given unto thee; but, remember that I forbid it"] it is made definitely clear. It is that the Lord said to Adam that if he wished to remain as he was in the garden, then he was not to eat the fruit, but if he desired to eat it and partake of death he was at liberty to do so. So really it was not in the true sense a transgression of a divine commandment. Adam made the wise decision, in fact the only decision that he could make. It was the divine plan from the very beginning that man should be placed on the earth and be subject to mortal conditions and pass through a probationary state. (*Answers to Gospel Questions*, Vol. 4, p. 81)

As mentioned previously, Eve has been especially maligned and criticized for her role in the Fall. However, we in The Church of Jesus Christ of Latter-day Saints honor and revere her for the unselfish choice she made. Perhaps you have noticed that she led out in partaking of the fruit of the tree of knowledge of good and evil (Genesis 3:6), and Adam followed. Elder John A. Widtsoe, of the Quorum of the Twelve, explained that this was an intentional, informed decision. He also explained how Adam and Eve, living in a state of innocence, could have understood enough to make an informed decision concerning the two commandments. Among other things, he reminds us that Adam and Eve walked and talked with God in the Garden and that they learned much during that time.

> Such was the problem before our first parents: to remain forever at selfish ease in the Garden of Eden, or to face unselfishly tribulation and death, in bringing to pass the purposes of the Lord for a host of waiting spirit children. They chose the latter.
>
> This they did with open eyes and minds as to consequences. The memory of their former estates may have been dimmed, but the gospel had been taught them during their sojourn in the Garden of Eden. They could not have been left in complete ignorance of the purpose of their creation. Brigham Young frankly said: "Adam was as conversant with his Father who placed him upon this earth as we are conversant with our earthly parents." (*Discourses of Brigham Young*, p. 104) The Prophet Joseph taught that "Adam received commandments and instructions from God; this was the order from the beginning." (*Teachings of the Prophet Joseph Smith* [*TPJS*], p. 168)
>
> The choice that they made raises Adam and Eve to pre-eminence among all who have come on earth. The Lord's plan was given life by them. They are indeed, as far as this earth is concerned, our loving father and mother. The "Fall" and the consequent redeeming act of Jesus became the most glorious events in the history of mankind. . . . The Lord had warned Adam and Eve of the hard battle with earth conditions if they chose to eat of the tree of the knowledge of good and evil. He would not subject his son and daughter to hardship and the death of their bodies unless it be of their own choice. They must choose for themselves. They chose wisely, in accord with the heavenly law of love for others. In life all must choose at times. Sometimes, two possibilities are good; neither is evil. Usually, however, one is of greater import than the other. When in doubt, each must choose that which concerns the good of others—the greater law—rather than that which chiefly benefits ourselves—the lesser law. The greater must be balanced against the lesser. The greater must be chosen whether it be law or thing. That was the choice made in Eden. . . . It is a thrilling thought that Adam and Eve were not coerced to begin God's work on earth. They chose to

do so, by the exercise of their free agency. . . . Considering our full knowledge of the purpose of the plan of salvation, and the reason for placing Adam and Eve on earth, the apparent contradiction in the story of the "Fall" vanishes. Instead the law of free agency, or individual choice, appears in distinct view. God's command is qualified by his great purpose to bless his children. Adam and Eve rise to the position of helpers in initiating the divine purpose on earth. They become partners with the Lord in making eternal joy possible for the hosts of heaven. . . . We, the children of Adam and Eve, may well be proud of our parentage. (*Evidences and Reconciliations*, pp. 193–195)

Encyclopedia of Mormonism summarizes Eve's role in the Fall as follows:

Satan was present to tempt Adam and Eve, much as he would try to thwart others in their divine missions: "and he sought also to beguile Eve, for he knew not the mind of God, wherefore he sought to destroy the world" (Moses 4:6). Eve faced the choice between selfish ease and unselfishly facing tribulation and death (*Evidences and Reconciliations*, by John A. Widtsoe, page 193). As befit her calling, she realized that there was no other way and deliberately chose mortal life so as to further the purpose of God and bring children into the world. (s.v. "Eve")

Elder Dallin H. Oaks taught about the vital contribution of Eve in partaking of the fruit and of the difference between *transgression* and *sin*.

It was Eve who first transgressed the limits of Eden in order to initiate the conditions of mortality. Her act, whatever its nature, was formally a transgression but eternally a glorious necessity to open the doorway toward eternal life. Adam showed his wisdom by doing the same. And thus Eve and "Adam fell that men might be" (2 Ne. 22:25).

Some Christians condemn Eve for her act, concluding that she and her daughters are somehow flawed by it. Not the Latter-day Saints! Informed by revelation, we celebrate Eve's act and honor her wisdom and courage in the great episode called the Fall (see Bruce R. McConkie, "Eve and the Fall," *Woman*, Salt Lake City: Deseret Book Co., 1979, pp. 67–68). Joseph Smith taught that it was not a "sin," because God had decreed it (see *The Words of Joseph Smith*, ed. Andrew F. Ehat and Lyndon W. Cook, Provo, Utah: Religious Studies Center, Brigham Young University, 1980, p. 63). Brigham Young declared, "We should never blame Mother Eve, not the least" (in *Journal of Discourses*, 13:145). Elder Joseph Fielding Smith said: "I never speak of the part Eve took in this fall as a sin, nor do I accuse Adam of a sin. . . . This was a transgression of the law, but not a sin . . . for it was something that Adam and Eve had to do!" (Joseph Fielding Smith, *Doctrines of Salvation*, comp. Bruce R. McConkie, 3 vols., Salt Lake City: Bookcraft, 1954–56, 1:114–15).

This suggested contrast between a *sin* and a *transgression* reminds us of the careful wording in the second article of faith: "We believe that men will be punished for their own sins, and not for Adam's transgression" (emphasis added). It also echoes a familiar distinction in the law. Some acts, like murder, are crimes because they are inherently wrong. Other acts, like operating without a license, are crimes only because they are legally prohibited. Under these distinctions, the act that produced the Fall was not a sin—inherently wrong—but a transgression—wrong because it was formally prohibited. These words are not always used to denote something different, but this distinction seems meaningful in the circumstances of the Fall. ("The Great Plan of Happiness," 73; part of this is also quoted in the *Old Testament Gospel Doctrine Teacher's Manual*, pp. 15–16)

Another question that might come up, based on the above quotes that Eve made a deliberate, unselfish choice, is how to deal with Paul's statement that Eve was deceived.

14 And Adam was not deceived, but the woman being deceived was in the transgression. (1 Timothy 2:14)

However, the Pearl of Great Price indicates that Satan "sought to beguile Eve," in other words, "tried" to deceive Eve, thus implying that he was not entirely successful.

6 And Satan put it into the heart of the serpent, (for he had drawn away many after him,) and he sought also to beguile Eve, for he knew not the mind of God, wherefore he sought to destroy the world. (Moses 4:6)

It may be that Satan did indeed deceive Eve in many ways, but "sought to" and failed to beguile her in the most important aspect of the situation, whether or not to remain in the Garden of Eden or to partake of the fruit and thus bring children into the world to further the Father's plan. Whatever the case, we will probably have to wait until we get a chance to talk to Eve herself, perhaps during the Millennium, for the complete account. There could be many ways in which she was deceived. Perhaps in the sense of not believing that mortality would be so difficult at times. Perhaps she had no idea what it would be like to care for twenty or thirty sick children when they all had the flu! Maybe she was deceived into thinking that old age with its attendant pains and disabilities would not be at all difficult. Actually, she couldn't have understood these physical struggles because she had no basis on which to judge, since she and her husband were not yet mortal, even though they had physical bodies at this point.

ADAM AND EVE BEAR TESTIMONY OF THE BENEFITS OF THE FALL

Sometime after they were cast out of the Garden of Eden, both Adam and Eve bore testimony of the benefits of the Fall and rejoiced that it had taken place and in the opportunities that it provided.

10 And in that day Adam blessed God and was filled, and began to prophesy concerning all the families of the earth, saying: Blessed be the name of God, for because of my transgression my eyes are opened, and in this life I shall have joy, and again in the flesh I shall see God.

11 And Eve, his wife, heard all these things and was glad, saying: Were it not for our transgression we never should have had seed, and never should have known good and evil, and the joy of our redemption, and the eternal life which God giveth unto all the obedient. (Moses 5:10–11)

As a result of the Fall, Adam and Eve and all their posterity became subject to both physical and spiritual death. Physical death is the separation of the mortal body from the spirit which gives it life. It prepares the way for resurrection, which is provided to all by the Atonement of Christ (1 Corinthians 15:22). Spiritual death means being cut off from the direct presence of God. It does not mean being completely cut off from any communication with Him or from any influence by Him. The term for completely dying as far as any spirituality is concerned, thus being cut off completely from God and His influence, is "second death" (Jacob 3:11; Alma 12:16, 32; 13:30).

In summary, vital blessings and benefits came as a result of the Fall. The Fall and the Atonement work together. The Fall was a planned step in our Father's plan for us. Heaven was not caught off guard or surprised by it (2 Nephi 2:24). We hold Adam and Eve in highest esteem for their unselfish role in instigating the Fall. The benefits of the Fall include:

1. Adam and Eve obtained mortal physical bodies.

2. Adam and Eve were able to have children, which means that we could come to earth.

3. Physical death came with its consequent resurrection resulting in immortality.

4. Knowledge of good and evil became available.

5. Spiritual death (being cut off from the direct physical presence of God) came, with the accompanying opportunities to walk by faith and prayer, scripture study, following the prophets, and so forth.

6. Misery and woe came upon mankind as part of our eternal education.

7. The Atonement of Christ came into play, overcoming the effects of personal sin through repentance and living the gospel of Jesus Christ.

8. The ground was cursed, causing Adam, Eve, and all of us to have to work, thus receiving the blessings and growth that accompany labor.

9. True joy became available.

10. The opportunity to grow and progress toward exaltation came to all. In other words, the Fall was the next step in the plan of happiness, bringing all of us the opportunity to continue progressing toward obtaining a glorified, resurrected physical body, and truly becoming like Heavenly Father.

CHAPTER 6

THE JEHOVAH
OF THE OLD TESTAMENT

The premortal Jesus Christ, as a spirit being, was the God of the Old Testament. As such, the Savior was generally known by the name Jehovah. He was often referred to as the God of Abraham, Isaac, and Jacob (Deuteronomy 1:8). The Bible Dictionary summarizes this.

> Jehovah. The covenant or proper name of the God of Israel. It denotes the "Unchangeable One," "the eternal I AM" (Ex. 6:3; Ps. 83:18; Isa. 12:2; 26:4). The original pronunciation of this name has possibly been lost, as the Jews, in reading, never mentioned it, but substituted one of the other names of God, usually Adonai. Probably it was pronounced Jahveh, or Yahveh. In the KJV, the Jewish custom has been followed, and the name is generally denoted by LORD or GOD, printed in small capitals.
> Jehovah is the premortal Jesus Christ and came to earth being born of Mary (see Mosiah 13:28; 15:1; 3 Ne. 15:1–5; D&C 110:1–10). Although Ex. 6:3 states that the God of Israel was not known by the name Jehovah before Moses' time, latter-day revelation tells us otherwise (Abr. 1:16; 2:8; cf. JST Ex. 6:3; see also Gen. 22:14). (BD, under "Jehovah")

The JST verse referred to in the quote from the Bible Dictionary, above, reminds us that Abraham, Isaac, and Jacob knew that Jehovah, or the premortal Jesus Christ, was the God of the Old Testament.

> 3 And I appeared unto Abraham, unto Isaac, and unto Jacob. *I am the Lord God* Almighty; *the Lord* Jehovah. *And was not my name* known *unto* them? (JST, Exodus 6:3)

It can be somewhat confusing when studying the Old Testament to determine whether references to "God" are referring to Heavenly Father or to the

Savior, the premortal Jehovah. We know that the Father was much involved in the Garden of Eden, but what about after the Fall of Adam and Eve? Who was it that commanded Abraham to sacrifice Isaac (Genesis 22:2)? Who was it that gave the Ten Commandments to Moses and wrote them on the stone tablets with His own finger (Exodus 20:3–17; 31:18)? Who was it that appeared to Isaiah and called him to serve as a prophet (Isaiah 6:1–13)? Joseph Fielding Smith gave a simple explanation to clear up this confusion.

> All revelation since the fall has come through Jesus Christ, who is the Jehovah of the Old Testament. In all of the scriptures, where God is mentioned and where he has appeared, it was Jehovah who talked with Abraham, with Noah, Enoch, Moses and all the prophets. He is the God of Israel, the Holy One of Israel; the one who led that nation out of Egyptian bondage, and who gave and fulfilled the law of Moses. (*Doctrines of Salvation*, Vol. 1, p. 27)

A clear example of the fact that the premortal Jesus Christ, as a personage of spirit, was the God of the Old Testament is found in the Book of Mormon when the Lord appeared to the brother of Jared. This experience took place at the time of the Tower of Babel (Genesis 11:1–9). Under the direction of the Lord, Jared, his brother, and their people were told to leave the wicked people who had been building the tower. They had arrived at the shores of the ocean and had constructed eight barges (Ether 2:16–22) for the crossing to the "land choice above all other lands" (Ether 2:15). Since they had been told that the barges would sometimes be submerged, they desired to have a source of light in each of them for such times.

The brother of Jared (Mahonri-Moriancumer) had "molten out of a rock sixteen small stones . . . white and clear, even as transparent glass" (Ether 3:1), and had taken them up to the top of a mountain. There, in mighty prayer, he humbly asked the Lord to touch the sixteen small stones so that they could use them to light the Jaredite ships during the ocean crossing. To his great astonishment, he saw the finger of the Lord, as the Savior reached out His hand and touched the small stones with His finger. After the brother of Jared had recovered sufficiently from seeing the finger of the Lord, Jesus showed him His spirit body.

> 6 And it came to pass that when the brother of Jared had said these words, behold, the Lord stretched forth his hand and touched the stones one by one with his finger. And the veil was taken from off the eyes of the brother of Jared, and he saw the finger of the Lord; and it was as the finger of a man, like unto flesh and blood; and the brother of Jared fell down before the Lord, for he was struck with fear.
> 7 And the Lord saw that the brother of Jared had fallen to the earth; and the Lord said unto him: Arise, why hast thou fallen?

8 And he saith unto the Lord: I saw the finger of the Lord, and I feared lest he should smite me; for I knew not that the Lord had flesh and blood.

Next, the premortal Jesus Christ explains that it is the faith of the brother of Jared that has enabled him to see Him.

9 And the Lord said unto him: Because of thy faith thou hast seen that I shall take upon me flesh and blood; and never has man come before me with such exceeding faith as thou hast; for were it not so ye could not have seen my finger. Sawest thou more than this?
10 And he answered: Nay; Lord, show thyself unto me.
11 And the Lord said unto him: Believest thou the words which I shall speak?
12 And he answered: Yea, Lord, I know that thou speakest the truth, for thou art a God of truth, and canst not lie.

Among other things, verse 13, next, teaches that the Atonement redeems us from the Fall and makes it possible for us to return to live in the presence of God.

13 And when he had said these words, behold, the Lord showed himself unto him, and said: Because thou knowest these things ye are redeemed from the fall; therefore ye are brought back into my presence; therefore I show myself unto you.
14 Behold, I am he who was prepared from the foundation of the world to re-deem my people. Behold, I am Jesus Christ. I am the Father and the Son. In me shall all mankind have life, and that eternally, even they who shall believe on my name; and they shall become my sons and my daughters.
15 And never have I showed myself unto man whom I have created, for never has man believed in me as thou hast. Seest thou that ye are created after mine own image? Yea, even all men were created in the beginning after mine own image.

In verse 16, He will explain that His spirit body looks like His mortal physical body will look like when He comes to earth.

16 Behold, this body, which ye now behold, is the body of my spirit; and man have I created after the body of my spirit; and even as I appear unto thee to be in the spirit will I appear unto my people in the flesh. (Ether 3:6–16)

In addition to being clearly taught that the premortal Jesus Christ was the God of the Old Testament by the above verses of scripture, we also come to understand that a spirit body looks like a physical body. The brother of Jared thought he was seeing the finger of a physical body of "flesh and blood" (verse 6), but it was actually the finger of the Savior's spirit body.

In the revelations recorded by Isaiah, we again see clearly that Jesus Christ is the God of the Old Testament, our Redeemer and Savior. Remember that

"LORD," written with small capital letters in the Latter-day Saint edition of the King James Version of the Bible (which we use as a Church in English speaking areas of the world), is a direct reference to Jehovah, or the premortal Jesus Christ, as stated in the Bible Dictionary under "Jehovah."

> 1 But now thus saith the LORD that created thee, O Jacob, and he that formed thee, O Israel, Fear not: for I have redeemed thee, I have called thee by thy name; thou art mine.
> 3 For I am the LORD thy God, the Holy One of Israel, thy Saviour: I gave Egypt for thy ransom, Ethiopia and Seba for thee.
> 11 I, even I, am the LORD; and beside me there is no saviour.
> 14 Thus saith the LORD, your redeemer, the Holy One of Israel; For your sake I have sent to Babylon, and have brought down all their nobles, and the Chaldeans, whose cry is in the ships.
> 15 I am the LORD, your Holy One, the creator of Israel, your King.
> 16 Thus saith the LORD, which maketh a way in the sea, and a path in the mighty waters. (Isaiah 43:1–16)

It is no wonder that the Jews, to whom He brought His gospel during His mortal ministry, were startled that He knew the Old Testament and the law of Moses so perfectly.

> 54 And when he was come into his own country, he taught them in their synagogue, insomuch that they were astonished, and said, Whence hath this man this wisdom, and these mighty works?
> 55 Is not this the carpenter's son? Is not his mother called Mary? And his brethren, James, and Joses, and Simon, and Judas?
> 56 And his sisters, are they not all with us? Whence then hath this man all these things? (Matthew 13:54–56)

> 14 Now about the midst of the feast Jesus went up into the temple, and taught.
> 15 And the Jews marveled, saying, How knoweth this man letters, having never learned? (John 7:14–15)

In summary, our oldest spirit brother, the firstborn spirit child of the Father (Colossians 1:13–15), our Redeemer who was chosen in the grand council in heaven (Moses 4:1–3; Abraham 3:27–28), the Creator of heaven and earth (Jacob 2:5), was also the God of the Old Testament.

CHAPTER 7

ATONEMENT SYMBOLISM IN THE OLD TESTAMENT

THE ATONEMENT WAS TAUGHT IN THE OLD TESTAMENT FIRST TO ADAM AND EVE

From the very beginning, in the Old Testament, the Atonement and its power to cleanse and heal were taught by the Savior through angels and prophets. It was often taught through symbolism. For example, after Adam and Eve had been cast out of the Garden of Eden, Adam was commanded to build an altar and offer sacrifices to the Lord. The instructions of the Lord to them and the teaching of the angel strongly teach the Atonement. As we quote the verses associated with this scene, watch for the following symbols and explanations:

The altar—symbolic of the cross, upon which the Savior was to be sacrificed.

The firstlings of the flocks—the firstborn males (Deuteronomy 15:19), symbolic of Christ, who was the "Firstborn" of the Father's spirit children (Colossians 1:15). These "firstlings" were to be "without blemish" (Exodus 12:5), symbolizing the perfect life of the Savior.

Faith-obedience—not blind obedience, rather, obeying because of faith in God.

The sacrifices—in similitude (symbolic) of the Savior, who would be sacrificed for all.

"Full of grace and truth"—the Savior's complete power to help us and the truths of His gospel.

Pay close attention now, as Adam and Eve first demonstrate humble faith-obedience, and then, as a result, are taught about the Atonement of Christ and how to gain its saving power in their own lives. Obedience is often called "the first law of heaven" because it leads to additional instruction and enlightenment from God. Note also that the Holy Ghost accompanies the teaching of the angel and bears witness to Adam and Eve that Jesus Christ is the "Only Begotten of the Father." He testifies to them that they can be redeemed through the Savior's Atonement, if they are willing.

> 4 And Adam and Eve, his wife, called upon the name of the Lord, and they heard the voice of the Lord from the way toward the Garden of Eden, speaking unto them, and they saw him not; for they were shut out from his presence.
> 5 And he gave unto them commandments, that they should worship the Lord their God, and should offer the firstlings of their flocks, for an offering unto the Lord. And Adam was obedient unto the commandments of the Lord.
> 6 And after many days an angel of the Lord appeared unto Adam, saying: Why dost thou offer sacrifices unto the Lord? And Adam said unto him: I know not, save the Lord commanded me.
> 7 And then the angel spake, saying: This thing is a similitude of the sacrifice of the Only Begotten of the Father, which is full of grace and truth.
> 8 Wherefore, thou shalt do all that thou doest in the name of the Son, and thou shalt repent and call upon God in the name of the Son forevermore.
> 9 And in that day the Holy Ghost fell upon Adam, which beareth record of the Father and the Son, saying: I am the Only Begotten of the Father from the beginning, henceforth and forever, that as thou hast fallen thou mayest be redeemed, and all mankind, even as many as will. (Moses 5:4–9)

THE ATONEMENT WAS TAUGHT TO THE CHILDREN OF ISRAEL

Through Moses, the premortal Jesus Christ taught the children of Israel about His future sacrifice for sin. He included much Atonement symbolism in the laws and sacrifices which He gave as a "schoolmaster" law (Galatians 3:24) to the Israelites, through His prophet Moses. This law was called the law of Moses, and was designed to prepare the people for the full gospel of Jesus Christ. An example of Atonement symbolism in the law of Moses can be seen when the Lord instituted the Passover. The Israelites were to be very selective in choosing a lamb so that the symbolism would be accurate.

> 5 Your lamb shall be without blemish, a male of the first year: ye shall take it out from the sheep, or from the goats. (Exodus 12:5)

They were clearly taught that they would be saved "by the blood of the Lamb" if they were obedient to the Lord's instruction about what to do with the lamb's blood.

7 And they shall take of the blood, and strike it on the two side posts and on the upper door post of the houses, wherein they shall eat it. (Exodus 12:7)

13 And the blood shall be to you for a token upon the houses where ye are: and when I see the blood, I will pass over you, and the plague shall not be upon you to destroy you, when I smite the land of Egypt. (Exodus 12:13)

It is interesting to note that, as part of the Feast of the Passover, the children of Israel were taught, in effect, that they were to hurry to "internalize" Christ in their lives and take necessary action to have His sacred blood protect them.

11 And thus shall ye eat it; with your loins girded, your shoes on your feet, and your staff in your hand; and ye shall eat it in haste: it is the LORD's passover. (Exodus 12:11)

In teaching about the Savior, Peter reminded his listeners that the Old Testament animal sacrifices were symbolic of Christ and His Atonement.

18 Forasmuch as ye know that ye were not redeemed with corruptible things, as silver and gold, from your vain conversation received by tradition from your fathers;
19 But with the precious blood of Christ, as of a lamb without blemish and without spot:
20 Who verily was foreordained before the foundation of the world, but was manifest in these last times for you. (1 Peter 1:18–20)

ATONEMENT SYMBOLISM IN LAW OF MOSES SACRIFICES

An example of such Atonement symbolism is found in the portion of the law of Moses which dealt with the cleansing of a leper. We will use some verses from Leviticus and include notes and commentary as we study specific verses. Until such symbolism is pointed out, it is missed by most of us as we read the Bible. Watch now as this segment of the law of Moses teaches the power of the Atonement to cleanse, heal, and set free.

1 And the LORD spake unto Moses, saying,
2 This shall be the law of the leper [*the rules for being made clean; symbolic of serious sin and great need for help and cleansing*] in the day of his cleansing [*symbolic of the desire to be made spiritually clean and pure*]: He shall be brought unto the priest [*authorized servant of God; bishop, stake president, who holds the keys of authority to act for God*]:
3 And the priest shall go forth out of the camp [*the person with leprosy did not have fellowship with the Lord's people and was required to live outside the main camp of the children of Israel; the bishop, symbolically, goes out of the way to help sinners*

who want to repent]; and the priest shall look, and, behold, if the plague of leprosy be healed in the leper [*the bishop/stake president serves as a judge to see if the repentant sinner is ready to return to full membership privileges*];

4 Then shall the priest command to take for him that is to be cleansed [*the person who has repented*] two birds [*one represents the Savior during His mortal mission, the other represents the person who has repented*] alive and clean, and cedar wood [*symbolic of the cross*], and scarlet [*associated with mocking Christ before his crucifixion, Mark 15:17*], and hyssop [*associated with Christ on the cross, John 19:29*]:

5 And the priest shall command that one of the birds [*symbolic of the Savior*] be killed in an earthen vessel [*Christ was sent to earth to die for us*] over running water [*Christ offers us "living water," the gospel of Jesus Christ—John 7:37–38—which cleanses us when we come unto Him*]:

6 As for the living bird [*representing the person who has repented*], he [*the priest; symbolic of the bishop, stake president, one who holds the keys of judging*] shall take it [*the living bird*], and the cedar wood, and the scarlet, and the hyssop [*all associated with the Atonement*], and shall dip them and the living bird in the blood of the bird that was killed over the running water [*representing the cleansing power of the Savior's blood which was shed for us*]:

7 And he shall sprinkle upon him that is to be cleansed from the leprosy [*symbolically, being cleansed from sin*] seven times [*seven is the number which, in biblical numeric symbolism, represents completeness, perfection*], and shall pronounce him clean [*he has been forgiven*], and shall let the living bird [*the person who has repented*] loose into the open field [*representing the wide open opportunities again available in the kingdom of God for the person who truly repents*].

8 And he that is to be cleansed shall wash his clothes [*symbolic of cleaning up your life from sinful ways and pursuits—compare with Isaiah 1:16*], and shave off all his hair [*symbolic of becoming like a newborn baby; fresh start*], and wash himself in water [*symbolic of baptism*], that he may be clean [*cleansed from sin*]: and after that he shall come into the camp [*rejoin the Lord's covenant people*], and shall tarry abroad out of his tent seven days.

9 But it shall be on the seventh day, that he shall shave all his hair off his head and his beard and his eyebrows, even all his hair he shall shave off [*symbolic of being "born again"*]: and he shall wash his clothes [*clean up his life, so his "garments" are "unspotted" from the world*], also he shall wash his flesh in water [*symbolic of baptism*], and he shall be clean [*a simple fact, namely that we can truly be cleansed and healed by the Savior's Atonement*].

10 And on the eighth day he shall take two he lambs without blemish [*symbolic of the Savior's perfect life*], and one ewe lamb of the first year without blemish, and three tenth deals of fine flour for a meat offering, mingled with oil [*pure olive oil, symbolic of healing, of light from Christ, of the Holy Ghost—D&C 45:55–57, of the Savior's suffering in Gethsemane (the "oil press") under the pressure and weight of our sins*], and one log of oil.

11 And the priest that maketh him clean [*symbolic of Christ*] shall present the man that is to be made clean, and those things, before the LORD, at the door of the tabernacle of the congregation:

12 And the priest shall take one he lamb [*symbolic of Christ*], and offer him for a trespass offering [*an atonement*], and the log of oil, and wave them for a wave offering [*see Bible Dictionary under "Feasts" for an explanation of several types of "offerings" associated with ritual feasts*] before the LORD:

13 And he shall slay the lamb in the place where he shall kill the sin offering and the burnt offering, in the holy place: for as the sin offering is the priest's, so is the trespass offering: it is most holy:

14 And the priest shall take some of the blood of the trespass offering [*the blood of the Lamb*], and the priest shall put it upon the tip of the right ear [*symbolic of hearing and obeying the Lord*] of him that is to be cleansed, and upon the thumb [*symbolic of actions, behaviors*], of his right hand [*the covenant hand; symbolic of making covenants with God*], and upon the great toe of his right foot [*symbolic of walking in the ways of God*]:

15 And the priest shall take some of the log of oil, and pour it into the palm of his own left hand:

16 And the priest shall dip his right finger in the oil that is in his left hand, and shall sprinkle of the oil with his finger seven [*symbolic of becoming perfect through Christ*] times before the LORD:

17 And of the rest of the oil that is in his hand shall the priest put upon the tip of the right ear of him that is to be cleansed, and upon the thumb of his right hand, and upon the great toe of his right foot, upon the blood of the trespass offering [*among many possible symbolisms, one can be that, as we take upon us the cleansing blood of Christ, through baptism, the Holy Ghost follows up by guiding us to hear, act, and walk in His ways*]:

18 And the remnant of the oil that is in the priest's hand he shall pour upon the head of him that is to be cleansed [*symbolic of being anointed in preparation for great blessings from the Lord*]: and the priest shall make an atonement for him before the LORD.

19 And the priest [*symbolizing the Savior*] shall offer the sin offering, and make an atonement for him that is to be cleansed from his uncleanness; and afterward he shall kill the burnt offering:

20 And the priest shall offer the burnt offering and the meat offering upon the altar: and the priest shall make an atonement for him, and he shall be clean. (Leviticus 14:1–20)

As you study the Old Testament, you will continue to see much of this Atonement symbolism, a reminder that, by design, the law of Moses kept Christ and His atoning sacrifice before the eyes of the people constantly.

"Types" of Christ

There are many "types" of Christ in the Old Testament. A "type" is a symbol of something else. The word *shadow* is also sometimes used in the scriptures to mean "symbolic of." Thus, the mission and Atonement of Jesus Christ are often taught through "types" and "shadows" in the scriptures. During part of his address to his people in the Book of Mormon, about 124 years before the birth of Christ, King Benjamin quoted an angel (Mosiah 3:2–3; 4:1) who had appeared to him the night before and given him a major message to deliver in his sermon the next day. Among other things, the angel spoke of "types and shadows," including many symbols of the Atonement given in the law of Moses.

14 Yet the Lord God saw that his people were a stiffnecked people, and he appointed unto them a law, even the law of Moses.

15 And many signs, and wonders, and types, and shadows showed he unto them, concerning his coming; and also holy prophets spake unto them concerning his coming; and yet they hardened their hearts, and understood not that the law of Moses availeth nothing except it were through the atonement of his blood. (Mosiah 3:14–15)

An example of a "type of Christ" is found in the account of Abraham and Isaac, after the Lord commanded Abraham to sacrifice his "only begotten son" by Sarah, through whom the Abrahamic covenant was to be perpetuated. Some Atonement symbolism found in this account includes:

Christ—the Only Begotten of the Father in the flesh (John 1:14).
Isaac—the only begotten of Abraham and Sarah (Genesis 22:2).

Christ—was allowed to be sacrificed by His Father.
Isaac—was to be sacrificed by his father.

Christ—carried the cross for His sacrifice (Luke 23:26).
Isaac—carried the wood for his sacrifice (Genesis 22:6).

Christ—gave His life voluntarily (John 10:18).
Isaac—volunteered to give his life (Abraham was too old to restrain him).

Abraham—symbolic of the Father.

The altar—symbolic of the cross upon which the Savior was crucified.

A ram—symbolic of the Savior, who was sacrificed that we might be spared and redeemed from sin. The Lord provided a ram for the sacrifice (Genesis 22:13) so that Isaac might be spared.

Another example of a "type" of Christ is found in the scriptural account of Joseph, who was sold into Egypt. There is much symbolism relating to the life and mission of Jesus Christ to redeem His people.

Christ—was sold for the price of a common slave (Matthew 26:15).
Joseph—was sold for the price of a common slave (Genesis 37:28).

Christ—was thirty years old when He began His formal mission to save His people (Luke 3:23).

Joseph—was thirty years old when he began his mission as prime minister of Egypt to save his people (Genesis 41:46).

Christ—used seven "days" or creative periods to create the earth in which to offer salvation to us (Genesis 1:1 to 2:2).

Joseph—used seven years to gather food to save his people (Genesis 41:46–48).

Christ—forgave His persecutors (Luke 23:34).

Joseph—forgave his persecutors (his brothers—Genesis 45:1–15).

CHAPTER 8

THE ANNUNCIATION

The Annunciation refers to the appearance of the angel Gabriel to Mary as he announced to her that she was to be the mother of the Son of God (Luke 1:26–38). Gabriel had already appeared to Zacharias and told him that he and his wife, Elizabeth, would be blessed to have a son (John the Baptist) who would prepare the way for the Savior (Luke 1:1–25). Picture in your mind the overwhelming feelings in the hearts of these humble, righteous souls, after Gabriel had carried out his mission. Zacharias and Elizabeth were both elderly, and Elizabeth was far past the age of child bearing. Now they would have a son who would prepare the way for the Son of God as He began His mortal mission (Luke 1:1–25). And imagine the thoughts and feelings in Mary's heart after Gabriel announced to her that she would be the mother of the Son of God (Luke 1:26–38). She was young, and espoused (engaged) to a wonderful man named Joseph (Matthew 1:18). And now the fulfillment of the numerous prophecies about the birth of Jesus Christ were to be fulfilled, and she was to be His mother.

Approximately four thousand years after the Fall of Adam and Eve, the time had arrived when the Savior Himself was to leave His exalted station as the Jehovah of the Old Testament, the Holy One of Israel, the God of Abraham, Isaac, and Jacob, and pass through the veil (Talmage, *Jesus the Christ*, p. 111), be born to Mary under the most humble circumstances as a helpless, new-born baby, and thus begin His mortal mission. The Creator of worlds without number, whose power and dominion could not be fathomed by man, would soon leave His glorious realm on high, enter a tiny body of flesh and blood, and begin His mission to atone, redeem, cleanse, and heal all who would come unto the Father through Him.

It is almost ironic that His mission of infinite importance would take place in such a small nation, barely 40 miles wide and close to 150 miles long, from north to south, and that His ultimate suffering for the sins of all (2 Nephi 9:21) would take place in a small garden, called Gethsemane, witnessed among mortals only by three weary Apostles (Matthew 26:37–46). As in all things, the humility of the Savior is evidenced here.

THE ANGEL GABRIEL

It is also interesting to think what a privilege and blessing it was for Gabriel to appear to them and announce that the time had finally come when the Son of God would come to earth for His mortal mission. Thanks to the Prophet Joseph Smith, we know that Gabriel was Noah (*TPJS*, p. 157), the Old Testament prophet who preached the gospel of Jesus Christ, including faith, repentance, baptism, and the gift of the Holy Ghost, to the wicked inhabitants of the earth for over 120 years preceding the Flood (Moses 8:17).

> 22 And God saw that the wickedness of men had become great in the earth; and every man was lifted up in the imagination of the thoughts of his heart, being only evil continually.
>
> 23 And it came to pass that Noah continued his preaching unto the people, saying: Hearken, and give heed unto my words;
>
> 24 Believe and repent of your sins and be baptized in the name of Jesus Christ, the Son of God, even as our fathers, and ye shall receive the Holy Ghost, that ye may have all things made manifest; and if ye do not this, the floods will come in upon you; nevertheless they hearkened not. (Moses 8:22–24)

Noah was rejected and ridiculed by almost all the people before the Flood. Now, over 2,200 years later, he was privileged to announce that the Savior, about Whom he had preached and Whom the people of his day rejected, was in very deed about to be born. The ancient prophecies that were rejected by the wicked were about to be fulfilled.

GABRIEL APPEARS TO ZACHARIAS

Let's turn to the scriptures in Luke for more detail about the faithful responses of Zacharias and Elizabeth, and also of Mary, to Gabriel's marvelous announcements. First, Zacharias and Elizabeth. Watch how startled amazement turns into faithful obedience and how both Zacharias and Elizabeth have the Holy Ghost come upon them and give them the power to prophesy. We will use the account in Luke, chapter 1. Zacharias and Elizabeth were both righteous and faithful, and Zacharias was an Aaronic Priesthood priest, whose turn had come to serve in the temple.

> 5 There was in the days of Herod, the king of Judæa, a certain priest [*in the Aaronic Priesthood*] named Zacharias, of the course of Abia [*a descendant of Aaron through Abijah*]: and his wife was of the daughters of Aaron [*was a descendant of Aaron*], and her name was Elisabeth.

The priests who served in the temple at the time of Christ were members of the Aaronic Priesthood. Zacharias was a righteous holder of this priesthood. Those men who fulfilled priestly duties at the temple at Jerusalem were divided into twenty-four groups or "courses," each group assigned to serve for one week at a time. Zacharias was a member of the eighth "course" or group. Each group had upwards of 1,400 men, so the privilege of officiating at the burning of incense in the temple might come once or never in the lifetime of a priest. (Talmage, *Jesus the Christ*, pp. 75–76)

> 6 And they were both righteous before God, walking in all the commandments and ordinances of the Lord blameless.
> 7 And they had no child, because that Elisabeth was barren [*had not been able to have children*], and they both were now well stricken in years [*were quite old and had given up on having children*].
> 8 And it came to pass, that while he [*Zacharias*] executed the priest's office [*carried out his duties in the temple*] before God in the order of his course,

>> 8 *And* while he executed the priest's office before God, in the order of his *priesthood*. (JST, Luke 1:8)

> 9 According to the custom of the priest's office, his lot was [*he had been selected*] to burn incense when he went into the temple of the Lord.

Since it was generally a once-in-a-lifetime opportunity for an Aaronic Priesthood priest to have the privilege of burning incense in the temple, as mentioned in the note above, this would have been a very humbling and important day for Zacharias.

> 10 And the whole multitude of the people were praying without [*outside of the temple, watching for the cloud of smoke from the incense to rise from the temple, and waiting for Zacharias to come back out in a few minutes*] at the time of incense.
> 11 And there appeared unto him [*Zacharias*] an angel of the Lord standing on the right side of the altar of incense.

This angel was Gabriel. He will also appear to Mary in a few months to tell her that she will be the mother of the Son of God. As mentioned previously, we are told that Gabriel is Noah. See Bible Dictionary, under "Gabriel."

12 And when Zacharias saw him, he was troubled, and fear fell upon him.
13 But the angel said unto him, Fear not, Zacharias: for thy prayer is heard; and thy wife Elisabeth shall bear thee a son, and thou shalt call his name John.

One of the important lessons we gain from verse 13, above, is that we should not give up praying for righteous desires of our hearts. The instruction by the angel to call their son John was very definite. Otherwise, they would very likely have named him Zacharias, after his father.

14 And thou shalt have joy and gladness; and many shall rejoice at his birth.

Next, the angel prophesies to Zacharias about the wonderful son he and Elizabeth will have, after having waited all these years.

15 For he shall be great in the sight of the Lord, and shall drink neither wine nor strong drink [*a sign that he was dedicated to a special calling*]; and he shall be filled with the Holy Ghost [*see D&C 84:27*], even from his mother's womb [*before he is born*].

Elder Bruce R. McConkie teaches us more about John the Baptist, as quoted in the *Doctrine and Covenants Student Manual*, page 183:

What concerns us above all else as to the coming of John, however, is that he came with power and authority. He first received his errand from the Lord. His was no ordinary message, and he was no unauthorized witness. He was called of God and sent by him, and he represented Deity in the words that he spoke and the baptisms he performed. He was a legal administrator whose words and acts were binding on earth and in heaven, and his hearers were bound, at the peril of their salvation, to believe his words and heed his counsels.

Luke says: "The word of God came unto John the son of Zacharias in the wilderness." Later John is to say: "He that sent me to baptize with water, the same said unto me," such and such things. (John 1:33.) Who sent him we do not know. We do know that "he was baptized while he was yet in his childhood [meaning, when he was eight years of age], and was ordained by the angel of God at the time he was eight days old unto this power [note it well, not to the Aaronic Priesthood, but] to overthrow the kingdom of the Jews, and to make straight the way of the Lord before the face of his people, to prepare them for the coming of the Lord, in whose hand is given all power." (D&C 84:24.) We do not know when he received the Aaronic Priesthood, but obviously it came to him after his baptism, at whatever age was proper, and before he was sent by one whom he does not name to preach and baptize with water. (*Mortal Messiah*, pp. 384–85)

16 And many of the children of Israel shall he turn to the Lord their God.
17 And he [John the Baptist] shall go before him [go ahead of Christ] in the spirit and power of Elias [one who prepares the way for even more important things; see *Teachings of the Prophet Joseph Smith*, pages 335–336; also see Bible Dictionary,

under "Elias"], to turn the hearts of the fathers to the children, and the disobedient to the wisdom of the just [righteous]; to make ready a people prepared for the Lord [Jesus].

It is easy to understand why Zacharias is humbly puzzled by the announcement of the angel, since he and Elizabeth are old, and she is well beyond the years when she could bear a child.

18 And Zacharias said unto the angel, Whereby [*how*] shall I know this? for I am an old man, and my wife well stricken in years [*we are beyond the years when we can have children*].
19 And the angel answering said unto him, I am Gabriel [*Noah; see note after verse 11 above*], that stand in the presence of God; and am sent to speak unto thee, and to shew thee these glad tidings.

While the limitation placed upon Zacharias, in verse 20, next, as a result of his hesitation to believe the words of the angel, might be viewed as a punishment, it might also be viewed as a kindness, as an assurance that he had indeed seen Gabriel and thus, that he and Elizabeth would surely have the promised son.

20 And, behold, thou shalt be dumb [*unable to talk*], and not able to speak, until the day that these things shall be performed [*until John is born*], because thou believest not my words, which shall be fulfilled in their season.
21 And the people waited for Zacharias, and marvelled that he tarried so long in the temple [*were wondering what was taking him so long*].
22 And when he came out, he could not speak unto them: and they perceived [*understood*] that he had seen a vision in the temple: for he beckoned unto them [*described with his hands that he had seen a vision*], and remained speechless.
23 And it came to pass, that, as soon as the days of his ministration were accomplished [*after his week of temple duties was over; see note after verse five above*], he departed to his own house.

Luke leaves it to our own imaginations to envision the scene that took place in the home of Zacharias and Elizabeth as he returned from his temple service and broke the good news to her.

24 And after those days his wife Elisabeth conceived, and hid herself five months, saying,
25 Thus hath the Lord dealt with me in the days wherein he looked on me, to take away my reproach among men [*to take away the social stigma of being childless*].

The Annunciation to Mary

Six months after Elizabeth conceived, Gabriel appeared to Mary to tell her that she would be the mother of Jesus Christ. Imagine what a joy it was to Noah, who preached the gospel and built the Ark in preparation for the Flood, to come back as the angel who had the privilege of announcing the coming birth of the Savior. We will continue using Luke, chapter 1.

26 And in the sixth month the angel Gabriel [*Noah; see note after verse 11 above*] was sent from God unto a city of Galilee, named Nazareth,

27 To a virgin espoused [*engaged, promised*] to a man whose name was Joseph, of the house of David [*who was a descendant of David*]; and the virgin's name was Mary.

Being "espoused" (verse 27, above) was a much stronger commitment than engagement is in our day. An espoused couple was bound by covenants to each other even before their marriage and the espousal could not be broken off except through formal action similar to divorce.

28 And the angel came in unto her, and said, Hail, thou that art highly favoured, the Lord is with thee: blessed art thou among women.

29 And when she saw him, she was troubled at his saying, and cast in her mind what manner of salutation this should be [*wondered what kind of a greeting this was*].

30 And the angel said unto her, Fear not, Mary: for thou hast found favour with God.

His Name Was to Be Jesus

31 And, behold, thou shalt conceive in thy womb, and bring forth a son, and shalt call his name Jesus.

Next, Gabriel gives Mary a brief description of her special Son. Mary would no doubt have recognized some of the ancient prophecies quoted by the angel, which would help her comprehend the significance of this announcement to her.

32 He shall be great, and shall be called the Son of the Highest [*the son of Heavenly Father*]: and the Lord God [*Heavenly Father*] shall give unto him the throne of his father [*ancestor*] David:

33 And he shall reign over the house of Jacob [*house of Israel; descendants of Jacob*] for ever; and of his kingdom there shall be no end.

34 Then said Mary unto the angel, How shall this be, seeing I know not a man [*I am a virgin*]?

35 And the angel answered and said unto her, The Holy Ghost shall come upon

thee, and the power of the Highest [*the highest member of the Godhead, in other words, the Father*] shall overshadow thee: therefore also that holy thing [*holy child*] which shall be born of thee shall be called the Son of God.

> 35 And the angel answered and said unto her, *Of* the Holy Ghost, and the power of the Highest. Therefore also, that holy *child* that shall be born of thee shall be called the Son of God. (JST, Luke 1:35)

Some people use verse 35, above, to suggest that the Holy Ghost is the father of Jesus. That is a completely false doctrine. Apostle James E. Talmage teaches the following:

> That Child to be born of Mary was begotten of Elohim, the Eternal Father, not in violation of natural law but in accordance with a higher manifestation thereof; and, the offspring from that association of supreme sanctity, celestial Sireship, and pure though mortal maternity, was of right to be called the "Son of the Highest." In His nature would be combined the powers of Godhood with the capacity and possibilities of mortality; and this through the ordinary operation of the fundamental law of heredity declared of God, demonstrated by science, and admitted by philosophy, that living beings shall propagate—after their kind. The Child Jesus was to inherit the physical, mental and spiritual traits, tendencies, and powers that characterized His parents—one immortal and glorified—God, the other human—woman. (*Jesus the Christ*, p. 81)

Next, Gabriel tells Mary that her elderly cousin Elizabeth (a relative, not necessarily a cousin—see Luke 1:36, footnote a, in the LDS edition of the King James Bible), is expecting a son.

> 36 And, behold, thy cousin Elisabeth, she hath also conceived a son in her old age: and this is the sixth month with her, who was called barren [*childless; Elizabeth is six months pregnant*].
> 37 For with God nothing shall be impossible.

MARY'S RESPONSE

There is probably not a greater example anywhere in scripture of humble faith and submission to the will of the Lord than the response given by Mary to the angel's announcement.

> 38 And Mary said, Behold the handmaid of the Lord; be it unto me according to thy word. And the angel departed from her.

MARY VISITS ELIZABETH

After Gabriel had appeared to Mary, she went to visit Elizabeth. Elizabeth was now six months pregnant with John the Baptist. When Mary entered Elizabeth's home, the baby responded to Mary's presence. Also, during that visit, the Holy Ghost came upon Elizabeth and she prophesied, bearing witness that everything Gabriel told Mary would be fulfilled.

> 39 And Mary arose in those days, and went into the hill country with haste [*hurried*], into a city of Juda;
>
> 40 And entered into the house of Zacharias, and saluted [*greeted*] Elisabeth.
>
> 41 And it came to pass, that, when Elisabeth heard the salutation [*greeting*] of Mary, the babe leaped in her womb [*little John the Baptist jumped inside of Elizabeth*]; and Elisabeth was filled with the Holy Ghost:

Apostle Bruce R. McConkie teaches some comforting doctrine regarding stillborn children based on verse 41 above. It is as follows:

> (The babe leaped in her womb). In this miraculous event the pattern is seen which a spirit follows in passing from his pre-existent first estate into mortality. The spirit enters the body at the time of quickening, months prior to the actual normal birth. The value and comfort attending a knowledge of this eternal truth is seen in connection with stillborn children. Since the spirit entered the body before birth, stillborn children will be resurrected and righteous parents shall enjoy their association in immortal glory. (*Doctrinal New Testament Commentary*, Vol. 1, pp. 84–85)

ELIZABETH PROPHESIES

Elizabeth will now exercise the gift of prophecy, which is one of the gifts of the Spirit, according to D&C 46:22.

> 42 And she [*Elizabeth*] spake out with a loud voice, and said, Blessed art thou [*Mary*] among women, and blessed is the fruit of thy womb [*the child who will be born to you*].
>
> 43 And whence is this to me, that the mother of my Lord should come to me [*how do I rate the privilege of having the mother of the Son of God come visit me*]?
>
> 44 For, lo, as soon as the voice of thy salutation [*greeting*] sounded in mine ears, the babe [*John*] leaped in my womb for joy.
>
> 45 And blessed is she that believed: for there shall be a performance of those things which were told her from the Lord [*everything promised to you will be fulfilled*].

MARY PROPHESIES

Next, we read of Mary's testimony and prophecy, which she gave while she was visiting Elizabeth. Immediately after Elizabeth had given her witness of Mary's sacred calling (Luke 1:41–45), Mary spoke of the fulfillment of ancient prophecies that were about to be fulfilled by her Son. Mary's words, recorded here in Luke 1:46–55, are often referred to in the Christian world as the "Magnificat."

> 46 And Mary said, My soul doth magnify [*praise*] the Lord,
> 47 And my spirit hath rejoiced in God my Saviour.
>
> 46 And my spirit *rejoiceth* in God my Savior. (JST, Luke 1:46)

It is touching to realize that Mary's baby would be her Savior as well as her child. From the verses we are reading here, it seems clear that she was well versed in the scriptures and understood that these prophecies pertained to the son whom she would now bear.

> 48 For he hath regarded [*seen, considered*] the low estate [humble condition] of his handmaiden [*servant*]: for, behold, from henceforth all generations shall call me blessed [*from now on, all people will know me and know how blessed I am*].
> 49 For he that is mighty [*God*] hath done to me great things; and holy is his name.
>
> 48 For he who is mighty hath done to me great things; and *I will magnify his holy name.* (JST Luke 1:48)

> 50 And his mercy is on them that fear [respect and obey] him from generation to generation.

In verses 51–55, we continue gaining marvelous insights into the depth of Mary's understanding concerning the coming Messiah.

> 51 He hath shewed [*demonstrated*] strength with his arm [*has shown His power*]; he hath scattered [*punished*] the proud in the imagination of their hearts [*because of their pride*].
> 52 He hath put down [*humbled*] the mighty from their seats [*positions of power*], and exalted them of low degree [*blessed and lifted up the humble*].
> 53 He hath filled the hungry [*those who "hunger and thirst after righteousness"; see Matthew 5:6*] with good things; and the rich [*the rich who are prideful*] he hath sent empty away.
> 54 He hath holpen [*helped*] his servant Israel [*the covenant people*], in remembrance of his mercy;
> 55 As he spake to our fathers [*ancestors*], to Abraham, and to his seed [*posterity*] for ever.

Verse 56 leads us to understand that Mary stayed with Zacharias and Elizabeth until about the time that John the Baptist was born to them. The scriptures are silent as to whether Mary was there when he was born. When she returned to Nazareth, she would have been about three months along with the Christ child.

> 56 And Mary abode with her [*stayed with Elizabeth*] about three months, and returned to her own house.

MARY RETURNS HOME

As you probably recall, Mary was already espoused to Joseph (Matthew 1:18). Many people use the word *engaged* to explain "espoused." However, among the Jews of that time, being espoused was a much more serious obligation than being engaged, in our day. During the espousal period, the bride-to-be lived with her family or friends and communication between her and her husband-to-be was carried on by a friend. The fact that Mary came back to town expecting a child presented a very difficult circumstance for both Mary and Joseph. In Jewish culture of the day, an unmarried woman found to be expecting a child was subject to being stoned to death, or, at the very least, subject to being publicly humiliated and shamed. And the man, to whom such a woman was espoused, would be expected to defend his honor and that of his parents and family by making a public announcement that the child was not his and that he was not immoral.

By the way, have you noticed that the angel waited until after Joseph made the decision to treat Mary with mercy and break off their espousal privately, before he appeared and gave Joseph the wonderful news that Mary was the virgin spoken of in prophecy? She was, in fact, the mother-to-be of the Son of God, and Joseph was to marry her.

> 19 Then Joseph her husband, being a just man, and not willing to make her a publick example, was minded to put her away privily.
> 20 But while he thought on these things, behold, the angel of the Lord appeared unto him in a dream, saying, Joseph, thou son of David, fear not to take unto thee Mary thy wife: for that which is conceived in her is of the Holy Ghost.
> 21 And she shall bring forth a son, and thou shalt call his name Jesus: for he shall save his people from their sins.
> 22 Now all this was done, that it might be fulfilled which was spoken of the Lord by the prophet, saying,
> 23 Behold, a virgin shall be with child, and shall bring forth a son, and they shall call his name Emmanuel, which being interpreted is, God with us. (Matthew 1:19–23)

Luke explains what is meant at the end of verse 20, above, where the angel said that Mary's child was "of the Holy Ghost." He says, in effect, that the Holy Ghost came upon Mary so that the divine conception could be accomplished. Luke wrote:

35 And the angel answered and said unto her, The Holy Ghost shall come upon thee, and the power of the Highest [*the Father*] shall overshadow thee: therefore also that holy thing [*the Christ child*] which shall be born of thee shall be called the Son of God. (Luke 1:35)

Picture if you will the joy in Joseph's heart as he arose from bed, quickly contacted Mary and told her that he now knew what she already knew, and that they were to marry immediately. And imagine the relief and joy in Mary's whole being as a terribly difficult situation brought about by obedience was transformed by the angel's revelation and instruction to Joseph. Also, have you noticed that Joseph and Mary did not have intimate relations until after Jesus was born? The phrase "knew her not," in verse 25, below, means "did not have sexual relations."

24 Then Joseph being raised from sleep did as the angel of the Lord had bidden him, and took unto him his wife:
25 And knew her not till she had brought forth her firstborn son: and he called his name Jesus. (Matthew 1:24–25)

After Jesus was born, Joseph and Mary went on to have at least six children of their own (see Mark 6:3). In fact, the Greek text of Mark 6:3 indicates that there were at least three sisters, plus the four brothers mentioned.

JOHN THE BAPTIST IS BORN

In due time, John the Baptist was born to Elizabeth. A crowd of family and friends gathered in the home of Zacharias and Elizabeth to celebrate the happy occasion.

57 Now Elisabeth's full time came that she should be delivered [*the time came for her to have her baby*]; and she brought forth a son.
58 And her neighbours and her cousins heard how the Lord had shewed [*showed*] great mercy upon her; and they rejoiced with her.

As you can see, in verse 59, next, the friends and neighbors of Zacharias and Elizabeth automatically assumed that their miraculous son would be named after his father. Remember, Zacharias has not been able to talk since the visit of Gabriel about nine months ago. Remember also that in verse 13, above, the angel instructed him to name his son John. Based on what we see in verse 60, he had told Elizabeth about the name and she held firm to that instruction from the angel, even when well-meaning people tried to talk her out of it.

59 And it came to pass, that on the eighth day they came to circumcise the child [*John*]; and they called him Zacharias, after the name of his father.

60 And his mother answered [*responded*] and said, Not so; but he shall be called John [*his name is not Zacharias; it is John!*].

61 And they said unto her, There is none of thy kindred that is called by this name. [*Why name him John? You have no relatives named John.*]

62 And they made signs to his father, how he would have him called [*asked Zacharias what the baby's name should be*].

Next, Zacharias confirms what Elizabeth had told them, and he is immediately able to speak again.

63 And he asked for a writing table [*because he was still unable to speak*], and wrote, saying, His name is John. And they marvelled all [*were all surprised*].

64 And his [*Zacharias's*] mouth was opened immediately, and his tongue loosed, and he spake, and praised God.

65 And fear [*awe*] came on all that dwelt round about them: and all these sayings were noised abroad [*were spread*] throughout all the hill country of Judæa.

66 And all they that heard them laid them up in their hearts, saying, What manner of child shall this be [*what kind of special child is John*]! And the hand of the Lord was with him.

ZACHARIAS PROPHESIES ABOUT JOHN

67 And his father Zacharias was filled with the Holy Ghost, and prophesied, saying,

68 Blessed be the Lord God of Israel [*we are grateful to God*]; for he hath visited [*come; helped*] and redeemed his people,

Zacharias is prophesying about the future as if it had already taken place. This is a common form of prophecy in the Bible.

69 And hath raised up an horn [*"horn" was symbolic of safety, strength, and protection in Jewish culture*] of salvation for us in the house of his servant David [*among us descendants of David*];

70 As he spake by the mouth of his holy prophets, which have been since the world began:

71 That we should be saved from our enemies, and from the hand of all that hate us;

72 To perform the mercy promised to our fathers [*ancestors*], and to remember [*fulfil*] his holy covenant;

73 The oath [*promise*] which he sware [*promised*] to our father [ancestor] Abraham,

74 That he would grant unto us, that we being delivered out of the hand of our enemies might serve him without fear [*without fear of being persecuted*],

75 In holiness and righteousness before him, all the days of our life.

76 And thou, child [*little John the Baptist*], shalt be called the prophet of the Highest [*God*]: for thou shalt go before the face of [*ahead of*] the Lord [*Jesus*] to prepare his ways;

77 To give knowledge of salvation unto his people by the remission of their sins,

78 Through the tender mercy of our God; whereby the dayspring [*rising sun, dawn*] from on high hath visited us [*this is the dawn of a new day for us*],

79 To give light to them that sit in darkness [*spiritual darkness*] and in the shadow of death, to guide our feet into the way of peace.

Next, Luke gives a very brief summary of John the Baptist's life from birth to the beginning of his mission to formally prepare the way for the Savior. He does something similar with respect to the life of Jesus, in Luke 2:40 and 52.

80 And the child [*John*] grew, and waxed strong [*gained strength*] in spirit, and was in [*lived in*] the deserts till the day of his shewing [*beginning of his mission*] unto Israel.

In summary, the angel Gabriel, who was Noah in the Old Testament, appeared to Zacharias and told him that he and his wife, Elizabeth, would be blessed with a son (John the Baptist) who would prepare the way before Jesus Christ, as He began His three-year formal mortal mission. When Elizabeth was in her sixth month of pregnancy with John the Baptist, Gabriel appeared to Mary and announced that she would be the mother of the Son of God. This is referred to as the Annunciation. Thus, the time had arrived for the Savior to enter mortality and bring to fruition His premortal covenant with the Father to carry out the Atonement.

CHAPTER 9

BORN TO THE VIRGIN MARY

As the time for His mortal mission drew near, think how it must have been for the Savior. Finally, He, the Redeemer chosen in the grand premortal council, was to experience mortality for Himself. After creating "worlds without number" for the Father, now He would actually be born on this one. Think how He must have felt, several years before His own birth, as Joseph's time came to leave the premortal spirit life and come to earth to be born. Was there a tender farewell scene where Jesus embraced Joseph, as they contemplated their future lives on earth together? Did Jesus express special gratitude for this humble and noble man who would be His wonderful stepfather, who would guard Him, who would protect Him and His mother, who would teach Him the carpenter's trade, who would provide a righteous home for Him and His mother, along with His half brothers and sisters?

What was it like when it came time for Mary, who would be His mortal mother, to leave our premortal heavenly home and enter the body that her own mortal mother was preparing for her? Did Mary and Jesus embrace and whisper "I love you" to each other as she departed? What thoughts were going through the Savior's mind, knowing that in just a few short years, He, too, would have the veil of forgetfulness drawn over His supreme mind and enter a state of helplessness and dependency upon Mary and Joseph?

We know from the scriptures that Jesus did, indeed, have the veil drawn over His mind as He came forth a newborn infant. He "grew, and waxed strong in spirit . . . and . . . increased in wisdom" (Luke 2:40, 52). Elder James E. Talmage explained this as follows:

He came among men to experience all the natural conditions of mortality; He was born as truly a dependent, helpless babe as is any other child; His infancy was in all common features as the infancy of others; His boyhood was actual boyhood, His development was as necessary and as real as that of all children. Over His mind had fallen the veil of forgetfulness common to all who are born to earth, by which the remembrance of primeval existence is shut off. The Child grew, and with growth there came to Him expansion of mind, development of faculties, and progression in power and understanding. (*Jesus the Christ*, p. 111)

TO BE BORN IN BETHLEHEM

The Old Testament prophet Micah had prophesied more than seven hundred years before the Savior's birth that Bethlehem, a small village of no particular importance commercially, would be the birthplace of the Messiah.

> 2 But thou, Beth-lehem Ephratah, though thou be little among the thousands of Judah, yet out of thee shall he [the Savior] come forth unto me that is to be ruler in Israel; whose goings forth have been from of old, from everlasting. (Micah 5:2)

This prophecy that the Messiah was to be born in the obscure village of Bethlehem seems to have been well known at the time of the birth of Christ. In fact, when the Wise Men approached King Herod to ask where the "King of the Jews" had been born (Matthew 2:2), the king's advisers had no trouble coming up with the answer that it was prophesied to be Bethlehem, which was about five miles south of Jerusalem.

> 4 And when he had gathered all the chief priests and scribes of the people together, he demanded of them where Christ should be born.
> 5 And they said unto him, In Bethlehem of Judæa: for thus it is written by the prophet,
> 6 And thou Bethlehem, in the land of Juda, art not the least among the princes of Juda: for out of thee shall come a Governor, that shall rule my people Israel. (Matthew 2:4–6)

THE JOURNEY FROM NAZARETH TO BETHLEHEM

As the time of the Savior's mortal birth drew near, Joseph and Mary were living in Nazareth, a village about 60 miles straight north of Bethlehem, but around 130–140 miles from Bethlehem, based on the common travel routes, avoiding Samaria, that Jews would likely take to go from Galilee into Judea. Nazareth was a town in the hill country of Galilee, and we suppose that it was there that Joseph received word of Caesar's decree that all his subjects were to register for purposes of being taxed. At that time, the Holy Land was part of the vast Mediterranean area ruled by Rome under Caesar Agustus (he ruled the Roman Empire for forty-five years from 31 BC to AD 14). Luke sets the stage for the difficult journey of Joseph and Mary to Bethlehem.

1 And it came to pass in those days, that there went out a decree from Cæsar Augustus, that all the world should be taxed.

2 (And this taxing was first made when Cyrenius was governor of Syria.)

3 And all went to be taxed, every one into his own city.

4 And Joseph also went up from Galilee, out of the city of Nazareth, into Judæa, unto the city of David, which is called Bethlehem; (because he was of the house and lineage of David:)

5 To be taxed with Mary his espoused wife, being great with child. (Luke 2:1–5)

James E. Talmage explains that, normally, Joseph could have registered right in Nazareth, but because of Jewish custom, he went to register in Bethlehem.

At that time a decree went out from Rome ordering a taxing of the people in all kingdoms and provinces tributary to the empire; the call was of general scope, it provided "that all the world should be taxed." The taxing herein referred to may properly be understood as an enrolment, or a registration, whereby a census of Roman subjects would be secured, upon which as a basis the taxation of the different peoples would be determined. This particular census was the second of three such general registrations recorded by historians as occurring at intervals of about twenty years. Had the census been taken by the usual Roman method, each person would have been enrolled at the town of his residence; but the Jewish custom, for which the Roman law had respect, necessitated registration at the cities or towns claimed by the respective families as their ancestral homes. As to whether the requirement was strictly mandatory that every family should thus register at the city of its ancestors, we need not be specially concerned; certain it is that Joseph and Mary went to Bethlehem, the city of David, to be inscribed under the imperial decree. (*Jesus the Christ*, pp. 91–92)

Thus, Joseph and Mary traveled to Bethlehem, the prophesied place of the Savior's birth. It may well be that Mary was already experiencing labor pains during this long journey. If so, it would have caused Joseph much additional worry and concern for the well-being of his young wife, above and beyond the normal worries of such travel with family. Before we continue with Joseph and Mary as they arrive in Bethlehem, we will go half a world away and listen in as Nephi is told that this is the night of the Savior's birth.

THE VOICE OF THE LORD TELLS NEPHI THE TIME FOR HIS BIRTH HAS COME

Remember that the enemies of the Church among the wicked Nephites in America had set a deadline for the fulfillment of the promised sign of the Savior's birth. There was to be a "day and a night and a day, as if it were one day," as foretold by Samuel the Lamanite about five years ago (Helaman 14:4), that would serve as unmistakable evidence that the Christ child had been born. If the sign did not come by the deadline, they would execute the believers. It had not yet come and the deadline was about up. The wicked were preparing for the imminent slaughter of the hated faithful believers in Christ. As Nephi bowed in sorrow and worry for his people, in fervent prayer, the voice of the Lord came to him with the joyous news.

> 13 Lift up your head and be of good cheer; for behold, the time is at hand, and on this night shall the sign be given, and on the morrow come I into the world, to show unto the world that I will fulfil all that which I have caused to be spoken by the mouth of my holy prophets.
>
> 14 Behold, I come unto my own, to fulfil all things which I have made known unto the children of men from the foundation of the world, and to do the will, both of the Father and of the Son—of the Father because of me, and of the Son because of my flesh. And behold, the time is at hand, and this night shall the sign be given. (3 Nephi 1:13–14)

Sure enough, as the sun went down, it did not get dark. The sign was given and the prophecy was fulfilled. Imagine the joy of Nephi and the joy and relief among the Nephite believers as their faithfulness against all odds was rewarded. Picture also the terror and confusion among the unbelievers as they faced the startling fact that they were wrong and wicked. Gratefully, many of these were converted and were baptized (1 Nephi 1:22–23). Thus, the Atonement worked for them, cleansing and healing them and giving them a fresh start.

The fact that this message to Nephi from the Savior was given the day before His birth leads us to suppose that it was likely given while Mary was in labor. Students of this part of the Book of Mormon often marvel at what a miracle it was that Jesus' spirit left His tiny body in Mary's womb to give this message to Nephi. However, we need to be a bit careful with this. While such a miracle is certainly possible with God, a careful reading of 3 Nephi 1:12 shows that it was "the voice of the Lord." With this in mind, we realize that there are perhaps several possibilities. The Lord could have left His body to be near Nephi and spoken to him that way. The Savior could have spoken from Bethlehem and used His power to have Nephi hear Him. The Holy Ghost, who can speak for the Son as if He were speaking (Moses 5:9), could have spoken to Nephi and delivered the Savior's message. Whatever the case, a marvelous manifestation was given to Nephi, and that night, when the sun went down, it remained as light as day, thus witnessing to the Nephites that the Son of God was to be born to Mary (Mosiah 3:8) the next day in Bethlehem. We will now return to Joseph and Mary.

No Room at the Inn

As worried Joseph and weary Mary arrived in Bethlehem, it must have been a relief to finally be at the end of the journey. But it is likely that this relief quickly changed to deep discouragement as Joseph's pleading inquiries for a room to stay in were repeatedly turned down. Throngs of people crowded the streets of the village, and the inns were full. It is interesting to note that the Bible, as it stands, mentions just one "inn" (Luke 2:7). However, the JST's use of the word "inns" (JST, Luke 2:7; see Luke 2:7, footnote b in the English version of the LDS edition of the King James Bible) thus indicates that Joseph enquired at several inns. Finally, arrangements were made for the most humble of accommodations in a stable, likely surrounded by domestic animals, with a manger that could serve as a bed for the newborn child. Perhaps you've noticed that the Bible gives very little detail about this scene. Thus, most everything we hear and see about it is based on tender and worshipful opinion and imagination of authors, artists, playwrights, filmmakers, and so forth, as to how things actually were. The eternally important matter is that the Son of God had now been born.

> 6 And so it was, that, while they were there, the days were accomplished that she should be delivered.
> 7 And she brought forth her firstborn son, and wrapped him in swaddling clothes, and laid him in a manger; because there was no room for them in the inn. (Luke 2:6–7)

Just a note about swaddling clothes. They were bands of cloth in which a newborn baby was wrapped. The baby was placed diagonally upon a square piece of cloth. The bottom corner of the square cloth was folded up to cover the baby's feet, and the side corners were folded in to cover the baby's sides. Then bands of cloth were wound around the baby to make a warm, comfortable bundle.

Shepherds See and Then Bear Witness

Even though we celebrate Christmas on the 25 of December, along with the majority of the Christian world, we understand that it was springtime when the Savior was born. President Spencer W. Kimball taught that Christ was born on April 6.

> "The hinge of history is on the door of a Bethlehem stable." (Ralph Sockman.) The name Jesus Christ and what it represents has been plowed deep into the history of the world, never to be uprooted. Christ was born on the sixth of April. ("'Why Call Me Lord, Lord, and Do Not the Things Which I Say?'" par. 9)

In one of the revelations given at the time of the official organization of the Church, which was specified by the Savior to take place on April 6, 1830, we see an implication that April 6 is of personal significance to Him.

> The rise of the Church of Christ in these last days, being one thousand eight hundred and thirty years since the coming of our Lord and Savior Jesus Christ in the flesh, it being regularly organized and established agreeable to the laws of our country, by the will and commandments of God, in the fourth month, and on the sixth day of the month which is called April. (D&C 20:1)

Thus, shepherds in the Bethlehem area would be grazing their sheep on the fresh new growth of spring and watching over them by night, when the Christ child was born. Certain of these shepherds had the great privilege of having an angel announce the birth of Christ to them, telling them that they would find Him in a manger.

> 8 And there were in the same country shepherds abiding in the field, keeping watch over their flock by night.
> 9 And, lo, the angel of the Lord came upon them, and the glory of the Lord shone round about them: and they were sore afraid.
> 10 And the angel said unto them, Fear not: for, behold, I bring you good tidings of great joy, which shall be to all people.
> 11 For unto you is born this day in the city of David a Saviour, which is Christ the Lord.
> 12 And this shall be a sign unto you; Ye shall find the babe wrapped in swaddling clothes, lying in a manger. (Luke 2:8–12)

This angel was joined by a vast multitude of angels singing praises and rejoicing in the holy birth.

> 13 And suddenly there was with the angel a multitude of the heavenly host praising God, and saying,
> 14 Glory to God in the highest, and on earth peace, good will toward men. (Luke 2:13–14)

When the shepherds recovered sufficiently from their initial fear and shock, they hurried to Bethlehem to see the newly born Son of God. And after having done so, they became witnesses to the glorious event and spread the word abroad.

> 15 And it came to pass, as the angels were gone away from them into heaven, the shepherds said one to another, Let us now go even unto Bethlehem, and see this thing which is come to pass, which the Lord hath made known unto us.
> 16 And they came with haste, and found Mary, and Joseph, and the babe lying in a manger.
> 17 And when they had seen it, they made known abroad the saying which was told them concerning this child. (Luke 2:15–17)

MARY KEPT THESE THINGS IN HER HEART

In spite of the fact that the shepherds had been told by angelic hosts that Mary's child was indeed the "Saviour, which is Christ the Lord" (Luke 2:11), and that they bore witness of their heavenly experience to many, we suppose that there must have been many things about this special child and His birth that Mary and Joseph could not share with those around them. To do so would be premature and no doubt invite ridicule and scorn, and perhaps even persecution. They both knew personally, by way of heavenly messages given them by angels, that this was the promised Messiah, the Son of the Most High God, the Redeemer, foretold in almost countless prophecies by ancient prophets of God. But to share more, discuss detail, explain more about who the child really was would not be wise. Luke summarizes this and much more in a simple phrase:

> But Mary kept all these things, and pondered them in her heart. (Luke 2:19)

JOSEPH AND MARY KEPT THE LAW OF MOSES

According to the law of Moses, all male children were to be circumcised (Leviticus 12:3), as a token of the covenant made by the Lord with Abraham (Genesis 17:9–12). This was the practice during Old Testament dispensations. The law of circumcision was done away with as the law of Moses was fulfilled by the Savior during His mortal mission (Galatians 5:1–6). Thus it was no longer required in the New Testament church, after Jesus established it. The custom among the Jews was to also give the child a name at the time of circumcision (BD, under "Circumcision"). Luke makes brief reference to these things as he gives his account of the Savior's earliest mortal days.

> 21 And when eight days were accomplished for the circumcising of the child, his name was called Jesus, which was so named of the angel before he was conceived in the womb. (Luke 2:21)

SIMEON AND ANNA IN THE TEMPLE

After waiting the forty days required by the law of Moses for purification, after the birth of a male child (Leviticus 12:2–4), Mary and Joseph took infant Jesus to the temple to dedicate Him to the Lord. Under the law of Moses, firstborn males were to be dedicated to the Lord.

> 1 And the LORD spake unto Moses, saying,
> 2 Sanctify unto me all the firstborn, whatsoever openeth the womb among the children of Israel, both of man and of beast: it is mine. (Exodus 13:1–2)

Can you see the symbolism in this? It is another example of Atonement symbolism in the law of Moses. It represented, among other things, that the "Firstborn" of the Father would be dedicated to carry out the work of the Father through His mission and Atonement. So it was that Joseph and Mary, faithful to the laws of God in their day, took Jesus to the temple to dedicate Him to the Lord. They purchased the required sacrifices and proceeded.

> 22 And when the days of her purification according to the law of Moses were accomplished, they brought him to Jerusalem, to present him to the Lord;
> 23 (As it is written in the law of the Lord, Every male that openeth the womb shall be called holy to the Lord;)
> 24 And to offer a sacrifice according to that which is said in the law of the Lord, A pair of turtledoves, or two young pigeons. (Luke 2:22–24)

While they were in the temple on this special occasion, a righteous man by the name of Simeon, who was apparently quite elderly, no doubt excitedly but reverently approached them and took the infant Jesus in his arms. Simeon had been promised through the Holy Ghost that he would not die until he had seen the promised Messiah in the flesh. With great joy and satisfaction, now that the promised blessing had been realized, Simeon exclaimed that he could now die in peace.

> 25 And, behold, there was a man in Jerusalem, whose name was Simeon; and the same man was just and devout, waiting for the consolation of Israel: and the Holy Ghost was upon him.
> 26 And it was revealed unto him by the Holy Ghost, that he should not see death, before he had seen the Lord's Christ.
> 27 And he came by the Spirit into the temple: and when the parents brought in the child Jesus, to do for him after the custom of the law,
> 28 Then took he him up in his arms, and blessed God, and said,
> 29 Lord, now lettest thou thy servant depart in peace, according to thy word:
> 30 For mine eyes have seen thy salvation,
> 31 Which thou hast prepared before the face of all people;
> 32 A light to lighten the Gentiles, and the glory of thy people Israel. (Luke 2:25–32)

It is evident in what Luke says next that he understood well that Mary was the mother of Jesus, but Joseph was not His father. This is a brief but significant verse of scripture bearing witness that Jesus Christ was the Son of God. Luke did not say "His father and mother," rather,

And Joseph and his mother marvelled at those things which were spoken of him. (Luke 2:33)

While the Spirit was upon Simeon, he continued, prophesying of the great mission of Mary's child and reminding us of the pain that she would yet go through as the mother of the Son of God.

34 And Simeon blessed them, and said unto Mary his mother, Behold, this child is set for the fall and rising again of many in Israel; and for a sign which shall be spoken against;
35 (Yea, a sword shall pierce through thy own soul also,) that the thoughts of many hearts may be revealed. (Luke 2:34–35)

The Joseph Smith Translation of the Bible makes changes to verse 35.

35 Yea, a spear shall pierce through *him to the wounding of thine own soul also*; that the thoughts of many hearts may be revealed. (JST, Luke 2:35)

Next, Luke tells us that an elderly woman, also in the temple at the same time, approached them just as Simeon was finishing his inspired utterances. She also witnessed to those present that this child was the Son of God. Her name was Anna, and she was from the tribe of Asher (one of the Twelve Tribes of Israel). Her husband had died seven years after they were married. If we understand Luke correctly, it appears that she was about eighty-four years old at this time.

36 And there was one Anna, a prophetess, the daughter of Phanuel, of the tribe of Aser: she was of a great age, and had lived with an husband seven years from her virginity;
37 And she was a widow of about fourscore and four years, which departed not from the temple, but served God with fastings and prayers night and day.
38 And she coming in that instant gave thanks likewise unto the Lord, and spake of him to all them that looked for redemption in Jerusalem. (Luke 2:36–38)

THE WISE MEN

The scriptures do not tell us how long after the birth of Jesus the Wise Men visited Him and presented their gifts to Him. Suffice it to say that by the time of their visit, He is referred to as a "young child" (Matthew 2:11 and 13) and Joseph and Mary along with the Christ child were living in a house somewhere in Bethlehem (Matthew 2:11). The scriptures are also silent as to the origins of the Wise Men, how many there were, their names, or much of anything else about them. It will be interesting to learn more about these great men, perhaps at the time of the Second Coming, when "all things" will be revealed (D&C 101:32). In the meantime we do know that they came from the East, that they had seen the new star, and were aware that it signaled the birth of the Son of God.

> 1 Now when Jesus was born in Bethlehem of Judæa in the days of Herod the king, behold, there came wise men from the east to Jerusalem,
> 2 Saying, Where is he that is born King of the Jews? for we have seen his star in the east, and are come to worship him. (Matthew 2:1–2)

The JST makes a significant change to verse 2, above. Notice what Joseph Smith substituted for "King of the Jews."

> 2 Saying, *Where is the child that is born, the Messiah* of the Jews? for we have seen his star in the east, and have come to worship him. (JST, Matthew 2:2)

King Herod was a cruel and hypocritical tyrant, much feared and hated by the Jews. James E. Talmage provides us with some background about him.

> Herod was professedly an adherent of the religion of Judah, though by birth an Idumean, by descent an Edomite or one of the posterity of Esau, all of whom the Jews hated; and of all Edomites not one was more bitterly detested than was Herod the king. He was tyrannical and merciless, sparing neither foe nor friend who came under suspicion of being a possible hindrance to his ambitious designs. He had his wife and several of his sons, as well as others of his blood kindred, cruelly murdered; and he put to death nearly all of the great national council, the Sanhedrin. His reign was one of revolting cruelty and unbridled oppression. Only when in danger of inciting a national revolt or in fear of incurring the displeasure of his imperial master, the Roman emperor, did he stay his hand in any undertaking. (*Jesus the Christ*, pp. 97–98)

When the Wise Men arrived in Jerusalem, they went to the palace of the king to seek directions as to the whereabouts of the Christ child in order to visit Him. Herod asked his advisors about the matter and they had no trouble coming up with the answer. The king then called the Wise Men to him, told them Bethlehem was the location of the Child's birth, asked some questions, and slyly asked them to inform him when they found the Holy Child so that he, too, could worship Him.

> 3 When Herod the king had heard these things, he was troubled, and all Jerusalem with him.
> 4 And when he had gathered all the chief priests and scribes of the people together, he demanded of them where Christ should be born.
> 5 And they said unto him, In Bethlehem of Judæa: for thus it is written by the prophet,
> 6 And thou Bethlehem, in the land of Juda, art not the least among the princes of Juda: for out of thee shall come a Governor, that shall rule my people Israel.
> 7 Then Herod, when he had privily called the wise men, enquired of them diligently what time the star appeared.
> 8 And he sent them to Bethlehem, and said, Go and search diligently for the young child; and when ye have found him, bring me word again, that I may come and worship him also. (Matthew 2:3–8)

The JST makes changes in verses 4–6, above.

> 4 And when he had gathered all the chief priests, and scribes of the people together, he demanded of them, *saying, Where is the place that is written of by the prophets, in which* Christ should be born? *For he greatly feared, yet he believed not the prophets.*
> 5 And they said unto him, It is written by the prophets, that he should be born in Bethlehem of Judea, *for thus have they said,*
> 6 *The word of the Lord came unto us, saying,* And thou Bethlehem, *which lieth* in the land of Judea, *in thee shall be born a prince, which* art not the least among the princes of Judea; for out of thee shall come the Messiah, who shall save my people Israel. (JST, Matthew 3:4–6)

The Wise Men were guided by a star to the house in which Joseph, Mary, and the young Child were then staying. Overjoyed when they arrived, these righteous men from the East then worshipped Him, presenting Him gifts of gold, frankincense, and myrrh. Perhaps it is the fact that Matthew mentions three specific gifts that gives rise to the often repeated but unsubstantiated notion that there were three of them. Gold was, of course, a very valuable gift. Frankincense and myrrh were likewise costly gifts and were highly prized for their use as pleasant smelling incense in this culture where sanitation was a concern and incense helped mask unpleasant odors. Also, it may well be that these gifts from the wise men helped pay expenses for the trip to Egypt, mentioned in Matthew 2:13.

9 When they had heard the king, they departed; and, lo, the star, which they saw
in the east, went before them, till it came and stood over where the young child
was.

10 When they saw the star, they rejoiced with exceeding great joy.

11 And when they were come into the house, they saw the young child with Mary
his mother, and fell down, and worshipped him: and when they had opened their
treasures, they presented unto him gifts; gold, and frankincense, and myrrh. (Matthew 2:9–11)

After visiting and worshipping the young Child, these humble men were
warned by God not to go back to Herod as requested by him and report their
visit to the Christ child and His current location. Rather, they were instructed to
leave the area by another route.

JOSEPH FOLLOWS THE LORD'S
COMMAND AND FLEES TO EGYPT

12 And being warned of God in a dream that they should not return to Herod,
they departed into their own country another way. (Matthew 2:12)

After the Wise Men left, Joseph was told by an angel in a dream to take
Jesus and His mother and flee to Egypt, where they would be out of Herod's
reach and where they were to remain until he received further word from God.
Joseph did not delay and the small family fled by night and traveled to Egypt
(Matthew 2:13–15). Matthew's account tells us that they remained in Egypt
until Joseph was told by an angel in a dream that Herod had died and it was
now safe to take his family back to the land of Israel (Matthew 2:19–20). Upon
returning, Joseph found out that Herod's son, Archelaus, was ruling in his place.
Consequently, Joseph took his small family to Galilee and settled in Nazareth,
rather than remaining in Judea (Matthew 2:21–23). By the way, have you noticed
what a good man Joseph was? He had the gift of "beholding of angels" (Moroni
10:14) through which he received messages from God. He was blessed with communication from God in dreams. And he was faithful and obedient to what he
was told in these revelations.

HEROD ORDERS THE SLAUGHTER OF
CHILDREN IN AND AROUND BETHLEHEM

King Herod was furious when he discovered that the Wise Men had disobeyed
his request to report back to him. As a result, he ordered the slaughter of all children
two years old and under in Bethlehem and the surrounding regions. According to
his calculations, based on what he had learned from the Wise Men, that action

should eliminate the Christ child and any threat to Herod's position as King from this supposed "King of the Jews" (Matthew 2:2).

> 16 Then Herod, when he saw that he was mocked of the wise men, was exceeding wroth, and sent forth, and slew all the children that were in Bethlehem, and in all the coasts thereof, from two years old and under, according to the time which he had diligently enquired of the wise men. (Matthew 2:16)

ZACHARIAS IS SLAIN FOR REFUSING TO DISCLOSE THE WHEREABOUTS OF YOUNG JOHN THE BAPTIST

At this time, John the Baptist was also a young child, just six months older than Jesus (Luke 1:36), and his parents apparently were living in the Bethlehem area. Joseph Smith informs us that John's father, Zacharias, was murdered by the soldiers of King Herod for refusing to disclose the whereabouts of young John.

> When Herod's edict went forth to destroy the young children, John was about six months older than Jesus, and came under this hellish edict, and Zacharias caused his mother to take him into the mountains, where he was raised on locusts and wild honey. When his father refused to disclose his hiding place, and being the officiating high priest at the Temple that year, was slain by Herod's order, between the porch and the altar. (*TPJS*, p. 261)

During the last week of His mortal mission, Jesus alluded to the murder of righteous Zacharias as He scolded the scribes and Pharisees for being hypocrites and persecuting and killing the prophets He had sent to them.

> 34 Wherefore, behold, I send unto you prophets, and wise men, and scribes: and some of them ye shall kill and crucify; and some of them shall ye scourge in your synagogues, and persecute them from city to city:
> 35 That upon you may come all the righteous blood shed upon the earth, from the blood of righteous Abel unto the blood of Zacharias son of Barachias, whom ye slew between the temple and the altar. (Matthew 23:34–35)

THE ONLY BEGOTTEN OF THE FATHER IN THE FLESH

In summary, in fulfillment of numerous prophecies given of His birth by ancient prophets of God from the beginning, and including one as recent as five years back, given by Samuel the Lamanite (Helaman 14:2), the "Only Begotten of the Father in the Flesh" had now entered mortality. He was the Son of God. As a result of His parentage, He had divine power over death as well as the ability to experience mortality and to die. A beautiful summary of these attributes of the Savior was given to King Benjamin by an angel. Subsequently, the King quoted the angel's testimony to his people during his farewell address to them.

5 For behold, the time cometh, and is not far distant, that with power, the Lord Omnipotent who reigneth, who was, and is from all eternity to all eternity, shall come down from heaven among the children of men, and shall dwell in a tabernacle of clay, and shall go forth amongst men, working mighty miracles, such as healing the sick, raising the dead, causing the lame to walk, the blind to receive their sight, and the deaf to hear, and curing all manner of diseases.

6 And he shall cast out devils, or the evil spirits which dwell in the hearts of the children of men.

7 And lo, he shall suffer temptations, and pain of body, hunger, thirst, and fatigue, even more than man can suffer, except it be unto death; for behold, blood cometh from every pore, so great shall be his anguish for the wickedness and the abominations of his people.

8 And he shall be called Jesus Christ, the Son of God, the Father of heaven and earth, the Creator of all things from the beginning; and his mother shall be called Mary. (Mosiah 3:5–8)

CHAPTER 10

THE SAVIOR'S YOUTH

Very little is known of the Savior's youth. We know that Joseph and Jesus' mother, Mary, lived in Nazareth, having settled there after returning from Egypt with the young child (Matthew 2:19–23).

JESUS HAD THE VEIL

In a very brief statement, Luke leads us to understand that when Jesus was born, He had the veil of forgetfulness drawn over His mind regarding His premortal life, such as is the case with all mortals.

> 52 And Jesus increased in wisdom and stature, and in favour with God and man. (Luke 2:52)

We learn from the Doctrine and Covenants that John the Baptist saw and taught much more about the Savior than is recorded in the Bible. The Baptist's teaching confirms what Luke recorded about growth and progress in the Savior's early mortal years.

> 11 And I, John, bear record that I beheld his glory, as the glory of the Only Begotten of the Father, full of grace and truth, even the Spirit of truth, which came and dwelt in the flesh, and dwelt among us.
> 12 And I, John, saw that he received not of the fulness at the first, but received grace for grace;
> 13 And he received not of the fulness at first, but continued from grace to grace, until he received a fulness;
> 14 And thus he was called the Son of God, because he received not of the fulness at the first.

15 And I, John, bear record, and lo, the heavens were opened, and the Holy Ghost descended upon him in the form of a dove, and sat upon him, and there came a voice out of heaven saying: This is my beloved Son.

16 And I, John, bear record that he received a fulness of the glory of the Father;

17 And he received all power, both in heaven and on earth, and the glory of the Father was with him, for he dwelt in him. (D&C 93:11–17)

Joseph Fielding Smith explained that these statements by Luke and John the Baptist clearly teach that Jesus had the veil over His mind when He was born.

Without doubt, Jesus came into the world subject to the same condition as was required of each of us—he forgot everything, and he had to grow from grace to grace. His forgetting, or having his former knowledge taken away, would be requisite just as it is in the case of each of us, to complete the present temporal existence. (*Doctrines of Salvation*, Vol. 3, p. 33)

Elder James E. Talmage taught that Jesus had a relatively normal infancy which included the veil.

He came among men to experience all the natural conditions of mortality; He was born as truly a dependent, helpless babe as is any other child; His infancy was in all common features as the infancy of others; His boyhood was actual boyhood, His development was as necessary and as real as that of all children. Over His mind had fallen the veil of forgetfulness common to all who are born to earth, by which the remembrance of primeval existence is shut off. The Child grew, and with growth there came to Him expansion of mind, development of faculties, and progression in power and understanding. His advancement was from one grace to another, not from gracelessness to grace; from good to greater good, not from evil to good, from favor with God to greater favor, not from estrangement because of sin to reconciliation through repentance and propitiation. (*Jesus the Christ*, p. 111)

NO NEED TO BE TAUGHT BY MAN

The JST adds three verses to Matthew, which would fit right after Matthew 2:23 in our King James Version of the Bible (the chapter and verse numbering are different in this part of the JST).

24 *And it came to pass that Jesus grew up with his brethren, and waxed strong, and waited upon the Lord for the time of his ministry to come.*

25 *And he served under his father, and he spake not as other men, neither could he be taught; for he needed not that any man should teach him.*

26 *And after many years, the hour of his ministry drew nigh. (JST, Matthew 3:24–26)*

JESUS TAUGHT IN THE TEMPLE AT AGE TWELVE

Joseph Smith taught that while still young, Jesus had tremendous capacity that reflected His divine heritage.

> When still a boy He had all the intelligence necessary to enable Him to rule and govern the kingdom of the Jews, and could reason with the wisest and most profound doctors of law and divinity, and make their theories and practice to appear like folly compared with the wisdom He possessed; but He was a boy only, and lacked physical strength even to defend His own person; and was subject to cold, to hunger and to death. (*TPJS*, p. 392)

According to the above quote by Joseph Smith, Jesus was capable, at an early age, of reasoning "with the wisest and most profound" leaders among the Jews. We see this in Luke's account of the young Jesus in the temple at Jerusalem when He was twelve.

By way of background and setting, Mary and Joseph were devout and faithful to the law of Moses. Thus, they traveled from Nazareth to Jerusalem each year for the Feast of Passover. This seven-day religious feast was celebrated annually by faithful Jews in March or April, to commemorate the angel of death "passing over" Israelite homes and flocks and sparing the life of the first-born of each when the Israelites were in Egyptian bondage (Bible Dictionary, under "Feasts").

You may recall that Pharaoh would not free the children of Israel, who were slaves. Moses warned him that the firstborn of the Egyptians would be slain by the Lord if he did not let them go. Pharaoh refused. In preparation for that event, the Israelites were instructed by the Lord to place lamb's blood on the doorposts and lintel (the horizontal beam at the top of the doorway) of their homes to avoid having their firstborn slain. There is Atonement symbolism here. The lamb's blood represents the Savior's blood, shed for us to set us free from sin and permanent death. The death of the firstborn symbolized the death of the Firstborn of the Father in the flesh in order to set the Lord's people free from the bondage of sin. Hyssop, in verse 22, next, is also associated with the crucifixion of the Savior (John 19:29).

> 21 Then Moses called for all the elders of Israel, and said unto them, Draw out and take you a lamb according to your families, and kill the passover.
> 22 And ye shall take a bunch of hyssop, and dip it in the blood that is in the bason, and strike the lintel and the two side posts with the blood that is in the bason; and none of you shall go out at the door of his house until the morning. (Exodus 12:21–22)

And so Joseph and Mary traveled to Jerusalem for Passover, along with Jesus and probably some of His half-brothers and sisters who might have been born by the time He was twelve years old.

> 41 Now his parents went to Jerusalem every year at the feast of the passover.
> 42 And when he was twelve years old, they went up to Jerusalem after the custom of the feast. (Luke 2:41–42)

When they had finished their Passover worship and other purposes of the trip, they departed for Nazareth, along with other friends and relatives in their company of travelers. They assumed that Jesus was with relatives or friends in the group.

> 43 And when they had fulfilled the days, as they returned, the child Jesus tarried behind in Jerusalem; and Joseph and his mother knew not of it.
> 44 But they, supposing him to have been in the company, went a day's journey; and they sought him among their kinsfolk and acquaintance. (Luke 2:43–44)

You can imagine Joseph and Mary's alarm as they later looked for Jesus among the travelers and did not find Him. They returned to Jerusalem and finally found Him in the Temple, after three days of frantic searching. Small wonder that Mary expressed their concern about His disappearance to Him. In the meantime, the learned scholars in the temple were astounded at Him and His knowledge and understanding.

> 45 And when they found him not, they turned back again to Jerusalem, seeking him.
> 46 And it came to pass, that after three days they found him in the temple, sitting in the midst of the doctors, both hearing them, and asking them questions.
> 47 And all that heard him were astonished at his understanding and answers.
> 48 And when they saw him, they were amazed: and his mother said unto him, Son, why hast thou thus dealt with us? behold, thy father and I have sought thee sorrowing. (Luke 2:45–48)

The Prophet Joseph Smith made a significant change to verse 46, above. As it stands in the Bible, it indicates that Jesus was being taught by these learned doctors of the law of Moses and the laws of the Jews, and was asking them questions. In the JST, we see that it was the other way around. Jesus was teaching them, and they were asking Him questions.

> 46 And it came to pass, that after three days they found him in the temple, sitting in the midst of the doctors, *and they were hearing him, and asking him* questions. (JST, Luke 2:46)

Having found Jesus in the temple, and being amazed at what was taking place, they nevertheless expressed their concern about the worry He had caused them. Mary and Joseph were puzzled by His response.

49 And he said unto them, How is it that ye sought me? wist ye not that I must be about my Father's business?
50 And they understood not the saying which he spake unto them.

James E. Talmage suggests that Jesus' response to His mother's mild scolding was not unkind or insensitive. Rather, it was a gentle reminder that He was, in fact, the Son of the Father and had a mission to perform here on the earth.

Let us not say that there was unkind rebuke or unfilial reproof in the answer of this most dutiful of sons to His mother. His reply was to Mary a reminder of what she seems to have forgotten for the moment—the facts in the matter of her Son's paternity. She had used the words "thy father and I"; and her Son's response had brought anew to her mind the truth that Joseph was not the Boy's father. She appears to have been astonished that One so young should so thoroughly understand His position with respect to herself. He had made plain to her the inadvertent inaccuracy of her words; His Father had not been seeking Him; for was He not even at that moment in His Father's house, and particularly engaged in His Father's business, the very work to which His Father had appointed Him? He had in no wise intimated a doubt as to Mary's maternal relationship to Himself; though He had indisputably shown that He recognized as His Father, not Joseph of Nazareth, but the God of Heaven. Both Mary and Joseph failed to comprehend the full import of His words. Though He understood the superior claim of duty based on His divine Sonship, and had shown to Mary that her authority as earthly mother was subordinate to that of His Immortal and divine Father, nevertheless He obeyed her. Interested as were the doctors in this remarkable Boy, much as He had given them to ponder over through His searching questions and wise answers, they could not detain Him, for the very law they professed to uphold enjoined strict obedience to parental authority. (*Jesus the Christ*, p. 115)

The scriptures are silent as to any other details of the Savior's youth, other than to say that He returned with Joseph and Mary to Nazareth and was subject to them.

51 And he went down with them, and came to Nazareth, and was subject unto them: but his mother kept all these sayings in her heart. (Luke 2:51)

The next time we see Jesus, He will be poised to begin His formal three-year mortal mission, which will culminate in His Atonement, including Gethsemane, the cross, and His resurrection.

CHAPTER 11

THE FIRST YEAR OF THE SAVIOR'S MORTAL MISSION

The formal mortal mission of the Savior spanned about three years. He began His ministry shortly before the Passover, when He was thirty years old, and concluded it on the Passover three years later. The events of the last week of His life took place during Passover. The fact that His formal ministry was launched at Passover time is significant because there is much Atonement symbolism in this religious feast and celebration. In order to set us free from the bondage of death and sin, the Savior, the Lamb of God, who was to be the final great sacrifice, came upon the scene in Jerusalem at the time when the Jews were celebrating the very feast that symbolically represented Him.

The Feast of Passover was a major religious occasion among the Jews, and the faithful came in multitudes to Jerusalem from far and near to celebrate and worship. As originally instituted, it included lambs (symbolic of Christ) that were sacrificed and were to be males without blemish, relatively young (Exodus 12:5), whose blood was shed (Exodus 12:6–7) but whose bones were not to be broken (Exodus 12:46). The feast also included eating unleavened bread, or bread without yeast, and also bitter herbs (Exodus 12:8). Yeast was symbolic of corruption and sin in the culture of ancient Israel. Avoiding yeast in order to be set free from the bondage of sin by the Lord is significant symbolism. And of course bread would become symbolic of Christ, who was without sin and was the "Bread of Life" (John 6:35), who would provide spiritual nourishment for those who followed Him faithfully. Bitter herbs symbolized the bitter bondage of sin. The meal was to be eaten in haste while the person was fully dressed and prepared for action (Exodus 12:11), symbolizing, among other things, the urgency of being set free from bondage by following God's commandments and counsel.

As mentioned above, the final week of the Savior's mortal life likewise took place during the Feast of Passover. His suffering in the Garden of Gethsemane and His crucifixion on the cross would be the last great sacrifice for sin, fulfilling the law of Moses, which pointed the way to Him.

Returning now to the first year of the Savior's formal mortal ministry, it is interesting to note that Matthew, Mark, Luke, and John recorded only eighteen events in the Master's life during this first year. They will record twenty-seven events in the second year of His ministry, and seventy-two in the third year (*The Life and Teachings of Jesus and His Apostles*, p. 32).

JOHN THE BAPTIST PREPARES THE WAY

John the Baptist was given the daunting task of preparing the way for the Messiah among apostate Israel. Jesus paid him a very high compliment when He said of him:

> 28 For I say unto you, Among those that are born of women there is not a greater prophet than John the Baptist: but he that is least in the kingdom of God is greater than he. (Luke 7:28)

The last phrase of verse 28, above, can cause some confusion. Joseph Smith explained it to mean, in effect, that He, Jesus Christ, who was considered by the apostate Jews to be the least in the kingdom of God, was nevertheless greater than John the Baptist. We will include the quote from Joseph Smith in which he explained the above verse and gave three reasons John the Baptist was given such a compliment.

> The question arose from the saying of Jesus—"Among those that are born of women there is not a greater prophet than John the Baptist; but he that is least in the kingdom of God is greater than he." How is it that John was considered one of the greatest prophets? His miracles could not have constituted his greatness.
>
> First. He was entrusted with a divine mission of preparing the way before the face of the Lord. Whoever had such a trust committed to him before or since? No man.
>
> Secondly. He was entrusted with the important mission, and it was required at his hands, to baptize the Son of Man. Whoever had the honor of doing that? Whoever had so great a privilege and glory? Whoever led the Son of God into the waters of baptism, and had the privilege of beholding the Holy Ghost descend in the form of a dove, or rather in the *sign* of the dove, in witness of that administration? The sign of the dove was instituted before the creation of the world, a witness for the Holy Ghost, and the devil cannot come in the sign of a dove. The Holy Ghost is a personage, and is in the form of a personage. It does not confine itself to the *form* of the dove, but in *sign* of the dove. The Holy Ghost cannot be transformed into a dove; but the sign of a dove was given to John to signify the truth of

the deed, as the dove is an emblem or token of truth and innocence.

Thirdly. John, at that time, was the only legal administrator in the affairs of the kingdom there was then on the earth, and holding the keys of power. The Jews had to obey his instructions or be damned, by their own law; and Christ Himself fulfilled all righteousness in becoming obedient to the law which he had given to Moses on the mount, and thereby magnified it and made it honorable, instead of destroying it. The son of Zacharias wrested the keys, the kingdom, the power, the glory from the Jews, by the holy anointing and decree of heaven, and these three reasons constitute him the greatest prophet born of a woman. (*TPJS*, pp. 275–76)

After giving three reasons John the Baptist was one of the greatest prophets ever, Joseph then explained the second phrase of Luke 7:28.

Second question:—How was the least in the kingdom of heaven greater than he? In reply I asked—Whom did Jesus have reference to as being the least? Jesus was looked upon as having the least claim in God's kingdom, and [seemingly] was least entitled to their credulity as a prophet; as though He had said—"He that is considered the least among you is greater than John—that is I myself." (*TPJS*, p. 276)

The Apostle John recorded another statement by Jesus in which He described John the Baptist as "a burning and a shining light" (John 5:35). Many great prophets of the past foretold the coming of John the Baptist, including Lehi, in 1 Nephi 10:7–10; Nephi, in 1 Nephi 11:27; 2 Nephi 31:4–18; Isaiah, in Isaiah 40:3; and the angel Gabriel (who was Noah—Bible Dictionary, under "Noah") in Luke 1:4–44.

John the Baptist was about six months older than Jesus (the Baptist's mother, Elizabeth, was six months pregnant when Mary visited her—Luke 1:36), and his mother fled with him to hide in the wilderness in order to escape the cruel edict of Herod, who, in a vain attempt to kill the Christ child, commanded that all children two years old and under in the Bethlehem area be killed (Matthew 2:16). In fact, as previously mentioned, John's father, Zacharias, gave his life to protect the whereabouts of his young son (Matthew 23:35; see page 90).

The Doctrine and Covenants gives a few more details about John the Baptist's early preparation for his unique mission.

28 For he was baptized while he was yet in his childhood, and was ordained by the angel of God at the time he was eight days old unto this power, to overthrow the kingdom of the Jews, and to make straight the way of the Lord before the face of his people, to prepare them for the coming of the Lord, in whose hand is given all power. (D&C 84:28)

Elder Bruce R. McConkie gave additional clarification to the revelation in the Doctrine and Covenants, referred to above, as follows:

We do know that "he was baptized while he was yet in his childhood [meaning, when he was eight years of age], and was ordained by the angel of God at the time he was eight days old unto this power [note it well, not to the Aaronic Priesthood, but] to overthrow the kingdom of the Jews, and to make straight the way of the Lord before the face of his people, to prepare them for the coming of the Lord, in whose hand is given all power." (D&C 84:24.) We do not know when he received the Aaronic Priesthood, but obviously it came to him after his baptism, at whatever age was proper, and before he was sent by one whom he does not name to preach and baptize with water." (*Mortal Messiah*, pp. 384–85)

When the time was right, "the word of God came unto John the son of Zacharias in the wilderness" (Luke 3:2), instructing him to come and begin actively preparing the way for the Savior. It had been prophesied that an "Elias," defined as "a title for one who is a forerunner" (Bible Dictionary, under "Elias") would come and prepare the way for the Lord. In this case, the "Elias" was John the Baptist. Isaiah prophesied of his coming. John the Baptist was the fulfillment of this prophecy.

3 The voice of him that crieth in the wilderness, Prepare ye the way of the LORD, make straight in the desert a highway for our God. (Isaiah 40:3)

Matthew verifies that John the Baptist was the fulfillment of Isaiah's prophecy as he sets the stage for the baptism of Jesus.

1 In those days came John the Baptist, preaching in the wilderness of Judæa,
2 And saying, Repent ye: for the kingdom of heaven is at hand.
3 For this is he that was spoken of by the prophet Esaias, saying, The voice of one crying in the wilderness, Prepare ye the way of the Lord, make his paths straight. (Matthew 3:1–3)

The Joseph Smith Translation makes a change that alters the whole meaning of verse 3, above. (This change is not cited in our current LDS edition of the King James Bible, but is included in the original text of the JST. There are a number of changes made by the Prophet Joseph Smith that are not included in our Bible because of space limitations.)

29 For *I am* he who was spoken of by the prophet Esaias, saying, The voice of one crying in the wilderness, Prepare ye the way of the Lord and make his paths straight. (JST, Matthew 3:29)

Remember that John had come from an upbringing in the wilderness and his clothing and food, as described by Matthew, reflected that difficult and Spartan existence.

4 And the same John had his raiment of camel's hair, and a leathern girdle about his loins; and his meat [*food*] was locusts and wild honey. (Matthew 3:4)

It is interesting to note that in spite of the rampant apostasy among the Jews at the time John began his mission to prepare the way for the Savior, he drew huge crowds who came to him to be baptized, confessing their sins (Matthew 3:5–6). This might well indicate that there were many who were honest in heart and who did not approve of the gross hypocrisy prevalent among the scribes and Pharisees, the Sadducees, and other religious leaders among the Jews at the time.

John the Baptist was a great and tender teacher. Luke gives us insight into the variety of people who came to the Baptist and responded to his invitation to repent and be baptized. After he had warned them not to rely on their righteous ancestor, Abraham, for salvation (Luke 3:8), and had counseled them to do good works, warning what would happen if they did not "bring forth good fruit" (Luke 3:9), several groups came to him and asked what they should do. These included the general population, some publicans (tax collectors) and some soldiers. Watch how John, as a master teacher, responded to each group.

10 And the people asked him, saying, What shall we do then?
11 He answereth and saith unto them, He that hath two coats, let him impart to him that hath none; and he that hath meat, let him do likewise.
12 Then came also publicans to be baptized, and said unto him, Master, what shall we do?
13 And he said unto them, Exact no more than that which is appointed you.
14 And the soldiers likewise demanded of him, saying, And what shall we do? And he said unto them, Do violence to no man, neither accuse any falsely; and be content with your wages. (Luke 3:10–14)

We gain additional insights into John's greatness as a teacher of righteousness and a witness of Jesus Christ from the Joseph Smith Translation of the Bible. The Prophet added a little over five verses that were left out of the Bible and fit at the end of Luke 3:4. The JST additions consist of verses 5 through 9, and include the phrase "For it is a day of power; yea," in verse 10.

5 *For behold, and lo, he shall come, as it is written in the book of the prophets, to take away the sins of the world, and to bring salvation unto the heathen nations, to gather together those who are lost, who are of the sheepfold of Israel;*
6 *Yea, even the dispersed and afflicted; and also to prepare the way, and make possible the preaching of the gospel unto the Gentiles;*
7 *And to be a light unto all who sit in darkness, unto the uttermost parts of the earth; to bring to pass the resurrection from the dead, and to ascend*

> *up on high, to dwell on the right hand of the Father,*
> 8 *Until the fulness of time, and the law and the testimony shall be sealed, and the keys of the kingdom shall be delivered up again unto the Father;*
> 9 *To administer justice unto all; to come down in judgment upon all, and to convince all the ungodly of their ungodly deeds, which they have committed; and all this in the day that he shall come;*
> 10 *For it is a day of power; yea, every valley shall be filled, and every mountain and hill shall be brought low; the crooked shall be made straight, and the rough ways made smooth.* (JST, Luke 3:5–10)

We gain yet more insights into John's message from the Doctrine and Covenants. From these verses, we understand that there is a considerable amount of information about John the Baptist that is missing from the Bible. The Savior Himself speaks about John the Baptist to Joseph Smith, and then quotes John bearing witness of Him.

> 6 And John saw and bore record of the fulness of my glory, and the fulness of John's record is hereafter to be revealed.
> 7 And he bore record, saying: I saw his glory, that he was in the beginning, before the world was;
> 8 Therefore, in the beginning the Word was, for he was the Word, even the messenger of salvation—
> 9 The light and the Redeemer of the world; the Spirit of truth, who came into the world, because the world was made by him, and in him was the life of men and the light of men.
> 10 The worlds were made by him; men were made by him; all things were made by him, and through him, and of him.
> 11 And I, John, bear record that I beheld his glory, as the glory of the Only Begotten of the Father, full of grace and truth, even the Spirit of truth, which came and dwelt in the flesh, and dwelt among us. (D&C 93:6–11)

Next, the Baptist explains, in effect, that Jesus had the veil over His memory of premortality in the beginning of His mortal life. He continued growing and progressing until He received a "fulness."

> 12 And I, John, saw that he received not of the fulness at the first, but received grace for grace;
> 13 And he received not of the fulness at first, but continued from grace to grace, until he received a fulness;
> 14 And thus he was called the Son of God, because he received not of the fulness at the first. (D&C 93:12–14)

The next verse of John's testimony bears witness to us that the Father as well as the Holy Ghost were present when John baptized the Savior.

15 And I, John, bear record, and lo, the heavens were opened, and the Holy Ghost descended upon him in the form of a dove, and sat upon him, and there came a voice out of heaven saying: This is my beloved Son. (D&C 9:15)

This revealed portion of the record of John the Baptist concludes with his testimony that Jesus continued on to receive all power, and that He and the Father worked in complete harmony and were in constant communication.

16 And I, John, bear record that he received a fulness of the glory of the Father;
17 And he received all power, both in heaven and on earth, and the glory of the Father was with him, for he dwelt in him.
18 And it shall come to pass, that if you are faithful you shall receive the fulness of the record of John. (D&C 93:16–18)

We will continue with the Savior's baptism, after making one observation about baptism itself, in conjunction with the large multitudes that flocked to John the Baptist.

BAPTISM WAS NOT NEW

In reading Matthew's introduction to the beginning of the mission of John the Baptist (Matthew 3:1–12), have you noticed that there was no expression of curiosity and wonder among the throngs at the fact that John was baptizing people? There is no mention at all of concern that he was saying a prayer and then immersing people in water. There is a good reason for this. Baptism was a common ordinance in ancient times (Bible Dictionary, under "Baptism"). In fact, a number of baptismal fonts are still found today among the ruins of ancient Israel. Adam was baptized (Moses 6:64–65). Noah taught baptism, along with the other first principles of the gospel before the Flood (Moses 8:24). Up until 3 Nephi, the Book of Mormon is an "Old Testament times" book of scripture and contains many examples of baptism long before the coming of John the Baptist and the Savior among the Jews. Paul speaks of baptism among the children of Israel (1 Corinthians 10:1–4).

John's major purpose, as reflected in his teaching and baptizing, was to prepare people's hearts and minds to accept Jesus as the Messiah. This is reflected in his humble teaching to the multitudes which followed him.

11 I indeed baptize you with water unto repentance: but he that cometh after me is mightier than I, whose shoes I am not worthy to bear: he shall baptize you with the Holy Ghost, and with fire. (Matthew 3:11)

By the way, fire, as used in verse 11, above, is symbolic of the Holy Ghost, and can refer, among other things, to the "burning" of our conscience, as He inspires us to repent and do better. It can also refer to the "burning" testimony and witness that the Holy Ghost gives us as He bears witness to our hearts and minds that the gospel is true and Jesus is the Christ.

THE BAPTISM OF JESUS

The first recorded public event of the Savior's adult life was His baptism by John the Baptist. The scriptures inform us that it took place "in Bethabara" (John 1:28), in the Jordan River near Jericho, about 25 miles from Jerusalem. John had been baptizing in that area. Matthew tells us what took place on that momentous day.

> 13 Then cometh Jesus from Galilee to Jordan unto John, to be baptized of him.
> 14 But John forbad him, saying, I have need to be baptized of thee, and comest thou to me?
> 15 And Jesus answering said unto him, Suffer [*allow*] it to be so now: for thus it becometh us to fulfil all righteousness [*it is necessary in order to fulfill the Father's will*]. Then he suffered him.
> 16 And Jesus, when he was baptized, went up straightway out of the water [*a reminder that He was baptized by immersion*]: and, lo, the heavens were opened unto him, and he saw the Spirit of God descending like a dove, and lighting upon him:
> 17 And lo a voice from heaven, saying, This is my beloved Son, in whom I am well pleased. (Matthew 3:13–17)

The JST adds a verse that is missing from the Bible, which fits in at the end of verse 15, above. It also makes changes to verses 15–17. The changes are indicated here by the use of italics. Remember, as previously mentioned, that verse numbers in the JST sometimes differ from our King James Version of the Bible because of inspired changes made by the Prophet Joseph Smith, including verses restored that were previously missing.

> 43 And Jesus, answering, said unto him, Suffer *me to be baptized of thee,* for thus it becometh us to fulfill all righteousness. Then he suffered him.
> 44 *And John went down into the water and baptized him.*
> 45 And Jesus when he was baptized, went up straightway out of the water; *and John saw,* and lo, the heavens were opened unto him, and he saw the Spirit of God descending like a dove and lighting upon *Jesus.*
> 46 And lo, *he heard* a voice from heaven, saying, This is my beloved Son, in whom I am well pleased. *Hear ye him.* (JST, Matthew 3:43–46)

We will take a moment here to quote Joseph Smith as he made a doctrinal clarification concerning the Holy Ghost, namely, that He does not occasionally transform Himself into a dove. He taught:

> The sign of the dove was instituted before the creation of the world, a witness for the Holy Ghost. . . . The Holy Ghost is a personage, and is in the form of a personage. It does not confine itself to the *form* of the dove, but in *sign* of the dove. The Holy Ghost cannot be transformed into a dove; but the sign of a dove was given to John to signify the truth of the deed, as the dove is an emblem or token of truth and innocence." (*TPJS*, pp. 275–76)

All three members of the Godhead were represented as separate and distinct personages at the baptism of the Savior. Jesus, of course, was there in person. John saw the Holy Ghost descending like a dove upon Christ. And the Father's voice was heard from heaven expressing His approval of His Son and instructing John to listen carefully to Him.

DID JESUS NEED BAPTISM?

Did Jesus actually need to be baptized, or did He simply submit to baptism in order to be an example to us for whom it is required? The answer is found in the Book of Mormon. Nephi spoke of this near the end of his own ministry, about 550 BC. He tells us that the Lord had shown him the future, and he saw John the Baptist baptize Jesus. He then points out that if the Savior, who was perfect, needed baptism, "how much more need have we, being unholy, to be baptized, yea, even by water!" (2 Nephi 31:4–5). Then, as the great teacher that he was, Nephi asks us a question:

> 6 And now, I would ask of you, my beloved brethren, wherein the Lamb of God did fulfil all righteousness in being baptized by water?
> 7 Know ye not that he was holy? (2 Nephi 31:6–7)

Having aroused our curiosity, Nephi then proceeds to give us the doctrine as to why Jesus was baptized. The first reason he gives is that obedience to this commandment of the Father was absolutely necessary for Him just as it is for us. Continuing with verse 7, above:

> 7 But notwithstanding he being holy, he showeth unto the children of men that, according to the flesh he humbleth himself before the Father, and witnesseth unto the Father that he would be obedient unto him in keeping his commandments. (2 Nephi 31:7)

The doctrine here is clear. Baptism is a commandment and a requirement for entry into the celestial glory (D&C 76:51). Those who are not baptized will be "damned" or "stopped" (Mark 16:16). Exceptions are "children who die before they arrive at the years of accountability" and who thus "are saved in the celestial kingdom of heaven" (D&C 137:10), plus some intellectually handicapped (D&C 29:50).

Continuing, Nephi gives another reason that the Savior, who was perfect, was baptized. It was to show us that there is not a large number of paths that can lead back to the presence of God. Rather, there is just one path, and one gate that leads into this path, namely, proper baptism:

> 9 And again, it showeth unto the children of men the straitness of the path, and the narrowness of the gate, by which they should enter. (2 Nephi 31:9)

A third important reason given by Nephi is that the Master set the example for all of us to follow:

> 9 He having set the example before them.
> 10 And he said unto the children of men: Follow thou me. Wherefore, my beloved brethren, can we follow Jesus save we shall be willing to keep the commandments of the Father? (2 Nephi 31:9–10)

TEMPTED BY THE DEVIL

In a revelation given to Joseph Smith, the Lord said, "I will give unto you a pattern in all things" (D&C 52:14). Patterns are mentioned in many other scriptures (Topical Guide, under "Pattern"). It seems to be a rather common pattern that Satan is extra forceful in tempting and pressing his wiles upon us just when we are about to embark on an important mission or calling in the work of God. Such was the case for young Joseph Smith when he went into the grove to pray and consequently received the First Vision (JS—History 1:15). This pattern was evident at the beginning of the Savior's mortal ministry. After being baptized by John the Baptist, Jesus went into the Wilderness of Judea to be with God. He "fasted forty days and forty nights" (Matthew 4:2). Satan's timing was, as usual, aimed to coincide with a time of extra potential for weakness, in this case when the Savior was extremely hungry. We will use Matthew's account and the JST corrections to it as we study this part of the beginning of Christ's mortal ministry. Matthew's account is an example of where the Bible is not translated correctly (Article of Faith 1:8).

> 1 Then was Jesus led up of the Spirit into the wilderness to be tempted of the devil. (Matthew 4:1)

> > 1 Then was Jesus led up of the Spirit into the wilderness to be *with God*. (JST, Matthew 4:1)

There is much doctrinal significance in the inspired change made by the Prophet Joseph Smith. Among other things, one important message we see here is that we are not to intentionally place ourselves in the path of temptation. The Savior prayed, "Lead us not into temptation" (Matthew 6:13). And if you look at Matthew 6:13, footnote b, in your Bible, you will see that "do not let us enter into temptation" is given as another translation of this phrase. We understand that temptation will come to us as a result of being here on earth (2 Nephi 2:11), but we should not deliberately place ourselves in tempting circumstances.

Thus, Jesus did not go into the wilderness so that Satan could tempt Him. But the devil did tempt Him, at a time of particular physical weakness because of hunger, just as he and his evil spirits tempt us, especially during times of extra weakness. Jesus went through everything we go through and much more, in order that "he may know according to the flesh how to succor his people according to their infirmities" (Alma 7:12).

> 2 And when he had fasted forty days and forty nights, he was afterward an hungred. (Matthew 4:2)

> > 2 And when he had fasted forty days and forty nights, *and had communed with God*, he was afterwards an hungered, *and was left to be tempted of the devil.* (JST, Matthew 4:2)

And so we see that Jesus went into the wilderness to be with God, fasted and communed with His Father, and then Satan came with his scheme to thwart the Savior's work at the onset of His ministry. Paul reminds us that part of the Savior's mortal experience was to be tempted, and that He was indeed tempted in all things with which we are tempted, yet, He did not yield to it.

> 18 For in that he himself hath suffered being tempted, he is able to succour [*help, nourish*] them that are tempted. (Hebrews 2:18)

> 15 For we have not an high priest [*Jesus is sometimes referred to as the "Great High Priest"*] which cannot be touched with the feeling of our infirmities [*in other words, we do not have a Savior who is unable to sympathize with our weaknesses*]; but was in all points tempted like as we are, yet without sin. (Hebrews 4:15)

The devil tempted the Savior with three major categories of sin, with which he likewise tempts us.

1. Physical appetites (Matthew 4:3)
2. Vanity and pride (Matthew 4:6)
3. Materialism and power (Matthew 4:9)

In addition, you will see another form of temptation associated with the above-mentioned temptations. It is the word *if* in verses 3, 6, and 9. The devil challenged Jesus to prove that He was indeed the Son of God. This "if" challenge can be a very effective tool for Satan as he likewise challenges us to "prove it." People often find themselves committing sin or taking foolish chances in order to respond to someone who is suggesting that they are not what they claim to be.

We will continue, using Matthew's account of the temptation of Christ by the devil, and include JST corrections. We will add some commentary within the verses.

> 3 And when the tempter [*Satan*] came to him, he said, If thou be the Son of God, command that these stones be made bread [*temptation to yield to physical appetite*].
> 4 But he answered and said, It is written [*in Deuteronomy 8:3*], Man shall not live by bread alone, but by every word that proceedeth out of the mouth of God.
> 5 Then the devil taketh him up into the holy city [*Jerusalem*], and setteth him on a pinnacle of the temple.

The JST makes an important correction here. The devil was not transporting Jesus, as if He were under his power and control.

> 5 Then *Jesus was taken* up into the holy city, and *the Spirit* setteth him on *the* pinnacle of the temple. (JST, Matthew 4:5)

Continuing with Matthew's account:

> 6 And saith unto him, If thou be the Son of God, cast thyself down: for it is written [*in Psalm 91:11–12*], He shall give his angels charge concerning thee: and in their hands they shall bear thee up, lest at any time thou dash thy foot against a stone [*temptation to yield to vanity, pride*].

Again, a JST correction:

> 6 *Then the devil came unto him and said,* If thou be the Son of God, cast thyself down, for it is written, He shall give his angels charge concerning thee, and in their hands they shall bear thee up, lest at any time thou dash thy foot against a stone. (JST, Matthew 4:6)

Did you notice that Satan quoted scripture here, as part of his temptation of Christ? It is important for us to realize that the devil knows them well and can use the scriptures in an attempt to further his evil causes. Perhaps you've noticed that he often uses the scriptures to cause contention between various religious groups.

7 Jesus said unto him, It is written again [*in Deuteronomy 6:16*], Thou shalt not tempt the Lord thy God.

Note that Jesus answers each temptation with a scriptural quote. This is a reminder of the power of the scriptures to safeguard us against successful temptation.

8 Again, the devil taketh him up into an exceeding high mountain, and sheweth him all the kingdoms of the world, and the glory of them.

Again, the JST teaches that it was the Spirit who was transporting the Savior here, not the devil.

8 *And again, Jesus was in the Spirit, and it* taketh him up into an exceeding high mountain, and showeth him all the kingdoms of the world and the glory of them. (JST, Matthew 4:8)

Next, the devil tempts Jesus with materialism. When you stop to think about it, this does not make much sense, since Christ is the Creator and "the earth is the Lord's, and the fulness thereof" (Psalm 24:1). Furthermore, Satan does not own a thing here to give us—a stark reminder that his promises are ultimately empty!

9 And saith unto him, All these things will I give thee, if thou wilt fall down and worship me [*temptation to yield to materialism and power*].

9 *And the devil came unto him again, and said*, All these things will I give unto thee, if thou wilt fall down and worship me. (JST, Matthew 4:9)

At the conclusion of these temptations, the Savior commanded Satan to depart, again quoting scripture.

10 Then saith Jesus unto him, Get thee hence [*leave Me*], Satan: for it is written [*in Deuteronomy 6:13*], Thou shalt worship the Lord thy God, and him only shalt thou serve.
11 Then the devil leaveth him, and, behold, angels came and ministered unto him.

The devil was unsuccessful in his attempts to stop Christ at the beginning of His formal three-year mission to preach the gospel and accomplish all His Father had sent Him here to do, including the Atonement. As you know, Satan will continue his efforts to stop God's work, and will resort to stirring up the people and the religious leaders of the Jews against the Master.

JOHN THE BAPTIST BEARS WITNESS OF CHRIST

After baptizing Jesus, John the Baptist was still preaching and baptizing in the area where he had baptized Him. To his followers and those who had come out of curiosity to see him, he bore strong witness of the divine mission of Jesus as the promised Messiah.

15 John [*the Baptist*] bare [*bore*] witness of him [*Christ*], and cried [*preached*], saying, This was he of whom I spake, He that cometh after me is preferred before me [*is higher in authority than I am*]: for he was before me.

> 15 John *bear* witness of him, and cried, saying, This *is* he of whom I spake; He *who* cometh after me, is preferred before me; for he was before me. (JST, John 1:15)

16 And of his fulness have all we received, and grace for grace.

> 16 *For in the beginning was the Word, even the Son, who is made flesh, and sent unto us by the will of the Father, And as many as believe on his name shall receive of his fulness.* And of his fulness have all we received, *even immortality and eternal life, through his grace.* (JST, John 1:16)

17 For the law [*law of Moses*] was given by Moses, but grace and truth [*salvation and exaltation*] came by Jesus Christ.

> 17 For the law was given *through* Moses, but *life* and truth came *through* Jesus Christ.
> 18 *For the law was after a carnal commandment, to the administration of death; but the gospel was after the power of an endless life, through Jesus Christ, the Only Begotten Son, who is in the bosom of the Father.* (JST, John 1:17–18)

Verse 17 and JST verse 18, above, are basically saying that the law of Moses was a schoolmaster law to help prepare the Israelites for the higher law which the Savior restored to earth. No one could be saved in celestial exaltation through the law of Moses. It is only through the full gospel, with all covenants and ordinances, that we can be exalted. By the way, this would not be a particularly popular thing for John the Baptist to say, because people of his day would look upon it as a "put down" for Moses, whom they considered to be their most important prophet. John the Baptist concluded this part of his testimony of Christ by making a statement that was not translated correctly in the Bible, and that many use against the Church.

> 18 No man hath seen God at any time; the only begotten Son, which is in the bosom of the Father, he hath declared him. (John 1:18)

The JST makes a vital change in restoring this verse to match the original statement by John the Baptist.

> 19 *And* no man hath seen God at any time, *except he hath borne record of the Son; for except it is through him no man can be saved.* (JST, John 1:19)

In the course of events, the Jewish leaders in Jerusalem, who were somewhat exasperated by John's work and widespread popularity, sent representatives to ask the Baptist, "Who art thou?" (John 1:19). He responded, telling them that he was the "Elias" who, according to prophecy, was to prepare the way for the Savior. But he assured them that he was "not the Christ" (John 1:20). By the way, "Christ" means "the anointed" or "Messiah" (Bible Dictionary, under "Christ").

The next day, Jesus came again to the location in which John was preaching and John again bore witness of Him to the multitude. What John was doing was very unselfish. He himself was popular and had many followers. Many men would be protective of their position and popularity and would be jealous of anyone who started taking their admirers away from them. But John is a humble prophet who gladly fulfills his mission to prepare the way for the Master and turn his followers over to Him. As you will see later, within this group of loyal followers of the Baptist are some who will become Apostles of the Savior. There are some translation mistakes in the Bible verses here that leave one wondering why John would not have recognized the Savior. He did, as the JST will point out.

> 29 The next day John seeth Jesus coming unto him, and saith, Behold the Lamb of God, which taketh away the sin of the world.
> 30 This is he of whom I said, After me cometh a man which is preferred before me: for he was before me.
> 31 And I knew him not: but that he should be made manifest to Israel, therefore am I come baptizing with water.
> 32 And John bare record, saying, I saw the Spirit descending from heaven like a dove, and it abode upon him.
> 33 And I knew him not: but he that sent me to baptize with water, the same said unto me, Upon whom thou shalt see the Spirit descending, and remaining on him, the same is he which baptizeth with the Holy Ghost.
> 34 And I saw, and bare record that this is the Son of God. (John 1:29–34)

The JST makes very significant changes, pointing out among other things that John the Baptist did recognize Jesus.

29 The next day John seeth Jesus coming unto him, and said; Behold the Lamb of God, who taketh away the sin of the world!

30 *And John bare record of him unto the people, saying,* This is he of whom I said; After me cometh a man who is preferred before me; for he was before me, and I knew him, *and* that he should be made manifest to Israel; therefore am I come baptizing with water.

31 And John bare record, saying; *When he was baptized of me,* I saw the Spirit descending from heaven like a dove, and it abode upon him.

32 And I knew him; *for* he *who* sent me to baptize with water, the same said unto me; Upon whom thou shalt see the Spirit descending, and remaining on him, the same is he who baptizeth with the Holy Ghost.

33 And I saw, and bare record that this is the Son of God.

34 *These things were done in Bethabara, beyond Jordan, where John was baptizing.* (JST, John 1:29–34)

TWO OF JOHN'S DISCIPLES FOLLOW JESUS

The next day, the Baptist and two of his loyal disciples (followers) were standing together when Jesus walked by. John, who had taught them about Jesus and borne witness often that He was the promised Savior, looked toward the Master as He walked by and said to these men, "Behold the Lamb of God" (John 1:36), in effect saying, "Brethren, you are looking at the Son of God, who will be sacrificed for the sins of the world." Upon hearing this, the two began following Jesus. One of the two was Andrew, Peter's brother (John 1:40). The other was John (John the beloved Apostle—*Jesus the Christ,* p. 140). It is interesting to note that John, the author of the Gospel of John, does not refer directly to himself by name in his writings; rather, he uses indirect references to himself. Examples are "the other disciple" (John 20:4) and "the disciple whom Jesus loved" (John 21:20).

As Andrew and John began following the Savior, He suddenly stopped, turned around toward them and asked what He could do for them (John 1:38). It appears that they were somewhat caught off guard. Perhaps embarrassed and at a loss for something to say, they quickly stammered, "Master, where dwellest thou?" (John 1:38). Of course we don't know if this was the situation, but it brings a smile to our faces when we consider that they apparently felt a bit awkward. Whatever the case, He was very kind to them and invited them to "come and see" (John 1:39).

It appears from the account in John that Andrew wanted to go and get his brother, Peter, at this point, and that Jesus waited for him to do so. Imagine Peter's astonishment when he met Jesus and the Master spoke to him, giving specifics about him and prophesying that he would become a "seer" (JST, John 1:42).

> 40 One of the two which heard John speak, and followed him, was Andrew, Simon Peter's brother.
> 41 He first findeth his own brother Simon [*Peter*], and saith unto him, We have found the Messias, which is, being interpreted, the Christ.
> 42 And he brought him to Jesus. And when Jesus beheld him, he said, Thou art Simon the son of Jona: thou shalt be called Cephas, which is by interpretation, A stone. (John 1:40–42)

>> 42 And he brought him to Jesus. And when Jesus beheld him, he said, Thou art Simon, the son of Jona, thou shalt be called Cephas, which is, by interpretation, *a seer, or* a stone. *And they were fishermen. And they straightway left all, and followed Jesus.* (JST, John 1:42)

All three, Andrew, John, and Peter, will be among the original Twelve Apostles chosen by Jesus.

To Galilee: More Future Apostles

At this point, the Savior expressed His desire to go to Galilee (in northern Israel; John 1:43). He spent approximately two of the three years of His mortal mission in Galilee, a province in the northwestern part of Palestine. Along the way, He met Philip (who will become one of the original twelve Apostles), "and saith unto him, Follow me" (John 1:43). Philip had a friend, Nathanael (usually known as Bartholomew, who will likewise become one of the original Twelve). Philip's excitement is evident as he tells Nathanael that they have found the Messiah. Nathanael had apparently had negative experience with residents of Nazareth, but it took but a moment for him to gain a testimony that Jesus was, indeed, the promised Messiah.

> 45 Philip findeth Nathanael, and saith unto him, We have found him, of whom Moses in the law, and the prophets, did write, Jesus of Nazareth, the son of Joseph.
> 46 And Nathanael said unto him, Can there any good thing come out of Nazareth? Philip saith unto him, Come and see.
> 47 Jesus saw Nathanael coming to him, and saith of him, Behold an Israelite indeed, in whom is no guile!

Nathanael, like Peter, was no doubt amazed that Jesus knew him so well. The Master demonstrated His divine power, as He not only read Nathanael's mind and heart, but also told him that He saw him under the fig tree where he was when Philip went to find him and bring him to see Jesus.

48 Nathanael saith unto him, Whence knowest thou me? Jesus answered and said unto him, Before that Philip called thee, when thou wast under the fig tree, I saw thee.

49 Nathanael answered and saith unto him, Rabbi, thou art the Son of God; thou art the King of Israel.

50 Jesus answered and said unto him, Because I said unto thee, I saw thee under the fig tree, believest thou? thou shalt see greater things than these.

51 And he saith unto him, Verily, verily, I say unto you, Hereafter ye shall see heaven open, and the angels of God ascending and descending upon the Son of man. (John 1:45–51)

It may be helpful to pause for a moment and discuss the phrase "Son of man" in verse 51, above. The correct term is "Son of Man" with the "m" in "man" capitalized. The complete phrase is "Son of Man of Holiness," meaning "Son of Heavenly Father." This is explained in Moses 6:57. For whatever reason, the printers of the King James Version of the Bible (the one the Church uses for English-speaking members) did not use an uppercase "m" for "man."

The Savior has now invited five future Apostles to follow Him: Andrew, John, Peter, Philip, and Nathanael (who is referred to by Matthew, Mark, and Luke as Bartholomew). You can find the names of all of the original Twelve in Luke 6:13–16.

THE FIRST RECORDED MIRACLE

Changing Water to Wine

The first recorded miracle by the Savior, according to John (John 2:11), was done at a marriage feast that was being held in Cana, a town about ten miles north of Nazareth, in Galilee. It is apparent that Jesus' mother, Mary, was much involved in the hosting of this celebration. Some have wondered if this could be Jesus' own marriage, thus providing scriptural evidence that He was married. Several factors combine to suggest that this marriage celebration does not provide such evidence. For one thing, in the culture of the day, the marriage would be held at the groom's hometown. If it were Jesus' wedding, it would have been held in Nazareth. Another thing against the notion that it was His wedding is that He and His disciples were invited to attend (verse 2). This would be a bit strange if He were the groom. Yet another factor is that the master of ceremonies of the festivities called the groom over to talk to him (verse 9), and there is no indication that this was Jesus. And finally, if it were Christ's wedding, one would expect the other Gospel writers to mention it. Whatever Mary's involvement was, she knew who her Son was, and when they ran out of wine, she requested His help. As you will see, the JST will make significant contributions to the Bible here.

> 1 And the third day there was a marriage in Cana of Galilee; and the mother of Jesus was there. (John 2:1)

>> 1 And on the third day *of the week*, there was a marriage in Cana of Galilee; and the mother of Jesus was there. (JST, John 2:1)

> 2 And both Jesus was called [*invited*], and his disciples, to the marriage.
> 3 And when they wanted [*lacked; ran out of*] wine, the mother of Jesus saith unto him, They have no wine.
> 4 Jesus saith unto her, Woman, what have I to do with thee? mine hour is not yet come. (John 2:2–4)

The JST change for verse four makes all the difference as to how Jesus responded to His mother's request.

> 4 Jesus said unto her, Woman, *what wilt thou have me to do for* thee? *that will I do; for* mine hour is not yet come. (JST, John 2:4)

"Woman" in verse 4 sounds disrespectful in our culture, but it is a term of high regard and respect in the culture of Jesus' day. We understand that the phrase "mine hour is not yet come" in verse 4 is a way of saying, in effect, that Jesus had not yet begun His formal mission. Perhaps it includes the idea that the time had not yet come in His plans to have large crowds following Him and His little group of disciples. Another possibility is that He was simply saying to His mother that He had plenty of time to do what she needed Him to do. Whatever the case, Mary, no doubt with great relief, instructed some of the others who were assisting with the feast to follow Jesus' instructions carefully.

> 5 His mother saith unto the servants, Whatsoever he saith unto you, do it.
> 6 And there were set there six waterpots of stone, after the manner of the purifying of the Jews, containing two or three firkins apiece. (John 2:5–6)

When we do the math, we see that this was apparently a rather large wedding celebration. Wedding feasts customarily lasted the better part of a week, and it appears that there were more guests than expected at this one. A "firkin" was a little more that 8 gallons (Bible Dictionary, under "Weights and Measures," then under "bath" and "firkin"). So, there were six containers, with a capacity of 16 to 24 gallons each (verse 6). This would make a total of about 96 to 144 gallons of water which Jesus turned into wine. Therefore, we sense that this was a rather unexpectedly large group, which apparently caught the host off guard when it came to having sufficient wine for the festivities. Imagine the looks on the servants' faces as they carried out the Master's instructions, next.

> 7 Jesus saith unto them, Fill the waterpots with water. And they filled them up to the brim.
> 8 And he saith unto them, Draw out now, and bear unto [*take the resulting drink to*] the governor [*master of ceremonies*] of the feast. And they bare it.
> 9 When the ruler of the feast had tasted the water that was made wine, and knew not whence it was: (but the servants which drew the water knew;) the governor of the feast called the bridegroom,
> 10 And saith unto him, Every man at the beginning doth set forth good wine; and when men have well drunk, then that which is worse: but thou hast kept the good wine until now.

As explained by the master of ceremonies to the groom in verse 10, it was the custom to save a little money on wine by serving the best first. Then when the guests had drunk enough to become less discriminating, less expensive wine was served to save on expenses. The master of ceremonies was surprised that the groom was serving the best wine at this point of the feast.

The JST emphasizes the role of this miracle in strengthening the testimonies and faith of the small group of disciples that was following the Savior at this point in His mission.

> 11 This beginning of miracles did Jesus in Cana of Galilee, and manifested forth his glory; and his disciples believed on him. (John 2:1–11)

> 11 This beginning of miracles did Jesus in Cana of Galilee, and manifested forth his glory; and *the faith of his disciples was strengthened in him.* (JST, John 2:11)

The changing of the water to wine is a strong reminder of the Savior's power over the elements. He can command and they obey, just as they did as He created the earth. He uses His powers to bless our lives. And He tenderly responded to the needs and desires of His mother, Mary, on this particularly occasion, even though it was apparently not in His plan to draw this type of attention to Himself this early in His mortal mission.

To Capernaum

The next recorded move of the Savior was to Capernaum, a town on the northern shore of the Sea of Galilee. It was a very busy, crowded, and prosperous area and was the home of Peter, Andrew, and Matthew. It was here that Jesus chose to live after turning water to wine at Cana. We will see many references to Capernaum, including many miracles performed here. In fact, the Master performed more miracles here than in any other place during His mortal ministry. But at this point near the beginning of His public ministry, there is just a one verse reference to it, indicating that the Savior was there for just a few days before traveling to Jerusalem in Judea for the Passover. The fact that there is no mention of Joseph in this verse leads us to wonder whether or not he has passed away by this time. We understand the word *brethren*, in verse 12, next, to mean family members, probably including some or all of His half-brothers and sisters who were mentioned by Mark (Mark 6:3).

> 12 After this he went down to Capernaum, he, and his mother, and his brethren, and his disciples: and they continued there not many days. (John 2:12)

TO JERUSALEM

The First Passover of His Ministry

At this point in time, the few recorded events of the Savior's adult life, including His baptism, calling some humble men to follow Him, and helping His mother by turning the water to wine at the marriage in Cana, have been relatively low key and private events. But now, as the time of the yearly Feast of the Passover in Jerusalem arrives, Jesus travels to Jerusalem. He will use the occasion to launch His formal three-year mortal mission in a very public manner. He will cleanse the temple, which has become a boisterous "house of merchandise" (John 2:16) rather than a house of God.

By way of brief review, the Feast of the Passover was an annual seven-day feast and celebration of great importance to the Jews. All who could went to Jerusalem for it. It was celebrated in March or April. Huge multitudes thronged the streets of Jerusalem. The worship associated with this feast included the shedding of lamb's blood, symbolic of the prophesied sacrifice of the Lamb of God. It celebrated the "passing over" of the angel of death over the houses and herds of the children of Israel, while slaying the firstborn among the men and animals of the Egyptians, who held the Israelites in bondage. The Passover was designed to emphasize that deliverance from bondage comes through the Lord (Exodus 12:12–14, 25–27). It was full of Atonement symbolism. And now the literal Lamb of God who, in three years, would offer Himself a sacrifice for all, was in Jerusalem and approaching the temple. His sacrifice at that time would mean that all would be set free from physical death, and could be set free from the bondage of sin if they choose to repent.

JESUS CLEANSES THE TEMPLE

The temple in Jerusalem was a focal point of this Passover worship. Money changers and merchants were set up in the outer courtyard or "temple grounds" and pressed the people to buy their wares and services. It had become big business for merchants to sell sacrificial animals and to exchange foreign money from pilgrims for temple coin. The spirit of proper worship was destroyed by the clamor and haggling involved in buying and selling animals and birds for the sacrifices. It was in this setting, on the first Passover of His mission, that Jesus cleansed the temple.

13 And the Jews' passover was at hand, and Jesus went up to Jerusalem,

14 And found in the temple those that sold oxen and sheep and doves, and the changers of money sitting:

15 And when he had made a scourge of small cords, he drove them all out of the temple, and the sheep, and the oxen; and poured out the changers' money, and overthrew the tables;

16 And said unto them that sold doves, Take these things hence; make not my Father's house an house of merchandise.

John mentions that when His disciples saw Jesus cleanse the Temple, they remembered that this scene had been prophesied anciently.

17 And his disciples remembered that it was written, The zeal of thine house hath eaten me up [*Psalm 69:9*]. (John 2:13–17)

Under normal circumstances, one would expect someone who had caused such a disruption to quickly flee the scene before the guards and soldiers who worked for the Jewish religious leaders could arrest him. But Jesus remained and fielded questions. It is not hard to imagine that His disciples might have been nervous for His welfare. It is also interesting to note that, rather than immediately arresting Him and taking Him away from the scene, the Jewish officials who interrogated Him, apparently suddenly cautious, asked about His authority to do what He had done.

18 Then answered [*responded*] the Jews and said unto him, What sign shewest thou unto us, seeing that thou doest these things? (John 2:18)

Jesus answered by saying, in effect, that His authority lies in the fact that He is the Son of God, the Messiah whom ancient prophets had foretold would be crucified and resurrected three days later. His interrogators completely missed the point.

19 Jesus answered and said unto them, Destroy this temple, and in three days I

will raise it up.

20 Then said the Jews, Forty and six years was this temple in building, and wilt thou rear it up in three days?

21 But he spake of the temple of his body. (John 2:19–21)

John indicates in verse 22, next, that when His disciples first heard Him give this prophecy, they also did not understand what He was saying. But later, when they saw the resurrected Lord, they remembered back to this scene and what He had said.

22 When therefore he was risen from the dead, his disciples remembered that he had said this unto them; and they believed the scripture, and the word which Jesus had said. (John 2:22)

It appears that the Jews did not take His warning seriously to make the temple a holy place again. After His triumphal entry into Jerusalem three years later (Matthew 21:1–11), He once again cleansed the temple (Matthew 21:12–13), during the final week of His life.

NICODEMUS

The Necessity of Baptism

A highly respected teacher among the Jews named Nicodemus approached Jesus by night and, in effect, asked to be taught. His request provided the setting for a vital truth to be taught by the Master. It is that baptism is necessary for entrance into the celestial kingdom (for those who are accountable—D&C 68:25; 137:10, 29:50). And baptism must be by "water and of the Spirit." Nicodemus was a Pharisee, and for the most part, the Pharisees opposed Jesus throughout His mortal mission. They lived the law of Moses strictly and wielded much power among the Jews. They believed in the resurrection, in spirits, and in angels. They avoided contact with anything to do with Gentiles and had a multitude of rules and laws which they lived with exactness. However, Nicodemus was obviously an exception. He was a humble man, probably many years older than Jesus, who addressed the Savior as "Rabbi," in this case a tender term of respect and humility. We will see more of Nicodemus later (John 7:50, 19:39).

1 There was a man of the Pharisees, named Nicodemus, a ruler of the Jews:

2 The same came to Jesus by night, and said unto him, Rabbi, we know that thou art a teacher come from God: for no man can do these miracles that thou doest, except God be with him. (John 3:1–2)

John records the Master's response to Nicodemus's invitation to teach him. Perhaps there is something missing here in the Bible which led specifically to this response by Jesus. Whatever the case, one of the core doctrines of the gospel of Jesus Christ is taught. We must be baptized and receive the gift of the Holy Ghost in order to return to live with God.

> 3 Jesus answered and said unto him, Verily, verily, I say unto thee, Except a man be born again, he cannot see the kingdom of God.
> 4 Nicodemus saith unto him, How can a man be born when he is old? can he enter the second time into his mother's womb, and be born?
> 5 Jesus answered, Verily, verily, I say unto thee, Except a man be born of water and of the Spirit, he cannot enter into the kingdom of God. (John 3:3–5)

Another thing that Nicodemus was taught during this learning session with Jesus was that the brass serpent that Moses was commanded to make and "set it upon a pole" (Numbers 21:8) symbolized the Savior and His Atonement. All people must look to Jesus Christ in order to be saved.

> 14 And as Moses lifted up the serpent in the wilderness, even so must the Son of man be lifted up:
> 15 That whosoever believeth in him should not perish, but have eternal life.
> 16 For God so loved the world, that he gave his only begotten Son, that whosoever believeth in him should not perish, but have everlasting life. (John 3:14–16)

Nephi taught more about the symbolism involved in the brass serpent that Moses was commanded to make and hold up before his people. Just as there was no other way for the children of Israel to be saved from the bites of the fiery serpents, other than through the brass serpent, so also there is no other means of salvation other than Jesus Christ.

> 20 And now, my brethren, I have spoken plainly that ye cannot err. And as the Lord God liveth that brought Israel up out of the land of Egypt, and gave unto Moses power that he should heal the nations after they had been bitten by the poisonous serpents, if they would cast their eyes unto the serpent which he did raise up before them, and also gave him power that he should smite the rock and the water should come forth; yea, behold I say unto you, that as these things are true, and as the Lord God liveth, there is none other name given under heaven save it be this Jesus Christ, of which I have spoken, whereby man can be saved. (2 Nephi 25:20)

During this conversation with Nicodemus, according to the JST, the Savior clearly introduced Himself to Nicodemus as the Messiah.

17 For God sent not his Son into the world to condemn the world; but that the world through him might be saved.
18 He that believeth on him is not condemned: but he that believeth not is condemned already, because he hath not believed in the name of the only begotten Son of God. (John 3:17–18)

> 18 He *who* believeth on him is not condemned; but he *who* believeth not is condemned already, because he hath not believed *on* the name of the *Only Begotten* Son of God, *which before was preached by the mouth of the holy prophets; for they testified of me.* (JST, John 3:18)

The JST addition, "testified of me," is a most significant addition, because it tells us that Jesus was telling Nicodemus clearly that he, Jesus, is the Son of God.

And so Nicodemus was taught by the Master that He is the only means of salvation, and baptism by water and the gift of the Holy Ghost are the only way through which we can come unto Christ. We do not know what the outcome of this conversation with Jesus was for Nicodemus, but we do know that he defended Jesus to the Pharisees (John 7:50) and that he assisted with the Savior's burial after the crucifixion (John 19:39).

THE SAVIOR'S EARLY MINISTRY IN JUDEA

The Apostle John informs us that sometime after the conversation with Nicodemus, the Savior took His disciples and went into the "land of Judea," which could also be termed "the Wilderness of Judea" (Bible Dictionary, under "Harmony of the Gospels"). There He did some baptizing. Judea was the southern province of Palestine in which Jerusalem was located.

> 22 After these things came Jesus and his disciples into the land of Judæa; and there he tarried with them, and baptized. (John 3:22)

For a short period of time, the missions of John the Baptist and Jesus overlapped.

> 23 And John [*the Baptist*] also was baptizing in Aenon near to Salim [*in the Jordan River, about halfway between the Sea of Galilee and the Dead Sea*], because there was much water there: and they came, and were baptized.
> 24 For John was not yet cast into prison [*the Baptist hadn't yet been put in prison*]. (John 3:23–24)

The fact that John the Baptist was baptizing in a place where there was "much water" is another reminder that he was baptizing by immersion. In fact, the word *baptize* means to immerse (Bible Dictionary, under "Baptism"). It appears that some of John the Baptist's followers might have become a bit jealous when they heard that Jesus was also baptizing, and that large crowds of people were coming to Him. Perhaps they are concerned that Jesus is taking some of John's popularity away from him. Just a reminder: the JST verses do not always have the same numbering as those of the Bible.

> 26 And they [*John's disciples*] came unto John, and said unto him, Rabbi [*"my master"; Bible Dictionary, under "Rabbi"*], he [*Jesus*] that was with thee beyond Jordan, to whom thou barest witness [*of whom you bore testimony*], behold, the same baptizeth, and all men come to him.

>> 27 And they came unto John, and said unto him, Rabbi, he *who* was with thee beyond Jordan, to whom thou bearest witness, behold, the same baptizeth, and *he receiveth of all people who* come *unto* him. (JST, John 3:27)

John's response to the concerns of his followers is a wonderful example of humility. He reminds his followers that he is not the Messiah. Rather, his calling is to prepare the way for the Lord. He will also tell them that he has great joy in his mission, which includes the privilege of listening to the Savior.

> 27 John answered and said, A man can receive nothing, except it be given him from heaven [*each of us only does the work assigned to us by God*].
> 28 Ye yourselves bear me witness [*you are my witnesses*], that I said, I am not the Christ, but that I am sent before him. [*In effect, saying that Jesus' mission is to be the Messiah. My mission is to prepare the way for Him.*]
> 29 He that hath the bride [*He to whom the Church belongs*] is the bridegroom [*Jesus*]: but the friend [*John the Baptist*] of the bridegroom, which standeth and heareth him, rejoiceth greatly because of the bridegroom's voice: this my joy therefore is fulfilled. [*In effect, John is saying that he is very happy just to be a friend of Jesus and to hear Him preaching.*] (John 3:27–29)

"HE MUST INCREASE, BUT I MUST DECREASE"

Verse 30, next, is one of most humble statements ever uttered. John the Baptist is telling his own disciples that the public's attention must now turn to the Son of God and His mortal mission, and that his own mission and popularity are drawing to a close. And he humbly accepts and advocates that fact.

> 30 He must increase, but I must decrease.
> 31 He [*Jesus*] that cometh from above [*from heaven*] is above all [*is in charge of all things here*]: he that is of the earth is earthly [*I am just an ordinary man*], and speaketh of the earth: he that cometh from heaven is above all. (John 3:30–31)

John Is Imprisoned

At some point during his preaching and preparing the way for the Savior, John the Baptist had called Herod the tetrarch to repentance for marrying his half-brother's wife, Herodias (Matthew 14:3–5). Herod was one of the three sons of Herod the Great, among whom the kingdom was divided after his death. Herod the Great died a few months after he issued the edict to kill all the children two years old and younger, in and around Bethlehem, in a vain attempt to destroy the Christ child. As a result of John's straightforward message to Herod the tetrarch, he had John put in prison (Luke 3:19–20). John will remain in prison for nearly a year, until Herodias succeeds in getting her husband to order his beheading (Mark 6:17–29). During the time that John was in prison, Jesus sent angels to visit him, according to the JST (Matthew 4:11, footnote a, in your English LDS edition of the King James Bible).

To Galilee

The growing popularity of Jesus in Judea was alarming to the Jewish religious leaders in Jerusalem, and opposition against Him began to mount.

> 1 When therefore the Lord knew how the Pharisees had heard that Jesus made and baptized more disciples than John,
> 2 (Though Jesus himself baptized not, but his disciples) (John 4:1–2)

Verse 2 above is a mistranslation in the Bible. The JST corrects this as follows (note that JST verses 2 and 4 have been left out of the Bible):

> 1 When therefore the Pharisees had heard that Jesus made and baptized more disciples than John,
> 2 They sought more diligently some means that they might put him to death; for many received John as a prophet, but they believed not on Jesus.
> 3 *Now the Lord knew this*, though *he* himself baptized not *so many as his* disciples;
> 4 For he suffered them for an example [*Jesus set the example for them*], preferring one another. (JST, John 4:1–4)

The Woman at the Well

After John was put in prison, Jesus departed for Galilee (Matthew 4:12). Samaria was directly between Judea and Galilee, and because most Jews despised the Samaritans and Samaritans despised Jews, it was a common practice to go around Samaria when traveling between Galilee and Judea. Note that, according to the JST, Jesus specifically told His disciples that it was necessary for Him to go through Samaria. We have the advantage of knowing that the woman at the well needed to meet Him and be converted.

> 3 He left Judæa, and departed again into Galilee.
> 4 And he must needs go through Samaria. (John 4:3–4)

> 6 *And said unto his disciples, I* must needs go through Samaria. (JST, John 4:6)

As the Master and His little company of leaders in training arrived at Jacob's well in Samaria, the disciples went into a nearby town to buy food. Alone, the Savior sat wearily on the well. It was about the sixth hour (about noon), and a woman came to draw water from the well. What happens next is both delightful and profoundly moving as we watch the Son of God, perhaps with a tired twinkle in His eye, engage this feisty and somewhat sharp-tongued woman in soul-saving conversation.

> 6 Now Jacob's well was there. Jesus therefore, being wearied with his journey, sat thus on the well: and it was about the sixth hour [*about noon*].
> 7 There cometh a woman of Samaria to draw water: Jesus saith unto her, Give me to drink [*please give Me a drink*].
> 8 (For his disciples were gone away unto the city to buy meat [*food, provisions*].)
> 9 Then saith the woman of Samaria unto him, How is it that thou, being a Jew, askest drink of me, which am a woman of Samaria? for the Jews have no dealings with the Samaritans. [*In other words, why would a Jew like You ask a Samaritan woman like me for a drink. Don't You know that Jews don't have anything to do with us?*] (John 4:6–9)

Watch, now, as the Savior gets her curiosity up.

> 10 Jesus answered and said unto her, If thou knewest the gift of God, and who it is that saith to thee, Give me to drink; thou wouldest have asked of him, and he would have given thee living water. [*In effect, if you knew about the gift Father in Heaven has for you, and who I am, you would have asked Me for a drink, and I would have given you "living water."*] (John 4:10)

The phrase "living water," in one form or another, was a familiar Old Testament phrase, having been used by Old Testament prophets to describe the blessings which flow from Jehovah to His faithful people (Jeremiah 2:13; Isaiah 8:6; 58:11).

> 11 The woman saith unto him, Sir, thou hast nothing to draw with, and the well is deep: from whence then hast thou that living water? [*Sir, You don't even have anything to get water out of the well. It is way too deep. So, just where do You think you are going to get me some of Your so-called "living water"?*]

12 Art thou greater than our father Jacob, which gave us the well, and drank thereof himself, and his children, and his cattle? [*In effect, do You think your "living water" is better than the water Jacob provided us here in this well? It was good enough for Jacob and his family and his animals. In other words, what makes You think Your water is better than the prophet Jacob's?*] (John 4:11–12)

Watch now as the Master Teacher takes her from being curious to a state of deep desire to partake of what He has to offer. She is still thinking of literal water, but the transition from the literal to the symbolical is about to take place in her mind.

13 Jesus answered and said unto her, Whosoever drinketh of this water shall thirst again [*will just get thirsty again*]:
14 But whosoever drinketh of the water that I shall give him shall never thirst [*will never be thirsty again*]; but the water that I shall give him shall be in him a well of water springing up into everlasting life [*eternal life*].
15 The woman saith unto him, Sir, give me this water, that I thirst not, neither come hither to draw. (John 4:13–15)

As you can see, the woman still doesn't get it. She thinks Jesus is talking about some kind of magical water that, when someone drinks it, he or she will never get thirsty again. She wants some so that she doesn't ever have to come to the well again and do the hard work of getting water. Watch how the Savior really gets her attention with what He says to her next. A wonderful teaching moment has been quickly generated by the Master Teacher! She is about to learn that He truly is "a prophet."

16 Jesus saith unto her, Go, call thy husband, and come hither [*go get your husband and bring him back here*].
17 The woman answered and said, I have no husband. Jesus said unto her, Thou hast well said, I have no husband [*you were certainly right when you said that you have no husband*]:
18 For thou hast had five husbands; and he whom thou now hast is not thy husband [*you are not married to the man you are living with now*]: in that saidst thou truly [*you were certainly telling the truth when you said you have no husband*].
19 The woman saith unto him, Sir, I perceive that thou art a prophet. [*Sir, it just dawned on me that you are a prophet.*] (John 4:16–19)

After additional conversation, it appears that it began to occur to her that it was prophesied that the Messiah would someday come to earth. Could this be Him? After she brings the subject up, Jesus tells her outright that He is indeed the Messiah.

25 The woman saith unto him, I know that Messias [*Messiah*] cometh, which is called Christ: when he is come, he will tell us all things. [*This*

woman is familiar with the prophecies about the coming of the Messiah, who will be known as Christ.]

26 Jesus saith unto her, I that speak unto thee am he [*the Messiah, Christ; the Jehovah of the Old Testament; John 4:26, footnote a, in the LDS edition of the King James Bible*].

> 28 Jesus said unto her, I who speak unto thee am *the Messias.* (JST, John 4:28)

27 And upon this [*just as Jesus finished saying this to the woman*] came his disciples, and marvelled [*were surprised*] that he talked with the woman [*that He would talk with a Samaritan woman*]: yet no man said, What seekest thou? or, Why talkest thou with her? [*But none of the disciples dared scold Him for so doing.*] (John 4:25–27)

The rather surprised and amazed Samaritan woman hurried back into the city and told the men that she had met a prophet at Jacob's Well who was no doubt the Messiah spoken of in the scriptures. They came to see Him for themselves with the result that many were converted.

39 And many of the Samaritans of that city believed on him for [*because of*] the saying of the woman, which testified, He told me all that ever I did.
40 So when the Samaritans were come unto him, they besought him that he would tarry with them [*they asked Him to stay with them*]: and he abode [*remained*] there two days.
41 And many more believed because of his own word;
42 And said unto the woman, Now we believe, not because of thy saying: for we have heard him ourselves, and know that this is indeed the Christ, the Saviour of the world.

The Savior stayed with these Samaritan converts for two days and then continued the journey to Galilee (John 4:43). Certainly one of the major messages in the account of the woman at the well, for us and for the future leaders of the New Testament church who were now traveling with the Savior, is that the gospel of Jesus Christ is for all people, regardless of who they are or where they live.

As Jesus and His disciples arrived in Galilee, He was welcomed enthusiastically by multitudes who had heard of His fame already. Many of them had been to the recent Feast of the Passover in Jerusalem themselves and had seen what He did there (John 4:45). The Jews in Galilee welcomed Him into their synagogues and praised Him (Luke 4:14–15).

TO CANA

Healing of the Nobleman's Son

As Jesus continued preaching in Galilee, He returned to Cana, where He had turned water to wine at the wedding feast (John 2:1–11), before attending the first Passover of His formal three-year ministry. In Cana, a certain nobleman approached Him and fervently requested that He come and heal his son who was "at the point of death" (John 4:47). First, we see the Lord test the man's motives to make sure they were pure (John 4:48–49). The nobleman was apparently not seeking a sign, in the negative sense. Next, we see the Savior's power to heal without being physically present at the sick person's side. The Creator said to the man, "Go thy way; thy son liveth" (John 4:50). The man had faith in what the Master said and set out to return home. Upon meeting his servants who were coming out to meet him, they gave him the good news that "[his] son liveth" (John 4:51). In answer to his question as to what time his son was healed, he discovered that the miracle took place at the same time Jesus had pronounced the healing, at about 1:00 PM the previous day (John 4:52–53). John calls this "the second miracle that Jesus did" after He had returned to Galilee from Judea and informs us that the nobleman's entire household was converted (John 4:53–54).

A NOTE ABOUT HEALINGS

The Savior said "all things bear record of me" (Moses 6:63). With this in mind, every time we read of a miracle of healing performed by Jesus, it can be a reminder to us of His power to cleanse and heal us spiritually through His Atonement. For example, when He healed the blind, literally, it was symbolic of His ability to heal our spiritual blindness. When He healed the lame, it can be considered symbolic of His ability to heal our inability to walk along the strait and narrow path toward salvation in celestial glory.

REJECTION AT NAZARETH

As He continued His early Galilean ministry, Jesus returned to His hometown of Nazareth where He entered the synagogue on the Sabbath and read some verses from Isaiah to the men who were there that day. We suppose that there was an extra large number in attendance that day due to the growing fame and popularity of Jesus. The passage from Isaiah is a prophecy of the Messiah. Jesus will read it and then pronounce that He is the fulfillment of it. By the way, on occasions, over many years of teaching, I have had students ask why Jesus didn't ever come right out and say that He was the Messiah. He did. We will first read the quote as recorded by Luke. Then we will read the original quote as recorded in Isaiah.

> 18 The Spirit of the Lord is upon me, because he hath anointed me to preach the gospel to the poor; he hath sent me to heal the brokenhearted, to preach deliverance to the captives, and recovering of sight to the blind, to set at liberty them that are bruised,
> 19 To preach the acceptable year of the Lord. (Luke 4:18–19)

> 1 The Spirit of the Lord God is upon me; because the LORD hath anointed me to preach good tidings unto the meek; he hath sent me to bind up the brokenhearted, to proclaim liberty to the captives, and the opening of the prison to them that are bound;
> 2 To proclaim the acceptable year of the LORD. (Isaiah 61:1–2)

Did you notice that these verses from Isaiah contain a brief summary of the Savior's mission and Atonement? The Atonement of Jesus Christ brings "good tidings" to the meek and humble who will accept the requirements of the Atonement. "Broken hearts" are healed by the Atonement. Those who are captives of Satan and in the bondage of sin are healed and set free by the Atonement. Those who have been "bruised" by bad choices are cleansed and healed by the Atonement.

Imagine the murmur that went through the synagogue when Jesus gave the Isaiah scroll back to the minister and announced:

> 21 This day is this scripture fulfilled in your ears. (Luke 4:21)

In other words, Jesus told them outright that He was the Savior, the fulfillment of Isaiah's prophecy. At first, there was quiet consideration of what the Savior had said, accompanied by admiration of His delivery (John 4:22). Then, the men in the synagogue started considering the fact that Jesus had grown up in their town. They knew His family. He couldn't be anyone that special. They began to murmur and say, "Is not this Joseph's son?" (John 4:22). Anger began to build, and ultimately the men became furious and cast the Creator of heaven and earth out of their synagogue and took Him to the edge of a cliff with the intent of throwing Him over (John 4:28–29), but He went "through the midst of them" and "came down to Capernaum" (John 4:30–31). It will be interesting someday to get the details of how He escaped this mob.

TO CAPERNAUM

When Jesus departed from the angry mob in Nazareth, He went to Capernaum, the hometown of Peter, Andrew, and Matthew, which was a prosperous and crowded Galilean town situated on the northern end of the Sea of Galilee. Luke informs us that He taught there on Sabbath days and that the people recognized that He taught with power and authority.

> 31 And came down to Capernaum, a city of Galilee, and taught them on the sabbath days.
> 32 And they were astonished at his doctrine: for his word was with power. (Luke 4:31–32)

Mark adds that the people were comparing the Savior's teaching with that of the scribes, who were the main teachers and interpreters of the law of Moses among the Jews of that day.

> 22 And they were astonished at his doctrine: for he taught them as one that had authority, and not as the scribes. (Mark 1:22)

JESUS CASTS OUT AN UNCLEAN SPIRIT

From what happens next in the synagogue at Capernaum, we see that evil spirits (the one third who were cast out of heaven— Revelation 12:4—and are here on earth tempting us) do not have the veil and that they readily recognized Jesus for who He was. We also see His power over Satan and his followers, and that when He commands them, they must obey.

> 23 And there was in their synagogue a man with an unclean spirit [*possessed by an evil spirit—Luke 4:33*]; and he [*the evil spirit*] cried out,
> 24 Saying, Let us alone; what have we to do with thee [*what business is it of Yours what we do?*], thou Jesus of Nazareth? art thou come to destroy us [*to ruin our opportunity to possess people*]? I know thee who thou art, the Holy One of God. (Mark 1:23–24)

From the wording in verses 23 and 24 above, it appears that this evil spirit is speaking for several of his colleague evil spirits as he questions Christ about what He is doing. The Messiah commands and is obeyed, much to the amazement of the onlookers. His fame continues to spread.

> 25 And Jesus rebuked him, saying, Hold thy peace [*Jesus doesn't want evil spirits bearing witness of Him*], and come out of him.
> 26 And when the unclean spirit had torn him [*severely shaken him*], and cried with a loud voice, he came out of him.

27 And they were all amazed, insomuch that they questioned among themselves, saying, What thing is this? what new doctrine is this? for with authority commandeth he even the unclean spirits, and they do obey him.

28 And immediately his fame spread abroad throughout all the region round about Galilee. (Mark 1:25–28)

THE CALLING OF PETER, ANDREW, JAMES, AND JOHN

The Master Teacher chose a setting on the shores of the Sea of Galilee to call Peter, Andrew, James, and John to be "fishers of men" (Matthew 4:19). This is not their call to serve as Apostles. That will come later (Matthew 10:1–4).

18 And Jesus, walking by the sea of Galilee, saw two brethren [*brothers*], Simon called Peter, and Andrew his brother, casting a net into the sea: for they were fishers [*fishermen; they earned their living by fishing*].

19 And he saith unto them, Follow me, and I will make you fishers of men.

20 And they straightway [*immediately*] left their nets, and followed him. (Matthew 4:18–20)

> 18 And he *said* unto them, *I am he of whom it is written by the prophets;* follow me, and I will make you fishers of men.
>
> 19 And they, believing on his words, left their net, and straightway followed him. (JST, Matthew 4:18–19)

From the JST changes given above, we can glean that Peter and Andrew knew the scriptures and the prophecies about the coming Messiah. They recognized what He was saying because they knew the scriptures. This can remind us, among other things, of the great value of reading and studying the scriptures ourselves.

21 And going on from thence [*from that place*], he saw other two brethren, James the son of Zebedee, and John his brother, in a ship with Zebedee their father, mending their nets; and he called them.

22 And they immediately left the ship and their father, and followed him. (Matthew 4:21–22)

CONTINUED TEACHING IN GALILEE

The Savior continued in Galilee, teaching the gospel and healing many who came to Him, drawing large crowds of people, including many from Jerusalem and other distant locations.

23 And Jesus went about all Galilee, teaching in their synagogues, and preaching the gospel of the kingdom, and healing all manner of sickness and all manner of disease among the people. (Matthew 4:23)

The JST adds an important lesson to the end of verse 23, above, about the necessity of believing. (Also, another reminder that the verse numbering in the JST is sometimes different than in the King James Version of the Bible.)

> 22 And Jesus went about all Galilee teaching in their synagogues, and preaching the gospel of the kingdom; and healing all manner of sickness, and all manner of diseases among the people *which believed on his name.* (JST, Matthew 4:22)

24 And his fame went throughout all Syria: and they brought unto him all sick people that were taken with [*who had*] divers [*various*] diseases and torments, and those which were possessed with devils, and those which were lunatick, and those that had the palsy; and he healed them.
25 And there followed him great multitudes of people from Galilee, and from Decapolis, and from Jerusalem, and from Judaea, and from beyond Jordan. (Matthew 4:24–25)

THE FIRST YEAR OF THE SAVIOR'S MISSION IS DRAWING TO A CLOSE

It would have taken a significant amount of time for Jesus to travel and preach and heal throughout "all Galilee" (verse 23, above). Thus, at this point in time, the first year of the Savior's three-year formal mortal mission is drawing to a close. He had become tremendously popular, and crowds from all over the area were constantly following Him around. In fact, at one point the crowds were pushing against Him so much that He got into a boat so that He could be out away from the throngs and then teach them.

> 1 And it came to pass, that, as the people pressed upon him [*crowded and pushed against Him*] to hear the word of God, he stood by the lake of Gennesaret [*the Sea of Galilee*],
> 2 And saw two ships standing by the lake: but the fishermen were gone out of them, and were washing their nets.
> 3 And he entered into one of the ships, which was Simon's [*which belonged to Peter*], and prayed [*asked*] him that he would thrust out a little from the land. And he sat down, and taught the people out of the ship. (Luke 5:1–3)

Next, Jesus taught Peter and his fellow fishermen an important lesson about His power to bless their temporal efforts, in preparation for an even more important lesson about the importance of helping the Savior save souls.

> 4 Now when he had left speaking, he said unto Simon [*Peter*], Launch out into the deep, and let down your nets for a draught [*a catch of fish*].
> 5 And Simon answering [*in response*] said unto him, Master, we have toiled [*worked hard fishing*] all the night, and have taken nothing: nevertheless at thy word I will let down the net. (Luke 5:4–5)

By way of information, it was the practice at this time for those who fished for a living on the Sea of Galilee to fish during the night.

> 6 And when they had this done, they inclosed a great multitude of fishes: and their net brake [*started to break; Luke 5:6, footnote a*].
> 7 And they beckoned [*waved*] unto their partners, which were in the other ship, that they should come and help them. And they came, and filled both the ships, so that they began to sink. (Luke 5:6–7)

There is beautiful symbolism here. As Peter and others follow the Savior's instructions in faith, they have great success in catching fish. Symbolically, as Peter and the others follow Christ, He will make them "fishers of men," and they will have a large "catch" of converts. See end of verse 10.

> 8 When Simon Peter saw it, he fell down at Jesus' knees [*very humble*], saying, Depart from me; for I am a sinful man, O Lord. [*I am not worthy to be in Thy presence.*]
> 9 For he was astonished, and all that were with him, at the draught [*catch*] of the fishes which they had taken:
> 10 And so was [*were*] also James, and John, the sons of Zebedee, which were partners with Simon [*Peter*]. And Jesus said unto Simon, Fear not; from henceforth [*from now on*] thou shalt catch men.
> 11 And when they had brought their ships to land, they forsook all [*left everything behind*], and followed him. (Luke 5:8–11)

The situation of these professional fishermen working all night, having nothing to show for it and then being told by the Master to try again, followed with startling success, will be repeated after the Savior's crucifixion and resurrection (John 21:1–6).

HEALING OF A LEPER

As Jesus continued His ministry in Galilee, a leper approached Him, requesting that He heal him. Leprosy is described in Webster's New World Dictionary, Second College Edition, 1980, as follows: "A chronic infectious disease . . . that attacks the skin, flesh, nerves, etc.; it is characterized by nodules, ulcers, white scaly scabs, deformities, and wasting of body parts." Leprosy was one of the most dreaded diseases of the time. It was greatly feared by others, and a person who had the disease was required by law to warn others to stay clear so they would not accidentally touch the leper and risk catching the disease. Lepers were social outcasts (Bible Dictionary, under "Leper" and "Leprosy").

40 And there came a leper to him, beseeching him, and kneeling down to him, and saying unto him, If thou wilt [*if it is Thy will*], thou canst make me clean [*heal me*].

41 And Jesus, moved with compassion, put forth his hand, and touched him, and saith unto him, I will; be thou clean.

42 And as soon as he had spoken, immediately the leprosy departed from him, and he was cleansed. (Mark 1:40–42)

Here, again, is beautiful Atonement symbolism. The symbolism is that Christ can cleanse and heal us from very serious illness, physical or spiritual, and make us whole. The Master instructed the healed man to show himself to the priest, as instructed by the law of Moses (Leviticus 14:2). Unfortunately, the man did not obey the Lord's firm command to keep this miracle to himself, except for showing himself to the priest. Consequently, Jesus was forced to leave that city.

43 And he straitly charged him [*very firmly told him not to tell anyone but the priest—verse 44*], and forthwith [*immediately*] sent him away;

44 And saith unto him, See thou say nothing to any man: but go thy way, shew thyself to the priest, and offer for thy cleansing those things which Moses commanded, for a testimony unto them.

45 But he [*the leper*] went out, and began to publish it much, and to blaze abroad the matter [*the leper went out and told everyone he could about his being healed*], insomuch that Jesus could no more openly enter into the city [*because so many people were crowding to see Him*], but was without [*outside of the city*] in desert places: and they came to him from every quarter.

CHAPTER 12

THE SECOND YEAR OF THE
SAVIOR'S MORTAL MISSION

As stated in the introduction to this work, chronologies of the events in the Savior's mortal ministry do not always agree completely with each other. With this in mind, we will start the second year of the Master's formal mortal mission with Jesus going from Galilee to Jerusalem for the Feast of the Passover, as stated in the New Testament student manual, p. 48. This trip to Jerusalem was apparently a brief one, after which the Master returned to Galilee.

JESUS COMES FROM GALILEE TO ATTEND
THE PASSOVER IN JERUSALEM

A Man Healed on the Sabbath

It is supposed by many Bible scholars that the feast spoken of by John was the Feast of the Passover.

> 1 After this there was a feast of the Jews; and Jesus went up to Jerusalem. (John 5:1)

While in Jerusalem for this feast, the Savior healed a man on the Sabbath, who had been crippled for thirty-eight years. After healing him, Jesus told him to take his bed with him as he left (John 5:5–9). When the Jews saw this man who had been healed, they were incensed at him for carrying his bed on the Sabbath and at Jesus for violating the Sabbath by healing someone on it. This is an example of how far away from the true gospel people can get when they no longer have and follow living prophets.

The Jewish religious leaders were so irate that they determined to put the Master to death for His Sabbath breaking.

> 15 The man departed, and told the Jews that it was Jesus, which had made him whole.
>
> 16 And therefore did the Jews persecute Jesus, and sought to slay him, because he had done these things on the sabbath day. (John 5:15–16)

JESUS BEARS STRONG WITNESS OF HIS MISSION AND OF THE FATHER, WHO SENT HIM

In response to the criticism of the Jews about healing on the Sabbath, Jesus gave a strong sermon about His mission and His relationship to the Father.

> 17 But Jesus answered them, My Father worketh hitherto, and I work [*in effect, My Father has done much of His work on the Sabbath, and I will continue to do so too*].
>
> 18 Therefore [*because of Jesus' reply*] the Jews sought the more [*even more*] to kill him, because he not only had broken the sabbath, but said also that God was his Father, making himself equal with God. (John 5:17–18)

In the next verses, Jesus humbly gives credit and honor to His Father and explains His relationship with the Father as They work together in complete harmony for the salvation of our souls.

> 19 Then answered Jesus and said unto them, Verily, verily, I say unto you, The Son can do nothing of himself, but what he seeth the Father do: for what things soever he [*the Father*] doeth, these also doeth the Son likewise. [*In other words, the Son does nothing that is not in complete harmony with the Father's will. See Mc-Conkie*, Doctrinal New Testament Commentary, *Vol. 1, p. 192.*]
>
> 20 For the Father loveth the Son, and sheweth [*shows*] him all things that himself doeth [*that He Himself does*]: and he will shew him greater [*more*] works than these, that ye may marvel.
>
> 21 For as the Father raiseth up the dead [*resurrects people*], and quickeneth them [*causes them to become alive spiritually*]; even so the Son [*Christ*] quickeneth [*gives eternal life to*] whom he will. (John 5:19–21)

Since every person who has ever been born on earth will be resurrected (1 Corinthians 15:22), or in other words, will be *quickened* the last phrase in verse 21 above cannot mean that Jesus will be selective as to whom He resurrects. Another scriptural use of the word *quicken* is "to be made alive spiritually," which, in turn, leads to eternal life (exaltation). As Jesus continues, He explains that He will be our final judge, and as such will give exaltation to "whom he will," according to the laws of justice and mercy.

22 For the Father judgeth no man, but hath committed all judgment unto the Son: [*The Father has given all the responsibility for final judgment to Jesus.*]
23 That all men should honour the Son, even as they honour the Father. He that honoureth not the Son honoureth not the Father which hath sent him.
24 Verily, verily, I say unto you, He that heareth my word, and believeth on him that sent me [*Heavenly Father*], hath everlasting life [*exaltation in the highest degree of glory in the celestial kingdom*], and shall not come into condemnation [*will not be stopped from eternal progress*]; but is passed from death unto life. (John 5:22–24)

The Master Teacher continues, explaining to these Jews who now seek His life that His mission extends beyond this world into the postmortal spirit world.

25 Verily, verily, I say unto you, The hour is coming, and now is, when the dead [*in the postmortal spirit world; 1 Peter 3:18–21, D&C 138*] shall hear the voice of the Son of God: and they that hear [*obey*] shall live [*receive exaltation*].
26 For as the Father hath life in himself [*is "an immortal, resurrected, exalted being," McConkie,* Doctrinal New Testament Commentary, *Vol. 1, p. 194*]; so hath he given to the Son to have life in himself [*Jesus has power over death*];
27 And hath given him authority to execute judgment also, because he is the Son of man [*the Son of God*]. [*See Moses 6:57 for an explanation of why Jesus is called the "Son of Man."*]
28 Marvel not at this: for the hour is coming, in the which all that are in the graves shall hear his voice,
29 And shall come forth [*everyone will be resurrected*]; they that have done good, unto the resurrection of life [*eternal life, exaltation*]; and they that have done evil, unto the resurrection of damnation [*those who will have limits placed on their progression; see D&C 76:112*]. (John 5:25–29)

The Savior continues, discussing the law of witnesses (John 5:31–32), and then reminds these Jewish leaders that John the Baptist also bore witness of Him and His mission.

33 Ye sent unto John [*the Baptist*], and he bare witness unto the truth.
34 But I receive not testimony from man: but these things I say, that ye might be saved.

35 And *he received not his testimony of [from] man, but of God, and ye yourselves say that he is a prophet, therefore ye ought to receive his testimony.* These things I say that ye might be saved. (JST, John 5:35)

35 He [*John the Baptist*] was a burning and a shining light: and ye were willing for a season to rejoice in his light.

36 But I have greater witness than that of John [*than that which John the Baptist gave of Me*]: for the works [*restoring the gospel, performing the Atonement, etc.*] which the Father hath given me to finish, the same works that I do, bear witness of me, that the Father hath sent me. (John 5:33–36)

> 37 But I have a greater witness than *the testimony* of John; for the works which the Father hath given me to finish, the same works that I do, bear witness of me, that the Father hath sent me. (JST, John 5:37)

37 And the Father himself, which hath sent me, hath borne witness of me. Ye [*the Jews*] have neither heard his voice at any time, nor seen his shape [*meaning that the Father has "shape," a resurrected, physical body; see D&C 130:22*].

> 38 And the Father himself who sent me, hath borne witness of me. *And verily I testify unto you, that* ye have never heard his voice at any time, nor seen his shape; (JST, John 5:38)

38 And ye [*the Jews*] have not his word abiding in you [*do not have the Father's gospel in your hearts*]: for whom he [*the Father*] hath sent, him ye believe not [*you refuse to believe Me, even though the Father sent Me*]. (John 5:37–38)

Verse 39, next, needs to be read carefully, in order to understand what is actually being said. Remember that the Master is addressing the hypocritical religious leaders of the Jews who are proud of their knowledge of the scriptures but who reject Him and violate the gospel constantly in their daily living.

> 39 Search the scriptures; for in them ye think ye have eternal life [*since you won't listen to Me, go ahead and keep studying your scriptures, the law of Moses, and so forth, without help, thus perpetuating your spiritual blindness; you think you can be saved that way; it won't work*]: and they are they which testify of me. [*If you understood the scriptures correctly, you would see that they testify of Me.*]

Next, Jesus gives these hypocrites a scathing rebuke for their intentional refusal to accept Him and for the widespread practice of priestcraft among them.

> 40 And ye will not [*you intentionally refuse to*] come to me, that ye might have life [*eternal life*].
>
> 41 I receive not honour from men. [*I am not honored by men like you are.*]
>
> 42 But I know you [*the Jews who are angry because Jesus healed the invalid on the Sabbath, and now want to kill Him; see verse 16 above*], that ye have not the love of God in you [*I know the evil which is in your hearts.*]
>
> 43 I am come [*have come*] in my Father's name, and ye receive me not [*you reject Me*]: if another shall come in his own name, him ye will receive. [*You accept false leaders and false prophets who build themselves up in the eyes of the people for per-*

sonal gain, who practice priestcraft; see Alma 1:12 and 16.]

44 How can ye believe, which receive honour one of another, and seek not the honour that cometh from God only? [*How can you believe and trust those who join together to build themselves up, rather than seeking God?*] (John 5:40–44)

As the Master continues, he tells these men that Moses himself will bear witness against them on Judgment Day because of how they maliciously twist and misinterpret his teachings for their own purposes.

45 Do not think that I will accuse you [*I will not even need to bear witness against you*] to the Father: there is one that accuseth you, even Moses, in whom ye trust [*because the teachings of Moses about Me, which you blatantly misinterpret and refuse to believe, will bear witness against you*].

46 For had ye believed Moses [*if you believed Moses, who clearly taught about Me*], ye would have believed me: for he wrote of me.

47 But if ye believe not his writings, how shall ye believe my words? [*If you won't believe Moses, how can you possibly believe Me?*]

Moses was the most important prophet in Jewish culture. In fact, the Jews were constantly angered by the fact that Jesus did not do things the way Moses taught, forgetting that many of the things Moses gave them were "schoolmaster" laws (Galatians 3:24), specifically designed to prepare them for the higher laws the Messiah would give them.

BACK TO GALILEE

With the Jewish religious leaders in Jerusalem actively seeking to take His life, Jesus departed again for Galilee.

THE CALLING AND ORDAINING OF THE TWELVE

In Galilee, the Lord called and ordained twelve men to serve as Apostles. With the exception of Judas Iscariot, these men would carry on the work of leading the Church and spreading the gospel after the Savior's crucifixion and resurrection. Mark gives us the names of the Twelve, as do Matthew and Luke (Matthew 10:1–4; Luke 6:12–16). We will use Mark's list here.

13 And he goeth up into a mountain, and calleth unto him whom he would: and they came unto him.

14 And he ordained twelve, that they should be with him, and that he might send them forth to preach,

15 And to have power to heal sicknesses, and to cast out devils:

16 And Simon he surnamed Peter;

17 And James the son of Zebedee, and John the brother of James; and he surnamed them Boanerges, which is, The sons of thunder:

18 And Andrew, and Philip, and Bartholomew, and Matthew, and Thomas, and James the son of Alphæus, and Thaddæus, and Simon the Canaanite,
19 And Judas Iscariot, which also betrayed him: and they went into an house. (Mark 3:13–19)

Jesus gave these twelve men extensive training in preparation for their missions (Matthew 10:5–42). It might be said that these verses in Matthew were the first "handbook of instructions" for Apostles in the New Testament Church. After giving these twelve newly called men this initial training and orientation, the Savior sent them out on missions (Mark 6:7–13; Luke 9:1–2). When they come back, they will have many questions and additional training will be very meaningful to them.

THE DIFFERENCE BETWEEN "DISCIPLES" AND "APOSTLES"

Elder James E. Talmage explained that *disciple* can refer to any faithful follower of Christ, whereas *Apostle* is a specific calling in the Melchizedek Priesthood to which a man is ordained, and that includes being a special witness of the Savior.

Discipleship is general; any follower of a man or devotee to a principle may be called a disciple. The Holy Apostleship is an office and calling belonging to the Higher or Melchizedek Priesthood, at once exalted and specific, comprising as a distinguishing function that of personal and special witness to the divinity of Jesus Christ as the one and only Redeemer and Savior of mankind. The apostleship is an individual bestowal, and as such is conferred only through ordination. (*Jesus the Christ*, p. 227)

THE SERMON ON THE MOUNT

The Sermon on the Mount was given in Galilee sometime near the beginning of the second year of the Savior's formal three-year ministry. It is one of the best known and most often quoted of His discourses, and comprises Matthew 5, 6, and 7 (compare with Luke 6:17–49). Many Christians consider these chapters to contain a series of desirable ethical behaviors, and indeed they do. But they are much more than that. As explained in 3 Nephi 12:1–2 as well as in JST Matthew 5:3–4, the righteous behaviors taught here by the Master are among those which enable baptized members of the Church to continue on the path after baptism to eventually obtain celestial glory and exaltation. The warnings and cautions given in the sermon help us avoid behaviors and attitudes that would prevent successfully returning to live in the presence of the Father forever. The Sermon on the Mount covers a wide range of gospel topics, doctrines, and principles.

As you will see, the JST makes significant contributions to our understanding of this sermon. Remember, as previously noted, the verse numbers for the JST are not always the same as the corresponding verses in the Bible because the Lord inspired the Prophet Joseph Smith to restore missing verses as well as to combine or separate some verses as they stand in the Bible. We will now begin with Matthew, chapter 5, joining the multitude which has gathered on a hillside in Galilee to listen to the Master Teacher.

MATTHEW 5

> 1 And seeing the multitudes, he went up into a mountain: and when he was set, his disciples came unto him:
> 2 And he opened his mouth, and taught them, saying. (Matthew 5:1–2)

The JST adds two complete verses (3 and 4) to Matthew 5:1–2 which are not found in the Bible.

> 1 And *Jesus*, seeing the multitudes, went up into a mountain; and when he was set *down*, his disciples came unto him;
> 2 And he opened his mouth, and taught them, saying,
> 3 *Blessed are they who shall believe on me; and again, more blessed are they who shall believe on your words, when ye shall testify that ye have seen me and that I am.*
> 4 *Yea, blessed are they who shall believe on your words, and come down into the depth of humility, and be baptized in my name; for they shall be visited with fire and the Holy Ghost, and shall receive a remission of their sins.* (JST, Matthew 5:1–4)

THE BEATITUDES

Verses 3–12 are often referred to as the Beatitudes, meaning "to be happy or blessed" (see Matthew 5, footnote 3a, in your Bible). In the Sermon on the Mount, they are instructions for continuing on to exaltation after baptism. If we follow these directions and develop these attributes, it will enable the Atonement of Jesus Christ to fully work in our lives. Notice that verses 3, 5, 8, 9, 10, and 12 all refer to heaven (celestial glory) in one way or another.

> 3 Blessed are the poor in spirit: for theirs is the kingdom of heaven [*celestial glory*].

> 5 Yea, blessed are the poor in spirit, *who come unto me*; for theirs is the kingdom of heaven. (JST, Matthew 5:5)

From the JST addition to verse 3, above, we are taught, among other things, that those who recognize that they are "poor in spirit," (in other words, who recognize that they are poor in spirituality) who repent and come unto Christ, can obtain celestial glory.

Verse 4, next, can have several meanings, including mourning for the loss of a loved one and being comforted by the Holy Ghost. But in the context of verse 3, above, one possible interpretation is that verse 4 is a continuation of the theme of repenting in order to come unto Christ. In other words, being truly sorry or "mourning" for sins committed.

> 4 Blessed are they that mourn: for they shall be comforted [*by the Holy Ghost*].
> 5 Blessed are the meek: for they shall inherit the earth [*this earth will become the celestial kingdom; see D&C 130:8–9*].
> 6 Blessed are they which do hunger and thirst after righteousness: for they shall be filled.
>
>> 8 *And* blessed are *all* they *that* do hunger and thirst after righteousness; for they shall be filled *with the Holy Ghost*. (JST, Matthew 5:8)

Have you noticed that when you truly "hunger and thirst after righteousness, the commandments are a joy rather than a burden to keep? Verse 7, next, is, in effect, a formula. Based on how we treat others, the script for our own judgment day is basically being written.

> 7 Blessed are the merciful: for they shall obtain mercy.
> 8 Blessed are the pure in heart: for they shall see God [*including when they are in the celestial kingdom*].
> 9 Blessed are the peacemakers: for they shall be called the children of God [*another term for those who inherit the celestial kingdom*].

The phrase "children of God," in verse 9, above, can also refer to faithful followers of Christ right here on earth—see Mosiah 5:7, which, of course, is another way of saying that they ultimately attain celestial glory. See also Psalm 82:6.

> 10 Blessed are they which are persecuted for righteousness' sake: for theirs is the kingdom of heaven [*celestial glory*].
> 11 Blessed are ye, when men shall revile you [*mock you, ridicule you for your righteous beliefs and lifestyle*], and persecute you, and shall say all manner of evil against you falsely, for my sake [*because you follow the Savior*].
> 12 Rejoice, and be exceeding glad: for great is your reward in heaven [*celestial glory*]: for so persecuted they the prophets which were before you [*who lived before you came to earth*].

14 *For ye shall have great joy*, and be exceeding glad; for great *shall be* your reward in heaven; for so persecuted they the prophets which were before you. (JST, Matthew 5:14)

13 Ye are the salt of the earth: but if the salt have lost his savour [*its ability to improve flavor; symbolic of the good that the righteous can do to improve the lives of others*], wherewith shall it be salted [*how will others here on earth be helped*]? it is thenceforth good for nothing, but to be cast out, and to be trodden under foot of men.

15 *Verily, verily, I say unto you, I give unto you to be* the salt of earth; but if the salt *shall* lose its savor, wherewith shall *the earth* be salted? *the salt shall* thenceforth *be* good for nothing, but to be cast out, and to be trodden under foot of men. (JST, Matthew 5:15)

14 Ye are the light of the world. A city that is set on an hill cannot be hid.

16 *Verily, verily, I say unto you, I give unto you to be* the light of the world; a city that is set on a hill cannot be hid. (JST, Matthew 5:16)

It is helpful to know that in the Holy Land, cities were built upon the hills, saving valuable land in the valleys for agricultural and pasture use. The wording in JST Matthew 5:16, above, reminds us of the responsibility of those who are given the blessings of Abraham, Isaac, and Jacob (as often stated in patriarchal blessings) to take the gospel and accompanying blessings of the priesthood to all the world—see Abraham 2:9–11.

15 Neither do men light a candle, and put it under a bushel [*a bushel basket*], but on a candlestick; and it giveth light unto all that are in the house.

17 *Behold*, do men light a candle and put it under a bushel? *Nay*, but on a candlestick; and it giveth light to all that are in the house. (JST, Matthew 5:17)

16 Let your light so shine before men, that they may see your good works, and glorify your Father which is in heaven.

18 *Therefore*, let your light so shine before *this world*, that they may see your good works, and glorify your Father *who* is in heaven. (JST, Matthew 5:18)

The topic now changes to the Savior's role with respect to the law of Moses, starting with verse 17, next. He is the fulfillment of the law of Moses, which was designed as a "schoolmaster" law, to point the minds and behaviors of the children of Israel and their descendants toward accepting the higher gospel that He would bring (Galatians 3:24). Misunderstanding of this issue, or deliberate refusal to accept Jesus as the fulfillment of Old Testament prophecies about the Messiah, led Jewish religious leaders to demand that the Master be crucified.

> 17 Think not that I am come to destroy the law [*of Moses*], or the prophets [*the Old Testament*]: I am not come to destroy, but to fulfil.
> 18 For verily I say unto you, Till heaven and earth pass, one jot or one tittle [*tiny bit*] shall in no wise pass from the law [*law of Moses*], till all be fulfilled.

> > 20 For verily I say unto you, *Heaven and earth must pass away, but* one jot or one tittle shall in no wise pass from the law, *until* all be fulfilled. (JST, Matthew 5:20)

Verse 19, next, is fair warning against those who deliberately twist the scriptures and teach others false doctrine for their own selfish purposes.

> 19 Whosoever therefore shall break one of these least commandments, and shall teach men so, he shall be called the least in the kingdom of heaven [*will not receive a great reward on Judgment Day; in other words, will be punished*]: but whosoever shall do and teach them, the same shall be called great in the kingdom of heaven [*will gain a great reward in the celestial kingdom*].

> > 21 Whosoever, therefore, shall break one of these least commandments, and shall teach men so *to do*, he shall *in no wise be saved* in the kingdom of heaven; but whosoever shall do and teach *these commandments of the law until it be fulfilled*, the same shall be called great, *and shall be saved* in the kingdom of heaven. (JST, Matthew 5:21)

In verse 20, next, the Master points out that the religious leaders of the Jews at the time claim to be living the laws of God, as embodied in the law of Moses, but are actually wicked men.

> 20 For I say unto you, That except your righteousness shall exceed the righteousness of the scribes [*Jewish religious leaders who explained and interpreted the scriptures*] and Pharisees [*an influential religious party among the Jews who adhered very strictly to the law of Moses*], ye shall in no case enter into the kingdom of heaven. [*This was a direct blow to the hypocritical scribes and Pharisees.*]

As mentioned above, the law of Moses had been given as a "schoolmaster" law (see Galatians 3:24) to bring the people to the point where they could accept Christ and His higher gospel teachings, which, if followed, would develop celestial qualities. Beginning with verse 21, next, we see the Savior teaching to help the people make the transition from the law of Moses to His full gospel.

> 21 Ye have heard that it was said by them of old time, Thou shalt not kill; and whosoever shall kill shall be in danger of the judgment [*punishments of God*]:

22 But I say unto you, That whosoever is angry with his brother without a cause [*both the JST and 3 Nephi 12:22 omit the phrase "without a cause"*] shall be in danger of the judgment: and whosoever shall say to his brother, Raca [*a term of derision, such as "You stupid idiot!" See Matthew 5, footnote 22d, in your Bible*], shall be in danger of the council: but whosoever shall say, Thou fool, shall be in danger of hell fire. [*In other words, don't put others down, as if you didn't have any imperfections yourself.*]

> 24 But I say unto you that whosoever is angry with his brother, shall be in danger of *his* judgment; and whosoever shall say to his brother, Raca, *or Rabcha*, shall be in danger of the council; *and* whosoever shall say *to his brother*, Thou fool, shall be in danger of hell fire. (JST, Matthew 5:24)

Some people believe that the word *fool* should never be used, because of the warning in verse 22, above. However, it appears from the scriptures that it is the behavior of demeaning people as if we had no faults or imperfections ourselves that is referred to here. The Apostle Paul uses "fools" in Romans 1:22 as well as in other places, and Nephi, son of Helaman, uses the word in Helaman 9:21.

Next, in the overall context of the Sermon on the Mount as emphasized by JST verse 25, below, we see that avoiding and overcoming contention are necessary qualities for coming unto Christ.

23 Therefore if thou bring thy gift to the altar, and there rememberest that thy brother hath ought against thee [*that you have contention with someone*];

> 23 Therefore, *if ye shall come unto me, or shall desire to come unto me, or* if thou bring thy gift to the altar, and there rememberest that thy brother hath aught against thee, (JST, Matthew 5:25)

24 Leave there thy gift before the altar, and go thy way; first be reconciled to [*make peace with*] thy brother, and then come and offer thy gift.
25 Agree with thine adversary [*make peace with the person you have contention with*] quickly, whiles thou art in the way with him [*while you have the opportunity*]; lest at any time the adversary deliver thee to the judge, and the judge deliver thee to the officer, and thou be cast into prison. [*If you don't try to make peace, it does a lot of damage to you, yourself.*]
26 Verily I say unto thee, Thou shalt by no means come out thence [*from the prison you put yourself into*], till thou hast paid the uttermost farthing. [*You will pay dearly for holding grudges in terms of lack of peace for yourself.*]

Next, the Savior teaches a higher law of chastity than was contained in the law of Moses.

27 Ye have heard that it was said by them of old time [*in the law of Moses*], Thou shalt not commit adultery:

28 But I say unto you, That whosoever looketh on a woman to lust after her hath committed adultery with her already in his heart.

Body parts mentioned in verses 29 and 30 are symbolic of choices, behaviors, associations with friends, sins, and so forth, that could cause you to lose salvation.

29 And if thy right eye [*symbolic of specific temptation, bad environment, friends, bad habit, specific sins, etc.*] offend thee [*puts you in spiritual danger*], pluck it out, and cast it from thee: for it is profitable for thee that one of thy members should perish, and not that thy whole body should be cast into hell.
30 And if thy right hand offend thee, cut it off, and cast it from thee: for it is profitable for thee that one of thy members should perish, and not that thy whole body should be cast into hell.

34 *And now this I speak, a parable concerning your sins; wherefore,* cast *them* from *you, that ye may not be hewn down and cast into the fire.* (JST, Mattew 5:34)

Verses 31 and 32, next, deal with divorce.

31 It hath been said, Whosoever shall put away [*divorce*] his wife, let him give her a writing of divorcement [*a legal divorce document*]:
32 But I say unto you, That whosoever shall put away [*divorce*] his wife, saving for [*except for*] the cause of fornication, causeth her to commit adultery: and whosoever shall marry her that is divorced committeth adultery.

Divorces were common and easy to obtain in the Savior's day. Clearly, marriage and family involve sacred promises which are very serious. In an ideal society, there would seldom, if ever, be a divorce. In cases where divorce has taken place, verse 32 can sometimes be misunderstood to teach that anyone who gets a divorce and then remarries is now living in adultery, except where fornication was involved in leading up to the divorce. This, of course, can present problems. A very important principle about following the Brethren (our First Presidency and Quorum of the Twelve) can be taught here. The principle is that the current practice of the Brethren, under the direction of the Lord, constitutes the correct interpretation of the scriptures. Even if you don't completely understand verse 32, you can understand the Brethren. The principle is defined by the question, "What do the Brethren do?" Do they ever allow a worthy divorced person to be sealed to a spouse in the temple? Answer: Yes. Would they allow such a thing if such sealing led automatically to adultery? Answer: No. It would be a mockery of most sacred ordinances. Conclusion: There must be some things we don't understand about verse 32.

With this in mind, we might wonder at the meaning of specific words in verse 32. For example, the word *fornication* is usually used with respect to sexual sin between unmarried individuals. Why, then, is it used in this verse where married people are involved? One possibility is that the word *fornication* is often used in the scriptures to mean total disloyalty, breaking covenants, and the like. See, for example, Revelation 14:8, 17:2, 19:2.

The word *adultery* is likewise often used in scripture in the sense of total disloyalty to God, breaking covenants, apostasy, and so forth. This is mentioned in the Bible Dictionary, in the back of your LDS edition of the King James Bible, under the topic, "Adultery," where it says: "While adultery is usually spoken of in the individual sense, it is sometimes used to illustrate the apostasy of a nation or a whole people from the ways of the Lord, such as Israel forsaking her God and going after strange gods and strange practices (Ex. 20:14; Jer. 3:7–10; Matt. 5:27–32; Luke 18:11)." Whatever the case, those who have gone through proper channels, working with their priesthood leaders and the General Authorities of the Church, and have remarried in a temple after a divorce, are not living in adultery. Rather, as they remain worthy and continue living in harmony with the gospel, they can look forward to exaltation and living in their family unit forever.

As we continue with the Sermon on the Mount, we see that the Savior dealt with virtually every aspect of daily life, counseling and instructing us in the things that could stand in the way of our attaining celestial exaltation, and exhorting us to develop righteous character traits. The sermon contains a major set of guidelines and goals for daily righteous living.

> 33 Again, ye have heard that it hath been said by them of old time, Thou shalt not forswear thyself [*commit perjury; make false or insincere promises*], but shalt perform unto the Lord thine oaths [*keep your word*]:
> 34 But I say unto you, Swear [*make contracts, promises, etc.*] not at all; neither by heaven; for it is God's throne:
> 35 Nor by the earth; for it is his footstool: neither by Jerusalem; for it is the city of the great King.
> 36 Neither shalt thou swear by thy head, because thou canst not make one hair white or black.

It was common among the Jews in the days of Christ to make agreements, contracts, and so forth, so complex that they were easy to get out of, legally. For instance, if one promised "by the full moon" that a chariot for sale was in top shape, and it wasn't, one could later say to the irate customer that the moon wasn't actually a full moon on the day of the contract, rather, was a day or two away from its full phase. Thus, the one giving his word was legally exempt from keeping it.

37 But let your communication be, Yea, yea; Nay, nay: for whatsoever is more than these cometh of evil. [*In other words, if you make a promise, keep it.*]

Verse 38, next, could be considered a rather high law, as given in Exodus 21:24–25, Leviticus 24:20, and elsewhere. In effect, it meant "only one eye for an eye, only one tooth for a tooth, only one cow for a cow, only one sheep for a sheep." Many people tended to get revenge, killing off a whole village in retaliation for the death of a sheep or other wrong against themselves. Now, the Savior will give a much higher law, a law requiring even more self-control and forgiving. Keeping such higher laws develops Christlike qualities in us. These higher laws are designed by the Lord to lead us along the path toward exaltation, as stated in verse 45, "That ye may be the children of [*successful followers of*] your Father which is in heaven": In other words, this is a vital part of our education toward becoming gods.

38 Ye have heard that it hath been said, An eye for an eye, and a tooth for a tooth:
39 But I say unto you, That ye resist not evil: but whosoever shall smite thee on thy right cheek, turn to him the other also.
40 And if any man will sue thee at the law, and take away thy coat, let him have thy cloke also.
41 And whosoever shall compel thee to go a mile, go with him twain.

Often, we tend to look at these verses and think in terms of extremes. For instance, if attacked by a mob intent on severely harming or killing us, we might be hesitant to give them a head start by "turning the other cheek." In fact, D&C 98:31 gives different instructions for situations where life is in immediate danger. If we look at the Savior's words here in the Sermon on the Mount in terms of daily living, we see that exercising self-control on our part and returning good for evil does much good in our relationships with others.

42 Give to him that asketh thee, and from him that would borrow of thee turn not thou away.
43 Ye have heard that it hath been said, Thou shalt love thy neighbour, and hate thine enemy.
44 But I say unto you, Love your enemies, bless them that curse you, do good to them that hate you, and pray for them which despitefully use you, and persecute you;
45 That ye may be the children of your Father which is in heaven [*that you may be received into celestial glory and become gods*]: for he maketh his sun to rise on

the evil and on the good, and sendeth rain on the just [*the righteous*] and on the unjust [*the wicked*]. [*He shows love and kindness for all.*]

46 For if ye love them which love you, what reward have ye? do not even the publicans the same? [*Publicans were Jews who worked for the Roman government as tax collectors. They were hated by the Jews and were excommunicated when they accepted such employment. See Bible Dictionary, under "Publicans"*]

47 And if ye salute your brethren only, what do ye more than others? do not even the publicans so?

As we become more successful in developing the Christlike qualities given in the above commandments, we draw closer to fulfilling the startling yet wonderful commandment given next in verse 48.

48 Be ye therefore perfect, even as your Father which is in heaven is perfect. [*The word* perfect, *as used here, means "complete," "finished," "fully developed," as stated in Matthew 5:48, footnote b. This denotes our actively pursuing the path leading to exaltation, eventually becoming "fully developed," in other words, becoming gods (D&C 132:20), and thus makes this commandment attainable for us.*]

50 *Ye are* therefore *commanded to be* perfect, even as your Father *who* is in heaven is perfect. (JST, Matthew 5:50)

MATTHEW 6

This next part of the Savior's sermon deals with the importance of proper motives for our worship and actions.

1 Take heed that ye do not your alms [*contributions to the poor, and so forth*] before men, to be seen of them [*your main motive for doing them*]: otherwise ye have no reward of your Father which is in heaven.

2 Therefore when thou doest thine alms, do not sound a trumpet before thee, as the hypocrites [*people who want to look righteous but do not want to be righteous*] do in the synagogues and in the streets, that they may have glory of men. Verily I say unto you, They have their reward [*the shallow reward of having people think they are righteous*].

3 But when thou doest alms, let not thy left hand know what thy right hand doeth:

4 That thine alms may be in secret: and thy Father which seeth in secret himself shall reward thee openly.

5 And when thou prayest, thou shalt not be as the hypocrites are: for they love to pray standing in the synagogues [*church buildings where the Jews worshiped*] and in the corners of the streets, that they may be seen of men. Verily I say unto you, They have their reward.

6 But thou, when thou prayest, enter into thy closet, and when thou hast shut thy door, pray to thy Father which is in secret; and thy Father which seeth in secret shall reward thee openly.

7 But when ye pray, use not vain [*useless, meaningless, ineffective*] repetitions, as the heathen [*non-Jews, non-Christians*] do: for they think that they shall be heard for their much speaking.

8 Be not ye therefore like unto them: for your Father knoweth what things ye have need of, before ye ask him.

The Savior now gives us what is commonly known as The Lord's Prayer. It is a beautiful example of prayer and may be considered to be one example of appropriate prayer, rather than a rigid form to be followed without deviation.

THE LORD'S PRAYER

9 After this manner therefore pray ye: Our Father which art in heaven, Hallowed [*sacred, holy*] be thy name.

10 Thy kingdom come. Thy will be done in earth, as it is in heaven.

11 Give us this day our daily bread.

12 And forgive us our debts [*sins, faults, offenses—see Matthew 6:12, footnote a*], as we forgive our debtors. [*This is an important formula for obtaining forgiveness for our own sins.*]

13 And lead us not into temptation [*we should avoid purposely putting ourselves into temptation*], but deliver us from evil: For thine is the kingdom, and the power, and the glory, for ever. Amen.

Next, the vital subject of forgiving others in order to be forgiven ourselves is taught. If you stop to think about it, God is very forgiving. People who properly repent of their sins are completely forgiven by the Lord (D&C 58:42). If we want to become gods (D&C 132:20), it is obvious that we will have to develop the capacity to be forgiving. Thus, what the Savior teaches next is vital to our salvation.

14 For if ye forgive men their trespasses [*their sins against you*], your heavenly Father will also forgive you:

15 But if ye forgive not men their trespasses, neither will your Father forgive your trespasses. [*This is a very simple guide to obtaining forgiveness ourselves.*]

The Savior now reminds us again that our internal motives are what really count in pursuing the path to exaltation.

16 Moreover when ye fast, be not, as the hypocrites, of a sad countenance: for they disfigure their faces, that they may appear unto men to fast. Verily I say unto you, They have their reward [*their reward is that people look at them and think that they are righteous*].

17 But thou, when thou fastest, anoint thine head, and wash thy face [*groom yourself to be presentable in public*];

18 That thou appear not unto men to fast, but unto thy Father which is in secret:

and thy Father, which seeth in secret, shall reward thee openly.

The Savior now reminds us that our priorities and energies need to be focused on things that have eternal value.

19 Lay not up for yourselves treasures upon earth, where moth and rust doth corrupt, and where thieves break through and steal:
20 But lay up for yourselves treasures in heaven, where neither moth nor rust doth corrupt, and where thieves do not break through nor steal:
21 For where your treasure is, there will your heart be also.

In the Book of Mormon, we find the following counsel about obtaining personal wealth which can go along with these teachings of the Savior about priorities, in the Sermon on the Mount:

17 Think of your brethren like unto yourselves, and be familiar with all and free with your substance, that they may be rich like unto you.
18 But before ye seek for riches, seek ye for the kingdom of God.
19 And after ye have obtained a hope in Christ ye shall obtain riches, if ye seek them; and ye will seek them for the intent to do good—to clothe the naked, and to feed the hungry, and to liberate the captive, and administer relief to the sick and the afflicted. (Jacob 2:17–19)

We now continue with the Sermon on the Mount, where the Master gives counsel about what we allow into our minds.

22 The light of the body is the eye: if therefore thine eye be single [*Matthew 6:22, footnote b, healthy, sincere, without improper motives*], thy whole body shall be full of light. [*What you watch, read, intentionally look at, etc., strongly affects your spiritual well-being.*]

22 Single *to the glory of God.* (JST, Matthew 6:22)

23 But if thine eye be evil [*intentionally takes in evil things*], thy whole body shall be full of darkness. If therefore the light that is in thee be darkness, how great is that darkness [*spiritual darkness*]!
24 No man can serve two masters: for either he will hate the one, and love the other; or else he will hold to the one, and despise the other. Ye cannot serve God and mammon [*worldly sins, pleasures, desires*].

INSTRUCTIONS TO THE APOSTLES

We learn from the wording in the JST, next, that the Savior now turns from the multitude and addresses verses 25–34 specifically to His Apostles and some disciples, telling them how they will be taken care of by the Father while on their missions. If you do not understand this, you might mistakenly consider some of the counsel in verses 25 to 34 to apply to all people. For example, you might quit working and trust the Lord to take care of you, thinking that if you have sufficient faith all your needs will be taken care of. Some individuals and groups have misapplied these verses in that way, with sad results.

> 25 *And, again, I say unto you, go ye into the world, and care not for the world; for the world will hate you, and will persecute you, and will turn you out of their synagogues.*
> 26 *Nevertheless, ye shall go forth from house to house, teaching the people; and I will go before you.*
> 27 *And your heavenly Father will provide for you, whatsoever things ye need for food, what ye shall eat; and for raiment, what ye shall wear or put on.* (JST, Matthew 6:25–27)

25 Therefore I say unto you [*the Savior's Apostles and disciples, who are now being given instructions to take the gospel to all the world*], Take no thought for your life, what ye shall eat, or what ye shall drink; nor yet for your body, what ye shall put on. Is not the life more than meat [*food; in our Bible's language, "meat" means food in general, "flesh" means meat as we use the word today*], and the body than raiment [*clothing*]?

26 Behold the fowls of the air: for they sow not [*don't plant crops*], neither do they reap [*harvest crops*], nor gather into barns [*nor store grain in barns*]; yet your heavenly Father feedeth them. Are ye [*the Savior's Apostles and disciples*] not much better than they?

27 Which of you by taking thought can add one cubit [*about 18 inches*] unto his stature [*physical height*]?

28 And why take ye thought for raiment [*clothing*]? Consider the lilies of the field, how they grow; they toil not, neither do they spin [*weave cloth*]:

29 And yet I say unto you, That even Solomon in all his glory was not arrayed [*dressed*] like one of these.

30 Wherefore, if God so clothe the grass of the field, which to day is, and to morrow is cast into the oven, shall he not much more clothe you, O ye of little faith?

Our full-time missionaries today operate under the same system, in the sense that all of their physical needs are met by contributions from others.

31 Therefore take no thought [*don't worry about your physical needs while on missions and doing My work*], saying, What shall we eat? or, What shall we drink? or, Wherewithal shall we be clothed?

32 (For after all these things do the Gentiles seek:) for your heavenly Father knoweth that ye have need of all these things.

33 But seek ye first the kingdom of God, and his righteousness; and all these things shall be added unto you. [*Cross-reference this with Jacob 2:17–19 as given between verses 20 and 21 above.*]

34 Take therefore no thought for the morrow: for the morrow shall take thought for the things of itself [*in other words, the Lord will take care of the Apostles' physi-*

cal needs while they are on missions]. Sufficient unto the day is the evil thereof. [*The New International Version of the Bible translates this sentence to read, "Each day has enough trouble of its own." In other words, the Apostles and disciples are being told that they will have enough daily troubles in preaching the gospel, without the distraction of worrying about their physical needs.*]

MATTHEW 7

Jesus begins this portion of the sermon with cautions about being judgmental of others. Obviously, there are situations in which we must judge, or we would constantly be victims of foolishness and deceit. As you will see, the JST adds important clarity to verse 1.

1 Judge not, that ye be not judged [*judged harshly by the Lord, based on the law of justice*].

> 1. *Now these are the words which Jesus taught his disciples that they should say unto the people.*
> 2. Judge not *unrighteously*, that ye be not judged: *but judge righteous judgment.* (JST, Matthew 7:1–2)

2 For with what judgment ye judge, ye shall be judged: and with what measure ye mete [*give out to others*], it shall be measured to you again.
3 And why beholdest thou the mote [*tiny speck; imperfection*] that is in thy brother's eye, but considerest not the beam [*large wooden beam; symbolic of shortcomings, faults*] that is in thine own eye?
4 Or how wilt thou say to thy brother, Let me pull out the mote out of thine eye; and, behold, a beam is in thine own eye?
5 Thou hypocrite, first cast out the beam out of thine own eye; and then shalt thou see clearly to cast out the mote out of thy brother's eye.

> 4 *And again, ye* [the Apostles, as mentioned in JST verse 1, above] *shall say unto them* [the people you will be teaching], *Why is it that thou* beholdest the mote that is in thy brother's eye, but considerest not the beam that is in thine own eye?
> 5 Or how wilt thou say to thy brother, Let me pull out the mote out of thine eye; *and canst not behold* a beam in thine own eye?
> 6 *And Jesus said unto his disciples, Beholdest thou the Scribes, and the Pharisees, and the Priests, and the Levites? They teach in their synagogues, but do not observe the law, nor the commandments; and all have gone out of the way, and are under sin.*
> 7 *Go thou and say unto them, Why teach ye men the law and the commandments, when ye yourselves are the children of corruption?*
> 8 *Say unto them,* Ye hypocrites, first cast out the beam out of thine own eye; and then shalt thou see clearly to cast out the mote out of thy brother's eye. (JST, Matthew 7:4–8)

Next, the Master gives cautions about sharing sacred things with others who cannot or will not respect and reverence them.

6 Give not that which is holy unto the dogs, neither cast ye your pearls before swine [*be careful with whom you share sacred things*], lest they trample them under their feet, and turn again and rend you [*they may turn on you and try to destroy your testimony*].

> 9 *Go ye into the world, saying unto all, Repent, for the kingdom of heaven has come nigh unto you.*
> 10 *And the mysteries of the kingdom ye shall keep within yourselves; for it is not meet to* give that which is holy unto the dogs; neither cast ye your pearls *unto* swine, lest they trample them under their feet.
> 11 *For the world cannot receive that which ye, yourselves, are not able to bear; wherefore ye shall not give your pearls unto them, lest they* turn again and rend you. (JST, Matthew 7:9–11)

As we diligently and humbly pursue our way on the "strait and narrow" path (Matthew 7:14, 1 Nephi 8:20) toward exaltation, we need much help and constant inspiration from above. The Lord next invites us to feel free to ask for help and guidance as we go along.

7 Ask, and it shall be given you; seek, and ye shall find; knock, and it shall be opened unto you: [*The words* ask, seek, *and* knock *remind us that work and effort are required on our part.*]
8 For every one that asketh receiveth; and he that seeketh findeth; and to him that knocketh it shall be opened.

> 12 *Say unto them, Ask of God;* ask, and it shall be given you; seek, and ye shall find; knock, and it shall be opened unto you.
> 13 For every one that asketh, receiveth; and he that seeketh, findeth; and *unto* him that knocketh, it shall be opened. (JST, Matthew 7:12–13)

There are verses missing from the Bible, here, which were replaced in the JST and provide important additional meaning and context.

> 14 *And then said his disciples unto him, they will say unto us, We ourselves are righteous, and need not that any man should teach us. God, we know, heard Moses and some of the prophets; but us he will not hear.*
> 15 *And they will say, We have the law for our salvation, and that is sufficient for us.*
> 16 *Then Jesus answered, and said unto his disciples, thus shall ye say unto them,*
> 17 *What man among you, having a son, and he shall be standing out, and shall say, Father, open thy house that I may come in and*

sup with thee, will not say, Come in, my son; for mine is thine, and thine is mine? (JST, Matthew 7:12–17)

9 Or what man is there of you, whom if his son ask bread, will he give him a stone?

10 Or if he ask a fish, will he give him a serpent?

11 If ye then, being evil, know how to give good gifts unto your children, how much more shall your Father which is in heaven give good things to them that ask him?

THE GOLDEN RULE

12 Therefore all things whatsoever ye would that men should do to you, do ye even so to them: for this is the law and the prophets [*the* law *means the first five books of the Old Testament;* prophets *means the inspired writings of Old Testament prophets; the meaning of the phrase "for this is the law and the prophets" is that a major focus of the law and the prophets was to teach us to be good to each other*].

13 Enter ye in at the strait gate [*spelled this way,* strait *means "narrow," reminding us that this gate has specific access, and requires focus, faith, repentance, baptism, and personal righteousness for entrance*]: for wide is the gate, and broad is the way, that leadeth to destruction, and many there be which go in thereat [*there are many ways to be wicked*]:

In the next verse we find the words *strait* and *narrow* used together. This is often referred to as "the strait and narrow path," meaning, in effect, the "narrow and narrowing path." The message here is that the more righteous you become, the more you restrict your behaviors away from evil and toward personal righteousness. The imagery is that the less you wander back and forth toward the outer edges of the path, seeing how close you can get to temptation and evil, the "narrower" your agency-chosen path becomes. There is a bit of a caution here: As you become more righteous, you discover inappropriate personal behaviors which you didn't even notice before. Sometimes, faithful Saints become discouraged and think "It's no use. I'll never be perfect!" as these so-called smaller imperfections come to light. Actually, you might want to rejoice in the fact that your path has become sufficiently narrow that you notice these imperfections. Then, go ahead and work on overcoming them.

14 Because strait is the gate, and narrow is the way, which leadeth unto life [*eternal life, exaltation*], and few there be that find it.

Next, we are given a simple but extremely important test by which we can detect false philosophies, dangerous teachings, bad examples, subtle deviations from truth, and so forth, that abound in the world around us.

15 Beware of false prophets [*anyone who teaches false philosophies, behaviors, etc., by word, example, deed, or whatever*], which come to you in sheep's clothing [*they*

seem harmless], but inwardly they are ravening [*very dangerous*] wolves.

16 Ye shall know them by their fruits [*what they ultimately produce*]. Do men gather grapes of thorns, or figs of thistles [*can you harvest good food from weeds*]?

17 Even so every good tree bringeth forth good fruit; but a corrupt tree bringeth forth evil fruit [Tree *is used here to symbolize people*].

18 A good tree cannot bring forth evil fruit, neither can a corrupt tree bring forth good fruit.

19 Every tree that bringeth not forth good fruit is hewn down, and cast into the fire [*symbolic of the burning of the wicked at the Second Coming; also symbolic of the final judgment*].

20 Wherefore [*therefore*] by their fruits ye shall know them.

The Master now emphasizes again that the gate is "strait" (narrow). In other words, we must keep the commandments in order to enter celestial glory.

21 Not every one that saith unto me, Lord, Lord, shall enter into the kingdom of heaven [*celestial glory*]; but he that doeth the will of my Father which is in heaven.

22 Many will say to me in that day [*judgment day*], Lord, Lord, have we not prophesied in thy name? and in thy name have cast out devils? and in thy name done many wonderful works?

23 And then will I profess unto them, I never knew you: depart from me, ye that work iniquity [*commit sin; disobey the laws of God*].

The JST makes a very important change to verse 23, above. It is not that the Savior does not know the wicked. Rather, it is the wicked who do not know the Savior!

And then will I *say, Ye never knew me*. (JST, Matthew 7:33)

The Master Teacher concludes His sermon on this beautiful hill in Galilee, with a story about two men. One, representing the wise and humble, diligently builds his house on a firm foundation, a rock, symbolic in the scriptures of Jesus Christ and His gospel (1 Samuel 2:2). The other man, representing the vain and foolish, builds his house upon the sand, which can symbolize the changing values and whims of men, and which does not provide a sure foundation when trouble comes. A major message here for us is that, if we are wise, we will carefully study the Savior's teachings given in this sermon and diligently apply them in our lives.

HOUSE BUILT ON A ROCK

24 Therefore whosoever heareth these sayings of mine, and doeth them, I will liken him unto a wise man, which built his house [*symbolic of his life*] upon a rock [*symbolic of Christ, who is the "Rock" of our salvation, see, for example, Hymn 258*]:

25 And the rain descended, and the floods came, and the winds blew [*trials and difficulties of life*], and beat upon that house [*his life*]; and it fell not: for it was founded upon a rock [*Christ*].

HOUSE BUILT ON SAND

26 And every one that heareth these sayings of mine [*in other words, who is accountable*], and doeth them not, shall be likened unto a foolish man, which built his house upon the sand [*worldly ways, priorities, philosophies, and so forth*]:
27 And the rain descended, and the floods came, and the winds blew, and beat upon that house [*his life*]; and it fell: and great was the fall of it.

Did you notice that the "rain descended, and the floods came, and the winds blew, and beat upon" both houses? In other words, trials and tribulation are a part of mortality for the righteous as well as the wicked. The outcome for us is determined by the foundation upon which we build.

28 And it came to pass, when Jesus had ended these sayings, the people were astonished at his doctrine:

> 36 And it came to pass when Jesus had ended these sayings *with his disciples*, the people were astonished at his doctrine; (JST, Matthew 7:36)

29 For he taught them as one having authority, and not as the scribes [*the main teachers and interpreters of the law among the Jews who rose in great opposition to the Savior; see Bible Dictionary, under "Scribes"*].

> 37 For he taught them as one having authority *from God*, and not as *having authority from* the scribes. (JST, Matthew 7:37)

HEALING OF THE CENTURION'S SERVANT

In Capernaum, a Roman centurion approached Jesus and humbly implored the Master to heal his servant (Matthew 8:5–6). A centurion was a Roman soldier in charge of one hundred soldiers and, thus, could wield great power over the Jews if he so desired. The Romans were Gentiles, and as such were falsely considered by the Jews to be inferior in the eyes of God. The Jews considered themselves to be God's only chosen people. All others, despite their best efforts, were considered by them to be second-class citizens in the Kingdom of God. This healing of the centurion's servant became the basis for the Savior's teaching that all people are equal in the sight of God and all must qualify themselves for salvation, through His Atonement. When Jesus told the Centurion that He would come to his home and heal the servant, the Roman's response demonstrated his humility and faith.

8 The centurion answered and said, Lord, I am not worthy that thou shouldest come under my roof: but speak the word only, and my servant shall be healed.

9 For I am a man under authority, having soldiers under me: and I say to this man, Go, and he goeth; and to another, Come, and he cometh; and to my servant, Do this, and he doeth it.

10 When Jesus heard it, he marvelled, and said to them that followed, Verily I say unto you, I have not found so great faith, no, not in Israel. (Matthew 8:8–10)

> 9 *And when they that followed him, heard this, they marveled, and* when Jesus heard this, he said unto them that followed, Verily I say unto you, I have not found so great faith, no, not in Israel. (JST, Matthew 8:9)

The next two verses contain the doctrine that the gospel is for all people regardless of their origins or status in life. And verse 13 gives the happy result of the Centurion's faith.

11 And I say unto you, That many shall come from the east and west [*many foreigners, including Gentiles*], and shall sit down with Abraham, and Isaac, and Jacob, in the kingdom of heaven [*will be saved along with Abraham, Isaac, and Jacob in celestial glory*].

12 But the children of the kingdom [*those Jews who considered themselves to be elite, above all other people*] shall be cast out into outer darkness [*probably not meaning into perdition, with Satan, rather, into the spirit world prison, as explained in Alma 40:11–13*]: there shall be weeping and gnashing of teeth.

13 And Jesus said unto the centurion, Go thy way; and as thou hast believed, so be it done unto thee. And his servant was healed in the selfsame hour.

A WIDOW'S SON IS RAISED FROM THE DEAD

Jesus and His disciples went to Nain, a city in southern Galilee, about ten miles southeast of Nazareth, with a large crowd following Him. As they approached the city gate, they saw a large funeral procession. It was a widow's only son who had died (Luke 7:11–12). The people with Him that day will plainly see that the Savior has power over life and death.

13 And when the Lord saw her, he had compassion on her, and said unto her, Weep not.

14 And he came and touched the bier [*the board being used to carry the dead man*]: and they [*the pallbearers*] that bare [*carried*] him stood still. And he said, Young man, I say unto thee, Arise.

15 And he that was dead sat up, and began to speak. And he delivered him [*turned him over*] to his mother. (Luke 7:13–15)

BACK IN CAPERNAUM: PETER'S MOTHER-IN-LAW IS HEALED

Back in Capernaum again, Jesus was in Peter's house. Peter's wife's mother lay ill with a fever. From what Matthew records, we understand that this good woman was anxious to help host the honored guests in Peter's home, and we suspect that it would have been terribly frustrating to her to be incapacitated by sickness at such a time.

> 14 And when Jesus was come into Peter's house, he saw his wife's mother laid, and sick of a fever.
> 15 And he touched her hand [*took hold of her hand—see Matthew 8:15, footnote a*], and the fever left her: and she arose, and ministered unto them. (Matthew 8:14–15)

One aspect of doctrinal significance attached to these verses is that Peter was married. The false doctrine of celibacy (believing that intentionally remaining single rather than marrying is a higher form of devotion to God than marriage), which is held to by some, is thus unsubstantiated by the Bible. Peter became the highest officer in the New Testament church after the Savior's resurrection and ascension into heaven (Acts 1:15), and he, of course, was married.

MANY MORE HEALINGS IN CAPERNAUM

In great anticipation and excitement, many are brought to the Master to heal while He is in Capernaum. Both His power over Satan's kingdom and His power to heal physical illness are demonstrated.

> 16 When the even [*evening*] was come, they brought unto him many that were possessed with devils: and he cast out the spirits with his word, and healed all that were sick [*symbolic of the Atonement's power to cleanse and heal*]:
> 17 That it might be fulfilled which was spoken by Esaias [*Isaiah*] the prophet, saying, Himself [*Christ*] took our infirmities, and bare our sicknesses [*see Isaiah 53:5, Alma 7:12*].

From the above verse and cross-references, we see again that the Savior's Atonement works not only for our sins, but also for our infirmities, meaning our shortcomings, imperfections, and so forth, as we strive to live righteously.

CALMING THE SEA

At this point, the throngs crowded and pressed such that the Master requested His disciples to get a ship and take Him to the other side of the Sea of Galilee. They did so, and being exhausted, Jesus slept so soundly that even a threatening storm that came up did not awaken Him. We are reminded that the Savior could get very, very tired and weary. In Mosiah 3:7, we read: "And lo, he shall suffer temptations, and pain of body, hunger, thirst, and fatigue, even more than man can suffer, except it be unto death."

It is not difficult to imagine His disciples' reluctance to wake Him as the storm intensified, but finally they did, feeling that they were in imminent danger of sinking and drowning. This moment is illustrated in our hymn 105, "Master the Tempest is Raging," which was written in honor of the Lord's power to calm the elements. In a sense, these Apostles are going through a rather intense "MTC" experience with the Master as their instructor. Their testimonies and understandings are still being strengthened and fortified and will be much enhanced by this experience with the Savior's power.

> 24 And, behold, there arose a great tempest [*storm*] in the sea, insomuch that the ship was covered with the waves: but he [*the Savior*] was asleep.
> 25 And his disciples came to him, and awoke him, saying, Lord, save us: we perish.
> 26 And he saith unto them, Why are ye fearful, O ye of little faith? Then he arose, and rebuked the winds and the sea; and there was a great calm.
> 27 But the men marvelled, saying, What manner of man is this, that even the winds and the sea obey him [*the disciples are still learning about the Savior and who He really is*]!

EVIL SPIRITS ENTER INTO SWINE

After the sea was calmed and the ship had arrived at the eastern shore of the Sea of Galilee, Matthew reports that two men possessed with devils confronted the Savior (Matthew 8:28). Mark and Luke record that there was one man (Mark 5:1–20; Luke 8:26–39). He cast the devils out and they entered into a herd of two-thousand swine (Mark 5:13). The swine went headlong into the sea and drowned (Matthew 8:28–32). Perhaps you have noticed that a rather quiet but consistent message of the Lord's mortal mission is that He has power over the kingdom of the devil. This is important knowledge. Without it, some come to believe that Satan is winning the battle and will ultimately triumph over God. He won't.

In a sad commentary on valuing materialism over things of the Spirit, the owners of the swine asked the Savior to leave, rather than inviting Him to stay and teach them His gospel. Apparently they didn't want another economic disaster and were thus blinded by material priorities to the eternal opportunity that stood before them.

> 34 And, behold, the whole city came out to meet Jesus: and when they saw him, they besought him that he would depart out of their coasts. (Matthew 8:34)

BACK TO CAPERNAUM
THE SAVIOR FORGIVES SINS

A Man with Palsy Is Healed

After the incident with the two men possessed of devils, and the drowning of the swine, the Savior again entered a ship, and He and those with Him went west across the Sea of Galilee back to Capernaum, which by now He was claiming as "his own city" (Matthew 9:1), since His hometown of Nazareth rejected Him (Matthew 4:13–16). While there, some people brought a man afflicted with palsy to Him to be healed. Initially, to their great surprise and perhaps some disappointment, He forgave the man's sins. In perspective, all of us have sins, and forgiveness of them is a far greater blessing that any physical healing could be.

> 2 And, behold, they brought to him a man sick of the palsy, lying on a bed: and Jesus seeing their faith said unto the sick of the palsy; Son, be of good cheer [*cheer up*]; thy sins be forgiven thee. (Matthew 9:2)

Among the onlookers at the time of this miracle were some scribes. Scribes were religious leaders among the Jews who claimed the right to interpret the scriptures and wielded great power in the Jewish culture. They were incensed when Jesus forgave the palsied man's sins. The drama that follows is spellbinding.

> 3 And, behold, certain of the scribes said within themselves, This man blasphemeth [*is acting with total disrespect for God and sacred things; a crime punishable by death in the Jewish society of the day*].
> 4 And Jesus knowing their thoughts [*the scribes' thoughts*] said, Wherefore [*why*] think ye evil in your hearts?
> 5 For whether [*which*] is easier, to say, Thy sins be forgiven thee; or to say, Arise, and walk? [*Any person could say "your sins are forgiven," because there is no immediate proof as to whether or not he speaks with authority. But, if a person says "arise and walk," there will be immediate evidence as to whether or not he is a fake.*]
> 6 But that ye may know that the Son of man [*the "Son of 'Man of Holiness.'" Man*

of Holiness is Heavenly Father's name in Adam's language—see Moses 6:57. In other words, Jesus is telling these scribes that He is the Son of God] hath power on earth to forgive sins, (then saith he to the sick of the palsy,) Arise, take up thy bed, and go unto thine house.

7 And he [*the man healed of palsy*] arose, and departed to his house.

> 5 For *is it not easier* to say, Thy sins be forgiven thee, *than to* say, Arise and walk?
>
> 6 But *I said this* that ye may know that the Son of man hath power on earth to forgive sins.
>
> 7 *Then Jesus said unto* the sick of the palsy, Arise, take up thy bed, and go unto thy house. (JST, Matthew 9:5–7)

8 But when the multitudes saw it, they marvelled, and glorified God, which had given such power unto men. (Matthew 9:3–8)

MATTHEW IS CALLED

After healing the man with palsy, Jesus went to the shore of the Sea of Galilee with large crowds following Him. As He passed by, he saw Matthew sitting at his tax collector's table, and called him to follow Him. "And he left all, rose up, and followed him" (Luke 5:28). He will eventualy become an Apostle. Matthew was a publican or tax collector, also known as Levi (Matthew 9:9; Mark 2:14). Publicans were despised by the people. There is a lesson for us in the fact that the Master called him to serve as an Apostle. The gospel is for all people, and there are good people in every nation and culture. Later, Matthew (Levi) hosted a great feast at his home in Capernaum in honor of Jesus. As always, at this point in the Savior's mortal ministry (this is near the midpoint of His three-year formal ministry), the scribes and Pharisees are watching Him closely, seeking to find justification for having Him arrested and executed. In fact, many of them have come all the way from Jerusalem to Galilee for this express purpose. Watch how these Jewish leaders avoid confronting Jesus directly, and instead direct their question to His disciples. Their question gave rise to a very well-known quote from the Savior in verse 31.

> 29 And Levi made him a great feast in his own house: and there was a great company of publicans and of others that sat down with them.
>
> 30 But their scribes and Pharisees murmured against his disciples, saying, Why do ye eat and drink with publicans [*tax collectors*] and sinners?
>
> 31 And Jesus answering said unto them, They that are whole need not a physician; but they that are sick.
>
> 32 I came not to call the righteous, but sinners to repentance. (Luke 5:29–32)

THE DAUGHTER OF JAIRUS RAISED FROM THE DEAD

A Woman with an Issue of Blood Is Healed

During the Savior's ministry in Galilee, we are seeing testimony after testimony of His power over the elements, over evil spirits, over disease and sickness of every kind. He has but to command and He is obeyed. He is obeyed by all, that is, except some people who exercise their agency to ignore or disobey Him. Now, we will once again witness His marvelous power over death, another symbolic testimony that He has power through His Atonement to bring resurrection to all (1 Corinthians 15:22).

A ruler of a synagogue in Capernaum named Jairus, no doubt going against extreme peer pressure from other Jewish religious leaders, humbly bowed at Jesus' feet and asked in faith for Him to heal his dying twelve-year-old daughter. As the Master went toward Jairus' home, huge crowds pressed and bumped against Him. Suddenly, He felt power go out of Him, and stopped and asked who had touched Him. Peter and the other disciples were a bit incredulous that He would even ask such a question, since so many people in the throng were touching and bumping into Him.

> 45 And Jesus said, Who touched me? When all denied [*nobody admitted touching him*], Peter and they that were with him said, Master, the multitude throng thee and press thee [*people in this crowd are bumping You and pressing against You constantly*], and sayest thou, Who touched me [*what do You mean, "who touched me"*]?
> 46 And Jesus said, Somebody hath touched me: for I perceive that virtue [*power; strength*] is gone out of me. (Luke 8:45–46)

When we go back a couple of verses we see that it was a woman who had spent all her money on doctor bills over the past twelve years, going from one physician to another as they tried in vain to heal her.

> 43 And a woman having an issue of blood twelve years [*who had been bleeding for twelve years*], which had spent all her living upon physicians, neither could be healed of any [*no doctors had successfully treated her illness*],
> 44 Came behind him, and touched the border of his garment [*robe, cloak*]: and immediately her issue of blood stanched [*the bleeding stopped*]. (Luke 8:43–44)

We are seeing a lesson in the power of faith here. Imagine the woman's relief when the Master mercifully put her at ease and explained to her that through her faith, she was healed.

47 And when the woman saw that she was not hid [*that she had been discovered*], she came trembling, and falling down before him, she declared unto him before [*in front of*] all the people for what cause [*the reason why*] she had touched him and how she was healed immediately.

48 And he said unto her, Daughter, be of good comfort: thy faith hath made thee whole [*healed*]; go in peace. (Luke 8:45–48)

While Jesus was talking with the woman who had been healed, someone came from Jairus' home and told him that his daughter had passed away and it was not necessary to impose further on the Master to come (Luke 8:49).

50 But when Jesus heard it, he answered [*responded to*] him, saying, Fear not: believe only [*just have faith*], and she shall be made whole [*will be healed*].

51 And when he came into the house, he suffered [*allowed*] no man to go in, save [*except*] Peter, and James, and John, and the father and the mother of the maiden.

52 And all wept, and bewailed her: but he said, Weep not; she is not dead, but sleepeth.

It was a common custom of the day to have a contingent of mourners bewail the death of a loved one. Apparently, by the time Jesus arrived at Jairus' home, such a group of mourners had already been gathered and had begun their loud wailing.

53 And they [*the mourners*] laughed him to scorn, knowing that she was dead.

54 And he put them all out [*sent the mourners out of the room*], and took her by the hand, and called, saying, Maid, arise.

55 And her spirit came again, and she arose straightway [*immediately*]: and he commanded to give her meat [*food*]. (Luke 8:50–55)

In the language of our King James Bible, "meat" means any type of food. "Flesh" means meat, as in beef, lamb, chicken, etc.

56 And her parents were astonished: but he charged [*instructed*] them that they should tell no man what was done. (Luke 8:56)

Some experiences with God are very private and personal and are to be kept to ourselves. Perhaps this is the reason the parents were so instructed by Jesus.

TWO BLIND MEN ARE HEALED

Symbolically, the healing of those who are physically blind can represent the Savior's power to heal those who are spiritually blind through His gospel and the power of His Atonement. As the Master left Jairus' household, having raised his young daughter back to life, two blind men in Capernaum followed Him, pleading with Him to heal them. Again we see emphasis on the role of faith in healings, and again we will see the Savior request that the healing be kept as a private kindness and not broadcast to the world at large. The healed blind men will fail to comply with His request. Matthew is the only writer of the Gospels who recorded this event.

> 27 And when Jesus departed thence [*from that place*], two blind men followed him, crying, and saying, Thou Son of David [*it was widely taught among the Jews that the Messiah would be a descendant of King David (Matthew 12:23); thus, these blind men were acknowledging Jesus as the promised Messiah*], have mercy on us.
> 28 And when he was come into the house, the blind men came to him: and Jesus saith unto them, Believe ye that I am able to do this? They said unto him, Yea, Lord.
> 29 Then touched he their eyes, saying, According to your faith be it unto you.
> 30 And their eyes were opened; and Jesus straitly charged them [*strictly instructed them*], saying, See that no man know it.
> 31 But they, when they were departed, spread abroad his fame in all that country. (Matthew 9:27–31)

A DEVIL IS CAST OUT OF A MAN

While still in Capernaum (more miracles were done in Capernaum during the Master's mortal mission than in any other city), the people brought a man to the Savior to be healed, who was possessed by a devil and could not speak.

> 32 As they went out, behold, they brought to him a dumb man [*one who could not speak*] possessed with a devil [*an evil spirit*].
> 33 And when the devil was cast out, the dumb spake: and the multitudes marvelled, saying, It was never so seen in Israel. (Matthew 9:32–34)

Perhaps as a reminder to us as to what lengths unbelievers will go to discredit the truth, both Matthew and Luke record that the Pharisees claimed that Jesus' power came from Satan.

> 34 But the Pharisees said, He casteth out devils through the prince of the devils [*the Pharisees, who seem good at missing the point, miss it again, and accuse Jesus of working for Satan and using the devil's power to cast out other devils*]. (Matthew 9:34)

15 But some of them said, He casteth out devils through Beelzebub the chief of the devils [*Jesus is using Satan's power to cast out evil spirits*]. (Luke 11:15)

THE PHARISEES ASK FOR A SIGN

As the Master continued His teaching and healing in Galilee, some scribes and Pharisees challenged Him by asking for a sign. His answer contained a scathing rebuke, indicative of their hypocrisy, and a prophecy of the three days that His body would lie in the tomb between His crucifixion and resurrection.

38 Then certain of the scribes [*interpreters of the religious laws among the Jews, usually Pharisees*] and of the Pharisees answered [*responded*], saying, Master, we would see a sign from thee [*show us a sign which proves that you are the Messiah, the Christ*].

39 But he answered and said unto them, An evil and adulterous generation seeketh after a sign; and there shall no sign be given to it, but the sign of the prophet Jonas [*if I do give you a sign, it will not be what you want, as in the case when Jonah was swallowed by the whale*]:

40 For as Jonas [*Jonah*] was three days and three nights in the whale's belly; so shall the Son of man [*I, Christ*] be three days and three nights in the heart of the earth [*My body will be in the tomb for three days and three nights*].

41 The men of Nineveh [*the city to which Jonah finally went and preached*] shall rise in judgment with this generation, and shall condemn it: because they repented at the preaching of Jonas [*Jonah*]; and, behold, a greater than Jonas is here [*the Son of God is here among you right now; you have no excuse for not repenting!*]. (Matthew 12:38–41)

These scribes and Pharisees do indeed understand that Jesus claims to be the Son of God. The Joseph Smith Translation of the Bible confirms the fact that these Jewish religious leaders had come to that realization somewhat earlier in Jesus' ministry.

21 *And then came certain men unto him, accusing him, saying, Why do ye receive sinners, seeing thou makest thyself the Son of God.* (JST, Mark 3:21)

JESUS' MOTHER AND BRETHREN SEEK TO SPEAK TO HIM

It appears that at this point in the Savior's response to the scribes and Pharisees, His mother and some other family members came and waited outside, desiring to speak to Him.

46 While he yet talked to the people, behold, his mother and his brethren [*Mary and some family members, see Matthew 12, footnote 46a, in your Bible*] stood without [*outside*], desiring to speak with him.

47 Then one [*someone*] said unto him, Behold [*look*], thy mother and thy brethren stand without, desiring to speak with thee.

48 But he answered and said unto him that told him, Who is my mother? and who are my brethren? [*In other words, who is my family? This is a teaching moment.*]

49 And he stretched forth his hand toward his disciples, and said, Behold [*you are seeing*] my mother and my brethren! [*My followers are my family. This answers the question Christ posed in verse 48. See also the answer in verse 50.*]

50 For whosoever shall do the will of my Father which is in heaven, the same is my brother, and sister, and mother. (Matthew 12:46–50)

The JST additions to verse 50, above, are very important because they remind us of His great love and concern for His mother and family members. By the way, this JST addition is one of those that was not included in our current LDS edition of the King James Bible. As previously mentioned, there are a number of JST additions not included because of lack of space. They can be found in the complete JST, which is available in or through most book stores that carry LDS books.

> 44 *And he gave them charge concerning her* [asked them to take good care of His mother], *saying, I go my way, for my Father hath sent me. And* whosoever shall do the will of my Father which is in heaven, the same is my brother, and sister, and mother. (JST, Matthew 12:44)

THE MASTER BEGINS TEACHING IN PARABLES

From this point on, the Master will do much of His teaching through the use of parables. A parable is a story which is used to teach us about real-life situations. The elements of the story represent actual things in people's lives. The Prophet Joseph Smith said: "I have a key by which I understand the scriptures. I enquire, what was the question which drew out the answer, or caused Jesus to utter the parable?" (*TPJS*, pp. 276–77). The Bible Dictionary gives a brief summary of why Jesus taught in parables.

During part of the Galilean ministry the record states that "without a parable spake he not unto them" (Mark 4:34). From our Lord's words (Matthew 13:13–15; Mark 4:12; Luke 8:10) we learn the reason for this method. It was to veil the meaning. The parable conveys to the hearer religious truth exactly in proportion to his faith and intelligence; to the dull and uninspired it is a mere story, "seeing they see not," while to the instructed and spiritual it reveals the mysteries or secrets of the kingdom of heaven. Thus it is that the parable exhibits the condition of all true knowledge. Only he who seeks finds. (Bible Dictionary, under "Parables")

There are eight parables recorded in Matthew, chapter 13, plus one recorded by Mark during this time period.

The Parable of the Sower

The Savior gave the parable of the sower from a ship near the shore of the Sea of Galilee. Because of the crowds which constantly followed Him now, He had entered a ship and had them push out a bit so that He could address the throngs who lined the banks (Matthew 13:1–2). Having situated Himself so that the people could hear Him, He taught them this parable, which pertains to the "seeds" of the gospel that He was "planting" and the various reactions of people to hearing the gospel message. He will provide the interpretation a little later.

3 And he spake many things unto them in parables, saying, Behold, a sower [*a farmer*] went forth to sow [*plant seeds*];

4 And when he sowed, some seeds fell by the way side, and the fowls [*birds*] came and devoured them up:

5 Some fell upon stony places [*where there was only a thin layer of soil, see Matthew. 13:5a*], where they had not much earth: and forthwith [*immediately*] they sprung up, because they had no deepness of earth:

6 And when the sun was up, they were scorched; and because they had no root, they withered away [*dried up and died*].

7 And some fell among thorns; and the thorns sprung up, and choked them:

8 But other fell into good ground, and brought forth fruit, some an hundredfold, [*produced a yield of a hundred times what was planted*] some sixtyfold, some thirtyfold. [*The Savior will explain this parable starting with verse 18.*]

9 Who hath ears to hear, let him hear [*those who are spiritually mature and in tune will understand what I am saying*]. (Matthew 13:3–9)

After His disciples asked Him why He was teaching in parables (Matthew 13:10), He answered their question (Matthew 13:11–17), and then gave the interpretation of this parable.

18 Hear ye therefore the parable of the sower [*I will explain the parable of the sower to you*].

19 When any one heareth the word of the kingdom [*the gospel*], and understandeth it not, then cometh the wicked one, and catcheth away that which was sown in his heart. This is he which received seed by the way side.

20 But he that received the seed into stony places, the same is he that heareth the word, and anon [*immediately*] with joy receiveth it;

21 Yet hath he not root in himself, but dureth [*lasts*] for a while: for when tribulation or persecution ariseth because of the word [*the gospel*], by and by he is offended.

22 He also that received seed among the thorns is he that heareth the word [*the gospel*]; and the care of this world, and the deceitfulness of riches, choke the word, and he becometh unfruitful [*does not remain faithful*].

23 But he that received seed into the good ground is he that heareth the word, and understandeth it; [*this takes work and commitment*] which also beareth fruit [*lives the gospel, remains faithful*], and bringeth forth, some an hundredfold, some sixty, some thirty. (Matthew 13:18–23)

> 21 But he that received seed into the good ground, is he that heareth the word and understandeth *and endureth*; which also beareth fruit, and bringeth forth, some an hundred-fold, some sixty, and some thirty. (JST, Matthew 13:21)

Joseph Smith gives additional insights about the parable of the sower as follows:

But listen to the explanation of the parable of the Sower: "When any one heareth the word of the Kingdom, and understandeth it not, then cometh the wicked one, and catcheth away that which was sown in his heart." Now mark the expression—that which was sown in his heart. This is he which receiveth seed by the way side. Men who have no principle of righteousness in themselves, and whose hearts are full of iniquity, and have no desire for the principles of truth, do not understand the word of truth when they hear it. The devil taketh away the word of truth out of their hearts, because there is no desire for righteousness in them. "But he that receiveth seed in stony places, the same is he that heareth the word, and anon, with joy receiveth it; yet hath he not root in himself, but dureth for a while; for when tribulation or persecution ariseth because of the word, by and by, he is offended. He also that receiveth seed among the thorns, is he that heareth the word; and the care of this world, and the deceitfulness of riches choke the word, and he becometh unfruitful. But he that received seed into the good ground, is he that heareth the word, and understandeth it, which also beareth fruit, and bringeth forth, some an hundred fold, some sixty, some thirty." Thus the Savior Himself explains unto His disciples the parable which He put forth, and left no mystery or darkness upon the minds of those who firmly believe on His words.

We draw the conclusion, then, that the very reason why the multitude, or the world, as they were designated by the Savior, did not receive an explanation upon His parables, was because of unbelief. To you, He says [*speaking to His disciples*] it is given to know the mysteries of the Kingdom of God. And why? Because of the faith and confidence they had in Him. (*TPJS*, p. 97)

THE PARABLE OF THE WHEAT AND THE TARES

A tare is a weed that looks very much like wheat while it is growing. Often, the roots of tares intertwine with the roots of the wheat while both are growing. When the two plants are mature, it is easy to tell the difference between wheat and tares.

24 Another parable put he forth unto them, saying, The kingdom of heaven is likened unto a man [*Christ, see verse 37*] which sowed [*planted*] good seed [*faithful followers of Christ, verse 38*] in his field [*the world, verse 38*]:

25 But while men slept, his enemy [*the devil, verse 39*] came and sowed tares [*wicked people, verse 38*] among the wheat [*faithful members of the Church*], and went his way. (Matthew 13:24–25)

26 But when the blade was sprung up, and brought forth fruit, then appeared the tares also.

27 So the servants of the householder [*Christ*] came and said unto him, Sir, didst not thou sow [*plant*] good seed [*wheat*] in thy field? from whence then hath it tares [*where did the tares come from*]?

28 He said unto them, An enemy hath done this. The servants said unto him, Wilt thou then that we go and gather them up [*would you like us to weed out the tares now*]?

29 But he said, Nay [*No*]; lest [*for fear that*] while ye gather up the tares, ye root up also the wheat with them. (Matthew 13:26–29)

There are several messages for us in verse 29, above. One message might be that there are often insincere and unrighteous members living among the righteous members of wards and branches of the Church. Another message could be that each of us has some "tares" in our own lives and personalities that we tend to weed out as our righteous attributes mature. Jacob 5:65–66, in the Book of Mormon, reminds us that as the good in people grows, the bad can gradually be cleared away. See also D&C 86:6. The Savior continued giving this parable. The JST makes a significant change in the order in which the final harvest takes place.

30 Let both grow together until the harvest: and in the time of harvest I will say to the reapers [*harvesters, angels in verse 39*], Gather ye together first the tares [*the wicked*], and bind them in bundles to burn them: but gather the wheat [*the righteous*] into my barn [*my kingdom*]. (Matthew 13:30)

29 Let both grow together until the harvest, and in the time of harvest, I will say to the reapers, Gather ye together first *the wheat into my barn; and the tares are bound in bundles to be burned.* (JST, Matthew 13:29)

At the request of the disciples, the Savior explained the parable of the wheat and the tares as follows:

> 36 Then Jesus sent the multitude away, and went into the house: and his disciples came unto him, saying, Declare [*explain*] unto us the parable of the tares of the field [*verses 24–30*].
>
> 37 He answered and said unto them, He that soweth [*plants*] the good seed [*wheat; righteousness*] is the Son of man [*Christ*];
>
> 38 The field is the world; the good seed are the children of the kingdom [*faithful members of the Church; the righteous*]; but the tares are the children of the wicked one [*followers of Satan; the wicked*];
>
> 39 The enemy that sowed them is the devil; the harvest is the end of the world; and the reapers [*harvesters*] are the angels.
>
> 40 As therefore the tares [*the wicked*] are gathered and burned in the fire; so shall it be in the end of this world [*the wicked will be burned at the Second Coming*]. (Matthew 13:36–40)

People often ask how the wicked will be burned. D&C 5:19 along with 2 Nephi 12:10, 19, and 21 explain that the wicked will be burned by the brightness of the glory of Christ, who comes in full glory at the time of the Second Coming. Those who are not wicked will be enabled to withstand the glory that will accompany the coming Lord, and thus, will not be consumed.

> 41 The Son of man [*Christ*] shall send forth his angels, and they shall gather out of his kingdom all things that offend, and them which do iniquity [*the wicked*];
>
> 42 And shall cast them into a furnace of fire [*the burning at the Second Coming—see note above*]: there shall be wailing [*bitter crying*] and gnashing [*grinding*] of teeth. (Matthew 13:41–42)

>> 39 The harvest is the end of the world, *or the destruction of the wicked.*
>>
>> 40 The reapers are the angels, *or the messengers sent of heaven.*
>>
>> 41 As, therefore, the tares are gathered and burned in the fire, so shall it be in the end of this world, *or the destruction of the wicked.*
>>
>> 42 *For in that day, before the Son of Man shall come,* he shall send forth his angels *and messengers of heaven.*
>>
>> 43 And they shall gather out of his kingdom all things that offend, and them which do iniquity, and shall cast them *out among the wicked; and* there shall be wailing and gnashing of teeth.
>>
>> 44 *For the world shall be burned with fire.* (JST, Matthew 13:39–44)

> 43 Then shall the righteous shine forth as the sun [*symbolic of celestial glory for the righteous Saints*] in the kingdom of their Father. Who hath ears to hear, let him hear [*those who are spiritually in tune will understand what I am saying*]. (Matthew 13:43)

As mentioned previously, both the JST, verse 29, and D&C 86:7 change the order of the harvesting. The correct order is that the wheat is gathered first. Then the tares are gathered, bundled [*bound*], and burned. This is significant doctrinally, because it indicates that, at the Second Coming, the righteous will be taken up first [*D&C 88:96*], and then the wicked will be burned.

THE PARABLE OF A CANDLE UNDER A BUSHEL

21 And he said unto them, Is a candle brought to be put under a bushel, or under a bed? and not to be set on a candlestick? [*In other words, should the light of the gospel be hidden from people? Answer: No.*]
22 For there is nothing hid, which shall not be manifested; neither was any thing kept secret, but that it should come abroad. [*All things will eventually be revealed to the righteous, who allow the "seed" to continue growing in their hearts and lives. See McConkie,* Doctrinal New Testament Commentary, *Vol. 1, p. 291.*]
23 If any man have ears to hear, let him hear [*you who are spiritually in tune, listen carefully to what I say*]. (Mark 4:21–23)

THE PARABLE OF THE MUSTARD SEED

31 Another parable put he forth unto them, saying, The kingdom of heaven is like to a grain of mustard seed, which a man took, and sowed in his field:
32 Which indeed is the least [*smallest*] of all seeds: but when it is grown, it is the greatest among herbs, and becometh a tree, so that the birds of the air [*symbolic of angels, see TPJS, p. 159*] come and lodge in the branches thereof. (Matthew 13:31–32)

Joseph Smith explained this parable.

And again, another parable put He forth unto them, having an allusion to the Kingdom that should be set up, just previous to or at the time of the harvest, which reads as follows—"The Kingdom of Heaven is like a grain of mustard seed, which a man took and sowed in his field: which indeed is the least of all seeds: but, when it is grown, it is the greatest among herbs, and becometh a tree, so that the birds of the air come and lodge in the branches thereof." Now we can discover plainly that this figure is given to represent the Church as it shall come forth in the last days." (*TPJS*, p. 98. For more of the Prophet's explanation, see *TPJS*, pp. 98–99 and p. 159.)

THE PARABLE OF THE LEAVEN

33 Another parable spake he unto them; The kingdom of heaven is like unto leaven [*an ingredient such as yeast, which, when mixed into bread dough, causes the whole loaf to rise*], which a woman took, and hid in three measures of meal, till the whole was leavened. (Matthew 13:33)

Joseph Smith explained that the leaven in verse 33 could be compared to the true Church as it expands into the whole world. (*TPJS*, pp. 100–102)

THE PARABLE OF THE TREASURE HID IN A FIELD

44 Again [*another parable*], the kingdom of heaven is like unto treasure hid in a field; the which when a man hath found, he hideth, and for joy thereof goeth and selleth all that he hath, and buyeth that field. [*It is worth the sacrificing of whatever it takes to join the Church and to remain faithful.*] (Matthew 13:44)

THE PARABLE OF THE PEARL OF GREAT PRICE

This parable is particularly special to members of the Church because from it, the name of our Pearl of Great Price is derived. The parable is a reminder that the gospel is more valuable than any earthly possession.

45 Again, the kingdom of heaven is like unto a merchant man, seeking goodly pearls:
46 Who, when he had found one pearl of great price, went and sold all that he had, and bought it. (Matthew 13:45–46)

THE PARABLE OF THE NET

It seems that in each ward and branch of the Church, there is often a wide variety of members, some faithful, some not, some representing the Church and the gospel of Jesus Christ very well to the public, and some who do considerable damage to the image of the Church. This next parable, among other things, explains that the "gospel net" gathers all kinds, and that it is a part of the plan.

47 Again, the kingdom of heaven is like unto a net, that was cast into the sea, and gathered of every kind. [*The missionary work of the Church gathers all kinds of converts, some sincere who remain faithful, others who are not sincere, and so forth. This verse also exemplifies that all people will get a chance to join with the Savior's Church, whether in this life or in the spirit world.*]
48 Which, when it was full, they drew to shore, and sat down, and gathered the good into vessels, but cast the bad away.

49 So shall it be at the end of the world: the angels shall come forth, and sever the wicked from among the just [*the righteous*],

50 And shall cast them [*the wicked*] into the furnace of fire [*the burning of the wicked*]: there shall be wailing [*bitter anguish*] and gnashing [*grinding*] of teeth [*symbolic of the extreme suffering of the wicked as they face the consequences of their evil choices*]. (Matthew 13:47–50)

> 50 *And the world is the children of the wicked.*
>
> 51 The angels shall come forth, and sever the wicked from among the just, and shall cast them *out into the world to be burned.* There shall be wailing and gnashing of teeth. (JST, Matthew 13:50–51)

51 Jesus saith unto them, Have ye understood all these things? They say unto him, Yea, Lord. (Matthew 13:51)

THE PARABLE OF THE SCRIBE WHO IS CONVERTED TO THE GOSPEL OF CHRIST

52 Then said he unto them, Therefore every scribe [*scribes were Jewish leaders, generally enemies of Christ, who determined correct interpretation of the scriptures among their people*] which is instructed unto the kingdom of heaven [*who has been converted and become a true follower of Christ, see Matthew 13:52, footnote b*] is like unto a man that is an householder, which bringeth forth [*throws out*] out of his treasure things new and old [*has to throw out many previously held beliefs; see Sperry Symposium, 1983, p. 101*]. (Matthew 13:52)

THE SECOND REJECTION AT NAZARETH

After He had finished teaching these parables, Jesus traveled from the Sea of Galilee to Nazareth. Remember that the last time He visited His hometown, He had been viciously rejected by the people there, who had taken Him out of the city to a cliff and attempted to throw Him over it (Luke 4:29). Their reason for treating Him so was that He had read to them Isaiah's prophecy about the Messiah (Isaiah 61:1–2) and had told them plainly that He was the fulfillment of that prophecy (Luke 4:16–21). That rejection had taken place during the first year of His ministry, and now, nearing the latter part of the second year of His mortal mission, He chose to go again to Nazareth. This time He again taught them in their synagogue and they were amazed at His wisdom and the tremendous miracles that He had performed. Yet, they again gave in to prejudice and disbelief that someone who had grown up among them could be the Messiah. Their lack of faith caused Him to leave without performing miracles similar to those He had done elsewhere.

54 And when he was come into his own country [*Nazareth*], he taught them in their synagogue, insomuch that they were astonished, and said, Whence hath this man this wisdom, and these mighty works?

55 Is not this the carpenter's son? is not his mother called Mary? and his brethren [*brothers, actually half-brothers*], James, and Joses, and Simon, and Judas?

56 And his sisters [*the Greek form of this word means three or more*], are they not all with us? Whence then hath this man all these things? [*Isn't this Joseph and Mary's son? We know the family. How could he possibly be saying and doing such incredible things?*]

57 And they were offended in him [*embarrassed and offended by what He was doing*]. But Jesus said unto them, A prophet is not without honour, save [*except*] in his own country, and in his own house.

58 And he did not many mighty works there because of their unbelief. (Matthew 13:54–58)

In Mark's Gospel (Mark 6:3), we see that they referred to Jesus as "the carpenter," suggesting that He had worked as a carpenter during His growing up years and possibly until He was thirty years old and began His formal mission. We also are told that He did perform a few healings in Nazareth.

1 And he went out from thence, and came into his own country; and his disciples follow him.

2 And when the sabbath day was come, he began to teach in the synagogue: and many hearing him were astonished, saying, From whence hath this man these things? and what wisdom is this which is given unto him, that even such mighty works are wrought by his hands?

3 Is not this the carpenter, the son of Mary, the brother of James, and Joses, and of Juda, and Simon? and are not his sisters here with us? And they were offended at him.

4 But Jesus said unto them, A prophet is not without honour, but in his own country, and among his own kin, and in his own house.

5 And he could there do no mighty work, save that he laid his hands upon a few sick folk, and healed *them*.

6 And he marvelled because of their unbelief. And he went round about the villages, teaching. (Mark 6:1–6)

THE DEATH OF JOHN THE BAPTIST

Herod the Tetrarch Fears That Jesus Is John the Baptist Come Back to Life

As the fame and influence of the Master gained more and more momentum among the people, Herod the tetrarch began to fear that Jesus was John the Baptist come back from the dead. At some point during the first year of the Savior's formal three-year mission, Herod had arrested the Baptist and placed him in prison (Matthew 14:3) in Machaerus in Perea. After he had been in prison for about a year, Herod's wife, Herodias, had succeeded in getting her husband to order him to be beheaded. Now he fears that Jesus, who has a large following, might be John the Baptist, somehow returned from the dead. Both Matthew and Mark tell us why she wanted John dead. He had called Herod to repentance for marrying her, because she was his half-brother Philip's wife. Remember that we are going back a bit in time here to see why Herod fears that Jesus is John the Baptist returned from the dead to cause him grief.

First, Matthew's account:

3 For Herod had laid hold on [*arrested*] John, and bound him, and put him in prison for Herodias' sake [*because of Herodias*], his brother Philip's wife. [*Herod was an immoral man who had married Herodias, his own half-brother's wife*].
4 For John [*the Baptist*] said unto him [*Herod the tetrarch*], It is not lawful for thee to have her.
5 And when he [*Herod*] would have put him [*John the Baptist*] to death, he feared the multitude, because they counted him as a prophet [*considered John the Baptist to be a prophet*]. (Matthew 14:3–5)

Mark's account:

17 For Herod himself had sent forth and laid hold upon [*arrested*] John, and bound him in prison for Herodias' sake [*as requested by Herodias*], his brother Philip's wife: for he had married her [*Herod had married his own half-brother's wife, Herodias*].
18 For John had said unto Herod, It is not lawful for thee to have thy brother's wife.
19 Therefore Herodias had a quarrel against him [*was very angry at John the Baptist*], and would have killed him; but she could not [*at first, she could not talk her husband, King Herod, into having John killed*]. (Mark 6:17–19)

We will use Mark's account for details as to how Herodias managed to force her husband to have John killed. It involved a birthday celebration for Herod and an unwise commitment from him during the party.

21 And when a convenient day was come, that Herod on his birthday made a supper to his lords, high captains, and chief estates of Galilee;
22 And when the daughter of the said Herodias [*the daughter's name was Salome; Bible Dictionary, under "Salome"*] came in, and danced, and pleased Herod and them that sat with him, the king said unto the damsel, Ask of me whatsoever thou wilt, and I will give it thee.
23 And he sware unto [*promised*] her, Whatsoever thou shalt ask of me, I will give it thee, unto the half of my kingdom.
24 And she went forth, and said unto her mother [*Herodias*], What shall I ask?

And she [*Herodias*] said, The head of John the Baptist.

25 And she [*Salome*] came in straightway [*immediately*] with haste unto the king, and asked, saying, I will that thou give me by and by [by and by *means "immediately" in Bible language*] in a charger [*on a platter*] the head of John the Baptist.

26 And the king was exceeding sorry; yet for his oath's sake [*because he had promised*], and for their sakes which sat with him [*because of peer pressure*], he would not reject her [*refuse granting her request*].

27 And immediately the king sent an executioner, and commanded his [*John the Baptist's*] head to be brought: and he [*the executioner*] went and beheaded him in the prison,

28 And brought his head in a charger, and gave it to the damsel [*Salome*]: and the damsel gave it to her mother [*Herodias*]. (Mark 6:21–28)

Now, some time later and with the growing popularity of Jesus worrying him, Herod is concerned about whether or not He is John.

9 And Herod said, John have I beheaded: but who is this, of whom I hear such things? And he desired to see him. (Luke 9:9)

Because we are blessed with continuing revelation through modern prophets, we know that John the Baptist was resurrected at the time of the Savior's resurrection (D&C 133:55). We also know that he came to Joseph Smith and Oliver Cowdery and conferred upon them the Aaronic Priesthood (D&C 13) and taught them how to baptize and ordain others to that priesthood (Joseph Smith—History 1:68–72). In tribute to this great man, the Savior said, "Among them that are born of women there hath not risen a greater than John the Baptist" (Matthew 11:11).

THE APOSTLES RETURN AND REPORT THEIR FIRST MISSION

Earlier, the Savior had sent the twelve Apostles out on missions. At this point in time, near the end of the second year or near the beginning of the third year of the Savior's formal ministry, we see them return and report to Him. They have had many experiences and now have many questions, based on actual experience, to ask the Master. There is often a significant difference between theory and actual practice, and these missions were an important part of the orientation and training of these Brethren which the Master was providing. Jesus invited them to come into a desert area where they could have privacy and time to continue discussing their missions with Him. Because of the large multitudes crowding around the Savior constantly, privacy was nearly impossible to come by.

30 And the apostles gathered themselves together unto Jesus, and told him all things, both what they had done, and what they had taught.

31 And he said unto them, Come ye yourselves apart into a desert place, and rest a while: for there were many coming and going, and they had no leisure so much as to eat. (Mark 6:30–31)

CHAPTER 13

THE THIRD YEAR OF THE SAVIOR'S MORTAL MISSION

By way of review, in the first year of the Savior's formal mortal mission, He gradually revealed His true identity to the Jews as the prophesied Messiah, the Son of God come to earth. The miracles He performed testified of His godhood, and provided opportunity to teach and preach the true gospel with the plan of salvation to select individuals as well as to large crowds. Multitudes began following Him, some sincere truth seekers, some just curious.

During the second year of His ministry, opposition from Jewish religious leaders mounted. Scribes and Pharisees were constantly watching, seeking opportunities to legally arrest Him and have Him killed. Because of the opposition from Jewish authorities in Jerusalem, Jesus spent most of His time in Galilee. During this period, He began teaching in parables and was rejected again at Nazareth. He also called and ordained the original Twelve Apostles. They were sent out on missions, then later returned and reported their experiences to the Master. Perhaps some of the most significant teaching the Savior was doing throughout this part of His mortal ministry, was that of training the Twelve to take over the leadership of the Church after His departure. They were, in effect, having an intense MTC experience.

Near the beginning of the third year of His mortal ministry, the Savior performed a very large-scale miracle: the feeding of 5,000 men plus women and children (Matthew 14:21). Sometime after the death of John the Baptist, Jesus invited His Apostles to meet with Him in a "desert place" where they could have some quiet time together, away from the constant press of the multitudes (Mark 6:31). However, some people saw them leaving on a ship for that place, and, successfully guessing where they were going, spread the word such that a vast multitude arrived at their destination before they did.

31 And he said unto them, Come ye yourselves apart into a desert place, and rest a while: for there were many coming and going, and they had no leisure so much as to eat.

32 And they departed into a desert place by ship privately.

33 And the people saw them departing, and many knew him, and ran afoot thither out of all cities, and outwent them [*got to the place before they did*], and came together unto him. (Mark 6:31–33)

THE FEEDING OF THE 5,000

Next, we see the Master's power, kindness, and compassion in action. One of the lessons we can learn from what He does now is that service is not always convenient and often requires a change of plans on our part. All four writers of the Gospels recorded this miracle (Matthew 14:16–21, Mark 6:33–44, Luke 9:11–17, John 6:5–14). It took place near Bethsaida (a city on the northeastern shore of the Sea of Galilee) and John mentions that it took place as the time of the Feast of the Passover in Jerusalem was approaching (John 6:4). Rather than going forward with the plans to have additional quiet training time with His Apostles, the Master, filled with compassion for the large crowd who had gathered, taught the multitude instead (Mark 6:34), and healed those who needed healing (Luke 9:11). Near the end of the day the Apostles expressed concern to the Lord that the people did not have food or provisions for eating and needed to be sent to nearby villages to address their food needs. He startled them by instructing them to feed the multitude, which, according to Matthew 14:21, consisted of 5,000 men plus women and children.

35 And when the day was now far spent, his disciples came unto him, and said, This is a desert place, and now the time is far passed [*the day is about over*]:

36 Send them away, that they may go into the country round about, and into the villages, and buy themselves bread: for they have nothing to eat.

37 He answered and said unto them, Give ye them to eat. And they say unto him, Shall we go and buy two hundred pennyworth of bread, and give them to eat?

As you can see in verse 37, above, they told Him that enough bread to feed such a crowd would cost two hundred pennies. A penny, or Greek denarius, was an average day's wage for a workman (see Mark 6:37, footnote a). In our day, assuming an average day's wage to be about $150, the cost of feeding the crowd which had gathered to hear the Savior, would be around $30,000 and would of course be overwhelming to the Apostles. With their full attention now focused on what He would say next:

38 He saith unto them, How many loaves [of bread] have ye? go and see. And when they knew, they say, Five, and two fishes.

Perhaps there is a subtle message that might easily be missed in verses 39–40, next. It is that in order to receive nourishment (spiritual "bread") from the Savior, we must become part of His kingdom, which is well-organized here on earth. Notice how He has His Apostles organize these people by hundreds and by fifties. This can remind us of the fact that He organizes us in wards and branches, in order that the "bread of life" (John 6:35) be made available to us.

39 And he commanded them to make all [the people] sit down by companies [groups] upon the green grass.
40 And they sat down in ranks, by hundreds, and by fifties.
41 And when he had taken the five loaves and the two fishes, he looked up to heaven, and blessed, and brake the loaves, and gave them to his disciples to set before them [the people]; and the two fishes divided he among them all.
42 And they did all eat, and were filled.

Verse 42, above, can certainly be symbolic of the fact that when we come unto Christ and partake of His nourishment for us, our spiritual need can be completely filled (exaltation).

43 And they took up [picked up the leftovers] twelve baskets full of the fragments [of bread—see John 6:13], and of the fishes.
44 And they that did eat of the loaves were about five thousand men [plus women and children; see Matthew 14:21]. (Mark 6:35–44)

THE MULTITUDE TRIES TO MAKE JESUS THEIR KING

After feeding the multitude and instructing that the leftovers be gathered, Jesus instructed His Apostles to enter a ship and go to the other side of the sea toward Capernaum (John 6:17) while He remained behind to dismiss the crowd (Matthew 14:22). What happened next is a sad commentary on the shallowness and greed that stands in the way of some people when it comes to understanding and accepting the Savior and His gospel.

14 Then those men, when they had seen the miracle that Jesus did [feeding the 5,000], said, This is of a truth that prophet that should come into the world.
15 When Jesus therefore perceived that they would come and take him by force, to make him a king, he departed again into a mountain himself alone. (John 6:14–15)

JESUS WALKS ON THE WATER AND CALMS THE SEA

After the feeding of the 5,000, Jesus had instructed His Apostles to take a ship and go across the sea to Capernaum (John 6:17) while He dismissed the multitude. Afterward, He went up into a mountain to pray (Mark 6:46). In the meantime, the Apostles, while rowing with all their might, had encountered a fierce wind that impeded their progress in the ship. John's account tells us:

> 19 So when they had rowed about five and twenty or thirty furlongs [*about three to four miles from shore*], they see Jesus walking on the sea, and drawing nigh [*getting close*] unto the ship: and they were afraid.
> 20 But he saith unto them, It is I; be not afraid.
> 21 Then they willingly received him into the ship: and immediately the ship was at the land whither they went [*the ship was suddenly at its destination, a miracle recorded only by John*]. (John 6:19–21)

Did you notice the additional miracle mentioned in verse 21, above? Perhaps there is an important lesson in it for us. After the weary Apostles had done all they could to arrive at the destination to which they were invited by the Master, and had toiled through the night to be obedient to His instruction, they still fell short. But when He came to them and calmed the sea, they were immediately taken to the desired destination. The Book of Mormon describes the pleasant doctrine that, after all we can do to live the gospel, the Savior takes us the rest of the way.

> 23 For we labor diligently to write, to persuade our children, and also our brethren, to believe in Christ, and to be reconciled to God; for we know that it is by grace that we are saved, after all we can do. (2 Nephi 25:23)

Mark's account gives additional details about the Apostles' unsuccessful efforts to be obedient, and about the Savior's help for them.

> 47 And when even [*evening*] was come, the ship was in the midst of the sea, and he alone on the land.
> 48 And he saw them toiling in rowing; for the wind was contrary unto them [*they were struggling to row against the wind and waves, still trying to get to their destination*]: and about the fourth watch of the night [*between about 3 AM and 6 AM*] he cometh unto them, walking upon the sea, and would have passed by them.

The JST makes a very helpful clarification to the last phrase of verse 48, above. From it we discover that Jesus intentionally acted as if He were going to walk on past them. He is the Master Teacher, and this certainly did get their attention and prepared them to be taught more about His power over the elements.

> 50 And about the fourth watch of the night he cometh unto them, walking upon the sea, *as if he would have* passed by them. (JST, Mark 6:50)

49 But when they saw him walking upon the sea, they supposed it had been a spirit [*ghost*], and cried out [*in fear*]:

The message given to these exhausted men in verse 50, next, is the same message the merciful Savior gives to all who are doing everything they can to come unto Him (these Apostles have been doing all in their power to row the boat against adversity in order to meet Him as instructed).

> 50 For [*because*] they all saw him, and were troubled [*very worried*]. And immediately he talked with them, and saith unto them, Be of good cheer [*be happy, rejoice, cheer up*]: it is I; be not afraid.

There is symbolism and comfort for us in these verses. We all go through storms of life and it is comforting to know that God is there to help and comfort us. He invites us to trust Him, cheer up and to stop being afraid.

> 51 And he went up unto them into the ship [*got into the ship*]; and the wind ceased: and they were sore [*very*] amazed in themselves beyond measure, and wondered. [*The Apostles were very surprised at the power Christ had over the wind and sea.*]
> 52 For they considered not the miracle of the loaves: for their heart was hardened. (Mark 6:47–51)

The miracle of feeding the 5,000 hadn't yet sunk into their hearts as far as their understanding of the Savior's power was concerned. We would do well not to criticize them for requiring time to learn about the Master's power. Rather, we ought to realize that these great men are in intense training now and are learning rapidly. The learning curve is steep!

The day following the feeding of the 5,000, the masses returned to the location where they had been fed by the Master the day before. They were disappointed to find that He and His Apostles were gone. Having guessed correctly that they had departed for Capernaum, these anxious souls arranged passage on available ships and went to find Jesus there.

> 22 The day following, when the people which stood on the other side of the sea [*near where they had been fed by the Master the day before*] saw that there was none other boat there, save [*except*] that one whereinto his disciples were entered, and that Jesus went not with his disciples into the boat, but that his disciples were

gone away alone; [*In other words, the next day the crowd came to see if Jesus was still there, so they could get Him to feed them again. They knew that the disciples had taken the only boat available the night before and had headed toward Capernaum without Jesus. At any rate, they saw that neither Jesus nor His disciples were there, so they determined to try to find them.*]

23 (Howbeit [*however*] there came other boats from Tiberias [*a large town built by Herod Antipas on the western shore of the Sea of Galilee*] nigh unto the place where they did eat bread [*some boats from Tiberias came that morning and came to shore near the site of the feeding of the 5,000*], after that the Lord had given thanks:)

24 When the people therefore saw that Jesus was not there, neither his disciples, they also took shipping [*got aboard the boats from Tiberias*], and came to Capernaum, seeking for Jesus. (John 6:22–24)

THE BREAD OF LIFE

The stage is now being set for one of the most significant and important doctrinal discourses given by the Master Teacher as He defines and describes His role as the One who can nourish and strengthen us and bring us unto the Father. It is often called the Bread of Life discourse or sermon.

When some of the spokesmen for the people who had been fed located the Master in Capernaum, they had a question for Him, but their motives were not pure. The JST makes this clear.

25 And when they had found him on the other side of the sea, they said unto him, Rabbi, when camest thou hither [*when did You come here*]?
26 Jesus answered them and said, Verily, verily [*this is very important; listen carefully!*], I say unto you, Ye seek me, not because ye saw the miracles, but because ye did eat of the loaves, and were filled. [*You are not looking for Me because you want to obey My gospel; you just want to be fed again. In other words, you are looking for Me for the wrong reasons.*]

> 26 Jesus answered them and said, Verily, verily, I say unto you, Ye seek me, *not because ye desire to keep my sayings, neither because ye saw the miracles*, but because ye did eat of the loaves and were filled. (JST, John 6:26)

27 Labour not for the meat which perisheth [*don't spend all your effort working for worldly things which do not last*], but for that meat [*food, symbolic of spiritual priorities*] which endureth unto everlasting life [*which brings exaltation*], which the Son of man [*Christ*] shall give unto you: for him hath God the Father sealed [*sent*]. (John 6:25–27)

Now begins a brief series of interesting questions and answers between the spiritually blind and insensitive people and the Master Teacher.

Question

28 Then said they unto him, What shall we do, that we might work the works of God? [*What would it take to teach us how to multiply loaves and fish?*] (John 6:28)

Answer

29 Jesus answered and said unto them, This is the work of God, that ye believe on him whom he hath sent. [*You must develop faith in Jesus Christ whom the Father has sent.*] (John 6:29)

Question

30 They said therefore unto him, What sign shewest thou then, that we may see, and believe thee? what dost thou work? [*They are getting a bit irritated that He is stalling and not teaching them how to multiply loaves and fishes. They challenge Him to show them a sign to prove to them that He has not lost the power which He had yesterday when He fed them.*]

31 Our fathers did eat manna in the desert; as it is written, He gave them bread from heaven to eat. [*In other words they seem to be taunting Jesus, saying in effect, "Moses gave our ancestors bread (manna) every day when he was their leader. What's the matter? Aren't You as capable as Moses?"*] (John 6:30–31)

What follows in verses 32–58 is commonly known as the Bread of Life discourse or sermon. It is well known and contains tremendous symbolism. Have you noticed that the Savior masterfully uses familiar objects and everyday settings as background for teaching gospel doctrines and principles? We see this method throughout His teaching.

Answer

32 Then Jesus said unto them, Verily, verily, I say unto you, Moses gave you not that bread from heaven [*Moses didn't give you that manna*]; but my Father giveth you the true bread [*symbolic of Christ*] from heaven.

33 For the bread of [*from*] God is he [*Christ*] which cometh down from heaven, and giveth life [*resurrection and the possibility of eternal life*] unto the world. (John 6:32–33)

Question

34 Then said they unto him, Lord, evermore give us this bread [*give us bread so we will never get hungry again*]. (John 6:34)

As you can see from verse 34, above, they still don't get the point (see also verse 52). They don't understand the symbolism that Christ and His gospel will nourish them spiritually here on earth and forever in celestial glory. Next, Jesus explains His role as the Redeemer, and that He has been sent to earth by the Father to enable us to return to Him. In effect, He is giving them a short course in the plan of salvation. In verse 35, we see the symbolic bread of life from which the sermon gets its name.

35 And Jesus said unto them, I am the bread of life: he that cometh to me shall never hunger [*spiritually*]; and he that believeth on me shall never thirst [*spiritually*].

36 But I said unto you, That ye also have seen me, and believe not.

37 All [*all the righteous people*] that the Father giveth me shall come to me; and him that cometh to me I will in no wise [*never*] cast out [*of my kingdom*].

38 For I came down from heaven, not to do mine own will, but the will of him [*the Father*] that sent me.

39 And this is the Father's will which hath sent me, that of all which he hath given me [*all the righteous saints*] I should lose nothing [*none of them*], but should raise it up again at the last day [*resurrect them in the resurrection of the righteous*].

40 And this is the will of him that sent me, that every one which seeth the Son, and believeth on him, may have everlasting life: and I will raise him up at the last day. (John 6:35–40)

> 40 And this is the will of him that sent me, that every one which seeth the Son, and believeth on him, may have everlasting life; *and I will raise him up in the resurrection of the just at the last day.* (JST, John 6:40)

The "resurrection of the just" as used in JST verse 40, above, is a term which means those who will attain exaltation, which is the highest degree of glory in the celestial kingdom. Sadly, as you can see from verses 41–42, next, these people still don't get it. They are typical of people who are so focused on material things that they can't see the spiritual.

> 41 The Jews then murmured at him, because he said, I am the bread which came down from heaven.
>
> 42 And they said, Is not this Jesus, the son of Joseph, whose father and mother we know? how is it then that he saith, I came down from heaven? [*How can Jesus have come down from heaven? We know His parents. We've known Him all His life.*]
>
> 43 Jesus therefore answered and said unto them, Murmur not among yourselves [*don't criticize Me among yourselves for saying what I've said*].
>
> 44 No man can come to me, except the Father which hath sent me draw him: and I will raise him up at the last day. (John 6:41–44)

The JST makes major changes to verse 44, above:

> 44 No man can come *unto* me, *except he doeth the will of my Father who hath sent me. And this is the will of him who hath sent me, that ye receive the Son; for the Father beareth record of him; and he who receiveth the testimony, and doeth the will of him who sent me, I will raise up in the resurrection of the just.* (JST, John 6:44)

45 It is written in the prophets [*in the Old Testament; Isaiah 54:13*], And they shall be all taught of God. Every man therefore that hath heard, and hath learned

of the Father, cometh unto me. [*Everyone who has properly understood Old Testament prophets will be motivated to come unto Me.*]

46 Not that any man hath seen the Father, save he which is of God [*except he who is worthy, such as Stephen in Acts 7:55–56*], he hath seen the Father.

47 Verily, verily, I say unto you, He that believeth on me [*Christ*] hath everlasting life [*will be exalted; will be placed into the highest degree of glory in the celestial kingdom and will become a god—see D&C 132:20*].

48 I am that bread of life. [*Symbolism: Jesus is the spiritual "bread" sent to us by the Father. When we eat it, that is, when we internalize it and make it part of our lives, we will be exalted.*]

49 Your fathers [*ancestors, mentioned in verse 31*] did eat manna in the wilderness, and are dead.

50 This is the bread [*symbolic of Christ's gospel and His Atonement*] which cometh down from heaven, that a man may eat thereof [*internalize it*], and not die [*not die spiritually*].

51 I am the living bread which came down from heaven: if any man eat of this bread, he shall live for ever [*shall have eternal life*]: and the bread that I will give is my flesh, which I will give for the life of the world. [*Jesus will sacrifice His body through suffering in the Garden of Gethsemane and crucifixion in order to accomplish the Atonement and provide resurrection for all and eternal life for those who qualify.*]

52 The Jews therefore strove [*argued*] among themselves, saying, How can this man give us his flesh to eat? [*They still don't get the point!*] (John 6:45–52)

Just as the Savior repeated the message time and time again in the previous verses, so He will repeat it several times in the next verses. He loves these spiritually insensitive people and is giving them every chance to understand that they must accept His Atonement and His gospel in order to be saved. They must symbolically "eat" Him ("he that eateth me," verse 57), that is, eat or internalize everything He is and everything He offers them and then make it a part of their lives in order to receive eternal life. Sadly, many of them will still not get the point, and will leave Him, even after so much repetition (verse 66).

53 Then Jesus said unto them, Verily, verily, I say unto you, Except [*unless*] ye eat the flesh of the Son of man [*Christ*], and drink his blood, ye have no life in you. [*Unless you internalize the Atonement and make it part of your lives, you will not have the life and light of the gospel here in mortality or in the world to come.*]

54 Whoso eateth my flesh, and drinketh my blood, hath eternal life; and I will raise him up at the last day. (John 6:53–54)

54 Whoso eateth my flesh, and drinketh my blood, hath eternal life; and I will raise him up *in the resurrection of the just at the last day.* (JST, John 6:54)

As you have no doubt noticed, there is much sacrament symbolism in the Savior's Bread of Life discourse. We see yet more of this beautiful symbolism that can help us appreciate and understand the sacrament better, as Jesus continues.

> 55 For my flesh is meat [*food; symbolic of spiritual food*] indeed, and my blood is drink [*symbolic of spiritual drink*] indeed.
> 56 He that eateth my flesh, and drinketh my blood, dwelleth in me, and I in him. [*He becomes one with Me, united with Me in the gospel.*]
> 57 As the living Father hath sent me, and I live by the Father: so he that eateth me [*internalizes My gospel*], even he shall live by me [*will be saved through living in accordance with My gospel*].
> 58 This is that bread which came down from heaven [*this is the Savior who was sent to earth from heaven*]: not as your fathers did eat manna [*physical nourishment*], and are dead: he that eateth of this bread [*spiritual nourishment*] shall live for ever [*will have eternal life, exaltation*].

As previously noted, John informs us that this sermon was given in the synagogue in Capernaum. Jesus spent so much time teaching and performing miracles in Capernaum that it became His adopted hometown, since His actual hometown, Nazareth, rejected Him. After hearing this discourse, many people stopped following Him.

> 59 These things said he in the synagogue, as he taught in Capernaum.
> 60 Many therefore of his disciples [*followers*], when they had heard this [*the Bread of Life Sermon*], said, This is an hard saying; who can hear it? [*This is too deep for us. Nobody can understand what He is saying.*]
> 61 When Jesus knew in himself that his disciples murmured at it, he said unto them, Doth this offend you [*are you bothered, offended by what I have taught about the Bread of Life*]?
> 62 What and if ye shall see the Son of man ascend up where he was before? [*Would it offend you if you saw Me go back up into heaven where I came from? Jesus will do exactly that after His resurrection.*]

Next, we are taught the necessity of having the help of the Holy Ghost in order to understand the message of salvation that the Savior is giving these people. This is an important reminder of the vital role the gift of the Holy Ghost plays in our lives. Those who do not have it cannot understand the importance nor the depth and beauty of these things.

> 63 It is the spirit that quickeneth [*it is the Holy Ghost that gives you understanding*]; the flesh profiteth nothing [*you can't possibly understand what Jesus just said, from an intellectual, academic basis*]: the words that I speak unto you, they are spirit [*spiritual*], and they are life [*they bring eternal life*].

64 But there are some of you that believe not. For Jesus knew from the beginning who they were that believed not, and who should betray him.

65 And he said, Therefore said I [*this is the reason I said*] unto you, that no man can come unto me, except it were given unto him of my Father. (John 6:63–65)

The JST makes an extremely important change here.

> 65 And he said, Therefore said I unto you, that no man can come unto me, except *he doeth the will of my Father who hath sent me.* (JST, John 6:65)

As you can see from verse 66, next, many people deserted Jesus after He gave the Bread of Life sermon.

66 From that time many of his disciples went back [*left him*], and walked no more with him.

67 Then said Jesus unto the twelve, Will ye also go away? [*Is this doctrine of the Bread of Life so hard to accept that you, too, will leave Me?*] (John 6:66–67)

Peter's response is so simple and beautiful! It is the right answer for each of us who is completely committed to follow the Savior by living His gospel.

68 Then Simon Peter answered him, Lord, to whom shall we go? thou hast the words of eternal life.

69 And we believe and are sure that thou art that Christ, the Son of the living God. (John 6:68–69)

Next, Jesus prophesied that one of the Twelve would betray Him. In verse 71, John explains to whom the Master was referring.

70 Jesus answered them, Have not I chosen you twelve, and one of you is a devil?

71 He spake of Judas Iscariot the son of Simon [*a different Simon than Peter the Apostle*]: for he it was that should [*would*] betray him, being one of the twelve. (John 6:70–71)

JESUS CONTINUES TEACHING IN GALILEE

John very briefly mentions that, after Jesus gave the Bread of Life discourse, the Master continued teaching in Galilee. He avoided going to Jerusalem for the time being because of plots among the Jews there to kill Him. Many chapters and verses in Matthew, Mark, and Luke will fill in the details.

1 After these things Jesus walked in Galilee: for he would not walk in Jewry, because the Jews sought to kill him. (John 7:1)

As Jesus continued this phase of His Galilean ministry, both Matthew and Mark record that He came to the Plain of Gennesaret, which was a fertile area on the northwest shore of the Sea of Galilee. When people in the surrounding area heard of His arrival, they brought their sick to Him to be healed. Many were restored to health by the simple act of touching the hem of His cloak. First, Matthew's account:

> 34 And when they were gone over, they came into the land of Gennesaret.
> 35 And when the men of that place had knowledge of him, they sent out into all that country round about, and brought unto him all that were diseased;
> 36 And besought him that they might only touch the hem of his garment: and as many as touched were made perfectly whole. (Matthew 14:34–36)

Now, Mark's account, with a little additional detail:

> 53 And when they had passed over, they came into the land of Gennesaret, and drew to the shore.
> 54 And when they were come out of the ship, straightway they knew him,
> 55 And ran through that whole region round about, and began to carry about in beds those that were sick, where they heard he was.
> 56 And whithersoever he entered, into villages, or cities, or country, they laid the sick in the streets, and besought him that they might touch if it were but the border of his garment: and as many as touched him were made whole. (Mark 6:53–56)

JEWISH LEADERS IN JERUSALEM SEND A DELEGATION TO GALILEE

At this point, the Jewish leaders in Jerusalem are very anxious to have Jesus killed. Their attempts to lure Him to Jerusalem have failed because He has remained in Galilee (John 7:1). Consequently, they now send a delegation of scribes and Pharisees all the way from Jerusalem to Galilee, instructed to trap Jesus into saying or doing something for which He could be legally arrested and put to death. The scribes were the most powerful and influential of these leaders. By the time the Savior came to earth for His mortal mission, the scribes had already wielded their influence upon Jewish life for several centuries. A description of their role in Jewish society follows:

> A foremost actor in a New Testament list of characters is the scribe. He is found in Jerusalem, Judea, and Galilee and is not new to Jewish life and culture. Present in Babylon and also throughout the dispersion, he is spokesman of the people; he is the sage; he is the man of wisdom, the rabbi who received his ordination by the laying on of hands. His ability to cross-examine and to question is renowned. Dignified and important, he is an aristocrat among the com-

mon people who have no knowledge of the law. Regarding faith and religious practice, he is the authority and the last word; and as a teacher of the law, as a judge in ecclesiastical courts, is the learned one who must be respected, whose judgment is infallible. He travels in the company of the Pharisees, yet he is not necessarily a member of this religious party. He holds office and has status. His worth is beyond that of all the common folk and they must honor him, for he is to be praised by God and by angels in heaven. In fact, so revered are his words regarding law and practice that he must be believed though his statements contradict all common sense, or though he pronounce that the sun does not shine at noon day when in fact it is visible to the naked eye. [Edersheim, *The Life and Times of Jesus the Messiah, 1:93–94.*]

We will use Matthew's account of this scene between the scribes and Pharisees and the Savior. You can see that as soon as they catch up with Him in Galilee, they immediately confront Him. Also, have you noticed that Jesus was kind and merciful to sinners, such as the woman taken in adultery (John 8:1–11), but blatant hypocrites drew scathing rebukes from Him? We will see this with the scribes and Pharisees here. There is no doubt an inherent warning here for all of us to avoid hypocrisy.

1 Then came to Jesus scribes and Pharisees [*religious leaders of the Jews*], which were of Jerusalem, saying,
2 Why do thy disciples transgress [*sin against*] the tradition of the elders [*laws and customs established over the centuries by Jewish religious leaders, not necessarily the laws of God*]? for they wash not their hands when they eat bread [*before eating a meal*]. (Matthew 15:1–2)

The Savior will now teach a major lesson, namely, that inner cleanliness of mind and spirit is far more important than outward physical cleanliness. Watch, as the Master calls their attention to their own hypocrisy for not taking care of their aged parents.

3 But he answered and said unto them, Why do ye also transgress the commandment of God by your tradition?
4 For God commanded, saying, Honour thy father and mother: and, He that curseth father or mother, let him die the death [*the penalty, given by Moses for failing to honor one's father and mother, was death*].
5 But ye say, Whosoever shall say to his father or his mother, It is a gift, by whatsoever thou [*the parents*] mightest be profited by me [*I have dedicated my money to God so I can't help you with it*];
6 And honour not his father or his mother, he shall be free [*of obligation to help his parents*]. Thus have ye made the commandment of God [*"Honor thy father and thy mother," Exodus 20:12*] of none effect by your tradition. (Matthew 15:3–6)

In the above verses, the Savior challenges the wicked practice, approved by the Jewish leaders, of avoiding taking care of their aging parents by dedicating their material means to God by saying "It is a gift" (verse 5, above), meaning that it is a gift to God (Bible Dictionary, under "Corban.") By formally saying this, they could make their material means, time, and so forth, off limits to their elderly parents who needed their help. This practice is called "Corban" in Mark 7:11.

7 Ye hypocrites [*people who want to appear righteous but like to do evil*], well did Esaias [*Isaiah*] prophesy of you, saying [*in Isaiah 29:13*],
8 This people draweth nigh unto me with their mouth, and honoureth me with their lips; but their heart is far from me.
9 But in vain [*it does no good*] they do worship me, teaching for doctrines the commandments of men.
10 And he called the multitude, and said unto them, Hear, and understand:
11 Not that which goeth into the mouth defileth a man; but that which cometh out of the mouth, this defileth a man. (Matthew 15:7–11)

This is a stinging rebuke to these wicked Jewish leaders. Jesus said to the multitudes who have gathered around within the hearing of the scribes and Pharisees, that the teachings which come out of the scribes' mouths and influence daily behavior of their people defile, or, in other words, make filthy. His disciples are worried about his bold scolding of the scribes and Pharisees as evidenced by the next verse. Watch His response to their concern.

12 Then came his disciples, and said unto him, Knowest thou that the Pharisees were offended, after they heard this saying?
13 But he answered and said, Every plant, which my heavenly Father hath not planted, shall be rooted up [*everything which is false will ultimately be exposed and destroyed*].
14 Let them alone: they be blind leaders of the blind. And if the blind lead the blind, both shall fall into the ditch [*ultimately, they and their followers will get caught up with*].

Peter quickly drops the concern about what Jesus said to the scribes and Pharisees and seeks understanding for himself and his fellow Apostles and disciples. These humble men are still being trained and will learn more now.

15 Then answered [*responded*] Peter and said unto him, Declare unto us this parable [*please explain what You just said*].
16 And Jesus said, Are ye also yet without understanding?
17 Do not ye yet understand, that whatsoever entereth in at the mouth goeth into the belly, and is cast out into the draught [*eventually leaves the body*]?
18 But those things which proceed out of the mouth come forth from the heart; and they defile [*make filthy*] the man [*because they show what he is really like*].
19 For out of the heart proceed evil thoughts, murders, adulteries, fornications,

thefts, false witness, blasphemies:

20 These are the things which defile a man: but to eat with unwashen hands [*verse 2*] defileth not a man.

Mark adds a few more sins to those that Matthew listed.

22 Thefts, covetousness, wickedness, deceit, lasciviousness, an evil eye, blasphemy, pride, foolishness:

23 All these evil things come from within, and defile the man. (Mark 7:22–23)

JESUS GOES TO TYRE AND SIDON

At this point in the third year of the Savior's formal mortal ministry, He and His disciples left the province of Galilee and went roughly 40–50 miles northwest to the coast of the Mediterranean Sea, through the region of Tyre and Sidon, two cities in Phoenicia (Matthew 15:21). The Phoenicians, who were known for their extensive commercial shipping, had a language that closely resembled Hebrew. While Jesus and the disciples were in that area, a Gentile woman approached the Master and requested that He heal her daughter who was possessed by an evil spirit. You may recall that Jesus limited His personal mortal ministry to the House of Israel, primarily the Jews (Matthew 15:24). After His resurrection, however, He instructed the Apostles that it was now time to take the gospel to all the world (Mark 16:15). There is a lesson in compassion for us in what happened next in the case of this Gentile woman.

24 And from thence [*there*] he arose, and went into the borders of Tyre and Sidon [*several miles north of the Sea of Galilee, on the coast of the Mediterranean Sea*], and entered into an house, and would have no man know it [*wanted to have some privacy*]: but he could not be hid. (Mark 7:24)

22 And from thence he arose, and went into the borders of Tyre and Sidon, and entered into a house, and *would that no man should come unto him.*

23 *But he could not deny them; for he had compassion upon all men.* (JST, Mark 7:22–23)

25 For a certain woman, whose young daughter had an unclean [*evil*] spirit, heard of him, and came and fell at his feet. (Mark 7:25)

We understand the "young" daughter to be over age eight, because D&C 29:46–47 tells us that Satan does not have power to tempt children until they begin to become accountable, which we know to be age eight (D&C 68:25–27). Next, Mark points out that the woman is a Gentile, by way of explanation to us for what the Savior says to her.

26 The woman was a Greek, a Syrophenician by nation; and she besought him [*pled with Him*] that he would cast forth the devil out of her daughter. 27 But Jesus said unto her, Let the children [*the Jews, the covenant people, Israel—see JST quoted next*] first be filled: for it is not meet [*appropriate*] to take the children's bread [*the gospel, intended for the Jews only at this time in God's plan*], and to cast it unto the dogs [*give it to the Gentiles*]. (Mark 7:26–27)

> 26 But Jesus said unto her, Let the children *of the kingdom* first be filled; for it is not meet to take the children's bread, and to cast it unto the dogs. (JST, Mark 7:26)

As mentioned previously, and as Jesus states here, His mortal mission was limited to the house of Israel, specifically, the Jews. This limitation will be done away with later, as exemplified by Mark 16:15 and also by Peter's dream in Acts 10:9–48. The word "dogs" in this context means "little dogs" or household pets (in other words, a term of endearment). A Bible scholar named Dummelow explains as follows:

> The rabbis often spoke of the Gentiles as dogs. . . . [Jesus] says not "dogs," but "little dogs," i.e. house-hold, favourite dogs, and the woman cleverly catches at the expression, arguing that if the Gentiles are household dogs, then it is only right that they should be fed with the crumbs that fall from their master's table. (Dummelow, Commentary, pp. 678–79)

> 28 And she answered and said unto him, Yes, Lord: yet the dogs under the table eat of the children's crumbs.
> 29 And he said unto her, For this saying [*you have talked Me into it (He probably said this with a twinkle in his eye)*] go thy way; the devil [*evil spirit*] is gone out of thy daughter.
> 30 And when she was come to her house, she found the devil gone out, and her daughter laid upon the bed. (Mark 7:28–30)

Matthew adds that the woman's faith was instrumental in the healing of her daughter.

> 28 Then Jesus answered and said unto her, O woman, great is thy faith: be it unto thee even as thou wilt. And her daughter was made whole from that very hour. (Matthew 15:28)

BACK TO GALILEE
MORE HEALINGS
Feeding of 4,000

Jesus returned again to Galilee, near the Sea of Galilee, where large multitudes followed Him, bringing their sick to Him for healing (Matthew 15:29–31; Mark 7:31–37). We suspect that this took a significant amount of time, because three days later, the multitude was still there. We see again the compassion of the Savior as well as another teaching and training opportunity for His disciples in what happened next. We are reminded that this compassion extends also to us.

> 1 In those days the multitude being very great [*large*], and having nothing to eat, Jesus called his disciples unto him, and saith unto them,
> 2 I have compassion on the multitude, because they have now been with me three days, and have nothing to eat:
> 3 And if I send them away fasting to their own houses, they will faint by the way: for divers [*some*] of them came from far.
> 4 And his disciples answered him, From whence can a man satisfy these men with bread here in the wilderness [*where could we get bread since there are no markets here in the wilderness*]?
> 5 And he asked them, How many loaves [*of bread*] have ye? And they said, Seven.
> 6 And he commanded the people to sit down on the ground: and he took the seven loaves, and gave thanks, and brake [*broke the loaves of bread into pieces*], and gave to his disciples to set before them [*to give to the people*]; and they did set them [*the pieces of bread*] before the people.
> 7 And they had a few small fishes: and he blessed, and commanded to set them also before them.
> 8 So they did eat, and were filled: and they took up of the broken meat [*food*] that was left seven baskets [*seven basketfuls of food were left over*]. (Mark 8:1–8)

One of the major messages for us in the above verses is that when we give the Savior what little we have, whether physical or spiritual efforts, He can make our efforts into much more than we can alone. The leftover food in verse 8, above, could symbolize the infinite blessings of exaltation for those who accept nourishment from the Master.

> 9 And they that had eaten were about four thousand [*in addition to women and children—Matthew 15:38*]: and he sent them away [*dismissed them to go home*]. (Mark 8:9)

THE WESTERN SIDE OF THE SEA OF GALILEE

Pharasees and Sadducees Join Forces to Trap Jesus

After feeding the 4,000, Jesus and His disciples entered a ship and traveled to the western shore of the Sea of Galilee to Magdala (Matthew 15:39), apparently known also as Dalmanutha (Mark 8:10). There, some Pharisees and Sadducees, traditionally bitter enemies of each other, confront the Master. These Jewish religious leaders have now joined forces to stop Him. They arrogantly ask Him for a sign. First, Matthew's account:

1 The Pharisees [*Jewish religious leaders who believed in resurrection*] also with the Sadducees [*Jewish religious leaders who did not believe in resurrection*] came, and tempting desired him that he would shew them a sign from heaven.

2 He answered and said unto them, When it is evening, ye say, It will be fair weather: for the sky is red.

3 And in the morning, It will be foul weather to day: for the sky is red and lowring [*threatening*], O ye hypocrites [*people who want to appear righteous but inwardly like to be evil*], ye can discern the face of the sky [*you can predict the weather by looking at the sky*]; but can ye not discern [*JST, tell*] the signs of the times [*the obvious fulfillment of prophecies about Christ's mortal ministry, which, if paid attention to, would present these hypocrites with sure evidence that this Jesus, against whom they were fighting, is the promised Messiah*]?

4 A wicked and adulterous generation seeketh after a sign; and there shall no sign be given unto it, but the sign of the prophet Jonas [*just as Jonah spent three days and three nights in the whale's belly, so also will Christ spend three days and three nights in the tomb, see JST, Mark 8:12*]. And he left them, and departed. (Matthew 16:1–4)

Now, Mark's account:

11 And the Pharisees [*Jewish religious leaders*] came forth, and began to question with him [*Jesus*], seeking of him a sign from heaven, tempting him [*to prove that he was from God*].

12 And he sighed deeply in his spirit, and saith, Why doth this generation [*the wicked people living in Israel at that time*] seek after a sign? verily I say unto you, There shall no sign be given unto this generation. (Mark 8:11–12)

> 12 *Verily I say unto you*, There shall no sign be give unto this generation, *save the sign of the prophet Jonah; for as Jonah was three days and three nights in the whale's belly, so likewise shall the Son of man be buried in the bowels of the earth.* (JST, Mark 8:12)

Luke points out the debilitating spiritual blindness which accompanied the hypocrisy in these Jewish religious leaders at the time of Christ. We see in this a warning to us to avoid hypocrisy ourselves.

56 Ye hypocrites, ye can discern the face of the sky [*you can predict the weather by looking at the signs in the sky*] and of the earth; but how is it that ye do not discern this time [*why are you so blind to the signs about the coming of Christ, which are all around you*]?

57 Yea, and why even of yourselves judge ye not what is right? [*These signs are so obvious that you should be able to tell what's going on without help!*] (Luke 12:56–57)

THE EASTERN SIDE OF THE SEA OF GALILEE

Beware of the Leaven of the Pharisees and Sadducees

After the confrontation with the Pharisees and Sadducees in Magdala, the Master and His disciples again boarded a ship and traveled to the eastern side of the Sea of Galilee (Mark 8:13; Matthew 16:5). Apparently in a hurry to leave the confrontation on the western shore, the disciples had forgotten to take provisions with them on the ship, other than one loaf of bread (Mark 8:14). These future leaders of the Church are still in intense training, and the Master Teacher chooses this time, when the disciples are concerned about physical nourishment, to teach a lesson on things that can corrupt our spirituality. At first these Apostles do not understand the Savior's teaching about the "leaven of the Pharisees." Leaven, or yeast, gradually affects the entire loaf of bread dough, and the "leaven" or false doctrines taught by the Pharisees can corrupt the whole person or society. Finally, they understand what the Savior is teaching them and another step in their personal growth is accomplished.

6 Then Jesus said unto them, Take heed and beware of the leaven of the Pharisees and of the Sadducees.

7 And they reasoned among themselves, saying, It is because we have taken no bread.

8 Which when Jesus perceived, he said unto them, O ye of little faith, why reason ye among yourselves, because ye have brought no bread [*you are missing the point*]?

9 Do ye not yet understand, neither remember the five loaves of the five thousand, and how many baskets ye took up [*Matthew 14:20*]?

10 Neither the seven loaves of the four thousand, and how many baskets ye took up [*Matthew 15:37*]?

11 How is it that ye do not understand that I spake it [*what I said about leaven, yeast*] not to you concerning bread, [*but, rather*] that ye should beware of [*watch out for*] the leaven [*influence*] of the Pharisees and of the Sadducees?

12 Then understood they [*the Apostles*] how that he bade them [*warned them*] not [*to*] beware of the leaven [*yeast*] of bread, but of the doctrine of the Pharisees and of the Sadducees. (Matthew 16:6–12)

It is helpful to know that *leaven* or *yeast* was symbolic of sin and corruption in the Jewish culture of the day. Thus, the Savior's choice of "leaven" in referring to the Pharisees and Sadducees had extra impact on the minds of His disciples.

BETHSAIDA

A Blind Man Is Healed in Stages

As the Savior continued this phase of His later Galilean ministry, He traveled to Bethsaida, a town near the northeast end of the Sea of Galilee. Mark records a rather rare physical healing by the Master in that a blind man was healed in stages there. There is likely symbolism for us in this.

22 And he cometh to Bethsaida; and they bring a blind man unto him, and besought [*asked*] him to touch him.

23 And he took the blind man by the hand, and led him out of the town; and when he had spit [*perhaps Jesus did this to help the man's faith, because the Jews had a belief that saliva had healing properties*] on his eyes, and put his hands upon him, he asked him if he saw ought [*anything*].

24 And he looked up, and said, I see men as trees, walking [*I can see, but not clearly*].

25 After that he put his hands again upon his eyes, and made him look up: and he was restored, and saw every man clearly. (Mark 8:22–25)

Perhaps this healing of the blind man in stages is symbolic of the fact that, usually, we are healed in stages. We grow "line upon line." We are gradually healed from our spiritual sicknesses such as lack of faith, meanness, inactivity, lack of charity, lustful thinking, and so forth, until we see "clearly" in spiritual matters, just as did the blind man in physical matters. Again, as in many other cases, the Master requested that the man keep this healing private.

26 And he sent him away to his house, saying, Neither go into the town, nor tell it [*that I healed you*] to any in the town. (Mark 8:26)

PETER BEARS STRONG TESTIMONY OF CHRIST

Keys of Sealing Are Promised

The Savior traveled farther north into Caesarea Philippi (Mark 8:27), a town near the headwaters of the Jordan River at the foot of Mount Hermon. It was here, as the Lord asked His disciples a vital question for all of us, that Peter bore his much-quoted testimony that Jesus was indeed the Messiah.

13 When Jesus came into the coasts of [*area around*] Caesarea Philippi [*about 15 to 20 miles north of the Sea of Galilee*], he asked his disciples, saying, Whom do men say that I the Son of man am?

14 And they said, Some say that thou art John the Baptist: some, Elias [*Elijah*]; and others, Jeremias [*Jeremiah*], or one of the prophets.

15 He saith unto them, But whom say ye that I am?

16 And Simon Peter answered and said, Thou art the Christ, the Son of the living God.

17 And Jesus answered and said unto him, Blessed art thou, Simon Bar-jona [*son of a man named Jona*]: for flesh and blood hath not revealed it unto thee, but my Father which is in heaven [*you have received your testimony of Me through revelation*]. (Matthew 16:13–17)

Next, during this wonderful teaching moment, the Master Teacher explains that true testimony comes by way of direct revelation, and He also teaches about priesthood keys.

18 And I say also unto thee, That thou art Peter, and upon this rock [*the "rock" of revelation, see TPJS, p. 274; also, Christ is the "rock" upon which the Church is based, see Matthew 16:18, footnote a*] I will build my church; and the gates of hell shall not prevail [*win*] against it. [*Satan's kingdom absolutely will not ultimately win against Christ's kingdom, a very comforting fact!*]

19 And I will give unto thee the keys [*including the sealing power*] of the kingdom of heaven [*Peter was authorized to serve as the President of the Church after the Savior left*]: and whatsoever thou shalt bind [*seal*] on earth shall be bound in heaven: and whatsoever thou shalt loose [*unseal*] on earth shall be loosed in heaven.

20 Then charged he his disciples that they should tell no man that he was Jesus the Christ. (Matthew 16:18–20)

It would seem that the instruction to the Apostles in verse 20, above, was temporary and for that particular time and circumstance. Perhaps they needed a bit of quiet time together for the Master to teach His disciples about His upcoming death (in about six months) and resurrection. Some Bible manuscripts say, in effect, "Don't go and tell anyone in the village."

JESUS BEGINS TO PROPHESY AND EMPHASIZE HIS UPCOMING CRUCIFIXION AND RESURRECTION

Peter Is Rebuked

At this time in the Savior's mortal mission, it is about six months before He will be crucified and resurrected. From this time forward, the Master begins to prophesy and emphasize to His disciples His upcoming death and resurrection. Peter, with typical energy of soul, strongly protests the idea that the Lord would be killed in Jerusalem. He is rebuked by the Messiah for attempting to stand in the way of the grand purpose for which He came to earth.

21 From that time forth began Jesus to shew unto his disciples, how that he must go unto Jerusalem, and suffer many things of the elders and chief priests and scribes, and be killed, and be raised again the third day.

22 Then Peter took him, and began to rebuke him, saying, Be it far from thee, Lord: this shall not be unto thee [*this can't happen to You!*].

23 But he turned, and said unto Peter, Get thee behind me, Satan: thou art an offence unto me: for thou savourest [*you cherish*] not the things that be of God, but those that be of men. [*You must not try to stop Me from following through with the Atonement.*]

THE TRANSFIGURATION OF CHRIST

Six days after Peter bore his strong witness of Jesus, saying "Thou art the Christ, the Son of the living God" (Matthew 16:16), the Savior took Peter, James, and John into a high mountain where He was transfigured before them. As you will see, this was a monumental event in the continued orientation and training of these three Apostles. As we join them now, through the eyes of the scriptures and the power of the Spirit, be aware that it is near October and the Savior will be crucified next April, thus finishing His mortal ministry. Peter, James, and John are already taking on the role of First Presidency. They will experience tremendous additional training now as the Master takes them with Him up on the mountain, which is referred to as the Mount of Transfiguration. There, they will see Christ transfigured before their eyes, will hear the Father's voice, and will see, among others, the great prophets Moses and Elijah, from whom they will receive additional priesthood keys. From JST Mark 9:3, we learn that John the Baptist was also there. We will use Matthew's account for our purposes here. Both Mark (Mark 9:2–13) and Luke (Luke 9:28–36) give accounts of the transfiguration of the Savior.

1 And after six days Jesus taketh Peter, James, and John his brother, and bringeth them up into an high mountain apart,

2 And was transfigured before them: and his face did shine as the sun, and his raiment [*clothing*] was white as the light.

3 And, behold, there appeared unto them Moses and Elias [*Elijah*] talking with him.

4 Then answered Peter [*Peter responded*], and said unto Jesus, Lord, it is good for us to be here: if thou wilt, let us make here three tabernacles [*small booths, typically used among the Jews for private worship during the annual Feast of Tabernacles*]; one for thee, and one for Moses, and one for Elias [*Elijah*].

5 While he yet spake, behold, a bright cloud overshadowed them: and behold a voice out of the cloud, which said, This is my beloved Son, in whom I am well pleased; hear ye him.

6 And when the disciples heard it, they fell on their face [*a show of humility*], and were sore [*very*] afraid.

7 And Jesus came and touched them, and said, Arise, and be not afraid.

8 And when they had lifted up their eyes, they saw no man, save [*except*] Jesus only. (Matthew 17:1–8)

Apostle Bruce R. McConkie summarizes what took place on the Mount of Transfiguration in the following quote:

From the New Testament accounts and from the added light revealed through Joseph Smith it appears evident that:

(1) Jesus singled out Peter, James, and John from the rest of the Twelve; took them upon an unnamed mountain; there he was transfigured before them, and they beheld his glory. Testifying later, John said, "We beheld his glory, the glory as of the only begotten of the Father" (John 1:14); and Peter, speaking of the same event, said they "were eyewitnesses of his majesty." (2 Pet. 1:16.)

(2) Peter, James, and John, were themselves "transfigured before him" (*Teachings*, p. 158), even as Moses, the Three Nephites, Joseph Smith, and many prophets of all ages have been transfigured, thus enabling them to entertain angels, see visions and comprehend the things of God. (*Mormon Doctrine*, pp. 725–26.)

(3) Moses and Elijah—two ancient prophets who were translated and taken to heaven without tasting death, so they could return with tangible bodies on this very occasion, an occasion preceding the day of resurrection—appeared on the mountain; and they and Jesus gave the keys of the kingdom to Peter, James, and John. (*TPJS*, p. 158.)

(4) John the Baptist, previously beheaded by Herod, apparently was also present. It may well be that other unnamed prophets, either coming as translated beings or as spirits from paradise, were also present.

(5) Peter, James, and John saw in vision the transfiguration of the earth, that is, they saw it renewed and returned to its paradisiacal state—an event that is to take place at the Second Coming when the millennial era is ushered in. (D&C 63:20–21; *Mormon Doctrine*, pp. 718–19.)

(6) It appears that Peter, James, and John received their own endowments while on the mountain. (*Doctrines of Salvation*, Vol. 2, p. 165.) Peter says that while there, they "received from God the Father honour and glory," seemingly bearing out this

conclusion. It also appears that it was while on the mount that they received the more sure word of prophecy, it then being revealed to them that they were sealed up unto eternal life. (2 Peter 1:16–19; D&C 131:5.)

(7) Apparently Jesus himself was strengthened and encouraged by Moses and Elijah so as to be prepared for the infinite sufferings and agony ahead of him in connection with working out the infinite and eternal atonement. (*Jesus the Christ,* p. 373.) Similar comfort had been given him by angelic visitants following his forty-day fast and its attendant temptations (Matt. 4:11), and an angel from heaven was yet to strengthen him when he would sweat great drops of blood in the Garden of Gethsemane. (Luke 22:42–44.)

(8) Certainly the three chosen apostles were taught in plainness "of his death and also his resurrection" (JST, Luke 9:31), teachings which would be of inestimable value to them in the trying days ahead.

(9) It should also have been apparent to them that the old dispensations of the past had faded away, that the law (of which Moses was the symbol) and the prophets (of whom Elijah was the typifying representative) were subject to Him whom they were now commanded to hear.

(10) Apparently God the Father, overshadowed and hidden by a cloud, was present on the mountain, although our Lord's three associates, as far as the record stipulates, heard only his voice and did not see his form. (*Doctrinal New Testament Commentary*, Vol. 1, p. 399.)

9 And as they came down from the mountain, Jesus charged [*instructed*] them, saying, Tell the vision to no man, until the Son of man be risen again from the dead.
10 And his disciples asked him, saying, Why then say the scribes that Elias must first come? (Matthew 17:9–10)

Here, in verse 10, Peter, James, and John seem to be asking the Savior to clear up some doctrinal confusion in their own minds about Elias. They had been taught by their scriptures that Elias would come and prepare the way for the Messiah. Yet, they had just seen Elias (Elijah) on the Mount and this was after the Savior had come; in fact, it was near the end of the Master's mortal ministry. It is helpful for us, as we study these scriptures, to be aware that the name "Elias" has many meanings (Bible Dictionary, p. 663). Thus, here, in this setting as explained by the Savior, Elias can mean John the Baptist who came before Jesus and prepared the way for him. It can also mean Elijah who ministered to Him on the Mount of Transfiguration and would yet appear in the Kirtland Temple (D&C 110:13–15). It is also helpful to read JST Matthew 17:10–14, quoted below as found in the back of our LDS edition of the Bible, concerning Elias.

11 And Jesus answered and said unto them, Elias truly shall first come, and restore all things.
12 But I say unto you, That Elias is come already, and they knew him not, but

have done unto him whatsoever they listed. Likewise shall also the Son of man suffer of them.

13 Then the disciples understood that he spake unto them of John the Baptist.

> 10 And Jesus answered and said unto them, Elias truly shall first come, and restore all things, *as the prophets have written.*
>
> 11 And again I say unto you that Elias has come already, concerning whom it is written, Behold, I will send my messenger, and he shall prepare the way before me; and they knew him not, and have done unto him, whatsoever they listed.
>
> 12 Likewise shall also the Son of man suffer of them.
>
> 13 But I say unto you, Who is Elias? Behold, this is Elias, whom I send to prepare the way before me.
>
> 14 Then the disciples understood that he spake unto them of John the Baptist, *and also of another who should come and restore all things, as it is written by the prophets.* (JST, Matthew 17:10–14)

With such a tremendous outpouring of blessings and witnesses of the Savior in their minds and hearts, Peter, James, and John will now continue their training under the direction of the Master. It will be an intense several months leading up to the last week of His life.

GALILEE

An Evil Spirit Is Cast Out

Luke tells us that the next day, after Jesus and the three chief Apostles had come down from the Mount of Transfiguration, a man begged the Lord to heal his son who was possessed by an evil spirit (Luke 9:37–39). The disciples had already tried to heal him, but without success (Luke 9:40; Matthew 17:16). The Master cast the devil out (Luke 9:41–42) and then explained why the disciples had not succeeded. Again, the issue was faith.

> 19 Then came the disciples to Jesus apart [*privately*], and said, Why could not we cast him out?
>
> 20 And Jesus said unto them, Because of your unbelief: for verily I say unto you, If ye have faith as a grain of mustard seed, ye shall say unto this mountain, Remove hence to yonder place; and it shall remove; and nothing shall be impossible unto you.
>
> 21 Howbeit [*however*] this kind goeth not out but by prayer and fasting. (Matthew 17:19–21)

GALILEE

The Master Prophesies Again of His Coming Death and Resurrection

As Jesus continued teaching and ministering in Galilee, He once again reminded His disciples of His coming betrayal, death, and resurrection (Matthew 17:22–23; Mark 9:30–32; Luke 9:43–45). It was extremely difficult for even His closest associates, the Apostles, to grasp and accept what He was telling them. In fact, John specifically mentions in his account that they did not understand Him then, but after His resurrection, they fully realized what He had been telling them all along about His death and resurrection.

> 16 These things understood not his disciples at the first: but when Jesus was glorified, then remembered they that these things were written of him, and that they had done these things unto him. (John 12:16)

CAPERNAUM

The Miracle of the Coin in a Fish's Mouth

Matthew is the only Gospel writer who mentions this miracle. It is another illustration and testimony of the Master's power over all creation. He and the disciples had come again into Capernaum, Peter's home town on the northern edge of the Sea of Galilee. While there, the temple tax collectors approached Peter and asked if Jesus was up to date on His payment of the temple tax.

> 24 And when they were come to Capernaum, they [*the temple tax collectors*] that received tribute money [*annual temple tax of a half shekel, required from every male, twenty years old and older*] came to Peter, and said, Doth not your master pay tribute [*the temple tax*]?
> 25 He saith, Yes. And when he [*Peter*] was come into the house, Jesus prevented him [*spoke to him first, before he had a chance to mention the temple tax to Jesus—see Matthew 17:25, footnote a, in your Bible*], saying, What thinkest thou, Simon [*here's a question for you, Peter*]? of whom [*from whom*] do the kings of the earth take custom [*collect taxes*] or tribute? of their own children, or of strangers [*others*]?
> 26 Peter saith unto him, Of strangers. Jesus saith unto him, Then are the children [*of kings*] free [*exempt*]. (Matthew 17:24–26)

There is a subtle play on words at work here. Jesus is the Son of the King (Heavenly Father). He is also the King, the Messiah. He is even the rightful political King of the Jews if the Romans had not been in political power at the time, because Joseph, Mary's husband, was the rightful heir to the political throne of the Jews. Thus, Jesus, as King and as the Son of the King (Elohim), should not have to pay this tax. Approaching it from another angle, since Jesus is a King in many ways, His children (his followers, the Apostles, etc.) including Peter, should not have to pay this tribute either.

27 Notwithstanding [*nevertheless*], lest we should offend them [*in order to keep the peace*], go thou to the sea [*Sea of Galilee, which is probably just a few hundred feet or less away*], and cast an hook [*go fishing*], and take up the fish that first cometh up [*the first one you catch*]; and when thou hast opened his mouth, thou shalt find a piece of money [*a one shekel (four-drachma) coin, the exact amount to pay the temple tax for Christ and Peter; see NIV Bible, Matthew 17:27*]: that take, and give unto them [*the temple tax collectors*] for me and thee. (Matthew 17:27)

Perhaps one of the important lessons we can learn from the example of the Savior here is that there are some things that we should do simply to keep the peace, whether or not what we do is completely fair to us.

GALILEE

Principles of Forgiving Others

After having responded to the question, "Who is the greatest in the kingdom of heaven?" asked by His disciples (Matthew 18:1–6; Mark 9:33–37; Luke 9:46–48), and taught regarding offenses, the Savior taught a major lesson on forgiving others. If we hope to have a pleasant judgment day, we must learn and apply these principles in our own lives.

15 Moreover if thy brother shall trespass against thee, go and tell him his fault between thee and him alone [*keep it private; don't gossip about it; see D&C 20:80*]: if he shall hear thee [*responds positively*], thou hast gained thy brother. (Matthew 18:15)

Gossip (implied in verse 15, above) can actually be a type of emotional terrorism, because it often claims innocent victims.

16 But if he will not hear thee [*will not accept your efforts to make peace*], then take with thee one or two more [*as witnesses that you have tried to work the matter out with him*], that in the mouth of two or three witnesses every word may be established [*this is known as the law of witnesses*].
17 And if he shall neglect to hear them [*if he won't respond favorably to that effort on your part*], tell it unto the church [*go to the authorities of the church*]: but if he neglect to hear the church, let him be unto thee as an heathen man and a publican [*go ahead and excommunicate him*]. (Matthew 18:16–17)

Next, Peter asks the Lord a question that no doubt has come up in each of our minds at one point or another in our lives.

21 Then came Peter to him, and said, Lord, how oft shall my brother sin against

me, and I forgive him? till seven times?

22 Jesus saith unto him, I say not unto thee, Until seven times: but, Until seventy times seven. [*In other words, forgive him every time he sins against you. See D&C 98:40.*] (Matthew 18:21–22)

This doctrine of forgiving is a most important one for our own salvation. When we forgive others, we free ourselves of the heavy burdens of hatred, grudges, bitterness, pity parties, and so forth. Nephi is a great example to us in 1 Nephi 7:21 where he "frankly forgave" his brothers. The Savior goes on now to teach Peter and all of us the importance of forgiving others if we want the Lord to forgive us.

THE PARABLE OF THE UNMERCIFUL SERVANT

23 Therefore is the kingdom of heaven likened unto a certain king, which would take account of his servants [*see who owes him how much*].

24 And when he had begun to reckon [*check the accounting records*], one was brought unto him, which owed him ten thousand talents. (Matthew 18:23–24)

One calculation of this amount, based on an average day's wage, yields a debt which would require 60,000,000 work days to pay off, which, of course, is an impossible debt to repay. A person who starts full-time work at age 15 and works six days a week for 55 years, would have 17,160 days of work in his or her lifetime.

25 But forasmuch as he had not to pay, his lord commanded him to be sold, and his wife, and children, and all that he had, and payment to be made. [*This can be symbolic of the fact that we would lose family and all that counts (see 2 Nephi 9:8–9) without the Atonement and its power to free us and cleanse us so that we can enter exaltation and dwell in family units forever.*]

26 The servant therefore fell down, and worshipped him, saying, Lord, have patience with me, and I will pay thee all.

27 Then the lord of that servant was moved with compassion, and loosed him, and forgave him the debt [*symbolic of the Atonement*].

Hypocrisy is one of the most damaging of all sins, both to the person who exemplifies it and to those affected by it.

28 But the same servant went out, and found one of his fellowservants, which owed him an hundred pence [*an amount equivalent to about 100 days' wages; see Matthew 20:2*]: and he laid hands on him, and took him by the throat, saying, Pay me that thou owest.

29 And his fellowservant fell down at his feet, and besought him, saying, Have patience with me, and I will pay thee all [*the exact words he himself had used as he begged for mercy in verse 26, above*].

30 And he would not [*he refused to be merciful to the person who owed him and couldn't pay*]: but went and cast him into prison, till he should pay the debt.

31 So when his fellowservants saw what was done, they were very sorry, and came and told unto their lord [*the king in verse 23*] all that was done.

32 Then his lord, after that he had called him [*the man who refused to forgive the relatively small debt of 100 days' wages*], said unto him, O thou wicked servant, I forgave thee all that debt, because thou desiredst me:

33 Shouldest not thou also have had compassion on thy fellowservant, even as I had pity on thee?

34 And his lord was wroth [*angry; righteous indignation*], and delivered him to the tormentors, till he should pay all that was due unto him [*symbolic of the law of justice*]. (Matthew 18:25–34)

Symbolically, *tormentors* would represent the punishment of the wicked who are eventually turned over to the buffetings of Satan (D&C 82:21) to pay for their own sins. Even after they have paid the penalty for their own sins, the highest degree of glory they can enter is the telestial (D&C 76:84–85). Also, this parable teaches the interplay between the Law of Justice and the Law of Mercy. The Law of Mercy allows us to be forgiven of unfathomable debt to God, through obedience to the gospel, including forgiving others. However, if we, through our actions, refuse the law of Mercy, then the Law of Justice takes over and we bear the burden of our sins as explained in D&C 19:15–18.

35 So likewise shall my heavenly Father do also unto you, if ye from your hearts forgive not every one his brother their trespasses. [*This is fair warning to us about forgiving others and quite an answer to Peter's question in verse 21, wherein he asked how often he should forgive others.*] (Matthew 18:35)

As part of the Master's teaching about the need to forgive others, He included parables about the worth of each soul. The parables of the lost sheep, the lost coin, and the prodigal son teach the value of each of His children to our loving Father in Heaven and to the Savior.

PARABLE OF THE LOST SHEEP

This parable is one of the best known given by the Savior. In it, the shepherd leaves the ninety and nine to find the one sheep that is lost. It is important to keep the context of this parable in mind as we study it. It is given to the Pharisees and scribes who have come to Galilee to find fault with Jesus in the hopes of gaining legal evidence with which to have Him arrested and killed. They were very strict about not associating with sinners, as a matter of religion. As reported in verse 2, these Jewish religious leaders are grumbling now because the Lord associates with sinners. We will use Luke's account here. He gives the background for the parable in verses 1 and 2.

1 Then drew near unto him all the publicans [*tax collectors*] and sinners for to hear him.
2 And the Pharisees and scribes murmured [*grumbled*], saying, This man receiveth [*accepts*] sinners, and eateth with them.
3 And he spake this parable unto them [*the grumbling Pharisees and scribes in verse 2*], saying,
4 What man of you, having an hundred sheep, if he lose one of them, doth not leave the ninety and nine in the wilderness, and go after that which is lost, until he find it? (Luke 15:1–4)

> 4 What man of you having a hundred sheep, if he lose one of them, doth not leave the ninety and nine, *and go into* the wilderness after that which is lost, until he find it? (JST, Luke 15:4)

5 And when he hath found it, he layeth it on his shoulders, rejoicing.
6 And when he cometh home, he calleth together his friends and neighbours, saying unto them, Rejoice with me; for I have found my sheep which was lost.
7 I say unto you, that likewise joy shall be in heaven over one sinner that repenteth, more than over ninety and nine just persons, which need no repentance. (Luke 15:5–7)

This parable can remind us of the quote from the Doctrine and Covenants dealing with the worth of souls. We will quote two verses:

10 Remember the worth of souls is great in the sight of God;
15 And if it so be that you should labor all your days in crying repentance unto this people, and bring, save it be one soul unto me, how great shall be your joy with him in the kingdom of my Father! (D&C 18:10, 15)

Reading verse 7 of Luke 15, above, could make a person feel bad that a repentant sinner makes heaven happier than a righteous person. One could almost be tempted to commit an occasional sin so as to bring more joy to heaven when he or she repents. But wait! That is not at all what verse 7 is saying. Using the Prophet Joseph Smith's explanation that the ninety nine "just persons" represent the Sadducees and Pharisees "that are so righteous; they will be damned anyhow"; (*TPJS*, pp. 277–78), we can then understand verse 7, in effect, as follows: "There is more joy in heaven over one humble sinner who repents, than over ninety nine self-righteous hypocrites like you Pharisees and Sadducees who claim to be just men who need no repentance!" Verse 7, then, is actually a scathing rebuke of these evil religious leaders of the Jews, whom the Savior called "whited sepulchres" (Matthew 23:27); in other words, whitewashed coffins which look clean on the outside, but inside are full of rot and filth.

THE PARABLE OF THE LOST COIN

This next parable likewise is in direct response to the criticism of the Pharisees and scribes in Luke 15:2, and reminds us that it is worth whatever effort is necessary to save one lost soul.

8 Either [*here is another example:*] what woman having ten pieces of silver [*equal to ten days' wages for a workman—see Luke 15, footnote 8a in your LDS edition of the King James Bible*] if she lose one piece, doth not light a candle, and sweep the house, and seek diligently till she find it?
9 And when she hath found it, she calleth her friends and her neighbours together, saying, Rejoice with me; for I have found the piece which I had lost.
10 Likewise, I say unto you, there is joy in the presence of the angels of God over one sinner that repenteth. (Luke 15:8–10)

THE PARABLE OF THE PRODIGAL SON

This parable is among the best-loved parables given by the Master Teacher. It is filled with rich imagery and symbolism along with deep emotion. We will suggest some possible symbolism. No doubt you will be able to come up with additional symbolism which would also fit in terms of gospel applications in our lives.

11 And he said, A certain man [*symbolic of God*] had two sons [*symbolic of different types of people*]:
12 And the younger of them said to his father, Father, give me the portion of goods that falleth to me [*give me my inheritance now, instead of waiting until you die; symbolism: I am not interested in future exaltation, but rather want to enjoy the ways of the world now*]. And he [*the father*] divided unto them his living [*divided up his property between his two sons; symbolism: our Father in Heaven respects our agency*].
13 And not many days after the younger son gathered all together [*put all his financial resources together*], and took his journey into a far country [*symbolism: he fell away from the Church and participated in the ways of the world*], and there wasted his substance [*financial resources; symbolism: his gospel heritage*] with riotous living [*symbolism: he wasted his potential for joy and happiness in the gospel for temporary worldly, sinful pleasures*].
14 And when he had spent all [*symbolism: when he was wasted away by his wicked lifestyle*], there arose a mighty famine in that land [*symbolism: Satan left him with no support, as taught in Alma 30:60*]; and he began to be in want [*in need, poverty, desperation*].
15 And he went and joined himself to [*got a job with*] a citizen of that country

[*symbolism: he didn't yet turn to God for help*]; and he sent him into his fields to feed swine. [*Feeding pigs was about the lowest, most humiliating job a person from Jewish culture could have; symbolism: he was totally humbled.*]

16 And he would fain have filled his belly with the husks that the swine did eat [*he got so hungry that even the carob tree pods he was feeding the pigs started to look good to him*]: and no man gave unto him [*no one gave him anything to help him in his poverty; symbolism: there was no worldly source of effective help for him*].

17 And when he came to himself [*came to his senses; symbolism: he started repenting*], he said, How many hired servants of my father's have bread enough and to spare, and I perish with hunger [*I am starving*]!

18 I will arise and go to my father, and will say unto him, Father, I have sinned against heaven, and before thee [*I have been wicked; symbolic of sincere confession*],

19 And am no more worthy to be called thy son [*symbolism: I am not worthy of exaltation*]: make me as [*let me be*] one of thy hired servants [*symbolism: let me go into one of the other degrees of glory*].

20 And he arose, and came to his father. But when he was yet a great way off [*still a long distance off*], his father saw him [*had been watching for him*], and had compassion, and ran, and fell on his neck [*hugged him*], and kissed him [*symbolism: the Father is merciful and kind and is anxious to "run" to us to help us return to Him*].

21 And the son said unto him, Father, I have sinned against heaven, and in thy sight, and am no more worthy to be called thy son [*symbolism: the son, thoroughly humbled by his wickedness, acknowledges his unworthiness to live with the Father in celestial exaltation*].

22 But the father said to his servants, Bring forth the best robe, and put it on him; and put a ring on his hand, and shoes on his feet:

23 And bring hither the fatted calf, and kill it; and let us eat, and be merry [*symbolic of joy and rejoicing on earth and in heaven when a sinner repents and returns*]:

24 For this my son was dead [*symbolic of being spiritually dead*], and is alive again [*symbolic of rebirth, through the Atonement*]; he was lost, and is found. And they began to be merry [*to celebrate*]. (Luke 15:11–24)

A question sometimes arises among members of the Church as to whether or not the returning prodigal son could ever repent sufficiently to gain exaltation, especially in view of his intentional wickedness. There is much symbolism in verse 22, above, which can help answer that question:

The Robe

Symbolic of royalty and status. It is also symbolic of acceptance by God, as in 2 Nephi 4:33 where Nephi says "O Lord, wilt thou encircle me around in the robe of thy righteousness! O Lord, wilt thou make a way for mine escape before mine enemies!" See also Isaiah 61:10. In Revelation 7:9, white robes are given to those who live in the presence of God (celestial glory). The "best robe" would be symbolic of potential for highest status, in other words, exaltation.

The Ring

Symbolic of authority to rule. Example: a signet ring which a king would use to stamp official documents and make them legal and binding.

The Shoes

Shoes were very expensive in the days of the Savior's ministry and were only worn by the wealthy and the rulers. Thus, shoes would be symbolic of wealth, power, and authority to rule.

Summary: The cultural symbolism in this verse would lead us to believe that the father was not only welcoming his wayward son back with open arms, but also that he was inviting him to repent and reestablish himself as a ruler in his household, symbolic of potential for exaltation. President David O. McKay, in April Conference, 1956, speaking of the prodigal son, said, "The Spirit of forgiveness will be operative" when the prodigal son comes to himself and repents. Elder Richard G. Scott, in October Conference 2000, "The Path to Peace and Joy" (*Ensign,* November 2000, 25–27), spoke of Alma the Younger and the four sons of Mosiah. He said they "were tragically wicked," and that there are no "second-class" citizens after true repentance. Said he, "If you have repented from serious transgression and mistakenly believe that you will always be a second-class citizen in the kingdom of God, learn that is not true."

Thus, the prodigal son does not have to remain a "second-class citizen" in the Father's kingdom. However, the older brother may have to change his attitude if he plans to retain his status in the Father's kingdom.

25 Now his elder son [*symbolic of a member who has been active all his life*] was in the field: and as he came and drew nigh [*near*] to the house, he heard musick and dancing.

26 And he called one of the servants, and asked what these things meant [*what is going on?*].

27 And he said unto him, Thy brother is come; and thy father hath killed the fatted calf, because he hath received him safe and sound.

28 And he was angry, and would not go in: [*This is hardly appropriate behavior for one who is supposed to be a faithful, righteous son.*] therefore came his father out, and intreated [*pleaded with*] him.

29 And he answering said to his father, Lo [*now see here!*], these many years do I serve thee, neither transgressed I at any time thy commandment: and yet thou never gavest me a kid, that I might make merry with my friends: [*you never killed even so much as a young goat for me to have a party with my friends!*]

30 But as soon as this thy son [*implies "thy son," not "my brother" anymore*] was come [*came home*], which hath devoured thy living with harlots [*wasted his*

inheritance with prostitutes], thou hast killed for him the fatted calf.

31 And he said unto him, Son, thou art ever with me, and all that I have is thine. [*This presupposes that the older son rethinks his attitude about his returning younger brother, repents, and helps him to get reestablished in his father's household.*]

32 It was meet [*needful, good*] that we should make merry [*celebrate*], and be glad: for this thy brother [*emphasizing that he is "your brother," not just "my son"*] was dead [*spiritually*], and is alive again [*has repented, is a new person*]; and was lost, and is found. (Luke 15:25–32)

An interesting exercise in a Church class might be to have students write the rest of the story in a verse or two, detailing what they hope the final outcome was between the two brothers. The author of this work hopes that it might be something to the effect that the elder son repented and changed his attitude, then offered to share his own resources with the younger brother so that he could build flocks and herds and establish his own place again. This is basically what the Nephites did for the people of Ammon (Alma 27:22).

CAPERNAUM? SEVENTY SENT FORTH

Judea? Seventy Return and Report

At this time, in the last half of the third year of His mortal ministry, the Savior continued organizing the priesthood officers of His Church by calling the Seventy, giving them instructions, and sending them out on missions in companionships of two (Luke 10:1–11). As was the case previously with the Twelve, this will be a time of learning and training. Later, the Seventy returned and reported their missions. As you have probably noticed, we are jumping around somewhat in Matthew, Mark, Luke, and John as we follow the basic chronology of the Savior's mortal ministry according to the Harmony given in the Bible Dictionary found in the back of the LDS edition of the King James Bible. For example, we have returned back to Luke 10 for the account of the Seventies given here.

17 And the seventy returned again with joy, saying, Lord, even the devils are subject unto us through thy name [*when we do it in the name of Jesus Christ*].

Next, Jesus tells the Seventy that He was there when Lucifer was cast out as a result of his rebellion—see Isaiah 14:12, Revelation 12:7–9, D&C 76:25–27. Among other things, the Savior is instructing these men in the fact that He has power and authority over Satan.

18 And he said unto them, I beheld [*saw*] Satan as lightning fall from heaven.

19 Behold, I give unto you power to tread on serpents and scorpions, and over

all the power of the enemy [*Satan and all who work with him in opposing the work of the Lord*]: and nothing shall by any means hurt you.

20 Notwithstanding [*nevertheless*] in this rejoice not [*don't get cocky or boastful*], that the spirits are subject unto you; but rather rejoice, because your names are written in heaven [*you will go to celestial glory*]. (Luke 10:17–20)

JERUSALEM

The Parable of the Good Samaritan

Having left His beloved Galilee, the Master had now set His mind toward Jerusalem, as recorded by Luke.

51 And it came to pass, when the time was come that he should be received up, he stedfastly set his face to go to Jerusalem. (Luke 9:51)

He will teach and perform many miracles in the last few months of His mortal ministry, going back and forth between Judea and Perea (east of Judea, across the Jordan River), and possibly Samaria. In Jerusalem, He will give the parable of the good Samaritan in response to a certain lawyer's question about who our "neighbor" is (Luke 10:25–29). The lawyer was trying to make himself look good by making Jesus look bad in front of the people who were listening. It is helpful to know that the Jews despised the Samaritans and the Samaritans generally despised and made fun of the Jews. Samaria (the land of the Samaritans) was between Judea (in southern Israel) and Galilee (in northern Israel). When the Ten Tribes of Israel, who lived in what became Samaria, were taken into captivity (about 721 BC) by the Assyrians, some Israelites were left behind and intermarried with the Assyrian soldiers who occupied that land. This intermarrying over the years led the Jews to despise the Samaritans for breaking the law of Moses in which marrying outside of covenant Israel was forbidden.

30 And Jesus answering [*responding to the lawyer's question*] said, A certain man went down from Jerusalem to Jericho, and fell among thieves [*was attacked by robbers*], which stripped him of his raiment [*clothing*], and wounded him, and departed, leaving him half dead.
31 And by chance there came down a certain priest [*Jewish priest*] that way: and when he saw him, he passed by on the other side.
32 And likewise a Levite [*another Jewish priest*], when he was at the place, came and looked on him, and passed by on the other side. (Luke 10:30–32)

33 And likewise a Levite, when he was at the place, came and looked *upon* him, and passed by on the other side *of the way; for they desired in their hearts that it might not be known that they had seen him.* (JST, Luke 10:33)

Just a reminder. As mentioned a number of times previously, all of the JST corrections and additions are not contained in our LDS edition of the Bible. There is not enough room for them, consequently there were some difficult decisions made by the Brethren as to what to include and what to leave out. The JST verse given above, which contains some more information about the priest and the Levite, is not in our Bible. In order to see all of the JST changes, you would need to purchase a copy of the complete JST from an LDS bookstore, check it out from a library, find it online, and so forth.

> 33 But a certain Samaritan [*a man from Samaria; as mentioned above, Samaritans were despised by the Jews*], as he journeyed, came where he was: and when he saw him, he had compassion on him,
> 34 And went to him, and bound up his wounds, pouring in oil and wine [*gave him first aid*], and set him on his own beast, and brought him to an inn, and took care of him.
> 35 And on the morrow when he departed, he took out two pence [*money representing two days' wages in that day*], and gave them to the host [*the innkeeper*], and said unto him, Take care of him; and whatsoever thou spendest more [*beyond what I have paid you*], when I come again, I will repay thee. (Luke 10:33–35)

Did you notice that it costs to be a "good Samaritan"? Certainly, that is one of the important messages for us in this parable. The Master now concludes the lesson by asking the lawyer a question.

> 36 Which now of these three, thinkest thou, was neighbour unto him that fell among the thieves?
> 37 And he [*the lawyer*] said, He that shewed [*showed*] mercy on him. Then said Jesus unto him, Go, and do thou likewise. (Luke 10:36–37)

BETHANY

Mary and Martha

Just outside of Jerusalem, near the Mount of Olives, was a village called Bethany in which two sisters, Mary and Martha, and their brother, Lazarus, lived. What happens now as Jesus pays them a visit is a rather well-known situation, in which Martha complains to Him that her sister, Mary, is not helping with the chores associated with preparing a meal for Him. What follows is a lesson by the Savior on priorities as well as on individual needs and personalities.

> 38 Now it came to pass, as they went, that he entered into a certain village [*Bethany*]: and a certain woman named Martha received him into her house.
> 39 And she had a sister called Mary, which also sat at Jesus' feet, and heard his word.

40 But Martha was cumbered about much serving [*very busy with all the details that needed attention in order to feed the Savior*], and came to him, and said [*complained*], Lord, dost thou not care that my sister hath left me to serve alone [*doesn't it bother you that Mary is not helping me*]? bid her therefore that she help me [*tell her to help me*].

41 And Jesus answered and said unto her, Martha, Martha, thou art careful and troubled about many things [*you are meticulous and always fuss over the tiniest details*]:

42 But one thing is needful: and Mary hath chosen that good part [*has chosen to listen to Me and My teachings*], which shall not be taken away from her [*which is a wise thing for her to be doing with her agency*]. (Luke 10:38–42)

Elder James E. Talmage, a member of the Quorum of the Twelve Apostles from 1911–33, spoke of this incident with Mary and Martha as follows:

> There was no reproof of Martha's desire to provide well; nor any sanction of possible neglect on Mary's part. We must suppose that Mary had been a willing helper before the Master's arrival; but now that He had come, she chose to remain with Him. Had she been culpably neglectful of her duty, Jesus would not have commended her course. He desired not well-served meals and material comforts only, but the company of the sisters, and above all their receptive attention to what He had to say. He had more to give them than they could possibly provide for Him. Jesus loved the two sisters and their brother as well. Both these women were devoted to Jesus, and each expressed herself in her own way. Martha was of a practical turn, concerned in material service; she was by nature hospitable and self-denying. Mary, contemplative and more spiritually inclined, showed her devotion through the service of companionship and appreciation. (*Jesus the Christ*, p. 433)

PEREA

A Crippled Woman Is Healed on the Sabbath

The Master continued ministering in Judea for a time, teaching about prayer (Luke 11:1–8), emphasizing the importance of living the gospel (Luke 11:27–28), warning against covetousness (Luke 12:13–21), and teaching the doctrine of repentance (Luke 13:1–5). He then traveled to Perea where He taught in a synagogue and healed a badly crippled woman on the Sabbath, which caused the ruler of that synagogue to become irate. Once again, we see how far astray people can go without guidance from living prophets.

10 And he was teaching in one of the synagogues on the sabbath.

11 And, behold, there was a woman which had a spirit of infirmity [*had been weak and sickly*] eighteen years, and was bowed together [*was bent over*], and could in no wise lift up herself [*could not straighten herself out at all*].

12 And when Jesus saw her, he called her to him, and said unto her, Woman, thou art loosed from thine infirmity [*you are set free from being crippled*].
13 And he laid his hands on her: and immediately she was made straight, and glorified [*praised*] God.
14 And the ruler of the synagogue answered [*responded*] with indignation [*anger*], because that Jesus had healed on the sabbath day, and said unto the people, There are six days in which men ought to work: in them therefore come and be healed, and not on the sabbath day. [*In other words, if you want to be healed in my synagogue, come on any of the six days of the week when work is permitted. But don't come to be healed on the Sabbath.*] (Luke 13:10–14)

Once again, we see the seriousness of hypocrisy as the Savior delivers a stinging rebuke and then teaches simple principles relating to the Sabbath.

15 The Lord then answered him, and said, Thou hypocrite, doth not each one of you on the sabbath loose [*untie*] his ox or his ass from the stall, and lead him away to watering?
16 And ought not this woman, being a daughter of Abraham, whom Satan hath bound, lo, these eighteen years, be loosed [*freed*] from this bond [*the bondage of being crippled*] on the sabbath day? [*You treat your beasts of burden better that you treat this woman.*]
17 And when he had said these things, all his adversaries [*opponents*] were ashamed: and all the people rejoiced for all the glorious things that were done by him. (Luke 13:15–17)

PEREA

The Parable of the Unjust Steward

At this point in Luke's account, the Savior is in Perea (east of the Jordan River and north of Jerusalem), and it is now the winter of 33 AD. As you have perhaps noticed, Luke's writing has much that was not included by Matthew, Mark, and John, relating to this period of the Master's ministry.

The Savior continued to teach in parables, teaching principles and doctrines that could be understood by those who were spiritually in tune but not by others. This next parable, known as the parable of the unjust steward, probably shouldn't be scrutinized for lots of details or various specific applications in our daily lives. Rather, it is probably best seen as a general message that people often are more resourceful in dealing with worldly situations than they are in working out their salvation. If we strain at finding detailed applications, we might come up with some that don't fit or that don't teach correct doctrine and lessons.

1 And he said also unto his disciples, There was a certain rich man, which had a steward [*a man in charge of all his business dealings*]; and the same was accused

unto him [*someone complained to the rich man*] that he [*the steward*] had wasted his goods [*was mismanaging the business*].

2 And he called him, and said unto him, How is it that I hear this of thee [*what's this I hear about you*]? give an account of thy stewardship [*give me a report on how the business is doing*]; for thou mayest be no longer steward [*I am going to fire you*].

3 Then the steward said within himself, What shall I do? for my lord taketh away from me the stewardship: I cannot dig [*I can't do manual labor*]; to beg I am ashamed [*I would be embarrassed to be a beggar*].

4 I am resolved what to do, that, when I am put out of the stewardship, they may receive me into their houses [*I have a plan, so that, after I am fired, I will have friends who will take care of me*].

5 So he called every one of his lord's debtors [*people who owed the owner money*] unto him, and said unto the first, How much owest thou unto my lord?

6 And he said, An hundred measures of oil. And he said unto him, Take thy bill, and sit down quickly, and write fifty [*if you pay now, I will settle for half of what you owe*].

7 Then said he to another, And how much owest thou? And he said, An hundred measures of wheat. And he said unto him, Take thy bill, and write fourscore [*eighty*].

8 And the lord commended [*congratulated*] the unjust steward, because he had done wisely: for the children of this world are in their generation wiser than the children of light [*often, people in business worry more about their future security on earth than members of the Church worry about their future security in heaven; see Talmage,* Jesus the Christ, *p. 463*]. (Luke 16:1–8)

PEREA

The Parable of Lazarus and the Rich Man

As background to this parable, which starts in Luke 16:19, it helps to know that the Pharisees had just attempted to publicly mock and ridicule Jesus (Luke 16:14). Their attempts to discredit Him are intensifying. And in reply, according to the JST, quoted here, next, He publicly warned them of their hypocrisy, and told them that they were adulterers and were perverting the right way of God. We understand that, among other evil practices, the Pharisees were secretly involved in marrying and divorcing to make their sexual conquests seem legal. The Savior said they were adulterers and strongly condemned them for this evil at the end of JST Luke 12:21. This verse, unfortunately, was left completely out of the Bible. As you can see, the last phrase of JST Luke 16:23 leads right up to the parable, as the Master tells them that the rich man in the parable represents them. Quoting from the JST:

21 *O fools! for you have said in your hearts, There is no God. And you pervert the right way; and the kingdom of heaven suffereth violence of*

you; and you persecute the meek; and in your violence you seek to destroy the kingdom; and ye take the children of the kingdom by force. Woe unto you, ye adulterers!

22 And they reviled him again, being angry for the saying, that they were adulterers.

23 But he continued, saying, Whosoever putteth away his wife, and marrieth another, committeth adultery; and whosoever marrieth her who is put away from her husband, committeth adultery. *Verily I say unto you, I will liken you unto the rich man.* (JST, Luke 16:21–23)

Now, the parable:

19 There was a certain rich man, which was clothed in purple and fine linen, and fared sumptuously [*lived in luxury*] every day:

20 And there was a certain beggar named Lazarus, which was laid at his gate, full of [*covered with*] sores,

21 And desiring to be fed with the crumbs which fell from the rich man's table: moreover the dogs came and licked his sores. [*Symbolizing that dogs take better care of beggars and people in need than the Pharisees do.*]

22 And it came to pass, that the beggar died, and was carried by the angels into Abraham's bosom [*was taken to paradise*]: the rich man also died, and was buried;

23 And in hell he lift up his eyes, being in torments, and seeth Abraham afar off, and Lazarus in his bosom [*Lazarus was with Abraham in paradise*].

24 And he cried and said, Father Abraham, have mercy on me, and send Lazarus, that he may dip the tip of his finger in water, and cool my tongue; for I am tormented in this flame [*it is miserable here in hell*].

25 But Abraham said, Son, remember that thou in thy lifetime receivedst thy good things, and likewise Lazarus evil things: but now he is comforted, and thou art tormented.

26 And beside all this, between us and you there is a great gulf fixed: so that they which would pass from hence to you cannot; neither can they pass to us, that would come from thence. (Luke 16:19–26)

This "gulf" or barrier between spirit prison and paradise was bridged by the Savior during the time that His body lay in the tomb and His spirit visited the righteous in paradise. There, in paradise, He set up and organized missionary work and authorized the righteous spirits in paradise to go to spirit prison and teach the gospel there. See D&C, section 138, 1 Peter 3:18 and 4:6.

Next in the parable, the rich man asks that Lazarus be sent to warn the man's brothers about what awaits them if they do not repent. One thing we can learn from this part of the parable is that the scriptures, accompanied by the witness of the Holy Ghost, are more effective in conversion than even a visit from an angel or a departed righteous spirit.

27 Then he said, I pray thee therefore, father [*Abraham*], that thou wouldest send him to my father's house [*to warn them about what has happened to me*]:

28 For I have five brethren [*brothers*]; that he [*Lazarus*] may testify unto them, lest they also come into this place of torment [*hell, spirit prison*].

29 Abraham saith unto him, They have Moses and the prophets; let them hear them. [*They have already been given that message through the writings of the prophets in the scriptures.*]

30 And he said, Nay, father Abraham [*they don't pay much attention to the scriptures*]: but if one went unto them from the dead, they will repent. [*That would scare them enough to repent.*]

31 And he said unto him, If they hear not Moses and the prophets [*if they ignore the scriptures*], neither will they be persuaded [*converted*], though one rose from the dead [*even if one came back from the dead to them*]. (Luke 16:27–31)

SAMARIA?

Ten Lepers Are Healed

Most Bible scholars believe that this miracle took place in Samaria, because the one leper who returned to thank the Master was a Samaritan. One of the major messages for us in this account is the importance of gratitude.

12 And as he entered into a certain village, there met him ten men that were lepers [*had leprosy*], which stood afar off [*by law they were not allowed to be near people who did not have leprosy*]:

13 And they lifted up their voices [*spoke loudly*], and said, Jesus, Master, have mercy on us.

14 And when he saw them, he said unto them, Go shew yourselves unto the priests [*as required by the law of Moses; see Leviticus 14:2*]. And it came to pass, that, as they went, they were cleansed [*healed*].

15 And one of them, when he saw that he was healed, turned back, and with a loud voice glorified [*praised*] God,

16 And fell down on his face at his feet [*humbly laid down at Jesus' feet—a sign of deep humility in Jewish culture*], giving him thanks: and he was a Samaritan. (Luke 17:11–16)

As previously mentioned, Samaritans were despised by Jews and Jews were despised by Samaritans (inhabitants of Samaria). Originally, about 700 years before Christ, the ancestors of the Samaritans were members of the tribes of Israel, especially Ephraim. When the Assyrians conquered the Ten Tribes and took them away into captivity, about 722 BC, Israelites who were permitted to remain ended up intermarrying with the occupational armies. This led to their being shunned by the Jews and developed into the long-standing ethnic dislike and hatred for Samaritans that was prevalent at the time of Christ's mortal ministry.

> 17 And Jesus answering said, Were there not ten cleansed [*healed*]? but where are the nine?
>
> 18 There are not found that returned to give glory to God, save this stranger [*foreigner, non Israelite; this may imply that the other nine lepers were Jews*].
>
> 19 And he said unto him, Arise, go thy way: thy faith hath made thee whole. (Luke 17:17–19)

SAMARIA?

The Parable of the Unjust Judge

One point of this parable, as given in verse 1, seems to be that some situations in life require that we continue to pray for desired blessings over a long period of time, and we shouldn't give up. Another lesson from this parable, according to verses 7–8, seems to be that the prayers of the Saints do not always stop persecution in its tracks, but such prayers will eventually be answered.

> 1 And he spake a parable unto them to this end [*with this purpose in mind*], that men ought always to pray, and not to faint [*give up*];
>
> 2 Saying, There was in a city a judge, which feared not God, neither regarded man:
>
> 3 And there was a widow in that city; and she came unto him, saying, Avenge me of mine adversary [*I have been wronged; please render judgment against my enemy*].
>
> 4 And he would not for a while: but afterward he said within himself, Though I fear not God, nor regard man [*even though I'm not afraid of God or man*];
>
> 5 Yet because this widow troubleth me [*keeps asking me for help*], I will avenge her [*grant her request*], lest [*for fear that*] by her continual coming she weary me.
>
> 6 And the Lord [*Jesus*] said, Hear [*pay attention to*] what the unjust judge saith.
>
> 7 And shall not God avenge his own elect [*will God not answer the prayers of His saints for justice*], which cry [*pray*] day and night unto him, though he bear long with them [*even if it takes a long time before He grants their request*]?
>
> 8 I tell you that he will avenge them speedily. Nevertheless when the Son of man [*Jesus*] cometh, shall he find faith on the earth?
>
>> 8 I tell you that he *will come, and when he does come*, he will avenge *his saints* speedily. Nevertheless, when the Son of man cometh, shall he find faith on the earth? (JST, Luke 18:8)

JERUSALEM

Jesus Attends the Feast of Tabernacles

We are indebted to John's Gospel for the account of several events that take place next, as the Savior attends the Feast of Tabernacles in Jerusalem. As mentioned previously, there is some uncertainty as to when these events occurred, in relationship to other events in the Master's ministry, but we will follow the Harmony of the Gospels given in the Bible Dictionary for our chronology.

The Feast of Tabernacles was held in the late fall at harvest time in Jerusalem. See Bible Dictionary, under "Feasts." It drew large crowds and was a week-long celebration of thanksgiving, which included daily animal sacrifices and a ceremony where people waved palm, myrtle, willow, and citrus branches toward the cardinal points of the compass (north, south, east, and west), symbolizing the presence of God throughout the universe. One additional day had been added to the celebration by the time of the Savior's mortal ministry.

From John 7:3–5, we sense a hint of criticism and disapproval on the part of Jesus' close relatives, likely including His own half-brothers, who do not believe in Him (verse 5), as they tell Him, in effect, that He really ought to go to Jerusalem for the Feast of Tabernacles so He can parade Himself in front of His disciples as well as huge numbers of people. There is a hint that these family members and close relatives were embarrassed that Jesus was part of their family. He indicates that they should go ahead to Jerusalem, but He will follow when He is ready, explaining why He will remain behind for a while.

> 6 Then Jesus said unto them, My time is not yet come [*perhaps meaning that the time for His atoning sacrifice in Jerusalem has not yet arrived—compare with Matthew 26:18*]: but your time is alway ready [*you can go to Jerusalem any time, so you go ahead and go for the Feast of Tabernacles*].
> 7 The world cannot hate you [*the people of the world don't hate you because you are just normal people and most of them don't even know you*]; but me it hateth, because I testify of it, that the works thereof are evil [*but they hate Me because I tell them they are wicked*].
> 8 Go ye up unto this feast [*the Feast of Tabernacles in Jerusalem*]: I go not up yet unto this feast; for my time is not yet full come [*it is not time for Me to go*]. (John 7:6–8)

When the time was right, He went to Jerusalem, but avoided situations in which He might be recognized, because the Jewish leaders were on the lookout for Him. Finally, in the middle of the week-long festivities, He went to the temple and taught openly (John 7:10–14). The people were amazed that He knew so much, not realizing or accepting that He was the Son of God and the Jehovah of the Old Testament.

> 15 And the Jews marvelled, saying, How knoweth this man letters, having never learned [*how does Jesus know so much; He hasn't had the formal training that our religious leaders have*]?
> 16 Jesus answered them, and said, My doctrine is not mine, but his that sent me. [*My Father is My teacher.*]
> 17 If any man will do his will, he shall know of the doctrine, whether it be of God, or whether I speak of myself. [*If anyone will live the gospel, he will find out that it is true.*] (John 7:15–17)

As Jesus continues teaching the crowds in the courtyard of the temple, some point out that He is the one whom the Pharisees want killed, and ask why they don't arrest Him.

> 25 Then said some of them of Jerusalem [*who were from Jerusalem*], Is not this he, whom they seek to kill?
> 26 But, lo, he speaketh boldly [*look, He is speaking out boldly in public*], and they [*the Pharisees and other Jewish leaders*] say nothing unto him. Do the rulers know indeed that this is the very Christ? [*Maybe they think He actually is Christ and are afraid of Him.*]
> 27 Howbeit [*regardless of what they think*] we know this man whence he is [*we know where Jesus comes from, namely Nazareth*]: but when Christ [*the promised Messiah*] cometh, no man knoweth whence he is [*no one will know where he comes from*]. (John 7:25–27)

The idea stated in verse 27, above, that no one would know where the true Christ came from, was a long-standing false tradition among the Jews. The situation intensifies as the Savior bears witness that the Father has sent Him. Many begin to believe Him.

> 28 Then cried Jesus in the temple [*Jesus spoke loudly so everyone could hear*] as he taught, saying, Ye both know me, and ye know whence I am: and I am not come of myself [*I have not come on My own*], but he that sent me is true, whom ye know not [*rather, I have been sent by the Father, whom you do not know because of your wickedness*].
> 29 But I know him: for I am from him, and he hath sent me.
> 30 Then they sought to take him [*wanted to arrest him*]: but no man laid hands on him, because his hour was not yet come. [*No one was able to seize him because it was not time yet for His trial and crucifixion.*]
> 31 And many of the people believed on him, and said, When Christ cometh, will he do more miracles than these which this man hath done? [*In other words, this has to be the Christ.*] (John 7:28–31)

Finally, the Pharisees and chief priests issue orders to arrest Jesus.

32 The Pharisees heard that the people murmured [*were saying*] such things concerning him; and the Pharisees and the chief priests sent officers to take him [*to arrest Him*].
33 Then said Jesus unto them, Yet a little while am I with you, and then I go unto him that sent me [*then I will return to My Father in Heaven*].
34 Ye shall seek me, and shall not find me: and where I am, thither [*there*] ye cannot come. (John 7:32–34)

Here again, as in so many other places, John is pointing out to us that we are watching a group of people who are very learned in the letter of the law and in the details of the scriptures but haven't a clue what it is really about, because they don't understand anything about the simple plan of salvation. Watch now, as they again stumble over details because they do not understand or accept the "big picture." This is a reminder to us of the importance of understanding the basics of the Father's plan for us.

35 Then said the Jews among themselves, Whither [*where*] will he go, that we shall not find him? will he go unto the dispersed among the Gentiles, and teach the Gentiles [*will He go to the Greeks and teach them; see John 7:35, footnote a*]?
36 What manner of saying is this that he said [*what does He mean by saying*], Ye shall seek me, and shall not find me: and where I am, thither ye cannot come? (John 7:35–36)

The worship and celebration associated with the Feast of Tabernacles continued through the rest of the week, with much extra excitement in the air because of the Master's presence and teaching in Jerusalem. Finally, the eighth and final day of the celebration, with its climactic finale arrived. Picture if you will, throngs of Jews crowding the grounds around the temple, watching in rapt attention as the traditional water from the stream of Siloam (symbolic of water drawn from the wells of salvation—see Isaiah 12:3) was carried to the altar and then poured upon it. Imagine it flowing down off it onto the ground, in a great ritual show symbolic of the living waters, including the Holy Ghost, which flow from the altar of God onto the earth to quench the spiritual thirst of the faithful—see Isaiah 44:3, 55:1. Perhaps, at that very moment, Jesus stood and with a loud voice spoke to the onlookers, saying, "If any man thirst, let him come unto me, and drink (verse 37, next)." There could not have been a more dramatic setting. Jesus was openly claiming to be the Messiah and to be the Jehovah of the Old Testament who had promised to give "living waters" to the faithful.

37 In the last day [*the eighth and final day of the Feast of Tabernacles, the climactic finale to the celebrating—see Bible Dictionary, under "Feasts"*], that great day [*the*

culmination] of the feast, Jesus stood and cried, saying, If any man thirst, let him come unto me, and drink.

38 He that believeth on me, as the scripture [*Isaiah 44:3, 55:1*] hath said, out of his belly shall flow rivers of living water.

John's original commentary about the Holy Ghost, given here, did not come through the various translations of the Bible in tact. But the JST restores it.

39 (But this spake he of the Spirit, which they that believe on him should receive: for the Holy Ghost was not yet given; because that Jesus was not yet glorified.) (John 7:37–39)

> 39 (But this spake he of the Spirit, which they that believe on him should receive; for the Holy Ghost was *promised unto them who believe, after that Jesus was glorified.*) (JST, John 7:39)

The phrase, "the Holy Ghost was not yet given," in verse 39 above, causes some to believe that the Holy Ghost was not here at all during the time Jesus was on earth for His mortal ministry. This is not the case. The Holy Ghost was obviously functioning and active on earth during that time. He attended the Savior's baptism. (Matthew 3:13–17) The Savior was "full of the Holy Ghost" in Luke 4:1. Thus, our understanding is that, while the Holy Ghost did function during Christ's mortal ministry, the full power of the Gift of the Holy Ghost was not here (Bible Dictionary, under "Holy Ghost").

After His magnificent appearance during the final day of celebration, proclaiming Himself to be the "living water," many people debated with each other as to who Jesus really was (John 7:40–43). Finally, the officers who had been instructed to arrest Jesus reluctantly returned to their leaders without Him.

45 Then came the officers [*soldiers*] to the chief priests and Pharisees [*Jewish religious leaders*]; and they said unto them, Why have ye not brought him [*why didn't you arrest Jesus*]?

46 The officers answered, Never man spake like this man [*nobody ever taught like He does*].

47 Then answered them the Pharisees [*then the Pharisees and chief priests said to the soldiers*], Are ye also deceived [*has Jesus got you fooled also*]?

48 Have any of the rulers or of the Pharisees believed on him [*have any of us rulers been deceived by him*]?

49 But this people who knoweth not the law are cursed. [*The people don't understand the teachings of Moses. That's why they are subject to being deceived by Jesus.*] (John 7:45–49)

JERUSALEM

Nicodemus Defends Jesus

Next, Nicodemus will defend Jesus before his peers, which is a very risky thing to do under the circumstances. Perhaps you remember that Nicodemus was the Pharisee who came to Jesus by night and was taught the necessity of baptism and the gift of the Holy Ghost (see John 3:1–21). He will also help Joseph from Aramathea prepare the body of the crucified Lord for burial (see John 19:39).

> 50 Nicodemus saith unto them, (he that came to Jesus by night, being one of them,) [*Nicodemus was a member of the Pharisees*]
> 51 Doth our law judge any man, before it hear him, and know what he doeth? [*Why are we violating our own laws? We haven't even given Jesus a fair trial and already we are judging Him.*]
> 52 They answered and said unto him, Art thou also of Galilee [*has He converted you too*]? Search, and look: for out of Galilee ariseth no prophet. [*Check the scriptures. There is no mention of a Prophet who comes from Galilee.*]
> 53 And every man went unto his own house.

THE TEMPLE AT JERUSALEM

The Woman Taken in Adultery

It is the day after the Feast of Tabernacles and there is still excitement in Jerusalem. Large crowds of people have gathered to listen to Jesus as He teaches in the courtyard of the temple. The scribes and Pharisees are very frustrated because, despite repeated attempts to discredit Jesus and get Him arrested, they continue to fail to reach their goal. John now reports yet another attempt to trap Him in His words. The Jewish leaders drag a woman taken in adultery to Jesus, in front of the crowd, and ask what He recommends be done to her. Their hope is that they can get Him to say something in opposition to the law of Moses concerning punishment for adultery, in order that they can have Him arrested. Watch, and see what happens.

> 1 Jesus went unto the mount of Olives [*just a few minutes' walk east of Jerusalem*].
> 2 And early in the morning he came again into the temple [*the courtyard of the temple*], and all the people came unto him; and he sat down, and taught them.
> 3 And the scribes and Pharisees brought unto him a woman taken in adultery; and when they had set her in the midst, (John 8:1–3)
>
>> 3 And the scribes and Pharisees brought unto him a woman taken in adultery; and when they had set her in the midst *of the people*, (JST, John 8:3)

4 They say unto him, Master, this woman was taken in adultery, in the very act [*we caught her right while she was doing it*]. (John 8:4)

One has to wonder why these Jewish leaders didn't also bring the man who was involved with this woman to the Savior. Perhaps he was one of their own. In JST Luke 16:21, Jesus called these leaders adulterers. We don't know if the man was a fellow Pharisee, but it is pure hypocrisy to single out the woman for embarrassment and humiliation, and let the man escape. Next, they continue setting the trap as they remind Him of what the law of Moses said regarding the matter, and then ask a question. Imagine how quiet it was as the crowd hushed in an attempt to watch and hear the Master's response. Imagine also how frightened and humiliated the woman was.

5 Now Moses in the law commanded us, that such should be stoned: but what sayest thou?
6 This they said, tempting him [*trying to lure Him into a trap*], that they might have to accuse him [*in order for them to build a legal case against Him*]. But Jesus stooped down, and with his finger wrote on the ground, as though he heard them not.
7 So when they continued [*kept*] asking him, he lifted up himself [*stood up*], and said unto them, He that is without sin among you [*perhaps implying whoever has not committed the same sin; see McConkie,* Doctrinal New Testament Commentary, *Vol. 1, p. 451*], let him first cast a stone at her.
8 And again he stooped down, and wrote on the ground.
9 And they which heard it, being convicted by their own conscience, went out one by one, beginning at the eldest, even unto the last: and Jesus was left alone, and the woman standing in the midst.
10 When Jesus had lifted up himself [*had stood up*], and saw none but the woman, he said unto her, Woman, where are those thine accusers? hath no man condemned thee? [*Where did the men go who wanted to stone you? Didn't any of them condemn you to death?*]
11 She said, No man, Lord. And Jesus said unto her, Neither do I condemn thee: go, and sin no more. (John 8:5–11)

> 11 She said, No man, Lord. And Jesus said unto her, Neither do I condemn thee; go, and sin no more. *And the woman glorified God from that hour, and believed on his name.* (JST, John 8:11)

Did you notice that Jesus did not forgive the woman at this point? Obviously, she has some serious repenting to do. But He did not condemn her meaning that she still had time and opportunity to repent. The Joseph Smith Translation, cited above, at the end of verse 11, confirms that she began repenting.

THE TEMPLE AT JERUSALEM
The Light of the World

As Jesus continued to teach the people in the courtyard of the temple, He used beautiful symbolism to illustrate His role in making salvation available to all who are willing to follow Him.

> 12 Then spake Jesus again unto them, saying, I am the light of the world: he that followeth me shall not walk in darkness [*spiritual darkness*], but shall have the light of life [*eternal life*]. (John 8:12)

The Pharisees continued to challenge Him, debating with Him about the law of witnesses in a vain attempt to stop His teaching (John 8:13–19). Still, no one attempted to arrest Him, as John points out.

> 20 These words spake Jesus in the treasury [*one of the temple buildings*], as he taught in the temple: and no man laid hands on him; for his hour was not yet come [*John is reminding us that the time for the Savior's arrest, trial, crucifixion, and resurrection was not yet here at this time*]. (John 8:20)

The Master continued teaching, prophesying His crucifixion, and reminding the people that unless they took advantage of His Atonement, they could not be forgiven of their sins and could not live in heaven with Him (John 8:21–31). He then concluded this part of His teaching with a brief but profound truth.

> 32 And ye shall know the truth, and the truth shall make you free (John 8:32).

Verse 32, above, contains a simple and powerful fact. The truth sets us free. For example, if people falsely believe that a baby who dies without baptism is forever damned from returning to heaven, they are set free by the truth in D&C 137:10, which teaches that little children are saved in the celestial kingdom. If one has lived a life of serious sin, and upon repenting and changing lifestyle, still believes that he or she will forever be a "second-class" citizen in the Church, Isaiah 1:18 will set him or her free from feelings of being permanently limited by past lifestyle. So will Elder Richard G. Scott's talk in October Conference, 2000, as previously referenced, set such persons "free." He taught: "If you have repented from serious transgression and mistakenly believe that you will always be a second-class citizen in the kingdom of God, learn that is not true."

After He had taught much more about who they were and who He is (John 7:33–58), the Jews finally came to clearly understand that Jesus claimed to be the God of the Old Testament, in other words, Jehovah. They were furious! It will be interesting someday to get the rest of the account as to how He escaped their attempts to stone Him.

> 59 Then took they up stones to cast at him: but Jesus hid himself, and went out of the temple, going through the midst of them, and so passed by.

JERUSALEM

A Blind Man Is Healed on the Sabbath

In the course of continuing events, Jesus will soon leave Jerusalem and spend additional time in Perea and elsewhere before returning to Jerusalem for the eventful final week of His mortal life. Before leaving Jerusalem this time, He and His disciples pass a blind man, which causes His Apostles to ask an important doctrinal question.

> 2 And his disciples asked him, saying, Master, who did sin, this man, or his parents, that he was born blind? (John 9:2)

It was a common false belief among the Jews in New Testament times that illness in general was caused by sin. The Savior straightens out this mistaken idea, and then bears witness that the Father sent Him to be the light of the world.

> 3 Jesus answered, Neither hath this man sinned, nor his parents: but that the works of God should be made manifest [*be shown*] in him.
> 4 I must work the works of him that sent me, while it is day: the night cometh, when no man can work. (John 9:3–4)

>> 4 I must work the works of him that sent me, while *I am with you; the time cometh when I shall have finished my work, then I go unto the Father.* (JST, John 9:4)

> 5 As long as I am in the world, I am the light of the world. (John 9:5)

The Master then healed the blind man, which caused no small stir among his neighbors and those who knew him (John 9:6–12). Since it was the Sabbath when the man was healed, the Pharisees soon became involved and tried to convince the former blind man that Jesus was of the devil because a man of God would not violate the Sabbath by healing someone on that holy day (John 9:13–17). The man was unimpressed by the efforts of these hypocritical spiritual leaders of the Jews to discredit Jesus, so they interrogated his parents as to whether or not he had truly been blind, and ultimately put more pressure on him (John 9:18–33). Perhaps one of the important lessons we can learn from this is that wickedness does not promote rational thought. Unsuccessful in their attempts to squelch this wonderful miracle, the Pharisees excommunicated the formerly blind man (John 9:34).

We see the tender mercy of the Savior next as He seeks out and introduces Himself to the previously blind man, who has been excommunicated by his Jewish religious leaders. The man humbly accepts the Master's message of salvation. Remember that the man had not seen the Savior so he did not know at first who He was. He was blind when Jesus anointed his eyes with clay and told him to go to the pool of Siloam and wash the clay from his eyes, at which point, away from the Master, he was healed (John 9:6–7).

35 Jesus heard that they had cast him out; and when he had found him, he said unto him, Dost thou believe on the Son of God?

36 He answered and said, Who is he, Lord, that I might believe on him?

37 And Jesus said unto him, Thou hast both seen him [*you are seeing Him now*], and it is he that talketh with thee. [*You are talking with Him now.*]

38 And he said, Lord, I believe. And he worshipped him. (John 9:35–38)

JERUSALEM

The Parable of the Good Shepherd

Next, the Master uses the imagery of a shepherd leading his sheep to illustrate that He is the Good Shepherd, and other, unauthorized shepherds (Pharisees and other false leaders) try to sneak in and lead the sheep astray. In the days of Jesus, it was a common practice for several shepherds to keep their sheep overnight in the same enclosure, so that only one guard would have to be on duty through the night. The next morning, each shepherd would come to the proper door of the enclosure, identify himself to the guard, and then literally call his own sheep to come out of the herd to him, often calling each of his sheep by its own name. His sheep recognized his voice and came out from the herd and followed him throughout the day as he led them to pasture and water. It is a fascinating sight in the Holy Land, even today, to see sheep following a shepherd who is leading his sheep, rather than herding them from behind.

1 Verily, verily, I say unto you, He that entereth not by the door into the sheepfold, but climbeth up some other way, the same is a thief and a robber [*is not authorized by God to lead the sheep; symbolic of Satan, apostates, and so forth, who try to lead us astray*].

2 But he [*Christ*] that entereth in by the door [*is authorized by God*] is the shepherd of the sheep.

3 To him the porter [*guard*] openeth; and the sheep hear his voice: and he calleth his own sheep by name, and leadeth them out.

4 And when he putteth forth his own sheep, he goeth before them [*leads them,*

rather than herding them], and the sheep follow him: for they know his voice.
5 And a stranger will they not follow, but will flee from him: for they know not the voice of strangers.
6 This parable spake Jesus unto them: but they understood not what things they were which he spake unto them. (John 10:1–6)

Next, Jesus explains the parable.

7 Then said Jesus unto them again, Verily, verily, I say unto you, I am the door of the sheep [*symbolic of the door to heaven*].
8 All that ever came before me are thieves and robbers [*any others who have come before Me and claim to be the doorway to heaven are false shepherds*]: but the sheep did not hear them [*My true followers don't come to them when they call*]. (John 10:7–8)

As Jesus continues explaining the meaning of the imagery in this parable, He teaches the clear doctrine that there is only one entrance into the kingdom of God, and He is that entrance, or door.

9 I am the door: by me if any man enter in, he shall be saved, and shall go in and out, and find pasture [*will be nourished by God*].
10 The thief [*symbolic of Satan, the wicked, and so forth*] cometh not, but for to steal, and to kill, and to destroy: I am come that they might have life [*to bring the faithful eternal life*], and that they might have it more abundantly.
11 I am the good shepherd: the good shepherd giveth his life for the sheep [*Jesus will give His life for us*].
12 But he that is an hireling [*a hired servant*], and not the shepherd, whose own the sheep are not [*who does not own the sheep*], seeth the wolf coming, and leaveth the sheep, and fleeth: and the wolf catcheth them, and scattereth the sheep.
13 The hireling fleeth [*runs away when danger comes*], because he is an hireling, and careth not for the sheep [*he doesn't love the sheep like the owner does*].
14 I am the good shepherd, and know my sheep, and am known of mine [*the Savior's true followers know His voice and come when He calls*].
15 As the Father knoweth me, even so know I the Father: and I lay down my life for the sheep [*Jesus will give His life for His people as He performs the Atonement*]. (John 10:9–15)

Next, the Lord mentions "other sheep."

16 And other sheep I have, which are not of this fold [*are not on this continent*]: them also I must bring, and they shall hear my voice; and there shall be one fold, and one shepherd [*all of my righteous followers will ultimately come together with me in celestial glory*]. (John 10:16)

We know from 3 Nephi 15:21 that Jesus was referring to the Nephites on the American continent, when He referred to "other sheep." We know also that there were yet other sheep besides the Nephites. To the Nephites, Jesus said, "I say unto you that I have other sheep, which are not of this land, neither of the land of Jerusalem" (3 Nephi 16:1). As we read 3 Nephi 17:4, we are told that Jesus was referring to the Lost Ten Tribes.

As the Savior continued teaching about the Good Shepherd, referring back to what He said in verse 11, above, He clearly taught that no one had the power to take His life from Him. Rather, He gave it voluntarily.

18 No man taketh it from me, but I lay it down of myself. I have power to lay it down [*to leave my body*], and I have power to take it again [*I have power to resurrect*]. This commandment have I received of my Father. [*This is what My Father asked Me to do.*]

PEREA

From Jerusalem, the Savior traveled again to Perea, east of the Jordan River, where the people flocked to hear Him and to have Him heal their sick (Matthew 19:1–2). As mentioned previously, these physical healings serve to remind us of the power of the Atonement of Jesus Christ to cleanse and heal us spiritually, which is the healing that counts eternally. And the wide variety of physical healings and cleansing from evil spirits performed by the Master can symbolize His power to heal us from a vast variety of spiritual ills.

Not surprisingly, the Pharisees follow Him to Perea, where they continue their efforts to trap Him into saying something for which they could have Him arrested. This time they choose to confront Him on the matter of divorce.

3 The Pharisees also came unto him, tempting him [*trying to trap him so they could arrest Him*], and saying unto him, Is it lawful for a man to put away [*divorce*] his wife for every cause?
4 And he answered and said unto them, Have ye not read, that he [*Heavenly Father*] which made them at the beginning made them male and female,
5 And said, For this cause [*marriage and family*] shall a man leave father and mother, and shall cleave to [*be faithful to*] his wife: and they twain [*two*] shall be one flesh?
6 Wherefore they are no more twain [*two people*], but one flesh [*one family unit*]. What therefore God hath joined together, let not man put asunder [*take apart*]. (Matthew 19:3–6)

As you can see, they are trying to pit the Master against the great lawgiver and prophet, Moses, who is very highly esteemed among the Jews at this time in the New Testament.

7 They say unto him, Why did Moses then command to give a writing of divorcement [*a legal certificate of divorce*], and to put her away [*divorce her*]?

8 He saith unto them, Moses because of the hardness of your hearts suffered [*allowed*] you to put away [*divorce*] your wives: but from the beginning it was not so.

9 And I say unto you, Whosoever shall put away his wife, except it be for fornication, and shall marry another, committeth adultery: and whoso marrieth her which is put away doth commit adultery. (Matthew 19:7–9)

You may wish to read the commentary about this topic, associated with the Sermon on the Mount, Matthew 5:31–32, in this book.

10 His disciples say unto him, If the case of the man be so with his wife, it is not good to marry [*if this is such a serious matter, it would be better not to risk getting married*].

11 But he said unto them, All men cannot receive this saying, save they to whom it is given.

12 For there are some eunuchs [*men who are physically unable to have children*], which were so born from their mother's womb: and there are some eunuchs, which were made eunuchs of men [*men who have been surgically rendered incapable of having children; see Bible Dictionary, under "Eunuch"*]: and there be eunuchs, which have made themselves eunuchs for the kingdom of heaven's sake. He that is able to receive it, let him receive it. (Matthew 19:10–12)

Verse 12, above, seems incomplete and fragmentary. We don't know what it really means. Concerning this verse, Apostle Bruce R. McConkie said, "Some added background and additional information is needed to understand fully what is meant by this teaching about eunuchs" (*Doctrinal New Testament Commentary*, Vol. 1, p. 549).

Once again, the Pharisees fail to stop the Master Teacher, and He continues this late Perean ministry. The people brought their children to Him to be blessed (Matthew 19:13–15), and He answered questions about requirements for eternal life for a rich young ruler (Matthew 19:16–26; Mark 10:17–27; Luke 18:18–27). In answer to Peter's question, He taught of the blessings that will attend those who sacrifice whatever is necessary in order to completely live the gospel, and He also taught the role of the Twelve in judging the tribes of Israel (Matthew 19:27–30).

PEREA

The Parable of the Laborers in the Vineyard
(The "Eleventh Hour" Parable)

As Jesus continued His later teaching in Perea, He gave this very significant parable which teaches, among other things, the merciful doctrine that those who come into the Church later in life, or who become active later in life, through their faithfulness thereafter can still be exalted in the celestial kingdom of God. It is a reminder that we will be judged by what we are, not what we have been, on the final day of judgment. The Parable of the Laborers is rich in symbolism. As is the case with most symbolism, there are many ways that it can be interpreted. We will present some possibilities here, for this parable.

> 1 For the kingdom of heaven [*celestial glory*] is like unto a man [*Heavenly Father*] that is an householder, which went out early in the morning to hire labourers [*faithful Saints who have been active in the Church all their lives*] into his vineyard [*the earth*].
> 2 And when he had agreed with the labourers for a penny a day [*full pay for a righteous mortal life; symbolic of exaltation*], he sent them into his vineyard [*the earth*]. (Matthew 20:1–2)

When we see the word *penny*, we think of a coin of very little worth. This misunderstanding can distract us as we read this parable. The King James Bible translators consistently used the word "penny" for "denarius." A denarius is a Roman silver coin (see Bible Dictionary, under "Money"). It was worth a day's wages and thus was a significant amount of money.

> 3 And he went out about the third hour, and saw others standing idle [*people who had not yet joined the Church or become active*] in the marketplace,
> 4 And said unto them; Go ye also into the vineyard [*"Join the Church, get active, go to work."*], and whatsoever is right I will give you [*"I will be fair with you."*]. And they went their way [*they joined the Church and remained faithful to the end of their lives*].
> 5 Again he went out about the sixth and ninth hour, and did likewise [*others joined the Church or became active later in their lives and remained faithful in the work*].
> 6 And about the eleventh hour he went out, and found others standing idle, and saith unto them, Why stand ye here all the day idle?
> 7 They say unto him, Because no man hath hired us. He saith unto them, Go ye also into the vineyard [*join the Church and remain faithful*]; and whatsoever is right, that shall ye receive.
> 8 So when even [*evening, in other words, life is over and judgment day has arrived*] was come, the lord of the vineyard [*Heavenly Father*] saith unto his steward [*Christ, who is the final judge—see John 5:22*], Call the labourers, and give them their hire [*give them their reward*], beginning from the last unto the first.
> 9 And when they came that were hired about the eleventh hour, they received every man a penny [*those who became faithful saints much later in life—not "deathbed" repentance—were given exaltation*]. (Matthew 20:3–9)

In these next verses, lifelong Saints are cautioned not to become jealous or feel unfairly treated since they have "bourne the burden and heat of the day" (verse 12), in other words, sacrificed and worked hard all their lives to be obedient, when they see converts or reactivated Saints get the same reward they have worked longer to achieve.

> 10 But when the first [*those who had been active all their lives*] came, they supposed that they should have received more; and they likewise received every man a penny.
>
> 11 And when they had received it, they murmured against the goodman of the house [*the Father*],
>
> 12 Saying, These last have wrought [*worked*] but one hour [*haven't worked nearly as long as we have to gain exaltation*], and thou hast made them equal unto us, which have borne the burden and heat of the day.
>
> 13 But he answered one of them, and said, Friend, I do thee no wrong: didst not thou agree with me for a penny [*exaltation*]?
>
> 14 Take that thine is [*take your exaltation—by the way, the Lord is being very patient with these complainers at this point; if they don't repent of this bad attitude, they will obviously lose their exaltation as indicated in verse 16*], and go thy way: I will give unto this last, even as unto thee.
>
> 15 Is it not lawful for me to do what I will with mine own? Is thine eye evil, because I am good [*are you jealous and sinning in your heart because I am forgiving and generous*]?
>
> 16 So the last shall be first, and the first last [*it is possible to lose exaltation because of a bad attitude such as that demonstrated by the workers in verses 10–15*]: for many be called, but few chosen [*all are in fact called or invited to become exalted, but not all make it*]. (Matthew 20:10–16)

JERUSALEM

The Feast of Dedication

In the winter before His crucifixion, Jesus returned to Jerusalem from Perea for the Feast of Dedication. This celebration consisted of eight days of festivities celebrating the dedication of a new altar of burnt offering in 165 BC, after the old one had been desecrated by Antiochus Epiphanes, the king of Syria in 168 BC. No fasting or mourning for any calamity of the past was allowed, which would mar the great gladness and rejoicing accompanying the celebration. Huge torches illuminated the streets and public gathering places in the city, and thus it became known as the Feast of Lights (Bible Dictionary, under "Feasts"). During this feast, Jesus once again openly declared that He was the prophesied Messiah, and the Jews once again tried to stone Him.

22 And it was at Jerusalem the feast of the dedication, and it was winter.

23 And Jesus walked in the temple in Solomon's porch.

24 Then came the Jews round about him, and said unto him, How long dost thou make us to doubt [*how long are You going to keep us wondering about who You really are*]? If thou be the Christ, tell us plainly.

25 Jesus answered them, I told you, and ye believed not [*I have told you many times and in many ways that I am Christ, but you won't believe Me*]: the works [*miracles and teaching*] that I do in my Father's name, they bear witness of me [*they tell you who I am*].

26 But ye believe not, because ye are not of my sheep, as I said unto you. [*You have been in apostasy so long that you no longer even recognize the voice of the Good Shepherd when He calls.*]

27 My sheep hear my voice, and I know them, and they follow me:

28 And I give unto them eternal life; and they shall never perish [*they will never suffer spiritual death*], neither shall any man pluck them out of my hand [*no one can take them away from Me.*].

Next, Jesus again bears witness of His Father, and teaches again the doctrine of unity as it applies to Him and the Father.

29 My Father, which gave them me, is greater than all; and no man is able to pluck them out of my Father's hand.

30 I and my Father are one. [*The Father and Son are completely united in all things.*] (John 10:22–30)

Next, the Jews accuse the Savior of blasphemy (mocking God) which, under their law, was a crime punishable by death. He will escape, leaving Jerusalem and returning to Perea (John 10:31–39), some thirty miles from Jerusalem. While in Perea, he will receive word that Lazarus, the brother of Mary and Martha, is sick and dying.

BETHANY

Lazarus Is Restored to Life

There was a tender friendship between the Master and Mary, Martha, and Lazarus, their brother, who lived in Bethany, just two miles or so from Jerusalem on the other side of the Mount of Olives. When the request came from the sisters for Him to come and heal Lazarus, the Savior waited another two days before leaving for Bethany (John 11:1–6). When He finally determined to go, His disciples reminded Him that the Jews in Jerusalem had just recently attempted to stone Him, and asked Him to rethink going (John 11:7–8). As the conversation continued, Jesus told them that Lazarus had died. In what happens next, among other things, we will gain even more appreciation for Thomas, one of the Apostles who is generally known as "doubting Thomas."

> 14 Then said Jesus unto them plainly, Lazarus is dead.
> 15 And I am glad for your sakes that I was not there, to the intent ye may believe [*in effect, I am glad he is dead, because what is going to happen will strengthen your testimonies*]; nevertheless let us go unto him.
> 16 Then said Thomas, which is called Didymus [*the twin*], unto his fellow disciples, Let us also go, that we may die with him. (John 11:14–16)

>> 16 Then said Thomas, which is called Didymus, unto his fellow disciples, Let us also go, that we may die with him; *for they feared lest the Jews should take Jesus and put him to death, for as yet they did not understand the power of God.* (JST, John 11:16)

As mentioned above, Thomas is usually referred to as "doubting Thomas," because he refused to believe that Jesus had been resurrected unless he could see Him personally and feel the wounds in His hands and side (John 20:25–28). Here we see Thomas in a much different light. He is a man of courage and conviction, and encourages the other disciples to join him in going to Jerusalem with Jesus so that they could all die with Him.

The miracle of restoring Lazarus back to life is another testimony of the Savior's power over life and death, and ultimately, the power of His atoning sacrifice to bring resurrection for all. Lazarus will not be resurrected at this time. After having been brought back to life, he will become a serious liability for the Pharisees because people will see him walking in the streets of Jerusalem, very much alive, and many more will believe that Christ is indeed the Messiah.

> 17 Then when Jesus came [*arrived in Bethany at Martha's house*], he found that he [*Lazarus*] had lain in the grave four days already.

Four days is very significant because of Jewish beliefs about death. They had a false belief that the spirit must remain by a dead person's body for three days. After that, the person is for sure dead. The fact that Lazarus had been dead for four days, and had already begun to stink (John 10:39) left no doubt in the minds of the mourners that he was very dead.

By the time the Savior and disciples arrived at the home of Martha and Mary, many had already arrived to comfort the grieving sisters. As Jesus talked to Martha, she chided Him mildly for not coming sooner, and then expressed her faith in His power to do whatever was needed (John 11:19–22). At that point, we see that this faithful woman had been well taught in the doctrines of the gospel and had a firm testimony.

23 Jesus saith unto her, Thy brother shall rise again.

24 Martha saith unto him, I know that he shall rise again in the resurrection at the last day. (John 11:23–24)

Verse 25, next, is a very well-known verse in the Bible. In a significant way, it is a very brief summary of the Savior's purpose and mission. Through His Atonement, all will be resurrected, and eternal life (exaltation) is made available to all, contingent on repenting and living the gospel.

25 Jesus said unto her, I am the resurrection, and the life [*in effect, I have power over death and can give eternal life*]: he that believeth in me, though he were dead, yet shall he live:

26 And whosoever liveth [*is spiritually alive*] and believeth in me shall never die [*spiritually*]. Believest thou this?

27 She saith unto him, Yea, Lord: I believe that thou art the Christ, the Son of God, which should come into the world. [*I believe that You are the promised Messiah.*] (John 11:25–27)

Next, a very tender and very powerful scene unfolds. Mary has become aware that the Master has arrived in the area. Verse 35 is the shortest verse in the Bible and is a reminder of the great kindness and compassion the Savior has for all of us.

32 Then when Mary was come where Jesus was, and saw him, she fell down at his feet, saying unto him, Lord, if thou hadst been here, my brother had not [*would not have*] died.

33 When Jesus therefore saw her weeping, and the Jews also weeping which came with her, he groaned in the spirit, and was troubled, [*This was a very emotional time for Him.*]

34 And said, Where have ye laid him [*where have you buried him*]? They said unto him, Lord, come and see.

35 Jesus wept. (John 11:32–35)

The Savior walked to the tomb where the body of Lazarus had been laid to rest, followed by a hushed crowd who were about to become eye witnesses to the power of the Son of God.

39 Jesus said, Take ye away the stone [*open the tomb*]. Martha, the sister of him that was dead, saith unto him, Lord, by this time he stinketh: for he hath been dead four days.

40 Jesus saith unto her, Said I not unto thee, that, if thou wouldest believe, thou shouldest see the glory of God [*you would see the power of God in action*]? (John 11:39–40)

As you have no doubt noticed, the Son humbly gives credit to the Father in all things, pointing our minds past Himself and to the Father. Here we see Him yet again bear witness of the Father.

41 Then they took away the stone from the place where the dead was laid. And Jesus lifted up his eyes, and said, Father, I thank thee that thou hast heard me.

42 And I knew that thou hearest me always: but because of the people which stand by I said it [*I said it out loud for the benefit of the people who have gathered around*], that they may believe that thou hast sent me.

43 And when he thus had spoken, he cried with a loud voice, Lazarus, come forth.

44 And he that was dead came forth, bound hand and foot with graveclothes: and his face was bound about with a napkin. Jesus saith unto them, Loose him [*unwrap him*], and let him go.

45 Then many of the Jews which came to Mary [*to comfort her*], and had seen the things which Jesus did, believed on him.

46 But some of them went their ways to the Pharisees, and told them what things Jesus had done. (John 11:41–46)

The Pharisees are beside themselves with frustration and anger. All their attempts to stop Jesus have failed. And now He has raised a man from the dead, and many people saw it happen. They will quickly convene a council of the leading Jewish religious leaders to determine what can be done about Him. As a result, He will once again leave the Jerusalem area and go about fifteen miles north to the city of Ephraim (John 11:47–54). As the time of the Feast of the Passover approaches, He will leave again for Jerusalem and begin the final week of His mortal life.

CHAPTER 14

THE LAST WEEK OF THE SAVIOR'S MORTAL MISSION, HIS SUFFERING IN THE GARDEN, CRUCIFIXION, VISIT TO THE POSTMORTAL SPIRIT WORLD, AND RESURRECTION

"To this end was I born" (John 18:37) might well summarize the final week of the Savior's life. It was Passover week, and the end of the third year of His mortal ministry. The season was late March or early April, and Jerusalem was once again filled to overflowing with worshipers from near and far. Preparations were being made for the symbolic sacrifices associated with the Passover rites. Sacrificial lambs were being purchased. Money changers were desecrating the temple. Sincere worshipers were preparing to commemorate the "passing over" of the destroying angel over the households of ancient Israel, and their redemption from Egyptian bondage. Symbolically, the blood of the Lamb of God had set them free from the bondage of sin and put them on the path toward the promised land. And now, in Jerusalem, the final stage was being set for the "great and last sacrifice" of the Son of God for the sins of all of God's children (Alma 34:14).

There was an extra air of excitement and anticipation this year. It was rumored that Jesus of Nazareth might attend, in defiance of the Jewish religious leaders who sought His life. Some felt He would come. Many thought He would not risk it.

> 55 And the Jews' passover was nigh at hand: and many went out of the country up to Jerusalem before the passover, to purify themselves.
> 56 Then sought they for Jesus, and spake among themselves, as they stood in the temple, What think ye, that he will not come to the feast?

357

> 57 Now both the chief priests and the Pharisees had given a commandment, that, if any man knew where he were, he should shew it, that they might take him. (John 11:55–57)

Not far from Jerusalem, the Firstborn of the Father, the Redeemer chosen in the grand premortal council, the Lamb slain before the foundation of the world, the Creator, the Great Jehovah, the Only Begotten of the Father in the flesh, walked a dusty road toward Jerusalem and set His face like flint (Isaiah 50:7) for what lay ahead of Him. His weary disciples, fearful for His safety in Jerusalem, accompanied Him. As He neared the city, as prophesied anciently (Zechariah 9:9), He requested that they secure a donkey for Him to ride into the streets of Jerusalem in what would become known as the Triumphal Entry.

While there is not complete agreement among Bible scholars as to the days of the week involved with the events of the last week, we will use the most commonly accepted calendar.

SUNDAY
JERUSALEM

The Triumphal Entry

All four of the Gospel writers, Matthew, Mark, Luke, and John, recorded the Triumphal Entry in their accounts. We will use Matthew's record, and add notes from the others.

> 1 And when they drew nigh [*near*] unto Jerusalem, and were come to Bethphage [*on the east side of the Mount of Olives*], unto the mount of Olives, then sent Jesus two disciples,
> 2 Saying unto them, Go into the village over against you [*ahead of you*], and straightway [*immediately*] ye shall find an ass tied, and a colt [*a young male donkey*] with her: loose them, and bring them unto me.
> 3 And if any man say ought unto you [*questions you about what you are doing*], ye shall say, The Lord hath need of them; and straightway [*immediately*] he will send them. (Matthew 21:1–3)

In Jewish culture and symbolism of that day, a donkey symbolized humility and submission. A horse, on the other hand, symbolized triumph and victory over enemies; in other words, military might and victory. Thus, the Savior's riding into Jerusalem on a donkey represents that He came in meekness and submission to the Father's will, and to the coming suffering and crucifixion needed to carry out the Atonement. At His Second Coming, He is prophetically represented as riding on a white horse (Revelation 19:11), which symbolizes His triumph and victory at that time over all enemies of righteousness, including Satan and his evil kingdom.

> 6 And the disciples went, and did as Jesus commanded them,
> 7 And brought the ass, and the colt, and put on them their clothes, and they set him thereon. (Matthew 21:6–7)

> > 5 . . . brought the *colt, and put on it their clothes; and Jesus took the colt and sat thereon; and they followed him.*" (JST, Matthew 21:5)

Have you ever noticed the miracle that just happened here? Luke 19:30 informs us that the colt had never been ridden before. Yet, the Master sat on it with no trouble from the colt, reminding us that Jesus has power over the animal kingdom too.

> 8 And a very great multitude spread their garments in the way [*along the path where Jesus rode*]; others cut down branches from the trees [*from palm trees—John 12:13*], and strawed [*spread*] them in the way. (Matthew 21:8)

In Jewish symbolism, palm branches symbolized triumph and victory. Thus, in cutting palm branches and excitedly waving them and spreading them on the ground in front of the Savior, the crowd was enthusiastically expressing their belief that Jesus would bring them military triumph and victory over their Roman enemies.

> 9 And the multitudes that went before, and that followed, cried, saying, Hosanna to the Son of David: Blessed is he that cometh in the name of the Lord; Hosanna in the highest.

The Hosanna Shout Today

In conjunction with the dedication of our temples today, we participate in what is known as the "Hosanna Shout." *Hosanna* means "Lord, save us now" (Bible Dictionary, under "Hosanna") .Another translation of Hosanna is "O, please, Jehovah, save (us) now, please!"

> During the dedication of the Kirtland Temple on March 27, 1836, Joseph Smith gave a dedicatory prayer. In the prayer (D&C 109), the Prophet pled with the Lord "that we may be clothed upon with robes of righteousness, with palms in our hands, and crowns of glory upon our heads, and reap eternal joy for all our sufferings." (D&C 109:76) The prayer was followed by the Saints standing and participating in the Hosanna Shout. Afterward, they sang *The Spirit of God Like a Fire is Burning* which includes the phrase, "Hosanna, Hosanna to God and the Lamb!" (See *Mormon Doctrine*, by Bruce R. McConkie, page 368, for more about the Hosanna Shout).

Today, worthy members are invited to bring clean, white handkerchiefs with them to temple dedications. These handkerchiefs are symbolic of palm branches, and represent victory and triumph over our enemies of sin and weakness through the Atonement of Christ.

> 10 And when he was come into Jerusalem, all the city was moved [*everyone in the city was excited about him*], saying, Who is this?
> 11 And the multitude said, This is Jesus the prophet of Nazareth of Galilee. (Matthew 21:10–11)

As you can see, the crowds were very excited. However, some of the Pharisees were deeply concerned at the high praise the people were giving Jesus, including saying that He was sent from God. Consequently, these leaders approached the Master and asked Him to have His followers stop saying such blasphemous things about Him.

> 39 And some of the Pharisees from among the multitude said unto him, Master, rebuke thy disciples.
> 40 And he answered and said unto them, I tell you that, if these should hold their peace, the stones would immediately cry out. (Luke 19:39–40)

SUNDAY

Jesus Weeps over Jerusalem

After entering Jerusalem, the Savior went to a vantage point where He and His disciples could see the city and there He wept over the city.

> 41 And when he was come near, he beheld the city, and wept over it,
> 42 Saying, If thou hadst known, even thou, at least in this thy day, the things which belong unto thy peace [*if only your inhabitants had been righteous and had done things which would have brought you peace*]! but now they are hid from thine eyes [*peace is no longer available*].
> 43 For the days shall come upon thee, that thine enemies shall cast a trench about thee, and compass thee round, and keep thee in on every side [*you will be attacked by enemy armies who will lay siege against you, dig trenches around you, and surround you*],
> 44 And shall lay thee even with the ground [*will tear you down to the ground*], and thy children [*inhabitants*] within thee; and they [*enemy armies*] shall not leave in thee one stone upon another; because thou knewest not the time of thy visitation [*because you would not acknowledge that your day of punishment would come*]. (Luke 19:41–44)

SUNDAY
JERUSALEM
The Father's Voice Is Heard

As the day continued, some Greeks approached Philip and requested to see Jesus (John 12:20–22). The arrangements were made and Jesus explained to them that the time had come for Him to give His life (John 12:23–24). During His discussion with these men and His Apostles, He got quite personal. Subsequently, the voice of the Father was heard by them.

> 27 Now is my soul troubled [*this is getting very difficult; see D&C 19:18*]; and what shall I say? Father, save me from this hour [*in effect, should I ask My Father to save Me from what I am now going to have to go suffer?*]: but for this cause [*the Atonement*] came I unto this hour [*to this point in My mortal life*].
> 28 Father, glorify thy name. Then came there a voice [*the Father's voice*] from heaven, saying, I have both glorified it, and will glorify it again.
> 29 The people therefore, that stood by, and heard it, said that it thundered: others said, An angel spake [*spoke*] to him.
> 30 Jesus answered and said, This voice came not because of me, but for your sakes. [*In other words, you were allowed to hear My Father's voice to strengthen you.*] (John 12:27–30)

SUNDAY EVENING
BETHANY

In a brief statement, Mark records that on Sunday evening, the Lord took the Twelve to Bethany (two miles from Jerusalem) and spent the night there.

> 11 And Jesus entered into Jerusalem, and into the temple: and when he had looked round about upon all things, and now the eventide was come, he went out unto Bethany with the twelve. (Mark 11:11)

MONDAY
NEAR BETHANY
Fig Tree Cursed

As the Savior and His Apostles left Bethany Monday morning, the training and orientation of His Apostles as future leaders of the New Testament church continued. The object of the training was a fig tree, and the lesson was completed the following morning.

> 12 And on the morrow, when they were come from Bethany, he was hungry:
> 13 And seeing a fig tree afar off having leaves [*in other words, appearing as if it*

was a productive tree with figs on it], he came, if haply [*to see if*] he might find any thing thereon: and when he came to it, he found nothing but leaves; for the time of figs was not yet.

14 And Jesus answered [*spoke*] and said unto it [*the fig tree*], No man eat fruit of thee hereafter for ever. And his disciples heard it. [*See more about this in verses 20–21.*] (Mark 11:12–14)

> 14 And on the morrow, when they *came* from Bethany he was hungry; and seeing a fig tree afar off having leaves, he came *to it with his disciples; and as they supposed, he came to it to see* if he might find anything thereon.
>
> 15 And when he came to it, *there was* nothing but leaves; for *as yet the figs were not ripe.*
>
> 16 And Jesus *spake* and said unto it, No man eat fruit of thee hereafter, forever. And the disciples heard *him.* (JST, Mark 11:14–16)

The next morning, as they again traveled the road from Bethany to Jerusalem, they saw the same fig tree and the Master Teacher concluded the lesson.

> 20 And in the morning, as they passed by, they saw the fig tree dried up from the roots. (Mark 11:20)

The fig tree is symbolic of the hypocritical Jewish religious leaders who pretend to look official but do not produce the fruit of the gospel. It is also symbolic of the Jewish nation, the covenant people, who are "barren" as far as the gospel is concerned (*Jesus the Christ*, p. 443).

> 21 And Peter calling to remembrance saith unto him, Master, behold, the fig tree which thou cursedst is withered away [*has dried up and died*]. (Mark 11:21)

Jesus will now use the fig tree incident to teach his disciples about the power of faith.

> 22 And Jesus answering saith unto them, Have faith in God.
>
> 23 For verily I say unto you, That whosoever shall say unto this mountain, Be thou removed, and be thou cast into the sea; and shall not doubt in his heart, but shall believe that those things which he saith shall come to pass; he shall have whatsoever he saith.
>
> 24 Therefore I say unto you, What things soever ye desire, when ye pray, believe that ye receive them, and ye shall have them. (Mark 11:22–24)

D&C 46:30 and 50:29–30 add to our understanding of this use of faith. In these Doctrine and Covenants verses we are instructed that in order to have this kind of faith, the Holy Ghost must inspire us as to what is permissible for us to ask. Next, beginning in verse 25, we are taught that in order to have the kind of faith spoken of in the above verses, we must forgive others. If we carry grudges in our heart, we can not have this type of faith. One of the major messages here is that, since we need the constant forgiveness of God in our lives, if we ask for it and do not forgive others, we are hypocrites and cannot have the help of the Holy Ghost to sufficiently strengthen our own faith.

> 25 And when ye stand praying [*when you are asking God for blessings and help*], forgive, if ye have ought [*anything*] against any: that your Father also which is in heaven may forgive you your trespasses. [*In other words, another message here is that if you want God to forgive your sins, you must forgive others.*]
> 26 But if ye do not forgive, neither will your Father which is in heaven forgive your trespasses. (Mark 11:25–26)

MONDAY
JERUSALEM

Cleansing of the Temple

At the beginning of His formal three-year mortal mission, one of the first things Jesus did was cleanse the Temple in Jerusalem during Passover (John 2:13–17). Now, at the end of His mortal ministry, He does it again. Those who desecrated that sacred structure had obviously not yet learned the needed lesson. While some chronologies place this event on Sunday, most consider it to have taken place on Monday.

> 12 And Jesus went into the temple of God, and cast out all them that sold and bought in the temple, and overthrew the tables of the moneychangers, and the seats of them that sold doves,
> 13 And said unto them, It is written [*in Isaiah 56:7*], My house shall be called the house of prayer; but ye have made it a den of thieves.
> 14 And the blind and the lame came to him in the temple; and he healed them. (Matthew 21:12–14)

Did you notice that Jesus didn't immediately leave the temple, after having cleansed it. No doubt there was potential danger to him from the authorities. Nevertheless, he remained for a considerable time to heal people who came to him. This must have been extremely frustrating to the Jewish religious leaders who "were sore displeased" (verse 15), and confronted Him about it (verse 16).

> 15 And when the chief priests and scribes [*Jewish religious leaders*] saw the wonderful things that he did, and the children crying in the temple, and saying, Hosanna to the Son of David [*the "Messiah"*]; they were sore [*very*] displeased, (Matthew 21:15)

13 Children *of the kingdom,* [*in other words, faithful members of the Church*] (JST, Matthew 21:13)

16 And said unto him, Hearest thou what these [*the "children of the kingdom" in verse 15*] say? [*In other words, do you realize how dangerous it is to you for them to be calling you the Messiah?*] And Jesus saith unto them, Yea; have ye never read, Out of the mouth of babes and sucklings thou hast perfected praise? [*In other words, among other possible interpretations, Jesus is saying "You are supposed to know the scriptures. Haven't you ever read that from childlike faithful members come true praises of God?"*] (Matthew 21:16)

TUESDAY
THE TEMPLE IN JERUSALEM
The Parable of the Two Sons

The next day, while continuing to teach in the temple in Jerusalem, the Master is again confronted by the Jewish religious leaders, who challenge His authority. In the course of His response, He gives more parables. In the parable of the two sons, given next, the second son represents the hypocritical Jewish religious leaders who claim to agree to do the work of the Lord, but do not do it.

28 But what think ye? A certain man had two sons; and he came to the first, and said, Son, go work to day in my vineyard.
29 He answered and said, I will not: but afterward he repented, and went.
30 And he came to the second, and said likewise. And he answered and said, I go, sir: and went not.
31 Whether of them twain [*which of the two*] did the will of his father? They say unto him, The first. Jesus saith unto them, Verily I say unto you, That the publicans [*hated Jewish tax collectors*] and the harlots [*prostitutes*] go into the kingdom of God before you [*are more likely to get to heaven than you are*].
32 For John [*the Baptist*] came unto you in the way of righteousness, and ye believed him not: but the publicans and the harlots [*sinners*] believed him [*repented*]: and ye, when ye had seen it, repented not afterward [*like the first son in the above parable*], that ye might believe him. (Matthew 21:28–32)

32 For John came unto you in the way of righteousness, *and bore record of me,* and ye believed him not; but the publicans and the harlots believed him; and ye, *afterward,* when ye had seen *me,* repented not, that ye might believe him.
33 *For he that believed not John concerning me, cannot believe me, except he first repent.*
34 *And except ye repent, the preaching of John shall condemn you at the day of judgment. And, again, hear another parable; for unto you that believe not, I speak in parables; that your unrighteousness may be rewarded unto you.* (JST, Matthew 21:32–33)

Tuesday
The Temple In Jerusalem
The Parable of the Wicked Husbandmen

Did you notice at the end of JST verse 34, above, the Savior spoke very plainly to these Jewish leaders who seek His life? Their accountability very likely increased at that point.

33 Hear another parable: There was a certain householder [*Heavenly Father*], which planted a vineyard [*had the earth created and put people on it*], and hedged it round about [*set up protections for them*], and digged a winepress in it [*prepared for a good harvest*], and built a tower [*so people could watch for enemies*], and let it out to husbandmen [*stewards who were supposed to take good care of it*], and went into a far country [*heaven*]:

34 And when the time of the fruit [*harvest time*] drew near, he sent his servants [*prophets*] to the husbandmen [*the Jewish religious leaders*], that they might receive the fruits of it.

35 And the husbandmen took his servants [*prophets*], and beat one, and killed another, and stoned another.

36 Again, he sent other servants [*prophets*] more than the first: and they [*the wicked husbandmen*] did unto them likewise.

37 But last of all he sent unto them his son [*Christ*], saying, They will reverence my son.

38 But when the husbandmen saw the son, they said among themselves, This is the heir; come, let us kill him, and let us seize on his inheritance.

39 And they caught him, and cast him out of the vineyard, and slew him [*crucified Him*]. (Matthew 21:33–39)

Now we see the question to which this parable has been leading.

40 When the lord [*Christ*] therefore of the vineyard cometh, what will he do unto those husbandmen? (Matthew 21:40)

The response by these leaders to the Lord's question comes next. They don't yet realize that He is referring to them.

41 They [*the chief priests and elders in verse 23*] say unto him [*Jesus*], He will miserably destroy those wicked men, and will let out his vineyard unto other husbandmen [*righteous religious leaders*], which shall render him the fruits in their seasons [*will bring righteous souls to Him at the time of harvest.*]

42 Jesus saith unto them, Did ye never read in the scriptures [*in Psalm 118:22–23*], The stone [*Christ*] which the builders rejected, the same is become the head of the corner [*the capstone or cornerstone*]: this is the Lord's doing, and it is marvellous in our eyes?

43 Therefore say I unto you [*Jewish religious leaders*], The kingdom of God shall

be taken from you, and given to a nation [*Gentiles*] bringing forth the fruits thereof [*who will bring the desired harvest of righteous souls to Me*].
44 And whosoever shall fall on this stone [*Christ*] shall be broken: but on whomsoever it shall fall, it will grind him to powder [*no one can ultimately stop the Lord's work*]. (Matthew 21:41–44)

Next, they finally get the message.

45 And when the chief priests and Pharisees had heard his parables, they perceived that he spake of them. (Matthew 21:45)

The phrase "they perceived that he spake of them" in verse 45 above, is very important to our understanding of what is going on here. Some people think that the Jewish religious leaders did not really understand who Jesus was. That is not true. They did indeed understand who Jesus was and set out to kill Him. This fact is confirmed again in JST Matthew 21:47, quoted after verse 46, below, where it says the same thing, "they perceived that he spake of them."

46 But when they sought to lay hands on him, they feared the multitude, because they took him for a prophet. [*They were afraid the people would mob them if they arrested Jesus.*]

The JST contains over two hundred added words of explanation for this parable. They are included here:

48 *And they said among themselves, Shall this man think that he alone can spoil this great kingdom* [the religious kingdom set up by these Jewish religious leaders for their own advantage]? *And they were angry with him*
49 But when they sought to lay hands on him, they feared the multitude, because they *learned that the multitude* took him for a prophet.
50 *And now his disciples came to him, and Jesus said unto them, Marvel ye at the words of the parable which I spake unto them?*
51 *Verily, I say unto you, I am the stone, and those wicked ones reject me.*
52 *I am the head of the corner. These Jews shall fall upon me, and shall be broken.*
53 *And the kingdom of God shall be taken from them, and shall be given to a nation bringing forth the fruits thereof;* [meaning the Gentiles.]
54 *Wherefore, on whomsoever this stone shall fall, it shall grind him to powder.*
55 *And when the Lord therefore of the vineyard cometh, he will destroy those miserable, wicked men, and will let again his vineyard unto other husbandmen, even in the last days* [the restoration through the Prophet Joseph Smith], *who shall render him the fruits in their seasons.*

56 *And then understood they the parable which he spake unto them, that the Gentiles* [the wicked Gentiles in the last days] *should be destroyed also, when the Lord should descend out of heaven* [the Second Coming] *to reign in his vineyard, which is the earth and the inhabitants thereof.* (JST, Matthew 21:48–56)

As Jesus continued His teaching on this Tuesday before the Friday of His crucifixion, the chief priests and elders of the Jews continued their attempts to stop Him. His next parable, the Parable of the marriage of the king's son (Matthew 22:1–14), was the last one directed specifically to these Jewish religious leaders and rulers who have been aggressively trying to trap Him all day. The parable was a direct warning to them and their predecessors who have killed past prophets and now seek to arrest and kill Jesus. After listening to this parable, the hypocritical leaders try another approach.

TUESDAY
THE TEMPLE IN JERUSALEM

"Render unto Caesar"

Hoping to trap Jesus by pitting Him against the Roman government on the topic of taxes, the rulers of the Jews send spies who pretend to be impressed with Jesus and His ministry and now press Him on the unpopular taxes required by Caesar. They hope He will say something that will cause the Romans to arrest Him.

20 And they [*the scribes, Pharisees and elders*] watched him, and sent forth spies, which should feign [*pretend*] themselves just [*righteous, sincere*] men, that they might take hold of his words [*catch Jesus saying something for which He could be arrested*], that so they might deliver him unto the power and authority of the governor [*the Roman governor, Pontius Pilate*].
21 And they [*the spies in verse 20*] asked him, saying, Master, we know that thou sayest and teachest rightly, neither acceptest thou the person of any [*You don't change Your teachings because of peer pressure*], but teachest the way of God truly: [*They were indeed pretending to be "just men," as instructed by their evil bosses in verse 20.*] (Luke 20:20–21)

Watch now as these cunning men attempt to get the Master in trouble with the Roman government. They have carefully worded a question.

22 Is it lawful [*legal*] for us to give tribute [*pay taxes*] unto Cæsar, or no?
23 But he perceived their craftiness, and said unto them, Why tempt ye me [*why are you trying to trick Me*]?
24 Shew [*pronounced "show"*] me a penny [*a Roman penny representing about a*

day's wage]. Whose image and superscription [*writing on the coin*] hath it? They answered and said, Cæsar's.

25 And he said unto them, Render [*pay*] therefore unto Cæsar the things which be Cæsar's, and unto God the things which be God's.

26 And they could not take hold of his words before the people [*their plot didn't work*]: and they marvelled [*were stunned*] at his answer, and held their peace [*kept quiet*]. (Luke 20:22–26)

TUESDAY
THE TEMPLE IN JERUSALEM

Eternal Marriage

Several groups of influential Jewish religious leaders, some who are normally bitter enemies toward each other, have now joined forces to stop Jesus. These include the chief priests, scribes, elders (Luke 20:1), the Herodians, who opposed the Roman government as well as the Pharisees (Mark 3:6; Bible Dictionary, under "Herodians"), and now the Sadducees (verse 23, next). The Sadducees did not believe in the resurrection, and were normally enemies of the Pharisees who did believe in it. The Sadducees now take the lead in attempting to trap Jesus. They try to get the Master to say something in opposition to the teaching of Moses on the topic of perpetuating families for brothers who have passed away. They will use the example of one wife and seven brothers.

23 The same day came to him the Sadducees, which say that there is no resurrection [*who do not believe in the resurrection*], and asked him,
24 Saying, Master, Moses said, If a man die, having no children, his brother shall marry his wife, and raise up seed unto his brother [*have children for his dead brother; plural marriage was in practice at this time in the Old and New Testament*].
25 Now there were with us seven brethren [*brothers*]: and the first, when he had married a wife, deceased [*died*], and, having no issue [*children*], left his wife unto his brother [*as required by the law of Moses—see Deuteronomy 25:5*]:
26 Likewise the second also, and the third, unto the seventh. [*Each of the six brothers likewise married her, but died, without her having any children.*]
27 And last of all the woman died also. (Matthew 22:23–27)

And now, the question designed by the Sadducees to discredit the Master.

28 Therefore in the resurrection whose wife shall she be of the seven? for they all had her [*had her as a wife*]. (Matthew 22:28)

Here we find a major doctrinal point. Many religions use these next two verses to prove that there is no such thing as eternal marriage and family in the next life. On the contrary, the simple fact that the Sadducees asked the Savior (in verse 28) whose wife she will be when they are all resurrected is strong evidence that the Savior had indeed preached the doctrine of marriage in the resurrection, or in other words, eternal marriage, for those who are worthy. Otherwise, their question would not make any sense at all!

29 Jesus answered and said unto them, Ye do err, not knowing the scriptures, nor the power of God.

30 For in the resurrection they neither marry, nor are given in marriage, but are as the angels of God in heaven [*refers to those who do not qualify for eternal marriage in this life or in the postmortal spirit world or during the Millennium—see D&C 132:15–17*]. (Matthew 22:29–30)

Here again, correct doctrine needs to be understood. After everyone from this earth is resurrected, there will be no more eternal marriages performed for them, because such marriages have to be done by mortals for themselves, or by mortals who serve as proxies for those who have died—see D&C 128:15 & 18. Brigham Young said: "And when the Millennium is over, . . . all the sons and daughters of Adam and Eve, down to the last of their posterity, who come within the reach of the clemency of the Gospel, [will] have been redeemed in hundreds of temples through the administration of their children as proxies for them" (*Discourses of Brigham Young*, p. 395). Since there will be no mortals left on earth after the resurrection is completed, there would be no one left to serve as proxies for eternal marriages.

31 But as touching the resurrection of the dead, have ye not read that which was spoken unto you by God, saying,

32 I am the God of Abraham, and the God of Isaac, and the God of Jacob [*quoting Exodus 3:6*]? God is not the God of the dead, but of the living. [*In other words, you Sadducees should believe in resurrection.*]

33 And when the multitude heard this, they were astonished at his doctrine. (Matthew 22:31–33)

After additional attempts to make Jesus look foolish in front of the people, the Jewish rulers no longer dared to continue confronting Him in public.

46 And no man was able to answer him a word, neither durst [*dared*] any man from that day forth ask him any more questions. [*It was getting pretty embarrassing trying to trap Jesus with questions because they lost out every time!*] (Matthew 22:46)

One of the major purposes of the pure gospel of Jesus Christ is to clearly expose all forms of evil so that sincere believers can recognize it for what it is and then avoid getting caught up in it. One of the most damaging and debilitating of all evils is that of hypocrisy. As Jesus continued His teaching from the temple grounds in Jerusalem on that Tuesday, He delivered a scathing denunciation of the hypocrisy of the scribes and Pharisees to the multitudes as well as to His disciples (Matthew 23:1–36). After that, He left the temple and with deep emotion mourned the wickedness of the people in Jerusalem and their coming destruction (Matthew 23:37–38). He would not teach the public any more. Rather, He spent the rest of the week teaching the Twelve.

TUESDAY
THE MOUNT OF OLIVES
Signs of the Second Coming

After departing from the Temple, and mourning for Jerusalem, the Master led His Apostles to the outskirts of Jerusalem where they ascended the Mount of Olives to a point from which they looked back on that wicked city. His disciples asked for more details about the coming destruction and He replied with a discourse containing many signs that would precede His Second Coming. Matthew (24:1–51), Mark (13:1–37), and Luke (12:37–48; 17:20–37; 21:5–38) all contain accounts of this sermon. Joseph Smith added about 450 additional words to Matthew 24, and rearranged the verse order in some cases. His inspired revision is found today in the JST as well as in the Pearl of Great Price where it appears as Joseph Smith—Matthew 1:1–55.

Many Christians in other churches place great importance on the signs of the times given in Matthew 24, and join with us in looking forward to the Second Coming.

> 1 And Jesus went out, and departed from the temple [*in Jerusalem*]: and his disciples came to him for to shew [*show*] him the buildings of the temple.
> 2 And Jesus said unto them, See ye not all these things? verily I say unto you, There shall not be left here one stone upon another, that shall not be thrown down. [*The temple will be destroyed. The Romans destroyed much, culminating with the final conquering of Jerusalem about AD 70.*]
> 3 And as he sat upon the mount of Olives [*located just outside of Jerusalem*], the disciples came unto him privately, saying, Tell us, when shall these things be [*the things Jesus had just prophesied*]? and what shall be the sign of thy coming, and of the end of the world? (Matthew 24:1–3)

The disciples asked Jesus two questions in verse 3, above: 1) "When shall these things be?" (meaning the things which will happen to Jerusalem, to the Jews, and to the early Christians following the crucifixion), and 2) "What shall be the sign of thy coming, and of the end of the world?" (meaning the "signs of the times" preceding his Second Coming).

4 And Jesus answered and said unto them, Take heed [*be careful*] that no man deceive you

5 For many shall come in my name, saying, I am Christ; and shall deceive many.

6 And ye shall hear of wars and rumours of wars: see that ye be not troubled [*don't let the signs of the times cause undue fear or panic in you*]: for all these things must come to pass, but the end is not yet.

7 For nation shall rise against nation, and kingdom against kingdom: and there shall be famines, and pestilences, and earthquakes, in divers [*various*] places.

8 All these are the beginning of sorrows.

9 Then shall they deliver you up to be afflicted, and shall kill you: and ye shall be hated of all nations for my name's sake.

10 And then shall many be offended [*many will leave the Church*], and shall betray one another, and shall hate one another.

11 And many false prophets shall rise, and shall deceive many. (Matthew 24:4–11)

Many people, when they read "false prophets" (verse 11, above), think only of ministers and preachers who teach false doctrines and philosophies. They would be wise to not limit their thinking to these types, but rather to include any influential individuals and groups who gather followers and lead them away from God. This can include politicians, movie stars, teachers, musicians, gang leaders, and so forth.

12 And because iniquity [*wickedness*] shall abound [*will be everywhere*], the love of many shall wax [*grow*] cold.

13 But he that shall endure unto the end, the same shall be saved.

14 And this gospel of the kingdom shall be preached in all the world for a witness unto all nations [*one of the last major signs which will happen before the Savior's Second Coming*]; and then shall the end [*of wickedness*] come. [*The Millennium will then begin*].

15 When ye therefore shall see the abomination of desolation, spoken of by Daniel the prophet [*in Daniel 11:31; 12:11*], stand in the holy place, (whoso readeth, let him understand:) (Matthew 24:12–15)

"Abomination of desolation" means terrible things which will cause much destruction and misery. The abomination of desolation spoken of by Daniel was to have two fulfillments. The first occurred in 70 AD when Titus, with his Roman legions, surrounded Jerusalem and laid siege to conquer the Jews. This siege resulted in much destruction with terrible human misery and loss of life. In the last days, the abomination of desolation will occur again (see Joseph Smith—Matthew 1:31–32), meaning that Jerusalem will again be under siege (see also Bible Dictionary, under "Abomination of Desolation").

16 Then let them which be in Judæa flee into the mountains: [*Many faithful*

Saints heeded this warning and fled to Pella, east of Samaria, and thus escaped the Romans.]

17 Let him which is on the housetop not come down to take any thing out of his house:

18 Neither let him which is in the field return back to take his clothes.

19 And woe unto them that are with child, and to them that give suck in those days!

20 But pray ye that your flight be not in the winter, neither on the sabbath day [*when city gates are closed*]:

21 For then shall be great tribulation, such as was not since the beginning of the world to this time, no, nor ever shall be.

22 And except those days should be shortened, there should no flesh be saved: but for the elect's sake those days shall be shortened [*the Lord will stop the destructions in time so that some covenant people will remain*].

23 [*Now, Jesus answers their second question—see note, verse 4.*] Then if any man shall say unto you, Lo, here is Christ, or there; believe it not.

24 For there shall arise false Christs, and false prophets, and shall shew [*show*] great signs and wonders; insomuch that, if it were possible, they shall deceive the very elect [*meaning those who have made covenants with God—see Joseph Smith—Matthew 1:22*].

25 Behold, I have told you before.

26 Wherefore if they [*false prophets, "gatherers," teachers, leaders, etc.*] shall say unto you, Behold, he [*Christ*] is in the desert; go not forth [*don't go to see him*]: behold, he is in the secret chambers; believe it not.

27 For as the lightning [lightning *is a mistake in the translation of the Bible, since lightning can come in any direction; it should be "as the light of the morning cometh out of the east"; see Joseph Smith—Matt. 1:26*] cometh out of the east, and shineth even unto the west; so shall also the coming of the Son of man be. [*In other words, when he comes for the actual Second Coming, everyone will see him. It will not be a low-key, quiet, secret coming as some false gatherers will suggest—see verse 26.*]

28 For wheresoever the carcase [*carcass*] is, there will the eagles be gathered together. (Matthew 24:16–28)

This is an unusual use of the word "carcase." Symbolically, in this context, it means "the body of the Church." In other words, the true Church with the true gospel. The eagles are converts, faithful members of the Church who will be gathered to the Church for nourishment in all parts of the world. See Joseph Smith—Matthew 1:27. In short, this verse prophesies of the gathering of Israel in the last days prior to the Second Coming (see also *Doctrinal New Testament Commentary*, Vol. 1, pp. 648–49).

29 Immediately after the tribulation of those days shall the sun be darkened, and the moon shall not give her light [*can refer to spiritual darkness as well as actual things in nature*], and the stars shall fall from heaven, and the powers of

the heavens shall be shaken:

30 And then shall appear the sign of the Son of man in heaven [*we don't yet know what this means*]: and then shall all the tribes of the earth mourn [*the wicked will mourn, but the righteous will rejoice—see 2 Nephi 9:14, D&C 88:96*], and they shall see the Son of man coming in the clouds of heaven with power and great glory. (Matthew 24:29–30)

Even those who caused the Savior's crucifixion, who are now in the world of departed spirits, will see him at this time. See Revelation 1:7.

31 [*As you can see, these verses are not all in chronological order.*] And he shall send his angels with a great sound of a trumpet, and they shall gather together his elect from the four winds, from one end of heaven to the other. [*This is the final gathering of the righteous.*]

The Parable of the Fig Tree

32 Now learn a parable of the fig tree; When his branch is yet tender, and putteth forth leaves, ye know that summer is nigh [*when a fruit tree starts putting on leaves, you know that summer is near*]:

33 So likewise ye, when ye shall see all these things [*signs of the times being fulfilled*], know that it [*the Second Coming*] is near, even at the doors.

34 Verily I say unto you, This generation [generation *can sometimes mean* dispensation] shall not pass, till all these things be fulfilled.

35 Heaven and earth shall pass away, but my words shall not pass away [*you can rely on My words completely!*].

36 But of that day and hour knoweth no man, no, not the angels of heaven, but my Father only. (Matthew 24:31–36)

On occasions we hear of people who claim to know when the Second Coming will be. Sometimes they gather others around them to await the exact day they have predicted He will come. Some say they don't know the hour and day, but they do know the month and year. Some say that the Brethren know, but are not allowed to tell us. Elder M. Russell Ballard, of the Quorum of the Twelve, taught the following:

I do not know when He is going to come again. As far as I know, none of my brethren in the Council of the Twelve or even in the First Presidency knows. And I would humbly suggest to you, my young brothers and sisters, that if we do not know, then nobody knows. (Speech given March 12, 1996, at a BYU Devotional)

37 But as the days of Noe [*Noah*] were, so shall also the coming of the Son of man [*Jesus*] be. [*Just as the wicked in the days of Noah did not believe the Flood would come, so also the wicked in the last days will not believe the Savior will come, and thus will be caught unprepared.*]

38 For as in the days that were before the flood they were eating and drinking, marrying and giving in marriage, until the day that Noe [*Noah*] entered into the ark,

39 And knew not until the flood came, and took them all away [*destroyed them*]; so shall also the coming of the Son of man [*Jesus*] be.

40 Then shall two be in the field; the one shall be taken, and the other left. [*One who is worthy will be taken up to meet Christ (see D&C 88:96) and the other who is not worthy will be left on earth to be destroyed at His coming.*]

41 Two women shall be grinding at the mill; the one shall be taken, and the other left.

42 Watch therefore: for ye know not what hour your Lord doth come.

43 But know this, that if the goodman [*symbolic of people who will be caught off guard by the Second Coming*] of the house had known in what watch [*the Jews divided the night into "watches" of about four hours each; Bible Dictionary, under "Watches"*] the thief would come, he would have watched [*would have been ready*], and would not have suffered [*allowed*] his house to be broken up.

44 Therefore be ye also ready: for in such an hour as ye think not the Son of man cometh. (Matthew 24:37–44)

In the next verses, the Savior, in effect, asks the disciples who they think will be saved at the Second Coming. He answers His own question and basically says that it will be those who are faithful to the gospel and who, as servants in the gospel, serve others with kindness and wisdom.

45 Who then is a faithful and wise servant, whom his lord hath made ruler over his household, to give them [*people under his jurisdiction*] meat [*food, nourishment*] in due season [*according to their needs*]?

46 Blessed is that servant, whom his lord when he cometh shall find so doing.

47 Verily I say unto you, That he shall make him ruler over all his goods. [*They will be exalted and will become gods. See D&C 84:38, D&C 132:20.*]

48 But and if that evil servant [*symbolic of the wicked in the last days*] shall say in his heart, My lord [*Christ*] delayeth his coming [*similar to the wicked in 3 Nephi 1*];

49 And shall begin to smite his fellowservants [*be mean and cruel to others*], and to eat and drink with the drunken [*participate in riotous living*];

50 The lord [*Christ*] of that servant shall come in a day when he looketh not for him, and in an hour that he is not aware of,

51 And shall cut him asunder [*destroy him*], and appoint him his portion [*put him in hell*] with the hypocrites [*people who want to appear righteous but like to do evil*]: there shall be weeping and gnashing of teeth [*grinding of teeth together in agony and misery*]. (Matthew 24:45–51)

TUESDAY
THE MOUNT OF OLIVES

The Parable of the Ten Virgins

Having answered the disciples' questions concerning the signs of His Second Coming, the Master now proceeds to give His Apostles a parable illustrating how to be prepared personally for His Second Coming. Obviously, this applies very much to each of us today.

> 1 Then [*the last days leading up to the time of the Second Coming*] shall the kingdom of heaven be likened unto ten virgins [*symbolic of members of the Church, see* Doctrinal New Testament Commentary, *Vol. 1, pp. 684–85*], which took their lamps, and went forth to meet the bridegroom [*"groom;" symbolic of Christ—see* Jesus the Christ, *p. 578*]. (Matthew 25:1)

>> 1 *And* then, *at that day, before the Son of man comes*, the kingdom of heaven *shall* be likened unto ten virgins, *who* took their lamps, and went forth to meet the bridegroom. (JST, Matthew 25:1)

> 2 And five of them were wise, and five were foolish.
> 3 They that were foolish took their lamps, and took no oil with them:
> 4 But the wise took oil in their vessels with their lamps. (Matthew 25:2–4)

Did you notice that all ten virgins had lamps with oil in them to begin with? But the five wise virgins carried flasks with extra oil and thus were able to endure to the end until the bridegroom (Christ) finally arrived.

> 5 While the bridegroom tarried, they all slumbered and slept.
> 6 And at midnight there was a cry made, Behold, the bridegroom cometh [*symbolic of the Second Coming*]; go ye out to meet him.
> 7 Then all those virgins arose, and trimmed their lamps.
> 8 And the foolish said unto the wise, Give us of your oil; for our lamps are gone out.
> 9 But the wise answered, saying, Not so; lest there be not enough for us and you: but go ye rather to them that sell, and buy for yourselves. (Matthew 25:5–9)

To some, it may seem that the five wise virgins were not living the gospel because they would not share their supplies of oil with the five foolish virgins. The point is that their extra oil is symbolic of personal worthiness and preparedness which the righteous cannot share or give to others, such as personal righteousness, church attendance, tithe paying, moral cleanliness, Sabbath observance, keeping the commandments, and so forth.

> 10 And while they [*the foolish virgins*] went to buy, the bridegroom came [*sadly, they were unprepared, unworthy, and could not get ready in time*]; and they that

were ready went in with him to the marriage [marriage *generally symbolizes making and keeping covenants with God; here, the marriage represents the Second Coming, see Talmage,* Jesus the Christ, *p. 578*]: and the door was shut.

11 Afterward came also the other virgins, saying, Lord, Lord, open to us.

12 But he answered and said, Verily I say unto you, I know you not. (Matthew 25:10–12)

The JST makes a very important change to verse 12, above. The Savior knows all of us, but not everyone knows Him.

> 11 But he answered and said, Verily I say unto you, *Ye* know *me* not. (JST, Matthew 25:11)

> 13 Watch therefore, for ye know neither the day nor the hour wherein the Son of man [*Christ*] cometh. (Matthew 25:13)

While they were still on the Mount of Olives, The Savior followed the parable of the ten virgins with two additional parables, which are likewise often referred to as "parables of preparation." These were the parable of the talents (Matthew 25:14–30) and the parable of the sheep and the goats (Matthew 25:31–46).

When Jesus had finished teaching these parables to His disciples, He again prophesied His crucifixion, which was now just three days away. The Passover feast was just two days away and would be held on Thursday evening. Can you imagine how these humble Apostles felt? They will probably not get much sleep over the next forty eight hours and it is small wonder that they will be so tired when the time comes for Jesus to go to the Garden of Gethsemane Thursday evening.

> 1 And it came to pass, when Jesus had finished all these sayings, he said unto his disciples,
> 2 Ye know that after two days is the feast of the passover, and the Son of man is betrayed to be crucified. (Matthew 26:1–2)

TUESDAY
JERUSALEM
The Plot at Caiaphas' Palace

Having failed miserably in all of their attempts to have Jesus legally arrested, or to incite the Romans against Him, the Jewish leaders now plot means to take Jesus illegally and kill Him. Mark informs us that this secret council took place two days before Passover (Mark 14:1–2). Matthew gives details.

3 Then assembled together the chief priests, and the scribes, and the elders of the people, unto the palace of the high priest, who was called Caiaphas,

4 And consulted that they might take Jesus by subtilty, and kill him. [*In other words, they plotted how they might arrest Jesus as quietly as possible so that they would not stir up the people and perhaps get mobbed themselves.*]

5 But they said, Not on the feast day, [*not on Thursday, the day of Passover*] lest there be an uproar among the people. (Matthew 26:3–5)

TUESDAY
BETHANY

A Woman Anoints Jesus for Burial

Most Bible chronologies place this event on Tuesday. It happened during a dinner hosted by a man named Simon the leper at his home in Bethany (Mark 14:3). We have no information about this Simon, other than that his home was in Bethany.

6 Now when Jesus was in Bethany [*about two miles east and south of Jerusalem*], in the house of Simon the leper. (Matthew 26:6)

It was the practice among the Jews to prepare the body of a deceased person for burial by putting sweet smelling ointments and spices on it, as explained in John 19:38–40. In verses 7–13, next, a woman anoints Jesus with costly ointment. Jesus is the Messiah. *Messiah* means "the Anointed One" (Bible Dictionary, under "Messiah"). It would seem that this woman understood what the disciples did not yet fully understand, and she symbolically "anointed" His body in preparation for His coming burial. This sheds light on the divine nature and spiritual sensitivity of women.

7 There came unto him a woman having an alabaster box of very precious ointment, and poured it on his head, as he sat at meat [*at dinner*].

8 But when his disciples saw it, they had indignation, saying, To what purpose is this waste [*why are you wasting this expensive ointment*]?

9 For this ointment might have been sold for much, and given to the poor.

10 When Jesus understood it, he said unto them, Why trouble ye the woman? for she hath wrought [*done*] a good work upon me.

11 For ye have the poor always with you; but me ye have not always. [*You need to keep things in perspective.*]

12 For in that she hath poured this ointment on my body, she did it for my burial. [*In other words, she understands that I will be crucified and buried now.*] (Matthew 26:7–12)

Next, the Master gives a prophecy about what this woman did.

13 Verily I say unto you, Wheresoever this gospel shall be preached in the whole world, there shall also this, that this woman hath done, be told for a memorial of her. (Matthew 26:13)

TUESDAY
JERUSALEM

Judas Iscariot Plots to Betray Jesus

Matthew records that after the dinner at the home of Simon the leper, Judas Iscariot went to the chief priests and bargained with them to betray Christ to them for thirty pieces of silver (Matthew 26:14–16). Luke adds a few more details.

2 And the chief priests and scribes sought how they might kill him; for they feared the people [were afraid of causing a riot by arresting Jesus].
3 Then entered Satan into Judas surnamed Iscariot, being of the number of the twelve [who was one of the Twelve Apostles].
4 And he went his way, and communed [plotted] with the chief priests and captains, how he might betray him [Jesus] unto them.
5 And they were glad, and covenanted to give him money [thirty pieces of silver—Matthew 26:15]. (Luke 22:2–5)

Thirty pieces of silver was the going price for an average slave in the culture of the day. Thus, it was an insult to Judas and demeaning to the Master to offer only the price of a common slave for Jesus.

6 And he [Judas] promised [agreed to the terms], and sought opportunity to betray him [Jesus] unto them in the absence of the multitude. [Judas looked for opportunities to betray Jesus quietly, out of sight of the public.] (Luke 22:6)

WEDNESDAY

There are no recorded events in the scriptures for Wednesday.

THURSDAY
JERUSALEM

Preparation for the Passover Meal

The first recorded event for Thursday was the preparation for the Passover meal that the Master and His Apostles would eat together that evening. This was the last Passover feast for Jesus during His mortal life. For hundreds of years, faithful Jews had kept the commandment given by Him, as Jehovah, to sacrifice a lamb during Passover in remembrance of His mercy to the Children of Israel in setting them free from Egyptian bondage. Tonight in the Garden of Gethsemane and tomorrow on the cross, He would give Himself as the "great and last sacrifice" (Alma 34:13) so that all might be set free from the bondage of physical death, and so that those who were willing to be obedient to His gospel could be set free from the bondage of sin. Now, the Son of God in the flesh would partake of the Passover meal, including a lamb sacrificed for that purpose, symbolic of Him, and then, shortly, would He become the Lamb sacrificed for all.

Have you noticed the miracles that took place in order to provide a place for the Master and His disciples to eat the Passover? These are yet another witness of Him to them and to us.

> 7 Then came the day of unleavened bread, when the passover must be killed. [*This is Thursday, the fifth day of the last week of the Savior's mortal life, when the actual feast of the Passover was eaten by the Jews.*]
> 8 And he [*Jesus*] sent Peter and John, saying, Go and prepare us the passover, that we may eat [*find a place for us to eat the Passover meal*].
> 9 And they said unto him, Where wilt thou that we prepare? (Luke 22:7–9)

Pay attention to the prophetic details which the Savior now provides as He directs Peter and John.

> 10 And he said unto them, Behold, when ye are entered into the city, there shall a man meet you, bearing a pitcher of water; follow him into the house where he entereth in.
> 11 And ye shall say unto the goodman [*owner*] of the house, The Master saith unto thee, Where is the guestchamber [*room*], where I shall eat the passover with my disciples?
> 12 And he shall shew [*show*] you a large upper room furnished: there make ready.
> 13 And they went, and found as he had said unto them: and they made ready the passover. (Luke 22:10–13)

THURSDAY
JERUSALEM
THE LAST SUPPER

Sacrament Introduced

It was evening and Jesus and the Apostles had gathered in the appointed place for their "last supper" together during the Savior's mortal life. It was during this Passover meal that He introduced the sacrament to them. It was also during this meal that He identified Judas Iscariot as the betrayer.

20 Now when the even [*evening*] was come, he sat down with the twelve.

21 And as they did eat, he said, Verily I say unto you, that one of you shall betray me.

22 And they were exceeding sorrowful, and began every one of them to say unto him, Lord, is it I?

23 And he answered and said, He that dippeth his hand with me in the dish, the same shall betray me.

24 The Son of man goeth as it is written of him [*I will perform the Atonement and be crucified as prophesied in the scriptures*]: but woe unto that man by whom the Son of man is betrayed! it had been good for that man if he had not been born. [*It would have been better for Judas Iscariot not to have been born.*]

25 Then Judas, which betrayed him, answered [*responded*] and said, Master, is it I? He said unto him, Thou hast said. (Matthew 26:20–25)

Many versions of the Bible give "Thou hast said" as "Yes" in one form or another, which fits with JST Mark 14:30 which says "And he said unto Judas Iscariot, What thou doest, do quickly; but beware of innocent blood." It is likely that this was a whispered conversation between Jesus and Judas because Matthew, Mark, Luke and John do not indicate that the other Apostles were aware of it. In the next verses, Jesus introduces the sacrament to His Apostles.

26 And as they were eating, Jesus took bread, and blessed it, and brake it, and gave it to the disciples, and said, Take, eat; this is my body [*this bread is symbolic of the Savior's body; when we partake of the sacrament bread, we are symbolically "internalizing" His gospel and making it a part of us*].

27 And he took the cup [*representing the blood which the Savior shed for our sins*], and gave thanks, and gave it to them, saying, Drink ye all of it [*not* part *of it, rather,* all *of it, symbolizing that we must fully accept Christ and His gospel and apply it in our lives*];

28 For this is my blood of the new testament [testament *means "covenant"; in other words, the new covenants associated with the full gospel which Christ had restored*], which is shed for many for the remission of sins.

29 But I say unto you, I will not drink henceforth of this fruit of the vine, until that day when I drink it new with you in my Father's kingdom. [*This is the last time the Master will partake of the sacrament with His disciples during His mortal life.*] (Matthew 26:26–29)

Important details are added in Mark's account of the introduction of the sacrament, accompanied by several JST changes and additions.

22 And as they did eat, Jesus took bread, and blessed, and brake it, and gave to them, and said, Take, eat: this is my body [*this represents My body*]. (Mark 14:22)

20 And as they did eat, Jesus took bread and blessed it, and brake, and gave to them, and said, *Take it, and eat.*

21 *Behold, this is for you to do in remembrance of my body; for*

as oft as ye do this ye will remember this hour that I was with you.
(JST, Mark 14:20–21)

23 And he took the cup, and when he had given thanks, he gave it to them: and they all drank of it.
24 And he said unto them, This is my blood [*this represents My blood*] of the new testament [*the new covenant, associated with the full gospel which Christ had restored*], which is shed for many. (Mark 14:23–24)

> 22 And he took the cup, and when he had given thanks, he gave it to them; and they all drank of it.
> 23 *And he said unto them, This is in remembrance of my blood which is shed for many, and the new testament which I give unto you; for of me ye shall bear record unto all the world.*
> 24 *And as oft as ye do this ordinance, ye will remember me in this hour that I was with you and drank with you of this cup, even the last time in my ministry.* (JST, Mark 14:22–24)

Next, in verse 25, the Master informs His disciples that the next time He will partake of the sacrament with them will be in the kingdom of God. You may wish to read D&C 27, beginning with verse 5, in which the Saviors speaks of a great sacrament meeting to be held in the future. Note that Mark 14:25 is footnoted in the Doctrine and Covenants as a cross-reference for D&C 27:5.

25 Verily I say unto you, I will drink no more of the fruit of the vine, until that day that I drink it new in the kingdom of God [*this is the last time the Savior will partake of the sacrament with them during His mortal life*]. (Mark 14:25)

> 25 Verily I say unto you, *Of this ye shall bear record; for* I will no more drink of the fruit of the vine *with you,* until that day that I drink it new in the kingdom of God. (JST, Mark 14:25)

THURSDAY
JERUSALEM

Jesus Washes the Apostles' Feet

Judas will soon leave the room where they have eaten the Passover meal, but before he leaves, the Redeemer, the great Jehovah, the Creator and Savior of worlds without number (D&C 76:24) will humbly wash the Apostles' feet in a tender demonstration of servant leadership. Notice Peter's response at first, and then see how quickly he changes his mind as he is taught a true principle. He is a wonderful example to all of us of immediate change upon learning a gospel truth.

4 He [Jesus] riseth from supper, and laid aside his garments; and took a towel, and girded himself.

5 After that he poureth water into a bason [*basin*], and began to wash the disciples' feet, and to wipe them with the towel wherewith he was girded. (John 13:4–5)

This must have been an especially emotional time, when the Master of all demonstrated that He was the servant of all. The washing of the dusty, tired feet of guests was a gesture of hospitality and service in the culture of the Jews. Among other things, the Savior was demonstrating by His actions that He was a humble servant to His Apostles.

6 Then cometh he to Simon Peter: and Peter saith unto him, Lord, dost thou wash my feet [*are You going to wash my feet too*]?

7 Jesus answered and said unto him, What I do thou knowest not now [*you don't understand now*]; but thou shalt know hereafter [*but later you will understand*].

8 Peter saith unto him, Thou shalt never wash my feet. [*Peter apparently felt that it was not necessary for Jesus to wash his feet—see JST below.*] Jesus answered him, If I wash thee not, thou hast no part with me. [*Symbolically, if he is not cleansed by the Savior, he will not be with Him in eternity.*] (John 13:6–8)

> 8 Peter saith unto him, Thou *needest not to* wash my feet. Jesus answered him, If I wash thee not, thou hast no part with me. (JST, John 13:8)

9 Simon Peter saith unto him, Lord, not my feet only, but also my hands and my head. [*In that case, please wash me completely.*]

10 Jesus saith to him [*Peter*], He that is washed [*is clean spiritually*] needeth not [*needs no more*] save [*except*] to wash his feet, but is clean every whit [*every bit. In other words, Peter, you are spiritually clean, and all I need to do is wash your tired dusty feet here this evening as a token of My being your servant; more is not necessary*]: and ye are clean, but not all [*you Apostles are "clean," except for Judas Iscariot—see verse 11*].

> 10 Jesus saith to him, He that *has* washed *his hands and his head*, needeth not save to wash his feet, but is clean every whit; and ye are clean, but not all. *Now this was the custom of the Jews under their law; wherefore, Jesus did this that the law might be fulfilled.* (JST, John 13:10)

11 For he knew who should [*would*] betray him; therefore said he, Ye are not all clean. (John 13:11)

THURSDAY
JERUSALEM

Jesus Teaches the Eleven

It is later Thursday evening, and, as soon as Judas Iscariot leaves (John 13:30), Jesus will expound many of the doctrines of the gospel to the remaining eleven Apostles (John 13:31–17:26). It will be, in effect, their final major instruction session in their three year "MTC" training before going on their missions to lead the Church after the Savior returns to heaven. John was the only one of the Gospel writers who recorded these teachings. You will no doubt recognize several of these teachings.

> 31 Therefore, when he was gone out [*when Judas had left*], Jesus said, Now is the Son of man [*the Son of God; Son of Man of Holiness; see Moses 6:57*] glorified, and God is glorified in him. [*The time has arrived for His Atonement, in which He will be glorified, and in which He will bring glory to His Father.*]
>
> 32 If God be glorified in him, God shall also glorify him in himself, and shall straightway [*right away*] glorify him.
>
> 33 Little children [*in effect, My dear Apostles, who still have much to learn*], yet a little while I am with you. Ye shall seek me: and as I said unto the Jews, Whither [*where*] I go, ye cannot come [*they cannot come to heaven with Him now*]; so now I say to you. (John 13:31–33)

Love One Another

> 34 A new commandment I give unto you [*He renews a very old commandment*], That ye love one another; as I have loved you, that ye also love one another.
>
> 35 By this shall all men know that ye are my disciples, if ye have love one to another. (John 13:34–35)

Did you catch how important it is to show love one to another, as taught in verse 35, above? The simple fact is that if we don't, we are not followers of Christ.

> 36 Simon Peter said unto him, Lord, whither goest thou? Jesus answered him, Whither I go [*where I am going*], thou canst not follow me now [*in other words, Peter can't follow Jesus to heaven now*]; but thou shalt follow me afterwards [*after he has finished his mission, he can come to heaven*]. (John 13:36)

We see Peter's basic boldness and courage in verse 37, next.

> 37 Peter said unto him, Lord, why cannot I follow thee now? I will lay down my life for thy sake. [*Peter apparently thinks Jesus is telling him that He, Jesus, must go it alone in Jerusalem, and Peter wants to stay close to Him and defend Him with his life if necessary.*] (John 13:37)

Before the Cock Crows

38 Jesus answered him, Wilt thou lay down thy life for my sake? Verily, verily, I say unto thee, The cock [*rooster*] shall not crow, till thou hast denied me thrice [*three times*]. (John 13:38)

Denying knowing the Savior is not the same as denying the Holy Ghost. Denying the Holy Ghost, as described in D&C 76:31–35, is an unforgivable sin. Peter's denying that he knows the Savior and has been one of His followers for three years is not unforgivable, though so doing brought Peter deep anguish and tears.

As mentioned previously, you may find many of the Savior's teachings here to be quite familiar. Many of these verses are quoted often in talks and lessons in the Church. As stated earlier, the Master is teaching His remaining eleven Apostles many things now before He goes to Gethsemane and then is betrayed and arrested. He senses the anxiety in the hearts of His humble and worried Apostles.

1 Let not your heart be troubled [*don't worry*]: ye believe in God [*the Father*], believe [*have faith*] also in me.
2 In my Father's house are many mansions: if it were not so, I would have told you. I go to prepare a place for you. (John 14:1–2)

Joseph Smith explained the meaning of verse 2, above, wherein it says "In my Father's house are many mansions." He said it should be, "In my Father's kingdom are many kingdoms." Also, "There are mansions for those who obey a celestial law, and there are other mansions for those who come short" (*TPJS*, p. 366). We know from D&C 76 that there are three degrees of glory, each of which has some degree of reward and glory. Even the telestial kingdom is so glorious that it "surpasses all understanding" (D&C 76:89). We know from D&C 131:1 that the celestial kingdom has three "mansions" or degrees. Thus, the Father's "house," or kingdom, does indeed have "many mansions" or categories. Verse 3, below, implies that Jesus will prepare a place in the highest mansion (exaltation) of His Father for His faithful Apostles, from whom He will shortly depart.

3 And if I go and prepare a place for you, I will come again, and receive you unto myself; that where I am, there ye may be also. (John 14:3)

3 And *when* I go, *I will* prepare a place for you, and come again and receive you unto myself; that where I am, ye may be also. (JST, John 14:3)

4 And whither I go ye know, and the way ye know. [*They have been taught where He is going, and how to get there themselves.*] (John 14:4)

These wonderful Apostles are still undergoing intensive training by the Savior. To those of us who are familiar with the concepts in these verses, because we have been taught them most of our lives or since we joined the Church, there may be a temptation to wonder why it is taking so much time and repetition for these brethren to catch on. We must remember that they grew up in an environment of apostate Judaism, a culture which is very foreign to these simple truths.

5 Thomas [*one of the Apostles*] saith unto him, Lord, we know not whither thou goest; and how can we know the way? [*We don't know where You are going, so how can we know the way to get there?*]

6 Jesus saith unto him, I am the way, the truth, and the life [*Christ has everything we need*]: no man cometh unto the Father, but by me [*except through Him*].

7 If ye had known me [*in effect, if you had truly known Me and understood Me and what I have been teaching you*], ye should have [*would have*] known my Father also: and from henceforth [*from now on*] ye know him, and have seen him [*because you have seen Me*].

8 Philip [*one of the Apostles*] saith unto him, Lord, shew us the Father, and it sufficeth us [*and that will be sufficient for us*].

9 Jesus saith unto him, Have I been so long time with you, and yet hast thou not known me [*and you still don't understand*], Philip? he that hath seen me hath seen the Father; and how sayest thou then [*so why do you say*], Shew [*show*] us the Father?

10 Believest thou not that I am in the Father, and the Father in me? the words that I speak unto you I speak not of myself: but the Father that dwelleth in me, he doeth the works. [*In effect, Don't you understand that the Father and I are a team and we work together in perfect unity? Everything I do is, in effect, what the Father is doing for you.*]

11 Believe me that I am in the Father, and the Father in me: or else believe me for the very works' sake. [*In effect, if you can't believe that I and my Father are perfectly unified in the work we do, at least believe Me because of the works you have seen and heard Me do, which could come from no one but the Father.*]

12 Verily, verily, I say unto you, He that believeth on me, the works that I do shall he do also; and greater [*additional*] works than these shall he do; because I go unto my Father. (John 14:5–12)

The word *greater* in verse 12 above, can have at least two meanings. In addition to meaning more significant or more spectacular or more powerful, higher, etc., it can also mean additional or on-going, continued, etc. It is used this way in D&C 7:5 where the Savior tells Peter that John the Beloved will stay on the earth until the Second Coming, and thus "do more, or a greater work" than he has done up to this point. For more on this, see Strong's *Exhaustive Concordance of the Bible*, word #3187, where greater is also defined as "more."

There is also another aspect of the word *greater* as used by the Master in this promise to His Apostles. When they are exalted, and have become gods, they will indeed do greater works, in the normal sense of the word. They will have spirit offspring, will create worlds, and as gods, will do even greater, more magnificent and higher things than they ever saw Christ do while He was among them. See Joseph Smith's teachings on this in *Lectures on Faith*, pp. 64–66.

13 And whatsoever ye shall ask in my name, that will I do, that the Father may be glorified in the Son.
14 If ye shall ask any thing in my name, I will do it. (John 14:13–14)

Verses 15–26, below, will speak of two different "Comforters." One of these Comforters is the Holy Ghost. The other is the Savior Himself and includes the Father on occasions. Verses 16, 17, and 26 speak of the Holy Ghost. Verses 18, 21, 23, and 28 speak of the Savior. (For more on this, see *TPJS*, pp. 149–51.)

15 If ye love me, keep my commandments.
16 And I will pray the Father, and he shall give you another Comforter [*the Holy Ghost—see McConkie,* Doctrinal New Testament Commentary, *Vol. 1, p. 737*], that he may abide [*be*] with you for ever;
17 Even the Spirit of truth; whom the world cannot receive [*the world, meaning those who are not members of the Church, cannot receive the Gift of the Holy Ghost*], because it seeth him not, neither knoweth him: but ye know him; for he dwelleth with you, and shall be in you.
18 I will not leave you comfortless: I [*Jesus*] will come to you. [*This is spoken of as the "Second Comforter." See McConkie,* Doctrinal New Testament Commentary, *Vol. 1, p. 738.*]
19 Yet a little while, and the world seeth me no more [*in effect, I will be crucified and gone, as far as most people are concerned*]; but ye see me [*you will see Me after I am resurrected*]: because I live [*resurrect*], ye shall live also. [*Because of the Atonement, they will resurrect also and have eternal life.*]
20 At that day ye shall know that I am in my Father, and ye in me, and I in you. [*Jesus is still responding to Thomas's question in verse 5 and to Philip's request in verse 8.*]
21 He that hath my commandments, and keepeth them, he it is that loveth me: and he that loveth me shall be loved of my Father, and I will love him, and will manifest myself to him [*as the "Second Comforter"*].
22 Judas [*one of the faithful Apostles*] saith unto him, not Iscariot [*not Judas Iscariot who has already left to betray Jesus*], Lord, how is it that thou wilt manifest thyself unto us, and not unto the world? (John 14:15–22)

22 Judas saith unto him, (not Iscariot,) Lord, how is it thou wilt manifest thyself unto us, and not unto the world? (JST, John 14:22)

23 Jesus answered and said unto him, If a man love me, he will keep my words: and my Father will love him, and we will come unto him [*the "Second Comforter," and make our abode with him*].

24 He that loveth me not keepeth not my sayings [*does not keep My commandments*]: and the word [*gospel*] which ye hear is not mine [*did not originate with Me*], but the Father's which sent me [*originated with the Father who sent me*].

25 These things have I spoken unto you, being yet present with you [*while He is still with them*]. (John 14:23–25)

In verse 26, next, the Master teaches two important functions of the Holy Ghost.

26 But the Comforter, which is the Holy Ghost, whom the Father will send in my name, he shall teach you all things, and bring all things to your remembrance, whatsoever I have said unto you.

Have you noticed that much of what the Savior is teaching His eleven remaining Apostles here is also vital for us, if we desire to qualify for His Atonement to truly cleanse and heal us from all our sins? Peace is one way that we can know if the Atonement is working for us.

27 Peace I leave with you, my peace I give unto you: not as the world giveth, give I unto you. Let not your heart be troubled, neither let it be afraid.

28 Ye have heard how I said unto you, I go away, and come again unto you. [*The Apostles had the Second Comforter for forty days, after Christ's resurrection; see Acts 1:3, as the Savior ministered personally to them and taught them.*] If ye loved me, ye would rejoice, because I said, I go unto the Father: for my Father is greater than I.

29 And now I have told you before it come to pass [*I have told you ahead of time that I will be arrested, tried, crucified and resurrected*], that [*so that*], when it is come to pass [*after it has all happened*], ye might believe.

30 Hereafter I will not talk much with you [*we can't keep talking much longer*]: for [*because*] the prince of this world cometh, and hath nothing in me. [*In effect, the Savior is saying, "We can't talk much longer because Satan is bringing Judas Iscariot and the high priests with their soldiers to arrest Me. Satan has no power over Me, but you are still vulnerable to his temptations."*] (John 14:26–30)

> 30 Hereafter I will not talk much with you; for the prince of *darkness, who is of this world*, cometh, *but hath no power over me, but he hath power over you*. (JST, John 14:30)

31 But that the world may know that I love the Father; and as the Father gave me commandment, even so I do [*Jesus is completely obedient to the Father*]. Arise, let us go hence [*let us go to the Garden of Gethsemane*]. (John 14:31)

> 31 *And I tell you these things, that ye* may know that I love the Father; and as the Father gave me commandment, even so I do. Arise, let us go hence. (JST, John 14:31)

THURSDAY
JERUSALEM

They Sang a Hymn

Mark 14:26 tells us that they sang a hymn at this point. Luke 22:39 tells us that Jesus then led His eleven remaining Apostles to the Mount of Olives. Matthew 26:36 informs us that they then went to Gethsemane, a garden with olive trees, near the foot of the Mount of Olives. The time is getting short, because, as Jesus knows, Judas Iscariot and the high priests and their soldiers will be coming shortly to arrest Him.

THURSDAY
THE MOUNT OF OLIVES

The True Vine

The time of His betrayal through Judas Iscariot is now even closer. Jesus next gives an allegory in which He illustrates the absolutely essential relationship between His Apostles and Himself and between Himself and His Father. In this, we are taught, among other things, that without the Savior, we would be like green branches cut off from the tree which provides nourishment to us. Without it, we would dry up and shrivel away.

> 1 I am the true vine [*grape vine; symbolic of the fact that the true gospel comes from Christ*], and my Father is the husbandman [*farmer, owner; symbolic of the fact that the Father owns the earth*]
> 2 Every branch [*branch growing from the vine; symbolic of people*] in me that beareth not fruit [*people who live wickedly*] he taketh away [*the wicked will be destroyed*]: and every branch [*every person*] that beareth fruit [*who lives righteously*], he purgeth it [*prunes it, cuts out inappropriate behaviors and sin, etc., nourishes it and shapes it*], that it may bring forth more fruit [*symbolic of continuing progress in the lives of the Saints*].
> 3 Now ye are clean [*you have become clean*] through the word [*through the gospel with the Atonement*] which I have spoken [*taught*] unto you.
> 4 Abide in me, and I in you [*stay connected with the True Vine and He will continue to nourish you*]. As the branch cannot bear fruit of itself, except it abide in [*stay attached to*] the vine; no more can ye, except ye abide in me. [*Just as a branch of a vine cannot live without remaining attached to the vine, so we cannot live righteous lives unless we stay connected to Him.*] (John 15:1–4)

The beautiful symbolism in verse 4 above is vitally important for us. How do we attach ourselves to the "vine" so that we can remain securely fastened to Christ? Answer: "Ye shall bind yourselves to act in all holiness before me" (D&C 43:9). How do we "bind" ourselves to the true vine (Christ, verse 1, above)? Answer: We make and keep covenants. Thus, by making covenants, we bind ourselves securely to the True Vine, receive constant nourishment from His roots, and are privileged to be pruned, shaped, and strengthened so that we can return to live with Him forever. Jesus continues this explanation in the next verses.

5 I am the vine, ye are the branches: He that abideth in me, and I in him, the same bringeth forth much fruit [*produces much good*]: for without me ye can do nothing.
6 If a man abide not in me, he is cast forth as a branch [*is cut off and thrown away*], and is withered [*and dries up*]; and men gather them, and cast them into the fire, and they are burned [*symbolic of the destruction of the wicked*].
7 If ye abide in me [*if we stay faithful to Him*], and my words abide in you [*and we are faithful to His gospel*], ye shall ask what ye will [*want*], and it shall be done unto you.
8 Herein is my Father glorified [*this is how His Father is glorified*], that ye bear much fruit; so shall ye be my disciples. [*This reminds us of Moses 1:39 which says "For behold, this is my work and my glory—to bring to pass the immortality and eternal life of man."*]
9 As the Father hath loved me, so have I loved you: continue ye in my love [*remain faithful to Him*].
10 If ye keep my commandments, ye shall abide in my love; even as I have kept my Father's commandments, and abide in his love.
11 These things have I spoken unto you, that my joy might remain in you, and that your joy might be full. (John 15:5–11)

As the Savior continues, He teaches about love (John 15:12–17) and then explains why the wicked hate the righteous.

18 If the world hate you, ye know that it hated me before it hated you. [*If they were not doing what is right, the world would not hate them.*]
19 If ye were of the world [*if you were worldly and wicked*], the world would love his own [*the world would love you because you would be just like they are*]: but because ye are not of the world, but I have chosen you out of the world, therefore [*that is why*] the world hateth you. (John 15:18–19)

At this point in His teaching, the Lord explains yet another major function of the Holy Ghost to His Apostles. They will soon be dependent on the special witness and teaching of the Holy Ghost, as we are, because the Master will not be with them constantly.

26 But when the Comforter [*the Holy Ghost*] is come, whom I will send unto you from the Father, even the Spirit of truth, which proceedeth from the Father, he shall testify of me. (John 15:26)

389

As the Savior continues His discourse before they arrive at the Garden of Gethsemane, He cautions the Eleven to avoid falling away because of the coming persecution upon them (John 16:1–4, 20–22), and He teaches them that, unless He leaves, they will not experience the full power and help of the Holy Ghost (John 16:7). He then explains more about the mission of the Holy Ghost, which will be a major source of strength for them.

13 Howbeit [*however*] when he [*the Holy Ghost*], the Spirit of truth, is come [*when the gift of the Holy Ghost has come upon you in full power*], he will guide you into all truth: for he shall not speak of himself; but whatsoever he shall hear [*from Heavenly Father and Jesus*], that shall he speak: and he will shew [*show*] you things to come.

14 He shall glorify me [*bear witness of Christ*]: for he shall receive of mine [*He gets His instructions from Me and My Father, see verse 15*], and shall shew it unto you.

15 All things that the Father hath are mine: therefore said I [*that is why I said*], that he shall take of mine, and shall shew it unto you. (John 16:13–15)

THURSDAY
THE MOUNT OF OLIVES

The Great Intercessory Prayer

It is still Thursday evening (see Talmage, *Jesus the Christ*, p. 593). Since there is so much that is coming together in the training of the Eleven at this point, we will provide another brief review. The Passover meal, known as the Last Supper, was eaten by Jesus and the Twelve. During the evening, Jesus introduced the sacrament and tenderly washed the Apostles' feet. Sometime during the evening, Judas Iscariot left to betray Jesus to the Jewish high priests and their soldiers. After Judas had left, Jesus began teaching the remaining eleven Apostles great doctrines which stretched their minds and strengthened their understandings. These teachings are recorded, beginning with John 13:31, and continuing to the end of John, chapter 16. Sometime, during or after this discourse, the Savior led the Eleven to the Mount of Olives, just outside of Jerusalem, where He "lifted up his eyes to heaven" and gave what is known as The Great Intercessory Prayer. It is recorded in John 17:1–26. In the first verses of the prayer, Jesus formally offers Himself as the great sacrifice for our sins, in order that we might have eternal life. He is the one who intercedes for us, allowing the law of mercy to act on our behalf. Thus, it is called the *intercessory* prayer.

1 These words spake Jesus, and lifted up his eyes to heaven, and said, Father, the hour is come [*the time to begin the Atonement has arrived*]; glorify thy Son, that thy Son also may glorify thee:

2 As thou hast given him [*Christ*] power over all flesh [*over all people*], that he

should give eternal life [*exaltation*] to as many as thou hast given him.

3 And this is life eternal, that they might know thee the only true God, and Jesus Christ, whom thou hast sent.

4 I have glorified thee on the earth: I have finished the work which thou gavest me to do.

5 And now, O Father, glorify thou me with thine own self with the glory which I had with thee before the world was. (John 17:1–5)

Next, in this prayer, the Savior emphasized that the Eleven were well prepared to take over the leadership of the Church (John 17:6–18) and then prayed for them and all who would believe their teaching and testimonies, that they would work together in unity and harmony, just as the Father and Son do, with continuing firm testimonies of the Father and the Son (John 17:19–26).

THURSDAY

His Suffering in Gethsemane

After finishing the Great Intercessory Prayer (John 17), the Master led His little band of faithful Apostles back down the Mount of Olives to a garden which He had often visited (John 18:2), which was named Gethsemane. It was here that the final suffering was to begin, for which He had volunteered in the grand premortal council (Moses 4:2; Abraham 3:27). It would conclude on the cross. From before the foundation of the earth, this place and this time were the focus of all the prophetic utterances and teachings about the Atonement. And it would be back to this time and place that all future teachings about the power of the Atonement to cleanse and heal, would direct the mind of the honest in heart.

Gethsemane means "oil press" (see online Wikipedia, under "Gethsemane") There is significant symbolism here. The Jews put olives into bags made of mesh fabric and placed them in a press to squeeze olive oil out of them. The first pressings yielded pure olive oil which was prized for many uses, including healing and giving light in lanterns. In fact, we consecrate it and use it to administer to the sick. The last pressing of the olives, under the tremendous pressure of additional weights added to the press, yielded a bitter, red liquid which can remind us of the "bitter cup" which the Savior partook of. Symbolically, the Savior is going into the "oil press" (Gethsemane) to submit to the "pressure" of all our sins which will "squeeze" His blood out in order that we might have the healing "oil" of the Atonement to heal us from our sins.

32 And they came to a place which was named Gethsemane: and he saith to his disciples, Sit ye here, while I shall pray.

33 And he taketh with him Peter and James and John [the "First Presidency"], and began to be sore amazed [astonished], and to be very heavy [with depression and anguish—see Mark 14:33, footnote b];
34 And saith unto them, My soul is exceeding sorrowful unto death: tarry ye here, and watch. (Mark 14:32–34)

> 36 And they came to a place which was named Gethsemane, which was a garden; and the disciples began to be sore amazed, and to be very heavy, and to complain in their hearts, wondering if this be the Messiah.
> 37 And Jesus knowing their hearts, said to his disciples, Sit ye here, while I shall pray.
> 38 And he taketh with him, Peter, and James, and John, and rebuked them, and said unto them, My soul is exceeding sorrowful, even unto death; tarry ye here and watch. (JST, Mark 14:36–38)

35 And he went forward a little, and fell on the ground, and prayed that, if it were possible, the hour might pass from him.
36 And he said, Abba [an intimate, personal, tender term; "Daddy" in the Aramaic language of New Testament times—Bible Dictionary, under "Abba"], Father, all things are possible unto thee; take away this cup from me: nevertheless not what I will, but what thou wilt. (Mark 14:35–36)

James E. Talmage describes the suffering of the Savior in Gethsemane as follows:

Christ's agony in the garden is unfathomable by the finite mind, both as to intensity and cause. The thought that He suffered through fear of death is untenable. Death to Him was preliminary to resurrection and triumphal return to the Father from whom He had come, and to a state of glory even beyond what He had before possessed; and, moreover, it was within His power to lay down His life voluntarily. He struggled and groaned under a burden such as no other being who has lived on earth might even conceive as possible. It was not physical pain, nor mental anguish alone, that caused Him to suffer such torture as to produce an extrusion of blood from every pore; but a spiritual agony of soul such as only God was capable of experiencing. No other man, however great his powers of physical or mental endurance, could have suffered so; for his human organism would have succumbed, and syncope would have produced unconsciousness and welcome oblivion. In that hour of anguish Christ met and overcame all the horrors that Satan, "the prince of this world" could inflict. The frightful struggle incident to the temptations immediately following the Lord's baptism was surpassed and overshadowed by this supreme contest with the powers of evil.

In some manner, actual and terribly real though to man incomprehensible, the Savior took upon Himself the burden of the sins of mankind from Adam to the end of the world. (Jesus the Christ, p. 613.)

37 And he cometh, and findeth them sleeping, and saith unto Peter, Simon, sleep-est thou? couldest not thou watch one hour?

38 Watch ye and pray, lest ye enter into temptation. The spirit truly is ready, but the flesh is weak.

39 And again he went away, and prayed, and spake the same words.

40 And when he returned, he found them asleep again, [for their eyes were heavy,] neither wist [knew] they what to answer him. (Mark 14:37–40)

No doubt these humble Apostles were very tired by this time of the week (Thursday night). It had been a difficult week for them, worrying about the Savior's safety and the plots to kill Him. No doubt they had had little sleep. Thus, it is easy to understand why "their eyes were heavy" in verse 40, above, meaning that they were very sleepy.

41 And he cometh the third time, and saith unto them, Sleep on now, and take your rest: it is enough, the hour is come [*the time for My arrest, trial and crucifixion is here*]; behold, the Son of man [*Christ*] is betrayed into the hands of sinners.

42 Rise up, let us go; lo, he [*Judas Iscariot*] that betrayeth me is at hand [*is com-ing*]. (Mark 14:41–42)

Luke adds some insights not mentioned by Matthew and Mark.

40 And when he was at the place [*the Garden of Gethsemane—see Matthew 26:36*], he said unto them, Pray that ye enter not into temptation.

41 And he was withdrawn from them about a stone's cast, and kneeled down, and prayed,

42 Saying, Father, if thou be willing, remove this cup from me: nevertheless not my will, but thine, be done.

43 And there appeared an angel unto him from heaven, strengthening him. [*Apostle Bruce R. McConkie suggested that this angel might be Michael (Adam); see April 1985 General Conference*].

44 And being in an agony he prayed more earnestly: and his sweat was as it were great drops of blood falling down to the ground. (Luke 22:40–44)

Verse 44, above, leaves some doubt as to whether or not the Savior actually bled from every pore. A close reading might make it appear that Luke, who was a physician (Colossians 4:14), may have been saying that the pain was so extreme that it was as if the Lord were sweating blood, not that He actually was. However, Mosiah 3:7 and D&C 19:18 clear up any doubt. He did bleed from every pore.

Thus, in a way that is completely beyond our ability to comprehend, the Redeemer suffered the sum total of all of the remorse, agony, and punish-ment associated with the sins of all humankind. He endured all of the physi-cal, mental, and spiritual pain and anguish required by the law of justice (2

Nephi 9:26). He described His suffering to Martin Harris as recorded in the Doctrine and Covenants.

15 Therefore I command you to repent—repent, lest I smite you by the rod of my mouth, and by my wrath, and by my anger, and your sufferings be sore— how sore you know not, how exquisite you know not, yea, how hard to bear you know not.

16 For behold, I, God, have suffered these things for all, that they might not suffer if they would repent;

17 But if they would not repent they must suffer even as I;

18 Which suffering caused myself, even God, the greatest of all, to tremble because of pain, and to bleed at every pore, and to suffer both body and spirit—and would that I might not drink the bitter cup, and shrink—

19 Nevertheless, glory be to the Father, and I partook and finished my preparations unto the children of men. (D&C 19:15–19)

We understand that the suffering in the Garden of Gethsemane occurred again on the cross. Speaking of the crucifixion, James E. Talmage wrote:

It seems, that in addition to the fearful suffering incident to crucifixion, the agony of Gethsemane had recurred, intensified beyond human power to endure. (*Jesus the Christ*, p. 661)

Who would want to reject such a gift from a loving Elder Brother, given at such infinite cost? According to Isaiah, all who accept His gift by joining His Church, repenting of their sins, and living His gospel, bring great satisfaction to Him.

11 He [*Jesus*] shall see of the travail of his soul [*the results of His suffering*], and shall be satisfied [*the Savior will have personal joy because of having performed the Atonement for us*]: by his knowledge [*by the knowledge He brings*] shall my righteous servant [*Christ*] justify many [*save many*]; for he shall bear their iniquities. (Isaiah 53:11)

THURSDAY
GETHSEMANE
Betrayed by a Kiss

When His agony in Gethsemane was completed, He returned to His exhausted disciples and eventually awakened them to accompany Him as He went to meet Judas Iscariot and the delegation of soldiers and others accompanying him.

45 Then cometh he to his disciples, and saith unto them, Sleep on now, and take your rest: behold, the hour is at hand [*the time has come*], and the Son of man

[*Christ—Moses 6:57*] is betrayed into the hands of sinners.

46 Rise, let us be going: behold, he [*Judas*] is at hand that doth betray me.

47 And while he yet spake, lo, Judas, one of the twelve, came, and with him a great multitude with swords and staves [*clubs*], from the chief priests and elders of the people. (Matthew 26:45–47)

It was prearranged between Judas and the representatives of the chief priests and elders that he would identify Jesus to them by giving the Master a kiss (Matthew 26:48). Thus they could be certain that they were arresting the right person. Judas did so and when they took hold of the Lord to take Him away, Peter took immediate action.

51 And, behold, one of them [*Peter*] which were with Jesus stretched out his hand, and drew his sword, and struck a servant of the high priest's, and smote off his ear. [*Jesus healed this man's ear; see Luke 22:51.*]

While we admire Peter's courage, the Master reprimanded him, reminding him that it was necessary for Him to continue with the Atonement (Matthew 26:52–54; John 18:10–11)). Those who arrested Him took Him away in the night for illegal trials before Jewish leaders. By this time, the Apostles had fled (Matthew 26:56) as had been prophesied earlier that evening by the Savior (Matthew 26:31).

THURSDAY NIGHT AND FRIDAY MORNING
JERUSALEM

The Lord Is on Trial

After His arrest, the Savior was bound and first taken for questioning to the house of Annas, the former high priest of the Jews for questioning (John 18:13, 19–21). During that questioning, one of the officers struck the Master, demanding that He address the former high priest with more respect (John 18:22–23). From the house of Annas, the Redeemer was sent across the courtyard to the house of Caiaphas, the ruling high priest (John 18:24). There, false witnesses were brought in but their false statements were so contradictory that even those wicked Jewish leaders could not accept them as evidence in their illegal night court (Mark 14:55–59). During this time, Jesus had remained silent. Finally, in exasperation, Caiaphas asked Him a direct question.

61 Art thou the Christ, the Son of the Blessed [*the Son of God*]?

62 And Jesus said, I am. (Mark 14:61–62)

Furious at the Master's answer, Caiaphas tore his own clothes in a sign of highest indignation and the illegal assembly pronounced Jesus worthy of death (Matthew 26:65–66). Then they spit on Him, blindfolded Him and hit Him on the face, calling on Him to use His powers to name the men who were striking Him (Luke 22:64–65).

In the early morning, arrangements were made to have Christ appear for trial before Pontius Pilate, the Roman governor of Judea (Mark 15:1; John 18:28–29). Pilate interrogated Him but found no cause to keep Him under arrest and said so (Luke 23:4). The Jewish leaders were outraged (Luke 23:5) with Pilate, who then thought of a way to get out of judging Jesus. He was aware that Herod, the governor of Galilee and Perea was in Jerusalem at the time, and, since Jesus was a Galilean (Luke 23:6), he determined to send Him to Herod to be judged (Luke 23:7). Herod was delighted to have the chance to see Jesus, and hoped He might entertain him by performing a miracle, but the Master remained completely silent (Luke 23:8–9). Finally, Herod's men mocked Him, "arrayed him in a gorgeous robe," and sent Him back to Pilate (Luke 23:10–11).

Before returning to the second appearance before Pilate, we will consider Peter's denial of knowing Jesus, and also the suicide of Judas Iscariot.

Peter's Denial of Knowing Jesus

We will someday know more about Peter's denial of knowing Christ, at the time of His trial. One thing is certain. He did not *deny* Christ in the sense of denying that He was the Messiah. Rather, he denied knowing Him.

> 69 Now Peter sat without [*outside of the trial room*] in the palace: and a damsel came unto him, saying, Thou also wast with Jesus of Galilee.
> 70 But he denied before them all, saying, I know not what thou sayest.
> 71 And when he was gone out into the porch, another maid saw him, and said unto them that were there, This fellow was also with Jesus of Nazareth.
> 72 And again he denied with an oath [*strongly*], I do not know the man [*Christ*].
> 73 And after a while came unto him they that stood by, and said to Peter, Surely thou also art one of them [*one of Christ's followers*]; for thy speech bewrayeth thee [*your Galilean accent gives you away*].
> 74 Then began he to curse and to swear, saying, I know not the man [*Jesus*]. And immediately the cock crew [*the rooster crowed*].
> 75 And Peter remembered the word of Jesus [*in Matthew 26:34*], which said unto him, Before the cock crow, thou shalt deny me thrice. And he went out, and wept bitterly. (Matthew 26:69–75)

James E. Talmage taught the following about this scene:

When Jesus was taken into custody in the Garden of Gethsemane, all the Eleven forsook Him and fled. This is not to be accounted as certain evidence of cowardice, for the Lord had indicated that they should go. Peter and at least one other disciple followed afar off; and, after the armed guard had entered the palace of the high priest with their Prisoner, Peter "went in, and sat with the servants to see the end." He was assisted in securing admittance by the unnamed disciple, who was on terms of acquaintanceship with the high priest. That other disciple was in all probability John, as may be inferred from the fact that he is mentioned only in the fourth Gospel, the author of which characteristically refers to himself anonymously.

While Jesus was before the Sanhedrists, Peter remained below with the servants. The attendant at the door was a young woman; her feminine suspicions had been aroused when she admitted Peter, and as he sat with a crowd in the palace court she came up, and having intently observed him, said: "Thou also wast with Jesus of Galilee." But Peter denied, averring he did not know Jesus. Peter was restless; his conscience and the fear of identification as one of the Lord's disciples troubled him. He left the crowd and sought partial seclusion in the porch; but there another maid spied him out, and said to those nearby: "This fellow was also with Jesus of Nazareth"; to which accusation Peter replied with an oath: "I do not know the man."

The April night was chilly, and an open fire had been made in the hall or court of the palace. Peter sat with others at the fire, thinking, perhaps, that brazen openness was better than skulking caution as a possible safeguard against detection. About an hour after his former denials, some of the men around the fire charged him with being a disciple of Jesus, and referred to his Galilean dialect as evidence that he was at least a fellow countryman with the high priest's Prisoner; but, most threatening of all, a kinsman of Malthus [Malchus—see John 18:10], whose ear Peter had slashed with the sword, asked peremptorily: "Did not I see thee in the garden with him?" Then Peter went so far in the course of falsehood upon which he had entered as to curse and swear, and to vehemently declare for the third time, "I know not the man." As the last profane falsehood left his lips, the clear notes of a crowing cock broke upon his ears, and the remembrance of his Lord's prediction welled up in his mind. Trembling in wretched realization of his perfidious cowardice, he turned from the crowd and met the gaze of the suffering Christ, who from the midst of the insolent mob looked into the face of His boastful, yet loving but weak apostle. Hastening from the palace, Peter went out into the night, weeping bitterly. As his later life attests, his tears were those of real contrition and true repentance." (*Jesus the Christ*, pp. 629–31)

The Death of Judas Iscariot

We do not know the ultimate fate of Judas Iscariot. Some think that he will be a son of perdition. Others feel that he did not have a strong enough testimony of the Savior to become such. The fact that he felt remorse (Matthew 27:4) suggests to some that he was not completely like Satan and his followers, who would gladly crucify Christ again (D&C 76:35), and therefore does not qualify to be with him forever. We will have to wait and see.

3 Then Judas, which had betrayed him, when he saw that he was condemned, repented himself [*changed his mind*], and brought again [*returned*] the thirty pieces of silver [*which he had been paid to betray Jesus*] to the chief priests and elders,
4 Saying, I have sinned in that I have betrayed the innocent blood. And they said, What is that to us? see thou to that [*that is your problem!*]. (Matthew 27:3–4)

5 And they said unto him, What is that to us? See thou to *it; thy sins be upon thee.* (JST, Matthew 27:5)

5 And he cast down the pieces of silver in the temple, and departed, and went and hanged himself.

6 And he cast down the pieces of silver in the temple, and departed, and went, and hanged himself *on a tree. And straightway he fell down, and his bowels gushed out, and he died.* (JST, Matthew 27:6)

6 And the chief priests took the silver pieces, and said, It is not lawful [*legal*] for to put them into the treasury, because it is the price of blood [*it is blood money, the price paid to have someone killed*].
7 And they took counsel [*talked it over*], and bought with them [*the thirty pieces of silver*] the potter's field, to bury strangers [*foreigners*] in. (Matthew 27:6–7)

We will now return to the trial before Pilate. Having failed in his attempt to get Herod to handle the case of the Jews vs. Jesus Christ, Pontius Pilate once again found himself facing the Master and His accusers. The Lord answered a question from Pilate, but refused to respond to the Jewish rulers.

11 And Jesus stood before the governor [*Pontius Pilate*]: and the governor asked him, saying, Art thou the King of the Jews? And Jesus said unto him, Thou sayest [*in other words, it is as you say, yes, I am; see John 18:37*].
12 And when he was accused of the chief priests and elders [*when the leaders of the Jews accused him in front of Pilate*], he answered nothing.
13 Then said Pilate unto him, Hearest thou not how many things they witness against thee [*don't you hear what they are accusing you of*]?
14 And he answered him to never a word [*Jesus did not reply*]; insomuch that the governor marvelled greatly [*was very surprised*]. (Matthew 27:11–14)

Next, Pilate thought to solve the situation by offering the Jews a choice between having Jesus released or releasing a notorious and dangerous criminal named Barabbas. The name *Barabbas* means "son of the father" (Bible Dictionary, under "Barabbas"). This may be symbolic in that the imposter, Satan, stirred up the multitude to demand the release of an imposter, Barabbas, while the true Son of the Father is punished for crimes which He did not commit. The leaders of the Jew persuaded them to demand the release of Barabbas (Matthew 27:15–21).

It is interesting to note that Pilate's wife had been told in a dream to warn her husband to have nothing to do with bringing harm to Jesus.

19 When he [*Pilate*] was set down on the judgment seat, his wife sent unto him, saying, Have thou nothing to do with that just [*innocent*] man [*Jesus*]: for I have suffered many things this day in a dream because of him. (Matthew 27:19)

Finally, Pilate yielded to the demands of the crowd and symbolically washed his hands of the whole affair. And, in a chilling moment of mob frenzy, the people voiced their willingness to be accountable for what happened to Jesus.

22 Pilate saith unto them, What shall I do then with Jesus which is called Christ? They all say unto him, Let him be crucified.
23 And the governor said, Why, what evil hath he done? But they cried out the more [*all the louder*], saying, Let him be crucified.
24 When Pilate saw that he could prevail nothing [*that he could not get the multitude to change their minds*], but that rather a tumult was made [*an uprising was in the making*], he took water, and washed his hands before the multitude, saying, I am innocent of the blood of this just [*innocent*] person: see ye to it [*it is on your heads now*].
25 Then answered all the people, and said, His blood be on us, and on our children. [*We and our children will take responsibility for killing Jesus.*] (Matthew 27:22–25)

Next, Pilate ordered the Savior to be scourged (Mark 15:15). Scourging was a very severe punishment and many prisoners did not live through it. It consisted of being whipped with a whip composed of leather thongs with bits of metal, bone, and the like, secured to the ends of the thongs.

26 Then released he Barabbas unto them: and when he had scourged [*whipped*] Jesus, he delivered him to be crucified. (Matthew 27:26)

After the scourging, Pilate's soldiers mocked the Lord and subjected Him to additional brutality.

16 And the soldiers led him away into the hall, called Prætorium [*a room in the governor's house*]; and they call together the whole band [*about six hundred Roman soldiers with a leader over them (McConkie, Doctrinal New Testament Commentary, Vol. 1, p. 781)*].
17 And they clothed him with purple [*in mockery of His claim to be "King of the Jews"*], and platted [*made, wove*] a crown of thorns, and put it about his head,
18 And began to salute him [*saying*], Hail, King of the Jews!

19 And they smote [*hit*] him on the head with a reed [*stick, mock scepter of kingly authority*], and did spit upon him, and bowing their knees worshipped him [*pretended to worship him*].

20 And when they had mocked him, they took off the purple from him, and put his own clothes on him, and led him out to crucify him. (Mark 15:16–20)

FRIDAY MORNING
OUTSIDE THE CITY WALL

The Crucifixion

Having brutally mocked and scourged our Savior, the authorities led Him outside the city wall toward a place on a nearby hill called Golgotha, where preparations for His crucifixion had been made. It takes little imagination to realize that the Savior's mortal body was very weak by this time. He had suffered untold agony and bled from every pore in Gethsemane. Soldiers and others had beaten and bruised Him mercilessly during mock trials, and the vicious scourging He suffered was often known to kill its victims before they were even taken out for crucifixion. Thus, a man in the crowd of onlookers, Simon from Cyrene (a city in northern Africa) was compelled to follow behind the Master, carrying His cross for Him (Luke 23:26).

While Matthew, Mark, Luke, and John all give accounts of the crucifixion, we will use Matthew's record here for the main narrative, along with additions from the JST and an occasional reference from the others. From each of their accounts, we can gain great appreciation for this portion of the Redeemer's atoning sacrifice and death for us.

> 33 And when they were come unto a place called Golgotha, that is to say, a place of a skull, (Matthew 27:33)

> > 35 And when they were come unto a place called Golgotha, (that is to say, a place of *burial*,) (JST, Matthew 27:35)

> 34 They gave him vinegar to drink mingled with gall [*designed to drug the victim of crucifixion to lessen the pain somewhat*—Jesus the Christ, *pages 654–55*]: and when he had tasted thereof, he would not drink.

> 35 And they crucified him, and parted his garments [*divided his clothing up among themselves*], casting lots: that it might be fulfilled which was spoken by the prophet [*Psalm 22:18*], They parted my garments among them, and upon my vesture [*clothing*] did they cast lots.

> 36 And sitting down they watched him there;

> 37 And set up over his head his accusation written, this is Jesus the King of the Jews. (Matthew 27:34–37)

> > 39 *And Pilate wrote a title, and put it on the cross, and the writing was,*

40 *Jesus of Nazareth*, the King of the Jews, *in letters of Greek, and Latin, and Hebrew.*

41 *And the chief priests said unto Pilate, It should be written and set up over his head, his accusation, This is he that said he was Jesus, the King of the Jews.*

42 *But Pilate answered and said, What I have written, I have written; let it alone.* (JST, Matthew 27:39–42)

38 Then were there two thieves crucified with him, one on the right hand, and another on the left.

39 And they that passed by reviled [*made fun of Him*] him, wagging their heads [*shaking their heads*],

40 And saying, Thou that destroyest the temple, and buildest it in three days, save thyself. If thou be the Son of God, come down from the cross. (Matthew 27:38–40)

These people obviously misunderstood what Jesus had said regarding the temple. What he said is found in John 2:19–21. He said that if they destroyed His body (the "temple of His body"), He would raise it up in three days (be resurrected in three days). By the time Jesus is on the cross, His statement has been misquoted and spread so that the mockers claim that He said He would destroy their massive temple in Jerusalem and rebuild it in three days.

41 Likewise also the chief priests mocking him, with the scribes and elders, said,

42 He saved others; himself he cannot save. If he be the King of Israel, let him now come down from the cross, and we will believe him.

43 He trusted in God; let him deliver him now, if he will have him: for he said, I am the Son of God.

44 The thieves also, which were crucified with him, cast the same in his teeth [*threw similar statements at Him*]. (Matthew 27:41–44)

The JST informs us that only one of the thieves railed against the Master.

47 *One of the thieves* also, which were crucified with him, cast the same in his teeth. *But the other rebuked him, saying, Dost thou not fear God, seeing thou art under the same condemnation; and this man is just, and hath not sinned; and he cried unto the Lord that he would save him.* (JST, Matthew 27:47)

Before we continue with Matthew's account, we will take a moment to consider Luke's record concerning the thief on the cross and correct doctrine regarding whether or not he was prepared for paradise.

43 And Jesus said unto him, Verily I say unto thee, To day shalt thou be with me in paradise. (Luke 23:43)

It is a common belief that the thief on the cross went to paradise. This is not the case. Our Bible Dictionary explains this. It says, "The Bible rendering is incorrect. The statement would more accurately read, 'Today shalt thou be with me in the world of spirits' since the thief was not ready for paradise." See Bible Dictionary, under "Paradise." No doubt, with his humble attitude, this thief accepted the gospel as taught by missionaries in the spirit prison (D&C 138). Now, we will return to Matthew's account.

> 45 Now from the sixth hour [*about noon*] there was darkness over all the land unto the ninth hour. (Matthew 27:45)

In the Jewish time system, the sixth hour would be about noon, the ninth hour would be about 3 AM in our time system. We understand that Jesus was nailed to the cross at the third hour, which would be about 9 AM.

> 46 And about the ninth hour Jesus cried with a loud voice, saying, Eli, Eli, lama sabachthani? that is to say, My God, my God, why hast thou forsaken me?

This was a very difficult time for the Savior, and incomprehensibly difficult for us to understand. Apparently, as part of the Atonement, Jesus had to experience what sinners do when they sin so much that the Spirit leaves them. At this point on the cross, we understand that all available help from the Father was withdrawn in order that the Savior might experience all things, including the withdrawal of the Spirit which grievous sinners experience.

Statements from the Cross

There are seven recorded statements made by the Savior from the cross. The references for these statements and the statements themselves are given here, and are in chronological order:

1. Luke 23:34: "Father, forgive them; for they know not what they do."

2. Luke 23:43: "Today shalt thou be with me in paradise."

3. John 19:26–27: "Woman, behold thy son!" "Behold thy mother!"

4. Matthew 27:46: "My God, my God, why hast thou forsaken me?"

5. John 19:28: "I thirst."

6. John 19:30: "It is finished."

7. Luke 23:46: "Father, into thy hands I commend my spirit."

We now continue with Matthew's account.

47 Some of them that stood there, when they heard that, said, This man calleth for Elias [*Elijah—see footnote 47a, in your Bible*].
48 And straightway [*immediately*] one of them ran, and took a spunge, and filled it with vinegar, and put it on a reed, and gave him to drink.
49 The rest said, Let be, let us see whether Elias [*Elijah*] will come to save him [*don't help him; let's see if Elijah comes to help Him*].
50 Jesus, when he had cried again with a loud voice, yielded up the ghost [*left His body, died*]. (Matthew 27:47–50)

> 54 Jesus when he had cried again with a loud voice, *saying, Father, it is finished, thy will is done,* yielded up the ghost. (JST, Matthew 27:54)

It startled some of the onlookers that Jesus had so much strength that He could speak so loudly. It appeared to them as if He had power to leave His body when He so chose, which indeed He did. We see this doctrine taught in John:

> 17 Therefore doth my Father love me, because I lay down my life, that I might take it again.
> 18 No man taketh it from me, but I lay it down of myself. I have power to lay it down, and I have power to take it again. This commandment have I received of my Father. (John 10:17–18)

51 And, behold, the veil of the temple [*in Jerusalem*] was rent in twain [*torn in two*] from the top to the bottom; and the earth did quake, and the rocks rent [*were torn apart*]; (Matthew 27:51)

Can you imagine what it must have been like for the Lord and Savior Jesus Christ to leave His pain-racked body and the heartless mocking and jeering onlookers, and then at the appropriate time, appear to the righteous spirits in paradise who awaited His arrival with joyous anticipation and loving reverence for Him (D&C 138:11–18)? It will be interesting someday to hear our Elder Brother express what He felt at that time, perhaps in a general conference during the Millennium or on some other special occasion.

Friday Evening
Near Jerusalem
The Lord's Burial

Among the Jews at this time in history, the days of the week, Monday, Tuesday, Wednesday, and so forth, went from about sundown to about sundown of the next day, rather than from midnight to midnight as is the case with our calendar system. Therefore, the Jewish religious leaders were very concerned about violating one of their laws which said people should not be crucified on the Sabbath. Their Sabbath (held on Saturday) would start at about six o'clock Friday evening. Jesus and the two thieves had been crucified at about nine that morning. Persons being crucified often lived two or three days. Therefore, these religious rulers of the Jews asked Pilate to have soldiers break the legs of the three "criminals" who were being crucified to kill them with additional pain and shock. This way, their expired bodies could be taken off their crosses in order to avoid violating the Sabbath. Pilate agreed and sent soldiers to do the deed.

> 31 The Jews therefore, because it was the preparation [*time to make preparations for the Sabbath*], that the bodies should not remain upon the cross on the sabbath day, (for that sabbath day was an high day,) besought Pilate that their legs might be broken, and that they might be taken away.
> 32 Then came the soldiers, and brake [*broke*] the legs of the first [*one of the thieves*], and of the other [*thief*] which was crucified with him.
> 33 But when they came to Jesus, and saw that he was dead already, they brake not his legs:
> 34 But one of the soldiers with a spear pierced his side, and forthwith came there out blood and water. (John 19:31–34)

As evening approached (Matthew 27:57), a righteous disciple of Christ named Joseph of Arimathea (from the city of Arimathea in Judea) who was also a member of the Jewish Sanhedrin (roughly equivalent to our senate), and who had refused to agree with the decision of that counsel to seek the death of Jesus (Luke 23:50–51), approached Pontius Pilate and asked for the body of the Savior. Pilate was surprised that Christ was dead, after so few hours on the cross, and sent a centurion to verify it. When the death had been confirmed, Pilate granted the request and Joseph took the body down from the cross (Mark 15:44–46) and placed it in an unused tomb that he had purchased for his own use (Matthew 27:59–60). Nicodemus, also a ruler of the Jews (John 3:1) and the one who had approached the Master by night at the beginning of His formal mortal ministry, and who had received a lesson on baptism (John

3:2–5), brought a large quantity of spices (myrrh and aloes) and assisted Joseph of Arimathea in preparing the Lord's body for burial (John 19:39–42). When they had cleaned the body and wrapped it in linen cloth with the spices, they rolled a large stone across the door of the tomb (Mark 15:46).

Some faithful women who had come with the Savior from Galilee (Mark 15:40–41; Matthew 27:61), followed Joseph and Nicodemus as they carried the body from the cross and laid it in the tomb, noting the location so that they could return to it on Sunday morning with additional spices and ointments (Luke 23:55–56). Since the Sabbath had arrived by this time Friday evening, they didn't dare do any more with the body. They would rest on the Sabbath and then return to the sepulchre to finish preparing the body for final burial on Sunday morning.

On Saturday morning, even though it was the Sabbath, the chief priests and Pharisees went to Pilate and requested that guards be placed by the tomb for fear that some of Christ's friends would steal the body in an attempt to make it look like His prophecy of His resurrection had come true. Pilate responded by telling them that, under his rule, they had been granted the privilege of having their own soldiers, and to send their own guards to the tomb to secure it. They did so, sealing the stone with a wax seal so that unauthorized entry could easily be detected, and setting a watch of their own soldiers to guard it (Matthew 27:62–66).

SATURDAY

Christ's Visit to the Postmortal Spirit World

As mentioned previously, it is no doubt beyond our ability to comprehend the joy in the Savior's heart as He left His physical body on the cross and entered the world of departed spirits. There, He was welcomed with "joy and gladness" by the spirits of the righteous in paradise who awaited His arrival (D&C 138:12–18). While His body lay in the tomb, He taught these faithful spirits of the dead the "everlasting gospel" with special emphasis on the doctrine of resurrection (D&C 138:19). This was of special interest to these individuals, including Adam and Eve, because they were to be resurrected with the Master on the coming Sunday morning. The long bondage (D&C 138:50) of being without their physical bodies was about to come to an end.

The Lord did not go in person to the wicked spirits there (D&C 138:20–22). After teaching and reviewing the plan of salvation with the righteous, He organized them into a marvelous missionary force to take the gospel to those in spirit prison (D&C 138:20–37). The message they were to preach was the same one that our missionaries today preach.

32 Thus was the gospel preached to those who had died in their sins, without a knowledge of the truth, or in transgression, having rejected the prophets.
33 These were taught faith in God, repentance from sin, vicarious baptism for the remission of sins, the gift of the Holy Ghost by the laying on of hands,
34 And all other principles of the gospel that were necessary for them to know in order to qualify themselves that they might be judged according to men in the flesh, but live according to God in the spirit. (D&C 138:32–34)

The great missionary work established by the Savior at that time continues today and is carried on by faithful members of the Church when they pass away.

SUNDAY
THE RESURRECTION OF JESUS CHRIST
Faithful Women Arrive at the Tomb

Very early Sunday morning (Mark 16:2), while it was yet dark (John 20:1) but nearing the first dim light of dawn (Matthew 28:1), the faithful, sorrowing women who had watched Joseph of Arimathea and Nicodemus make preliminary preparations of the Savior's body for burial Friday evening (John 19:38–42; Luke 23:50–56) arrived at the tomb with sweet spices with which to finish preparing His body for final burial (Mark 16:1). As they had walked toward the sepulchre, they had discussed the problem of getting someone to roll away the large stone that blocked the entrance to the tomb. As they arrived at the site, to their surprise and dismay, it was already rolled away (Mark 16:3–4). Their concern soon changed to amazement and joy as two angels explained what had happened earlier that morning.

1 In the end of the sabbath [*Saturday*], as it began to dawn toward the first day of the week [*Sunday*], came Mary Magdalene and the other Mary to see the sepulchre.
2 And, behold, there was a great earthquake: for the angel of the Lord descended from heaven, and came and rolled back the stone from the door, and sat upon it. (Matthew 28:1–2)

> 2 And behold, there *had been* a great earthquake; for *two angels* of the Lord descended from heaven, and came and rolled back the stone from the door, and sat upon it. (JST, Matthew 28:2)

3 His countenance [*face*] was like lightning, and his raiment [*clothing*] white as snow:

4 And for fear of him the keepers [*guards*] did shake, and became as dead men.
5 And the angel answered and said unto the women, Fear not ye: for I know that ye seek Jesus, which was crucified. (Matthew 28:3–5)

> 3 And *their* countenance was like lightning, and *their* raiment white as snow; and for fear of *them* the keepers did shake, and became as *though they were dead*.
> 4 And the *angels* answered and said unto the women, Fear not ye; for *we* know that ye seek Jesus *who* was crucified. (JST, Matthew 28:3–4)

6 He is not here: for he is risen [*resurrected*], as he said. Come, see the place where the Lord lay. (Matthew 28:6)

Peter and John Run to the Tomb

Having entered the empty tomb and seen for themselves that the Master's body was not there, and having heard the explanation from the two angels (Luke 24:1–5), they hurried to tell the eleven Apostles (Luke 24:9). They had been told by the angels to tell them that Jesus had been resurrected and that the disciples were to go to Galilee where they would see Him (Matthew 28:7) as He had previously instructed them (Matthew 26:32). Upon hearing the women's report, the initial reaction of the disciples was disbelief (Luke 24:11). But Peter and John ran to the tomb to see for themselves. John outran Peter, but waited for him at the site and then Peter was the first to enter the empty sepulchre.

> 3 Peter therefore went forth, and that other disciple [*John*], and came to the sepulchre.
> 4 So they ran both together: and the other disciple did outrun Peter [*John outran Peter*], and came first to the sepulchre.
> 5 And he stooping down, and looking in, saw the linen clothes lying; yet went he not in. [*John waited for Peter to arrive.*]
> 6 Then cometh Simon Peter following him, and went into the sepulchre [*tomb*], and seeth the linen clothes lie [*saw the strips of linen which Joseph and Nicodemus had used to wrap the Savior's body in*],
> 7 And the napkin [*burial cloth*], that was about [*was wrapped around*] his head, not lying with the linen clothes, but wrapped together [*folded*] in a place by itself.
> 8 Then went in also that other disciple [*John*], which came first to the sepulchre, and he saw, and believed.
> 9 For as yet they knew not [*did not understand*] the scripture, that he must rise again from the dead [*as John explained in John 12:16*]. (John 20:3–9)

As indicated in verses 8–9, above, it was at this point in time that John came to believe that Jesus had actually been resurrected. Up to that point, even though the Master had told them He would rise from the dead, it had not become a part of their active understanding.

Cover-up Conspiracy of the Guards and Jewish Leaders

In the meantime, Matthew informs us of a scene that was playing itself out in Jerusalem with the guards who were on duty at the tomb very early that morning when the stone was rolled away by the angels. The lies generated by that conspiracy were still in circulation at the time Matthew wrote his Gospel.

11 Now when they were going [*while the women were going to tell the Apostles*], behold, some of the watch [*soldiers who had been assigned to guard the tomb*] came into the city, and shewed [*told*] unto the chief priests all the things that were done.
12 And when they [*the chief priests*] were assembled with the elders, and had taken counsel [*had plotted together*], they gave large money [*bribes*] unto the soldiers,
13 Saying, Say ye, His disciples came by night, and stole him away while we slept. [*In other words, lie about what happened.*]
14 And if this [*news of Jesus' body being gone from the tomb and angels saying that he is resurrected*] come to the governor's ears, we will persuade him [*we will handle Pilate*], and secure you [*protect you from being executed for leaving your post while on guard duty*].
15 So they [*the soldiers*] took the money [*the bribes*], and did as they were taught: and this saying [*story*] is commonly reported among the Jews until this day. (Matthew 28:11–15)

Mary Magdalene Sees the Resurrected Lord

Mark informs us that the first mortal to see the resurrected Lord was Mary Magdalene (Mark 16:9). She had apparently followed Peter and John as they ran back to the garden tomb to see for themselves that the stone had been rolled away and the Master's body was gone (John 20:1–10). After they had gone, she remained outside of the tomb weeping. She had been at the tomb with the other women earlier that morning when the two angels said "he is risen" (Mark 16:6). But in her distraught state of mind, the message had apparently not yet become reality with her. What follows now is a very tender scene for both Mary and the Lord.

11 But Mary [*Mary Magdalene—John 20:1*] stood without [*outside*] at the sepulchre weeping: and as she wept, she stooped down, and looked into the sepulchre,
12 And seeth two angels in white sitting, the one at the head, and the other at the feet, where the body of Jesus had lain.

13 And they say unto her, Woman, why weepest thou? She saith unto them, Because they have taken away my Lord, and I know not where they have laid him. 14 And when she had thus said, she turned herself back [*away from the angels*], and saw Jesus standing, and knew not [*did not notice*] that it was Jesus.

15 Jesus saith unto her, Woman, why weepest thou? whom seekest thou? She, supposing him to be the gardener, saith unto him, Sir, if thou have borne him hence [*if you have taken His body somewhere*], tell me where thou hast laid him, and I will take him away.

16 Jesus saith unto her, Mary. She turned herself, and saith unto him, Rabboni; which is to say, Master. (John 20:11–16)

It is apparent that Mary's overriding concern at this moment is worry as to where the Savior's body has been taken. After turning away from the tomb and the two angels therein, she sees a man whom she assumes is the caretaker. The question comes up as to why she did not immediately recognize Jesus. Several possibilities exist. One is that she had been crying and was so distraught that she didn't even take a good look at Jesus at first. Another possibility is that she hadn't turned all the way around from the tomb. She "turned herself back" from the tomb and the angels in verse 14, yet she "turned herself" in verse 16, implying that she had not turned completely toward where Jesus was standing when she first turned from the tomb. Whatever the explanation, when Jesus said "Mary," she recognized His voice, apparently looked again, and her sorrow was over.

17 Jesus saith unto her, Touch me not; for I am not yet ascended to my Father: but go to my brethren, and say unto them, I ascend unto my Father, and your Father; and to my God, and your God. (John 20:17)

> 17 Jesus saith unto her, *Hold* me not; for I am not yet ascended to my Father; but go to my brethren, and say unto them, I ascend unto my Father, and your Father; and to my God, and your God. (JST, John 20:17)

18 Mary Magdalene came and told the disciples that she had seen the Lord, and that he had spoken these things unto her. (John 20:17)

Other Women See the Lord

Sometime in the course of events on this momentous day, the Savior appeared to the women who had come to the tomb earlier that morning, and they were allowed to touch His feet.

9 And as they went to tell his disciples, behold, Jesus met them, saying, All hail [*a greeting*]. And they came and held him by the feet, and worshipped him. (Matthew 28:9)

Two on the Way to Emmaus

Luke tells about two disciples who were sadly disappointed in the death of Jesus and were discussing their feelings that He apparently was not all He claimed to be as they walked to the town of Emmaus. It is a fascinating account of the role of true doctrine about Christ and the witness of the Holy Ghost in the conversion process.

> 13 And, behold, two of them [*two of Christ's disciples, not Apostles*] went that same day to a village called Emmaus, which was from Jerusalem about three-score furlongs [*about seven miles from Jerusalem*].
> 14 And they talked together of all these things which had happened.
> 15 And it came to pass, that, while they communed together and reasoned, Jesus himself drew near, and went [*started walking*] with them.
> 16 But their eyes were holden that they should not know him. [*Jesus kept them from recognizing Him yet.*]
> 17 And he said unto them, What manner of communications are these that ye have one to another, as ye walk, and are sad [*what are you talking about that makes you so sad*]?
> 18 And the one of them, whose name was Cleopas, answering said unto him, Art thou only a stranger in Jerusalem, and hast not known the things which are come to pass therein these days? [*You must have just arrived or You would know the tragic things which have happened here in recent days.*]
> 19 And he said unto them, What things? And they said unto him, Concerning Jesus of Nazareth, which [*who*] was a prophet mighty in deed and word [*powerful in actions and teaching*] before God and all the people:
> 20 And how the chief priests and our rulers delivered him [*turned Him over*] to be condemned to death, and have crucified him. (Luke 24:13–20)

As these two disciples of the Master continue chatting with this Stranger who has joined them, you can feel their disappointment as they express to Him their dashed hopes.

> 21 But we trusted that it had been he which should have redeemed Israel [*we were hoping that He would turn out to be the promised Messiah who would free us from our enemies*]: and beside all this, to day is the third day since these things were done [*and besides that, it has been three days now since He was crucified*]. (Luke 24:21)

We see from verses 22–24, next, that these two disciples were among "all the rest" in Luke 24:9 when the breathless women excitedly told the eleven Apostles and others what the angels at the tomb had told them.

> 22 Yea, and certain women also of our company [*of our group of followers of Jesus*] made us astonished [*told us an amazing story*], which were early at the sepulchre [*who went to the tomb early this morning*];

23 And when they found not his body, they came, saying, that they had also seen a vision of angels, which [*who*] said that he was alive.

24 And certain of them [*Peter and John—see John 20:2–8*] which were with us went to the sepulchre, and found it even so as the women had said [*found the tomb empty, just like the women said*]: but him they saw not [*but Peter and John didn't see Christ*]. (Luke 24:22–24)

The implication here is that since Peter and John didn't see Jesus, and the women's account couldn't be trusted because of the emotional state they were in, the whole thing about Jesus has turned out to be a big disappointment for these two disciples on the road to Emmaus. Watch now as the resurrected Christ uses the power of the scriptures and true doctrine to teach a firm lesson on faith, reminding these disappointed disciples of the numerous prophecies in the Old Testament which match what has just happened.

25 Then he said unto them, O fools, and slow of heart to believe all that the prophets [*such as Isaiah and Jeremiah*] have spoken:

26 Ought not Christ to have suffered these things, and to enter into his glory? [*In other words, why is it so hard to believe that Jesus was the Christ, and that He suffered, died, was resurrected, and has entered into His glory in heaven?*]

27 And beginning at Moses and all the prophets [*starting with the writings of Moses (Genesis, Exodus, Leviticus, Numbers and Deuteronomy) and continuing with the other Old Testament prophets*], he expounded unto them [*taught them*] in all the scriptures the things concerning himself.

28 And they drew nigh [*near*] unto the village [*Emmaus*], whither they went [*which was their destination*]: and he made as though he would have gone further [*indicated that He was going to go farther*].

29 But they constrained him [*begged Him*], saying, Abide [*stay*] with us: for it is toward evening, and the day is far spent. And he went in to tarry [*stay*] with them.

30 And it came to pass, as he sat at meat [*supper*] with them, he took bread, and blessed it, and brake, and gave to them.

31 And their eyes were opened, and they knew him; and he vanished out of their sight. (Luke 24:25–31)

Next, we see that the witness of the Holy Ghost had become active during the time that the Savior was teaching them.

32 And they said one to another, Did not our heart burn within us, while he talked with us by the way [*along the way*], and while he opened [*explained*] to us the scriptures?

33 And they rose up the same hour, and returned to Jerusalem, and found the eleven gathered together, and them [*other members*] that were with them,

34 Saying, The Lord is risen indeed, and hath appeared to Simon [*Peter*].

35 And they [*the two disciples to whom Jesus had appeared on the way to Emmaus*] told what things were done in the way [*as they walked along the road*], and how he

411

was known of them in breaking of bread [*how they finally recognized Jesus when He served them supper*]. (Luke 24:25–35)

Christ Appears to Many Gathered in Jerusalem

Later on Sunday evening, a number of disciples had gathered in a room in Jerusalem (John 20:19) and were discussing the events and personal experiences of the day (Luke 24:34). The two disciples returned from Emmaus, entered the room, and excitedly told of the appearance of the Savior to them (Luke 24:13–35). While they were reporting their experience, the Lord Himself appeared. From what took place next, we gain knowledge about resurrected bodies and we are given yet another lesson on the necessity of the Atonement.

36 And as they thus spake, Jesus himself stood in the midst of them, and saith unto them, Peace be unto you.

37 But they were terrified and affrighted, and supposed that they had seen a spirit [*thought they were seeing a ghost*].

38 And he said unto them, Why are ye troubled? and why do thoughts arise in your hearts?

39 Behold [*look at*] my hands and my feet, that it is I myself: handle me, and see; for a spirit hath not flesh and bones, as ye see me have.

40 And when he had thus spoken, he shewed them his hands and his feet. (Luke 24:36–40)

A major doctrine is taught in verses 39–40, above, namely that the Savior now has a resurrected body of flesh and bone. The same is true of the Father. The Doctrine and Covenants confirms this.

22 The Father has a body of flesh and bones as tangible as man's; the Son also; but the Holy Ghost has not a body of flesh and bones, but is a personage of Spirit. Were it not so, the Holy Ghost could not dwell in us. (D&C 130:22)

Among other doctrines given next, as the Master demonstrates that He is not a ghost, we find that resurrected beings can eat mortal food.

41 And while they yet believed not for joy [*they were so happy they could hardly believe what was happening*], and wondered [*marveled*], he said unto them, Have ye here any meat [*do you have any food*]?

42 And they gave him a piece of a broiled fish, and of an honeycomb.

43 And he took it, and did eat before them [*before their eyes*].

44 And he said unto them, These are [*this is what I meant by*] the words which I spake unto you, while I was yet with you, that all things must be fulfilled, which were written in the law of Moses, and in the prophets, and in the psalms [*in other words, the Old Testament*], concerning me. (Luke 24:41–44)

The Savior now teaches a concise summary of His mission and Atonement.

45 Then opened he their understanding, that they might understand the scriptures, [*then He taught them.*]

46 And said unto them, Thus it is written, and thus it behoved Christ to suffer [*Christ had to suffer*], and to rise from the dead the third day:

47 And that repentance and remission of sins should be preached in his name among all nations, beginning at Jerusalem. [*The Atonement had to be accomplished, in order that repentance and remission of sins could be made available to all people, beginning at Jerusalem.*]

48 And ye are witnesses of these things.

49 And, behold, I send the promise of my Father upon you: but tarry ye [*wait*] in the city of Jerusalem, until ye be endued with [*clothed with, endowed with*] power from on high. (Luke 24:45–49)

Thomas Doubts

One of the eleven Apostles, Thomas, was absent when the Savior appeared to the others and invited them to feel His hands and feet (Luke 24:36–39). Upon being told about the marvelous manifestation experienced by the others, Thomas refused to believe it (John 20:24–25). Eight days later, the Lord appeared to them again and mercifully invited Thomas to have a similar experience.

26 And after eight days again his disciples were within [*inside the house*], and Thomas with them: then came Jesus, the doors being shut, and stood in the midst, and said, Peace be unto you.

27 Then saith he to Thomas, Reach hither [*here*] thy finger, and behold [*look at*] my hands; and reach hither thy hand, and thrust it into my side: and be not faithless, but believing.

28 And Thomas answered and said unto him, My Lord and my God.

29 Jesus saith unto him, Thomas, because thou hast seen me, thou hast believed: blessed are they that have not seen, and yet have believed. (John 20:26–29)

Others Were Resurrected with the Savior

We are taught that all of the righteous, who are worthy of celestial glory, from Adam and Eve down to the time of the Savior's resurrection, were resurrected with Him. This would include John the Baptist. Speaking of the resurrection at the time of Christ's resurrection, the Doctrine and Covenants teaches:

54 Yea, and Enoch also, and they who were with him; the prophets who were before him; and Noah also, and they who were before him; and Moses also, and they who were before him;

55 And from Moses to Elijah, and from Elijah to John [*the Baptist*], who were with Christ in his resurrection, and the holy apostles, with Abraham, Isaac, and Jacob, shall be in the presence of the Lamb. (D&C 133:54–55)

The Lord Meets the Apostles in Galilee

The Master had told the Apostles to meet Him in Galilee (Matthew 26:32), and the faithful women who had seen the angels at the empty tomb had been instructed to remind them that they were to go to Galilee where the Master would meet them (Mark 16:7). No doubt with this in mind, after a few days in Jerusalem, Peter and the others left for Galilee. When they arrived by the Sea of Galilee, Peter said "I go a fishing" and the others went with him (John 21:3).

> 1 After these things Jesus shewed [*showed*] himself again to the disciples at the sea of Tiberias [*the Sea of Galilee*]; and on this wise shewed he himself [*and this is how He showed himself to them*].
> 2 There were together Simon Peter, and Thomas called Didymus, and Nathanael of Cana in Galilee, and the sons of Zebedee [*James and John*], and two other of his disciples.
> 3 Simon Peter saith unto them, I go a fishing. They say unto him, We also go with thee. They went forth, and entered into a ship immediately; and that night they caught nothing. (John 21:1–3)

In the days of Jesus, it was common for fishermen to fish at night on the Sea of Galilee, when the fishing was best. Peter, having been a professional fisherman on that lake before the Savior said "come follow me," has now taken his fellow disciples and they have fished all night with absolutely no success. The sons of Zebedee, verse 2 above, were James and John, and they, too, had been professional fishermen, before being called by Jesus to follow Him. It must have been extra frustrating for these professionals to have zero success fishing. Watch now as the Savior gets their attention. Perhaps it is appropriate to imagine a bit of a smile on His face and a twinkle in His eye.

> 4 But when the morning was now come, Jesus stood on the shore: but the disciples knew not that it was Jesus. [*He was apparently far enough away that they didn't recognize Him.*]
> 5 Then Jesus saith unto them, Children, have ye any meat [*have you caught any fish*]? They answered him, No.
> 6 And he said unto them, Cast the net on the right side of the ship, and ye shall find. They cast therefore, and now they were not able to draw it [*bring it in*] for the multitude [*because of the large number*] of fishes. (John 21:4–6)

As already mentioned, these tired disciples had had absolutely no success fishing throughout the night. This stranger on the shore had asked them if they had had any luck. He then told them to simply cast their net overboard on the other side of the ship. Perhaps there are few things more irritating to professionals than having a stranger tell them how to do their work. Nevertheless, they did what He said and, as John says, suddenly the net filled with so many fish (153 big fish, see verse 11) that they could hardly pull it in.

This sounds familiar. An almost identical thing had happened three years ago when Jesus first called Peter, Andrew, James, and John (see Luke 5:1–11). Jesus had come by, and because of the crowd, had requested that Peter take Him a little way out from the shore in his ship. When He was through speaking to the crowd, He told Peter to go out farther into the lake and let down his nets. Peter replied that they had fished all night with no success, but, since Jesus said to do it, he did. Their net filled with so many fish that it began to break. James and John quickly brought their ship out to help, and the large number of fish almost sank both ships. Now, the same thing is happening again. Could it be the Master who is on the shore now?

> 7 Therefore that disciple whom Jesus loved [*in other words, John, the Beloved Apostle*] saith unto Peter, It is the Lord. Now when Simon Peter heard that it was the Lord, he girt his fisher's coat unto him, (for he was naked [*stripped to the waist*],) and did cast himself into the sea [*Peter jumped in and swam to shore, a distance of about 300 feet—see verse 8*].
> 8 And the other disciples came in a little ship; (for they were not far from land, but as it were two hundred cubits [*about a hundred yards*],) dragging the net with fishes.
> 9 As soon then as they were come to land, they saw a fire of coals there, and fish laid thereon, and bread. (John 21:7–9)

This is a very touching scene. No one could be busier than the Savior. Yet He had taken the time to cook breakfast for His weary, discouraged disciples who had fished all night with no success.

> 10 Jesus saith unto them, Bring of the fish which ye have now caught.
> 11 Simon Peter went up, and drew the net to land full of great [*large*] fishes, an hundred and fifty and three: and for all there were so many, yet was not the net broken. (John 21:10–11)

There is symbolism here. Jesus told the Apostles, when He called them, that He would make them "fishers of men" (Matthew 4:19). The fact that the Savior helped them have such success with actual fish is symbolic of the fact that He will help them have great success in bringing souls into the gospel net and unto the Father.

> 12 Jesus saith unto them, Come and dine. And none of the disciples durst ask him, Who art thou? knowing that it was the Lord.
> 13 Jesus then cometh, and taketh bread, and giveth them, and fish likewise.
> 14 This is now the third time that Jesus shewed himself to his disciples, after that he was risen from the dead. (John 21:12–14)

The Savior's Ascension into Heaven

After continuing to instruct and teach His Apostles and disciples for forty days after His resurrection (Acts 1:3), the time finally came for His ascension into Heaven. Luke tells us that He took His disciples to Bethany and then was taken up (Luke 24:50–53). Later, Luke, who also wrote Acts, records a few more details of His departure from the disciples into heaven.

> 9 And when he had spoken these things, while they beheld, he was taken up; and a cloud received him out of their sight.
>
> 10 And while they looked stedfastly toward heaven as he went up, behold, two men stood by them in white apparel;
>
> 11 Which also said, Ye men of Galilee, why stand ye gazing up into heaven? this same Jesus, which is taken up from you into heaven, shall so come in like manner as ye have seen him go into heaven. (Acts 1:9–11)

An so it is that He will come again, "in power and great glory" (D&C 56:18), at the time of the Second Coming.

CHAPTER 15

THE CLEANSING AND HEALING
POWER OF THE ATONEMENT

In this chapter, the emphasis will be on the marvelous and miraculous power of the Atonement of Jesus Christ to cleanse and heal, such that we can press forward in our lives with bright hope and optimism, having been "born again" (John 3:3–5) through Christ. Many examples and applications from real life situations that I have encountered over the years will be used, and the discussion will often tend to be somewhat informal. While several examples will show the effectiveness of correct application of the Atonement, some will be given that demonstrate unnecessary prolonging of pain and remorse that comes from misunderstanding.

WHO REMEMBERS SINS NO MORE?

Many years ago a student lingered at the end of one of the seminary classes I was teaching. It was obvious that she had a question and desired privacy in which to ask it. After the other students had left the room, she quietly asked if it was true that once you have been forgiven, you won't remember the sin anymore. Her concern was the same as that of many other students and members over the years who have asked the same basic question: "Is it true that, once you have been forgiven, you will no longer remember the sin?" The answer is no. Such an incorrect belief can be a very discouraging and damaging false doctrine.

As she continued, she explained that one of her teachers some time ago in a church class had taught that as long as we can remember a sin, it is evidence that we have not yet been forgiven. I gently asked her if she remembered Alma in the Book of Mormon and how he had recounted his rebellion days to his son Helaman (Alma 36). She had studied the Book of Mormon in a previous seminary year and did remember. I invited her to turn with me to Alma 36, and we read some of the verses together, including:

12 But I was racked with eternal torment, for my soul was harrowed up to the greatest degree and racked with all my sins.

13 Yea, I did remember all my sins and iniquities, for which I was tormented with the pains of hell; yea, I saw that I had rebelled against my God, and that I had not kept his holy commandments.

14 Yea, and I had murdered many of his children, or rather led them away unto destruction; yea, and in fine so great had been my iniquities, that the very thought of coming into the presence of my God did rack my soul with inexpressible horror.

15 Oh, thought I, that I could be banished and become extinct both soul and body, that I might not be brought to stand in the presence of my God, to be judged of my deeds.

16 And now, for three days and for three nights was I racked, even with the pains of a damned soul. (Alma 36:12–16)

After we read these verses, I asked her if she thought Alma could still remember his sins, long after he had been forgiven. With a look of relief on her face, she answered that he obviously could. We then turned to Mosiah in the Book of Mormon where we are told that Alma had become president of the Church among the Nephites (Mosiah 29:42). We also turned to Alma (45:18–19) where Helaman suggests that Alma was taken up to heaven. The point of turning to these verses, of course, was to point out that Alma the Younger was without a doubt completely forgiven. The Atonement had cleansed him and healed him spiritually, yet he could remember the past. Having established that point, we then returned to Alma 36 to see what it was that he could no longer "remember." We read:

17 And it came to pass that as I was thus racked with torment, while I was harrowed up by the memory of my many sins, behold, I remembered also to have heard my father prophesy unto the people concerning the coming of one Jesus Christ, a Son of God, to atone for the sins of the world.

18 Now, as my mind caught hold upon this thought, I cried within my heart: O Jesus, thou Son of God, have mercy on me, who am in the gall of bitterness, and am encircled about by the everlasting chains of death.

19 And now, behold, when I thought this, I could remember my pains no more; yea, I was harrowed up by the memory of my sins no more. (Alma 36:17–19)

Did you catch the answer in verse 19? She did. It was the pain and constant agony of soul, the lack of peace and tranquility that were no longer present in his life. He could remember his sins, and even the pain he experienced because of them. But, he "could remember his pain no more," meaning, in context, that the pain was gone and no longer plagued him constantly. We then read carefully to see what replaced this pain and anguish of soul in Alma.

> 20 And oh, what joy, and what marvelous light I did behold; yea, my soul was filled with joy as exceeding as was my pain!
> 21 Yea, I say unto you, my son, that there could be nothing so exquisite and so bitter as were my pains. Yea, and again I say unto you, my son, that on the other hand, there can be nothing so exquisite and sweet as was my joy.
> 22 Yea, methought I saw, even as our father Lehi saw, God sitting upon his throne, surrounded with numberless concourses of angels, in the attitude of singing and praising their God; yea, and my soul did long to be there.
> 23 But behold, my limbs did receive their strength again, and I stood upon my feet, and did manifest unto the people that I had been born of God.
> 24 Yea, and from that time even until now, I have labored without ceasing, that I might bring souls unto repentance; that I might bring them to taste of the exceeding joy of which I did taste; that they might also be born of God, and be filled with the Holy Ghost. (Alma 36:20–24)

Did you see the things that replaced his pain? "Joy" (v. 20), "marvelous light" (v. 20), "soul was filled with joy" (v.20), "exquisite and sweet . . . joy" (v.21), his "soul did long to be" with God (v. 22), "exceeding joy" (v. 24).

Having discussed the marvelous cleansing and healing that comes through the Atonement of Jesus Christ, which replaces torment and anguish of soul upon repenting, we considered possible sources for the false belief that, when truly forgiven, one remembers the sins no more. We concluded that one possibility for this sometimes tragic misunderstanding might be that people take D&C 58:42, which applies to the Lord, and misapply it to us instead.

> 42 Behold, he who has repented of his sins, the same is forgiven, and I, the Lord, remember them no more.
> 43 By this ye may know if a man repenteth of his sins—behold, he will confess them and forsake them. (D&C 58:42–43)

It is the Lord who will remember our sins "no more." And we are the ones who will remember our "pains no more," meaning, in the context of Alma's statement, that the painful conscience pangs of serious sin will no longer plague us. It is the Lord who will not bring our sins up to us anymore, including on Judgment Day. It is we who are blessed by the Atonement to not have our sins "harrow up" (or tear up) our daily peace and hope for the future with God.

At the conclusion of our chat, my student left, much relieved and appreciating the pure doctrine taught by the Savior, that the truth will set us free from many types of burdens, including the bondage of misunderstanding.

32 And ye shall know the truth, and the truth shall make you free. (John 8:32)

The truth for this student on that occasion, and for all of us, is that through the Atonement of Jesus Christ, we can be cleansed, healed, and have newness of life, while still remembering our past sins as a deterrent against repeating them.

A RATHER WONDERFUL PROBLEM

Over the course of my service as a bishop and also over many years of serving as a stake president, I often ran into a rather wonderful problem associated with the cleansing and healing power of the Atonement. The story went something like this: An individual had committed serious sin and, as a result, had lost membership in the Church through appropriate disciplinary action. In the course of sincere, deep repentance, with the required "godly sorrow" spoken of by Paul (2 Corinthians 7:10), the individual had eventually been rebaptized. Temple blessings had been restored, and great peace and joy had come into the heart and soul.

However, some months following the joys of their rebaptism, restoration of blessings, and full membership privileges and blessings, a few of these wonderful Saints would come into my office deeply concerned about their standing before God. In each case, the conversation went something like this:

> "I thought I was doing so well, but now I see so many things in my life that need fixing. I didn't even notice them before, but now they are everywhere! It has become very discouraging."

My response was, "Great!" As you can imagine, that response was completely unexpected and made the individual wonder if I had failed to understand what had just been said to me. I quickly continued the conversation by explaining that now that these faithful Saints were doing so well, the Holy Ghost was pointing out things that they had failed to notice before. They were being given more light and knowledge by the Spirit than ever before. As a result, they were seeing smaller things in their lives that needed attention. They were being "fine tuned" to be comfortable in the presence of God. Thus, what was happening to them now was a very good sign that they were making wonderful progress. There is a verse of scripture in the Book of Mormon, in the account of Lehi's dream, which explains this process.

20 And I also beheld a strait and narrow path, which came along by the rod of iron, even to the tree by which I stood; and it also led by the head of the fountain, unto a large and spacious field, as if it had been a world. (1 Nephi 8:20)

Have you ever noticed that *strait* and *narrow* are basically the same thing? *Strait* means "narrow," and, of course, *narrow* means "narrow." Years ago, a colleague of mine pointed out to us in a faculty meeting that the phrase "strait and narrow path" means, in effect, "narrow and narrowing path." He continued, explaining that the path leading back to God is narrow, requiring specific righteous choices and obedience in order to remain firmly on it. As we progress and draw closer to God, we tend to make the path along which we are walking toward Him narrower and narrower. In other words, we watch our words and thoughts and deeds (Mosiah 4:30) more carefully, trying to be more Christlike. We don't allow ourselves to do things that are "on the edge" or questionable, nearly as much as we used to. As we tighten our obedience to God's commandments and to the promptings of the Holy Ghost, we receive more light and knowledge from above, which serve to illuminate our path more brightly. Thus, things in our lives show up that we hadn't even noticed before. Rather than being discouraged by this, we can look upon it as a sign that we are making significant progress toward returning home to our Father in Heaven.

WHAT ABOUT THE ABUSED AND THE ABUSERS?

Another situation that came up in the course of many years of serving as a judge in Israel was that of serious abuse. The individual, who had gone through the repentance process, including Church disciplinary action, and had returned in the course of time to full membership privileges, would say, in effect, "I felt so good, but now I realize that I can't ever be completely forgiven." When I asked why, the response was basically, "Because of the damage I did to others. They are still struggling because of what I did. I don't think they will ever recover."

This conversation does bring up some serious questions. What about victims of grievous sin? What about the sinner who committed the abuse? Can the Atonement cleanse and heal both? The answer to the last question is yes. The answer is rooted in the fact that God is completely fair. He is just (Mosiah 3:18). Our modern prophets have clearly taught that victims of someone's grievous sin are not guilty of sin themselves.

Victims of abuse should seek help immediately, normally from their bishop or branch president. His first responsibility is to help those who have been abused and to protect those who may be vulnerable to future abuse.

Victims of abuse should be assured that they are not to blame for the harmful behavior of others. They do not need to feel guilt. If they have been a victim of rape or other sexual abuse, whether they have been abused by an acquaintance, a stranger, or even a family member, victims of sexual abuse are not guilty of sexual sin. (Church Web Page, lds.org/Gospel Library/Gospel Topics, under "Abuse.")

Furthermore, our modern prophets and Apostles have also taught that those guilty of committing abuse can be forgiven, through deep and sincere repentance.

Those who have been abusive in any relationship are urged to repent of their sin, to plead with the Lord for forgiveness, and to ask for forgiveness from those who have been harmed. Those who have been abusive should also speak with their bishop or branch president so he can help them through the repentance process and, if necessary, help them receive additional counseling or other assistance. Part of the repentance process may also include accepting whatever penalties are imposed by law. (Church Web Page, lds.org/Gospel Library/Gospel Topics, under "Abuse.")

What if victims of abuse are unable to fully recover and heal in this life? The answer, in the context of the plan of salvation, is that God is completely fair, and they will be healed when they die and arrive in the world of departed spirits. Then, they will be given completely fair opportunities to understand, accept, and live the gospel under normal circumstances, if they so choose, before Judgment Day. The doctrine that victims of abuse and other heinous sins and deception will "be reclaimed" is clearly taught in the Doctrine and Covenants.

7 Behold, verily I say unto you, there are hypocrites among you, who have deceived some, which has given the adversary power; but behold such shall be reclaimed. (D&C 50:7)

Can you imagine the comfort that this sweet doctrine brought into the hearts of the members who came to my office once again burdened by what they had done, yet had been forgiven of? The major message here is that the Atonement of Jesus Christ is infinite. Indeed, it can and does take care of things we cannot repair ourselves. Thus, burdens too heavy to bear are lifted by the Savior from the victim, and can be lifted from the abuser.

BUT BISHOP, I DID CONFESS

An obstacle to being cleansed and healed by the Savior's Atonement some-times comes in the form illustrated in the next example. A person is in the bishop's office, saying, "But bishop, I did confess the sin. What more do you want? My friend in another ward did the same thing I did, and his bishop didn't place any restrictions on him or make him do any more formal repenting after he confessed. I think you ought to give me back my temple recommend so I can attend my cousin's temple wedding next Friday."

What is missing? Many things, but especially the humility and change of heart that come with godly sorrow. Unfortunately, some members of the Church, and indeed, some members of other Christian faiths, have the mis-taken idea that confession of sins committed is all that is required for forgive-ness. Depending on the individual, confession can include deep sorrow and desire for change, or, it can merely be lip-service, following the letter of the law with no internal motivation for change. Successful change and rebirth (being "born again") are often accompanied by pain, without which true change is not made. Listen to what Paul says about this, as he teaches us how to qualify for the gift of the Atonement. Pay special attention to verses 4 and 6.

> 4 Therefore we are buried with him by baptism into death: that like as Christ was raised up from the dead by the glory of the Father, even so we also should walk in newness of life [*the symbolism of baptism includes burying our old selves and coming forth out of the water as a new person with new opportunities, through the Savior's Atonement*].
> 5 For if we have been planted together in the likeness of his death, we shall be also in the likeness of his resurrection:
> 6 Knowing this, that our old man [*our old way of being*] is crucified [*the use of* crucified *here implies that pain accompanies true change*] with him, that the body of sin might be destroyed [*that our sins might be done away with*], that henceforth we should not serve sin. (Romans 6:4–6)

In 2 Corinthians, Paul refers to the beneficial pain that accompanies sin as "godly sorrow." We will read his words about this in a moment, but first, a com-ment about rescuing individuals prematurely from the consequences of their sinful behaviors. It is sometimes tempting for parents to "rescue" their children too soon from the consequences of sin and misbehavior, before the consequences can create needed change. They sometimes intervene when their child has mis-behaved at school or elsewhere, taking the side of the errant child against the authorities who are responsible to administer the needed discipline. Thus, the parents stand in the way of appropriate consequences and train their offspring to avoid beneficial change. While serving as a stake president, I counseled our bishops to avoid rescuing members of their wards too soon, which could minimize or nullify the beneficial effects of godly sorrow.

Let's read now and see what Paul taught concerning godly sorrow. We will add a number of comments and explanations within and between the verses.

10 For godly sorrow worketh repentance to salvation [*causes us to repent and thus enables us to obtain exaltation*] not to be repented of [*and leaves us with no regrets*]: but the sorrow of the world [*being sorry you got caught, or sorry because you are embarrassed, or sorry that your opportunity to continue committing that sin has been taken away*] worketh death [*leads to spiritual death*].

Next, Paul describes some components of godly sorrow which make it so wonderfully effective in cleansing us from sin and leading us to change and becoming more righteous.

11 For behold this selfsame thing [*this godly sorrow, the very thing I'm teaching you about, namely*], that ye sorrowed [*were sorry for sins*] after a godly sort [*in the way God wants you to be*], what carefulness [*sincerity, anxiety*] it wrought [*caused*] in you, yea, what clearing of yourselves [*eagerness to become clear of the sin*], yea, what indignation [*irritation, anger at yourself for committing the sin*], yea, what fear [*alarm*], yea, what vehement desire [*strong desire to change*], yea, what zeal [*enthusiasm to change*], yea, what revenge [*punishment; suffering whatever is necessary to make permanent change*]! In all things ye have approved yourselves to be clear in this matter [*in everything you have done you have demonstrated that you understand the principle of godly sorrow*].

When a person has godly sorrow, it makes no difference what another bishop requires of one of his members, or what another person does under seemingly similar circumstances. It makes no difference what else is required. The person humbly faces his or her own sins head on and, with the help of the Savior's Atonement, does whatever is required to be set free of the bondage of sin and "walk in newness of life (Romans 6:4).

THE SCOPE OF THE SAVIOR'S ATONEMENT

Does It Work for Other Worlds Also?

This is a question asked often by students and members throughout the years. The answer is yes, and lies in the fact that the Atonement of Jesus Christ is the central theme of the universe! Moses points out to us that all things bear testimony of Christ.

63 And behold, all things have their likeness, and all things are created and made to bear record of me, both things which are temporal, and things which are spiritual; things which are in the heavens above, and things which are on the

earth, and things which are in the earth, and things which are under the earth, both above and beneath: all things bear record of me. (Moses 6:63)

How many worlds has our Savior created for the Father, and how many of them benefit from His Atonement? Again, the answers are found in the scriptures. First, let's consider how many other worlds are out there. Another way of putting it might be, is there life in outer space?

33 And worlds without number have I created; and I also created them for mine own purpose; and by the Son I created them, which is mine Only Begotten.
35 But only an account of this earth, and the inhabitants thereof, give I unto you. For behold, there are many worlds that have passed away by the word of my power. And there are many that now stand, and innumerable are they unto man; but all things are numbered unto me, for they are mine and I know them. (Moses 1:33 and 35)

The answer is that our Savior has created "worlds without number," and there is indeed life in outer space, since there are "many worlds . . . that now stand." Next, the question is whether or not our Savior's Atonement works for the inhabitants of all of these other worlds. The Doctrine and Covenants has the answer. Bearing their witness of the Savior, Joseph Smith and Sidney Rigdon taught:

22 And now, after the many testimonies which have been given of him, this is the testimony, last of all, which we give of him: That he lives!
23 For we saw him, even on the right hand of God; and we heard the voice bearing record that he is the Only Begotten of the Father—
24 That by him, and through him, and of him, the worlds are and were created, and the inhabitants thereof are begotten sons and daughters unto God. (D&C 76:22–24)

Did you see the answer to whether or not our Savior's Atonement works for other worlds also, as found in verse 24, above? It lies in the phrase, "and the inhabitants thereof [*of all the other worlds*] are begotten sons and daughters unto God." What does "begotten sons and daughters unto God" mean? Simply that "by him and through him," all of the inhabitants of those other worlds can be brought back unto God the Father to live with Him forever, if they, too, live the gospel. Since we are all "begotten sons and daughters" *of* the Father, as spirit children (see Proclamation on the Family, para. 2), becoming "begotten sons and daughters *unto* God" (italics added for emphasis) means being brought back into the presence of the Father through the Atonement of Jesus Christ. Thus, the Atonement that the Savior worked out upon our world works also for the inhabitants of all of Heavenly Father's worlds, past, present, and future.

Some might question whether or not the above interpretation of D&C 76:24 is correct. The Prophet Joseph Smith wrote a poetic version of section 76 of the Doctrine and Covenants, which was published in Nauvoo, Illinois, in February 1843 (published in the *Times and Seasons*, vol. 4, February 1, 1843, pages 82–85). The lines which correspond to D&C 76:24 are as follows:

19 And I heard a great voice, bearing record from heav'n,

He's the Saviour, and only begotten of God—

By him, of him, and through him, the worlds were all made,

Even all that career in the heavens so broad, [*the word* career *means to "course" or "orbit"*]

20 Whose inhabitants, too, from the first to the last, Are sav'd by the very same Savior of ours:

Once we understand the scope and reach of the Savior's infinite Atonement, the question sometimes arises as to whether or not He has to be born, raised, crucified, and resurrected on each of those other planets. The answer is no. The Doctrine and Covenants teaches that He will visit other worlds, which will include visiting them for their millenniums (D&C 88:51–61). Paul explained that we die but once (Hebrews 9:27).

For additional clarification on the doctrine that the Savior will visit other worlds for their millenniums, we will quote from the *Doctrine and Covenants Student Manual*, used by the Institutes of Religion of the Church. The quote is given in explanation of D&C 88:51–61.

Moses saw in vision that the Savior had created many worlds like this earth that were also inhabited (see Moses 1:27–29). The inhabitants of these worlds are sons and daughters of God and are precious in his sight. The Savior is responsible for these creations and visits them in their times and seasons. Elder Orson Pratt explained: "The Lord wanted to represent these kingdoms so that we could understand what he desired to impart, and he gave it as a parable, in order to assist our weak comprehensions. . . . Says the interrogator—"I do not comprehend this idea of the Lord's withdrawing from one and going to another." In order to comprehend this let us come back to our own globe. Do we not expect that the Lord will, by and by, come and visit us and stay a little while, about a thousand years. Yes, and then we shall be made glad with the joy of the countenance of our Lord. He will be among us, and will be our King, and he will reign as a King of kings and Lord of lords. He will have a throne in Zion, and another in the Temple at Jerusalem, and he will have with him the twelve disciples who were with him during his ministry at Jerusalem; and they will eat and drink with him at his table; and all the people of this globe who are counted worthy to be called Zion, the pure in heart, will be made glad by the countenance of their Lord for a thousand years, during which the earth will rest. Then what? He withdraws. What for? To fulfill other purposes; for he has other worlds or creations and other sons and daughters, perhaps just as good as those dwelling on this planet, and they, as well as we, will be visited, and they will be made glad with the countenance of their Lord. Thus he will go, in the time and in the season thereof, from kingdom to kingdom or from world to world, causing the pure in heart, the Zion that is taken from these creations, to rejoice in his presence.

"But there is another thing I want you to understand. This will not be kept up to all eternity, it is merely a preparation for something still greater. And what is that? By and by, when each of these creations has fulfilled the measure and bounds set and the times given for its continuance in a temporal state, it and its inhabitants who are worthy will be made celestial and glorified together. Then, from that time henceforth and for ever, there will be no intervening veil between God and his people who are sanctified and glorified, and he will not be under the necessity of withdrawing from one to go and visit another, because they will all be in his presence." (*Journal of Discourses*, 17:331–32) (*Doctrine and Covenants Student Manual*, p. 201)

And so it is that the doctrine is clear. The Savior's Atonement, which He carried out upon our earth, brings cleansing and healing and the opportunity for exaltation to all of the inhabitants of all of the Father's worlds who will humbly live the gospel of Jesus Christ.

How Completely Can the Atonement Cleanse and Heal?

For the answer to this, we will turn to the Old Testament and the teachings of Isaiah. His writings are rich in Atonement imagery and symbolism. Isaiah is the prophet who is most quoted by the Savior in the scriptures. We will use part of Isaiah, chapter 1, for our purposes here. Isaiah is speaking to the very wicked people of his own day. Some people feel that their sins are beyond the reach of the Atonement. If you feel this way or someone you know feels this way, listen carefully to Isaiah. Keep in mind that what we will be reading in verses 1–17 is background and setting for the marvelous truth taught in verse 18, which teaches:

18 Come now, and let us reason together, saith the LORD: though your sins be as scarlet, they shall be as white as snow; though they be red like crimson, they shall be as wool. (Isaiah 1:18)

Watch how wicked and depraved these people are, as we read from verse 2 through verse 15. And remember that Isaiah's message is that the Atonement can

OUR SAVIOR'S LIFE AND MISSION TO REDEEM AND GIVE HOPE

still work for them! We will include notes and commentary as we go along. First, in verse 2, the Lord states the problem.

> 2 Hear, O heavens, and give ear, O earth: for the Lord hath spoken, I have nourished and brought up children, and they have rebelled against me.
>
> 3 The ox knoweth his owner, and the ass his master's crib [*manger*]: but Israel doth not know [*know God*], my people doth not consider [*think seriously, in other words, Israel, animals are wiser than you are!*].
>
> 4 Ah sinful nation, a people laden with iniquity [*loaded down with wickedness*], a seed of evildoers, children that are corrupters: they have forsaken the Lord, they have provoked the Holy One of Israel unto anger, they are gone away backward [*retrogressing; they are "in the world" and "of the world"*].
>
> 5 Why should ye be stricken any more [*why do you keep asking for more punishment*]? ye will revolt more and more: the whole head [*leadership*] is sick, and the whole heart faint [*the people are diseased; in other words, spiritually sick*].

As Isaiah continues, the theme is that the whole nation is riddled with wickedness and is thus completely spiritually sick. He uses repetition to drive home that point.

> 6 From the sole of the foot even unto the head there is no soundness in it [*you are completely sick*]; but wounds, and bruises, and putrifying [*filled with spirit pus*] sores [*symbolically saying that the people are spiritually beaten down and infected with sin*]: they have not been closed, neither bound up, neither mollified with ointment [*you are sick and you don't even care; you won't try the simplest first aid (the Atonement of Christ)*].

Next, Isaiah uses a technique quite often used by Old Testament prophets. These great men of God often spoke prophetically of the future as if it had already happened. Watch as Isaiah uses this technique next, as he prophesies of the impending captivity of these wicked people.

> 7 Your country is desolate, your cities are burned with fire: your land, strangers [*foreigners*] devour it in your presence, and it is desolate as overthrown by strangers [*foreigners, specifically the Assyrians*].
>
> 8 And the daughter of Zion [*Israel*] is left as a cottage in a vineyard [*temporary, rather flimsy shade structure in the garden, built of straw and leaves*], as a lodge in a garden of cucumbers, as a besieged city [*your defense against your enemies is about as secure as a flimsy shade shack in a garden*].
>
> 9 Except the Lord of hosts had left unto us a very small remnant [*if God hadn't intervened and saved a few of Israel*], we should have been as Sodom, and we should have been like unto Gomorrah [*completely destroyed*].

Next, Isaiah asks these extremely wicked people why they even attempt to appear religious. First, he specifically addresses their leaders who are leading out in pursuing wickedness themselves.

10 Hear the word of the Lord, ye rulers of Sodom [*Listen up, you wicked leaders!*]; give ear unto the law of our God, ye people of Gomorrah [*Sodom and Gomorrah symbolize total wickedness*].

11 To what purpose is the multitude of your sacrifices unto me [*what good are your insincere, empty religious rituals*]? saith the Lord: I am full [*I've had it to here!*] of the burnt offerings of rams, and the fat of fed beasts; and I delight not in the blood of bullocks, or of lambs, or of he goats [*proper religious worship under the law of Moses*].

12 When ye come to appear before me, who hath required this at your hand, to tread my courts [*who authorized you hypocrites to act religious and worship Me*]?

13 Bring no more vain [*useless*] oblations [*offerings*]; incense is an abomination unto me; the new moons [*special Sabbath ritual at beginning of month—Bible Dictionary, under "New Moon"*] and sabbaths, the calling of assemblies, I cannot [*I can't stand it!*] away with; it is iniquity, even the solemn meeting [*solemn assembly*].

14 Your new moons and your appointed feasts [*your hypocritical worship*] my soul hateth: they are a trouble unto me; I am weary to bear them.

15 And when ye spread forth your hands [*when you pray*], I will hide mine eyes from you: yea, when ye make many prayers, I will not hear: your hands are full of blood [*bloodshed; murder—see Isaiah 1:21*].

Next, in spite of the gross wickedness of these people, as described by Isaiah, they are invited by a merciful Savior to repent and return to Him. The wonderful message here is that if you want to repent but you think your sins have put you beyond the reach of the Savior's Atonement, think again.

16 Wash you [*be baptized*], make you clean; put away the evil of your doings from before mine eyes [*repent*]; cease to do evil;

17 Learn to do well [*don't just cease to do evil, but replace evil with good*]; seek judgment [*be fair*], relieve the oppressed, judge the fatherless [*be kind and fair to them*], plead for [*stand up for, defend*] the widow.

Verse 18, next, is among the best known of all quotes from Isaiah. With verses 1–15 as a backdrop, this verse wonderfully and clearly teaches the power of the Atonement of Jesus Christ to cleanse and heal, completely.

18 Come now, and let us reason together, saith the Lord: though your sins be as scarlet [*cloth dyed with scarlet, a colorfast dye*], they shall be as white as snow [*even though you think your sins are "colorfast," the Atonement can cleanse you*]; though they be red like crimson, they shall be as wool [*a long process is required to get wool white, but it can be done*].

AT WHAT PRICE DID THE SAVIOR PROVIDE THIS CLEANSING AND HEALING?

What kind of a price did the Savior pay in order that sins we might consider to be "colorfast" can be "white as snow?" What did He go through so that "scarlet" sins, "crimson" sins, and daily smaller sins that nevertheless need cleansing, can be completely repented of? What price did He pay so that we can be completely cleansed and healed? Many scripture references answer this question. His suffering in the Garden of Gethsemane and on the cross are described, for example, in the Doctrine and Covenants:

> 15 Therefore I command you to repent—repent, lest I smite you by the rod of my mouth, and by my wrath, and by my anger, and your sufferings be sore—how sore you know not, how exquisite you know not, yea, how hard to bear you know not.
> 16 For behold, I, God, have suffered these things for all, that they might not suffer if they would repent;
> 17 But if they would not repent they must suffer even as I;
> 18 Which suffering caused myself, even God, the greatest of all, to tremble because of pain, and to bleed at every pore, and to suffer both body and spirit—and would that I might not drink the bitter cup, and shrink—
> 19 Nevertheless, glory be to the Father, and I partook and finished my preparations unto the children of men. (D&C 19:15–19)

One phrase, however, in a verse of scripture reminding us of what the Savior went through for us, seems not to be noticed by many. We will quote the verse here.

> 6 I gave my back to the smiter, and my cheeks to them that plucked off the hair. I hid not my face from shame and spitting. (2 Nephi 7:6; see also Isaiah 50:6)

The phrase is "my cheeks to them that plucked off the hair." Did you know that, among the cruel torture inflicted upon the Savior by His tormentors was that of pulling out His beard? This terrible abuse is discussed briefly by a Bible scholar in reference to Isaiah 50:6:

> In addition, the servant [*symbolizing Christ*] gave his cheeks to those who pluck out the hair. The reference is to those who deliberately give the most heinous and degrading of insults. The Oriental regarded the beard as a sign of freedom and respect, and to pluck out the hair of the beard (for *cheek* in effect would refer to a beard) is to show utter contempt. (Young, *The Book of Isaiah*, 1992, p. 300)

Thus, our Lord and Savior Jesus Christ went through incomprehensible and unfathomable suffering in order to give us the gift of cleansing and healing from our sins. One of the greatest expressions of gratitude to Him on our part is to accept His gift through repenting, such that the gift is fully effective in our lives. In somewhat of an understatement, Isaiah says that the Savior was "satisfied" by what His sacrifice did for us.

11 He [*Christ*] shall see of the travail of his soul [*His agony and suffering for us*], and shall be satisfied: by his knowledge shall my righteous servant justify [*save*] many; for he shall bear their iniquities. (Isaiah 53:11)

In a statement by the Savior Himself, we get the sense that He gets great satisfaction indeed in the results of His Atonement for us. He loves to be merciful and bless us with choice blessings. When we use our agency to qualify for the blessings of the Atonement, it enables Him to "delight" in blessing us.

5 For thus saith the Lord—I, the Lord, am merciful and gracious unto those who fear me, and delight to honor those who serve me in righteousness and in truth unto the end.
6 Great shall be their reward and eternal shall be their glory. (D&C 76:5–6)

Confidence before the Lord

As discussed at the beginning of this chapter, Alma describes the joy that replaces the pain of sin, once the Atonement has worked its miracle (Alma 36:19–24). One of the aspects of the Atonement's power to heal, that we did not mention at that time, is found in Alma 36:28. It is humble confidence in one's standing with the Lord, which allows us to plan on making it to exaltation. Pay close attention to what Alma says in the first phrase of this verse.

28 And I know that he will raise me up at the last day, to dwell with him in glory; yea, and I will praise him forever, for he has brought our fathers out of Egypt, and he has swallowed up the Egyptians in the Red Sea; and he led them by his power into the promised land; yea, and he has delivered them out of bondage and captivity from time to time. (Alma 36:28)

Allow the Atonement to Work for You

It was my observation as a bishop and stake president that sometimes members who had been involved in grievous sin did not feel worthy to feel so good, after they had gone through the requirements of repentance and had been cleansed by the Atonement. Perhaps it is one of Satan's effective tools to press the false notion upon such individuals that it is not fair to those who have not committed serious sin that they should join them in feeling worthy and whole. In fact, the false notion of not being worthy to feel good about one's spiritual standing with God, after appropriate repentance, regardless of the gravity of sins committed, seems to be far too prevalent. It is a vital step in the repentance process to accept the miracle of forgiveness from the Savior when He offers it. The devil would have us believe otherwise. Enos, in the Book of Mormon, was actually startled by how effective and complete the Atonement can be in cleansing and healing. His example is important. He simply accepted it, according to verse 6.

> 5 And there came a voice unto me, saying: Enos, thy sins are forgiven thee, and thou shalt be blessed.
> 6 And I, Enos, knew that God could not lie; wherefore, my guilt was swept away.
> 7 And I said: Lord, how is it done?
> 8 And he said unto me: Because of thy faith in Christ, whom thou hast never before heard nor seen. And many years pass away before he shall manifest himself in the flesh; wherefore, go to, thy faith hath made thee whole. (Enos 1:5–8)

At one point in King Benjamin's preparation for continuing to address his people, it appears that an angel addressed this issue of holding back a bit in fully accepting the cleansing and renewal provided by the Atonement. Pay close attention to the instructions of the angel to righteous King Benjamin. The message was given personally to the King, and was to be given by him to the people.

> 4 For the Lord hath heard thy prayers, and hath judged of thy righteousness, and hath sent me to declare unto thee that thou mayest rejoice; and that thou mayest declare unto thy people, that they may also be filled with joy. (Mosiah 3:4)

Did you see the message? It was "thou mayest rejoice." And he was to declare to his people that "they may also be filled with joy." Among other things, that message encourages us to allow the Atonement to work for us and to rejoice in its blessings upon us.

WHAT WOULD HAVE HAPPENED WITHOUT THE ATONEMENT?

The absolute necessity of the Atonement of Jesus Christ is pointed out by Jacob, in the Book of Mormon, as he instructs his people about how it works for them. Most of us are aware that without the Atonement, we would not be resurrected. But Jacob also points out that without it we would have become devils.

> 7 Wherefore, it must needs be an infinite atonement—save it should be an infinite atonement this corruption [*mortal body*] could not put on incorruption

[*could not be resurrected*]. Wherefore, the first judgment [*the Fall of Adam and Eve*] which came upon man must needs have remained to an endless duration [*without the Atonement, the effects of the Fall would have lasted forever*]. And if so, this flesh [*our mortal bodies*] must have laid down to rot and to crumble to its mother earth, to rise no more.

8 O the wisdom of God, his mercy and grace! For behold, if the flesh should rise no more our spirits must become [*would have become*] subject to that angel who fell from before the presence of the Eternal God, and became the devil, to rise no more.

9 And our spirits must have [*would have*] become like unto him, and we become devils, angels to a devil, to be shut out from the presence of our God, and to remain with the father of lies [*Satan*], in misery, like unto himself; yea, to that being who beguiled our first parents, who transformeth himself nigh unto an angel of light, and stirreth up the children of men unto secret combinations of murder and all manner of secret works of darkness. (2 Nephi 9:7–9)

"AFTER ALL WE CAN DO"

It is quite possible to become discouraged by overemphasizing a word in a wonderful verse in the Book of Mormon.

23 For we labor diligently to write, to persuade our children, and also our brethren, to believe in Christ, and to be reconciled to God; for we know that it is by grace that we are saved, after all we can do. (2 Nephi 25:23)

If we place undo emphasis on *all*, it can lead us to believe that we must be a "walking nervous breakdown" in order to be a faithful Latter-day Saint. However, if we emphasize *we*, it provides a healthy balance between what we can sincerely do with honest hearts, and the grace or help of the Savior that ultimately cleanses us from sin and enables us to return to the presence of the Father. Occasionally we meet members of the Church who get so caught up in trying to be perfect that they are forever serious, sad, and often depressed. They worry so much about their faults and imperfections that they fail to enjoy the journey. The Atonement, properly understood and accessed, enables us to find much happiness and enjoyment along the road through life, in spite of trials and tribulations along the way. The Prophet Joseph Smith reminded us that we are not expected to attain perfection during this life. In fact, he taught that it would be a great while after we die before we finish qualifying for exaltation.

When you climb up a ladder, you must begin at the bottom, and ascend step by step, until you arrive at the top; and so it is with the principles of the gospel—you must begin with the first, and go on until you learn all the principles of exaltation. But it will be a great while after you have passed through the veil before you will have learned them. It is not all to be comprehended in this world; it will be a great work to learn our salvation and exaltation even beyond the grave. (*TPJS*, p. 348)

Elder Dallin H. Oaks counseled members of the Church to avoid getting caught up in the discouragement that can accompany unrealistic goals for perfection in this life.

> Another idea that is powerful to lift us from discouragement is that the work of the Church…is an eternal work. Not all problems…are fixed in mortality. The work of salvation goes on beyond the veil of death, and we should not be too apprehensive about incompleteness within the limits of mortality. (Conference Report, "Powerful Ideas," October 1995)

WHAT MUST WE DO TO ENABLE THE SAVIOR TO MAKE US CLEAN?

We could go on for some time giving many correct answers, including keep the commandments, follow the Brethren, read the scriptures, say our prayers, serve one another, keep the Sabbath day holy, pay our tithing, be nice, and on and on. And each answer would be correct as a part of a wonderful body of commandments and teachings designed to promote our happiness here on earth as well as provide growth toward exaltation and lead us back into the presence of God. Since all faithful Saints and all who desire to become faithful are striving constantly to do these and many other good things, there must be some simple, basic answer that provides encouragement for the honest in heart, without being overwhelming. There must be some simple principle which gives us confidence that we can qualify to have the Savior make us clean. There is. It is the principle of improvement. It is taught in Alma. We often miss it as we study these verses because we are usually paying close attention to the dangers of procrastination.

> 33 And now, as I said unto you before, as ye have had so many witnesses, there-fore, I beseech of you that ye do not procrastinate the day of your repentance until the end; for after this day of life, which is given us to prepare for eternity, behold, if we do not improve our time while in this life, then cometh the night of darkness wherein there can be no labor performed.
> 36 And this I know, because the Lord hath said he dwelleth not in unholy temples, but in the hearts of the righteous doth he dwell; yea, and he has also said that the righteous shall sit down in his kingdom, to go no more out; but their garments should be made white through the blood of the Lamb. (Alma 34:33, 36)

The word *improve* in verse 33, above, becomes a key word. If we "do not improve," we are in trouble. On the other hand, if we continue improving, sincerely, we enable the Savior to make us clean through the Atonement (v. 36). Elder Marvin J. Ashton of the Quorum of the Twelve taught that the emphasis in the gospel of Christ is on direction and diligence, not necessarily on speed. He taught the importance of continuing improvement. In a general conference address, he taught:

> The speed with which we head along the strait and narrow path isn't as important as the direction in which we are traveling. (Conference Report, "On "Being Worthy," April 1989)

Being made clean, we are "spotless" (2 Nephi 33:7). Being spotless, we are allowed to be in the presence of God,

HOW GOOD DO WE HAVE TO BE?

Over the years, many students have asked how good we have to be at the end of this life in order to return to the presence of God. A question led to a discussion which served to lead to an answer. The question is this: In order to be in the presence of God, do you need to be "perfect," or do you need to be "spotless?" Before we answer this question, perhaps we should ask which of the following statements is correct:

1 "No imperfect thing can dwell in the presence of God."

or

2 "No unclean thing can dwell in the presence of God."

There are many scriptural references which will provide the correct answer for us, for example (italics added for emphasis):

> 21 Wherefore, if ye have sought to do wickedly in the days of your probation, then ye are found unclean before the judgment-seat of God; and *no unclean thing can dwell with God*; wherefore, ye must be cast off forever. (1 Nephi 10:21)

> 25 But behold, ye have rejected the truth, and rebelled against your holy God; and even at this time, instead of laying up for yourselves treasures *in heaven*, where nothing doth corrupt, and *where nothing can come which is unclean*, ye are heaping up for yourselves wrath against the day of judgment. (Helaman 8:25)

> 19 And *no unclean thing can enter into his kingdom*; therefore nothing entereth into his rest save it be those who have washed their garments in my blood, because of their faith, and the repentance of all their sins, and their faithfulness unto the end. (3 Nephi 27:19)

The answer, repeated over and over again in the scriptures, is that no *unclean* thing can return into the presence of God. In other words, we must be "spotless," not "perfect." This is very good news! It is summarized by Nephi as follows (italics added for emphasis):

> 7 I have charity for my people, and great faith in Christ that I shall meet *many souls spotless* at his judgment-seat. (2 Nephi 33:7)

If we get mixed up in our thinking between "spotless" and "perfect," and decide that we have to be perfect, it can lead to much discouragement and can lead some members to the point where they quit trying to live the gospel. With the help of the Savior and the Atonement, we can all get to the point where we can be made clean, or spotless, and thus qualify to enter back into the presence of God. Christ was the only one who was perfect during mortality, and perfection will come along in due time for us after we have passed through the veil.

In summary, the Atonement of Jesus Christ has infinite power to cleanse and heal. Without it, we would be completely, hopelessly lost. With it, we can "press forward with . . . a perfect brightness of hope" (2 Nephi 31:20) toward exaltation with God and Christ forever. We can be optimists. We have to be honestly striving to be righteous. We must participate in the saving ordinances of the gospel. No matter where we are along the path which leads to the presence of the Father, if we want to be good, and we are sincerely improving, then we enable the Savior to make us clean. And thus, we can meet Christ and be welcomed into His presence with the Father.

CHAPTER 16

THE RESURRECTED SAVIOR'S
APPEARANCE TO THE NEPHITES

In this chapter we will very briefly review the Savior's visit to the Nephites after His resurrection, as He teaches them how to obtain the full blessings of His recently completed Atonement. As we study His ministry and instructions to them, we are likewise directed in the path that leads to the cleansing, healing, and saving power of His atoning sacrifice.

In a pattern that foreshadows the events of the yet future Second Coming in our dispensation, the wicked on the American Continent were destroyed "in about the space of three hours" (3 Nephi 8:19) in conjunction with the Lord's crucifixion near Jerusalem. Those who were not destroyed were "the more righteous part of the people" (3 Nephi 10:12). So it will be in our day at the time of the Lord's Second Coming. The wicked will be destroyed, and the "more righteous," meaning those who are living a terrestrial or a celestial lifestyle at the time, will be spared and will join Him for the Millennium.

It was "soon after the ascension of Christ" (3 Nephi 10:18) and after the absolute darkness that covered the land "for the space of three days" (Helaman 14:27) that He appeared to the Nephites and began a glorious period of teaching and blessing which led to 200 years of peace among them. Those who survived the destruction had the rare privilege of hearing the Father's voice introduce His resurrected Son to them (3 Nephi 11:3–7; *Gospel Doctrine Teacher's Manual*, 2004, p. 166), and also the privilege of seeing the resurrected Lord Himself descend out of heaven into their midst (3 Nephi 11:8–11). During their time with Him they were taught how they could receive the full blessings of the cleansing and healing power of His Atonement.

AVOID CONTENTION

After inviting 2,500 people (3 Nephi 17:25) to come to Him one by one and feel the wound in His side and the prints of the nails in His hands and feet (3 Nephi 11:15), one of His first major messages to them was to avoid contention (3 Nephi 11:22–30). Since we live in a day when contention is rampant, and in fact deliberately fostered by many, this message is crucial for us if we desire to have the Atonement work in our lives.

FAITH, REPENTANCE, BAPTISM, GIFT OF THE HOLY GHOST

Christ clearly taught the first principles of the gospel as the means for us to build our lives upon the "rock" of Jesus Christ (3 Nephi 11:32–40).

HOW TO CONTINUE PROGRESSING AFTER BAPTISM

In 3 Nephi 12:1–2, the Savior taught that the sermon He gave next (similar to the Sermon on the Mount) is a guide for members of the Church to follow after baptism, to help them successfully live the gospel and qualify for exaltation (3 Nephi 12–14).

THE LAW OF MOSES WAS FULFILLED BY CHRIST

A very important message of the Lord to the Nephites was that the law of Moses had been fulfilled by Him and that they were now to live His full gospel in order to receive eternal life, which is another term for exaltation (3 Nephi 15:2–10).

THE SON OF GOD HONORS HIS FATHER

After addressing the multitude, the Lord turned to the Twelve whom He had chosen (3 Nephi 11:18–22; 12:1) and repeatedly emphasized that He was acting under the direction of the Father and that all glory and honor belongs to Him (3 Nephi 15:13–25). In fact, if you count the references to the Father in these few verses, you will see at least nine.

OTHER SHEEP

As He continued teaching and instructing the Nephites, the Savior mentioned that He had told some of the Jews in the Holy Land that He has other sheep (John 10:16). Then He went on to explain that the Nephites were the "other sheep" (3 Nephi 15:21), and that there were yet other sheep whom He would visit (3 Nephi 16:1–3). He later explained that these were the lost Ten Tribes (3 Nephi 17:4).

Ponder and Pray for Understanding

A crucial message for us is found in 3 Nephi 17, as we strive to live the gospel and qualify for the full power of the Atonement in our lives. After having taught much to the Nephites, the Lord noted that they were having difficulty absorbing all of the things He was teaching them. Consequently, He instructed them to go home and "ponder upon the things which I have said, and ask of the Father, in my name, that ye may understand" (3 Nephi 17:3).

The Savior's Mercy and Compassion

After instructing the people to go home and ponder and pray about the things He had already taught them, Jesus saw that they were willing to be obedient, but that they hoped He would stay longer (3 Nephi 17:5–6). Consequently, with His own emotions running full, He invited them to bring any sick among them to Him and He would heal them, which He did (3 Nephi 17:7–9). Following that, as many as could work their way through the crowd came to Him and bowed down at His feet, bathing them with their tears (3 Nephi 17:10). Next, He commanded that their little children be brought to Him, and He blessed them one by one. Much of what transpired at this time could not even be written (3 Nephi 17:11–24).

The Sacrament

Next, the Master instituted the sacrament among these people as a vital step in their continuing worship and progress toward exaltation (3 Nephi 18:1–14). The emblems of the sacrament represent the body and the blood sacrificed for us by the Savior in the Garden of Gethsemane and on the cross. The covenants we make and renew as we partake of the sacrament are critical for us as we strive to be cleansed and healed from our sins. We gain a sense of its importance, in the Doctrine and Covenants, where the Lord instructed that we "meet together often" to partake of it (D&C 20:75).

In 3 Nephi 18:28–30, the Lord instructed His newly called Twelve in how to deal appropriately with those who are not worthy to partake of the sacrament. Then, He gave brief instructions to them about excommunication when necessary (3 Nephi 18:31) and about the importance of continuing to fellowship and welcome all, including those restricted by disciplinary action, to the public meetings of the Church (3 Nephi 18:31–32).

Finally, having stayed far beyond His planned timetable, the Savior said, "And now I go unto the Father" (3 Nephi 18:35). As He prepared to leave, He ministered one by one to each of the twelve disciples He had chosen, and then departed (3 Nephi 18:35–39).

EFFORTS TO MAKE THE GOSPEL AVAILABLE TO OTHERS

At the end of the first day of teaching and blessing the Nephites, the Savior ascended into heaven, after having told them that He would return the next day (3 Nephi 18:39; 19:2). All through the night, the people contacted as many others as possible so that they also could come to where the Savior would meet them again in the morning (3 Nephi 19:2–3). In the morning, with great anticipation, the multitude gathered at the site and awaited the arrival of the Lord. While they were waiting, the Twelve (who were Apostles, according to Joseph Smith—*History of the Church*, Salt Lake City: Deseret Book, 1978; vol. 4, p. 538) organized them into twelve groups and began teaching them (3 Nephi 19:4–6). This was no doubt according to plan and part of the orientation and training that the Savior was giving these twelve special men.

Many in the multitude had not been in attendance on the previous day when the Savior first appeared to the 2,500. Consequently, the Twelve taught the "same words which Jesus had spoken—nothing varying from the words which Jesus had spoken" (3 Nephi 19:8) to prepare them for the Master's message on this day.

THE NEPHITE TWELVE ARE REBAPTIZED

With the fulfilling of the law of Moses (3 Nephi 15:4–8) and the establishment of the full Church of Jesus Christ, the Twelve were rebaptized into the newly restored Church of Jesus Christ, and the Holy Ghost fell upon them (3 Nephi 19:12–13). Afterward, they received the ministering of angels (3 Nephi 19:14). Joseph Fielding Smith explained why they were rebaptized.

> When Christ appeared to the Nephites on this continent, he commanded them to be baptized, although they had been baptized previously for the remission of their sins. We read how Nephi beheld angels who came and ministered to him daily; how he baptized all who came to be baptized for the remission of sins; how he organized the Church; and how he even raised his brother from the dead, since he held the priesthood. Then we read that the Savior commanded Nephi and the people to be baptized again, because he had organized anew the Church under the gospel. Before that it had been organized under the law [*law of Moses*].
> (*Doctrines of Salvation*, 2:336)

THE SAVIOR APPEARS AGAIN THE NEXT DAY

As the angels ministered to the Twelve, Jesus returned as promised and ministered to them. What followed was a lesson to the Twelve and to the multitude on the Holy Ghost and prayer (3 Nephi 19:15–35). Among other things, we are reminded that both the gift of the Holy Ghost and much prayer are essential elements in the righteous life that leads to exaltation. It is through the guidance of the Holy Ghost that we are led to make the Atonement effective in our lives.

THE MULTITUDE IS MIRACULOUSLY FED

As the day continued, the Savior miraculously provided bread and wine to feed the multitude (3 Nephi 20:1–6). This reminds us of His feeding of the 5,000 men plus women and children in Galilee during His mortal ministry (Matthew 14:15–21), as well as the feeding of the 4,000 men plus women and children some time later (Matthew 15:32–38). After feeding the Nephite multitude, He again administered the sacrament (3 Nephi 20:8).

THE GATHERING OF ISRAEL IN THE LAST DAYS

One of the prominent signs of the times is the "literal gathering of Israel" (Article of Faith 1:10) in the last days. This was a major topic for much of the Lord's remaining time with the Nephites (3 Nephi 20:10 through 22:17). In addition to being physically gathered to the Church, a vital part of this gathering is that of being gathered unto Christ whose mission is to bring us back to the Father. We are witnessing this great gathering to the gospel which is underway in our day.

As He taught them about the gathering, the Savior explained that the coming forth of the Book of Mormon would be a very specific sign that the last days gathering had begun. The Book of Mormon is a major tool for bringing people to Christ (3 Nephi 21:1–2).

STUDY THE WRITINGS OF ISAIAH

Have you wondered why the Master would refer to the writings of Isaiah and then tell the Nephites, "Yea, a commandment I give unto you that ye search these things diligently; for great are the words of Isaiah" (3 Nephi 23:1)? What special benefit might there be for us in studying the teachings of Isaiah? Nephi gave an answer to this question as he spoke to his brothers. He mentioned two major reasons for studying Isaiah's words. We will use italics to point out the answers to the question.

> 23 And I did read many things unto them which were written in the books of Moses; but that I might *more fully persuade them to believe in the Lord their Redeemer* I did read unto them that which was written by the prophet Isaiah; for I did liken all scriptures unto us, that it might be for our profit and learning.
>
> 24 Wherefore I spake unto them, saying: Hear ye the words of the prophet, ye who are a remnant of the house of Israel, a branch who have been broken off; hear ye the words of the prophet, which were written unto all the house of Israel, and liken them unto yourselves, *that ye may have hope* as well as your brethren from whom ye have been broken off; for after this manner has the prophet written. (1 Nephi 19:23–24)

In summary, we see that Isaiah's teachings bear strong witness of Christ and thus provide hope and optimism to us for salvation.

PAY TITHES AND OFFERINGS

As the Lord continued His teaching of the Nephites, He repeated the revelation given to Malachi about 400 BC (Malachi 3 and 4) and had them write it down (3 Nephi 24:1). Since Lehi left Jerusalem in 600 BC, which was 200 years before Malachi's time, the Nephites did not have Malachi's record with them in the contents of the brass plates. Therefore, the Master dictated it to them and they wrote it down (3 Nephi 24:1). Among other things, it stressed the payment of tithes and offerings and the blessings that come to full-tithe payers.

> 10 Bring ye all the tithes into the storehouse, that there may be meat in my house; and prove me now herewith, saith the Lord of Hosts, if I will not open you the windows of heaven, and pour you out a blessing that there shall not be room enough to receive it.
>
> 11 And I will rebuke the devourer for your sakes, and he shall not destroy the fruits of your ground; neither shall your vine cast her fruit before the time in the fields, saith the Lord of Hosts. (3 Nephi 24:10–11)

THE COMING OF ELIJAH BEFORE THE SECOND COMING

Jesus quoted the fourth chapter of Malachi (3 Nephi 25), which deals with the burning of the wicked at the Second Coming and the fact that the righteous have no need to fear it (3 Nephi 25:1–2). It also tells of the coming of Elijah in the last days to restore the keys of sealing families together for eternity (3 Nephi 25:5–6). While we have no record in the Book of Mormon that the righteous of that day participated in temple ordinances, including sealing families, the implication is here that they did. It may be that a record of this is in the sealed portion of the gold plates. We don't know at present, and will have to wait for future revelation on this topic. We do know that Elijah came in our day, to the Kirtland Temple, and restored the keys of sealing (D&C 110:13–16).

Jesus Expounds All Things from the Beginning to the End

After He had finished teaching the words of Malachi, the Savior "did expound all things, even from the beginning until the time that he should come in his glory" (3 Nephi 26:3). This was, no doubt, a crowning discourse in the Lord's work to enable these people to use their agency to take full advantage of His Atonement. Mormon explains that he couldn't even record "a hundredth part" in his record of what the Master taught in this discourse (3 Nephi 26:6–8). He goes on to say that Jesus Christ taught the Nephites for three days and then visited them often afterward (3 Nephi 26:12–13).

They Shared with Each Other

In a brief statement, Mormon explains that the people "had all things common among them, every man dealing justly, one with another" (3 Nephi 26:19). We understand that one of the qualifications for living in celestial glory is the ability to get along with each other in this way (D&C 82:19).

The Name of the Church

In the days after the Savior had finished teaching and had departed, a disagreement arose among the people as to what the name of the newly established church should be. While the disciples were praying about the matter, Jesus appeared to them and explained that the Church should carry His name (3 Nephi 27:2–8). In our day, at the time of the Restoration, many different names for the Church were used until the Master gave a specific revelation on the matter.

4 For thus shall my church be called in the last days, even The Church of Jesus Christ of Latter-day Saints. (D&C 115:4)

The Savior Reviews the Power of His Atonement

After addressing the issue of the name of the Church, Jesus reviewed again the purposes of His atoning sacrifice for us.

13 Behold I have given unto you my gospel, and this is the gospel which I have given unto you—that I came into the world to do the will of my Father, because my Father sent me.

14 And my Father sent me that I might be lifted up upon the cross; and after that I had been lifted up upon the cross, that I might draw all men unto me, that as I have been lifted up by men even so should men be lifted up by the Father, to stand before me, to be judged of their works, whether they be good or whether they be evil—

15 And for this cause have I been lifted up; therefore, according to the power of the Father I will draw all men unto me, that they may be judged according to their works. (3 Nephi 27:13–15)

Next, He explains the cleansing power of the Atonement.

16 And it shall come to pass, that whoso repenteth and is baptized in my name shall be filled; and if he endureth to the end, behold, him will I hold guiltless before my Father at that day when I shall stand to judge the world.

19 And no unclean thing can enter into his kingdom; therefore nothing entereth into his rest save it be those who have washed their garments in my blood, because of their faith, and the repentance of all their sins, and their faithfulness unto the end.

20 Now this is the commandment: Repent, all ye ends of the earth, and come unto me and be baptized in my name, that ye may be sanctified by the reception of the Holy Ghost, that ye may stand spotless before me at the last day. (3 Nephi 27:16, 19–20)

In conclusion, Jesus Christ appeared to the Nephites on the American continent after His resurrection, restored His true Church among them, and taught them His gospel. His recurring focus with them was how they could become clean and worthy to return to the Father through the cleansing and healing power of His Atonement.

CHAPTER 17

THE SAVIOR'S CONTINUING MINISTRY TO BRING US BACK TO THE FATHER

In this concluding chapter of the book, we will very briefly consider the Savior's continuing ministry to make the Atonement available to all, thus bringing our Father's children who are willing to live the gospel, back to Him. We will pay particular attention to Him in His role as our Advocate, and in His role as our final Judge.

THE APPEARANCE OF THE FATHER AND SON TO JOSEPH SMITH

For many centuries after His crucifixion and resurrection in the Holy Land, and after His visit to the Nephites on the American Continent, apostasy reigned. The Church on both hemispheres had fallen away and spiritual darkness took over. In the Old World, this period of history is referred to as the "dark ages." We have no scriptural accounts for that dismal period of the earth's history. Not only did God's children lose the light and knowledge of the true gospel along with its saving ordinances, but they also lost many basics associated with the true gospel such as scientific truths, laws of health and sanitation, and rules of behavior that foster healthy governments and societies.

Finally, in the spring of 1820, the light of truth and intelligence burst forth once again upon the earth with the appearance of the Father and the Son to young Joseph Smith. The Prophet later described it as "a beautiful, clear day, early in the spring of eighteen hundred and twenty" (Joseph Smith—History 1:14). After the Father had introduced His Son to Joseph, Jesus answered his question and set things in motion for the restoration of His true church once again upon the earth (Joseph Smith—History 1:17–20).

In the course of the Restoration, the Savior appeared many times. Included in these manifestations was His appearance to Joseph Smith and Sidney Rigdon in the John Johnson home at Hiram, Ohio, when the revelation was given revealing details about the three degrees of glory and perdition (D&C 76). He appeared on Easter Sunday, April 3, 1836, to Joseph Smith and Oliver Cowdery in the Kirtland Temple and accepted that first temple of this dispensation, which had been built at such high cost and sacrifice of the Saints. On numerous occasions, the voice of Jesus Christ was heard by the Prophet Joseph Smith and others, reminding us of His deep personal involvement in making His gospel available on earth once again.

THE SAVIOR IS IN OUR MIDST TODAY

One of the sobering and yet wonderful facts of the ministry of the Savior is that He is often among us. He has said, "I am in your midst" (D&C 29:5) and "I am in your midst and ye cannot see me" (D&C 38:7). His personal ministry to many individuals is a matter of private and sacred testimony, and continues today. His ongoing revelation to our living prophets today is sure, and is witnessed by the Holy Ghost to faithful Saints throughout the world.

THE SECOND COMING

The Second Coming is yet future but will occur in this dispensation, the dispensation of the fulness of times. When that time arrives, the Savior will once again come to earth, this time "with power and great glory" (Matthew 24:30), to reign on earth for a thousand years (Revelation 20:4). The wicked will be destroyed by His glory (2 Nephi 12:10, 19, 21), and the faithful Saints who are on the earth at the time of His coming will be "quickened and caught up to meet him" (D&C 88:96) as He comes. It will be a precious privilege beyond imagination for these Saints to be in His personal presence and feel of His glory as they return to earth to finish out their mortal lives during the first years of the Millennium.

THE MILLENNIUM

One of the major purposes of the Millennium will be that of ordinance work for all who are worthy but have not yet received the saving ordinances of the gospel of Jesus Christ. Those who have not yet had a fair opportunity to hear, understand, accept, or reject the full gospel of Jesus Christ will be given it at sometime during the thousand years. The Savior Himself will rule and reign as "KING OF KINGS AND LORD OF LORDS" (Revelation 19:16) and will ensure that all of the blessings of His infinite Atonement are made available to those who are worthy. It will be a time of peace and beauty, harmony and pleasant cooperation.

THE FINAL JUDGMENT

Because of the Atonement of Jesus Christ, it is possible to have a very pleasant final judgment. John the Apostle informs us that Jesus Christ will be our final Judge.

> 22 For the Father judgeth no man, but hath committed all judgment unto the Son. (John 5:22)

Elsewhere in the scriptures, we read that Jesus is our Advocate. In the context of what we are discussing here, another term for *advocate* would be "lawyer."

> 28 For he hath answered the ends of the law, and he claimeth all those who have faith in him; and they who have faith in him will cleave unto every good thing; wherefore he advocateth the cause of the children of men; and he dwelleth eternally in the heavens. (Moroni 7:28)

> 5 Lift up your hearts and be glad, for I am in your midst, and am your advocate with the Father; and it is his good will to give you the kingdom. (D&C 29:5)

> 3 Listen to him who is the advocate with the Father, who is pleading your cause before him. (D&C 45:3)

Thus, in effect, Jesus is both our lawyer who is representing us on Judgment Day, and He is our final judge. This is a rather wonderful combination. Just think what would happen if you were in a court of law as a defendant, and, as it turned out, the court had appointed your lawyer to also be your judge. This example presupposes that your lawyer knows you have done everything in your power to make amends and that you are qualified to be acquitted. Thus, he presents your case fairly and then takes the bench and, as your judge, sets you free.

In our example, the Savior is our Advocate and our Redeemer. He knows of our sincere repentance and honest efforts to live the gospel, and He has paid the price of our sins, "after all we can do" (2 Nephi 25:23). Now, as we approach the judgment bar of God, He becomes our Judge, welcomes us, and pronounces us worthy, because of His Atonement, to enter celestial glory and receive exaltation. Our final judgment has proceeded as described by Nephi in the Book of Mormon:

> 9 The righteous shall have a perfect knowledge of their enjoyment, and their righteousness, being clothed with purity, yea, even with the robe of righteousness. (2 Nephi 9:14)

When Finished, the Savior Will Turn the Kingdom Over to the Father

Basically, the Savior's mission is to provide resurrection for all, and to enable the Father's sons and daughters who are willing to live the gospel to return to His presence and live there eternally as exalted beings (Moses 1:39). After the Millennium is over and the "little season" at the end of it is completed with its accompanying defeat of Satan and his hosts (D&C 88:111–114), and after the final resurrection and after the Savior has completed all of the work of the final judgment, this earth will be celestialized and will become the celestial kingdom for its inhabitants who are judged worthy of that glory (D&C 130:9–11). Then the "earth will be rolled back into the presence of God, and crowned with celestial glory" (*TPJS* p 181). In other words, it will be taken from its present position in this solar system and moved back into the interstellar neighborhood where Heavenly Father lives. Then, its inhabitants will literally be back in the Father's presence. Abraham, the great prophet and astronomer, taught that the celestial planet on which the Father resides is near Kolob (Abraham 3:3; see also Abraham, Explanation, Facsimile No. 2, Fig. 2).

Thus, at that point, the Savior's mission to bring us back into the presence of the Father will have been completed. The Firstborn of the Father, our Elder Brother, the Redeemer chosen in the grand premortal council, the Creator, the Jehovah of the Old Testament, the Messiah, the Only Begotten of the Father in the flesh, the Resurrected Lord, the King of Kings and Lord of Lords, Our Advocate with the Father, will present the kingdom to the Father, spotless. The Doctrine and Covenants explains this as follows:

> 106 Until the fulness of times, when Christ shall have subdued all enemies under his feet, and shall have perfected his work;
>
> 107 When he shall deliver up the kingdom, and present it unto the Father, spotless, saying: I have overcome and have trodden the wine-press alone, even the wine-press of the fierceness of the wrath of Almighty God.
>
> 108 Then shall he be crowned with the crown of his glory, to sit on the throne of his power to reign forever and ever. (D&C 76:106–108)

Sources

Bible Dictionary, at the back of the English version of the LDS Bible. (BD)

Doctrine and Covenants Student Manual. Salt Lake City: The Church of Jesus Christ of Latter-day Saints, 1981.

Doctrines of the Gospel Student Manual. Salt Lake City: The Church of Jesus Christ of Latter-day Saints, 1986.

Edersheim, Alfred. *The Life and Times of Jesus the Messiah.* London: Longmans, Green and Co., 1883.

Encyclopedia of Mormonism. Edited by Daniel H. Ludlow. 5 vols. New York: Macmillan, 1992.

Hinckley, Gordon B. *Faith: The Essence of True Religion.* Salt Lake City: Deseret Book, 1989.

Holland, Jeffrey R. "This Do in Remembrance of Me." In Conference Report, October 1995.

Kimball, Spencer W. "The Blessings and Responsibilities of Womanhood." *Ensign.* March 1976.

—. "'Why Call me Lord, Lord, and Do Not the Things Which I Say?'" In Conference Report, April 1975.

McConkie, Bruce R. *Doctrinal New Testament Commentary,* 3 vols. Salt Lake City: Bookcraft, 1975.

—.*Mormon Doctrine.* Salt Lake City: Bookcraft, 1977.

—. *The Mortal Messiah.* Salt Lake City: Deseret Book, 1979.

Nielsen, Kent. "People on Other Worlds." *New Era*. April 1971.

Oaks, Dallin H. "The Great Plan of Happiness." In Conference Report, October 1993.

Old Testament Gospel Doctrine Teacher's Manual. Salt Lake City: The Church of Jesus Christ of Latter-day Saints, 2001.

Old Testament Student Manual: Genesis–2 Samuel. Salt Lake City: The Church of Jesus Christ of Latter-day Saints, 1981.

Smith, Joseph. *History of The Church of Jesus Christ of Latter-day Saints*. Edited by B. H. Roberts. 2d ed. rev., 7 vols. Salt Lake City: The Church of Jesus Christ of Latter-day Saints, 1932–1951. (HC)

—–. *Teachings of the Prophet Joseph Smith*, selected by Joseph Fielding Smith. Salt Lake City: Deseret Book, 1976. (*TPJS*)

—–. *The Words of Joseph Smith: The Contemporary Accounts of the Nauvoo Discourses of the Prophet Joseph*, compiled and edited by Andrew F. Ehat and Lyndon W. Cook. Provo, Utah: BYU Religious Studies Center, 1980. (*Words of Joseph Smith*)

Smith, Joseph F. *Gospel Doctrine: Selections from the Sermons and Writings of Joseph F. Smith*, compiled by John A. Widtsoe. Salt Lake City: Deseret Book, 1939.

Smith, Joseph Fielding. *Answers to Gospel Questions*. Compiled by Joseph Fielding Smith. 5 vols. Salt Lake City: Deseret Book, 1957–1966.

—–. *Doctrines of Salvation*. Compiled by Bruce R. McConkie. 3 vols. Salt Lake City: Bookcraft, 1954–1956.

—–. *The Way to Perfection*. Salt Lake City: Genealogical Society of Utah, 1949.

Sperry Symposium, Salt Lake City: Randall Book Company, 1983.

Talmage, James E. *Jesus the Christ*. Salt Lake City: Deseret Book, 1982.

—–. *The Articles of Faith*. Salt Lake City: Deseret Book, 1981.

Teachings of Presidents of the Church—Joseph Smith. Salt Lake City: The Church of Jesus Christ of Latter-day Saints, 2007.

"The Family: A Proclamation to the World." *Ensign*. November 1995, 102. (Proclamation on the Family)

The First Presidency, Heber J. Grant and counselors. "The Mormon View of Evolution." *Improvement Era*. September 1925.

The Joseph Smith Translation of the Bible. (JST)

The Life and Teachings of Jesus and His Apostles. New Testament student manual. Salt Lake City: The Church of Jesus Christ of Latter-day Saints, 1979.

Webster's New World Dictionary, Second College Edition. New York: Simon and Schuster, 1980.

Widtsoe, John A. *Evidences and Reconciliations.* Salt Lake City: Bookcraft, 1960.

Young, Edward J. *The Book of Isaiah,* vol 3. Grand Rapids, MI: WM. B. Eerdmans Publishing, 1992.

NOTES

NOTES

ABOUT THE AUTHOR

David J. Ridges taught for the Church Educational System for thirty-five years and taught for several years at BYU Campus Education Week. He taught adult religion classes, Especially for Youth, and Know Your Religion classes for BYU Continuing Education for many years. He has also served as a curriculum writer for Sunday School, Seminary, and institute of religion manuals.

He has served in many callings in the Church, including Gospel Doctrine teacher, bishop, stake president, and patriarch. He and Sister Ridges have served two full-time eighteen-month CES missions. He has written over 40 books, including study guides for Isaiah, the book of Revelation, the Old Testament, New Testament, Book of Mormon, Doctrine and Covenants, and Pearl of Great Price.

Brother Ridges and his wife, Janette, are the parents of six children, have 17 grandchildren, and make their home in Springville, Utah.

Scan to visit

www.davidjridges.com